**Understanding Language
Understanding**

Language, Speech, and Communication

Statistical Language Learning, Eugene Charniak, 1994
The Development of Speech Perception, edited by Judith Goodman and Howard C. Nusbaum, 1994
Construal, Lyn Frazier and Charles Clifton, Jr., 1995
The Generative Lexicon, James Pustejovsky, 1996
The Origins of Grammar: Evidence from Early Language Comprehension, Kathy Hirsch-Pasek and Roberta Michnick Golinkoff, 1996
Language and Space, edited by Paul Bloom, Mary A. Peterson, Lynn Nadel, and Merrill F. Garrett, 1996
Corpus Processing for Lexical Acquisition, edited by Branimir Boguraev and James Pustejovsky, 1996
Methods for Assessing Children's Syntax, edited by Dana McDaniel, Cecile McKee, and Helen Smith Cairns, 1996
The Balancing Act: Combining Symbolic and Statistical Approaches to Language, edited by Judith Klavans and Philip Resnik, 1996
The Discovery of Spoken Language, Peter W. Jusczyk, 1996
Lexical Competence, Diego Marconi, 1997
Finite-State Language Processing, edited by Emmanuel Roche and Yves Schabes, 1997
Children with Specific Language Impairment, Laurence B. Leonard, 1997
Type-Logical Semantics, Bob Carpenter, 1997
Statistical Methods for Speech Recognition, Frederick Jelinek, 1997
WordNet: An Electronic Lexical Database, Christiane Fellbaum, 1998
WordNet 1.6 CD-ROM, edited by Christiane Fellbaum, 1998
Investigations in Universal Grammar: A Guide to Experiments on the Acquisition of Syntax and Semantics, Stephen Crain and Rosalind Thornton, 1998
A Prosodic Model of Sign Language Phonology, Diane Brentari, 1998
Language Form and Language Function, Frederick J. Newmeyer, 1998
Working with Glue: Resource Accounting and Semantic Interpretation in Lexical Functional Grammar, edited by Mary Dalrymple, 1998
Understanding Language Understanding: Computational Models of Reading, edited by Ashwin Ram and Kenneth Moorman

Understanding Language Understanding

Computational Models of Reading

edited by
Ashwin Ram and Kenneth Moorman

A Bradford Book
The MIT Press
Cambridge, Massachusetts
London, England

© 1999 Massachusetts Institute of Technology

All rights reserved. No part of this book may be reproduced in any form by any electronic or mechanical means (including photocopying, recording, or information storage and retrieval) without permission in writing from the publisher.

This book was set in Times New Roman on the Monotype 'Prism Plus' Imagesetter by Asco Trade Typesetting Ltd., Hong Kong.
Printed and bound in the United States of America.

Library of Congress Cataloging-in-Publication Data

Understanding language understanding : computational models of reading
 / edited by Ashwin Ram and Kenneth Moorman.
    p.   cm. — (Language, speech, and communication)
 "A Bradford book."
 Includes bibliographical references and index.
 ISBN 0-262-18192-4 (hc : alk. paper)
 1. Psycholinguistics—Data processing. 2. Reading—Data processing. 3. Comprehension—Data processing. I. Ram, Ashwin.
II. Moorman, Kenneth. III. Series.
P37.5.D37U53   1999
401′.9′0285—dc21   98-39141
                                                                    CIP

Contents

About the Editors   vii

About the Authors   ix

Foreword by Walter Kintsch   xv

Chapter 1
Introduction: Toward a Theory of Reading and Understanding   1

Ashwin Ram and Kenneth Moorman

Chapter 2
Cognition and Fiction   11

William J. Rapaport and Stuart C. Shapiro

Chapter 3
Sentence Processing in Understanding: Interaction and Integration of Knowledge Sources   27

Kavi Mahesh, Kurt P. Eiselt, and Jennifer K. Holbrook

Chapter 4
Capturing the Contents of Complex Narratives   73

Eric Domeshek, Eric Jones, and Ashwin Ram

Chapter 5
Retrieval from Episodic Memory by Inferencing and Disambiguation   107

Trent E. Lange and Charles M. Wharton

Chapter 6
A Connectionist Model of Narrative Comprehension   181

Mark C. Langston, Tom Trabasso, and Joseph P. Magliano

Chapter 7
Importance of Text Struture in Everyday Reading   227

Bonnie J. F. Meyer

Chapter 8
A Theory of Questions and Question Asking   253

Ashwin Ram

Chapter 9
Semantic Correspondence Theory   299

Justin Peterson and Dorrit Billman

Chapter 10
Creativity in Reading: Understanding Novel Concepts   359

Kenneth Moorman and Ashwin Ram

Chapter 11
On the Intersection of Story Understanding and Learning   397

Michael T. Cox and Ashwin Ram

Chapter 12
Information Extraction as a Stepping Stone toward Story Understanding   435

Ellen Riloff

Chapter 13
Text Processing and Narrative Worlds   461

Richard J. Gerrig

Chapter 14
Computational Models of Reading and Understanding: What Good Are They?   483

Charles R. Fletcher

Index   491

About the Editors

Ashwin Ram is an associate professor in the College of Computing of the Georgia Institute of Technology, an associate professor of Cognitive Science, and an adjunct professor in the School of Psychology. He received his BTech in electrical engineering from the Indian Institute of Technology, New Delhi, in 1982 and his MS in computer science from the University of Illinois at Urbana-Champaign in 1984. He received his PhD degree from Yale University for his dissertation *Question-Driven Understanding: An Integrated Theory of Story Understanding, Memory, and Learning* in 1989. Dr. Ram's research interests lie in the areas of artificial intelligence and cognitive science, with an emphasis on machine learning, case-based reasoning, natural language understanding, and cognitive multimedia, and he has several research publications in these areas. He is a coeditor of a book on *Goal-Driven Learning*, published by MIT Press/Bradford Books. Dr. Ram is a member of the editorial boards of the *Journal of the Learning Sciences* and the *International Journal of Applied Intelligence*, and an associate of *Brain and Behavioral Sciences*. He is a member of the technical advisory board of the EduTech Institute. He cochaired the 1994 Annual Conference of the Cognitive Science Society, the 1994 AAAI Spring Symposium on Goal-Driven Learning, the 1995 AAAI Fall Symposium on Adaptation of Knowledge for Reuse, and the 1996 FLAIRS Special Track on Real-World Natural Language Understanding. His current address is: College of Computing, Georgia Institute of Technology, Atlanta, GA 30332-0280 (ashwin@cc.gatech.edu, *http://www.cc.gatech.edu/faculty/ashwin/*).

Kenneth Moorman is an assistant professor of computer science at Transylvania University. He received his BA in computer science and mathematics from Translyvania University in 1991, his MSc in computer science from the Georgia Institute of Technology in 1996, and his PhD in computer science from the Georgia Institute of Technology in 1997 for his dissertation on creative reading. While at Georgia Tech, Dr. Moorman was a Hertz Fellow from 1991 to 1996. His current research interests include natural language processing, real-world reading, creativity, learning, memory, and robotics. He is a member of AAAI, the Cognitive Science Society, the International Reading Association, and the ACM. Dr. Moorman cochaired the 1996 FLAIRS Special Track on Real-World Natural Language Understanding. His current address is: Transylvania University, 300 North Broadway, Lexington, KY 40508 (kmoorman@mail.transy.edu, *http://www.transy.edu/homepages/kmoorman/*).

About the Authors

Dorrit Billman is an associate professor in the School of Psychology at the Georgia Institute of Technology, a member of the Cognitive Science faculty, and an adjunct professor of computing. She received her PhD from the University of Michigan in 1983 and was previously on the faculty of the University of Pennsylvania. Her research interests focus on the relation between language and thought, on the relation between verbs and events representation, and on the principles or biases guiding concept learning. Her current address is: School of Psychology, Georgia Institute of Technology, Atlanta, GA 30332-0170 (billman@cc.gatech.edu, *http://www.gatech.edu/psychology/billman.htm*).

Michael T. Cox is currently an assistant professor in the Department of Computer Science and Engineering at Wright State University, Dayton, OH. He received his PhD in Computer Science from the Georgia Institute of Technology, Atlanta, in 1996 and his undergraduate (highest honors) from the same in 1986. From 1996 to 1998 he was a postdoctoral fellow in the Computer Science Department at Carnegie Mellon University in Pittsburgh working on the PRODIGY project. His research interests include case-based (analogical) reasoning, mixed-inititative planning, understanding (situation assessment), introspection, and learning. More specifically, he is interested in how goals interact with and influence these broader cognitive processes. His approach to research follows both artificial intelligence and cognitive science directions.

Eric Domeshek is an assistant professor in the Computer Science Department at Northwestern University, and a member of the Institute for the Learning Sciences. He received his PhD from Yale University in 1992. His research interests include artificial intelligence and cognitive science, focusing on case-based reasoning, representation design, human-computer systems, and educational applications. He is especially interested in rich media, such as video and graphics, and complex cognitive processes, such as design. His current address is: Institute for the Learning

Sciences, Northwestern University, 1890 Maple Ave., Suite 300, Evanston, IL 60201 (domeshek@ils.nwu.edu, *http://www.ils.nwu.edu/~domeshek*).

Kurt Eiselt is the assistant dean of the College of Computing at the Georgia Institute of Technology, a member of the Cognitive Science faculty, and an adjunct professor of Psychology. He received his PhD in Information and Computer Science from the University of California, Irvine, in 1989. His research interests include cognitive science, natural language understanding, and computational psycholinguistics. His current address is: College of Computing, Georgia Institute of Technology, Atlanta, GA 30332-0280 (eiselt@cc.gatech.edu, *http://www.cc.gatech.edu/aimosaic/faculty/eiselt.html*).

Charles R. (Randy) Fletcher is an associate professor of psychology at the University of Minnesota. He teaches courses in cognitive science and the psychology of language and conducts research on the psychological processes involved in understanding and remembering texts. Most of his research has focused on the roles of attention and memory in the comprehension and recall of simple narratives, though lately his interests have broadened to include mathematical proofs and spatial descriptions. He has a BA in psychology from the University of California, Berkeley, and a PhD in psychology from the University of Colorado, Boulder. His current address is: Department of Psychology, University of Minnesota, 75 East River Rd., Minneapolis, MN 55455-0344 (randy@text3.psych.umn.edu, *http://text2.psych.umn.edu/RandyHomePage.htmld/*).

Jennifer Holbrook is a research staff member in the EduTech Institute at the Georgia Institute of Technology. She received her PhD in psychology from the University of California, Irvine, in 1989. Her research interests in psycholinguistics include ambiguity resolution, comparison of unilingual and multilingual language users, computational psycholinguistics, and natural language understanding applications. Her current address is: EduTech Institute, College of Computing, Georgia Institute of Technology, Atlanta, GA 30332 (holbrook@cc.gatech.edu).

Eric Jones is a senior member of technical staff at Alphatech, Inc. From 1992 to 1996 he was a member of academic staff in the Department of Computer Science at Victoria University of Wellington, New Zealand. He received his PhD from Yale University in 1992 for his dissertation *The Flexible Use of Abstract Knowledge in Planning*. He also has degrees in mathematics and geography from the University of Otago, New Zealand. His research interests include intelligent database retrieval, case-based reasoning, natural language processing, and machine learning. His current address is: Alphatech, Inc., 50 Mall Rd., Burlington, MA 01803 (eric.jones@alphatech.com).

About the Authors

Richard Gerrig is an associate professor in the Department of Psychology, State University of New York, Stony Brook. He received his PhD from Stanford University in 1984. His book, *Experiencing Narrative Worlds*, was published in 1993 by Yale University Press. His research interests include cognitive experiences of narratives and the understanding of speaker's meaning. His current address is: Department of Psychology, State University of New York, Stony Brook, Stony Brook, NY 11794-2500 (rgerrig@psych1.psy.sunysb.edu).

Trent Lange is a PhD candidate in the Computer Science Department of the University of California, Los Angeles. His research interests include natural language understanding, models of human memory, connectionist networks, and cognitive science. Recent interests include statistical models for stock market arbitrage. His current address is: Artificial Intelligence Lab, Computer Science Department, University of California, Los Angeles, CA 90024 (lange@cs.ucla.edu).

Mark Langston is a PhD candidate in Cognitive Psychology at the University of Chicago. His interests include inference generation, memory, and discourse comprehension. His current research focuses on the dynamic organizational aspects of short- and long-term memory during the on-line comprehension of text, and the development of computational models that simulate these processes. He is also employed with IBM as a systems analyst. His current address is: Department of Psychology, University of Chicago, 5848 S. University Ave., Chicago, IL 60615 (fugue@ccp.spc.uchicago.edu, *http://www.ccp.uchicago.edu/~fugue/vitae.html*).

Joe Magliano is currently an assistant professor at Northern Illinois University. He received his BA (1987) in psychology from the University of Dayton, and his MS (1990) and PhD (1992) from Memphis State University in cognitive psychology. He also was a postdoctoral fellow at the University of Chicago from 1993 to 1996. The focus of his current research is on the question of how people understand events as they experience them over time, such as those conveyed in written discourse and in film. He is specifically interested in how readers and viewers construct coherent representations for a story. His current address is: Department of Psychology, Northern Illinois University, DeKalb, IL 60115 (jmagliano@niu.edu).

Kavi Mahesh is a senior computational linguist at Oracle Corporation. His chapter was written while he was a research scientist and an adjunct assistant professor at the Computing Research Laboratory in New Mexico State University. He received his PhD in computer science from Georgia Institute of Technology in 1995. His research interests include natural language understanding, text processing, summarization, ontologies, and knowledge bases. His current address is: Oracle Corporation, 500 Oracle Parkway, MS 659510, Redwood Shores, CA 94065 (kmahesh@us.oracle.com, *http://crl.nmsu.edu/users/mahesh/*).

Bonnie J. F. Meyer is a professor in the Department of Educational Psychology, School Psychology, and Special Education at The Pennsylvania State University and member of the Faculty of Gerontology at the Gerontology Center at The University of Georgia. She received her PhD from Cornell University in 1974. Her research interests include reading comprehension, discourse analysis, prose learning, and learning, memory, problem solving, and decision making across the adult life span. Her current address is: Department of Educational Psychology, School Psychology, and Special Education, Penn State, 204 Cedar Bldg., University Park, PA 16802 (bjm8@psu.edu, *http://www2.ed.psu.edu/espse/staff/bonnie/bonnie.htm*).

Justin Peterson is a system vice president developing architectures for global mangement systems at Citibank. Previously he was in the AI group at Bell Atlantic, formerly NYNEX, Science Technology Research Lab. He received his PhD at Georgia Institute of Technology in 1996. His research interests include the application of natural language processing systems to electronic banking systems. His current address is: 111 Wall Street, 12th floor Zone 4, New York, NY 10043 (justin.peterson@citicorp.com).

William J. Rapaport is an associate professor of computer science, adjunct professor of philosophy, and a member of the Center for Cognitive Science, all at State University of New York, Buffalo. He received his PhD from Indiana University in 1976. His research interests are in cognitive science, knowledge representation, and computational linguistics. His current address is: Department of Computer Science, SUNY Buffalo, Buffalo, NY 14260-2000 (rapaport@cs.buffalo.edu, *http://www.cs.buffalo.edu/pub/WWW/faculty/rapaport/*).

Ellen Riloff is an assistant professor of computer science at the University of Utah. She received her PhD from the University of Massachusetts in 1994. Her research interests include natural language understanding, artificial intelligence, and information retrieval. Her current address is: Department of Computer Science, University of Utah, Salt Lake City, UT 84112 (riloff@cs.utah.edu, *http://www.cs.utah.edu/~riloff*)

Stuart C. Shapiro is professor and chair of the Department of Computer Science and a member of the Center for Cognitive Science at the State University of New York, Buffalo. He is a fellow of the American Association for Artificial Intelligence, and a past chair of ACM's Special Interest Group on Artificial Intelligence. He received his PhD from the University of Wisconsin, Madison, in 1971. His research interests include knowledge representation, reasoning, and natural language processing. His current address is: Department of Computer Science, University at Buffalo, Buffalo, NY 14260-2000 (shapiro@cs.buffalo.edu, *http://www.cs.buffalo.edu/~shapiro/*).

About the Authors

Tom Trabasso is the Irving B. Harris Professor of Psychology at The University of Chicago. His interests are on discourse analysis and comprehension. His focus has been on the analysis and understanding of narratives. He and his colleagues have investigated the role that causal inferences play in the construction of coherent understanding of narrative texts. His current address is: Department of Psychology, University of Chicago, 5848 S. University Ave., Chicago, IL 60637 (tomt@cicero.uchicago.edu, *http://www.ccp.uchicago.edu/faculty/Thomas Trabasso/*).

Charles M. Wharton is a research fellow in the Language Section of The National Institute of Deafness and Communication Disorders, The National Institutes of Health. He received his PhD from UCLA in 1993. His research interests focus on using functional neuroimaging to understand the neuroanatomy of reasoning, abstract mental representation, and cognition and emotion. His current address is: Language Section, Bldg. 10, room 5N118A, NIDCD, NIH, Bethesda, MD 20892 (wharton@codon.nih.gov).

Foreword

Without language, neither human intelligence nor our existence as social beings would be conceivable. Language is surely a central characteristic among those that are distinctly human. Therefore it is no surprise that the study of language has fascinated scholars for a very long time. Indeed some of the hotly disputed current issues in the study of language, such as the conflict between formal approaches that stress structure and order and informal, observational approaches that stress the flexibility and context dependency of language, had been well formulated two thousand years ago. So is there nothing new under the sun in the study of language? A perusal of the present volume will convince the reader that this is by no means so, that a number of very important changes have occurred. For almost all of history, philosophers and linguists have focused on language as an object of analysis. They were interested in describing and analyzing the product language, whether this product was spoken discourse or written texts, accumulating a huge amount of important and useful knowledge about language in this way. Only in the last few decades have we begun to consider not just the product but also the processes by which we comprehend and use language. The present volume exemplifies this research strategy. It is a strategy that seeks not to replace linguistic or semantic analysis but to complement and enrich it. Moreover it is a strategy that holds a great deal of promise because it combines the insights arising from the analysis of language as an object with a new set of constraints based on psychological and computational considerations. The data that psychologists have collected in their laboratories about language processing and the results that researchers in natural language processing have amassed about the properties and requirements of computational procedures provide a new look at language and help us to gain a new level of understanding that was not possible before.

Until now the conditions for studying the process of language understanding did not exist. Psychologists needed to develop and refine their research methods, and the computers and computational methods needed simply were not available earlier. In fact there has been considerable interest in the process of understanding for some time among a school of literary criticism that focused on the reception of a poem or literary text by the reader, that is, on the process of understanding the text rather than on the text itself. However, their only tools were intuition and phenomenological analysis, which were insufficient to build an objective, convincing case. The computational approach, whose strength and promise are well demonstrated by the chapters in the present volume, has changed all of that, making it possible to construct processing theories that are objective and testable and that can be powerful tools to investigate language understanding processes.

There are several distinctive features of this volume that set it apart from other work on reading and understanding, even work with a computational emphasis. First, the editors have paid a great deal of attention to the integration of computational approaches and psychological research. Thus some of the chapters here are explicitly concerned with psychological data and models whose primary goal is to simulate human understanding processes. But even the chapters that focus directly on computational issues are also informed and constrained by what we know about human comprehension. Another important theme that runs through this book is the emphasis on knowledge representation and the role of knowledge in comprehension. Some of the toughest problems for computational models of understanding lie here. The contributors to this volume are vigorously exploring these problems and offer a variety of potential solutions. Finally special note should be taken of the authors' attempts to deal explicitly with reading goals in the context of computational modeling. People don't read and understand in a vacuum but always for some reason, and their goals are important determinants of the reading process that have all too often been neglected in the past.

Why focus on reading, one might ask, why not study language understanding in general? Are not conversation and discussion equally interesting and important as reading? They certainly are, but there are good reasons for an initial focus on reading because a number of serious scientific problems can be avoided in that way. It is not possible to model conversation successfully without explicitly including the whole physical and interpersonal situation in which the conversation in embedded—which is not easily done. In contrast, written texts are designed to stand on their own, be understandable by readers whom the author cannot know beforehand and in situations the author cannot anticipate. Authors must make assumptions about the knowledge background and goals of their readers, but they can neglect many factors that play crucial roles in conversations. Hence reading comprehension, for all its complexity, is more readily analyzed than a conversation.

For the most part the chapters in this book deal with short and simple texts. Thus our literary critic might not find much here, for it is a long way from a simple story to high literature. However, this is a young field, and starting with relatively simple though natural text is clearly the right research strategy to use. Furthermore it is apparent in several of the chapters that the process of scaling up has already begun—both scaling up to complex, even literary texts, and to longer texts. In this effort the present approaches may someday be complemented by another research tradition in natural language understanding that relies on statistical techniques and the analysis of large corpora. Eventually these different research enterprises might be combined, adding processing constraints to the statistical approaches and enabling computational process models to scale up.

Computational models of understanding are rapidly developing. The present volume will do much to focus this development and even accelerate it. It will also contribute to further the collaboration between computational modeling and the psychological study of language. Reading research is a broad and interdisciplinary field, and computational modeling must find its place in this varied landscape. It has much to offer to the more traditional approaches in the reading area, but it can also profit from the rich experience of the older approaches. The present volume demonstrates that continued interdisciplinary cooperation can pay off handsomely.

Walter Kintsch

Understanding Language Understanding

Chapter 1
Introduction: ... and Kenneth
Reading

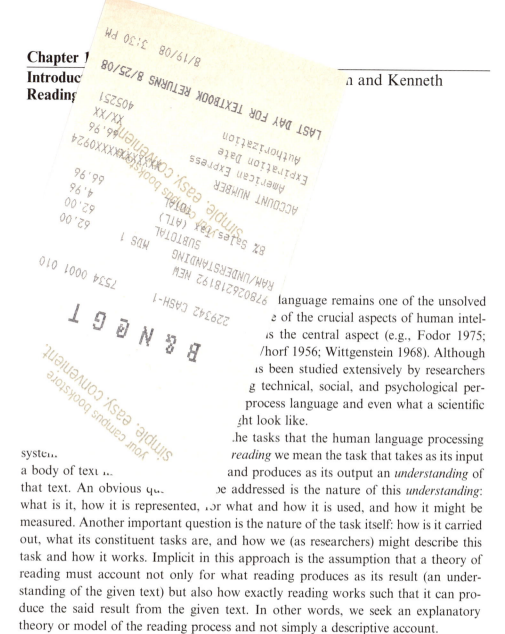

... language remains one of the unsolved ... e of the crucial aspects of human intelligence ... is the central aspect (e.g., Fodor 1975; ... /horf 1956; Wittgenstein 1968). Although ... is been studied extensively by researchers ... g technical, social, and psychological perspectives ... process language and even what a scientific ... ght look like.

... the tasks that the human language processing system ... *reading* we mean the task that takes as its input a body of text ... and produces as its output an *understanding* of that text. An obvious q... be addressed is the nature of this *understanding*: what is it, how it is represented, for what and how it is used, and how it might be measured. Another important question is the nature of the task itself: how is it carried out, what its constituent tasks are, and how we (as researchers) might describe this task and how it works. Implicit in this approach is the assumption that a theory of reading must account not only for what reading produces as its result (an understanding of the given text) but also how exactly reading works such that it can produce the said result from the given text. In other words, we seek an explanatory theory or model of the reading process and not simply a descriptive account.

Our goal is to address the problem of reading comprehension—processing and understanding a natural language text, narrative or story. This constrains our endeavor in two ways. First, an account of reading must explain how the reader can understand text, that is, understand the situations described in the text, explain who did what to whom, and how, and why, and construct a coherent interpretation of the text that "makes sense." A theory that focuses, for example, only on syntactic parsing of sentences is, by this metric, not a theory of reading comprehension or text understanding, although it might certainly be an important piece of a complete theory. The second constraint is that an account of reading must explain how the reader can understand "real" natural language texts—narratives, stories, newspaper articles, dialogues, advertisements, and so on. This rules out models that focus only on the processing of single sentences taken out of context or of small researcher-constructed "stories." Although such models are certainly important in that they provide crucial stepping stones toward the "big picture" and may even be a piece of the complete theory of reading, they do not by themselves constitute a satisfactory account of the human reading capability. Methodologically, of course, researchers must often concentrate on narrower subtasks of the reading process (e.g., syntactic parsing, explanation construction, or belief modeling) and/or on a narrower range of textual inputs (e.g., individual sentences, short newspaper articles, or simple question-and-answer scenarios); the point is that the eventual goal of the endeavor that has come to be known as *natural language processing* (NLP) is to produce a theory of reading comprehension "in the large."

1.2 Assumptions

What might a theory of reading look like? We make two assumptions in this volume. First, a scientific understanding of how agents read is best expressed in terms of a *functional-computational-representational* model of the reading process.[2] By *functional* we mean that the process will be defined in terms of its inputs and outputs and that it may be decomposed into one or more interactive subtasks and further sub-subtasks which, in turn, will be defined in terms of their inputs and outputs as well as their interactions with each other. Once defined, the theory will also explain how exactly each subtask works such that it can perform its function of transforming its inputs into its outputs. By *computational* we mean that this transformation will be described using an information-processing or computational model—an explanatory, step-by-step account of how exactly the reading system (human or machine) can derive the required outputs from the given inputs. By convention, this account will be written down using the language of computer algorithms and implemented using a computer program which can be executed to provide evidence that the model does what is claimed of it. This requirement forces the theory to be described precisely and provides a means for experimentation; these and other benefits of the "computational psychology" or "cognitive modeling" approach will be discussed below. Finally by *representational* we mean that the reading process is expected to make use of extensive background knowledge in order to understand a text and produce as its output

Introduction

some description of the information conveyed by the text; both the background knowledge and output description will be represented in some manner inside the reading system. The form, content, and organization of these representations is as much a research issue as is the process that utilizes and produces them.

The second assumption underlying this volume is that inasmuch as a theory of reading is concerned with accounting for the human ability to read, it is important that the functions, processes, and representations postulated by the theory, and the behaviors exhibited by the model, be cognitively plausible and justified to the extent possible through psychological experimentation. Where it is not possible to obtain detailed psychological data to verify or refute fine-grained assumptions of a theory, these assumptions may be justified in teleological terms (e.g., computational, functional, ecological, evolutionary, or philosophical arguments for why a subsystem works the way it does) or at least via a sufficiency argument that demonstrates that the proposed model is able to produce the behaviors that are being accounted for (e.g., see Ram and Jones 1995). This demonstration is facilitated by the presence of an executable computer model.

1.3 Modeling Approach

Before we visit the reading task in more detail, let us discuss the computational modeling approach that we will take to address this task. It is probably the case that many of the models described in this volume will appear too limited to appear to be actually "reading" the texts which they are given in the full sense of the word. Then what purpose do such models serve? In the computational modeling approach, the model itself is not the end of the research cycle; instead, the model is used as a tool by the researcher in order to refine the overarching theory behind it. As Margaret Boden expressed it (Boden 1986):

> ... artificial intelligence is the use of programs as tools in the study of intelligent processes, tools that help in the discovery of the thinking-procedures and epistemological structures employed by intelligent creatures.

As a tool, then, what power does the computational model give to the intelligence researcher? Boden suggests a set of what she calls *Lovelace questions* which explore the "usefulness" of computer modeling with respect to the study of creativity (see Boden 1991). These questions are easily adapted to be applicable to the study of reading as well.

First, can a computational model ever perform in a way such that it appears to read and understand? The answer to this is yes, as many of the models depicted in this volume will show, albeit perhaps in a manner or domain that is narrower than the full human reading capacity can handle. However, this is an uninteresting question. After all, ELIZA (Weizenbaum 1966) *appeared* to comprehend quite a bit using nothing more than simple pattern matching, substitution, and a human willingness to believe. The ways in which we tend to measure the appearance of cognitive ability are now more strict, but even then most of the models here will at least appear to be performing some aspect of reading.

If the first question is not that interesting, a reasonable followup might be: Can a computational model ever *really* be able to read and understand material? Unfortunately, it is not clear exactly how one can distinguish "true" comprehension from the mere appearance of comprehension; thus this question is best left to computational philosophers.

If the appearance of comprehension is uninteresting and the reality of comprehension is beyond the scope this volume, where does that leave us? The issue is not whether an implemented computer program can actually read and understand text but whether building such programs is a reasonable way to approach the problem of producing an explanatory theory of reading and understanding. The third Lovelace question therefore is the one we will concentrate on: Can computational models help us understand how human reading is possible? We believe the answer to be yes for a number of reasons:

- The computational model can act as a sufficiency argument for the theory. In other words, if the model is an accurate instantiation of the theory and if the model appears to perform some aspect of reading, then the model shows that the claims of the theory are sufficient for explaining that aspect of reading.
- The computational model requires the researcher to be precise in the specification of the theory, not only in what the tasks are and what they do but also in how exactly they work. It is often easy to "believe" an assumption to be true; when that assumption is implemented, it is revealed whether it is true or not. As Hintzman states (Hintzman 1991):

... an assertion can be so intuitively compelling that it is accepted without close examination. In these cases, it may take a formal model to convince researchers that the assertion is wrong, and even then the belief may be hard to kill.

This is not meant to imply that researchers intentionally misbelieve assumptions that they hold dear; Hintzman goes on to point out that models are useful in illuminating theories because researchers are subject to a number of reasoning flaws, such as not being able to track a large number of variables simultaneously or being biased to accepting often heard statements as true.

- The computational model gives the researcher a solid basis on which to perform empirical evaluation. Through rigorous experimentation with the model, the research

Introduction

can evaluate the power of the theory in question. This evaluation of the model can also lead to refinement of the theory. As Cohen states (Cohen 1995):

> Studying [computer] systems is not very different from studying moderately intelligent animals such as rats. One obliges the agent (rat or program) to perform a task according to an experimental protocol, observing and analyzing the macro- and micro-structure of its behavior. Afterword, if the subject is a rat, its head is opened up or chopped off; and if it is a program, its innards are fiddled with.

If the model does something unexpected, then the theory can be modified and the model re-evaluated. The unexpected behavior might represent an inadequacy in the theory or sometimes even an unusual success.

- The researcher interested in psychological theory derives an additional benefit: the behaviors produced by the model can be compared with psychological data. This allows the cognitive basis or plausibility of the theory to be evaluated. Often experimentation with the model provides predictions that can be evaluated through additional psychological experiments.
- The model allows the researcher to test the assumptions of the theory—which ones are warranted, which ones are *ad hoc*, which ones are simply wrong. The model forces the researcher to critically examine why the theory works at an empirical level.
- Finally the model can allow the researcher to generalize the theory. Cohen uses coherent explanations as an example (Cohen 1995). If one builds a model that produces coherent explanations, one can then examine that model to determine precisely what aspects of it are responsible for its behavior. Once this is done, one is able to manipulate the model in ways that can test the predictions of the underlying theory and generalize the causal mechanisms involved. For example, one might be able to reuse a portion of the model for a task other than reading which requires the construction of coherent explanations.

Reading is a large, complicated, and ill-defined cognitive behavior, and one that is extremely difficult to capture theoretically. However, for the above reasons, computational modeling is a promising approach toward this problem. Even if implemented models are still primitive with respect to human performance, the endeavor of theorizing about, building, evaluating, and revising these models can add significantly to our knowledge of the human reading capacity.

1.4 Tasks of Reading

A theory of reading, as we have defined it, must deal with a wide range of issues and account for a wide range of behaviors and capabilities. Consider the following example (Henry 1986), which is the first paragraph of a longer story:

One dollar and eighty-seven cents. That was all. And sixty cents of it was in pennies. Pennies saved one and two at a time by bulldozing the grocer and the vegetable man and the butcher until one's cheeks burned with the silent imputation of parsimony that such close dealing implied. Three times Della counted it. One dollar and eighty-seven cents. And the next day would be Christmas.

Some of the pieces of this puzzle include:

- *Processing words and sentences.* The starting point for reading is the input of the words in a sentence, word by word, sentence by sentence. Before anything can be understood about the story, for example, the English text has to be processed at this low level. Much research in natural language processing is concerned with how word meanings are looked up (what does *parsimony* mean?), how ambiguous words are disambiguated (which meaning of *close* should be applied?), how the meanings of the words in a sentence are combined into a meaning for the sentence as a whole, how anaphora are resolved (in the second sentence, what does *that* refer to?), what the role of various punctuation is, what the tense of the sentence is, when and how a reader might go back and re-read some text, and so on. This area of the field is often called *sentence processing*, though in real-world texts there is also the need to deal with sentence fragments, such as *one dollar and eighty-seven cents*.

- *Drawing inferences.* Natural language texts leave much as an exercise to the reader. One of the most important tasks the reader must carry out is to determine hidden meanings and make explicit what was left implicit in the text. In order to do this, the reader must draw on the context provided by the text that has been read so far, by the external situation that the reader is in, and by the overarching task that the reader is carrying out. The reader must also draw on background knowledge about the world in general and the reader's past experiences—for example, why is the amount of money Della has in the story and the fact that the next day is Christmas important pieces of related information? Much of the research in this area is concerned with *knowledge representation*—how contextual and background knowledge is encoded; with *memory*—how this knowledge is organized such that it can be retrieved at the appropriate moment using the available cues (many of you reading the example probably recognized it as *Gifts of the Magi* and retrieved the gist of the remainder of the story); and with *abduction*—how background knowledge and current context can be brought together to enable the reader to draw plausible inferences from the material in the text.

- *Dealing with novelty.* It is almost a definitional characteristic of natural languages that they possess a great deal of novelty by virtue of their flexibility and constant redefinition through cultural and social agreement. This novelty can range from the introduction of novel words or the metaphorical reuse of words in new contexts to the description of unfamiliar or novel concepts through the use of language. Consider

Introduction 7

the example story. Many readers will be unfamiliar with the word *imputation* but will not have difficulty arriving at a reasonable meaning for it, based on the context. On the other hand, consider the use of the term *bulldoze*. Even readers unfamiliar with the usage given in the story can arrive at a reasonable interpretation based on what they know about literal *bulldozing* and given the the rest of the paragraph. Thus reading research has also been concerned with issues of *learning, metaphor, analogy,* and *creativity*.

- *Controlling the process.* People do not read in a vacuum; they read for a purpose, be it entertainment, information seeking, or communication. During the reading process, they are also concerned with other goals, activities, and occurrences in the world around them which demand attention. It follows that reading is an extremely flexible process; one can quickly skim a newspaper article on the train while commuting to work in the morning, or read a mystery novel and allocate much attention to details of the plot while skipping over lengthy descriptions of the setting, or read in great detail a carefully constructed argument in an editorial that one has been asked to write a response to for a term paper. For example, there is probably no one who read the example paragraph word by word. Instead, the average way to read a bit of text like that is to read *almost* every word, skimming the rest. This would be more evident on a longer piece of course. There is less research into this aspect of reading, but some research has been concerned with *situated reading*—how the reading task interacts with, and is affected by, the larger context in which it is carried out; *focus of attention*—how a reader pays different amounts of attention on different aspects of the text, switching dynamically between skimming and in-depth processing; and *meta-reasoning*—reasoning about the reading process itself.

The chapters in this volume span this range of tasks that reading research has been concerned with. We begin with Rapaport and Shapiro's discussion (chapter 2) of cognitive models of reading and the relationship between cognition and fiction. They explore the epistemological questions of how a cognitive agent could represent fictional entities and their properties, and reason about such entities, and their relationship with nonfictional entities, during the course of reading a story. Following this, Mahesh, Eiselt, and Holbrook (chapter 3) discuss psycholinguistic issues in sentence processing, focusing in particular on how multiple types of information, such as syntactic and semantic information, can be integrated while understanding a sentence. They present a computational model that can resolve ambiguous interpretations of a sentence and recover from conclusions that turn out to be erroneous. Next, Domeshek, Jones, and Ram (chapter 4) discuss issues of form, content, and organization in knowledge representation. They discuss how a reader can represent the meaning of a text as well as the inferential knowledge that is required to understand the text. Wharton and Lange (chapter 5) discuss how a reader's episodic memory might be organized and deployed to provide support for the reader's inferential processes. They argue that the process by which some text is understood should be integrated with the process by which it is used to recall relevant information from memory, and present a computational model of the combined process. Trabasso, Langston, and Magliano (chapter 6) further the discussion of inference, presenting a model of text comprehension along with psychological data supporting their model. They explore the differences between on-line processing during text comprehension and off-line processing after the text has been read.

Following these chapters, we turn our attention to issues of contextualization of the reading processes in the structure of the text as well as the overarching tasks that the reader is engaged in. Meyer (chapter 7) discusses how the reader can use the structure of the text to support the comprehension of that text. Different genres of text are read in different ways because the individual characteristics of the readers interact with the individual characteristics of the texts and of the authors of those texts. Ram (chapter 8) discusses the influence of the reader's learning goals on the manner and depth to which the text is processed. He presents a model of reading as an active process in which the reader subjectively processes the text while seeking information, creating hypotheses, asking questions, and pursuing interesting ideas.

We then move on to discuss issues of learning and creativity. Peterson and Billman (chapter 9) present a model that explains how a reader handles linguistic novelty. They present a computational model that can read and interpret sentences containing novel verbs using underlying semantic information about the language. Moorman and Ram (chapter 10) discuss a model of creative understanding which enables a reader to comprehend texts that contain novel concepts. They show how a reader can creatively understand novel concepts in a science fiction story using analogical reasoning and problem reformulation supported by a principled representation of knowledge. Cox and Ram (chapter 11) discuss parallels between reading and learning, arguing that there are many similarities between these two tasks: identification of interesting input, elaboration of input concepts, determination of the agent's goals, and determination and execution of the strategies to be used to process the input in pursuit of those goals.

While this volume is primarily concerned with functional-computational-representational models of reading, be they symbolic or distributed (e.g., connectionist) models, Riloff (chapter 12) presents a number of alternative recent approaches which both share much with the previous models and deviate from many of the assumptions underlying these models. She argues that information extraction approaches, concerned with identifying and extracting specific types of information from text rather than in-depth knowledge-intensive analysis of text, can provide significant leverage in story understanding. Gerrig (chapter 13) discusses what human reading is really like and provides several directions that future research on reading will need to pursue. He describes the reader's experience of being transported into the narrative world of a text and mentally participating in that narrative world during the reading process. Finally Fletcher (chapter 14) concludes with his perspective on the endeavor of building computational models of reading, such as those presented in this volume, arguing that it is productive to invest resources and intellectual energy in this enterprise.

Notes

1. A *natural language* is a language that has evolved through use in a social system (e.g., English, Spanish, French, or Hindi) as opposed to one that has been designed by people for a specific purpose (e.g., Fortran or Java). Languages that are engineered but evolve through social action (e.g., Esperanto, American Sign Language, and Klingon) are also examples of natural languages.

2. This does not imply that all research into reading or natural language processing must necessarily involve computational modeling; on the contrary, a range of psychological, social, and computational research is needed to work toward the common goal of producing a detailed functional-computational-representational model of reading.

References

Boden, M. A. 1986. *Artificial Intelligence and Natural Man*, 2d ed. New York: Basic Books.

Boden, M. A. 1991. *The Creative Mind: Myths and Mechanisms*. New York: Basic Books.

Cohen, P. R. 1995. *Empirical Methods for Artificial Intelligence*. Cambridge: MIT Press.

Fodor, J. A. 1975. *The Language of Thought*. New York: Thomas Y. Crowell.

Henry, O. 1986. Gifts of the magi. In Paul J. Horowitz, ed., *Collected Stories of O. Henry*. New York: Avenel Books.

Hintzman, D. L. 1991. Why are formal models useful in psychology? In William E. Hockley and Stephen Lewandowsky, eds., *Relating Theory and Data: Essays on Human Memory in Honor of Bennet B. Murdock*. Hillsdale, NJ: Lawrence Erlbaum.

Johnson, M. 1987. *The Body in the Mind: Bodily Basis of Meaning, Imagination, and Reason*. Chicago: University of Chicago Press.

Lakoff, G., and M. Johnson. 1980. *Metaphors We Live By*. Chicago: University of Chicago Press.

Ram, A., and E. Jones. 1995. Foundations of *Foundations of Artificial Intelligence*. *Philosophical Psychology* 8: 193–99.

Weizenbaum, J. 1966. ELIZA—A computer program for the study of natural language communication between man and machine. *Communications of the ACM* 9: 36–45.

Whorf, B. L. 1956. Science and linguistics. In J. B. Carroll, ed., *Language, Thought, and Reality*. Cambridge: MIT Press.

Wittgenstein, L. 1968. *Philosophical Investigations*, trans. G. E. M. Anscombe. New York: Macmillan.

Chapter 2
Cognition and Fiction

William J. Rapaport and
Stuart C. Shapiro

2.1 Computational Philosophy of Fiction

This is an essay in *computational philosophy*, the investigation of philosophical issues using computational methods as well as the application of philosophy to problems in computer science. The philosophical issues we will explore include predication and fiction. The computational issues are primarily in artificial intelligence (AI).

"Knowledge" representation is the study of the representation of information in an AI system; since the information need not be true—especially if the information is from fiction—a more accurate name would be "belief" representation (see Rapaport 1992). In a companion piece to this chapter (Shapiro and Rapaport 1995), we looked at how predication is represented in a "knowledge"-representation system when it is used for cognitive modeling and natural-language competence (by which we mean both natural-language understanding and generation; see Shapiro and Rapaport 1991). The present chapter discusses appropriate means of representing fictional items, fictional predication, and propositions from fiction in such a system. We briefly survey four philosophical ontological theories of fiction and sketch an epistemological theory of fiction using a story operator and rules for allowing propositions to "migrate" into and out of story "spaces."

2.2 Fictional Predication

Our colleagues and we have been investigating how a cognitive agent is able to read a narrative and comprehend the indexical information in it: *where* the events described in the narrative are taking place (i.e., where in the "story world"—a semantic domain corresponding to the syntactic narrative text), *when* they take place (in the time line of the story world), *who* the participants in these events are (the characters in the story world), and *from whose point of view* the events and characters are described (see Duchan et al. 1995).

In order to do this, a reader (human or machine) has to be able to (1) read a narrative (in particular, a fictional narrative), (2) construct a mental representation or model of the story and the story world, and (3) use that mental model to understand and to answer questions about the story. To construct the mental model, she will need to contribute something to her understanding of the narrative. One contribution is in the form of the "deictic center"—a data structure that contains the indexical information needed to track the who, when, and where.

Another contribution is background knowledge about the *real* world. For instance, in reading a novel about the Civil War, a reader would presumably bring to her understanding of it some knowledge of the Civil War, such as that Abraham Lincoln was the sixteenth president of the United States and was assassinated in 1865, even if that information is not explicitly stated in the novel. The novel might go on to make other claims about Lincoln, such as that he was tall or that he had a particular conversation with General Grant on a particular day in 1860 (even if, in fact, they never talked on that day—this is a novel, after all). Such a claim would probably not be inconsistent with anything the reader antecedently believed about Lincoln. But some claims in the novel might be inconsistent in this way (e.g., if she read that Lincoln was re-elected to a third term in 1868). So the reader has to be able to represent the information presented in the narrative, keep it suitably segregated from her background knowledge, yet be able to have information from her antecedent real-world beliefs "migrate" into her model of the story world as well as have information from the story world "migrate" back into her store of beliefs about the real world: There must be a semi-"permeable membrane" separating these two subspaces of her mental model (see Yordy 1990–91: 2).

There have been a number of theories in philosophy about the nature of fictional objects. All of these are *ontological* theories concerned with such questions as: What are fictional objects? How are properties predicated of them? How are fictional objects related to nonfictional ones? However, for the purposes of our project, we need to be more concerned with "epistemological" or processing/computational/interpretive issues: How does a reader understand a (fictional) narrative? How does a reader decide whether and to what extent it *is* fictional? How does a reader construct a mental model of the story world? How does a reader represent fictional entities and the properties predicated of them? How do readers integrate their knowledge of the real world with what they read in the narrative? And so on. Some of these are, indeed, ontological issues, but they are what we have elsewhere termed issues in "epistemological ontology" (Rapaport 1985–86): Corresponding to the purely or *metaphysically* ontological question, "What *are* fictional objects?", we ask the *epistemologically* ontological question, "How does a cognitive agent *represent* fictional objects?" And corresponding to the purely ontological question, "How are properties *predicated* of fictional objects?", we ask the epistemologically ontological question, "How does a cognitive agent *represent* the predication of properties of fictional objects?"

In this chapter we examine several philosophical theories of fiction to see what aspects of them are useful for our cognitive/computational project, and we propose a representation scheme that satisfactorily answers most of the kinds of questions raised above (and that incorporates an exciting, if counterintuitive, proposal for the remaining questions). Our scheme is implemented in SNePS, an intensional, propositional, semantic-network "knowledge"-representation and reasoning system that is used for research in AI and in cognitive science. (The uninitiated reader will benefit from reading the companion article, Shapiro and Rapaport 1995.) Specifically, the proposed representation scheme is to embed the propositions of the fictional narrative in a "story operator" that is formally akin to the belief representations we already have in SNePS (Rapaport 1986; Wiebe and Rapaport 1986; Rapaport, Shapiro, and Wiebe 1997). We will show how SNePS's propositional and fully intensional nature, plus the story operator, allow the best aspects of the philosophical theories to be implemented.

2.2.1 Four Ontological Theories of Fiction

Let us begin by briefly surveying four (out of many, many more) philosophical theories of the ontological status of fictional objects. We will not be concerned so much with criticizing them (though we will mention some difficulties they have) as we will with finding what aspects of them might be useful for our, rather different, purposes.

2.2.1.1 Castañeda's Theory Hector-Neri Castañeda's theory of guises and consubstantiation is an all-encompassing theory of the objects of thought as well as of the objects in the world (Castañeda 1972/1974, 1975ab, 1977, 1980, 1989); it includes a theory of fictional objects (Castañeda 1979, 1989). We have discussed the full theory in more detail elsewhere (Rapaport 1978, 1985b), so we will content ourselves with a presentation of his theory of fiction here.

Castañeda takes a uniform viewpoint, with which we agree: All objects in fiction are to be treated alike, whether they are "real" or "fictional" (see Scholes 1968, Rapaport 1985a). They are, in his terminology, "guises," that is to say, roughly, intensional objects of thought. But there are different modes of predication of properties to guises. Thus, if one reads in a narrative about the Civil War that Lincoln died in 1865, this would be analyzed in his theory as a "consubstantiation" (C*) of two guises, the guise c{being Lincoln} (i.e., the intensional object of thought whose sole internal property is *being Lincoln*) and the guise c{being Lincoln, having died in 1865} (i.e., the intensional object of thought whose sole internal properties are *being Lincoln* and *having died in 1865*):

C*(c{being Lincoln}, c{being Lincoln, having died in 1865})

Consubstantiation is an existence-entailing equivalence relation. On the other hand, if one reads another narrative, in which the author has stated that Lincoln was re-elected in 1868, this would be analyzed as a "consociation" (C**) of two guises:

C**(c{being Lincoln}, c{being Lincoln, having being re-elected in 1868})

Consociation is an equivalence relation, not entailing existence, among guises that are "joined together" in a mind. But it is the *same* Lincoln (i.e., c{being Lincoln}) in both cases.

That is a rather drastic oversimplification, but it raises the following concern: How is the reader to decide whether a sentence read in the course of a narrative is to be analyzed by consubstantiation or by consociation? In fact, we would claim, the uniformity with respect to the *objects* should be extended to the mode of predication: All predications in narrative are consociational, even the "true" ones.

Castañeda also admits the existence of "story operators" into his theory but finds them otiose. A story operator is a (usually modal) operator that prefixes all sentences in a narrative: 'In story S, it is the case that φ'. Not all theorists of fiction find them attractive (see Rapaport 1976, 1985a), but as Castañeda points out, one can hardly deny that they exist: One can take the operator to be the title page of the narrative! His claim is that story operators fail to account for the interesting or problematic aspects of fiction.

An example in the context of SNePS might clarify things a bit. Consider the situation illustrated in figure 2.1. Suppose that the reader has a background belief ("world knowledge," as we might say) that

(1) George Washington was the first president.

This would be analyzed as a consubstantiation. Suppose next that the cognitive agent reads in a narrative that

(2) George Washington chopped down a cherry tree.

This would be analyzed as a consociation. The *processing* problem is this: If both sentences were to have occurred in the narrative, they would have to be treated *alike*, using the *same* mode of predication, namely consociation. But this is a reasonable modification of Castañeda's theory, and there are no other problems so far, so all is well.

Background belief:
(1) GW was the first president   (C*)
Narrative claim:
(2) GW chopped down a cherry tree   (C**)

Processing problem:
In narrative, both have to be treated alike;
same mode of predication (C**)

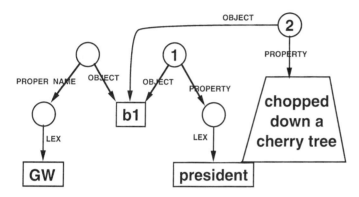

Figure 2.1
A narrative for Castaneda's theory.

2.2.1.2 Lewis's Theory David Lewis's theory of fiction (Lewis 1978) makes essential use of the story operator, and despite earlier misgivings about them (see the references above), we now find that they have a useful role to play. But Lewis's version has some problems. He allows his story operator to be dropped *by way of abbreviation*. Thus we might say

Sherlock Holmes lived at 221B Baker Street,

but what we really mean is, for instance,

In *The Hound of the Baskervilles*, Sherlock Holmes lived at 221B Baker Street,

since, after all, the former is false and the latter is true.

There is an evident advantage to this, for it enables us to distinguish between "facts" about fictional and nonfictional entities: a worthy endeavor, and one that the reader must be able to do. In fact she will do it much the way that Lewis recommends. Consider the following argument:

Lived-at (221B Baker St., Sherlock Holmes)
221B Baker St. = a bank
∴ Lived-at (a bank, Sherlock Holmes)

Although the first premise is true in the story world (but false or truth-valueless in the real world), and the second is factually true (see Rule 1989), the conclusion is false in both the real world and the story world. But *merely* replacing the story operator won't help:

In *The Hound of the Baskervilles*, Lived-at (221B Baker St., Sherlock Holmes)
221B Baker St. = a bank
∴ In *The Hound of the Baskervilles*, Lived-at (a bank, Sherlock Holmes)

fares no better, since 221B Baker St. is *not* a bank in *The Hound of the Baskervilles*. Nor does:

In *The Hound of the Baskervilles*, Lived-at (221B Baker St., Sherlock Holmes)
221B Baker St. = a bank
∴ Lived-at (a bank, Sherlock Holmes)

fare any better, since the conclusion is false with or without the story operator. But a *uniform* application of the story operator works fine:

In *The Hound of the Baskervilles*, Lived-at (221B Baker St., Sherlock Holmes)
In *The Hound of the Baskervilles*, 221B Baker St. = a bank
∴ In *The Hound of the Baskervilles*, Lived-at (a bank, Sherlock Holmes)

and

Lived-at (221B Baker St., Sherlock Holmes)
221B Baker St. = a bank
∴ Lived-at (a bank, Sherlock Holmes)

are both valid, albeit unsound: The former is unsound because the second premise is false; the latter is unsound because the first premise is false.

The difficulty with Lewis's proposal is that

Sherlock Holmes is fictional

is false no matter how you slice it. It's false *with* the story operator restored, since *within the story* Holmes is as real as anyone is. And it's false (or at least truth-valueless) *without* it, since 'Sherlock Holmes' is a nondenoting expression. This difficulty is unacceptable.

2.2.1.3 Parsons's Theory Terence Parsons's theory of fiction (Parsons 1975, 1980) is based on his theory of nonexistent objects. In contrast to Castañeda, whose theory has one kind of property but two modes of predication, Parsons's has two kinds of properties (nuclear and extranuclear) but only one mode of predication. Rather than rehearse his full theory of fiction here (see Rapaport 1985a for a summary and critique), we will focus on a distinction he makes between "native," "immigrant," and "surrogate" fictional objects.

Native fictional objects are, roughly, those who originate in the story in which they are found, such as Sherlock Holmes in *The Hound of the Baskervilles*. Immigrant fictional objects are, roughly, those who have migrated into a story from elsewhere, such as London in *The Hound of the Baskervilles* or Sherlock Holmes in *The Seven-Per-Cent Solution* (Meyer 1974). But, of course, the London of *The Hound of the Baskervilles* has properties that the real London lacks (and vice versa), which raises obvious difficulties. So the London-of-*The-Hound-of-the-Baskervilles* is a surrogate fictional object distinct from the real London.

Such distinctions can be made and are no doubt useful. But there are a number of questions that have to be answered before one can accept them: Which London did Conan Doyle discuss? Which London did Sherlock Holmes and Dr. Watson discuss? When is one discussing London and when the London-of-*The-Hound-of-the-Baskervilles*? In general, how does the reader distinguish properties of the "real" London from properties of the London-of-*The-Hound-of-the-Baskervilles*? These are questions that can be dealt with, we believe, in the SNePS proposal to be introduced below.

2.2.1.4 Van Inwagen's Theory The final theory of fictional objects in our brief survey is one that we find quite congenial in many respects, though it, too, falls short. Peter van Inwagen's theory (Van Inwagen 1977), like Castañeda's, distinguishes between two modes of predication, and like Lewis's, it uses something like a story operator.

Van Inwagen's two modes of predication are "predication" and "ascription." 'Sherlock Holmes is fictional' expresses a property *predicated of* an existing theoretical entity of literary criticism, namely Sherlock Holmes. (Other kinds of theoretical entities of literary criticism include novels, short stories, etc.) In contrast, 'Sherlock Holmes is a detective' expresses (perhaps elliptically) a property *ascribed to* the same theoretical entity of literary criticism *in* a work of fiction:

A(detective, Sherlock Holmes, *The Hound of the Baskervilles*).

Note that the story is not strictly speaking a logical operator, but an essential argument place in a three-place predication relation.

There are two problems with this otherwise quite nice theory. They are, we believe, not serious problems and could be easily gotten around. First, in "Sherlock Holmes

Confronts Modern Logic" (Hintikka and Hintikka 1983), the authors call Holmes a "great detective" (p. 155). According to van Inwagen's theory, contrary to what one might expect, it is *not* the case that

A (great detective, Sherlock Holmes, "Sherlock Holmes Confronts Modern Logic").

Why? Because "Sherlock Holmes Confronts Modern Logic" is not literature and hence not a theoretical entity of literary criticism. This strikes us as an unnecessary aspect of van Inwagen's theory.

Second, assume that in *War and Peace* it is stated that Napoleon is vain.[1] But, according to van Inwagen's theory and again contrary to what one might expect, it is *not* the case that

A(vain, Napoleon, *War and Peace*),

because Napoleon is not a theoretical entity of literary criticism! Again, this strikes us as unnecessary.

2.2.2 A SNePS Approach to Fiction

In order for our computational cognitive agent (we call her 'Cassie') to read a narrative, the representations she should construct will include a story operator (as in Lewis's or van Inwagen's theory), only one mode of predication (as in Parsons's theory), and only one kind of property (as in Castañeda's theory). Since, at the time of writing, this theory is only beginning to be implemented, there is a strong possibility that this will prove insufficient: The one addition that we can foresee (urged in earlier writings, e.g., Rapaport 1976, 1985a, and suggested in conversation by Johan Lammens) is the need to distinguish between real-world entities and their surrogates, but it must be kept in mind that all entities represented in the mind of our reader are just that—entities in her mind—*not* entities some of which are real and some of which are fictional.

The story operator will set up a "story space" that is formally equivalent to a belief space (see Rapaport 1986; Wiebe and Rapaport 1986; Shapiro and Rapaport 1991, 1995; Rapaport, Shapiro, and Wiebe 1997). It will allow the reader to distinguish her own beliefs about London from (her beliefs about) claims made about London in a story in precisely the same way that belief spaces allow our computational cognitive agent to distinguish her own beliefs about John from her beliefs about Mary's beliefs about John (as in Shapiro and Rapaport 1995, fig. 2b; see Rapaport 1986; Shapiro and Rapaport 1987; Rapaport, Shapiro, and Wiebe 1997).

But how should this be handled? Consider figure 2.2. Suppose that one of Cassie's background beliefs is that Lincoln died in 1865 and that she reads in a narrative that Lincoln was re-elected in 1868. There is a processing problem: Cassie, our computa-

Background belief:
(1) Lincoln died in 1865.
Narrative claim:
(2) Lincoln was re-elected in 1868.

Processing problem: inconsistency

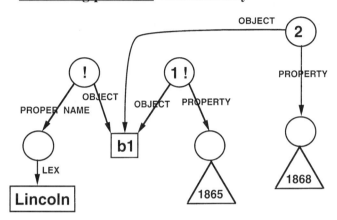

Figure 2.2
A processing problem for Cassie.

tional cognitive agent, is faced with an inconsistency. There are two solutions. First, the SNePS Belief Revision system (SNeBR; Martins and Shapiro 1988)—a facility for detecting and removing inconsistent beliefs—can be invoked. The detection of the inconsistency will cause a split to be made into two (consistent) contexts. But note that the net effect of this is to embed the second statement (the re-election in 1868) in a story operator. So we could start with a story operator in the first place. This is the second solution, as shown in figure 2.3. (Implementations of the first solution are given in Rapaport 1991 and Rapaport and Shapiro 1995.)

But now let's complicate the data a bit. Consider figure 2.4. Suppose that Cassie's background beliefs include both that Lincoln was the sixteenth president and that Lincoln died in 1865, and suppose once again that she reads in a narrative that Lincoln was re-elected in 1868. The processing "problem" here (it is not really a problem) is that we want the first of the reader's two background beliefs to "migrate into" the story world. The reason that this is not a problem is that those first two background beliefs are *the reader's* beliefs and the third is not. The first one (that Lincoln was sixteenth president) is both believed by the reader *and* is in the story world.

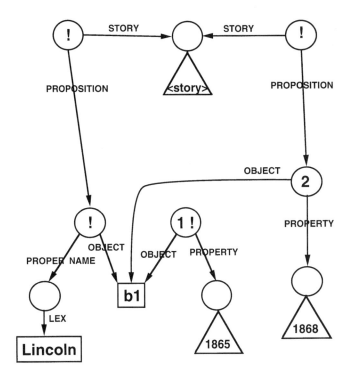

Figure 2.3
A solution using a story operator.

Consider figure 2.1 again. If Cassie knows that she is reading a narrative, we want it to be the case that she believes (1) (that Washington was the first president), and we want both (1) and (2) (that he chopped down the cherry tree) to be in the story world. How do we accomplish this? Under the first solution, *all propositions from the narrative will be placed in a story context.* Under the second solution, we *start* with a story operator on (2). In general, we will put a story operator on *all* narrative predications.

But then we face two problems: Background beliefs of the reader are normally brought to bear on understanding the story, as we saw in figure 2.2. And we often come to learn (or, at least, come to have beliefs) about the real world from reading fictional narratives. Thus we need to have two rules, which we will put roughly, but boldly, as follows:

(R1) Propositions *outside* the story space established by the story context or the story operator (i.e., antecedently believed by the reader) are assumed, *when necessary*, to hold *within* that story space *by default* but *defeasibly*.

Background beliefs:
(1) Lincoln was the 16th president.
(2) Lincoln died in 1865.
Narrative claim:
(3) Lincoln was re-elected in 1868.

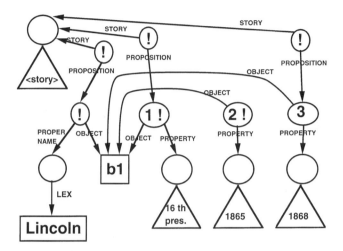

Figure 2.4
A more complex narrative.

(R2) Propositions *inside* the story space are assumed, *when necessary*, to hold *outside* that story space *by default* but *defeasibly*.

Some comments: The "when necessary" clause is there to prevent an explosion in the size of belief and story spaces. The migrations permitted by these two rules would only take place on an as-needed basis for understanding the story or for understanding the world around us. The "by default" clause is there for obvious reasons: We wouldn't want to have Lincoln's dying in 1865 migrate into a narrative in which he is re-elected in 1868. The "defeasibly" clause is there to undo any damage that might be done at a later point in the narrative if such a migration had taken place, innocently, at an earlier point. Rule (R1) (or such refinements of it as will, no doubt, be necessary as implementation of the theory proceeds) aids in our understanding of the story. Rule (R2) (or such refinements of it as will also, no doubt, be necessary as implementation of the theory proceeds) allows us to enlarge our views of the world from reading literature, while also allowing us to segregate our real-world beliefs from our story-world beliefs. In this manner we can facilitate the membrane whose

**1. Sherlock Holmes is fictional.
2. Sherlock Holmes is a detective.**

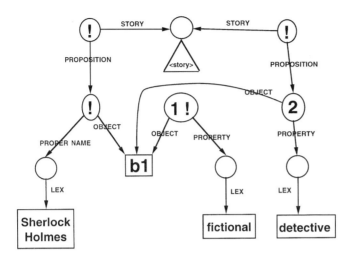

Figure 2.5
Handling the problem with Lewis's theory.

semi-permeability allows us to understand narratives using our world knowledge, and to *learn* from narratives—indeed, *to understand the real world in terms of narratives* (see Bruner 1990).

We will close with three final remarks. First, to see how the story operator solves the problem with Lewis's theory, look at figure 2.5. (How it solves the problems with van Inwagen's are left as exercises for the reader.) Second, in figures 2.1 to 2.5, we have used the linguist's triangle to hide irrelevant details; however, figure 2.6 shows how the story operator looks in detail. Finally two demo runs of preliminary implementations using SNeBR are presented in Rapaport (1991) and in a longer version of this paper (Rapaport and Shapiro 1995: 118–27).

2.3 Conclusion

This brings to an end our essay in computational philosophy. We have explored knowledge-representation and reasoning issues surrounding fictional entities and their fictional (and nonfictional) properties, as well as their "interaction" with non-fictional entities. We have shown how a reader (human or machine) could read a

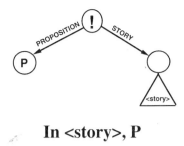

In <story>, P

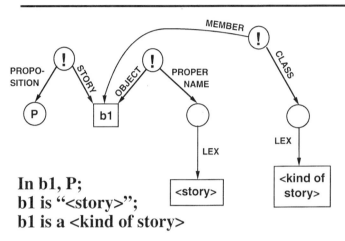

In b1, P;
b1 is "<story>";
b1 is a <kind of story>

Figure 2.6
Details of the story operator.

narrative and construct and reason about her mental model of the story expressed by the narrative, and how information can selectively flow between general "real-world" knowledge and story-world knowledge.

Notes

The work presented here was done in collaboration with the members of the SNePS Research Group and the Center for Cognitive Science at State University of New York at Buffalo. We are grateful for their contributions and comments, especially those of Jürgen Haas, Susan Haller, Johan Lammens, Sandra L. Peters, and Janyce M. Wiebe. This research was supported in part by the National Science Foundation under grant IRI-8610517. Versions of this chapter were presented by Rapaport at the 1989 Conference on Problems and Changes in the Concept of Predication (University of California Humanities Research Institute, University of California at Irvine) and the First Annual SNePS Workshop (SUNY Buffalo; Kumar 1990). Previous versions of this chapter appeared in Rapaport (1990) and as part of Rapaport (1991). The present version is a slightly edited abridgment of Rapaport and Shapiro (1995).

1. It may in fact be so stated; one of the coauthors confesses to not (yet) having read it; the other has read it but does not recall whether it is so stated. It might suffice for van Inwagen's example that it follow (logically) from what is stated in *War and Peace* that Napoleon is vain; no matter.

References

Bruner, J. 1990. *Acts of Meaning*. Cambridge: Harvard University Press.

Castañeda, H.-N. 1972. Thinking and the structure of the world. *Philosophia* 4 (1974): 3–40; reprinted in 1975 in *Critica* 6 (1972): 43–86.

Castañeda, H.-N. 1975a. Identity and sameness. *Philosophia* 5: 121–50.

Castañeda, H.-N. 1975b. *Thinking and Doing: The Philosophical Foundations of Institutions*. Dordrecht: D. Reidel.

Castañeda, H.-N. 1977. Perception, belief, and the structure of physical objects and consciousness. *Synthese* 35: 285–351.

Castañeda, H.-N. 1979. Fiction and reality: Their fundamental connections; an essay on the ontology of total experience. *Poetics* 8: 31–62.

Castañeda, H.-N. 1980. Reference, reality, and perceptual fields. *Proceedings and Addresses of the American Philosophical Association* 53: 763–823.

Castañeda, H.-N. 1989. *Thinking, Language, and Experience*. Minneapolis: University of Minnesota Press.

Duchan, J. F., G. A. Bruder, and L. E. Hewitt, eds. 1995. *Deixis in Narrative: A Cognitive Science Perspective*. Hillsdale, NJ: Lawrence Erlbaum.

Hintikka, J., and M. B. Hintikka, 1983. Sherlock Holmes confronts modern logic. In U. Eco and T. A. Sebeok, eds., *The Sign of Three*. Bloomington: Indiana University Press, pp. 154–69.

Kumar, D., ed. 1990. *Current Trends in SNePS—Semantic Network Processing System*. Lecture Notes in Artificial Intelligence, no. 437. Berlin: Springer-Verlag.

Lewis, D. 1978. Truth in fiction. *American Philosophical Quarterly* 15: 37–46.

Martins, J., and S. C. Shapiro. 1988. A model for belief revision. *Artificial Intelligence* 35: 25–79.

Meyer, N. 1974. *The Seven-per-Cent Solution: Being a Reprint from the Reminiscences of John H. Watson, M.D., as edited by Nicholas Meyer*. New York: Dutton.

Parsons, T. 1975. A Meinongian analysis of fictional objects. *Grazer Philosophische Studien* 1: 73–86.

Parsons, T. 1980. *Nonexistent Objects*. New Haven: Yale University Press.

Rapaport, W. J. 1976. *Intentionality and the Structure of Existence*. PhD dissertation. Bloomington: Indiana University Department of Philosophy.

Rapaport, W. J. 1978. Meinongian theories and a Russellian paradox. *Noûs* 12: 153–80; errata, *Noûs* 13 (1979): 125.

Rapaport, W. J. 1985a. To be and not to be. *Noûs* 19: 255–71.

Rapaport, W. J. 1985b. Meinongian semantics for propositional semantic networks. *Proceedings of the 23rd Annual Meeting of the Association for Computational Linguistics* (*University of Chicago*). Morristown, NJ: Association for Computational Linguistics, pp. 43–48.

Rapaport, W. J. 1985–86. Non-existent objects and epistemological ontology. *Grazer Philosophische Studien* 25/26: 61–95; reprinted in Rudolf Haller, ed., *Non-existence and Predication*. Amsterdam: Rodopi, 1986.

Rapaport, W. J. 1986. Logical foundations for belief representation. *Cognitive Science* 10: 371–422.

Rapaport, W. J. 1990. Representing fiction in SNePS. In D. Kumar, ed., *Current Trends in SNePS—Semantic Network Processing System*. Lecture Notes in Artificial Intelligence, no. 437. Berlin: Springer-Verlag, pp. 107–21.

Rapaport, W. J. 1991. Predication, fiction, and artificial intelligence. *Topoi* 10: 79–111.

Rapaport, W. J. 1992. Belief representation systems. In S. C. Shapiro, ed., *Encyclopedia of Artificial Intelligence*, 2d ed. New York: Wiley, pp. 98–110.

Rapaport, W. J., and S. C. Shapiro. 1995. Cognition and fiction. In J. Felson Duchan, G. A. Bruder, and L. E. Hewitt, eds., *Deixis in Narrative: A Cognitive Science Perspective*. Hillsdale, NJ: Lawrence Erlbaum, pp. 107–28.

Rapaport, W. J., S. C. Shapiro, and J. M. Wiebe. 1997. Quasi-indexicals and knowledge reports. *Cognitive Science* 21: 63–107.

Rule, S. 1989. Sherlock Holmes's mail: Not too mysterious. *The New York Times* (5 November): 20.

Scholes, R. 1968. *Elements of Fiction*. New York: Oxford University Press.

Shapiro, S. C., and W. J. Rapaport, 1987. SNePS considered as a fully intensional propositional semantic network. In N. Cercone and G. McCalla, eds., *The Knowledge Frontier: Essays in the Representation of Knowledge*. New York: Springer-Verlag, pp. 262–315; shorter version appeared in *Proceedings of the 5th National Conference on Artificial Intelligence (AAAI-86, Philadelphia)*. Los Altos, CA: Morgan Kaufmann, 1986, 278–83; revised short version appeared as "A fully intensional propositional semantic network," in Leslie Burkholder, ed., *Philosophy and the Computer*. Boulder, CO: Westview Press, pp. 75–91.

Shapiro, S. C., and W. J. Rapaport. 1991. Models and minds: Knowledge representation for natural-language competence. In R. Cummins and J. Pollock eds., *Philosophy and AI: Essays at the Interface*. Cambridge: MIT Press, pp. 215–59.

Shapiro, S. C., and W. J. Rapaport, 1995. An introduction to a computational reader of narratives. In J. F. Duchan, G. A. Bruder, and L. E. Hewitt, eds., *Deixis in Narrative: A Cognitive Science Perspective*. Hillsdale, NJ: Lawrence Erlbaum, pp. 79–105.

Van Inwagen, P. 1977. Creatures of fiction. *American Philosophical Quarterly* 14: 299–308.

Wiebe, J. M., and W. J. Rapaport, 1986. Representing *de re* and *de dicto* belief reports in discourse and narrative. *Proceedings of the IEEE* 74: 1405–13.

Yordy, J. 1990–91. Teaching Hal to read: Algorithmic approaches. *Scientiae: Magazine of the [SUNY Buffalo] Faculty of Natural Sciences and Mathematics* 4.2 (Winter): 2–3.

Chapter 3

Sentence Processing in Understanding: Interaction and Integration of Knowledge Sources

Kavi Mahesh, Kurt P. Eiselt, and Jennifer K. Holbrook

3.1 Why Sentence Processing

The primary input to an understanding system is a natural language text. Natural language is a system of interconnecting and overlapping levels of structure and meaning. The ordering of words and structuring of phrases provide important clues to the meaning and purpose of the text, over and above the meanings of the words themselves. As a result an understanding system must process the words and phrases and their order and structuring in order to attempt a higher-level understanding of the text. Yet many extant models of higher-level text understanding do not process natural language texts directly; rather, they work with a so-called internal representation of text which they try to understand at a higher level. We offer another view: that processing the base unit of text, the individual sentence, provides the basis for the richest possible understanding of an input text. In this chapter we focus on the problem of understanding individual sentences and present a contemporary design for a sentence processor that provides the necessary grounding for an understanding system to work from input texts.

Language researchers in a variety of disciplines have long agreed that the fundamental meaning unit of spoken and written language is the sentence. While the individual word is the smallest unit of language that conveys meaning, the structure of a sentence provides far more precise meaning than a set of unconnected words can provide. Of course sentences themselves are embedded within the larger structure of the text, and natural language understanding also requires additional knowledge of intersentential interactions, such as reference and ellipsis, as well as knowledge of discourse structures. Therefore the task of text processing has many levels, which must be taken into account to successfully understand an input text.

Moreover these multiple levels of language understanding are highly interrelated. For example, the problems of sentence understanding, such as word sense ambiguity or various forms of underspecification, often cannot be resolved by a stand-alone sentence processor. The solutions require feedback from such higher-level processing of the text as discourse structure and pragmatics. A computational model of understanding that uses a stand-alone sentence processor will have both a weaker sentence processor and a poorer level of overall understanding. As such, it is particularly important for computational modeling of understanding to include the design of a sentence processor that can interact with higher-level processing at the appropriate points in processing to improve the performance of higher-level understanding.

Although most computational modeling of language understanding is carried out in English, multilingual aspects of understanding further highlight the role of a sentence processor. Presumably models of higher-level text understanding transfer well to other natural languages. It is the sentence processor that must deal with language-specific idiosyncrasies to enable higher-level understanding and, eventually, to facilitate language translation.

While our primary focus in this chapter is on computational models of sentence understanding, this model is firmly based in a contemporary psycholinguistic account of human text comprehension, particularly sentence processing, lexical and syntactic disambiguation. We take this approach because it is the human cognitive structure within which natural language developed, and it is through this structure that the text which a computational model is developed to understand is produced. The human cognitive structure has regularities and limitations that shape how natural language can be produced and comprehended. Therefore we also raise issues concerned with the psycholinguistics of sentence understanding throughout the chapter. From a psycholinguistic point of view, there is ample evidence that the human understanding system pays attention to sentence structure and extracts clues from it. Evidence for phenomena such as garden-path sentences illustrate the need for a sentence processing theory in a complete cognitive model of reading and understanding.

3.2 Introduction to Sentence Understanding

The majority of unresolved issues in accounts of both human and machine sentence understanding are concerned with the questions of when each of the various types of knowledge, such as syntactic and semantic knowledge, should be applied in processing a sentence and how the different types of knowledge should be integrated to select the most appropriate interpretation(s) of a sentence in its context. From a computational point of view, it is important to find good answers to these two questions because natural language processors need to be able to apply the right types of knowledge at the right times to reduce local ambiguity and produce unique interpretations without demanding unreasonable amounts of complete and specific knowledge of the domain or context. These issues are equally important from the point of view of psychological modeling of human sentence processing. How should the model apply each type of knowledge and how and when should it make decisions using the knowledge in order to explain the variety of human behaviors in sentence processing that are documented in psycholinguistic literature?

In psycholinguistics two theories of human sentence processing predict very different kinds of cognitive structure and on-line processing behavior. One theory is that language processing is done by multiple, independent *modules*, each acting on a different level of language understanding (e.g., looking up word meanings occurs separately from deciding on the boundaries of a verb phrase). There is experimental evidence the sentence processor shows modular behaviors in some situations where only some types of knowledge seem to have been applied to make decisions, delaying the application of other types of knowledge. A second theory is that language processing is more integrated, or *interactive*. There is experimental evidence that in some processing tasks, the sentence processor seems to have made decisions by immediately integrating different types of knowledge. These two views have produced a whole body of psychological experiments supporting each view and computational models explaining each set of behaviors continuing the *modularity debate* for many years (Crain and Steedman 1985; Fodor 1987; Frazier 1987; Marslen-Wilson and Tyler 1987; Tanenhaus, Dell, and Carlson 1987).

A number of models of sentence understanding, both psychological (cognitive) models and computational models, have been proposed to address the above questions. In general, models of sentence processing have either accounted primarily for the application of one type of knowledge to resolve certain types of ambiguities or, from a cognitive point of view, have only explained certain kinds of behaviors observed in human sentence processing. For example, there are many modularity-based models that only deal with the use of syntactic knowledge to resolve syntactic ambiguities, as well as models that only account for immediate interactions between syntax and semantics in human sentence processing, ignoring modular effects entirely.

Our answers to the above questions are derived from both psycholinguistic results from a variety of studies and computational considerations of sentence processing architectures. Essentially we present a computational model of sentence understanding called COMPERE[1] (Mahesh 1995) that is a true implementation of the *integrated processing hypothesis*. This model not only minimizes the amount of local ambiguity encountered in processing a sentence by applying syntactic and semantic knowledge at the right times, it also attempts to explain seemingly contradictory human behavior in sentence understanding by showing how arbitration between syntax and semantics accounts for both modular and interactive behaviors.

3.2.1 Issues in Sentence Understanding

In this chapter we ask the following specific questions regarding the use of knowledge to derive unique interpretations of sentences:

1. How are the different types of knowledge integrated in sentence processing?[2] How are conflicts, if any, among them resolved?
2. When are decisions made to resolve an ambiguity by selecting from the set of possible interpretations? When should the sentence processor attempt to make a decision in order to minimize local ambiguity and working memory requirements?
3. What happens when previously made decisions lead to an error? How does the sentence processor recover from different types of errors?

We know that a sentence processor must use its syntactic, semantic, lexical, conceptual, and other knowledge in order to resolve ambiguities in sentences. How are these different types of knowledge represented and applied in sentence processing? For example, are they integrated a priori in various combinations, or are they represented and applied separately but integrated dynamically during sentence interpretation? What happens when different types of knowledge are in conflict with each other when it comes to determining a unique interpretation for a sentence?

In sentence processing the time (or location in the sentence) at which the processor attempts to resolve an ambiguity makes considerable differences in the amount of local ambiguity that the processor must struggle with. For example, if the processor does not resolve an ambiguity even after it has the information necessary to resolve the ambiguity, it will be dealing with more ambiguity than it would have had it resolved the ambiguity using the available information. On the other hand, if the processor attempts to make a decision even before it has the right knowledge that enables it do so, it suffers from one of two problems. It either increases the amount of ambiguity by considering each of the alternatives at that ambiguity and, being unable to select one, adds the ambiguity to the current interpretation, or makes a decision that is not justified by any piece of knowledge and runs into possible errors at later times. If the processor attempts to resolve an ambiguity exactly at the point when the necessary information becomes available, it neither carries along ambiguities longer than necessary nor adds to the ambiguity by considering alternative possibilities that it has no information to choose from.

Despite applying a variety of types of knowledge and despite applying them at the right time, the sentence processor is bound to run into errors. This is because the information necessary to resolve an ambiguity convincingly may become available only much later in processing a sentence. The processor is forced to make the best decision given the knowledge that is currently available to it, either for lack of resources or because of the need to make early commitments and produce incremental interpretations in order to avoid combinatorial multiplications of ambiguities. What happens when an error is detected? How does the sentence processor recover from the error and change the interpretation by switching to another interpretation or repairing the current interpretation?

In the rest of this chapter, we begin with a functional analysis of the task of sentence understanding as a distinct (but not entirely independent) subtask of reading. We then turn to an analysis of different possibilities in syntax-semantics interactions and different architectures for sentence understanding and introduce the need for an arbitration mechanism in implementing integrated processing. The next two sections present the basic processes of syntactic and core semantic analyses. The following section describes COMPERE as a true implementation of integrated processing, before concluding the chapter with a brief discussion of how a sentence understander may be situated in an overall model of understanding.

3.3 Sentence Understanding: The Task

From a functional point of view, sentence understanding is an information processing task that efficiently converts an input sentence to an internal representation of the structure and meaning of the sentence. Such an analysis of the sentence understanding task can be used to show, independently of any psychological evidence about human sentence processing, the need for incremental interpretation and communication between syntactic and semantic processes during sentence understanding.

3.3.1 The Input

The input to a sentence understander is a sentence (complete or not, grammatical or otherwise) in a natural language. Though sentences can be of different types such as interrogative or exclamatory, we only consider declarative sentences in this chapter. We do not pay attention to punctuation either. The input is thus a sentence that can be characterized as a linear sequence of words in a natural language. The sentence may contain a rich structure such as relative and embedded clauses and prepositional adjuncts as well as a rich meaning, perhaps with many types of ambiguities in word and sentence meanings.

3.3.2 The Output

The output of the sentence understanding task is much less well defined than the input. In the absence of a situation, a specific task for which natural language processing is being carried out, the output of sentence understanding can only be said to have those kinds of information that are deemed useful in a large variety of tasks. Exactly what these kinds of information are depends on the theory of meaning or semantics employed. A minimalist approach specifies the components of the output of sentence understanding that would have the essential elements of the outputs demanded by most situating tasks. Our analysis of the sentence understanding task attempts to ensure that enhancing the output of the task does not negate the commitments made by our model of sentence understanding. As we will see later in our discussion of semantics, we simply adopt an event-oriented semantics and define the output of sentence understanding to be a set of events, objects, their properties, and the thematic role relationships between the events and the objects. This semantics leaves out other components of meaning such as temporal and spatial relationships, aspect, and modality (e.g., Frawley 1992) for possible extensions if necessary.

For example, consider the input sentence

(1) The bugs moved into the lounge.

The output of sentence understanding for this input may be

- the syntactic structure of the sentence showing that "the bugs" was the subject noun phrase for the main verb "move" (in past tense) to which is attached the prepositional phrase "into the lounge" where the noun phrase "the lounge" is headed by the preposition "into"; and
- the core semantics of the sentence that says that INSECTS were the Agent of a MOVE event and the LOUNGE was the Location (or Destination, to be more specific) of the event.

3.3.3 Problems in Sentence Understanding

Why is sentence understanding hard given that it is simply a task of mapping an input sentence to an output representation of its meaning? The reason is, it is a many-to-many mapping. The mapping is neither unique nor unambiguous. Moreover parts of what needs to be in the output are completely left out from the input information. Not everything that is in the input is relevant to the output either. These features of natural language lead to its classical problems of ambiguity, incompleteness (e.g., reference, ellipsis), and vagueness (or indirectness). Successful mapping can only be achieved by using a variety of knowledge, whose application and interactions can be fairly complex.

Among the problems listed above, incompleteness and indirectness tend to fall outside the scope of basic sentence understanding, since they generally involve discourse analysis. In this chapter we focus on the problem of ambiguity for the most part.

Ambiguity is the problem of one input mapping to more than one output. For example, a word might map to more than one meaning, or there may be more than one way of composing a sequence of words to form a whole meaning. Ambiguities can be resolved by applying many types of knowledge. Knowledge helps to reduce the ambiguity by eliminating one or more of the possible mappings for a given input. However, there is no single type of knowledge that always resolves a particular type of ambiguity. For instance, knowledge of the grammar of the language does help in reducing ambiguities in word meanings but cannot always do so by itself. Other types of knowledge such as the semantic context may be necessary at other times to resolve the same kind of ambiguity in word meanings. It is this problem of the need for different types of knowledge at different times and situations that makes the problem of sentence processing a hard one. Ambiguity resolution in light of the functional or cognitive constraints on sentence understanding requires complex interactions between the different types of knowledge available to the sentence understander.

There are many types of ambiguities, including syntactic and semantic ambiguities, lexical and structural ambiguities, and local and global ambiguities. In this chapter we use the following types of ambiguities to illustrate central issues in sentence understanding:

- *Lexical semantic or word sense ambiguity* occurs when a word has more than one meaning (or sense) for the same syntactic category (or part of speech). For example, "bug" can mean either INSECT or a secretly installed MICROPHONE.
- *Structural syntactic or attachment ambiguity* occurs when two or more syntactic units (e.g., words or phrases) can be composed syntactically in more than one way according to the grammar of the natural language. For example, in sentence (1) above, given only the first three words, "the bugs moved...," the noun phrase (NP) "the bugs" and the verb phrase (VP) "moved" can be composed either in a simple subject-object construct or in a more complex structure where "moved" (short for "which were moved") starts a reduced-relative clause attached to the NP.

Either of the above ambiguities may be local in a sentence meaning information present in the later parts of the sentence eliminate the ambiguity or global with respect to the sentence. It must also be noted here that syntactic ambiguities often require semantic or conceptual knowledge to resolve, and vice versa.

3.3.4 Knowledge Sources Used in Sentence Understanding

Several kinds of knowledge, both language-specific and extra-linguistic, are necessary to map the input sentence to the output representation of its meaning, resolving any ambiguities in the mapping. A natural language is a set of conventions for communicating meaning between the generator and the comprehender. Types of linguistic knowledge are merely distinct types of regularities that one can observe in a natural language. A sentence in a natural language can be looked at as a structured collection of cues to the meaning intended to be communicated. The regularities in the cues and how the cues map to meanings differ from language to language. As such, the discussion of knowledge sources here is somewhat specific to English and its close relatives.

The following types of knowledge are often useful in basic sentence understanding:

- *Word meanings.* Meanings of open class or content words (e.g., nouns, verbs, and adjectives) and closed class or function words (e.g., prepositions and conjunctions) in a natural language.
- *Word category information.* The parts of speech that can be assigned to a particular word.
- *Syntactic structure or grammar.* Knowledge of the ways in which words can be structured to form sentences that are grammatical in the language.
- *Semantic knowledge.* Knowledge of how individual word meanings can be composed to construct larger units of meaning. The ways in which word meanings can be composed semantically do not always correspond to the ways in which the words themselves can be composed syntactically.
- *Conceptual knowledge.* Knowledge of the relationships (both taxonomic and otherwise) among different meanings (or concepts) in the world, independent of the natural language under consideration.

Lexical and Nonlexical Knowledge One can look at a completely orthogonal partitioning of linguistic (and other) knowledge and divide all knowledge used in natural language understanding into lexical and nonlexical knowledge. Lexical knowledge is the knowledge that is specific to a particular word—knowledge that is found in the lexical entry of the word.[3] This word-specific lexical knowledge can be any type of knowledge and typically includes syntactic category information, meaning(s) of the word(s), subcategory information, subcategorization information, thematic grids (Carlson and Tanenhaus 1988), and so on. Nonlexical knowledge is knowledge, mostly syntactic and semantic, that is not specific to a particular word and hence is not tied to any lexical entry. For instance, knowledge of a grammar, or how a thematic role combines with others, typically falls under such general knowledge. Conceptual world knowledge is also mostly nonlexical.

3.3.5 Example
To illustrate the task of sentence understanding, consider the sentence

(2) The bugs moved into the lounge were found quickly.

Given this input, the task of understanding this sentence is to choose the appropriate meanings of the words "bugs," "moved," "lounge," "found," and "quickly" and compose those meanings to form a meaning for the entire sentence. Consider the task of word meaning selection for the word "bugs." Lexical entry retrieval for the word "bugs" tells us that the word has two possible syntactic categories: noun and verb. In order to perform a word category selection, we need to determine the syntactic structure of the sentence at least up to that word. Syntactic analysis tells us that after seeing the determiner "The," we are expecting a noun to follow, not a verb. Using this syntactic context, we can select the noun category for "bugs." Word sense disambiguation is now the task of choosing between the two possible meanings of the noun form of "bugs": INSECT bugs and electronic MICROPHONES (see table 3.1). Though the INSECT meaning may be more common than the MICROPHONE meaning in many contexts, such frequency information does not always correctly resolve the word sense ambiguity. At this point in sentence understanding, we do not have the semantic information to perform word sense disambiguation. Our best bet is to postpone that task and move ahead in reading the sentence. That is, we carry along both meanings of the noun "bugs" as we read the next word(s).

After analyzing the next word "moved," we try to compose the meanings of the words "bugs" and "moved." Syntactically there are two ways of composing these two parts of the sentence (in a direct attachment or through a reduced-relative clause, as noted earlier). Semantically either meaning of "bugs" is compatible with the relative clause attachment, the corresponding semantic composition being that of a theme role for the meanings of "bugs" in the MOVE event. However, only the INSECT meaning of "bugs" is compatible with the direct attachment, since only INSECT "bugs" are in the class of animate objects that can move themselves (i.e., be agents of MOVE events, as per a piece of conceptual knowledge). This ambiguity is resolved at this point in favor of the direct attachment, since there is a syntactic preference for the attachment that completes the sentence structure by filling the expectation for a verb phrase. As a result of this choice, the MICROPHONE meaning of "bugs" is deactivated, since it is incompatible with the composition selected by syntactic analysis.

The analysis proceeds further to produce the composite meaning of the first part of the sentence "The bugs moved into the lounge." However, at this point, there is no grammatical way of composing the meaning of the next word "were" within the existing sentence structure. Assuming that the sentence is syntactically correct (i.e., grammatical), we can hypothesize that an erroneous decision has been made. Going back and looking at previous decisions, we find that we decided to compose "bugs" and "moved" by making "moved" the main verb. We can identify that this is the error by noting that we do not currently have a way of attaching the new verb phrase containing "were" and the decision to make "moved" the main verb was another attachment of a verb phrase (with the verb "moved"). Perhaps if we made a different decision at that earlier, related choice, there would be room left in the syntactic structures to compose the meaning of the phrase starting with "were." We do this by *repairing* the previous syntactic structures. We attach "moved" (and the meaning of "into the lounge" which has already been composed with the meaning of "moved") as a reduced relative clause to "bugs" and thereby *recover from the error*. We now have room for composing the meaning of "were found" with the earlier meanings.

In this process of error recovery, while removing the previous attachment of "moved" with "bugs," we reconsider our associated decision of deactivating the MICROPHONE meaning of "bugs." Since there is no longer a reason to rule out the MICROPHONE meaning as either type of "bugs" can be the themes of being MOVED by someone else, we now bring back the deactivated meaning of "bugs." Thus we reintroduce the ambiguity in the meaning of "bugs" and undo the word sense disambiguation performed earlier.[4] This example not only shows the need for the *error recovery* subtask, it also shows some of the complexities in the interactions between these tasks. Much of this would not be necessary, but for the functionally (and cognitively) motivated constraint of incremental interpretation (see below). Table 3.1 shows the intermediate results of processing this example after every word.

3.3.6 Functional Constraints on Sentence Understanding

Based on purely functional considerations, we can list several constraints on when knowledge is applied and decisions made in a model of sentence understanding.

Table 3.1
Semantics after each word of sentence 2

Part	After word	Semantics
a	"The"	
b	"bugs"	INSECT, MICROPHONE
c	"moved"	INSECT: Agent of MOVE: Event
d	"into"	Same as above
e	"the"	Same as above
f	"lounge"	Same as above and LOUNGE: Location of MOVE: Event
g	"were"	INSECT, MICROPHONE: Theme of MOVE: Event LOUNGE: Location of MOVE: Event
h	"found"	INSECT, MICROPHONE: Theme of MOVE: Event; LOUNGE: Location of MOVE: Event
i	"quickly"	INSECT, MICROPHONE: Theme of FIND: Event; Same as above

Sentence Processing in Understanding 37

3.3.6.1 Eager Selection *The sentence processor strives to select a unique interpretation whenever the information necessary to do so is available to it.* The sentence processor does not simply produce all possible interpretations and let an external agent select the best. Selection (or ambiguity resolution) is a part of the job of language understanding. Many connectionist models of language comprehension (e.g., McClelland and Kawamoto 1986) as well as parsing algorithms such as Earley's (1970) algorithm (which is considered an efficient combination of bottom-up and top-down parsing) violate this principle. They simply present a set of possible interpretations and let an external agent pick a suitable interpretation.

The principle of eager selection (sometimes also called *early commitment*) is close to the *first analysis* principle of Frazier (1987) which states that the language processor always selects one interpretation in the first analysis based on syntactic criteria alone. However, the eager selection principle is less stringent; it does not require that the processor pursue and present exactly one interpretation at all times even when the information to select from among them is not available.

3.3.6.2 Incremental Interpretation *The language processor produces incremental interpretations.* There are both computational and cognitive motivations for proposing a sentence processing architecture in which syntactic and semantic processing communicate with each other incrementally during sentence comprehension. From a functional point of view, the mapping from the input sentence to its syntactic structure or to its semantic representation is underconstrained and highly ambiguous. The subtask of semantic (or word meaning) composition in the absence of syntactic guidance is largely combinatorial. Similarly the assignment of unique syntactic structure is often impossible without semantic feedback that helps constrain the possible structures. Because of the problem of ambiguity and the consequent combinatorial explosion of the number of possible interpretations of a sentence, syntactic and semantic analyses must communicate with each other incrementally and provide information to each other that will help reduce the number of interpretations being considered by the other. Incremental communication between syntax and semantics can produce incremental interpretations of a sentence while adequately handling the different kinds of ambiguities in a natural language.

From a cognitive point of view, experimental results in psycholinguistics have demonstrated a number of phenomena such as immediate semantic influence on syntactic garden paths, error recovery, delayed decisions, and early commitment. These behaviors can only be explained by an architecture that permits incremental interaction between syntax and semantics.

Along with the eager selection principle above, the principle of incrementality demands that the language processor must select as unambiguous an interpretation as possible incrementally (e.g., after each word) instead of only at the end of the sentence. This principle has also been called the *principle of incremental comprehension* by Crocker (1993), the *on-line principle* by Jurafsky (1991), and *immediacy of interpretation* by Just and Carpenter (1980, 1987). It was also a primary objective behind the development of language understanding programs such as IPP (Lebowitz 1983).

3.3.6.3 Integrated Processing *The language processor applies a piece of knowledge of any type (syntactic, semantic, conceptual, lexical, etc.) as soon as it is available* (called the *integrated processing hypothesis* by Birnbaum 1986; Schank, Lebowitz, and Birnbaum 1980). Incremental selection requires integrated processing. If a piece of knowledge was available and the language processor did not use it, it would not be able to reduce the set of possible interpretations using the piece of knowledge or it would not be able to do so at a time when it was already possible. Thus incremental selection precludes the processor from applying just one or a few types of knowledge initially and applying other types of information only later in processing the input.

Apart from the above functional motivation for integrated processing, there is a large body of evidence for integrated processing in psycholinguistic literature. A number of studies have shown that the human language understander shows immediate effects of syntactic preferences, of semantic feedback, of conceptual priming, of the context, of referential success or failure, and so on. For example, the same principle is stated differently as the *immediate semantic decision hypothesis* in some psycholinguistic studies (e.g., Stowe 1991).[5]

3.3.6.4 Functional Independence *The language processor is able to apply a piece of knowledge of any type at a point independently of whether or not other types of knowledge are available (or accessible) at that point.* Functional independence (e.g., Caramazza and Berndt 1978; Eiselt 1989) between different knowledge sources is entailed by the integrated processing principle. As long as there are situations in which some kinds of knowledge are useful for making rational decisions but other knowledge sources are unavailable or unusable for some reason, the integrated processing principle requires that the ones that are useful be applicable and hence independent of those that are not. Since such situations do occur in language processing, integrated processing entails the independent applicability of each knowledge source.

3.3.6.5 Determinism *The language processor does not make any commitment (e.g., a selection) unless it has a piece of knowledge that supports the commitment.* In other words, the language processor does not make random selections. This is the counterpart of integrated processing. The language processor not only applies every piece of knowledge that is available to it, it does not make any bindings or selections when it has no information substantiating such decisions. Determinism might require delaying decisions when necessary information is not available yet. For example, this principle precludes the use of a top-down parser which makes initial commitments without any information in support of the commitments and later backtracks until its blind commitments turn out to be the right ones. Such a top-down parser is used in models of language processing based on the Augmented Transition Network (ATN) model (e.g., the LUNAR system by Woods 1973).

Determinism does not guarantee that the sentence processor never makes a mistake. Often a decision that was justified by available knowledge at one point in a sentence will turn out to be in error when later parts of the sentence bring in conflicting information. Hence the ability to recover from errors (without having to reprocess the input from the beginning) is an essential requirement for sentence understanders.

The five constraints above dictate that a model of language processing must make commitments to particular interpretations, make those commitments incrementally in processing the input, make commitments only when there is some knowledge that justifies the commitments, make the commitments as soon as a supporting piece of knowledge is available, and must be able to use any type of knowledge independently of other types. The five principles together ensure that a model based on them is not just a linguistic or analytical model of language comprehension but a cognitive model of the *process* of language comprehension.

3.4 Syntax-Semantics Interactions

Syntactic and semantic analyses are needed for both word meaning selection and word meaning composition. However, neither syntactic nor semantic analysis can be done independently of the other because of ambiguities. In this section we analyze the issue of syntax-semantics communication and what it has to say about the control of processing in sentence understanding.

3.4.1 Need for Independent Knowledge Sources
In addition to the functional and cognitive constraints, we want a model of sentence comprehension to be computationally minimal. That is, it should perform its task with the fewest types and least amount of knowledge and with the minimal set of processing mechanisms that will enable sentence comprehension. Such a minimal processor can be said to have a high degree of generativity because it can deal with a variety of input sentences using only a concise representation of the requisite

knowledge. Maintaining such generativity entails independence between different sources of knowledge as described below. Combining knowledge obtained from these separate sources dynamically during sentence interpretation in turn requires incremental communication between syntax and semantics.

To illustrate the need for independent representation of different types of knowledge and their dynamic integration during sentence interpretation, let us examine an alternative to the above solution that would not require incremental communication between separable syntactic and semantic processes.

Integrated Representations By independently representing and processing each type of knowledge used in language understanding, we can maximize the generativity of the language processor. Otherwise, the processor would be specific to some particular sublanguage in some domain. For example, one can combine the regularities a priori for a particular domain or a particular sublanguage in the form of a semantic grammar or some other integrated construction. But by combining two kinds of regularities in predetermined ways, the language processor loses certain other combinations of the independent pieces.

For example, one piece of syntactic knowledge tells us that, given a subject noun phrase followed by a verb that has a subcategory ambiguity, being in either a simple past tense form or a past participle form, we prefer the simple past form since this would satisfy the expectation for a main verb and thereby complete the sentence structure. A piece of semantic knowledge tells us that subject noun phrases in active voice sentences take up agent roles if the event represented by the verb accepts the subject noun as an agent. A piece of conceptual knowledge tells us that for a verb such as "teach," the agent must be an adult human being. We could either represent these three pieces of knowledge independently as stated above or combine them into an integrated representation for the particular situation of the verb "teach." That is, we could say "if the subject noun of "teach" in an active voice sentence is an adult, then prefer the simple past tense form of "taught"; otherwise, prefer the past participle form." If we do that, how could the sentence processor understand sentence (3) below?

(3) The children taught at the academy.

In this sentence the conceptual knowledge is violated and "children" does take up the agent role though it does not represent adult human beings. Since there is a strong syntactic preference for assigning a complete syntactic structure to the full sentence, the conceptual preference for a nonagent role for "children" must be disregarded. The integrated rule would exclude this particular composition of the meanings involved. If we represent them as independent pieces of knowledge, we could combine them during processing to account for the presence or absence of garden-path effects in sentences (4) and (5) below, but also understand the above sentence (3).[6]

(4) The officers taught at the academy were very demanding.

(5) The courses taught at the academy were very demanding.

Once we decide to represent different types of knowledge independently of one another, there must be a way of combining them dynamically during sentence processing in order to adhere to the integrated processing principle and use all types of available information as soon as possible in making sentence processing decisions. This dynamic combination cannot be deferred until the end and must be incremental as required by the other functional and cognitive reasons above.

3.4.2 Sentence Processing Architectures

The sentence processor must combine information coming from semantic and conceptual analyses with syntactic interpretations. Top-down and bottom-up influences arising from syntactic sources of knowledge can be combined in a parsing algorithm (see section 3.5). However, the parsing algorithm merely identifies the points when the communication ought to occur but doesn't tell us how the communication is handled or how conflicts are resolved in the best interests of the functional and cognitive constraints on the behavior of the sentence interpreter. Such communication between syntax and semantics is also necessary to account for psycholinguistic evidence for immediate interaction, delayed decisions, early commitment, and error recovery (e.g., Carpenter and Daneman 1981; Crain and Steedman 1985; Eiselt and Holbrook 1991; Frazier 1987; Stowe 1991; Tyler and Marslen-Wilson 1977).

There have been many computational architectures proposed in various models of sentence understanding to integrate syntax, semantics, and other components:

Sequential Architecture Models of sentence understanding can be classified as sequential, integrated, or parallel models depending on how their knowledge representations and different processes relate to each other. In a sequential architecture, a "lower-level" process does not get any feedback from a "higher-level" process. Each level receives the output of processing at the previous lower level and sends out its output to its next higher level. Traditionally the task of language understanding has been decomposed into the analyses of syntax, semantics, and pragmatics which are arranged in a syntax-first sequential architecture. Such a sequential model has the advantage of accounting for the fast, autonomous processing at syntactic and other earlier stages. However, the communication is one-way and the processing at the lower levels cannot take advantage of results or knowledge available through analyses being carried out at higher levels.

Integrated Architecture The integrated processing principle (Birnbaum 1986; Birnbaum 1989; Schank et al. 1980) states that the language processor applies syntactic, semantic, and other kinds of knowledge at the earliest opportunity in processing a piece of text. However, integrated models of language understanding have assumed more than just this; they employ integrated representations of knowledge, not just the integration of the information provided by the representations during processing. They do not retain independence in the use of the different kinds of knowledge. Though the principle itself is called the integrated *processing* principle, the integration has always been modeled in the representation itself. The only example of a model that integrated independently represented syntactic and semantic knowledge dynamically during processing is Lytinen's (1984; 1987) MOPTRANS model which was a sequential semantics-first model. In fact, as we have seen earlier, the integrated processing principle entails functional independence between the different knowledge sources. However, previous implementations of integrated processing did not support functional independence with the exception of MOPTRANS which was a sequential model. It is in this sense that we claim COMPERE to be a true implementation of the integrated processing principle.

Parallel Architecture Parallel architectures retain independent representations of different kinds of knowledge and yet support on-line interaction between them. Parallel models can adhere to the integrated processing principle without having to sacrifice the independence between the uses of different kinds of knowledge.

Syntax and semantics can be placed in parallel in several different ways. Different parallel configurations yield different degrees of control on the communication between syntax and semantics:

- *Uncontrolled interaction.* The simplest parallel configuration is one in which syntactic and semantic processes interact with each other continuously without any monitoring, arbitration, or even translation. If the two processes shared the same language to represent information and the same operations to manipulate the information, then they could interact with each other in this fashion. This has been the mechanism used in certain connectionist models such as the one by Waltz and Pollack (1985). However, it remains to be seen that an uncontrolled interaction between processing mechanisms such as spreading activation can actually model the variety of interactions between syntax and semantics observed in human sentence processing (e.g., Frazier 1987; Marslen-Wilson and Tyler 1987; Stowe 1991). Even from a computational point of view, it is neither clear that such processing mechanisms can deal with the complexities of linguistic structure nor that they can effectively reduce the degree of local ambiguity encountered by a sentence interpreter.

Sentence Processing in Understanding 43

- *Interaction through a translator.* Another parallel configuration between syntax and semantics is one where there is a bidirectional translator between syntactic and semantic processes. This gives syntax and semantics the freedom to use their own internal representations and processes. In other words, this architecture does permit representational modularity between the modules. This mode of communication, again, does not provide any control on the interaction. Problems with translation include lack of control in resolving conflicts, lack of a guarantee that resulting interpretations are consistent (especially during and after an error recovery operation), and the lack of a declarative representation of intermediate decisions for use in error recovery.

- *Interaction through a blackboard.* In a blackboard configuration there is no direct communication between syntax and semantics. The two processes communicate with each other by writing onto and reading from a common representation called the blackboard (e.g., Erman et al. 1980; Nii 1989; Reddy, Erman, and Neely 1973). This configuration does not guarantee that communication actually occurs because each process might very well disregard what the other wrote. By a proper design of the representations on the blackboard, however, it may be possible to guarantee consistency of results. However, it still does not give the sentence processor any control over the resolution of conflicts between syntactic and semantic preferences. Moreover the blackboard can be overwritten, and there is no record of intermediate decisions with a resulting difficulty in implementing error recovery.

- *Controlled interaction through an arbitrator.* In an arbitrator configuration, syntactic and semantic processes perform their analyses and send their results (e.g., alternative interpretations and preferences for each of them) to the central arbitrator. The arbitrator controls the interactions between the processes by synchronizing the processes, providing feedback from one process to the other, resolving any conflicts by selecting the alternative that is best overall (see figure 3.7 for the algorithm), and retaining alternatives not presently selected for later error recovery, apart from translating between the different representations.

3.4.3 Issues in Syntax-Semantics Communication

We have seen that syntactic and semantic processing in our model of incremental sentence comprehension communicate with each other through a single arbitrating mechanism and declarative intermediate representations that facilitate error recovery. Given these constraints, the three main issues in syntax-semantics communication that the model must address can be summarized as below:

- *When to communicate.* At what points in time (in terms of the word position in the input sentence) should syntax and semantics communicate? When should the arbitrator arbitrate between syntax and semantics? The answer to this question determines how we mix bottom-up and top-down processing in the parsing algorithm. This issue is further addressed in section 3.5.

• *What to communicate about.* What are the contents and representations of syntactic interpretations, word meanings, and semantic roles? What information is used to arbitrate between syntax and semantics? These questions are addressed in section 3.6.

• *How to arbitrate.* How does the arbitrator decide? What does it do when there are conflicts between the preferences of syntax and semantics? How does error recovery happen? How long are alternatives retained? These questions are addressed in sections 3.6 and 3.7.

3.5 Syntactic Analysis

A sentence is an ordered sequence of words in a language. The sentence processor needs to select appropriate meanings for words and combine them to form the meaning of the sentence as a whole. Syntactic knowledge, or grammar, tells the sentence processor which meanings to select and attempt to compose, avoiding an exhaustive search for all possible compositions of all word meanings. Syntactic analysis is the process of identifying the compositions licensed by the grammar of the language. It adds hierarchy to the left-to-right order in the words in a sentence. As we move each level up in the hierarchy, it tells us what units at the lower levels combine with what other units to form bigger meanings. Thus, given a sentence and a grammar for the natural language, the task of syntactic analysis is to output a parse tree (or a parse forest, if there is no single tree for the sentence) that identifies which units need to be composed with which others and in what left-to-right order at each level in the tree.

Semantic processing makes use of these recommendations and those from other sources of knowledge and attempts to make compositions and arrive at a sentence meaning. Since neither grammatical nor semantic knowledge guarantees unique compositions of word meanings all the time, ambiguities of composition (as distinct from ambiguities of selection, e.g., lexical ambiguities) exist in both syntax and semantics. That is, there are often multiple ways of composing word meanings according to syntactic or semantic knowledge. In order to deal with the ambiguities and meet the set of functional and cognitive constraints on the sentence understander, syntactic analysis should communicate with the semantic processing so as to produce the right sequence of decisions and commitments in sentence processing. Syntactic analysis should not only communicate incrementally with semantics, it should do so at the right points or times in processing a sentence.[7] The times at which the communication occurs are determined by the usefulness of the communication between syntax and semantics.[8] Communication is useful if it eliminates certain alternatives and leads to a reduction in the number of choices being considered by syntax and semantics.

Syntax and semantics should interact only at those times when one can provide some information to the other to help reduce the number of choices being considered. This can happen only at or after syntactic analysis has reached a decision point at which semantics could have information to make communication useful. For instance, the parser should not interact with the semantic analyzer until it has completed analyzing a unit that carries some part of the meaning of the sentence, such as a content word. Only then can semantics provide useful feedback perhaps using selectional preferences for fillers of thematic roles. An alternative is to eliminate the question of deciding when to communicate by proposing integrated representations of grammatical and semantic knowledge as in semantic grammars or in integrated understanders. Such an approach loses heavily on the generativity of the language analyzer and would work only in a limited, familiar domain.

The choice of points in syntactic analysis at which to communicate with semantics is determined by the points at which syntactic analysis makes commitments to structure (i.e., commitments to particular compositions of words). This is in turn determined by the choice of parsing algorithm employed for performing syntactic analysis. A parsing strategy must be designed that communicates with semantics precisely at those points at which semantics begins to have the necessary information to provide helpful feedback. For this purpose pure bottom-up parsing turns out to be too circumspect since it waits until the end of a phrase to posit any attachment. Pure top-down parsing, on the other hand, is too eager and makes its commitments too early for semantics to say anything about those attachments. The resulting backtracking in a top-down parser complicates the issue of semantic interaction significantly. A combination strategy called *left-corner* (LC) parsing is a good middle ground, making expectations for required constituents from the leftmost unit of a phrase, but waiting to see the left corner before committing to a bigger syntactic unit. In LC parsing the leftmost child (i.e., the left corner) of a phrase is analyzed bottom-up, the phrase is projected upward from the leftmost child, and other children of the phrase are projected top-down from the phrase.

While LC parsing defines when to project top-down, it does not tell us when to make attachments. That is, it does not tell when to attempt to attach the phrase projected from its left corner to higher-level syntactic units. Should it be done immediately after the phrase has been formed from its left corner, or after the phrase is complete with all its children, or at some intermediate point? Since ambiguities arise in making attachments and since semantics could help resolve such ambiguities, the points at which semantics can help the syntactic parser determine when the parser should attempt to make such attachments.

LC parsing defines a range of parsing strategies in the spectrum of parsing algorithms (figure 3.2) along the "eagerness" dimension (Abney and Johnson 1991). The two ends of this dimension are purely bottom-up (i.e., most circumspect) and purely top-down (i.e., most eager) parsers. Different LC parsers result from the choice of arc enumeration strategies employed in enumerating the nodes in a parse tree. In arc eager LC (AELC) parsing, a node in the parse tree is linked to its parent without waiting to see all of its children. Arc standard LC (ASLC) parsing, on the other hand, waits for all the children before making attachments. While this distinction vanishes for pure bottom-up or top-down parsing, it makes a big difference for LC parsing.

In this section, an intermediate point in the LC parsing spectrum between ASLC and AELC strategies called *head-signaled left-corner parsing* (HSLC) is presented. The proposed point produces the right sequence of decisions for incremental interaction with semantics. In this strategy a node is linked to its parent as soon as all the required children of the node are analyzed, without waiting for other optional children to the right. The required units are predefined syntactically for each phrase; they are not necessarily the same as the semantic head of the phrase (e.g., N is the required unit for NP, V for VP, and *NP* for *PP*). HSLC makes the parser wait for required units before interacting with semantics but does not wait for optional adjuncts, such as PP adjuncts to NPs or VPs.

3.5.1 Parsing Strategies

Different parsing algorithms differ in the order in which they traverse the tree structures representing the compositions of words as they build those structures. The criterion used in selecting the right parsing algorithm for COMPERE is one of making *maximal commitments with justifiable bases.* That is, at a particular point in the sentence, we would want COMPERE to make the maximal set of commitments so as to minimize the number of alternatives being pursued at that point as long as those commitments are justified by some piece of knowledge. We would want to avoid making unjustified commitments that lead to unwarranted backtracking, in order to meet the functionally and psychologically derived constraints on the time course of sentence processing decisions.

Knowledge sources that justify syntactic commitments include the syntactic category (or part of speech) of a word, subcategorization (or predicate argument structure) information, grammatical information, and preferences arising from syntactic structures (e.g., minimal attachment or right association), semantic relations, and

Sentence Processing in Understanding 47

pragmatics. These types of information can be used as preferences in resolving category or attachment ambiguities. Justifications arising from semantic and conceptual preferences are handled by means of incremental communication between syntax and semantics. Those arising from syntactic expectations and structural preferences are integrated with bottom-up syntactic information by the syntactic parsing algorithm. The parsing algorithm determines when and how such information is used to make justified early commitments and thereby eliminate certain alternatives from immediate consideration.

3.5.1.1 Two Constraints from Human Parsers Models of human language processing must take into account two constraining factors arising from both the nature of natural languages and the nature of the human processing system: *local ambiguities* and *memory requirements*. Natural languages are full of local ambiguities that use memory by making the processor hold on to multiple intermediate interpretations. However, the human processing system has a limited memory capacity. A cognitive model of parsing must therefore devise a parsing algorithm that keeps memory requirements to a minimum by reducing the amount of local ambiguity it must deal with. For example, the human parser is unable to comprehend deeply center-embedded constructions while being able to parse left- and right-branching structures with ease. Using this empirical evidence, Abney and Johnson (1991) have shown that in order to minimize both space requirements and local ambiguities in an incremental parser, the parsing strategy can neither be bottom-up nor top-down. They showed that an intermediate, uniform, syntax-directed parsing strategy known as left-corner parsing has the right properties along the dimensions of both local ambiguity and minimum space requirements. However, a pure left-corner parsing strategy does not build the syntactic structure in an order suitable for incremental semantic comprehension. We present an alternative parsing strategy, *head-signaled left-corner parsing*, that retains the local ambiguity and memory requirement virtues of left-corner parsing and integrates them with the virtues of head-driven parsing that are compatible with incremental semantic comprehension.[9]

3.5.1.2 Different Parsing Strategies A *parsing strategy* is a way of enumerating the nodes in a parse tree. There are three basic parsing strategies that correspond to the three basic patterns of tree traversal: top-down (pre-order), bottom-up (post-order), and left-corner parsing (in-order traversal).

There are non-syntax-directed parsing strategies such as *head-driven parsing*. In head-driven parsing, every phrase has a distinguished child called the head. A parent node is enumerated immediately after its head is enumerated. We will see the advantages of head-driven parsing for incremental semantic interpretation below.

In any of the strategies above, one can make a distinction between an arc-eager strategy and an arc-standard strategy with consequent differences in space requirements and local ambiguity. A parser is said to be *arc eager* if it attaches a pair of nodes as soon as both nodes are available regardless of whether their children have been enumerated or not. A parser is said to be *arc standard* if it either attaches two enumerated nodes when none of the subtree under the nodes has been enumerated, or when all of the subtrees rooted at the nodes have been enumerated. These two strategies are identical for a top-down or bottom-up parsing strategy. However, they are not identical for an intermediate strategy such as left-corner parsing. An arc eager strategy may lead to a reduction in space requirements but never requires more space than its arc standard counterpart. This reduction is accompanied by an increase in local ambiguity for the arc eager strategy.

Natural languages allow many ways of constructing a syntactic unit by appending or inserting optional constituents to a simpler structure. Each syntactic structure has at least one *required* unit and zero or more *optional* units. This distinction between optional and required units is a very important one when it comes to syntactic processing, especially when syntactic processing is supposed to be interacting incrementally with semantic processing. Optional constituents can be to the left of the required parts (e.g., an adjective in an NP) or to the right of an already completed phrase (e.g., a PP attached to an NP). One of the required constituents of a phrase is called the *head* of the phrase (often called the *semantic head*). The head provides the core meaning of the phrase; the other required and optional constituents modify the meaning of the head. For example, N is the head of an NP, V that of VP, and VP that of S (in an event-centered semantics as described in section 3.6).

3.5.2 Problems with Left-Corner Parsing

Though left-corner parsing is a combination of bottom-up and top-down parsing strategies, it still has problems with incremental communication with semantics. Consider the enumeration of a parse tree with an optional adjunct by arc eager left-corner parsing (figure 3.1a). There is a local ambiguity at the point of attaching the PP: its parent could be either the NP or the VP. This parsing strategy, being eager to make commitments, proceeds to deal with this local ambiguity as soon as it sees the preposition. However, semantics is unable to help syntax resolve this local attachment ambiguity, since the head of the NP in the PP is as yet unknown. The meaning of the prepositional object is unavailable for the semantic interpreter to decide which of the two attachments is semantically feasible.[10]

If only the parser had waited until it had seen the head, it could have sought the help of semantics in resolving this ambiguity. It could have avoided wasteful processing of parallel interpretations, or it could have avoided some errors and back-

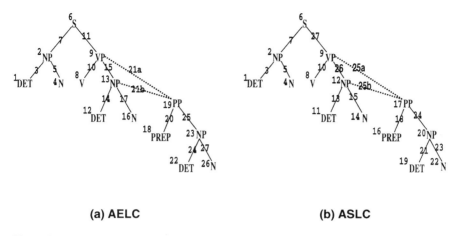

(a) AELC **(b) ASLC**

Figure 3.1
(a) Arc-eager left-corner parsing is too eager; (b) arc-standard left-corner parsing is too circumspect.

tracking which would have resulted if the parser tried a first analysis derived from a structural preference.

An arc standard left-corner parser would perhaps fare better. Consider the same tree enumerated by such a parser (figure 3.1b). It can be seen that the arc standard left-corner parser violates the principle of incremental interpretation. It does not provide a maximal partial semantic interpretation where it could have if only it had been a little less circumspect. For instance, after seeing the V, the event described by the V could have been semantically related to the subject NP by building the link between the VP and the S (figure 3.1b). This parser, however, did not permit that at least until after the direct object of the V was composed with the V. In other words, link number 27 between the VP and the S in figure 3.1b was built only after those between the PP and the NP/VP, number 25, and that between the object NP and the VP, number 26.

From the above analysis, it is fairly obvious that what we need for an incremental semantic interpreter that minimizes local ambiguities is a parsing strategy that is intermediate to an arc eager and an arc standard left-corner parser. It is also obvious that it is the head of a phrase that defines the announce point for interaction with semantics. The head marks the point at which semantics could provide useful advice for syntactic decision making. As seen above, if we take the eager extreme and attempt to communicate all the time, semantics will be unable to help before the head and unable to alleviate the increase in local ambiguity resulting from early commitment (figure 3.1a).

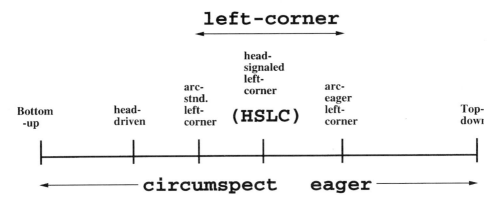

Figure 3.2
Relative positions of parsing strategies.

3.5.3 Head-Signaled Left-Corner Parsing (HSLC Parsing)

Left-corner parsing provides a neat way to combine bottom-up and top-down strategies: generate the left branch bottom-up, go up a level, and then project top-down to the other branches. Left-corner parsing is however an incomplete specification of a parsing strategy unlike pure bottom-up or top-down parsing. An arc eager left-corner strategy turns out to be rather too eager when incremental semantic interpretation is considered. An arc standard left-corner strategy, on the other hand, happens to be too circumspect. Between these two ends, left-corner strategies define a range of parsing strategies that are all between bottom-up and top-down strategies. A point within this range defined by the semantic head of the phrase is the left-corner parsing strategy that has the right computational properties in terms of space requirements and local ambiguities for incremental semantic interpretation. This is called *head-signaled left-corner parsing*. (See figure 3.2 for the positions of different parsers on a scale from bottom-up to top-down parsing.) The HSLC algorithm (figure 3.4) generates the parent from the left branch, always attaches a node further up after seeing its head, and does not wait for other constituents after the head to make attachments.

Figure 3.4 shows the HSLC parsing algorithm and figure 3.3 illustrates graphically the data structures described in figure 3.4.

The enumeration produced by this strategy is shown in figure 3.5. This is different from a pure head-driven parsing in that it permits the generation of a parent from just its left branch no matter if this branch is the head of the parent node or not. Head-driven parsing would behave like a bottom-up parser, waiting until later, if the left-branch was not a head. The eagerness licensed by the left-corner strategy in such a situation is valuable in the following way. It permits the generation of the parent

Sentence Processing in Understanding

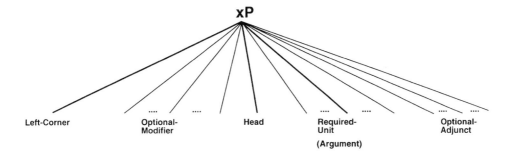

(a) Constituents of a Phrase.

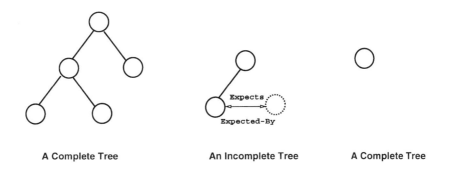

(b) A Forest of Parse Trees

Figure 3.3
An illustration of data structures in HSLC parsing.

and the associated predictions immediately after the left branch. These expectations can be used to resolve local structural and lexical ambiguities in the right branches to follow. For instance, such a preference for an expected structure helps produce a minimal attachment behavior without having to count the number of nodes in the tree.

Consider a PP attachment ambiguity and the tree traversal labelings produced by different LC parsers shown in figures 3.1a and b and figure 3.5. It can be seen from figure 3.1a that AELC attempts to attach the PP to the VP or NP even before the

Data Structures

Tree: An *n*-ary tree of *nodes*.

Node: A record

Children: ordered list of children nodes

Parent: parent node

Expects: node that is expected by this node

Expected-by: node that expects this node

Lexical-entry: lexical entry of the word from which
                this node was created

Head: head child node for the phrase this node represents

Complete-p: Is this node (phrase) complete?

Algorithm HSLC

Given a grammar and an empty set as the initial forest of parse trees,

For each word,

Add a new node T_w to the current forest of trees $\{T_i\}$

    for each category in the lexical entry of the word;

    mark T_w as a complete subtree;

Repeat until there are no more complete trees that can be attached
to other trees,

    Propose attachments for a complete subtree T_j

        to a T_i that is expecting T_j, or

        to a T_i as an optional constituent, or

        to a new T_k to be created if T_j can be

    the left corner (leftmost child) of T_k;

Select an attachment by consulting semantics (see the description of role
assignment in section 3.6) and arbitrating (see Algorithm Arbitrate
in figure 3.7) and attach;

    If a new T_k was created, add it to the forest, and

        make expectations for required units of T_k;

    If a T_i in the forest has just seen its head,

        Mark the T_i as a complete subtree.

Figure 3.4
HSLC algorithm.

noun in the PP has been seen. At this time, semantics cannot provide useful feedback, since it has no information on the role filler for a thematic role to evaluate it against known selectional preferences for that role filler. Thus AELC is too eager for interactive semantics. ASLC, on the other hand, does not attempt to attach the VP to the S until the very end (figure 3.1b). Thus even the thematic role of the subject NP remains unresolved until the very end. ASLC is too circumspect for interactive semantics. HSLC on the other hand, attempts to make attachments at the right time for interaction with semantics (figure 3.5).

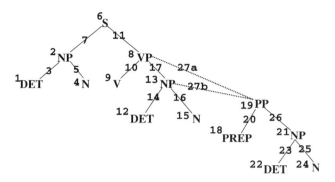

Figure 3.5
HSLC: Head-signaled left-corner parsing.

At first sight, it might appear that HSLC parsing is not quite a neat strategy, since it says one has to wait for the semantic head to make attachments. However it is more uniform than arc-eager left-corner parsing in the wake of attachment ambiguities. Left-corner parsing requires the parser to wait until every child of the left branch has been enumerated but the arc eager strategy requires the parser to proceed to make attachments for the right branches without waiting for the descendants of the right branches. That is, the parser waits even on optional adjuncts on the left branch but does not even wait for required descendants on the right branches. An arc standard strategy would result in far greater uniformity but, as we have seen earlier, arc standard is too bottom-up for incremental interpretation. HSLC, on the other hand, requires the parser to wait until the head is parsed to make further *attachments* on any branch. It is left-corner only because the parent is *generated* from the left branch no matter what.

It might also be argued that waiting for the semantic head kills the independence of syntax. However, HSLC does not require the parser to wait for particular meanings or lexical strings; it simply requires waiting until the head has been parsed. Heads are grammatically defined syntactic entities, since they are defined for each phrase in a language irrespective of particular lexical items.

It can be shown that HSLC retains the advantages of left-corner parsing in minimizing both local ambiguities and memory requirements for syntactic constructs permitted in natural languages. It can also be shown that HSLC is not the same as any of the related parsers such as head-corner parsing and parsers based on categorical grammars (Mahesh 1995).

In summary, we used computational arguments based on space requirements and local ambiguities to argue that there is a parsing strategy in the range defined by left-corner parsing that has the right set of properties for modeling incremental syntax-semantics interactions. We showed that the two extremes of left-corner parsing defined by arc-eager and arc-standard strategies are both unsuitable for syntax-semantics interactions. The left-corner parser was impregnated with the head-drivenness of a head-driven parser to define a middle point in left-corner parsing. The resulting parsing strategy, called head-signaled left-corner parsing, possesses the right space-requirement and local ambiguity properties. In this algorithm, the pathways of parsing are laid out by the left-corner strategy with the head-driven strategy providing the "stop and go" signals for interactions with semantics at the crossroads of parsing decisions.

3.6 Core Semantic Analysis

The semantic component of a natural language is about linguistic meaning. Core semantic analysis is the process of extracting *literal, decontextualized, grammatical meaning* (Frawley 1992). Core semantics is not only more precise than a nonliteral (inferential, metaphoric, implied, etc.), a contextual, or a conceptual (as opposed to grammatical) theory of semantics, but it also provides an output representation that is of potential use to many situated reasoners with their own nonlinguistic (or extra-linguistic), contextual, or conceptual ontologies and inference mechanisms. The theory of semantics presented here is closest to the view of meaning as conceptual structure (Frawley 1992) in an internal representation that precedes contextually or culturally appropriate meanings. The primary mechanism for meaning selection and composition employed here is the use of *selectional preferences*.

3.6.1 Elements of Core Semantics

The semantic component of a sentence is comprised of the following core elements of meaning:

1. *Entities* or *objects*. The things in the conceptual space that are temporally stable and typically appear as nouns.
2. *Events*. The temporally sensitive things in the conceptual space that are typically encoded as verbs.
3. *Thematic roles*. Thematic roles are the relationships between entities and events. They are the semantics of the roles entities play in events. Thematic roles represent the participant, causal, spatial, or purposive roles that objects (and other events) play in events. Thematic roles are based on the fundamental notion of predication.
4. *Spatial roles*. The spatial relationships between objects.

5. *Aspect.* The nontemporal, internal contour of an event. Aspect is the way an event is distributed through the time frame in which the event occurs.
6. *Tense and time.* The semantics of how a language encodes time.
7. *Modality and negation.* Modality is the element of semantics that is concerned with the factual status of a statement. For instance, this involves the negation, possibility, and obligational entailments of statements.
8. *Modification.* This final element of linguistic semantics encompasses all relationships between objects that can be called properties, qualities, or modifiers of conceptual entities.

In the examples of this chapter, we focus only on objects, events, and thematic roles. Certain elements of modification have been captured using the generic *state* role as described below. However, incorporating the other elements above is not expected to cause any conceptual problem in COMPERE, since its representations and processes have been designed with the entire set of semantic elements above in mind. For instance, one could add the semantics of spatial relationships by adding the necessary spatial roles and the intermediate roles that link them to the spatial prepositions. Such enhancement is particularly feasible because of a uniform representation of all semantic elements in the form of *semantic roles.*

All the above eight elements of semantics are uniformly represented in COMPERE in terms of semantic roles. This notion of semantic roles is an extension of thematic roles viewed as predication where semantic roles form a set of predicates that represent any of the eight elements of semantic representation. Such a uniform representation (Mahesh and Eiselt 1994) enables COMPERE to apply the same set of operations to all semantic elements such as the operations carried out during error recovery. A standard set of thematic roles includes at least the following roles (Allen 1987; Frawley 1992): agent, instrument, experiencer, beneficiary, theme, location, co-agent, and co-theme.

3.6.2 Semantic Processing

A functional analysis of sentence understanding reveals two main tasks, word sense disambiguation and word meaning composition, that are accomplished in part by semantic processing. Given the notions of semantic roles, these two tasks can be achieved by the method of role assignment as follows:

Word sense disambiguation. Whenever a role assignment is made, the word meanings associated with the roles are checked against any constraints on that role assignment. Any meanings that are not compatible with the assignment are deactivated and retained for possible later use in error recovery (see Mahesh 1995 for further details and examples; also see Eiselt 1989). Thus only those meanings that are compatible with the role assignment are selected. The process of role assignment is described in further detail below.

Word meaning composition. Word meanings are composed by filling one word meaning in a role of another meaning. For instance, many thematic roles help compose the meanings of the objects with that of the event, modifier roles may compose the meanings of two objects, and so on. This composition is performed using syntactic guidance as described below to constrain the search in the role assignment process.

3.6.2.1 Role Assignment and Syntactic Guidance

In COMPERE's theory of sentence processing, role assignment is the primary operation in semantic processing. Portions of the input sentence are assigned primitive roles by lexical information (e.g., syntactic category). These primitive roles of words are assigned to bigger syntactic units by syntactic analysis. Each bigger syntactic unit acquires its role from its head child.

When a role is propagated from a head child to its parent, it is composed with any roles of other children of the parent. This composition also results in a composition of the word meanings of the modifier and the head. For example, the meaning and role of a prepositional phrase attached to a noun phrase are composed with the meaning and role of the head noun of the noun phrase.

Syntactic compositions do not always lead to unique semantic roles. Other types of knowledge must be used to figure out how the suggested pair of roles should be composed. Such knowledge might be of a variety of types, such as conceptual selectional preferences on role assignments or other linguistic cues.

The above process of role assignment and composition can be viewed as "semantic parsing" that produces a *role tree*, a hierarchy similar to a parse tree, rooted at the role of the head meaning of the sentence with other word meanings in the sentence hanging off roles in the interior of the tree.

The semantic parsing algorithm used in COMPERE is a simple head-driven parsing algorithm very similar to the HSLC parser applied to syntactic processing (Mahesh 1995). The only difference is that no left-corner projection is done in semantic parsing since there is no particular advantage for doing that in semantics in terms of reducing ambiguity.

3.6.2.2 Syntax-Semantics Consistency and Correspondence

It is important in sentence processing to ensure that there is consistency between syntactic and semantic interpretations at all times. It is also important to ensure consistency between syntactic and semantic representations during and after an error recovery operation. During error recovery certain commitments made either in syntax or in semantics must be undone. Such deletion of a role assignment in syntax must be followed by a recovery operation that performs corresponding deletions or changes in semantics and vice versa.

In COMPERE, consistency before, during, and after error recovery is maintained with the help of role assignments. Every syntactic unit in a parse tree has links to semantic roles that it corresponds to and vice versa. These links maintained during role assignment and composition operations are used to determine which parts of the other representation are affected when a change is made to a part of a syntactic or a semantic representation. The links provide a declarative representation of every decision that was made during processing. Using them, COMPERE can figure out what changes in one representation are necessitated by a change made to another representation. It can examine the constraints based on the satisfaction of which a particular role was assigned and *repair* its interpretations instead of having to rebuild them by reprocessing the input.

3.6.2.3 Arbitration and Conflict Resolution When there is an ambiguity, it is possible that syntactic and semantic knowledge will assign different preferences to the various interpretations, leading to conflicts between syntax and semantics. The arbitrating process makes the selection between alternative interpretations and resolves any conflicts.

Since syntactic and semantic role assignments are proposed using respective knowledge and since the arbitrator examines both before it selects an interpretation, it effectively combines or integrates different types of information in sentence processing. Information of different kinds (e.g., syntactic and semantic preferences) can be combined either as continuous numerical values or as discrete qualitative values. Since there is no clear way to determine how to combine real-number preferences of different kinds (e.g., whether a syntactic preference of 2.3 is stronger or weaker than a semantic preference of 3.2), nor is there a way to figure out what those real numbers must be in a particular situation, we have adopted discrete qualitative values for preferences in COMPERE. However, even while combining discrete values, we run into the problem of comparing values for preferences of different types. COMPERE's arbitrating algorithm avoids this problem of combining dissimilar values by merely ranking preferences of each kind and choosing the interpretation that has the highest preference in both syntax and semantics. When there is a real conflict (i.e., when the syntactically preferred interpretation is rejected by semantics, and vice versa), the arbitrator simply delays the selection and pursues multiple interpretations until some new information enables it to resolve the conflict away. The arbitration algorithm for combining discrete values is presented in section 3.7, along with a description of the COMPERE system.

It may be noted that the arbitrator is the unified process in COMPERE that carries out both ambiguity resolution and error recovery. Recovery from an error is accomplished by the arbitrator by re-examining the alternative interpretations in the light of the new information that led to the detection of the error. It is important to note that this process of arbitration is neither syntactic processing nor semantic processing. It is the unified process that is common to both syntactic and semantic decision making.

3.7 COMPERE: A True Implementation of Integrated Processing

In this section we present COMPERE as a true model of integrated processing in sentence understanding and illustrate its knowledge representations and algorithms.

3.7.1 Knowledge Representation
COMPERE represents syntactic and semantic knowledge separately but uniformly.

Lexical Knowledge   Each word has a set of one or more lexical entries in the lexicon, one for each category of the word. Each lexical entry is a frame and includes the word itself, the syntactic category of the word, subcategory information (this might include the number and person of a noun, the tense of a verb, etc.), the meaning(s) of the word (for that category), and the semantic role that corresponds to the word (mostly for closed-class words like prepositions). COMPERE's lexical representation is similar to those used in LFG (lexical functional grammar) formalisms (Bresnan and Kaplan 1982; Sells 1985). However, unlike in LFG, COMPERE does not require lexicalized semantic knowledge or syntax-semantics mappings defined a priori and stored in the lexical entry of each word. Instead, it uses general, nonlexical semantic knowledge and applies an arbitration algorithm to determine the mappings from syntax to semantics dynamically.

Syntactic Knowledge   Syntactic knowledge is mainly comprised of phrase-structure rules. However, the rules in COMPERE's syntactic knowledge are reversed from the standard representation and indexed differently so that they can be accessed efficiently by the left-corner parser. The rules also have preconditions on subcategories, expectations, and other information attached to them and thereby extend the grammar beyond context-free grammars to capture the context sensitiveness of natural languages.

Semantic Knowledge   Semantic analysis in COMPERE is based on thematic roles. A standard set of thematic roles is extended by introducing intermediate roles that link syntactic structures to their thematic roles (Mahesh 1995). These intermediate roles help maintain declarative representations of the sentence interpretation process in all its stages. Each role is linked to the syntactic structure (i.e., the node in the parse tree that corresponds to the role) on the one side and the conceptual meaning (i.e., the word meaning that is the filler for the role) on the other. The representation of roles is by design very similar in content and form to the representation of grammar rules in syntax (Mahesh 1995).

Conceptual Knowledge   Content words such as nouns and verbs have their meanings represented in conceptual units that state how the concept relates to other concepts. Concepts are organized in multiple hierarchies, each hierarchy being a generalization-specialization structure between related concepts. A concept also specifies its relations to other concepts by stating the selectional preferences for classes of concepts that can fill particular role relationships with the concept. For example, the event TEACH has selectional preferences on its agent role for adult human beings. Objects fall into different hierarchies of concepts, which tell us whether a particular concept is animate or not, whether it is an abstract entity or a physical object, and so on. COMPERE's conceptual knowledge was built only for the purpose of demonstration and included only those concepts and distinctions between them that were necessary for the example sentences that COMPERE was tested with.[11]

Working Memory   COMPERE maintains a working memory to keep track of the interpretation(s) it has built and to be able to access the syntactic and semantic interpretations for the initial parts of the sentence while processing the later parts. A sample working memory with syntactic and semantic structures is shown in figure 3.6.

Since COMPERE arbitrates between several possible attachments proposed by both syntax and semantics, before making an attachment, it needs to hold on to proposed attachments in the working memory. COMPERE's arbitrator passes on a syntactic attachment proposal to semantics and combines the corresponding semantic proposal(s) with the syntactic one to form a complex "proposal complex." Its use in arbitration is described below.

3.7.2   Sentence Processing Methods

We describe the syntactic parsing and semantic role assignment algorithms briefly by listing the major modules in their implementations and focus mainly on the arbitration algorithm. Further details of COMPERE's methods can be found in Mahesh (1995).

The important methods in the HSLC parsing algorithm are (1) deciding when to attempt to attach a syntactic unit to a parent unit, (2) proposing possible attachments, (3) selecting a subset of the proposed attachments, and (4) making the attachment(s). This enumeration does not include other minor steps such as creating instances for word categories.

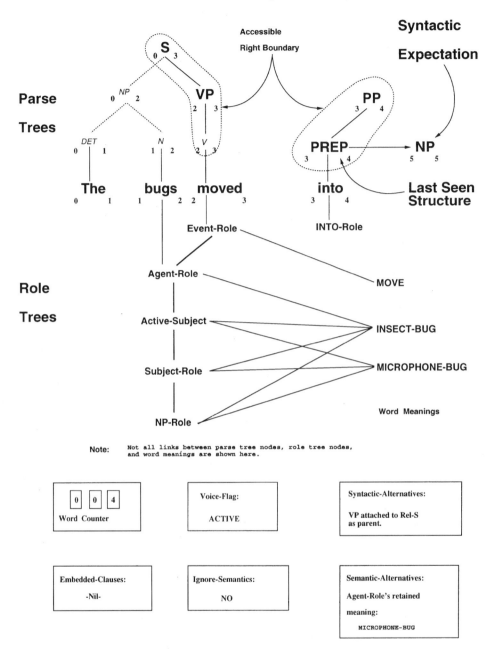

Figure 3.6
COMPERE's working memory.

Implementing role assignment in semantics involves the following steps: (1) deciding when to make role attachments, (2) generating semantic attachment proposals, (3) selecting among the proposed role assignments, and (4) making the assignments. Deciding when to make role assignments is already taken care of by the HSLC parsing algorithm. Role attachments are attempted whenever a head-complete syntactic unit is being attached to a parent unit. The only other time COMPERE might want to attempt role attachments is when there is no composition suggested by syntax, such as when the input is ungrammatical.

Given a set of proposed syntactic attachments, COMPERE evaluates the semantic feasibility of each of those attachments. This results in the generation of one or more possible semantic attachment proposals corresponding to the syntactic attachment proposals. The arbitration algorithm selects from this set of pairs of syntactic and semantic attachment proposals, a subset that the sentence processor needs to actually pursue and make attachments.

3.7.2.1 Arbitration Having generated the semantic attachment proposals (or rejections for that matter) corresponding to syntactic attachment proposals, COMPERE arbitrates between the different syntactic and semantic alternatives and preferences. Arbitration is really a task of combining information arising from disparate sources of knowledge. Unless these distinct knowledge sources are always benign, the arbitrator must weigh the preferences against each other in order to select the alternative that is "best" overall. A fundamental problem in doing this is determining a projection from one scale of preferences to another. If the two scales are merged, then the preferences can be combined using arithmetic operations.[12] How do we know for instance whether a level 2 preference in syntax is higher or lower than a level 1 in semantics? Since these preferences embody conceptual knowledge as well, such a projection could perhaps only be derived from analyses of a corpus of texts or a domain and the application task in which sentence interpretation is situated. The arbitration algorithm presented below is a simpler one where this problem of projecting one scale of preference to line it up with another is avoided altogether. As a result the arbitrator might appear to be slightly biased, favoring syntax a bit more than semantics, but this has not been a problem at all in COMPERE. The arbitration algorithm described below is also well suited to explaining the psychological data on ambiguity resolution and error recovery (Holbrook, Eiselt, and Mahesh 1992; Mahesh and Eiselt 1994; Stowe 1991).

While mathematical approaches for doing arbitration using real-numbered preferences and various theories of probabilities have been proposed for integrating information from multiple knowledge sources, such precision has not been necessary for COMPERE to produce acceptable sentence processing behaviors. However, it is duly

Data Structures
Proposal Complex: A record
Nodes: two nodes to be syntactically composed
Syn-Pref: syntactic preference level
Roles: role pairs being semantically composed
Sem-Pref: semantic preference levels for role pairs

Algorithm Arbitrate
Given a set of feasible compositions $\{P_i\}$
where each P_i is a proposal complex:
Sort the set of P_is in decreasing order of Syn-Pref;
Partition the sorted list into equivalence classes E_j
of P_is of equal Syn-Pref;
For each partition E_j,
   Sort the P_is in E_j in decreasing order of
   the maximum Sem-Pref in a P_i;
Select the first E_j with a positive maximum Sem-Pref;
Else if no such E_j exists,
   select the first partition in the sorted list E_1
   (syntactically most preferred);
Select from the chosen partition E_j those P_is
that have the maximum Sem-Pref among the P_is in that E_j.

Figure 3.7
Arbitration algorithm.

noted that the arbitration algorithm presented here could be seen as an approximation to one using real-numbered preferences. A propitious aspect of using only discrete levels of preferences is that COMPERE does not have to deal with the question of where those real numbers originate from or how they can be acquired or learned.

The arbitration algorithm shown in figure 3.7 selects the highest preferred interpretation that both syntax and semantics agree on. It may be noted that this algorithm implicitly allows delayed decisions: Whenever semantics has equal preferences (whether positive, zero, or negative), it allows the selection of all the alternatives with equal preference so that they are all pursued until disambiguated later by new information. If semantics has a positive preference for at least one syntactic proposal, such a proposal is selected. If semantics has no preference for or against any syntactic attachment, the most preferred syntactic attachment is selected. If, on the other hand, semantics rejects all syntactic proposals, one or more of the most preferred syntactic proposals are still selected, thereby allowing syntax to override semantics and produce an interpretation instead of none at all.

To illustrate the workings of the arbitration algorithm, consider a benign and a conflict situation in syntax-semantics interactions.

Sentence Processing in Understanding

Arbitration: A benign situation

(4) The officers taught at the academy were very demanding.

Consider, for example, sentence (4) above with an ambiguity in composing the verb "taught" with the subject NP "The officers." It is clear that in this case there is a strong syntactic preference for the main verb attachment. This attachment satisfies the syntactic expectation for a VP and completes the sentence while the reduced-relative attachment does not. Since semantics has equal preferences for either attachment ("officers" can be teachers or be taught by others), arbitration is trivial in this case and the main verb attachment is selected at this point.

Arbitration: A conflict situation

(5) The courses taught at the academy were very demanding.

Considering sentence (5) above, on the other hand, we see that though the syntactic preferences remain the same as in the previous example, semantics now has a negative preference for the main verb attachment (i.e., semantics rejects this attachment proposal, since "courses" cannot be the agents of "taught"). Thus in this case the reduced-relative attachment is selected by the arbitrator.

3.7.2.2 Resolving Lexical Semantic Ambiguities Lexical semantic (or word sense) ambiguities do not lend themselves to be construed as a choice in some form of attachment. As such, separate methods are necessary to resolve lexical semantic ambiguities. COMPERE has the following additional methods that work in conjunction with the arbitration algorithm to choose contextually appropriate word meanings:

- *Deactivate Meanings.* This method is called whenever a role attachment is made. It deactivates any word meanings that are not compatible with the role attachment being made. Any meaning that violates one or more selectional preferences are taken out of the set of conceptual meanings for the structure being attached. These meanings are retained as alternative meanings for their potential recall during later error recovery processes.
- *Reactivate Retained Meanings.* This method is applied during an error recovery operation. It reexamines any deactivated meaning in the new context and brings back any meaning that is now appropriate because the selectional constraint that eliminated it in the first place is not present in the new context. If there are new selectional constraints, on the other hand, this method might use the service of Deactivate Meanings to remove some of the previously active meanings. Thus COMPERE has the capacity to switch conceptual meanings appropriately as the syntactic or semantic structure of the interpretation changes.

Indiscreet retention of unselected alternatives could soon become prohibitive with hundreds of alternatives retained for some sentences. COMPERE uses a simple heuristic to decide when to retain an alternative and when it can safely discard an unselected proposal:

- *Retain only accessible alternatives.* Only alternatives for attachments that are currently accessible by being on the right-hand boundary of a parse tree are retained. As a subtree moves to interior parts of a tree, alternatives associated with nodes on that subtree are discarded. This greatly reduces the number of alternatives retained for error recovery. This rule is based on a hypothesis that not only is a right-hand boundary the only accessible part for making attachments, it is also the only part accessible for repairing the parse forest during error recovery. This hypothesis has not been contradicted by any sentence COMPERE has been tested with.

3.7.2.3 Implementation of Error Recovery Algorithms In its attempts to produce incremental interpretations and also be deterministic to the extent possible, COMPERE sometimes commits errors in both syntactic and semantic interpretation.[13] However, it has the ability to recover from errors in both syntax and semantics. There are several specific error recovery methods that it employs for reinterpreting the sentence without reprocessing it entirely.

Though the essential mechanism for error recovery is obviously backtracking to a previously unselected alternative, COMPERE's error recovery methods are more than plain chronological backtracking. The alternatives are stored in the working memory as already mentioned. Error recovery methods pick out the appropriate alternatives from this memory using the information available from the error situation without having to search through unrelated alternatives. Error situations and the corresponding recovery methods can be of three basic kinds:

Composition Failure When a new word meaning cannot be composed with the existing interpretations either syntactically or semantically, then we have a composition failure. Assuming that the sentence itself is always correct, COMPERE looks at its alternatives to see if reinterpreting the initial part of the sentence using one of the retained alternatives results in a new interpretation with which the new word meaning can be composed successfully. Since the new structure that could not be composed is available in this type of error, COMPERE searches the memory of alternatives for precisely that which involves an alternative composition of a previous structure of the same kind. This heuristic search process is not the same as either chronological or dependency-directed backtracking. It does not go back and reexamine every decision that was made in processing the sentence. Furthermore, although it is similar to dependency-directed backtracking, it is not dependency directed because there was no explicit knowledge of a causal dependency between the previous decision and the present error.

(2) The bugs moved into the lounge were found quickly.

For example, consider sentence (2) above and the error situation upon reading the word "were." This is a composition failure where there is no way to compose the meaning of "were" with the previous part of the sentence. At this point there are three retained syntactic alternatives. COMPERE does not examine or pursue each one of these. From the present error situation it knows that the error occurred because of a lack of place to attach the new VP. Hence it looks for alternatives for attaching previous VP's. It selects the reduced-relative alternative for "moved" and repairs the parse forest and associated semantic role assignments. This results in a correct interpretation through an error recovery process without complete reprocessing of the input sentence. For instance, the prepositional phrase "into the lounge" and its semantic role in its parent VP are never modified in any manner during this recovery.

Incompleteness Failure When a syntactic or semantic structure remains incomplete (e.g., at the end of the sentence where there are no more words to be processed), the result is an incompleteness failure. In such a situation COMPERE analyzes the required units for the incomplete sentence or phrase to be completed, which are also the expected units at that point, and picks out alternatives from its working memory that involve compositions of structures, which are still on the right boundary and hence are accessible at this time, that are of the same type as the required unit(s). COMPERE explores such alternatives to see if reinterpreting them removes the error by producing complete structures. Here again the same heuristic is employed to search the retained alternatives although the error situation is different from the previous one.

(3) The children taught at the academy.

For example, consider sentence (3) above. COMPERE has pursued a reduced-relative interpretation until the end of the sentence since there is a conceptual constraint in TEACH that does not allow "children" to fill an agent role in it. In this interpretation, "children" fill an experiencer role in the event (i.e., "the children who were taught at..."). However, at the end of the sentence, the sentence structure is incomplete, still waiting for its head VP. COMPERE selects the main verb alternative for "taught" from among the alternatives retained at this point and repairs the structure to obtain a complete sentence structure with a corresponding meaning. In this interpretation the "children" fill an agent role in the TEACH event, overriding the selectional constraint on the agent of TEACH. COMPERE accomplishes this by telling its arbitrator to disregard semantic constraints and go ahead considering only syntactic preferences. Such a change in strategy necessary to model this type of error recovery behavior is possible in COMPERE because its architecture has a unified arbitrator. The arbitrator provides the necessary control over syntax-semantics interaction to enable recovery from such conflicts and errors. Once again, error recovery was accomplished through repair and reinterpretation, not reprocessing of the entire sentence.

Recovery Induced Errors It is also possible that recovering from one error causes a decision made previously to be revoked or altered. For instance, reinterpreting a syntactic structure might annul a previous word sense disambiguation. In sentence (2) above at the time of the composition failure, the word "bugs" was disambiguated to mean only an INSECT, the MICROPHONE meaning being deactivated and retained as an alternative (see table 3.1). After repair and recovery from the error, however, there is no longer a reason to reject the latter meaning of "bugs." COMPERE reexamines the active and deactivated meanings of the structures involved in error recovery, which are also the structures whose roles are reassigned, to see their current status as per the new constraints coming from the new role assignments. This process is done concurrently with the role (re)assignment process to ensure consistency between the syntactic and semantic interpretations at all times. For example, in (2), both the INSECT and the MICROPHONE meanings are made active upon error recovery. As a result the previously resolved word sense ambiguity is "unresolved."

Note that though COMPERE is capable of recovering from the types of errors described above, the program (i.e., its "state") does not change in any manner after it encounters an error and recovers from it. For example, it behaves the same way over and over again making the same errors and recovering from them when presented with a sequence of sentences that lead the processor to the similar errors. COMPERE differs from human sentence processors in this respect, since the human processor appears to be at least aware of difficulties encountered in recovering from certain errors. However, in order to model such an "awareness" in a program, it appears that having a single process acting as a unified arbitrator is a definite advantage in keeping a record of the additional decisions and arbitrations it had to perform in order to recover from the error and change the behavior of the program in subsequent processing.

3.7.3 COMPERE, the Program

COMPERE, the computational model of sentence understanding, has been implemented and tested with a variety of sentences containing syntactic and semantic ambiguities, including the examples used in this chapter. A graphical user interface to

COMPERE allows the user to process a sentence and see the words being processed, the current syntactic output (i.e., parse trees), and the current semantic output (role bindings and word meanings) in separate windows. A key feature of the interface is that it allows the user to stop COMPERE after each word to see a clear graphical demonstration of incremental processing capabilities, garden-path effects, and error recoveries.

The program is designed so that syntactic processing can be separated from semantic processing. By setting a single flag, COMPERE can be made to run as a syntactic parser only or as a semantic processor that interprets directly from lexical entries of words without depending on a syntactic parse of the input sentence. This feature allows one to see clearly the functional independence between syntax and semantics in COMPERE.

COMPERE's program includes a simple grammar for English, a small lexicon, and a limited amount of semantic knowledge. The lexicon has recently been extended to include over 600 English words. COMPERE's grammar has 31 categories (or nonterminals) with 1 to 8 "rules" per category covering a variety of phrase, clause, and sentence structures. COMPERE's semantics has 34 roles with 1 to 7 "rules" per role. Its conceptual knowledge has over 500 concepts in several hierarchies. COMPERE runs fairly fast, taking less than a second to process a word on average.

COMPERE has been tested with 20 to 25 types of sentences with various syntactic constructs and various combinations of syntactic and semantic ambiguities, both lexical and structural. COMPERE has also been integrated with the ISAAC story understanding system and tested with some complete stories which are short science fiction stories (Moorman and Ram 1994).

3.8 Sentence Processor Situated in a Text Understander

An understanding system without a cooperating sentence processor is limited to behaving as though the input text was a mere set of its content words (i.e., nouns, verbs, adjectives, and adverbs). It misses all of the clues to meaning that arise from a sentence level analysis of word order, morphology, parts of speech, syntax, and closed class elements (e.g., prepositions). While it has been demonstrated by many early understanding systems that having appropriate knowledge structures in memory can compensate partially for this loss, it is commonly accepted that a sentence processor becomes more and more inevitable when one attempts to scale such systems to understanding of open domain texts from the real world.

In designing COMPERE, we have always recognized that sentence understanding is a subtask to be situated in a bigger task such as reading. In fact, as noted above, COMPERE has already been integrated with the ISAAC story reading system. We believe that the design of COMPERE facilitates such integration in the following ways:

- COMPERE provides incremental output, including incremental semantic output, that enable tasks such as reading to apply other methods and knowledge at the earliest opportunity.
- COMPERE does not demand complete knowledge of any kind. It produces an interpretation that can be used by other tasks even when some knowledge is missing or the input is less than perfect. Unlike COMPERE, most syntactic parsers, for example, reject even slightly ungrammatical sentences and provide no output for use by other tasks.
- COMPERE has a central arbitrator that combines syntactic and semantic information. The arbitration algorithm can be extended easily to accept additional kinds of information, thereby enabling other tasks in reading to provide incremental feedback to the sentence understander.
- COMPERE is not specific to any particular domain, corpus, or knowledge base. It does not demand complete knowledge of scripts or other knowledge structures for a domain. Thus it can be easily integrated with domain-specific modules, if any, in a reading system.

Moreover, the exercise in integrating COMPERE with ISAAC has already demonstrated that COMPERE's lexicon, grammar, and conceptual knowledge can be extended to increase the coverage of sentences that it can process. It is also modular in design. For example, if a different parsing algorithm was found better for another natural language, COMPERE's HSLC algorithm can be replaced with ease.

3.9 Conclusion

Sentence processing is an important part of language understanding. A model of understanding, whether computational or cognitive, must not only include a model of sentence-level processing, it must also explain when and how higher level understanding processes interact with sentence processing.

Sentence processors are often designed in isolation to solve particular problems in sentence analysis, such as prepositional attachment ambiguities or word sense disambiguation. It is critical in developing computational models of understanding to design a sentence processor that performs both syntactic and semantic analyses and extracts all of the information necessary for higher-level understanding. In this chapter we have presented such a design in COMPERE which enables effective interaction with higher-level understanding processes.

We believe that COMPERE is one of the few models that meets many of the functional and cognitive constraints on sentence understanding set forth in this chapter (in section 3.3.6). In particular, it is a true implementation of integrated processing that supports incremental interactions between syntax and semantics, yet retains sufficient control over the interactions, through its arbitrator, to resolve conflicts and recover from errors.

Certainly there are many unresolved and controversial issues in sentence understanding, in terms of both computational and cognitive modeling. Yet we believe that sentence understanding technology is ripe enough to be applied in the service of solving bigger problems like story understanding and reading.

Notes

Many parts of this chapter are taken from the PhD thesis of the first author (Mahesh 1995).

1. Cognitive Model of Parsing and Error Recovery. A *compere* is one who introduces and interlinks items of an entertainment, according to *Chambers Twentieth Century Dictionary*.

2. One could ask a more basic question, What are the different types of knowledge that play a role in language understanding? We do not raise this question here. Instead, we assume that knowledge sources commonly employed in linguistics, psycholinguistics, computational linguistics, and natural language processing, such as syntax and semantics, are essential for resolving ambiguities in sentences. See an introductory textbook such as the one by Allen (1987) or Grishman (1986) for a good explanation of the role of syntax and semantics in natural language understanding.

3. Actually the word as the basic lexical unit is a somewhat loose characterization, since sometimes we use phrasal lexicons where commonly occurring phrases have lexical knowledge associated with them.

4. From this example, note that we can also derive a psychological prediction generated by the COMPERE model that a word sense ambiguity, as in the "bugs" example, remains unresolved at the end of the sentence, even though it was resolved temporarily until the resolution was found to be in error.

5. It may also be noted that given the goal of incremental selection, and the fact that all types of knowledge can be of help in reducing ambiguity in language processing, the integrated processing principle is merely a restatement of the principle of rationality (Newell 1981).

6. See Mahesh (1995) for a discussion of the psycholinguistic implications of how COMPERE deals with sentence (3) above.

7. Time here refers to points in the sentence (e.g., after word 2 from the left), not the micro-level time in processing a particular word. The latter demands a finer level of analysis than this chapter attempts and falls into modularity arguments such as those given by Fodor (1983).

8. Semantics in this section refers to semantic as well as conceptual knowledge.

9. While COMPERE's head-signaled left-corner parsing has the virtue of keeping memory requirements to a minimum, no limit has been placed on available memory in the implementation.

10. One could argue that there are other sources of information such as statistical information from a corpus, lexical subcategorizations of the verb for particular prepositions, or contextual biases that enable a justified early commitment immediately after the preposition. See the discussion on flexible parsing in Mahesh (1995) for possible improvements to the parsing algorithm to account for the above sources of information.

11. For more elaborate representations of conceptual knowledge, see the discussion of Mikrokosmos ontology in Mahesh (1996), for example.

12. It may be noted that certain connectionist networks do precisely this by having a merged single scale of activation levels to start with so that arbitration is in a sense automatic.

13. These errors do not occur because of incorrect algorithms or bugs in COMPERE's implementation. They are due to the fact that COMPERE makes its incremental decisions based on the information it has at its access at the time of decision, but sometimes information available later in processing a sentence proves a previous decision incorrect.

References

Abney, S. P., and M. Johnson. 1991. Memory requirements and local ambiguities of parsing strategies. *Journal of Psycholinguistic Research* 20: 233–50.

Allen, J. 1987. *Natural Language Understanding*. Menlo Park, CA: Benjamin/Cummings.

Birnbaum, L. 1986. *Integrated Processing in Planning and Understanding*. PhD thesis. Research report 489. Yale University, Department of Computer Science, New Haven.

Birnbaum, L. 1989. A critical look at the foundations of autonomous syntactic analysis. In *Proceedings of the Eleventh Annual Conference of the Cognitive Science Society*, pp. 99–106, Ann Arbor, MI. Cognitive Science Society.

Bresnan, J., and R. Kaplan. 1982. Introduction: Grammars as mental representations of language. In J. Bresnan ed., *The Mental Representation of Grammatical Relations*. Cambridge: MIT Press.

Caramazza, A., and R. S. Berndt. 1978. Semantic and syntactic processes in aphasia: A review of the literature. *Psychological Bulletin* 85: 898–918.

Carlson, G. N., and M. K. Tanenhaus. 1988. Thematic roles and language comprehension. In W. Wilkins, ed., *Syntax and Semantics*, vol. 21, *Thematic Relations*. San Diego: Academic Press.

Carpenter, P. A., and M. Daneman. 1981. Lexical retrieval and error recovery in reading: A model based on eye fixations. *Journal of Verbal Learning and Verbal Behavior* 20: 137–60.

Crain, S., and M. Steedman. 1985. On not being led up the garden path: The use of context by the psychological syntax processor. In D. R. Dowty, L. Karttunen, and A. M. Zwicky, eds; *Natural Language Parsing: Psychological, Computational, and Theoretical Perspectives*. Cambridge: Cambridge University Press.

Crocker, M. W. 1993. Properties of the principle-based sentence processor. In *Proceedings of the Fifteenth Annual Conference of the Cognitive Science Society*. Hillsdale, NJ: Lawrence Erlbaum, pp. 371–76.

Earley, J. 1970. An efficient context-free parsing algorithm. *Communications of ACM* 13: 94–102.

Eiselt, K. P. 1989. *Inference Processing and Error Recovery in Sentence Understanding*. PhD thesis. Technical report 89-24. University of California, Irvine.

Eiselt, K. P., and J. K. Holbrook. 1991. Toward a unified theory of lexical error recovery. In *Proceedings of the Thirteenth Annual Conference of the Cognitive Science Society*, Chicago. Cognitive Science Society.

Erman, L., F. Hayes-Roth, V. Lesser, and D. Reddy. 1980. The hearsay-ii speech understanding system: Integrating knowledge to resolve uncertainty. *ACM Computing Survey* 12: 213–53.

Fodor, J. A. 1983. *The Modularity of Mind*. Cambridge: MIT Press.

Fodor, J. A. 1987. Modules, frames, fridgeons, sleeping dogs, and the music of the spheres. In J. L. Garfield, ed., *Modularity in Knowledge Representation and Natural-Language Understanding*. Cambridge: MIT Press.

Frawley, W. 1992. *Linguistic Semantics*. Hillsdale, NJ: Lawrence Erlbaum.

Frazier, L. 1987. Theories of sentence processing. In J. L. Garfield ed., *Modularity in Knowledge Representation and Natural Language Understanding*. Cambridge: MIT Press.

Grishman, R. 1986. *Computational Linguistics: An Introduction*. Cambridge: Cambridge University Press.

Holbrook, J. K., K. P. Eiselt, and K. Mahesh. 1992. A unified process model of syntactic and semantic error recovery in sentence understanding. In *Proceedings of the Fourteenth Annual Conference of the Cognitive Science Society*, pp. 195–200, Bloomington, IN. Cognitive Science Society.

Jurafsky, D. 1991. An on-line model of human sentence interpretation. In *Proceedings of the Thirteenth Annual Conference of the Cognitive Science Society*, 449–54, Chicago. Cognitive Science Society.

Just, M. A., and P. Carpenter. 1980. A theory of reading: From eye fixations to comprehension. *Psychological Review* 87: 329–54.

Just, M. A., and P. Carpenter. 1987. *The psychology of reading and language comprehension*. Needham Heights, MA: Allyn and Bacon.

Lebowitz, M. 1983. Memory-based parsing. *Artificial Intelligence* 21: 363–404.

Lytinen, S. L. 1984. *The Organization of Knowledge in a Multi-lingual Integrated Parser*. PhD thesis. Research report 340. Yale University, Department of Computer Science, New Haven.

Lytinen, S. L. 1987. Integrating syntax and semantics. In S. Nirenburg, ed., *Machine Translation, Theoretical and Methodological Issues*. Cambridge: Cambridge University Press, pp. 302–16.

Mahesh, K. 1995. *Syntax-Semantics Interaction in Sentence Understanding*. PhD thesis. Technical report GIT-CC-95/10. College of Computing, Georgia Institute of Technology, Atlanta.

Mahesh, K. 1996. Ontology development: Ideology and methodology. Technical report MCCS-96-292. Computing Research Laboratory, New Mexico State University, Las Cruces.

Mahesh, K., and K. Eiselt. 1994. Uniform representations for syntax-semantics arbitration. In *Proceedings of the Sixteenth Annual Conference of the Cognitive Science Society*. Hillsdale, NJ: Lawrence Erlbaum, pp. 589–94.

Marslen-Wilson, W., and L. K. Tyler. 1987. Against modularity. In J. L. Garfield, ed., *Modularity in Knowledge Representation and Natural-Language Understanding*. Cambridge: MIT Press.

McClelland, J. L., and H. Kawamoto. 1986. Mechanisms of sentence processing: Assigning roles to constituents. In J. L. McClelland, D. E. Rumelhart, and the PDP Research Group, eds., *Parallel Distributed Processing. Explorations in the microstructure of cognition,* vol. 2, *Psychological and Biological Models*. Cambridge: MIT Press.

Moorman, K., and A. Ram. 1994. Integrating creativity and reading: A functional approach. In *Proceedings of the Sixteenth Annual Conference of the Cognitive Science Society*. Hillsdale, NJ: Lawrence Erlbaum, pp. 646–51.

Newell, A. 1981. The knowledge level. *AI Magazine* 2: 1–20. Presidential Address, American Association for Artificial Intelligence AAAI80, Stanford University, 19 August 1980.

Nii, H. P. (1989). Blackboard systems. In A. Barr, P. R. Cohen, and E. A. Feigenbaum, eds., *The Handbook of Artificial Intelligence*, vol. 4. Reading, MA: Addison-Wesley, pp. 1–82.

Reddy, D., L. Erman, and R. Neely. 1973. A model and a system for machine recognition of speech. *IEEE Transactions on Audio and Electroacoustics* 21: 229–38.

Schank, R. C., M. Lebowitz, and L. Birnbaum. 1980. An integrated understander. *American Journal of Computational Linguistics* 6: 13–30.

Sells, P. 1985. Lectures on contemporary syntactic theories. Center for the Study of Language and Information. Stanford University.

Stowe, L. A. 1991. Ambiguity resolution: Behavioral evidence for a delay. In *Proceedings of the Thirteenth Annual Conference of the Cognitive Science Society*, pp. 257–62. Cognitive Science Society.

Tanenhaus, M. K., G. S. Dell, and G. Carlson. 1987. Context effects in lexical processing: A connectionist approach to modularity. In J. L. Garfield, ed., *Modularity in Knowledge Representation and Natural-Language Understanding*. Cambridge: MIT Press.

Tyler, L. K., and W. D. Marslen-Wilson. 1977. The on-line effects of semantic context on syntactic processing. *Journal of Verbal Learning and Verbal Behavior* 16: 683–92.

Waltz, D. L., and J. B. Pollack. 1985. Massively parallel parsing: A strongly interactive model of natural language interpretation. *Cognitive Science* 9: 51–74.

Woods, W. A. 1973. An experimental parsing system for transition network grammars. In R. Rustin, ed., *Courant Computer Science Symposium* 8: *Natural Language Processing*. New York: Algorithmics Press.

Chapter 4
Capturing the Contents of Complex Narratives

Eric Domeshek, Eric Jones, and Ashwin Ram

4.1 Language and Representation

Dave: "Hal. Please open the pod bay door."
HAL: "I'm sorry Dave. I can't do that."[1]

Thirty years after this first appeared on screen, a simple exchange between desperate man and homicidal machine remains fiction—not a threatening reality. Building machines that can kill is easy. Building machines that can *perceive a need* to kill is another matter. The point is not to dwell on HAL's character flaws or tragic situation but rather to explore why a machine with HAL's facility for assessing situations, choosing actions, and communicating with humans remains elusive.

Researchers in natural language processing (NLP) can readily enumerate the difficulties of participating in, or even understanding, this snippet of dialogue. Understanding what is going on means understanding how words refer to things and (potential) actions in the world, it means understanding the motives behind utterances and the plans that people are likely to be pursuing, it means being able to figure out what actions agents might take as circumstances change around them, and it means understanding the conventions of normal conversation.

The sort of artificial intelligence (AI) and cognitive science that has concerned itself with tasks such as understanding natural language has long been wedded to some notion of *knowledge representation*. Conventional symbolic models of cognition would posit that anyone able to understand Dave's request must have some internal representation of the spaceship and its portals, the operations of opening and closing those portals, and Dave's physical location with respect to the spacecraft and its portals. Similarly, to understand what HAL says requires knowing who HAL and Dave are, how Dave feels about HAL, where HAL is located, and what is likely to happen to HAL if Dave is let in, or to Dave if HAL shuts him out. That requisite "knowing" is again modeled as possession of appropriate internal representations of these facts, attitudes, and likelihoods.

4.1.1 Why Have Representation?

Representation is central to cognitive modeling and AI for many reasons. To understand why, we should start by considering what is meant by the term "representation." Most obviously and essentially, a representation is a surrogate, or stand-in, for something else. In the case of a "mental representation" we are talking about surrogates for things in the world as well as for beliefs, attitudes, and emotions; these stand-ins are supposed to be physically instantiated somehow in the brain, allowing their manipulation by the mind. In the case of "knowledge representation" we are talking about computer models of mental representations. Again, these are surrogates for things in the world and for ideas; only this time they are physically instantiated in a computer memory, allowing them to be manipulated by mechanized computational processes. The first reason to posit representations, then, is because we cannot get actual *things* into a mind (or a computer) and because, when it comes to generating *ideas*, we can only imagine (or implement) thought processes that have some physical (or computational) basis.

But language is itself a form of representation; computers, for instance, can store and manipulate strings of characters making up words, phrases, sentences, and whole texts. Why do we need anything else to account for mentation in human or machine? One major reason might be called "cognitive economy." There are simply too many different natural language expressions that have approximately the same meaning (even limiting our consideration to a single language, such as English). Dave might very well have happened to say something other than "Please open the pod bay door"; he could equally well have uttered any of a large number of other equivalent sentences: "Please let me into the pod bay," "Please open the airlock," or simply "Let me in." Furthermore, under normal circumstances, he might shortly thereafter have made a logically related request such as "Please close the pod bay door," or "Please close the hatch," or just "Close it up."

A minimal requirement for any mental model is the intelligence to reliably say whether or not some fact presented to the model is something it already knew. The need to perform this kind of reasoning arises constantly during natural language understanding, during the resolution of anaphora, and when determining whether a new utterance reiterates, elaborates, or contradicts an earlier one. If, for instance, the reader knows "the pod bay door is closed" (expressed as that English phrase), they must be able to reliably determine that "the pod bay door is not open" constitutes the same already known fact, and that "the door of the pod bay" probably refers to the same object as "the pod bay door." They also must recognize that "the pod bay door is locked" builds on the previous knowledge about the pod bay door, while "the pod bay door is gaping" contradicts it. A natural approach is to begin by translating all the different ways of expressing these ideas into a *canonical form*: a form in which expressions with a similar meaning have more or less the same representation. A canonical representation makes it easy to compare old and new facts.

Language has other "problems" that drive cognitive modelers to use knowledge representations. Not only can many different phrases mean the same thing, but a single word or phrase can mean many different things. Ambiguity and imprecision in language can be powerful tools in argumentation or in art, but as properties of a language for automated reasoning, they introduce needless complications. Although meanings may shift in predictable ways with the larger contexts in which a word or phrase is used, it would clearly be better to avoid spending time checking the context every time a symbol is referenced. Thus it is preferable to have a simpler *compositional semantics* in which the meaning of a larger expression is built up in a straightforward way from the meanings of its parts, rather than having the meanings of the parts shift depending on the larger expressions in which they are embedded. Again, a natural approach is to begin by translating natural language utterances into a representation that has a suitable semantics.

4.1.1.1 Need for Inference What kinds of manipulations might it be necessary to perform on mental contents? We have already suggested simply comparing assertions to see if they are familiar, consistent, or contradictory. That is pretty minimal intelligence. More generally, a system should be able to *draw inferences* from what it is told in order to recognize explicitly some of what was implicit in available information. In story understanding, inference is required to establish narrative coherence, to explain the actions of the participants in terms of their plans, goals, and underlying motivations, and to answer questions about the story. The necessity of inference was first recognized long ago when early NLP programs had to infer causal and motivational connections to make sense of simple pairs of sentences like "John hit Mary," and "Mary cried" (e.g., Schank 1975).

In physical symbol systems, inference is typically implemented as a process of rule application, based on matching representational patterns and instantiating representational templates. A representation encoding that a person "John" propelled a hard physical object into a person "Mary" with notable force matches the antecedent for a rule, which when applied produces as its conclusion a representation of the belief that the person "Mary" is probably feeling pain. Another rule can make the common-sense causal connection between the expectation that "Mary" is feeling pain, and the second sentence's encoding of the fact that "Mary" cried.

The need for inference further underscores the importance of canonical representations. If representations are canonical, it is possible to dramatically reduce the number of inference rules that a system requires. Lacking a canonical representation, essentially the same inferential knowledge must be encoded many times, once for each distinct but semantically equivalent representation of an inference rule antecedent.

Our *2001* excerpt is substantially more complex than the simple story about John and Mary. For instance, the reader knows that the pod bay door is closed and that Dave is outside the ship; therefore given an understanding of solid materials, containers, and portals, it is reasonable to conclude that Dave cannot get inside the ship. Given further understandings about outer space, space ships, and biology, the reader knows that Dave cannot live long if he doesn't get back inside the ship. Finally, given expectations about human desires, confirmed by observations of repeated escalating demands for entrance, the reader can conclude that Dave wants to continue living and is upset by HAL's behavior.

All of this analysis is inferential extension of the much more limited data presented by the observed situation. A viewer or reader of *2001* receives only information about the conversation and its context, yet manages to understand how Dave (and HAL) are feeling and to form expectations of what they are likely to do next.

4.1.1.2 Theories of Representation and Inference Traditional theories of representation and inference in AI have for the most part operated within the framework of model-theoretic semantics (e.g., McCarthy 1968; McDermott 1978; Hayes 1978). These approaches are attractive because they stake out mathematically clear definitions about what it means to represent anything at all and because they come with guarantees about the ability to derive only truthful conclusions from truthful premises (or to derive plausible conclusions from plausible premises, depending on the particular theory). Unfortunately, preoccupation with these mathematical properties seems to have left relatively little time for many researchers to delve deeply into other aspects required for a useful representational system.

In computational modeling, commitment to some formalism is unavoidable. But rather than dwell on the mathematical properties of a formal system, our preferred focus for theories of representation and inference is on different, functionally oriented questions: What content needs to be represented to support some particular behavior? How can fragmentary inputs be pieced together into reasonable elaborated conclusions and expectations? How should the content be organized so that the right knowledge comes to hand at the right times?

Compared to formal semanticists, we adopt a looser, more pragmatic, approach to thinking about representation and inference. Representations do not capture truth by bearing some strict correspondence to the real world. Instead, we seek representations that support a fairly informal causal account of people's and systems' behavior:

We observe that people's behavior is often appropriate to their circumstances, and we want the same to be true for AI systems we construct. As cognitive scientists, in order to account for the observed fact that people often behave appropriately, we posit that people possess internal representations that correlate with significant aspects of situations. All we require are arguments that people can identify these representational features in the real world with fair reliability, and that their behavior is more often appropriate when such features are considered. As computer scientists, we build systems that operate over the same kinds of internal representations.

4.1.1.3 Aspects of Representation Knowledge representation is concerned with encoding a range of types of information, such as facts, heuristics, associations, procedures, plans, constraints, concepts, experiences, causal models, commonsense knowledge, beliefs, and so on. In accomplishing such an encoding, any AI system must take a stand on three fundamental aspects of representations: their form, content, and organization. *Form* covers issues such as the syntax of representation languages and their embodiment in physical structure (e.g., computer memory and accompanying procedures). Although we may want to de-emphasize issues of form, we cannot totally ignore them if we want a functioning, testable mechanized model. *Content* refers to the distinctions made by a representation and its underlying ontology: the dimensions along which it carves up the world. *Organization* implies that there are interesting associations and access paths among the contents of a knowledge base; the totality of a knowledge representation system is better thought of as a memory honed through a history of goal-directed task pursuit, than as a simple unstructured laundry list of knowledge.

Consider, for example, the problem of representing the domain of economics. A content issue is whether or not to include the law of supply and demand (indeed, whether to include "supply" and "demand" as entities in the ontology in the first place) and at what level of detail the law should be expressed. There are two corresponding issues of representational form: (1) whether the chosen representational syntax is sufficiently powerful to encode the desired content, and (2) whether this syntax is well suited to the reasoning process that will operate over the representations. A related issue of representational organization is whether a particular physical encoding of the representation allows the reasoning process to readily locate the law in memory under appropriate circumstances. In English, for example, the law of supply and demand can be encoded using the sentence, "Other things remaining equal, the price of a commodity is directly proportional to its demand and inversely proportional to its supply." In the language of mathematics, the same law can be encoded using an algebraic equation, $P_i \alpha D_i / S_i$. Other representations are also possible, for example, using probabilistic models or diagrams.

These different expressions of the law of supply and demand cover much the same territory. However, the *form* of each representation is different, having distinct syntactic structure and supporting the use of different kinds of representation elements (e.g., English words vs. mathematical symbols). The *content* of each representation also differs, both in the level of detail in which it describes the law of supply and demand and in the aspects of the law on which it focuses. A probabilistic model of supply and demand, for example, can be expected to include information about the extent to which actual supply and demand varies from idealized supply-demand curves. This information is only hinted at the English version ("other things remaining equal") and is missing altogether from the algebraic version.

It is also important to note that some formalisms are much better suited than others to encoding particular kinds of content. While it is certainly possible to represent quantitative probabilistic information using English, such information is more naturally and concisely stated using the language of probability theory, which is also much more amenable to formal reasoning.

In the remained of this section, we will elaborate on what we mean by the form, content, and organization of representation systems. We will then use these representational issues as the organizing principle for the balance of the chapter.

4.1.2 What Is Representational Form?

Throughout this chapter we restrict our attention to symbolic representational systems. That means a system starts with a set of symbols, each interpreted as having some more or less fixed meaning. Most often, when there are clusters of related meanings to be represented—such as "I want you to open the door," "I want you to close the door," "You want me to close the door"—we prefer to design the representational system so that the shared components are assigned symbols, and the variations in meaning are accounted for by different ways in which those symbols are combined. Thus, for instance, there might be symbols **me**, **you**, **open**, **close**, and **door** representing the obvious related concepts; there also might be a single structure for grouping those symbols to express the several related ideas above: (**you, open, door**), (**you, close, door**), (**me, close, door**).

One aspect of representational form, then, is the allowable structures for combining symbols. This is the syntax of the representation system, which may vary from simple and uniform to highly complex with many distinctions among the kinds of symbols there are and the ways they can be combined.

Another aspect of representational form is the model underlying the formalism—that is, the way that onlookers are supposed to think about the system. Popular representational models include first-order logic, frames, and semantic networks. For the most part, these various models are interconvertible (can capture equivalent distinctions), but different models do suggest different syntaxes (Hayes 1978). More important, different models suggest different processes and most especially suggest different organizational strategies. This issue will come up again in section 4.1.4.

The final aspect of representational form is the actual implementation of the system in some computational substrate (e.g., data structures in a computer). Again, basic aspects of a system's implementation are usually suggested by the system's underlying model: to implement propositions, it is natural to start with a list of tuples; to implement frames, it is natural to start with properties attached to symbols; to implement semantic nets, it is natural to start with something like typed pointers. However, all of these implementation biases are just starting points, and ultimately the underlying structures may become much more complicated, since they are honed to support the most common operations suggested by the models.

We will give all three of these aspects of representational form relatively short shrift in this chapter. There is more to say, but if the question for this book is "How do you understand complex texts?" relatively little of the answer depends on which form you choose for your representations.

4.1.3 What Is Representational Content?

The critical aspect of knowledge representation in support of reading and understanding is the range of content that can be represented. In NLP circles the results of attending to this issue are often called *content theories*. A content theory includes several kinds of specific representational commitments: (1) a basic ontology dividing descriptive terms into several classes, (2) some core symbols and their meanings in important closed ontological classes, (3) ways of combining symbols from the various classes, and (4) inferences that can be drawn from specified patterns of symbol structures. A content theory specifies exactly how a system could represent some range of meanings, and it is interesting to the extent that it covers a sizable and useful range.

The canonical example of a content theory is Schank's original conceptual dependency (CD) theory (Schank 1975). CD started with distinctions among actions, states, things, and causal linkages; introduced eleven core symbols to represent primitive actions plus a handful more to represent causal connections; provided rules for how to combine these ingredients into meaningful descriptions; and enumerated a core set of inferences licensed by patterns using these symbols. The symbol **ptrans** was defined to represent the action of physical movement; the symbol **at-loc** was defined to represent the state of something being located somewhere. An action like **ptrans** could be performed by some agent on some object and take that object from some initial position to some final position. An inference from **ptrans** was that if some object was **ptrans**ed to a location, then that object was known to be **at-loc** the designated place.

Since CD was proposed, many other content theories have been elaborated covering areas such as motivation (Carbonell 1979; Ram 1989; Domeshek 1990), planning (McDermott 1985), social relations (Seifert 1987; Domeshek 1992), emotions (Ortony, Cllore, and Collins 1988), questions (Ram 1989), and so on.

It is important, to distinguish these content theories from a larger class of "theories" prevalent in AI research—*domain theories*. Every symbolic AI system requires some commitment to representational ontology, specific symbols, combination rules, and inferences. However, quite often the point of building the system is to demonstrate a domain-independent technique (e.g., least-commitment planning) rather than to accomplish a task requiring deep domain knowledge (e.g., reading and paraphrasing a narrative). In these cases, what is being reasoned about is secondary (which often translates to "unimportant"). You can study planning in "blocks world" or in "job-shop world" or in "kitchen world." So long as you are studying planning, rather than paying attention to cooking, manufacturing, or (for some unknown reason) block-stacking, the representations you develop for these domains are likely to remain shallow. Such toy domain theories are not interesting content theories. Or to put it another way, as Larry Birnbaum, the originator of the concept, suggested: "A content theory is a domain theory you can be proud of."

4.1.4 What Is Representational Organization?

The last of our three views on representation focuses on how a system gets access to relevant symbol structures at the right time. The importance of organizing a large body of representations became apparent as it was noticed that, contrary to what happened when people learned, early AI systems almost always got slower as they were given more information to work with. Representation systems that simply accumulated big sets of facts without regard for how they should be organized to support their intended task quickly proved to be a dead end. In NLP, systems began to take their cues from human memory (e.g., Schank 1982).

It is critical to understand that performance problems of unorganized memories are not simply minor inconveniences. No matter what model of reasoning is employed, understanding requires searching through a large space of possible interpretations; it is crucial that this search be conducted as efficiently as possible. The MARGIE system (Rieger 1975) provides an early example of a system whose search process suffers from a poor memory organization. Interpretations in MARGIE are causal chains that link together the actions in a story and render them coherent. The system works by conducting bi-directional search for causal chains linking each pair of action representations. At each stage of the search, the system attempts to link a chain originating from one action to a chain originating from another. A *combinatorial explosion* of inference results because at each stage there are many possible ways to extend the chain and an ever-increasing number of possible ways to link chains together. For many stories, MARGIE is intractably inefficient.

Equally problematic, there are often many possible causal chains linking the actions in a story, only a few of which constitute plausible interpretations. Even though any single link in a chain may be plausible if considered in isolation, considered jointly they may form a very improbable chain. There is nothing in MARGIE's representations of real-world knowledge that allows the system to assess the relative plausibility of alternative interpretations.

As inference chains get longer, the understanding process quickly becomes intractable, and the problem of choosing between alternative interpretations becomes acute. Inference chains must be kept short, and the number of viable options at each step must be kept small. First-principles reasoning from large collections of very simple facts cannot be the norm.

People rarely seem to engage in extended first-principles reasoning where they plod through elaborate extended reasoning chains. Especially when working in domains that they know well, people tend to analyzed situations in a few large leaps and jump right on to a reasonable response. Representational organization, then, refers to ways of structuring and indexing the knowledge needed for natural language understanding with the aim of producing this kind of behavior. In section 4.3 we will discuss past approaches to helping systems take the right reasoning steps and to take large steps.

4.2 Representational Content

This section lays out the criteria for content theories in considerable detail, sketches some typical ways of carving up the world into content clusters to be represented, and discusses one such cluster in some depth.

4.2.1 Desirable Properties of Representational Content

We take Birnbaum's definition as our starting point: "*A content theory is a domain theory you can be proud of.*" We have already said a bit about what a domain theory is: It constitutes a set of representational commitments to an ontology, some core symbols, rules of symbol-structure combination, and inferences. We have said that such a theory is interesting to the extent that it covers a sizable and useful range of possible meanings, and we gave CD as an example of such a theory. It is difficult to construct wide-ranging, useful representational theories, especially ones that are also reasonably usable, compact, and efficient. Even approximating these criteria justifies a certain amount of pride, and claim to the label "content theory."

In total, we have identified eleven interrelated criteria for a good content theory. Some of these were introduced in section 4.1, when we justified the use of an internal representation other than natural language. The first four are actually constraints on the relationship between representational form and content: (1) Expressions should be unambiguous (one meaning per symbol-structure), (2) syntactically distinct expressions should be semantically distinct (one symbol-structure per meaning), (3) similar but nonidentical meanings should have similar representations, and (4) the representation's semantics should be compositional in a straightforward way (related meanings share structure).

The next two criteria support reasoning at multiple levels of detail: (5) a content theory should allow representations to be elaborated as needed to encode the distinctions required at any stage of processing, and (6) a coding trick called *reification* should be supported to facilitate this task. The next two criteria are required to ensure a content theory is interesting: a content theory should (7) cover a wide ranging territory, and (8) cover territory that is actually useful for supporting some desired task. The last three criteria are practical constraints: it is preferable to have systems that are (9) more easily used by their intended audiences, (10) more compact, and (11) more efficient in processing. We elaborate on each of these criteria below.

1. Unambiguous Real-world situations are almost always open to a variety of interpretations, and the input to a cognitive system (e.g., a natural language text describing a situation) is typically rife with ambiguities. Nonetheless, once a system builds an internal representations of a situation based on some input, it seems better to avoid having to repeatedly invest a lot of effort in figuring our what that representation means. A system in which the internal symbol **buy** can mean both purchase (as in "John bought a book from Mary") and belief (as in "I don't buy that") will need to perform additional computations to determine what inferences follow from a formula such as **(Sam, buy, X)**.

As can be seen from this example, the need to resolve ambiguities is driven in large part by considerations of inferential efficiency. If the applicability of a bundle of inferences depends on a distinction between two possible interpretations, it makes sense to perform the inferences necessary to disambiguate up front and to cache the result.

Of course there will be circumstances in which a system *cannot* settle on a single interpretation, in which case the system may need to explicitly carry around multiple alternate descriptions. However, the most common kind of meaning multiplicity— that based on lack of detail (often referred to as *vagueness*)—can be compactly encoded in most systems using abstract concepts. For instance, if a text mentions someone but does not reveal their gender, then a system can use a vague term such as **person** in place of an explicit disjunction of the more specific concepts **man** and **woman**.

Finally it is important to emphasize that not all ambiguities matter. A system need only concern itself with those ambiguities whose resolution is important to the task at hand, either because the user has an interest in the results of disambiguation or because the applicability of important inferences hangs upon the result.

2. Canonical Just as it simplifies processing to ensure that there is only one meaning per symbol-structure, so too it is advantageous to ensure that as far as possible, there is only one symbol-structure per meaning. This is just the issue of canonical form again, which was first raised in section 4.1. Canonical representations bring two computational benefits. First, it is easy to compare or match up representations with similar meanings. Second, so long as there is only one way to encode a meaning, a system developer need write only one version of any inference rule sensitive to that meaning (or a system need learn only one rule version).

Having said that, it is nevertheless frequently convenient to define a new symbol as a shorthand for a longer expression with equivalent meaning. For example, the concept **woman** can be defined as a **person** with **gender female**. Concept definitions can allow compact representation of complex situations, which brings a number of benefits, as discussed below (criterion 7). Sowa (1984) presents an algorithm for *type contraction* that uses concept definitions to compute a maximally compact representation of a situation.

The issue of definitions is also closely tied up with the issues of vagueness and ambiguity. While abstract concepts allow compact encodings in the face of vagueness, once a system has more information, it ought to be able to revise its representation to use the most specific term available: Upon learning that a mystery character is female, a system should reclassify her as a **woman** rather than a **person** so as to trigger inferences that follow from her being a woman.

The drive for canonical representations should not be confused with a related issue of co-reference. Sometimes it is useful to construct two distinct representations of the same object or situation. Co-referential representations can still be canonical if each representation picks out different aspects of the object or situation to which it refers. It can be useful to introduce explicit representations of co-reference and to specify inference strategies for reasoning with multiple descriptions; the interested reader is referred to (Jones 1992).

3. Commensurable Not only should different meanings have different representations, but similar or related meanings should have similar or related representations. This property of representations facilitates partial matching of related pieces of knowledge, such as is required to determine whether two representations may be co-referential or to answer questions. For example, if the system knows that "John drove home" and is then asked whether "John went home," it is easier to match the question to the assertion if the two are represented in syntactically similar ways. One standard strategy is to arrange related concepts in an abstraction hierarchy: for example, "John went home" might be represented using the concept **ptrans**, "John drove home" using the concept **drive**, and **drive** asserted to be a subclass of **ptrans**. Partial matching can then be designed to allow objects at different levels in the abstraction hierarchy to match one another.

Knowledge can also be provided for relating concepts in different parts of an abstraction hierarchy (i.e., concepts neither being an abstraction of the other). For example, rules can be provided that allow a representation of a terrorist attack to be described as an illegal activity, a goal conflict, a political statement, and so forth (Jones 1992).

4. Compositional We want the interpretation of compound representations to be a reasonably simple function of the interpretations of their components and of the ways in which the components are combined. While we may lack a crisp definition of "reasonably simple," reasonable and unreasonable exemplars are easy to recognize. It should always be straightforward for the system to determine the intended interpretation of individual symbols no matter what context they appear in; the same should be true for larger symbol patterns.

There are two ways that this is accomplished in practice. The traditional approach is to take symbols and symbol patterns to represent essentially the same concept in all contexts (though their modal status as fact, belief, hypothetical, desire, fear, or existence in the past, present, or future may be malleable). A more recent approach is to formalize the notion of context itself and provide explicit representations for reasoning about contexts and interpretations within a context (Guha 1991; McCarthy 1993; Buvac 1996).

5. Elaboration The representation of a piece of knowledge should be at a level of detail and explicitness that is appropriate for the task at hand. Different levels of detail are sometimes appropriate at different stages of reasoning, so it should be possible to *elaborate* a representation on demand: that is, to replace or augment it with a more detailed representation that makes explicit further relevant distinctions.

Consider, for example, representing the utterance, "Please open the pod bay door." This may be represented using a predicate such as **open**; alternatively, it may be represented in more detail by making the sequence of actions explicit: "move to the door," then "reach out and grasp the door handle," then "pull the door handle toward you," and so on. While the former may be appropriate when instructing a human (or an intelligent robot in a science fiction movie) who has the knowledge required to understand the command and act on it, the latter, more detailed representation might be required when issuing a sequence of commands to an actual robot. In addition, if the system is to reason about whether it can (or should) open the door as instructed, or what the effects of that action might be, it must be able to decompose **open** (or **move**, **reach**, and **pull**) into finer-grained representations.

Elaboration may simply involve unpacking concept definitions (which Sowa 1984 calls *type expansion*, the inverse of his type contraction operation), or it may involve more complex reasoning such as planning, in which a system must project plausible consequences of intended actions.

6. Reification The need to be able to reason at multiple levels of detail leads directly to another, somewhat technical, constraint on representation design. A powerful strategy for elaborating a representation is to introduce a token that stands for the referent of the original representation and then predicate new properties of it. This proposal goes back to Davidson (1967), and it is a leading idea behind frame-based representations of complex situations. Instead of representing the event of opening the pod bay door using a formula such as **open(HAL, pod-bay-door)**, a new object **s** is introduced to represent the situation of opening the door, together with the assertions **actor(s) = HAL**, **object(s) = pod-bay-door**, and **open(s)**, or syntactic variants of these. (For example, in a frame-based representation a *frame* **s** is introduced with *slots* **actor** and **object**; **HAL** and **pod-bay-door** are *fillers* of these slots.)

The new object **s** is said to reify the original two-place predicate **open**. Reification has the benefit of making it easy to further elaborate the representation of the door-opening episode as needed. For example, if the time at which the door is opened becomes important (perhaps because of concerns about Dave's air supply), this information can easily be added to the representation as a new assertion of the form **time(s) = t**. In contrast, there is no straightforward way to add this kind of information to the original, unreified representation.

Many existing knowledge representation system do not take the idea of reification far enough. Most frame-based representational languages take slots as primitive and incapable of elaboration: For example, the symbol **actor** in **actor(s) = HAL** is treated as primitive. Instead, the formalism should provide a way to represent the meanings of predicates, relations, slots, or links as first-class representational objects in their own right so that properties can be explicitly predicated of them.

Reification of arbitrary representations is useful for another reason: It provides a way to represent goals beliefs, and other propositional attitudes regarding these relationships within a first-order framework. For example, "Dave believes that the time that the pod bay door opened was 1800 hours" can be represented by further reifying the relevant temporal relation **time(s) = 1800-hrs** by introducing a new token, **t** say, together with the assertions **situation(t) = s**, **time-of(t) = 1800-hrs**, and **temporal-relation(t)**. Dave's belief can then be represented as **believes(Dave, t)**. Wilensky (1992) provides a good discussion of the issues involved in reification; Hobbs et al.'s (1993) Tacitus system introduces a convenient notation for relating reified and unreified representations in a logic-based framework.

7. Coverage   The representational formalism must provide a means for expressing the range of facts, concepts, generalizations, theories, relationships, rules, and ideas that the content theory demands. Two considerations flow from this requirement. First, the basic machinery for representation must be sufficiently powerful. For example, if beliefs or goals need to be explicitly represented, then mechanisms for representing propositional attitudes of this kind must be provided.

Second, the representation must make the necessary content distinctions. In this regard it is interesting to note that specific content theories are rarely equivalent in their expressive power. Only infrequently do we find two competing content theories claiming to cover the same territory. Such duplication is largely limited to a few choice attractive niches (e.g., the physically foundational categories like *time*, *space*, *substances*, and *processes*, or some psychologically foundational categories like *emotions*). When multiple content theories do cover approximately the same ground, battles among them are usually fought over which ones can describe particular tricky situations, which can distinguish among subtly divergent situations, which ones can support more reasonable inferences, and which can support inference more efficiently. The debate between point-based (Vilain and Kautz 1986) and interval-based (Allen 1983) representations for temporal events provides one example of this kind of head-to-head competition between content theories (although for an elegant unified framework, see Meiri 1991).

8. Useful   The ability to describe, distinguish among, or reason about all situations is not equally valuable (to some users, for some purposes). Some situations may occur only rarely, some situations may occur frequently but be of no importance to anyone modeling reasoning, some distinctions make no difference for many practical decisions, some inferences are true but irrelevant, and some relevant inferences may be too expensive to pursue in practice. The bottom line is that when researchers invest in designing ever more elaborate expressive representational systems, they should ensure that the elaborated representations are good for something.

One way to ensure usefulness is to always have some task in mind when designing representations. Powerful content theories are generally developed in the context of systems that actually perform some task. Ideally these systems' abilities to perform their tasks are dependent on their having chosen to represent content that is useful for those tasks. Of course some content is more generally useful than other. The reason content theories of basic physics concepts are so common is that basic physics (at least naive physics) is relevant in so many situations. The same can be said for basic mental and social concepts. Nonetheless, it turns out these nonphysical domains have been less common targets for content theories, perhaps because they are harder to formalize than physical concepts.

9. Usable Not all content theories are equally usable. Researchers and other practitioners must be able to construct systems that do some job using the specified content encoding. Some theories require users to specify more detail than they really care about to describe a situation, or force the user to break up the description into odd chunks. Facilities for elaboration, reification, and reasoning with multiple descriptions can go a long way toward alleviating these concerns. Syntactic sugar and clever interface design can also go a long way to improving the usability of any given system.

The sociology of the field plays an important role in affecting usability, for a theory's usability depends not only on its intrinsic merits but also on the background of the potential user. Some encodings make more sense than others to particular classes of users: When describing the physical world, formally educated engineers might prefer systems with clear connections to differential equations. When describing the everyday social world, an NLP researcher who grew up with CD might prefer a system that is presented as an extension of that earlier theory.

10. Compact A pretheoretical commitment to Occam's razor, concern for learnability, and recognition of limited (researcher) memory and attention drive us to seek compact theories. An unambiguous system is limited to one meaning per symbol. But compositionality allows us to build up complex compound meanings out of a smaller set of components. Most content theories are based on a limited set of primitive symbols and relationships in which those symbols can be combined. CD, for instance, limited itself to a dozen primitive acts, and four main causal relations.[2] Given a pair of systems in which a comparable range of meanings can ultimately be represented the system relying on fewer primitive symbols and relationships is more economical and thus is generally preferred.

11. Efficient While we do not want excess baggage in our theory, we do want the concepts to be appropriate to the situations that are common and tasks that must frequently be performed. If "betrayal" is a theme that comes up often enough in a system's reading, then the system probably ought to have a concept to represent it directly (rather than having to do all its reasoning in terms of complex expressions describing agents, relationships, goals, and actions done for the benefit of one party at the expense of the other). Given the right concepts, common ideas can be expressed compactly, and common chains of reasoning can be kept short (Hayes 1978).

While there are many representational languages in use, including languages based on logic, frames, production rules, and semantic networks, these tend to be syntactic variants of each other in that information expressed in one is for the most part easily translated into another. For example, slots in a frame representation and links in a semantic network can correspond to predicates or functions in a logical representation. However, the art of knowledge representation is not so much about choosing the appropriate language as it is about developing the structure and relationships between the objects to be represented. The requirements listed above apply to this enterprise regardless of the specific language chosen, as do the corresponding limitations that accrue from violating these requirements.

These requirements are not absolute, however, since in many cases their absence can be made up by clever algorithmic machinery. Ambiguous representations, for example, can be disambiguated, and noncanonical representations can be handled by sophisticated partial matchers. In fact the human natural language understanding system presumably has precisely such machinery in order to reason with natural language, which in fact does violate many of these representational desiderata. However, the use of such machinery carries with it various costs, including computational time, effort, and the danger of being wrong. Adhering to these desiderata to the extent possible simplifies the design of representations and intelligent systems.

4.2.2 Kinds of Content Needing Representation (An Ontology)

To understand everyday events in typical narratives, a broad range of basic representations may be required. One reasonable initial partition of commonsense knowledge identifies three major categories: **physical**, **mental**, and **social** knowledge. Of these, representations of the physical world are the best developed. Scientific and engineering models have been built and tested for centuries; qualitative and "naive" approximations have, over the last few decades, been a mainstay of AI researchers interested in supporting engineering applications. The best summary of AI representations of the physical world can be found in (Davis 1990). However, in typical stories the primary causal structure is tied to agents' intentions, not to physics—the most interesting aspects of the physical world are its interactions with people's everyday goals.

To start representing the mental and social aspects of the world, we need a notion of **agent**: a goal-pursuing actor. The centrality of agents in narratives ensures that the primary form of causation tying together the typical story is *intentional* causation. Representations for agents must allow for individual agents, with their varied interests and capabilities, as well as group agents that also vary in their composition and cohesion. Whatever the agent, we need a way to characterize that which is stable and predictable about the agent's intentional structure. The standard representation form for this task is the **theme** (Schank and Abelson 1977). Themes roughly correspond to personality traits and the constraints of social relationships. Thus a first step toward understanding what is going on in the excerpt from *2001* requires us to represent the astronaut Dave and the computer HAL as agents and to assign them themes such as "be-alive" (suggesting self-preservation goals), and for Dave "be-explorer" (suggesting he may take risks, and be particularly resourceful).

Themes serve primarily as organizers of other intentional constructs such as **goals**, **plans**, and **priorities**, which constitute the core representations of the mental world. Goals are intentional attitudes toward world states, but there is more to say about them than simply that some agent "wants" some random state of the world to hold. When studying the recognizable classes of agents that appear in most narratives, there are recognizable and predictable states about which they are likely to care: biological states, such as health, hunger, and sex-drive; social states, such as status, power, love, respect; and so on. Furthermore goals neither materialize out of thin air nor vanish without consequences. Goals have histories of pursuit, frustration, and satisfaction; goals recur under predictable circumstances; goals can implicate other agents and be affected by their actions. An effective representation of goals must take all these factors into account. Thus it is an interesting aspect of Dave and HAL's situation that they have previously been cordial "colleagues," with HAL as the clear "subordinate," and that it is only Dave's intent to "disable" HAL that awakens the "self-preservation" goal that leads HAL to try "disabling" Dave. Here novel goals that conflict with prior relationships arise in response to new threats.

Representations of mental constructs cover other states with motivational importance. There are, for instance, a wide range of situational **assessments** (Domeshek 1992, ch. 8) that enter into intentional analysis: What **attitude**s do agents hold about their own or related agents goals? What form of **volition** led to salient actions? Could the agents make accurate **predictions** of their actions relevant effects? Was an action taken with the **intent** of producing certain impacts on active goals? **Emotions**, too, are key components of mental life and can usefully be reasoned about in interpreting narratives (Dyer 1982). There is also the vast generic territory of **beliefs** (which, since one can have beliefs about pretty much anything, can encompass pretty much any other kind of representation). Finally the most abstract (and in some ways most interesting) knowledge that agents can possess are plan generation/repair **strategies** and various forms of **meta-knowledge** characterizing how mental processes work; these form the focus of section 4.2.3.

The last of our three domains is the social world. What is most interesting about the social world is its pervasive influence on intentions, so there are many connections to the mental constructs outlined already. In particular, there are many social goals and plans, and there are a wide range of interpersonal themes (or social relationships). These are similar to the themes, goals, and plans discusses earlier, but with the added dimension that they all involve states or actions in which other agents play a role. Generally, other agents become important when they are linked through participation in **social-units** and **social-situations**. Social-units are relatively stable configurations a agents in long-term relationships, such as families, friendships, or companies. Social-situations are more ephemeral, often goal-directed configurations of agents, such as eating at a restaurant, riding in a cab, and many other script situations. Expected sequences of themes can be characterized as stereotypical **threads**, knowledge of which allows us to recognize common patterns and interesting variations (e.g., the romantic relationship thread that follows a path from acquaintance, through dating, engagement, and on to marriage, but then diverts to divorce).

There is another common but orthogonal partition of the space of representations into three different categories: **things**, **states**, and **events**. Things are the tangible entities that can be said to exist in the world. The ubiquitous **John** and **Mary** are both things, respectively, members of the thing classes **man** and **woman** which are subclasses of **person**. **Person**, in turn, is usually treated as that most interesting class of things: goal-pursuing agents. States are ways of describing most of the intangible properties and relationships that hold in the world over various stretches of time. **John** (for some period) has the property that he is **age** 24; for an indefinite period **John** is in the social relationship of **brother-of** to **Mary**; yesterday **John** was **at-loc Mary**. Events, finally, are the occasions of state change: it is, for instance, occurrences of the CD primitive act **ptrans** that lead to new states of **at-loc**.

The distinction between states and events is to a large extent a matter of useful conventions. Though **ptrans** describes the act of something moving, it is also easy, and sometimes useful, to think about an object being in a state of motion. Most actions take discernible time. Nonetheless, it is a useful convention to talk about events as different from, and responsible for the creation of states. First of all, people talk and think that way, and so systems need to be able to understand what people are talking about and how they are reasoning. Second, understanders can often profitably focus on *change*, and events serve as a focal point for reasoning about the causes of change. In particular, **actions** are the class of events where responsibility can be assigned to some **agent**. As noted earlier, reasoning about intentional agents (to understand them, to predict their actions, to influence them) is central to our ability to function in what is largely a socially defined world.

Understanding stories involving human characters requires a theory of motivational analysis, which a system can use to construct volitional explanations describing the planning behavior of agents. The representation of a story must, among other things, describe the planning process that an agent goes through when considering whether to perform the action that he or she is observed to perform in the text. One approach is to create a **decision model** that encodes the planning decisions of a character in a story (Ram 1989). A decision model relates proposed actions of the character to the **outcomes** of those actions, and to the **goals**, **beliefs**, **emotional states**, and **social states** of the character, as well as to the **priorities** or **orderings** among the goals. A decision model captures the **decision process** that the character goes through in considering her goals, priorities, and likely outcomes of the actions in deciding which (if any) actions to perform.

In one chapter we cannot hope to preset all the existing content theories covering all the basic categories laid out in the previous section. Instead, we now given an informal account of a small ontology for representing planning strategies and meta-knowledge, to give a sense for the territory. As already noted, the core representations required to capture the gist of most narratives are those that record the intentional structure underlying agents' actions; what makes people (and stories about people) interesting is the potential for clever and unexpected ways of dealing with the complex web of desires that their social entanglements weave for them. Section 4.2.3, then, describes content theories for planning strategies and meta-knowledge that enable the creation of interesting solutions to novel problems.

4.2.3 Planning Strategies and Meta-knowledge

In order to model an agent's reasoning processes in detail, it is useful to develop representations of reasoning itself. Such representations can help process texts that require an understanding of who did what and why. Less obviously, such representations also facilitate learning. Specifically, one way for an agent (be it a character in a story or the understanding system itself) to learn from experience is to model its own successes and failures and analyze them to determine both what it needs to learn and how to learn it (Ram and Cox 1994; Ram and Leake 1995). A reasoning system that can do this in a general manner must be able to reflect on its own internals. Determining why a failure occurred, for example, often involves not just analyzing a plan of action that the system created, or understanding the events in the world that resulted from it, but also understanding the reasoning process by which the plan was created and the knowledge used in that reasoning process.

Modeling reasoning in its most general sense as the goal-driven processing of an input using some knowledge in the context of a performance task entails developing representations for the **goals**, **mental processes**, **mental states** or **knowledge states**, and the **environment** of the agent. These must be represented explicitly if they are to be reasoned about by the agent (or by an external observer). In addition, since goals, strategies, and knowledge must be organized in some fashion to facilitate access, the agent (or the observer) may need to represent and reason about the **heuristics** or **indexes** used for **goal selection**, mental process or **strategy selection**, and **knowledge selection**. Likewise, to model the process by which an agent determines which inputs to attend to or process in what detail, it may be necessary to develop representations for **input selection** as well. For example, in order to represent why John forgot to fill up his car with gas before embarking on a long trip, one would need to be able to distinguish between several possibilities (Cox and Ram 1992):

- *Missing knowledge.* Did John not know that cars must have gas before they can operate?
- *Misindexed knowledge.* Did John just not recall, at the time of planning his trip, that cars need gas?
- *Missing goal.* Did John not generate the goal of filling up with gas before he set out?
- *Misindexed goal.* Did John generate the goal of filling up with gas but then not remember that goal as he set out (perhaps he took a detour to withdraw money from the ATM and didn't drive by the gas station which he had expected would jog his memory)?

These possibilities can get more complex; for example, perhaps John should not have expected to remember to fill up with gas by virtue of driving by a gas station and should have chosen some other strategy for remembering this important goal instead (e.g., writing it down). Every situation of text need not be represented in such grueling detail, of course; the point is that the representational ontology must allow these and other possibilities to be described should it become necessary to reason about them. This requires the ability to represent an agent's reasoning processes in much the same manner as their decision-making processes. As discussed earlier, a decision model encodes how an agent considers relevant goals, goal priorities, and expected outcomes of performing an action before deciding whether or not to perform that action. Meta-reasoning can be represented in a similar manner (Cox 1996). A set of states, priorities, and the expected strategy outcome determine a reasoner's decision of a processing strategy. Based on general knowledge, the current representation of the situation, and relevant inferences that can be drawn from this knowledge, the agent chooses a particular reasoning strategy. Once executed, a strategy may produce further reasoning, requiring additional strategy decisions.

Reasoning can thus be modeled as a sequence of **decide-compute stages** in which the agent performs **input analysis, goal specification** and **goal selection, processing strategy selection**, and **processing strategy execution**.[3] These stages can be decomposed and concatenated to form larger and more complex chains of reasoning. In addition to representing the reasoning process, it is useful to represent the outcomes of this process. One way to do this is to represent a **reasoning success** in which the **expected outcome** of the four-stage reasoning process is equal to the **actual outcome**, as well as various types of **reasoning failures**, including **unexpected success, contradiction, expectation failure, false expectation**, and **impasse**. These failures can be due to problems with **missing, incorrect**, or **misindexed knowledge, strategies, goals**, or **input**. Combinations of these can represent familiar mental phenomena as forgetting of being "stumped"; see Cox (1996) for details. Analysis of reasoning at this level of detail not only can help an understander achieve a deeper level of understanding of a story or situation but also can help an agent analyze its own successes and failures in order to determine what, when, whether, and how to learn (Ram and Cox 1994; Ram, Cox, and Narayanan 1995; Ram and Leake 1995; Ram, Narayanan, and Cox 1995).

4.3 Representational Organization

It has often been argued that a truly intelligent understanding system will require a very large knowledge base of past experience. Existing systems for natural language understanding operate in only very narrow domains, such as terrorist attacks in Latin America or chip fabrication, and are only required to answer a limited range of questions about their inputs (e.g., see Sundheim 1991). Much larger knowledge bases will be needed to scale up natural language understanding to less restricted domains and tasks. As the size of a knowledge base increases, it rapidly becomes essential to organize its representations so that relevant knowledge can be efficiently retrieved at the right time.

For systems of even moderate size, attention to representational organization is critical. In section 4.1.4 we discussed efficiency problems of the MARGIE system (Rieger 1975) stemming from its simplistic memory organization. As a more recent example, the Tacitus system (Hobbs et al. 1993) is almost impractically slow, again because its designers paid little attention to how its knowledge should be organized. Knowledge in Tacitus is encoded as Horn clauses in a uniform database equipped with only simple indexing mechanisms. Tacitus uses backward chaining to produce an abductive proof of the "logical form" of the input. These proofs are often quite elaborate, and the branching factor at each stage of backward chaining is large; a combinatorial explosion of inference inevitably results.

No matter what kind of interpretation is produced by story understanding—be it a causal chain, a proof tree, or something else—two general problems arise. First, it is simply too expensive to construct a suitable interpretation from scratch by piecing together small fragments (inference rules, Horn clauses, or whatever) using a process of unguided search. Second, there are almost always many possible interpretations, most of which are wildly implausible and only a few of which merit serious consideration. Additional knowledge is needed so that plausible interpretations can be efficiently computed without wasting effort on implausible ones. One way to supply this knowledge is to specify a suitable memory organization—an appropriate structuring of the system's knowledge base.

4.3.1 Desirable Properties of Representational Organization

The principal function of a memory organization is to guide inference, so issues of memory organization cannot be decoupled from discussions of inference strategies. In particular, the utility of a memory organization should be evaluated by examining the extent to which it facilitates two key tasks that inference subserves:

1. Efficiently constructing plausible interpretations.
2. Distinguishing plausible interpretations from implausible ones.

A memory organization necessarily channels a system's inference into a constrained set of allowable patterns, which can both limit the expressive power of the system's representations and restrict the system's ability to fully exploit the intended content of its representations. In evaluating a memory organization, we must also take such limitations into account.

4.3.2 Object-Centered Design

If a system is told that something has moved (**ptrans**ed), it ought not consider everything it knows to see if there is any connection to movement. Almost any system with a modicum of sense should limit its attention to concepts known to be related, such as **at-loc** (being at a location). More generally, a first step in the construction of a sensible memory organization is to index all relational knowledge in terms of the objects of the relations; this establishes associative links among the objects, and those links carry as their labels the relation names. This fundamental principle of *object-centered design* underpins many popular notations for knowledge representation, in particular, frames and so-called semantic networks. The associative links that object-centered representations provide can be used to focus search for relevant inferential knowledge.

The forms of object-centered representations directly reflect the structure of the access paths in their computer implementations. For example, frame structures are often written as graphs whose nodes are frames, connected to one another by labeled, directed arcs representing the slots. The frame at the endpoint of an arc is the filler of the corresponding slot. These graph structures mirror the access paths in memory that frame structures provide: given a pointer to a frame, all slots and fillers associated with the frame are instantly accessible. At this basic level, issues of memory organization are tightly coupled to issues of representational form.

It is important to emphasize that an object-centered design is only a small part of an adequate solution to the problems of memory organization. Even searching through the smaller set of concepts directly associated with a **ptrans** can still be too time-consuming, especially if the search is unguided. A system is better off if it has already activated a larger template in which the **ptrans** is expected; this may reduce or even obviate the need for further reasoning about this "new" fact. Organize representations can help ensure that the right expectations are active; this can help channel reasoning in more directed streams, and sometimes it can help avoid the need for reasoning entirely.

4.3.3 Template-Based Approaches

From the 1970s to the present day, much of the research into the organization of computer memories has been informed by theories of human memory. Starting from the observation that human reasoning appears to involve large inferential leaps, it is natural to suppose that human memory is organized into large chunks and that understanding can to a first approximation be modeled as a process of retrieving and instantiating appropriate chunks.

This suggests the following general approach to memory organization: Specify templates packaging up large patterns of inference that have often proved useful in the past. Interpretations that don't match a template can simply be ignored. This approach to memory organization transforms the combinatorially explosive task of searching through a huge, deep space of inference chains into a potentially more constrained task of searching through a shallow space of large templates.

For simple understanding tasks in narrow domains, template-based approaches can go a long way toward addressing the problem of efficiently constructing plausible interpretations. In particular, if the total number of templates can be kept small, and if stories are simple enough that only one template is needed per story (or per segment of a story), then it is easy to make the interpretation process efficient, and distinguishing plausible from implausible interpretations reduces to the simple problem of determining which of the available templates fits the story best.

One of the earliest systems of this kind, the SAM system (Cullingford 1978), employed templates called *scripts*. A script packages up a stereotyped sequence of events in a particular setting, such as dining at a restaurant, shopping at a supermarket, taking a plane trip, or visiting a doctor. Each event in a script is represented by a subtemplate called a *scene*. Causal relationships between scenes are also represented. For SAM and other script-based systems, story understanding consists in retrieving and activating appropriate scripts and then using their contents to tightly constrain processing of the rest of the story. Consider the following story.

John went out to a restaurant with Mary last night. The waiter brought him a menu and an extensive wine list. He selected a steak and a Chateau de Beaucastel 1990. When he paid, he noticed he was running low on cash. So he stopped by a cash machine on the way home.

In processing this story, a script-based system would retrieve and activate a restaurant-dining script, and possibly a cash-machine-visit script as well. Scripts are retrieved using cues such as physical settling that predict their applicability. For example, the word *restaurant* in the first sentence of the above story suggests that a restaurant-dining script may be appropriate.

Once a script has been activated, it supplies expectations that guide processing of further inputs. The phrase *selected a steak*, for example, is interpreted as picking an item from a menu, since this interpretation is consistent with the scene in the script in which food is ordered; the phrase is not interpreted as (for example) picking a steak off a supermarket shelf. In other words, having activated a restaurant-dining script, an *order-food* scene is expected, and this expectation guides the interpretation process.

Of course a story about restaurants may not explicitly mention every scene of a typical restaurant-dining experience. For example, our story does not describe John's eating his steak, even though it is reasonable to assume that he did so. The expectations that guide interpretation of inputs can also supply "gap-filling" inferences to answer questions about events not explicitly mentioned in a story. If asked whether John ate his steak, a script-based system can use its expectations about eating to answer *yes, probably*.

More generally, script application can be viewed as a form of pattern completion: Events mentioned in a story are fitted into the pattern that a script template defines; this template is then fleshed out into a complete pattern. Both expectation-guided interpretation and gap-filling inferences can be viewed as forms of pattern completion.

Script-based views of language processing have the benefit of accounting for a number of peculiarities of language use. For example, our story makes definite reference to *the waiter*, even though there is no prior mention of a waiter. This seems to defy conventional rules of grammar, which dictate that the definite article should not be used to introduce new material. In this context, however, definite reference is not in the least odd, and its acceptability can be explained by positing that a restaurant-dining script is activated as the first sentence of the story is processed. The activated script sets up an expectation that a waiter may exist in the context of the story; this expectation renders definite reference acceptable.

A script can be thought of as caching a long chain of causal inferences connecting a sequence of events. Retrieving and applying a script thus obviates the need for expensive inference to construct this inference chain from scratch. But a script is more than a mere inference cache: It also implicitly encodes additional information about the plausibility of the inference chain it packages. Few if any of the links in the chain could be confidently hypothesized in the absence of prior knowledge about the broader activity that the script describes. For example, the role of menus in restaurant dining is determined in large part by the social conventions governing ordinary behavior at a restaurant. The inference that picking an item from a list of food possibilities should lead a waiter to bring you some food is only plausible in light of knowledge about conventional behavior at restaurants. Scripts thus address both of the key tasks of memory organization: They facilitate efficient construction of plausible interpretations, and they help distinguish plausible from implausible interpretations.

Script-based approaches to memory organization are not without their shortcomings, however. First of all, scripts needlessly duplicate information. Visiting a doctor and visiting a dentist are similar activities in many ways, but a script-based system requires completely independent structures for each. A more economical approach is to arrange scripts and their components into an abstraction hierarchy, storing information common to similar scripts at as high a level of abstraction as possible in the hierarchy.

This organizational principle gave rise to a different kind of template: the *memory organization packet* or MOP (Schank 1982). A "professional-office-visit" MOP, for example, might contain scenes encoding the general sequence of events associated with visiting both doctors and dentists, including getting to the office, sitting in the waiting room, receiving treatment in an inner office, paying, and leaving. A MOP for visiting a doctor then need only specify those features of a doctor's visit that differ from a generic professional office visit.

MOPs inherit from scripts a restriction on their content: They can only represent stereotypical sequences of events. This is both their greatest strength and their greatest weakness. Such content restrictions are often perfectly acceptable for story understanding systems that operate in narrow domains. For example, the most successful systems in recent message understanding conference (MUC) competitions (e.g., DoD 1996) were all essentially MOP or script based. The aim of such systems is to extract from the input answers to a simple, fixed set of questions. The MUC competitions have demonstrated that systems with good performance can be constructed by specifying scripts or MOP's whose expectations correspond to these questions.

However, scripts and MOPs are not always well-suited to less restricted understanding tasks. In particular, event sequences are ill-suited to representing the rich goal-subgoal structure that underpins much human activity. Consider the following two-sentence "story":

Bill was hungry. He picked up the Michelin guide.

To understand this story, it is necessary to realize that being hungry sets up the goal of wanting to eat, that going to a restaurant is way of satisfying that goal, that to go to a restaurant one has to decide on a restaurant, that one way to decide on a restaurant is to pick from a list of restaurants, that one way to find out a list of restaurants is to read a guidebook (e.g., the Michelin guide), that holding a book enables reading it, and that picking something up is a way to achieve holding it. Understanding this story thus involves piecing together a long chain of goal-plan-subgoal-subplan relationships, which are simply not stereotypical sequences of events.

It is possible of course to enrich template representations to incorporate explicit goal-plan relationships, and a number of systems have taken such an approach, for example, the PAM system (Wilensky 1978) and various systems built by Charniak's group, for example (Charniak 1988). Charniak employs the generic term *schema* to refer to any template for natural language understanding, irrespective of its content: Schemas can represent event sequences, goal-plan relationships, and even complex physical objects. Schemas can package up large patterns of inference like scripts, or they can package up only a few related facts, in which case their content resembles atomic inference rules. While scripts and MOP-based approaches are characterized in large part by restrictions on representational content, schema-based reasoning is characterized by the abductive reasoning process used to apply schemas to inputs (Charniak and McDermott 1986; Charniak 1988).

Texts such as our story about the Michelin guide seem to indicate that scaling up natural language understanding to less restricted domains at the very least requires being able to reason with large collections of schemalike templates. But two familiar problems of memory organization immediately arise. First, at each stage of reasoning it must be possible to efficiently sort through a large collection of schemas and work out which ones are relevant to the current story. Second, as illustrated above, story understanding can require constructing long chains of reasoning involving multiple schemas. In other words, the prospect of a combinatorial explosion of inference once again reappears. Although schemas can allow reasoning to proceed in larger chunks, it seems that there is still no escaping the need for multi-step inference.

At this point there are two possible options: Abandon schema-based representations and try something else, or find better ways to focus schema-based reasoning. Examining the first option for a moment, one possible alternative is to turn to case-based reasoning in which a large collection of representations of specific stories serves as the main knowledge base. Case-based understanding proceeds by retrieving a story that matches the current input as closely as possible, and then adapting it to resolve any mismatches. This new approach to memory organization and reasoning again transforms the search space that a natural language understander must explore in constructing plausible interpretations. Retrieving an appropriate case now involves sorting through a large collection of past cases, while adaptation involves an inference process that mutates the representation of an old story to fit a new one.

4.3.4 The Indexing Problem

Whether or not a case-based approach is adopted, the problem remains that it is necessary to be able to efficiently select appropriate knowledge structures (cases or schemas) from a large memory of such items—that is, to quickly determine which knowledge structures in memory are most relevant to constructing a plausible interpretation of the input. This is known as the *indexing problem*, and it remains an area of active research with many unsolved aspects. Any proposed solution to the indexing problem must address three issues:

1. *Content of indexes.* The relevance of a knowledge structure to a story is determined by comparing the input—a partial interpretation of a story—to key features of the knowledge structure. The latter can be thought of as an *index label* for storing the knowledge structure in memory (Schank 1982; Domeshek 1992; Kolodner 1993). How is the content of index labels to be determined?

2. *Partial matching.* If the match between an index label and the input is exact, then the knowledge structure with that label may be safely assumed to apply. Matches are seldom exact, however, and assessment of relevance generally involves some form of partial matching. How should knowledge structures be partially matched against inputs to determine their plausibility in the context of a given story?

3. *Indexing technology.* What concrete data structures and algorithms are to be used to efficiently implement partial matching? This last issue is hardware-dependent. On serial hardware, a key challenge is to make retrieval faster than linear in the number of knowledge structures in memory; on massively parallel hardware, it may be easy to achieve between than linear performance. Indexing technology is beyond the scope of this chapter, but the interested reader is referred to Kolodner (1993).

A simple strategy for indexing and retrieval of templates is to begin by filtering out all templates that are logically inconsistent with the input. For example, *John walked into the doctor's waiting room* is consistent with a scene of a professional-office-visit MOP but inconsistent with any scene of a restaurant-dining MOP, so the restaurant-dining MOP can be rejected. If this approach is used, then conceptually at least, the entire template is its own index label, and templates are matched against inputs by a process of *abductive matching* (Charniak 1988). Having retrieved a subset of templates consistent with the input, a number of heuristics can then be applied to further narrow the possibilities. One might, for example, prefer partial matches between a template and a story that introduce fewer new objects or that confirm more specific expectations of the template.

Consistency, however, is seldom a black-and-white issue, so completely ruling out knowledge structures that at first glance seem to be inconsistent with the input may later on turn out to be a mistake. Furthermore, heuristics such as minimizing the number of new objects introduced are really proxies for true estimates of plausibility, and it is easy to construct counterexamples that violate any particular heuristic. One way to address this problem is to ground assessment of plausibility in Bayesian probability theory (Charniak and Goldman 1989; Charniak and Shimoney 1990). On this view the aim of story understanding is to compute a maximally probable explanation of the words of the story. Recent research provides compelling evidence in support of a Bayesian formulation of causal and taxonomic knowledge (Pearl 1988). To the extent that interpretations of stories are explanations constructed from such knowledge, Bayesian approaches seem to have gotten something right; at the very least they place the ad hoc heuristics of earlier systems on a firmer footing.

On the other hand, Bayesian approaches to explanation suffer from several troubling philosophical difficulties (e.g., see Pearl 1988, sec. 5.6). Furthermore, Bayesian reasoning over non-singly connected knowledge structures quickly becomes intractable as the size of knowledge structures increases. This seems to call for an alternative form of reasoning that approximates a Bayesian approach at least in the commonest cases, or for a convincing demonstration that suitably rich representations can be constructed in networks that are close to singly connected. The study of such options is an active area of current research (e.g., see Koller 1997).

It is interesting to note that in the final analysis, the requirements of memory organization lead to new constraints on representational content. An effective memory organization requires good indexing, good indexing requires a reliable scheme for partial matching, and reliable partial matching seems to require explicit representations for reasoning about plausibility. Although templates implicitly encode some of the necessary information, scaling up to less constrained understanding tasks appears to require rather more than this. In particular, comparing the relative plausibilities of alternative hypotheses involving different templates (or composites constructed from more than one template) necessitates explicit reasoning about plausibility. Similar considerations hold for case-based approaches.

4.4 State of the Art and Future of the Art

Representation is unavoidably central to symbolic models of cognition. Efforts to date have uncovered many constraints on what is required of effective representations, and have generated an imposing and useful repertoire of representational conventions at the levels of form, content, and organization. But neither the constraints on representation nor the inventory is yet complete. What we have is useful—it might, for example, help us understand why Dave ultimately disconnects HAL—but it is a long way from allowing us to understand Clarke and Kubrick's overall message when they made the movie *2001*. It is a safe bet that representation design will remain a fertile field for the foreseeable future.

The continuing importance of work on representation design is not just a consequence of representation's central role in our models of cognition. The work summarized here shares another common assumption: that researchers and designers need to be involved in the creation of representational systems. This assumption is rooted in two observations. If we do not design the representations ourselves, then we are at a serious disadvantage when it comes to understanding how our systems work. Even worse, if we do not design representations for our systems, then those systems are not likely to work—at least on interesting problems. The fact is that most interesting problems require a lot of knowledge represented in an appropriate form, and learning useful knowledge in a usable form is, in general, a very hard problem. Experience suggests that it is nearly impossible for a system to learn what it needs to know to accomplish some task, unless it already knows a great deal; in particular, learning requires a representational base in which the new knowledge can be expressed as a simple extension or a small perturbation. In the current state of the art, it is hard to learn something if you don't know pretty much what you want to learn.

Ultimately we want systems that can master new domains on their own. This means not only accumulating the knowledge of some domain, it means developing the concepts in which to express that knowledge. As a first step toward this long-term goal, much current research in natural language processing is focused on developing knowledge acquisition and machine learning tools to streamline and supplement the laborious process of developing hand-coded representations. In particular, corpus-based machine learning tools are already starting to automatically or semiautomatically generate broad-but-shallow domain theories to support a range of useful tasks such as lexical disambiguation.

For quite some time, however, hand-analysis of representations and spoon-feeding of knowledge will continue to play a critical role. Although it may be possible to develop shallow domain theories automatically, no one has any idea how to automate the development of the kinds of rich, deep content theories and detailed causal knowledge needed to process complex narratives.

Meanwhile, work on story understanding both relies on and contributes to work on representation. Many of the theories, models, and systems described in this volume attest to the intimate synergy of representational theory and processing practice. Armed with the background knowledge outlined in this chapter, you should be able to construct interesting interpretations of the stories contained in the rest of this book. Go ahead and build some new representations for yourself.

Notes

1. From the movie *2001: A Space Odyssey*, directed by Stanley Kubrick, written by Kubrick and Arthur C. Clarke. In the movie, HAL, an intelligent computer controlling the spaceship, becomes psychotic and attempts to murder Dave, an astronaut, by locking him out of the ship.

2. CD did not, however, set any serious limit on the states that could be introduced to describe situations, and there was no suggestion that one could ever catalog the objects in the world.

3. Learning can in turn be modeled as a similar process involving **failure analysis**, **learning goal specification**, **learning strategy selection**, and **learning strategy selection**; see chapter 11 in this volume.

References

Allen, J. 1983. Maintaining knowledge about temporal intervals. *Communications of the ACM* 26: 832–43.

Buvac, S. 1996. Quantificational logic of context. In *Proceedings of the Thirteenth National Conference on Artificial Intelligence*. Menlo Park, CA: AAAI Press.

Carbonell, J. 1979. *Subjective Understanding: Computer Models of Belief Systems*. PhD thesis. Yale University, New Haven.

Charniak, E. 1988. Motivation analysis, abductive unification, and nonmonotonic equality. *Artificial Intelligence* 34: 275–95.

Charniak, E., and D. McDermott. 1986. *Introduction to Artificial Intelligence*. Reading, MA: Addison-Wesley.

Charniak, E., and R. Goldman. 1989. A semantics for probabilistic quantifier-free first-order language, with particular application to story understanding. In *Proceedings of the Eleventh Joint Conference on Artificial Intelligence*. San Mateo, CA: Morgan Kaufmann, pp. 1074–79.

Charniak, E., and S. Shimoney. 1990. Probabilistic semantics for cost-based abduction. In *Proceedings of the Eighth National Conference on Artificial Intelligence*. Menlo Park, CA: AAAI Press, pp. 106–111.

Cox, M. T., and A. Ram. 1992. An explicit representation of forgetting. In J. W. Brahan and G. E. Lasker, eds., *Proceedings of the Sixth International Conference on Systems Research, Informatics and Cybernetics*, Vol. 2: *Advances in Artificial Intelligence—Theory and Applications*. Windsor, Ontario, Canada: International Institute for Advanced Studies in Systems Research and Cybernetics, pp. 115–20.

Cox, M. T. 1996. *Introspective Multistrategy Learning: Constructing a Learning Strategy under Reasoning Failure*. PhD thesis. Technical report GIT-CC-96/06, College of Computing, Georgia Institute of Technology, Atlanta.

Cullingford, R. 1978. *Script Application: Computer Understanding of Newspaper Stories*. PhD thesis. Yale University, New Haven.

Davidson, D. 1967. The logical form of action sentences. In Nicholas Rescher, ed., *The Logic of Decision and Action*. Pittsburgh: Pittsburgh University Press, 81–95.

Davis, E. 1990. *Representations of Commonsense Knowledge*. San Mateo, CA: Morgan Kaufmann.

Domeshek, E. 1990. Volition and advice: Suggesting strategies for fixing problems in social situations. In *Proceedings of the Twelfth Annual Conference of the Cognitive Science Society*. Hillsdale, NJ: Lawrence Erlbaum, pp. 844–51.

Domeshek, E. 1992. *Do the Right Thing: A Component Theory for Indexing Stories as Social Advice*. PhD thesis. Yale University, New Haven. Available as Northwestern University ILS Technical report 39.

Dyer, M. G. 1982. *In-depth Understanding: A Computer Model of Integrated Processing for Narrative Comprehension*. PhD thesis. Research report 116. Yale University, New Haven.

Guha, R. 1991. *Contexts: A Formalization and Some Applications*. PhD thesis. Stanford University. Available as Report STAN-CS-91-1399-Thesis.

Hayes, P. 1978. The naive physics manifesto. In D. Michie, ed., *Expert Systems in the Micro-Electronic Age*. Edinburgh: Edinburgh University Press.

Hobbs, J., M. Stickel, D. Appelt, and P. Martin. 1993. Interpretation as abduction. *Artificial Intelligence* 63: 69–142

Jones, E. 1992. *The Flexible Use of Abstract Knowledge in Planning*. PhD thesis. Yale University, New Haven. Available as Northwestern University ILS Technical report 28.

Kolodner, J. 1993. *Case-Based Reasoning*. San Mateo, CA: Morgan Kaufmann.

Koller, D. 1997. A probabilistic frame-based representation language. Stanford University memorandum.

McCarthy, J. 1968. Programs with common sense. In M. Minsky, ed., *Semantic Information Processing*. Cambridge: MIT Press, pp. 403–418.

McCarthy, J. 1993. Notes on formalizing context. In *Proceedings of the Thirteenth Joint Conference on Artificial Intelligence*. San Mateo, CA: Morgan Kaufmann, pp. 555–60.

McDermott, D. 1978. Tarskian semantics, or no notation without denotation! *Cognitive Science* 6: 101–55.

McDermott, D. 1985. Reasoning about plans. In J. R. Hobbs, and R. C. Moore, eds., *Formal Theories of the Commonsense World*. Norwood, NJ: Ablex.

Meiri, I. 1991. Combining qualitative and quantitative constraints in temporal reasoning. In *Proceedings of the Ninth National Conference on Artificial Intelligence*. Menlo Park, CA: AAAI Press, pp. 260–67.

Ortony, A., G. Cllore, and A. Collins. 1988. *The Cognitive Structure of Emotions*. Cambridge: Cambridge University Press.

Pearl, J. 1988. *Probabilistic Reasoning in Intelligent Systems*. San Francisco: Morgan Kaufmann.

Ram, A. 1989. *Question-Driven Understanding: An Integrated Theory of Story Understanding, Memory and Learning*. PhD thesis. Yale University, New Haven. Available as Yale AI Technical report 710.

Ram, A., and M. T. Cox. 1994. Using introspective reasoning to select learning strategies. In R. S. Michalski and G. Tecuci, eds., *Machine Learning: A Multistrategy Approach*, vol. 4. San Mateo, CA: Morgan Kaufmann, pp. 349–77.

Ram, A., and D. B. Leake. 1995. Learning, goals, and learning goals. In A. Ram and D. B. Leake, eds., *Goal-Driven Learning*. Cambridge: MIT Press.

Ram, A., M. T. Cox, and S. Narayanan. 1995. Goal-driven learning in multistrategy reasoning and learning systems. In A. Ram and D. B. Leake, eds., *Goal-Driven Learning*. Cambridge: MIT Press, pp. 421–37.

Ram, A., S. Narayanan, and M. T. Cox. 1995. Learning to troubleshoot: Multistrategy learning of diagnostic knowledge for a real-world problem solving task. *Cognitive Science* 19: 289–340.

Reiger, C. 1975. Conceptual memory. In R. Schank, ed., *Conceptual Information Processing*. Amsterdam: North Holland.

Schank, R. C. 1975. *Conceptual Information Processing*, vol. 3, *Fundamental Studies in Computer Science*. Amsterdam: North Holland.

Schank, R. C. 1982. *Dynamic Memory: A Theory of Reminding and Learning in Computers and People*. Cambridge: Cambridge University Press.

Schank, R. C., and R. Abelson. 1977. *Scripts, Plans, Goals and Understanding: An Inquiry into Human Knowledge Structures*. Hillsdale, NJ: Lawrence Erlbaum.

Seifert, C. 1987. *Mental Representation of Social Knowledge: A Computational Approach to Reasoning about Relationships*. PhD thesis. Yale University, New Haven.

Sowa, J. 1984. *Conceptual Structure: Information Processing in Mind and Machine*. Reading, MA: Addison-Wesley.

Sundheim, B. 1991. Overview of the third message understanding evaluation and conference. In United States, Department of Defense, Defense Advanced Research Projects Agency, *Proceedings of the Third Message Understanding Conference (MUC-3)*. San Mateo, CA: Morgan Kaufmann, pp. 3–16.

United States, Department of Defense, Defense Advanced Research Projects Agency. 1996. *Proceedings of the Sixth Message Understanding Conference (MUC-6)*. San Mateo, CA: Morgan Kaufmann.

Vilain, M., and H. Kautz. 1986. Constraint propagation algorithms for temporal reasoning. In *Proceedings of the Fifth National Conference on Artificial Intelligence*. Menlo Park, CA: AAAI Press, pp. 377–82.

Wilensky, R. 1978. *Understanding Goal-Based Stories*. PhD thesis. Yale University, New Haven.

Wilensky, R. 1992. Sentences, situations, and propositions. In J. Sowa, ed., *Principles of Semantics Networks: Explorations in the Representation of Knowledge*. San Mateo, CA: Morgan Kaufmann, pp. 157–90.

Chapter 5
Retrieval from Episodic Memory by Inferencing and Disambiguation

Trent E. Lange and Charles M. Wharton

5.1 Introduction

The most parsimonious account of language comprehension and episodic reminding is that they amount to different views of the same mechanism (Schank 1982, 23). Consider the following:

There were sightings of Great Whites off Newport, but Jeff wasn't concerned. The surfer was eaten by the fish. They found his board with a big chunk cut out. (**Killer Shark**)

In reading this passage, we may be reminded of analogous stories of people being eaten by sharks or, more abstractly, of others who knowingly ventured into mortal danger and suffered the consequences (e.g., skiers who ignored warnings and were buried under avalanches). Why do these remindings occur? To comprehend this passage, a reader must find structures in memory that will provide important inferred information, such as the goals and plans of story characters and the characteristic features of events and locations. Thus, in the process of constructing the meaning of a text passage, we may be reminded of similar episodes because these episodes were understood with (and have became associated with) the same knowledge structures.

Despite the apparent connectedness of comprehension and memory, artificial intelligence simulations of memory retrieval have usually modeled reminding separately from story and language understanding. While this approach may make accounts of each phenomena more manageable, it is undeniable that real-world retrieval cues are the product of the comprehension process. Further the manner in

Reprinted, with minor updates, from "REMIND: Retrieval from Episodic Memory by INferencing and Disambiguation," in J. Barnden and K. Holyoak, eds., *Advances in Connectionist and Neural Computation Theory*, vol. 2, *Analogical Connections*, Norwood, NJ: Ablex.

which a fully elaborated scene interpretation, or discourse model (Kintsch 1988), is constructed from an explicit textual representation will influence what is retrieved from memory. Thus, we believe that a model that integrates the process by which a cue is understood with the process by which it is used to recall information from memory can make an important contribution to the understanding of episodic memory retrieval.

In this chapter we describe REMIND (Retrieval from Episodic Memory through INferencing and Disambiguation), a structured connectionist spreading-activation model that integrates language understanding and memory retrieval. We start by giving an overview of the comprehension and reminding processes that REMIND models. We then summarize relevant psychological and artificial intelligence (AI) investigations of sentential comprehension, word sense selection, inference generation, and episodic reminding. Next we describe and demonstrate how the model performs language understanding and memory retrieval. We conclude by showing several examples to illustrate REMIND's inferencing and reminding abilities and compare them with those of other AI and psychological models of episodic reminding.

5.1.1 Aspects of Reminding

All researchers agree that people tend to be reminded of episodes from memory that are somehow similar to a cue story or thought, as opposed to being reminded of episodes that are completely dissimilar. However, much debate has concerned whether memory retrieval is affected by surface similarity, thematic similarity or a combination of both (Hammond, Seifert, and Gray 1991; Wharton et al. 1994; Wharton, Holyoak, and Lange 1996). Surface, or *superficial*, similarity between a cue story and an episode occurs when both share similar features, such as similar actors, places, or actions. Thematic, or *analogical*, similarity occurs when episode representations mostly share the same abstract goals, plans, roles, causal structures, belief, and attitudes. It is generally assumed that thematic remindings are more useful than surface remindings for a problem-solver because thematically similar remindings are likely to contain information most relevant to the problem at hand. Different computational models of memory retrieval have made use of surface and abstract similarities to varying degrees, but empirical evidence from cognitive psychology indicates that both types of similarities have an important effect on the episodes of which people are reminded.

There is overwhelming psychological evidence that human memory retrieval is highly sensitive to the degree of surface feature overlap between the cue and long-term memory episodes (Gentner, Rattermann, and Forbus 1993; see discussion in

Gentner 1989, 226–33). In the case of **Killer Shark**, a person would likely be reminded of other stories that also involve Great Whites, surfers, surf boards, Newport, or eating because these stories contain concepts that are semantically associated to individual lexical items in this story. In general, people tend to recall stories that have a large semantic overlap with what they are currently thinking about.

While the influence of surface similarity on remindings has generally been agreed upon, the effect of thematic similarity on memory retrieval is still a matter for debate. The most robust finding in the analogy literature is that people often fail to retrieve analogous, but superficially dissimilar, targets (e.g., Gick and Holyoak 1980; Keane 1988; Ross 1987; Seifert et al. 1986; Spencer and Weisberg 1986). Gentner et al. (1993) have found reliable retrieval advantages for cue/target story pairs that shared similar concrete nouns but no analogical similarity in comparison with story pairs that, conversely, were analogically similar but shared no similar concrete nouns. In the context of their SME model of analogical mapping, these findings led Falkenhainer, Forbus, and Gentner (1989, 35) to propose that memory access is determined by object-attribute similarity (mere-appearance rules), but not the relational similarity between cues and targets.

Intuitively, however, using only the surface features of a text does not seem to tell the whole story of memory retrieval. In fact it misses most of the story—the actual meaning that a person infers to understand the surface features. Using only the surface features for memory retrieval in **Killer Shark**, for example, would miss the important inferences that the surfer took his surfboard out into the waters off Newport, that he did so despite being warned of the danger, and that he was therefore killed in a vicious fashion by a shark. These inferences would seem to be at least as important cues as surface features such as "sightings," "Great White," and "eaten." Even more valuable, from a planning perspective, is the ability to access episodes by more abstract features inferred from the text, so that the memories can be useful in other contexts. For example, recall of the planning failure caused by ignoring the danger warning in **Killer Shark** could literally be life-saving to a person who was about to ignore another life-threatening situation (e.g., warning of avalanches).

Such an approach is taken by many AI models of episodic reminding (e.g., Kolodner 1984) and case-based reasoning (e.g., Hammond 1989; Kolodner, Simpson, and Sycara 1985; Owens 1989; Schank and Leake 1989). Because of their problem-solving orientation, such models generally attempt to retrieve the episode from memory that is most likely to help them in their current task. To do this, they search memory using intelligent indexing methods for the best-matching episodes that share an analogous structure of goals, plans, enablements, or failures with the current problem situation, depending on the reasoning task. Almost all case-based reasoning models use highly structured representations of episodes (or cases) that include not only their surface features but also abstract features and structures that allow them to be retrieved at useful times.

Case-based reasoning models have received indirect support from several psychological experiments. For example, the notion that inferred explanations for the reason something failed will cause people to think of other episodes with similar failures was tested by Read and Cesa (1990). These authors found that when subjects were asked to give reasons for unexpected events in stories, they were reminded of previously read stories that had analogous outcomes. Similarly, in contrast to the claims of Falkenhainer et al. (1989), several empirical studies have shown that reminding is sensitive to cue/target analogical or thematic similarity at least in some cases (Gentner et al. 1993, exp. 1; Gick and McGarry 1992; Holyoak and Koh 1987; Johnson and Seifert 1992; Ross 1989; Wharton et al. 1994, 1996). In two experiments in Wharton et al. (1994), subjects studied a number of pairs of two competing passages, such as **Killer Shark** and the following:

Larry had never had sushi before. His friends bet $20 he couldn't eat everything on the plate, but they lost. The sailor consumed the fish.

The individual words of the competing passages were equally associated with the reminding cues (e.g., *The diver devoured the eel*), but only one of the competing passages shared an analogous sentence with the cue (e.g., *The sailor consumed the fish*). Wharton et al. (1994) found that analogous passages were recalled more frequently than disanalogous passages when surface similarities were equated, especially when there was more than one related story in memory. In a methodologically similar experiment, Wharton et al. (1996) found that target stories sharing the same abstract theme with a superficially unrelated cue were more likely to be retrieved than competing stories that shared only a moderately related theme with the cue.

In general, psychological evidence seems to support a theory of reminding in which surface similarities between a cue and the target episodes in memory form a major basis for retrieval, but for which deeper structural similarities and abstract meanings inferred during the understanding and planning process also play an important part.

5.1.2 Need for Integrating Reminding and Understanding
As mentioned previously, most psychological and artificial intelligence models of memory retrieval and language understanding have looked at the processes of comprehension and retrieval in isolation. Due to the enormous complexity of human memory retrieval and language comprehension and the limited understanding that we have of them, such an approach has been necessary to make any progress at all. Models of analogical retrieval and case-based retrieval are usually given a complete representation of the input cues, a representation that is either explicitly or implicitly

assumed to be the result of general comprehension or reasoning processes. Similarly, models of language understanding (see Schank and Abelson 1977; Dyer, 1983; Kintsch 1988; Norvig 1989) have generally performed only language understanding, and not episodic retrieval. The exceptions that perform both (e.g., Lebowitz 1980; Kolodner 1984) have generally implemented the understanding and reminding processes as relatively separate modules using a conventional language parser to understand the story and passing its output representation to the reminding model as a cue.

We believe that building an *integrated* model of language understanding and episodic memory retrieval will allow insights into the processes of both that cannot be gained by modeling them separately. The relationship between language comprehension and episodic reminding is neither simple nor unidirectional. Not only does reading or hearing something occasionally cause one to be reminded of similar episodes, but those remindings themselves can have an important effect on subsequent reasoning and comprehension. For example, Ross and Bradshaw (1994) had subjects read stories with more than one plausible thematic interpretation. They found that thematic interpretations (and reading times) of these stories were influenced by superficial reminding cues to earlier stories with unambiguous themes (see also Read and Cesa, 1991).

An integrated model is perhaps the only way to successfully model some of the more subtle aspects of this interaction. Given that almost all English language word have multiple senses (e.g., river bank, money bank, blood bank), accounting for how individual words are semantically disambiguated is important for a theory of reminding. If the ambiguous sentence *John shot some bucks* is read in a context in which a forest is being talked about, a likely interpretation is that John shot a few deer with a gun (Waltz and Pollack 1985). However, if the same sentence is read in a context involving casinos, a more likely interpretation is that John lost some money while gambling. Although it has yet to be demonstrated empirically, the different interpretations reached by language understanders in different contexts should also affect what episodes they recall. In the first context, one would likely be reminded of episodes involving hunting, whereas in the second context, one would be likely to be reminded of episodes involving gambling—an obvious effect of the understanding process on reminding. More telling, however, is that the stories one is reminded of themselves affect the context in which subsequent sentences are read. For example, the context of the forest itself could have been activated by having just recalled a particular trip to a national forest after a discussion about vacations. Such priming effects could only be explained by an integrated model in which the understanding and reminding processes interact with and directly affect each other.

Finally modeling episodic reminding and discourse understanding within an integrated model imposes important constraints on the types of processing and knowledge that can be used in either mechanism. If reminding cues are the direct result of the language comprehension process, then the type of indexes that those cues contain is limited to the information that the normal understanding process can (and does) infer. Without modeling this integration and thereby constraining the representations used as recall cues, reminding models are in danger of using information (or input) that might not normally be available for retrieval. For example, some case-based reasoning models routinely assume that the representations of cue stories contain high-level thematic inferences. This is because such inferences are necessary for getting the cross-contextual remindings that these models need for analogical transfer and problem-solving to take place. However, it is not necessarily reasonable to assume that people always recognize the high-level themes in the stories they read. This seemed to have been the case in a study by Seifert et al. (1986) in which subjects read two stories that were either superficially dissimilar instantiations of the same theme (e.g., closing the barn door after the horse has gotten out), or instantiations of two different themes. When subjects simply read these stories, there was no evidence for cross-contextual reminding in a speeded recognition task. However, when the subjects were instructed to pay special attention to the thematic structure of the target stories (and therefore were presumably more likely to recognize or infer their abstract themes), an effect of the similar thematic structure on reminding was found. Only by building an integrated model of language comprehension and reminding can one expect to model the specific circumstances under which understanders infer and can use thematic information in probing memory.

5.1.3 Overview of REMIND

To explore how comprehension and reminding processes interact, we have developed REMIND, a spreading-activation model that integrates language understanding and memory retrieval. REMIND is initially given a syntactic representation of a short input text as a memory cue. Using general knowledge stored in its long-term memory, REMIND constructs an elaborated interpretation of the cue, and then retrieves the sentence or episode that is most similar to the surface and inferred features of that interpretation. REMIND is a model of the type of deliberate, nonaccidental reminding that would occur when one intentionally uses a cue to probe memory, as in attempting to remember an analogous solution to a current problem. While REMIND does not currently model unintentional memory reminding, we are optimistic that much of what we have developed will generalize to such a theory.

REMIND's structured spreading-activation networks encode world knowledge about concepts and general knowledge rules for inferencing in the same way as ROBIN (Lange and Dyer 1989; Lange 1992), a structured connectionist model that performs some of the high-level inferencing and disambiguation processes needed for natural language understanding. REMIND's networks also contain representations of prior episodes, such as *Fred put his car in the car wash before his date with Wilma* (**Car Wash**) and *Billy put his* Playboy *under the bed so his mother wouldn't see it and spank him* (**Dirty Magazine**). The representations of these episodes are the actual plan/goal analysis (or discourse model) that was inferred by the network when input for them was first presented to the network to be understood. These prior episodes are indexed into the semantic comprehension network through connections with all the knowledge structures with which they were understood.

To perform retrieval, REMIND is given a short text passage to use as a deliberate memory cue, such as *John put the pot inside the dishwasher because company was coming* (**Dinner Party**). Units in the network representing the cue and its syntactic bindings are clamped to high levels of activation, which then spreads through the network. By propagating *signature* activation, the network makes the different possible inferences that might explain the input (Lange and Dyer 1989; see section 5.3). For example, one of the multiple interpretation paths that gets inferred as a possible explanation for John putting the pot inside the dishwasher in **Dinner Party** is that John was trying to clean the pot to satisfy his goal of having everything ready for entertaining his guests. Other interpretations concurrently activated include the possibilities that he was trying to store the pot or hide it. Activation spreads until the network settles, and the units representing the most plausible set of inferences has the most activation. The final most highly activated chain of inferences represents the network's disambiguated plan/goal interpretation of the cue.

Because the units representing long-term memory episodes are connected within the network, an important side effect of the understanding process is that episodes having concepts related to the elaborated cue also become highly activated. This includes episodes related because there is superficial semantic overlap with the cue (e.g., episodes involving other kitchen appliances or guests) and episodes related abstractly because they share similar inferred plans and goals of their actors (e.g., the **Car Wash** episode becomes activated after receiving the **Dinner Party** cue because both share the inferences that a person was trying to Clean something in preparation for an Entertainment act). After the network settles, the episode that received the most activation from the cue's interpretation and surrounding context becomes the most highly activated, and is therefore retrieved as the best match for the cue.

REMIND is thus an integrated model in which a single mechanism drives both the language understanding and memory retrieval processes. The same spreading-activation mechanism that infers a single coherent interpretation of a cue also activates the episodes the model retrieves from memory. Activation of these episodes combines evidence from both the surface semantics of the input (i.e., different possible word and phrase meanings) and the deeper thematic inferences made from the input so that the recalled episodes depend on surface and analogical similarities with the cue. Further, because all representations of the cue and target episodes used in memory retrieval are constructed from inferences made by the language understanding portion of the model, REMIND predicts that the ability to recall analogous episodes directly depends on the context and level of processing when the input was originally understood. Finally, because both inferencing and memory retrieval occur within a single integrated network, the context in which interpretations are formed affects the episodes that are retrieved, which in turn influence the context in which disambiguation and interpretation of input cues takes place. Thus text comprehension and memory retrieval processes are tightly coupled and strongly affect each other.

5.1.4 Language Understanding and High-Level Inferencing

The part of the natural language understanding process that REMIND concentrates on is the problem of *high-level inferencing* (Lange and Dyer 1989). Because everything that REMIND infers becomes part of the representation of the cue, high-level inferencing is also the basis of its ability to recall analogous memory episodes. High-level inferencing is the use of knowledge and rules about the world to build new beliefs about what is true. To understand a text, a reader must often make multiple inferences to understand the motives of actors and to causally connect actions that are unrelated on the basis of surface semantics alone. Complicating the inference process is the fact that language is often both lexically and conceptually ambiguous. A sentence that serves as a good example of many of the problems of high-level inferencing is the following:

John put the pot inside the dishwasher because the police were coming. (**Hiding Pot**)

Contrast this with the **Dinner Party** example mentioned earlier (*John put the pot inside the dishwasher because company was coming*). In **Dinner Party**, most people would infer that John transferred a Cooking-Pot inside a dishwasher to get the Cooking-Pot clean. In **Hiding Pot**, however, it seems more likely that John was trying to hide his Marijuana from the police. In this case there are conflicts in the interpretation suggested by the first clause by itself (that John was cleaning a cooking pot) and the final interpretation suggested by the first clause combined with the second clause (that John was hiding marijuana). This reinterpretation requires inferences like those shown in table 5.1 to understand the most probable causal relationship between the actions in **Hiding Pot**.

To understand episodes such as **Dinner Party** and **Hiding Pot**, a system must be able to dynamically make chains of inferences and temporarily maintain them with a variable-binding mechanism. For example, a system must know about the general

Table 5.1

Types of inferences needed to understand the sentence *John put the pot inside the dishwasher because the police were coming.* (**Hiding Pot**)

I1:	If the police see John's marijuana, then they will know that he possesses an illegal object (since marijuana is an illegal substance).
I2:	If the police know that John is in possession of an illegal object, then they will arrest him, since possessing an illegal object is a crime.
I3:	John does not want to get arrested.
I4:	John has the goal of stopping the police from seeing his marijuana.
I5:	The police coming results in them being in the proximity of John and his marijuana.
I6:	The police being in the proximity of John's marijuana enables them to see it.
I7:	John's putting the marijuana inside the dishwasher results in the marijuana being inside the dishwasher.
I8:	The marijuana is inside an opaque object (the dishwasher).
I9:	Since the marijuana is inside an opaque object, the police cannot see it, thus satisfying John's goal.

concept (or frame) of an actor transferring himself to a location (*coming*). To initially represent the phrase *police were coming* in **Hiding Pot**, the system must be able to temporarily maintain a particular instantiation of this Transfer-Self frame in which the Actor role (a variable) is bound to Police and the Location role is bound to some unknown location (which should later be inferred to be the location of John). The system must also have the general knowledge that when an actor transfers himself to a location, he ends up in the proximity of that location, which might be represented as the rule:

```
R1: (Actor X Transfer-Self Location Y)
 == results-in ==> (Actor X Proximity-Of Object Y)
```

Applying this rule to the instantiation of the police Transfer-Self would allow the system to make inference I5 in table 5.1, that the police will be in the proximity of John and his marijuana. Another rule the system must have to understand **Hiding Pot** is that an actor must be in the proximity of an object in order to see it:

```
R2: (Actor X Proximity-Of Object Y)
 == precondition-for ==> (Actor X See-Object Object Y)
```

If rule R2 is applied to the new knowledge that the Police will be in the proximity of John, then the system infers that there is the potential for the Police to see John and his marijuana (I6). The rest of the inferences in table 5.1 required to understand **Hiding Pot** are the result of the application of similar knowledge rules about the world.

Even the ability to maintain variable bindings and apply general knowledge rules of the above sort is often insufficient for language understanding and other high-level cognitive tasks. This is because language is often ambiguous, as **Hiding Pot** illustrates, with several possible interpretations that must be discriminated. One of the fundamental problems in high-level inferencing is thus that of *frame selection* (Lytinen 1984; Lange and Dyer 1989). When should a system make inferences from a given frame instantiation? And when conflicting rules apply to a given frame instantiation, which should be selected? Only a system that can handle these problems will be able to address the following critical subparts of the frame selection problem:

Word-sense disambiguation. Choosing the contextually appropriate meaning of a word. In **Dinner Party** the word *pot* refers to a Cooking-Pot, but when **Hiding Pot** is presented, the evidence is that the interpretation should change to Marijuana.

Inferencing. Applying causal knowledge to understand the results of actions and the motives of actors. There is nothing in **Hiding Pot** that explicitly states that the police might see the pot (I6), or even that the police will be in proximity of it and John (I5). Nor is it explicitly stated what the police will do if they see he possesses Marijuana (I1, I2). Each of these assumptions must be inferred from the facts specified in the text.

Concept refinement. Instantiating a more appropriate specific frame from a general one. In **Dinner Party** the fact that the pot was put inside a dishwasher tells us more than the simple knowledge that it was put inside a container. In contrast, the salient point in **Hiding Pot** is that it is inside of an opaque object (I8), which allows us to infer that the police will not be able to see it (I9).

Plan/goal analysis. Recognizing the plan an actor is using to fulfill his goals. In **Dinner Party** John has put the pot into the dishwasher as part of the $Dishwasher-Cleaning script (a stereotypical sequences of actions) to satisfy his goal of getting the pot clean, perhaps itself serving as part of his plan to prepare for company coming over. In **Hiding Pot**, however, it appears that John has put the pot into the dishwasher to satisfy his subgoal of hiding the pot from the police (I4), which is part of his overall goal of avoiding arrest (I3).

High-level inferencing is complicated by the effect of additional context, which often causes a *reinterpretation* to competing frames. For example, the interpretation of **Hiding Pot** can change again if the next sentence is

P3: They were coming over for dinner in half an hour.

P3 provides more evidence for the possibility that John was trying to clean the pot to prepare for dinner, perhaps causing the word *pot* to be reinterpreted back to Cooking-Pot, as in **Dinner Party**. These examples clearly point out two subproblems of frame selection, those of *frame commitment* and *reinterpretation*. When should a system commit to one interpretation over another? And if it does commit to one interpretation, how does new context cause that interpretation to change?

The issues of word-sense disambiguation and inferencing have been relatively well explored in psychological experiments. Experiments have shown that many potential meanings of a word (e.g., Cooking-Pot, Marijuana, and Planting-Pot for the word *pot*) are primed immediately after the word is read—causing subjects, for example, to respond more quickly to words closely related to each of the meanings than to nonprimed words (Swinney 1979; Till, Mross, and Kintsch 1988). However, after no more than a second, the contextually appropriate meaning of the word becomes significantly more primed than the nonappropriate meanings. The meaning of the ambiguous word becomes constrained by the lexical environment in which it appears, which is crucial to the selection of its contextually appropriate sense (Glucksberg, Kreuz, and Rho 1986; Till, Mross, and Kintsch 1988).

Semantic reinterpretation is necessary when an old lexical interpretation is no longer appropriate to a new linguistic context. While there have been very few studies of this phenomenon, it would seem reasonable that previously activated word meanings would not immediately decay to baseline activation. This residual activation might play a role in the ability to reinterpret word meanings when new linguistic contexts are encountered, as in **Hiding Pot**.

5.2 Related Models of Comprehension and Memory Retrieval

In REMIND the understanding mechanism constructs an elaborated interpretation of its input that not only serves as the model's representation of the meaning of the text; it is also used as a cue for episodic memory retrieval. The language-understanding component of the system must be able to (1) perform the high-level inferencing necessary to create a causal plan/goal analysis of the cue, (2) dynamically store the complex structured cue representation, and (3) perform lexical disambiguation (and possible reinterpretation) to select the most contextually appropriate representation. Thus the brunt of the work in an integrated language understanding and memory retrieval system falls upon the language understanding part of the model. In this section we discuss several related symbolic and connectionist approaches to these language understanding problems and give a brief overview of previous models of memory retrieval.

5.2.1 Symbolic Rule-Based Systems
Symbolic rule-based systems have been the most successful AI models at performing the high-level inferencing necessary for natural language understanding. A good example is BORIS (Dyer 1983), a program for modeling in-depth understanding of

relatively long and complex stories. BORIS has a symbolic knowledge base containing knowledge structures representing various actions, plans, goals, emotional affects, and methods for avoiding planning failures. When a story is read in, BORIS fires rules from its knowledge base to infer additional story information. This allows BORIS to form an elaborated representation of the story, about which it can then answer questions. Other models that have successfully approached complex parts of the language understanding process have all had similar types of knowledge representation and rule-firing capabilities (see Schank and Abelson 1977; Lebowitz 1980; Wilensky 1983; Lytinen 1984; Reeves 1991).

While traditional symbolic models have demonstrated an ability to understand relatively complex stories (albeit in limited domains), these models encounter difficulty when trying to resolve and reinterpret ambiguous input. One solution has been to use expectation-based conceptual analyzers, as in such models as CA (Riesbeck 1975) and BORIS (Dyer 1983). These systems use bottom-up or top-down *requests* or *demons* that are activated as words are read in. A word is disambiguated when one of the request rules fires. An example of a bottom-up request that might be used to disambiguate the word *pot* would be:

```
If the context involves Cleaning,
    then interpret pot as a Cooking-Pot.
```

Once such a request is fired, the interpretation chosen is generally used throughout the rest of the inferencing process, and the word is thrown away. However, this makes it impossible to reinterpret the word if the context changes, such as in **Hiding Pot**. A partial answer might be to keep words around in case a new context causes another disambiguation request to fire. However, this solution creates a different problem—how to decide between conflicting disambiguation rules. For example, one cannot simply specify that the *pot* disambiguation request involving the Police context always has a higher priority than the request involving the Cleaning context, because police can be in the same place as cooking pots (e.g., if **Hiding Pot** was followed by *They were coming over for dinner in half an hour*). As the amount of knowledge stored in the system grows, the number of disambiguation requests needed grows with them, producing even more conflicts. Moreover, because rule application in traditional symbolic models is fundamentally serial, these systems dramatically slow down as the number of inferencing and disambiguation rules increases.

Partially because they avoid such problems, connectionist networks have significant potential advantages over traditional symbolic approaches to language understanding. Their conceptual knowledge is stored entirely in an interconnected network of units whose states are computed in parallel. The activation of these units is calculated solely by local update functions which are based on their previous state and the other units to which they are connected. As a result a major portion of the understanding process is potentially controlled by a relatively simple, local spreading-activation mechanism instead of by a large collection of brittle and possibly ad hoc rules.

5.2.2 Marker-Passing Networks
Marker-passing models operate by spreading symbolic markers in parallel across labeled semantic networks in which concepts are represented by individual nodes. Possible interpretations of the input are formed when marker propagation results in a path of units connecting words and concepts from the input text. Like rule-based systems, marker-passing systems are able to perform much of the high-level inferencing necessary for language understanding because of the symbolic information held in their markers and networks (see Charniak 1986; Riesbeck and Martin 1986; Granger, Eiselt, and Holbrook 1986; Norvig 1989; Kitano, Tomabechi, and Levin 1989). The primary advantage of marker-passing networks over traditional symbolic, rule-based systems is that their massively parallel marker-passing process allows them to generate all of the different possible interpretations of a text in parallel. This is a tremendous advantage for ambiguous texts such as **Hiding Pot** and for more complex stories.

Marker-passing systems have many of the same problems as traditional symbolic systems in performing disambiguation and reinterpretation. Because of the generally all-or-none symbolic nature of the inference paths generated by the marker-passing process, these systems have problems choosing the most contextually sensible interpretation out of all the paths that they generate. Most marker-passing models attempt to deal with this problem by using a separate symbolic path evaluation mechanism to select the best interpretation. Unfortunately, the marker-passing process generally creates an extremely large number of *spurious* (i.e., unimportant or logically impossible) inference paths, which often represent over 90 percent of the paths generated even for small networks (Charniak 1986). As network size increases to include more world knowledge, there is a corresponding explosion in the number of paths generated. Because path evaluation mechanisms work serially, marker-passing systems' advantage of generating inference paths in parallel is substantially diminished. This explosion of generated connections and the generally all-or-none nature of marker-passing inference paths become especially difficult problems when applying marker-passing systems to ambiguous natural language texts (Lange 1992).[1]

5.2.3 Distributed Connectionist Networks
Distributed connectionist (or PDP) models represent knowledge as patterns of activation within massively parallel networks of simple processing elements. Distributed

connectionist models have many desirable properties, such as learning rules that allow stochastic category generalization, noise-resistant associative retrieval, and robustness against damage (see Rumelhart, Hinton, and McClelland 1986).

A good example of how distributed connectionist models have been used to model language understanding is provided by the case-role assignment model of McClelland and Kawamoto (1986). The main task of their model is to learn to assign proper semantic case roles for sentences. For example, given the syntactic surface form of the sentence *The boy broke the window*, their network is trained to place the semantic microfeature representation of Boy in the units representing the Agent role on the output layer, whereas given *The rock broke the window*, it is trained to place the representation of Rock in the Instrument role. Their network is also trained to perform lexical disambiguation, for example, mapping the pattern for the word *bat* to a Baseball-Bat for sentences such as *The boy hit the ball with the bat*, and to a Flying-Bat for sentences such as *The bat flew*. Once the input/output pairs have been learned, the network exhibits a certain amount of generalization by mapping the case roles and performing lexical disambiguation for new inputs that are similar to the training sentences.

One of the main limitations of McClelland and Kawamato's model for language understanding is that it can only successfully analyze direct one-step mappings from the input to the output. This limits the model to sentences that can be understood and disambiguated based solely on the surface semantics of the input. Two distributed connectionist models that get around this limitation are those of Miikkulainen and Dyer (1991) and St. John (1992). Both models use *recurrent networks* with a hidden layer of units whose activation pattern essentially stores the state (or "gestalt") of the stories being understood. This allows them to learn to process more complex texts based on stereotypical scripts and scriptlike stories (Schank and Abelson 1977). Both models have the lexical disambiguation abilities of McClelland and Kawamoto's model but are also able to infer unmentioned story events and role-fillers from the script that has been recognized by the hidden layer.

Unfortunately, there may be significant problems in scaling distributed connectionist models to handle more complex language. Both the Miikkulainen-Dyer and the St. John model work by resolving constraints from the context of the input to recognize one of their trained scripts and to instantiate it with the bindings of the particular input story. However, much of language understanding involves the inference of causal relationships between events for completely novel stories in which no script or previously trained input/output pair can be recognized. This requires *dynamic inferencing*—producing chains of inferences over simple known rules, with each inference resulting in a potentially novel intermediate state (Touretzky 1990). Most important, the problem of ambiguity and the exponential number of potential causal connections between two or more events requires that multiple paths be explored in parallel (the forte of marker-passing networks). It remains to be seen whether a single blended activation pattern across the bank of hidden units in a recurrent network can solve this problem by simultaneously holding and making dynamic inferences for multiple, never-before encountered interpretation chains.

Other distributed models explicitly encode variables and rules, such as the models of Touretzky and Hinton (1988) and Dolan and Smolensky (1989). Consequently such *rule-implementing* distributed models are able to perform some of the dynamic inferencing necessary for language understanding. However, the types of rules they can currently encode are generally limited. More important, like traditional rule-based systems, they are *serial at the knowledge level*—namely they can fire only one rule at a time. As previously mentioned, this is a serious drawback for natural language understanding, particularly for ambiguous text, in which the often large number of multiple alternative inference paths must be explored in parallel (Lange 1992).

5.2.4 Structured Spreading-Activation Models

Structured (or localist) spreading-activation models are connectionist models that represent knowledge in semantic networks like those of marker-passing networks, but in which the nodes are simple numeric units with weighted interconnections. The activation on each conceptual node generally represents the amount of *evidence* available for its concept in a given context. As in marker-passing networks, structured connectionist networks have the potential to pursue multiple candidate interpretations of a story in parallel (i.e., be parallel at the knowledge level) as each interpretation is represented by activation in different local areas of the network. Unlike pure marker-passing networks, however, the evidential nature of structured spreading-activation networks make them ideally suited to perform lexical disambiguation. Disambiguation is achieved automatically as related concepts under consideration provide graded activation evidence and feedback to one another in a form of constraint relaxation (see Cottrell and Small 1982; Waltz and Pollack 1985; Kintsch 1988).

As an example of how structured connectionist models process language and perform disambiguation, consider the sentence:

The astronomer married the star. **(Star-Marriage)**

The word *star* could easily be disambiguated to Movie-Star by a symbolic rule-based system having selectional restrictions (even astronomers cannot marry celestial bodies, except perhaps metaphorically). However, many readers report this and similar sentences as cognitive doubletakes because *astronomer* initially primes the Celestial-Body

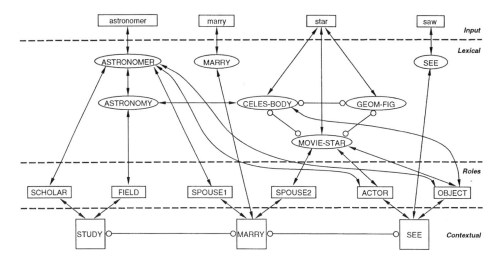

Figure 5.1
Localist spreading-activation network based on Waltz and Pollack (1985). Lines with arrows are excitatory connections; lines ending with open circles are inhibitory.

interpretation. Figure 5.1 shows an extended version of the semantic portion of the structured network Waltz and Pollack (1985) built to process **Star-Marriage** and illustrate this effect. After the input units for **Star-Marriage** are clamped to a high level of activation, the Celestial-Body interpretation of *star* initially acquires more activation than the Movie-Star interpretation because of priming from Astronomer through Astronomy (figure 5.2). However, Movie-Star eventually wins out because activation feedback over the semantic connections from the Marry unit to Movie-Star outweighs that spreading from Astronomer to Celestial-Body.

Until recently the applicability of structured connectionist models to natural language understanding has been severely hampered because of their difficulties representing dynamic role-bindings and performing inferencing. The basic problem is that the evidential activation on structured networks' conceptual units gives no clue as to *where* that evidence came from. For example, the network of figure 5.1 has no way to distinguish between the sentences *The astronomer saw the star* and *The star saw the astronomer*, despite the crucial difference that the role-bindings make in their interpretation. More important, without a mechanism to represent such dynamic bindings, they cannot propagate bindings to make the chains of inferences necessary for understanding more complex texts. Thus, unlike marker-passing systems, most structured connectionist models have been limited to simple language processing tasks that can be resolved solely on the surface semantics of the input.

Retrieval from Episodic Memory

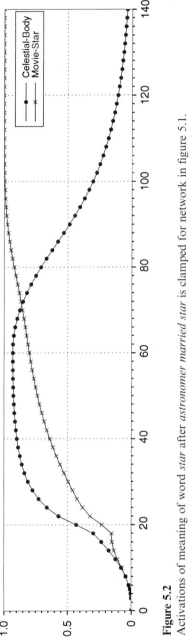

Figure 5.2
Activations of meaning of word *star* after *astronomer married star* is clamped for network in figure 5.1.

A way of compensating for the lack of dynamic inferencing abilities in spreading-activation networks is to use a symbolic processing mechanism external to the spreading-activation networks themselves to perform the variable binding and inferencing necessary for language understanding. Such a spreading-activation/symbolic hybrid has been used in Kintsch's (1988) construction-integration model of language comprehension. This system uses a traditional symbolic production system to build symbolic representations of the alternative interpretations of a text. These representations are then used to construct a spreading-activation network in which the different interpretations compete to integrate contextual constraints. The integration of constraints with spreading-activation in the network allow Kintsch's model to correctly disambiguate and interpret input sentences. A somewhat similar approach is taken by ACT* (Anderson 1983), a psychologically based spreading-activation model of language understanding, fact encoding and retrieval, and procedure encoding and retrieval. Kintsch's and Anderson's models both illustrate many of the impressive emergent properties of spreading-activation networks for modeling realistic language understanding, such as their ability to model the time course of lexical disambiguation in a way consistent with psychological evidence (e.g., Swinney 1979). However, if a mechanism internal to the networks (instead of an external symbolic production system) could be found to construct text inferences, the parsimony and psychological realism of structured spreading-activation networks would be greatly increased.

Recently a number of researchers have shown how structured connectionist models can handle some variable binding and inferencing abilities within the networks themselves (e.g., Barnden 1990; Holldobler 1990; Shastri and Ajjanagadde 1993; Sun 1993). Most of these models, however, have not been applied to language understanding and have no mechanisms for handling ambiguity. An exception is ROBIN (Lange and Dyer 1989), a structured spreading-activation model that propagates *signatures* (activation patterns that identify the concept bound to a role) in order to generate all possible interpretations of an input text in parallel. At the same time ROBIN uses the network's evidential constraint satisfaction to perform lexical disambiguation and selection of the contextually most plausible interpretation. Thus ROBIN is able to perform high-level inferencing and disambiguation within the structure of a single network, without the need for external symbolic processing. Given these abilities, such a structured spreading-activation model seems a promising place to start for building an integrated language understanding and memory retrieval model.

5.2.5 Memory Retrieval Models

The process of memory retrieval has generally been explored in isolation from the process of language understanding. Storage and retrieval of complex episodes requires many of the same abilities to represent and handle structural relationships and variable bindings that natural language understanding does. Because connectionist models have had difficulties handling complex structural relationships in general, few attempts have been made to build connectionist retrieval models for the type of high-level episodes discussed in this paper. Nonetheless, a few models have shown the potential value of connectionist models for memory storage and retrieval. For example, COPYCAT (Hofstadter and Mitchell 1994) uses connectionist constraint-satisfaction in solving letter-string analogy problems. Although the retrieval portion of COPYCAT only retrieves simple concepts and not memory episodes, it seems to exhibit some of the fluidity of concepts and perception apparent in human analogical reasoning. Miikkulainen (1993) shows how a variant of distributed connectionist topological feature maps (Kohonen 1984) can be used to store and retrieve the script-based stories that it has understood using recurrent distributed networks. Besides showing how purely distributed connectionist models can store and retrieve multiple-sentence episodes, Miikkulainen's model exhibits a number of features of human episodic memory, such as certain kinds of memory confusions and recency effects. Although connectionist models such as COPYCAT and Miikkulainen's DISCERN are currently able to store only relatively simple or stereotypical episodes, they do illustrate their promise for psychologically plausible memory retrieval.

As for natural language understanding, symbolic models have had the greatest success in modeling retrieval of complex, high-level memory episodes. Case-based reasoning (CBR) models (cf. Hammond 1989; Riesbeck and Schank 1989) form the largest class of symbolic memory retrieval models. In CBR models memory access is performed by recognition of meaningful *index patterns* in the input that allow retrieval of the episodes (or cases) most likely to help them solve their current problem. An analysis phase is usually performed to determine the indices that are most important for finding relevant cases for a particular problem, such as cases that share similar plans, goals, enabling preconditions, or explanation failures. In addition CBR models are usually careful to retrieve *only* those cases that will help find a solution, explicitly rejecting cases that do not. CBR models are therefore generally models of expert reasoning within a given domain of expertise, rather than models of general human reminding. It is quite possible that expert memory retrieval may be satisfactorily modeled by such methods. However, general reminding seems to be substantially messier, being affected by not only by the sort of useful abstract indexes used in CBR models but also by superficial semantic similarities that often lead to quite *inexpert* remindings. Further the problem of selecting and recognizing appropriate indexes becomes substantially more difficult when reading ambiguous texts outside of limited expert domains.

General, nonexpert reminding has been modeled in systems such as ARCS (Thagard et al. 1990) and MAC/FAC (Gentner and Forbus 1991). These systems model retrieval without using specific indexing methods. Instead, they retrieve episodes whose representations share superficial semantic similarities with retrieval cues, with varying degrees of preference toward retrieval of episodes that are also analogically similar or structurally consistent. However, unlike most CBR models, these systems do not specify how they construct the representation of retrieval cues from a source input or text and so cannot explain how inferences and comprehension affect reminding.

Theoretically REMIND lies somewhere between case-based reasoning models and general analogical retrieval models such as ARCS and MAC/FAC. Like ARCS and MAC/FAC, REMIND is meant to be a psychologically-plausible model of general human reminding, and therefore takes into account the prevalence of superficial feature similarities in remindings. However, we believe that many of the types of high-level planning and thematic knowledge structures used as indexes in case-based reasoning systems also have an important effect on reminding. REMIND is thus partially an attempt to bridge the gap between case-based and analogical retrieval models. As it turns out, this gap is naturally bridged when the same spreading-activation mechanism is used to both understand cues and to retrieve episodes from memory. Using the same mechanism for both processes causes retrieval to be affected by all levels that a text was understood with, as hypothesized by Schank (1982). This is the case in REMIND, in which the understanding mechanism is given the superficial features and actions of a text and attempts to explain them by inferring the plans and goals being used—causing long-term memory episodes to be activated by both.

5.3 Language Understanding in REMIND

REMIND is a structured spreading-activation model that integrates language understanding and memory retrieval. It is an extension of ROBIN (Lange and Dyer 1989; Lange 1992), a structured connectionist model that performs high-level inferencing and disambiguation to build interpretations of syntactically parsed input for short texts such as **Hiding Pot** and **Dirty Magazine**. These interpretations are then added to the network to encode the model's long-term memory episodes.

In REMIND memory retrieval is a natural side effect of using spreading-activation to perform language understanding. The knowledge structures used to understand an input cue activate similar episodes that were understood and stored in the network earlier. For example, **Dirty Magazine** becomes active when **Hiding Pot** is being understood because both involve hiding to avoid punishment. An episode is retrieved

Retrieval from Episodic Memory

from memory when there are enough similarities between it and a cue's interpretation to cause it to become the most highly active episode in the network. Because both inferencing and memory retrieval occur within a single spreading-activation network, these processes strongly interact and affect each other, as appears to be the case in human memory. In this section we give an overview of how REMIND performs high-level text inferencing and disambiguation. A more detailed description is provided in Lange and Dyer (1989).

5.3.1 Knowledge Given to REMIND

REMIND, like ROBIN, uses structured networks of simple connectionist units to encode semantic networks of frames representing world knowledge. Each frame has one or more roles, with each role having expectations and selectional restrictions on its fillers. General knowledge rules used for inferencing are encoded as interconnected pathways between corresponding roles. The knowledge base of frames and rules consists of the causal dependencies relating actions, plans, goals, and scripts (Schank and Abelson 1977) necessary for understanding stories in a limited domain. The knowledge base is hand-built, as in most structured connectionist models. However, there is no information in the knowledge base about specific episodes (e.g., **Hiding Pot**, **Dinner Party**, and **Dirty Magazine**) that the networks will be used to understand.

Table 5.2 gives an example of how knowledge is defined in REMIND. It defines the conceptual frame Inside-Of, which represents the general state of one object being inside of another. Inside-Of has three roles: an Object that is inside of something (which must be a Physical-Object), a Location that the Object is inside of (which must be a Container-Object), and a Planner that may have caused the state to be reached (which must be a Human). The rest of table 5.2 defines Inside-Of's *relations* to other frames. The knowledge represented here is that it is (1) directly accessed by the phrase ⟨S_is inside of_DO⟩ (as in *The fork is inside of the dishwasher*), (2) a Result-Of the action Transfer-Inside, and (3) has several possible concept refinement frames: Inside-Of-Dishwasher, Inside-Of-Opaque and Inside-Of-Carwash.

Refinements (short for concept refinements, an inverse of the *is-a* relation) of frames are useful because they allow more specific inferences to be made when role-bindings are known (Lytinen 1984). For example, if the network has inferred that a cooking utensil is inside of a dishwasher (Inside-Of-Dishwasher), a likely inference is that it is about to cleaned. If the network has inferred that any object is inside of an opaque object (Inside-Of-Opaque), the network can infer that the object is blocked from sight. When multiple frames are defined as alternatives for a given relation to a frame, as in the multiple refinements of Inside-Of, they are defined as *mutually exclusive* relations that compete for selection as the relation's instantiation at any given

Table 5.2
Simplified definition of the frame representing the state Inside-Of

Frame	Inside-Of state			
:Roles	(Object	(Physical-Object	0.05))	
	(Location	(Container-Object	0.30))	
	(Planner	(Human	0.05))	
:Phrase	(<S_is inside of_DO>	1.0 (Object Subject)	(Location Direct-Object))	
:Result-Of	(Transfer-Inside	1.0 (Object Object)	(Location Location)	(Planner Actor))
:Refinements	(Inside-Of-Dishwasher	1.0 (Object Object)	(Location Location)	(Planner Planner))
	(Inside-Of-Opaque	1.0 (Object Object)	(Location Location)	(Planner Planner))
	(Inside-Of-Carwash	1.0 (Object Object)	(Location Location)	(Planner Planner)))

Retrieval from Episodic Memory

time. For example, although there are multiple possible plans-for the goal of Satisfy-Hunger ($Restaurant, $Eat-At-Home, etc.), generally only one will be used as the plan for a *given* instance of somebody wanting to satisfy his hunger in a particular story.

The relations and their role correspondences shown in table 5.2 also define the network's general knowledge rules, such as the following:

```
R3: (Subject X ⟨S_is inside of_DO⟩ Direct-Obj Y)
 == phrase ==>
    (Object X Inside-Of Location Y)
```

(The phrase "X is inside of Y" means that object X is inside of object Y.)

```
R4: (Actor X Transfer-Inside Object Y Location Z)
 == results-in ==>
    (Object Y Inside-Of Location Z Planner X)
```

(When an actor X transfers an object Y into a location Z, then object Y is inside of location Z.)

Finally the numbers in table 5.2 represent the connection weights (ranging from 0 to 1) from each of the related concepts to Inside-Of, and they are chosen on the basis of how much evidence they provide. For example, if an object has just been transferred inside of something else (Transfer-Inside), then the network can definitely infer that the object is Inside-Of it. Therefore the weight from Transfer-Inside to Inside-Of is maximal (1.0). If something that is a container (Container-Obj) has been mentioned in a story, then there is some, though not certain, evidence that something is inside of it, so a corresponding middling weight of 0.3 from Container-Obj to Inside -Of's Location role is given. On the other hand, a very small weight (0.05) is given from Physical-Object to Inside-Of's Object role, since mere mention of any particular physical object does not very strongly imply Inside-Of. The actual weights chosen are clearly arbitrary. What is important is that they be in a *range* reflecting the amount of evidence the concepts provide for their related concepts in a certain knowledge base.

5.3.2 Structure of REMIND

The knowledge given to REMIND is used to *construct* the network before any processing begins. As with other structured connectionist models, a single node in the network represents each frame or role. Relations between concepts are represented by weighted connections between the nodes. Activation on frame and role nodes is *evidential*, corresponding to the amount of evidence available from the current context for that concept. However, as described earlier, simply representing the amount of evidence available for a concept is not sufficient for complex inferencing tasks. Solving the variable binding problem requires a way to *identify* the concept that is

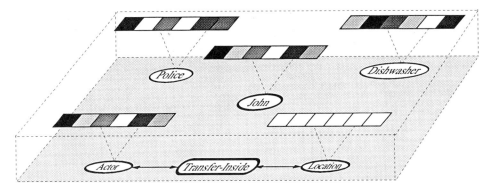

Figure 5.3
Examples of signature patterns (banks of units on top plane) for concepts (ovals on lower plan). Actor and location roles and of the Transfer-Inside frame and their binding units are also shown.

dynamically bound to a role. Furthermore the network's structure must allow such role-bindings to propagate across the network to dynamically instantiate inference paths and form an elaborated representation of the input.

5.3.3 Variable Binding with Signatures

Representation of variables and role-bindings is performed in REMIND by network structure that processes *signatures*—activation patterns that uniquely identify the concept bound to a role (Lange and Dyer 1989). Every concept in the network has a set of *signature units* that output its signature, a constant activation pattern different from all other signatures. A dynamic binding exists when a role or variable's *binding units* have an activation pattern matching the activation pattern of the bound concept's signature.

An example of signatures is shown in figure 5.3, which shows the concept nodes for the concepts Police, John, and Dishwasher (on the lower plane) and their associated signature units (banks of units on the top plane). Here signatures are shown as unique six-unit distributed patterns, with different levels of activation being represented by different levels of gray. The figure also shows some of the units for the frame Transfer-Inside and their activation values when its Actor is bound to John. The *virtual binding* of Transfer-Inside's Actor role to John is represented by the fact that its binding units have the same activation pattern as John's signature. The binding banks for the Location role have no activation because this role is currently unbound. The complete Transfer-Inside frame is represented in the network by the group of units that include the conceptual unit Transfer-Inside, a conceptual unit for each of its roles (the

Object role not shown), and the binding units for each of its roles. The same binding units could, at another time, hold a different virtual binding, simply by having the activation pattern of another concept's signature.

In general, signatures can be uniquely identifying activation patterns of any size. Ideally signatures are distributed activation patterns (e.g., made up of semantic microfeatures) that are themselves reduced semantic representations of the concept for which they stand (figure 5.3). Having the signatures represented as distributed activation patterns carrying semantic information may allow their future use as inputs for local distributed learning mechanisms after they have been propagated for inferencing (Lange and Dyer 1989). For simplicity, however, REMIND's simulations are currently run with signatures simply being unique arbitrarily-generated scalar values (e.g., 6.8 for Marijuana and 9.2 for Cooking-Pot).

5.3.4 Propagation of Signatures for Inferencing

The most important feature of signatures is that they can be propagated without change across long paths of binding units to dynamically instantiate candidate inference paths. Figure 5.4 shows how the network's structure accomplishes this and automatically propagates signatures to fire rules (e.g., R4). Evidential activation for disambiguation is spread through the paths between conceptual units on the bottom plane, such as Transfer-Inside and its Object role. Signature activation for dynamic role-bindings is spread across the parallel paths of corresponding binding units (solid black circles) on the top plane. For simplicity, the signatures in the figure are uniquely identifying scalar values. Units and connections for the Actor, Planner, and Location roles are not shown. As shown here, there are actually multiple binding units per role to allow simultaneous propagation of ambiguous bindings, such as the multiple meanings of the word *pot*. In general, this requires that there be as many binding units per role as there are possible meanings of the most ambiguous word in the network.

Initially there is no activation on any of the conceptual or binding units in the network. When input for a phrase such as *John put the pot inside the dishwasher* (**P1**) is presented, the lexical concept nodes for each of the words in the phrase are clamped to a high level of evidential activation. This directly provides activation for the concepts John, Transfer-Inside, Cooking-Pot, Marijuana, and Dishwasher. To represent the role-bindings given by phrase **P1**, the binding units of each of Transfer-Inside's roles are clamped to the signatures of the concepts bound to them. For example, the binding units of Transfer-Inside's Object are clamped to the signature activations (6.8 and 9.2) of Marijuana and Cooking-Pot, representing the candidate bindings from the word *pot* (figure 5.4).[2] An alternative input, such as *George put the cake inside the oven*, would be represented by clamping the signatures of its bindings

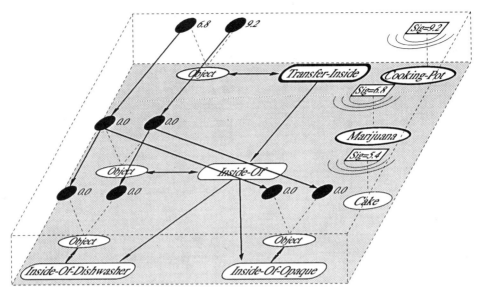

Figure 5.4
Simplified ROBIN/REMIND network segment showing parallel paths over which evidential activation (bottom plane) and signature activation (top plane) are spread for making inferences. The figure shows the initial activation and clamping for the first phrase of **Hiding Pot** (*John put the pot inside the dishwasher*). Signature nodes (outlined rectangles) and binding nodes (solid black circles) are in the top plane. Thickness of conceptual node boundaries (ovals) in the bottom plane represents their levels of evidential activation. Node names do not affect the spread of activation in any way. They are used only to initially set up the network's structure and to aid in analysis.

(i.e., George, Cake, and Oven) instead. A completely different set of inferences would then ensue.

The activation of the network's conceptual units is equal to the weighted sum of their inputs plus their previous activation times a decay rate, similar to the activation function of previous structured networks. However, the activation of the binding units is equal to the maximum of their unit-weighted inputs so that signatures can be propagated without alteration. Binding units calculate their activation as the maximum of their inputs because this preserves their signature input value even when the signature can be inferred from more than one direction. The actual relative signature activation values do not matter because gated connections (not shown) ensure that two different signatures do not reach the same binding node.

As activation starts to spread after the initial clamped activation values in figure 5.4, Inside-Of receives evidential activation from Transfer-Inside, representing the strong

Retrieval from Episodic Memory   133

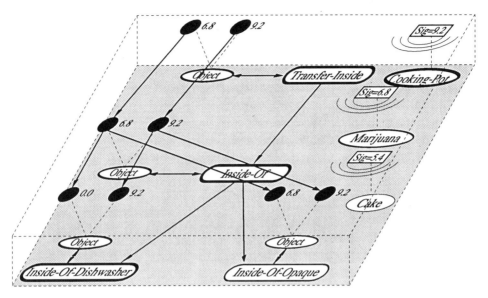

Figure 5.5
Simplified ROBIN/REMIND network segment showing activation midway through processing **Hiding Pot**. At this time Cooking-Pot and Inside-Of-Dishwasher have higher evidential activations than Marijuana and Inside-Of-Opaque, as is illustrated by their thicker ovals.

evidence that something is now inside of something else. Concurrently the signature activations on the binding units of Transfer-Inside's Object propagate to the corresponding binding units of Inside-Of's Object (figure 5.5) because each of the binding units calculates its activation as the maximum of its inputs. For example, Inside-Of's left Object binding unit has only one input connection, that from the corresponding left Object binding unit of Transfer-Inside. Since the connection has a unit weight and the left Object binding unit of Transfer-Inside has an activation of 6.8, Inside-Of's left Object binding unit also becomes 6.8 (Marijuana's signature), since 6.8 is its maximum (and in this case only) input. The potential binding of Cooking-Pot (signature 9.2) to Inside-Of's right Object binding unit propagates at the same time, as do the bindings of Inside-Of's Planner role to the signature of John and its Location role to the signature of Dishwasher.

By propagating signature activations from the binding nodes of Transfer-Inside to the binding nodes of Inside-Of, the network has made its first inference. Because of the signatures now on Inside-Of's binding nodes, the network not only represents that something is inside of something else but also represents exactly which thing is inside the other. REMIND continues to make subsequent inferences from the activations of this new knowledge. Evidential and signature activation spreads, in parallel, from

Inside-Of to its refinements Inside-Of-Dishwasher and Inside-Of-Opaque and their corresponding binding units (see figure 5.5), on through the rest of the network.[3] Figure 5.6 shows an overview of the signature bindings in a portion of the network after presentation of the input for the rest of **Hiding Pot** (*because the police were coming*) is presented, and the network eventually settles. The network has made inferences I1-I9 of table 5.1, with most being shown in the figure.

5.3.5 Disambiguation and Reinterpretation

REMIND's propagation of signature activations dynamically instantiates candidate inference paths in parallel in much the same way as marker-passing systems and the structured connectionist binding mechanisms of Shastri and Ajjanagadde (1998) and Sun (1998). However, as described earlier, natural language understanding requires more than simple basic variable binding and rule-firing capabilities—it also requires the ability to resolve ambiguities and select between the large number of candidate inference paths instantiated by rule-firing. This is handled in REMIND by the evidential activation that spreads in parallel with signature bindings.

If this were a marker-passing system constructing an internal representation of **Hiding Pot**, an external symbolic path evaluator would have to be used to select between the dishwasher cleaning path and the longer hiding path connecting John's Transfer-Inside to the Police's Transfer-Self. At the end of processing the path evaluator would also have to recognize that Marijuana should be selected over the Cooking-Pot and Planting-Pot bindings throughout the network.

Such disambiguation is performed entirely within REMIND's network without resorting to a separate path-evaluation module. Instead, the evidential portion of the network (figure 5.5) decides between the competing inference paths that have been instantiated by signature activation. The activations of the conceptual frame nodes are always approximately proportional to the amount of evidence available for them in the current context from their bindings and related frames. REMIND's interpretation of its input is the most highly activated path of frame units and their bindings when the network settles.[4]

Often there are multiple possible competing interpretations for a given frame. This occurs when there are multiple plans to achieve a goal or multiple refinements for a frame (e.g., the Inside-Of-Dishwasher and Inside-Of-Opaque refinements of Inside-Of). In these cases the most highly activated interpretation that has been instantiated with compatible signature role-bindings is chosen as part of the inference path. Similarly, when there are multiple possible bindings for a role, the binding chosen at any given time is the one whose concept has the highest level of evidential activation.

Figure 5.7 illustrates how evidential activation works through constraint satisfaction to disambiguate meanings and interpretations. The evidential activations of the

Retrieval from Episodic Memory 135

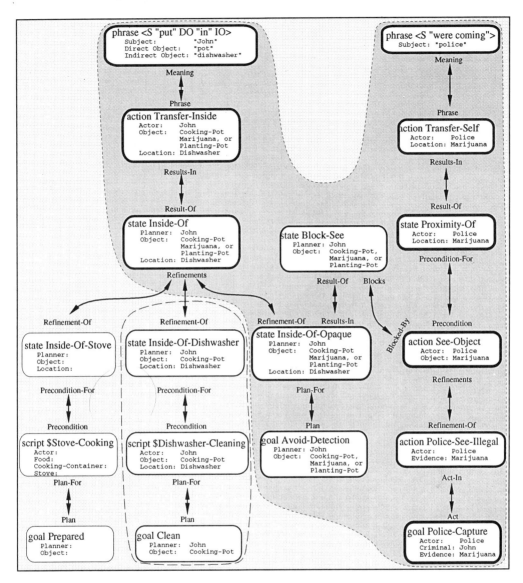

Figure 5.6
Overview of a small portion of a ROBIN/REMIND network showing inferences made after clamping of inputs for phrases P1 and P2 of **Hiding Pot**. Thickness of frame boundaries shows the amount of evidential activation on the frames conceptual nodes. Role fillers shown are the ones dynamically instantiated by propagation of signature activation over the roles' binding nodes (as in figure 5.5). Darkly shaded area indicates the most highly activated path of frames representing the network's interpretation of the input. Dashed area shows the discarded dishwasher-cleaning interpretation. Frames outside of both areas show a small portion of the rest of the network that received no evidential or signature activation.

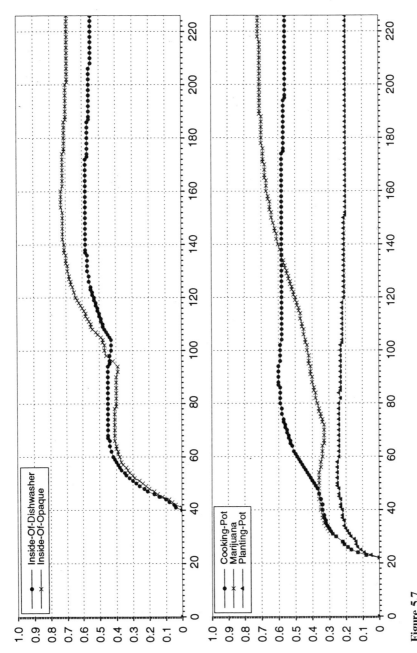

Figure 5.7
Evidential activations for meanings of *pot* and of competing refinements of Inside-Of after presentation of *John put the pot inside the dishwasher* (**P1**) at cycles 1 through 31 and *the police were coming* (**P2**) at cycles 51 through 61.

competing meanings of *pot* and refinements of Inside-Of change during the processing of **Hiding Pot**. Initially there is more evidence for the interpretation that John was trying to clean a cooking pot. This is shown by the fact that after Inside-Of-Dishwasher becomes activated at about cycle 60, Cooking-Pot becomes more highly activated than Marijuana or Planting-Pot. Input for the second phrase of **Hiding Pot** (*because the police were coming*) is presented at cycles 51 through 61. The evidential activation levels shown by the thickness of conceptual node boundaries in figure 5.5 correspond to the activations at cycle 90. The inferences about the police propagate through Transfer-Self, Proximity-Of, See-Object, and Block-See, until they reach Inside-Of-Opaque (see figure 5.6). This occurs at about cycle 95. By about cycle 160, reinforcement from the Block/See/Police/Capture path causes Inside-Of-Opaque to become more activated than Inside-Of-Dishwasher, and Marijuana to become more highly activated than Cooking-Pot. Thus REMIND's interpretation of **Hiding Pot** is that John was trying to avoid detection of his Marijuana from the police by hiding it inside of an opaque dishwasher. The final inference path interpretation is shown in the darkly shaded area of figure 5.6.

5.3.6 Activation Control

A major issue for all structured connectionist networks is controlling the spread of activation. Other spreading-activation models have usually addressed this problem by using direct inhibitory connections between competing concepts (e.g., between meanings of *star* in Waltz and Pollack's network in figure 5.2). For inferencing tasks, however, the inhibitory connections that these networks use are usually semantically unjustifiable and combinatorially explosive. The biggest problem, however, is that they are *winner-take-all networks*, acting to kill the activations of input interpretations that do not win the competition. This becomes a problem when a new context arises that makes an alternative interpretation more plausible. With the activations of the alternative interpretations killed by the inhibition from the false winner, it is exceedingly difficult for the activation from the new context to revive the correct one. The automatic reinterpretation capabilities of the networks are thus sabotaged.

In contrast, REMIND, like ROBIN, has no inhibitory links between competing concepts. It instead uses a group of units that acts as a global inhibition mechanism. These *global inhibition* units serve to inhibit by equal proportions (normalize) all concepts in the network when their average activation becomes too high. The concepts in the network are thus free to keep an activation level relative to the amount of evidence in their favor. Global inhibition nodes are similar to the regulator units used by Touretzky and Hinton (1988), except that their regulator units are *subtractive inhibitory*, subtracting a constant amount of activation from all nodes and implementing a winner-take-all network, while REMIND's global inhibition nodes are *short-circuiting inhibitory*, controlling the spread of activation, but leaving *relative* values of evidential activation unchanged.

As opposed to driving the losers activations down to 0 using winner-take-all networks, REMIND's short-circuiting global inhibition mechanism allows all concepts in the network to hold a level of evidential activation relative to the amount of evidence in their favor. Letting losing interpretations keep activation proportional to their evidence enables REMIND to easily perform reinterpretation. When new context enters the network that favors an alternative interpretation over a previous one, it boosts the new interpretations relative levels of evidential activation—often being enough to cause the new interpretation to become most highly activated. This occurs in **Hiding Pot**, in which the evidence from **P1** (*John put the pot inside the dishwasher*) initially favors Cooking-Pot. However, after evidence from the inferences of **P2** (*the police were coming*) is introduced, Marijuana's activation increases enough so that the network reinterprets *pot* as Marijuana.

5.3.7 Elimination of Crosstalk: Interaction of Signature and Evidential Activation

The use of signatures and evidential activation is a partial solution to the variable binding and inferencing problems of structured connectionist networks. However, the highly complex, overlapping, and ambiguous knowledge needed for language understanding (and eventual memory retrieval) requires more than simple integration of a variable binding mechanism and a standard evidential spreading-activation network. In particular, the problem of *crosstalk* inherent to all spreading-activation networks makes it crucial that the two paths of activation interact so that the dynamic variable bindings in the network control and channel the spread of activation (Lange 1992). This section gives a brief overview of some of the problems of crosstalk for language understanding and how REMIND solves them. The reader interested mainly in memory retrieval may skip to the next section.

Crosstalk occurs when activation spreads from one area of a network into another area when it should not. This often provides unsupported activation evidence to a subset of network nodes and therefore disrupts the contextual disambiguation of the network. This can especially become a problem as networks get bigger and begin to have larger areas activated from inferences, as in REMIND. As an example, consider the following sentence:

John ate some rice before he went to church on Sunday morning. (**Church Service**)

The most probable interpretation of **Church Service** is that John had rice for breakfast before he went to attend services at church ($Church-Service). However, in a normal spreading-activation network, crosstalk from the combined activity of Rice and Church can cause $Wedding to become more highly activated than $Church-Service, since $Church-Service would only receive evidence from Church. This is an example of crosstalk from *logically unrelated inferences*. In general, Rice in the context of a Church should provide evidence for $Wedding. However, in the case of **Church Service**, Rice should not lead to the inference that a $Wedding is occurring, because the Rice is being eaten and not thrown.

One of the main potential sources of crosstalk in spreading-activation networks is that of *spurious*, or *logically impossible* inferences, which is also a problem in many marker-passing systems. In **Church Service** an inference path connecting the Ingesting of the Rice to $Wedding would be spurious, since the actions of eating and going to church are not causally related. As another example, consider the sentence

After Bill put the omelet on the stove, he put the bowl inside the dishwasher.
(**Cook-and-Clean**)

The most likely interpretation of **Cook-and-Clean** is that after Bill cooked his omelet, he put the bowl in the dishwasher so that he could clean it. Inside-Of-Dishwasher with Bill as the Actor and Bowl as the Object should be the winning refinement of Inside-Of. However, if Inside-Of-Stove (a refinement of Inside-Of leading to cooking inferences) is allowed to combine activation from Inside-Of with that from Stove, then Inside-Of-Stove could become more activated than Inside-Of-Dishwasher. The network might then might make the impossible inference that Bill was trying to cook something in the bowl even though he put it in the dishwasher.

REMIND's network structure controls such spurious, logically impossible inferences by enforcing *selectional restrictions*, or binding constraints, on role-fillers. Selectional restrictions on role-fillers are defined in the knowledge base (e.g., table 5.2), and encode knowledge such as that only Cooking-Utensils and Eating-Utensils are typically cleaned in dishwashers and that the Location of a dishwasher cleaning is a Dishwasher. The network structure enforces selectional restrictions by stopping activation from spreading to frames and roles whose selectional restrictions are violated. To perform this, each connection between binding units is actually a multiplicative connection that is gated by another unit calculating whether the signature is a legal one (cf. sigma pi units in Rumelhart, Hinton, and McClelland 1986). The effect of this selectional restriction structure can be seen in the lower part of figure 5.5. Here the network has recognized that Marijuana (6.8), the signature on the left binding node of Inside-Of's Object, violates Inside-Of-Dishwasher's Object's selectional restrictions. The gated connection (not shown) therefore does not allow Marijuana's signature to propagate to Inside-Of-Dishwasher's Object binding node, since only Cooking-Utensils and Eating-Utensils are cleaned in dishwashers. However, the network calculates that Cooking-Pot (9.2) does match the selectional restrictions. Cooking-Pot is allowed to propagate as a possible Object of Inside-Of-Dishwasher (figure 5.5). Though not shown, the network recognizes selectional restriction violations basically by having units that compare the bindings' signatures to those of the expected signatures.

In other cases, the role-fillers' selectional restrictions on a frame are completely violated. For instance, Inside-Of-Stove and Inside-Of-Carwash are impossible interpretations for **Hiding Pot** and **Cook-And-Clean**, since the pot was put inside of a dishwasher and not a stove or car wash. In these cases signature bindings interact with evidential activation so that the violated frames are completely stopped from receiving activation. Thus selection restrictions dramatically reduce the number of spurious, logically impossible inference paths generated by the propagation of signatures—and thereby allows REMIND to avoid one of the major pitfalls of simple marker-passing systems.

Another basic problem of structured connectionist networks is using the dynamic bindings of case role information to perform lexical disambiguation. For example, normal structured networks cannot distinguish between the sentences *The astronomer saw the star* and *The star saw the astronomer*. Signatures partially solve this problem by allowing the network to represent the bindings of the two sentences differently and keep track of who is seeing whom. However, if these bindings do not have an effect on the spread of evidential activation, then they do not help disambiguate between the meanings of *star*. For example, the extended Waltz and Pollack (1985) network of figure 5.1 disambiguates the word *star* in *The astronomer saw the star* to a Celestial-Body, because Celestial-Body receives activation through hard-coded connections from both Astronomy and Sees Object. Unfortunately, when presented with *The star saw the astronomer*, the network does almost exactly the same thing. Celestial-Body again ends up with more activation than Movie-Star because it is still receiving activation from the hard-coded connection from See's Object. This occurs even though Celestial-Body is not bound to See's Object in this story (see analysis in Lange 1992). This is an example where the default, hard-coded case role connections that work in the general case can fail catastrophically in specific instances where the actual variable bindings are known.

ROBIN and REMIND solve this problem and use dynamic role-binding information to perform lexical disambiguation by using gated connections that give them a temporary *virtual structure* specific to the network's current dynamic bindings. These connections feed evidential activation back from frames *only* to concepts that are actually bound to their roles with signature activation. For example, in the case of *The star saw the astronomer*, only the signature of Movie-Star reaches the Actor role of See. Celestial-Body does not, since it violates See's selectional restrictions (celestial bodies have no eyes and cannot see). Since frames only feed evidential activation back to the objects that are bound to their roles, Movie-Star therefore receives evidential activation from See's Object. Celestial-Body does not, and so Movie-Star wins as the interpretation of *star*.

The combination of selection restrictions and the channeling of evidential activation through the virtual role-binding structure solve the problems of crosstalk exemplified by **Cook-And-Clean** and **Church Service**. In **Cook-And-Clean**, the Inside-Of-Stove and stove cooking frames that might otherwise have won do not receive signature or evidential activation because their selectional restrictions are violated. In **Church Service**, the evidential activation from Rice goes to the eating frame that it is bound to and to the breakfast frames those bindings reach, and not (aside from a small amount of biasing activation) to the $Wedding frames. In both cases REMIND's structure avoids normal spreading-activation networks' crosstalk problems and allows it to arrive at the most plausible interpretation. REMIND's virtual structure is also often key to disambiguating more complex stories such as **Hiding Pot**. As shown in figure 5.6, only Cooking-Pot reaches the $Dishwasher-Cleaning frames and receives evidential activation from them. Similarly only Marijuana reaches and receives evidential activation from the Police-Capture frames. Thus frames supported by contextual evidence of the network's inferences and bindings become more activated than their competitors, and so they are more likely to be chosen as part of REMIND's interpretation of its input.

Finally it is important to note that the evidential activation of the network also affects the spread of signatures. Signatures stop spreading to frames when the frames' evidential activation drops below threshold. This stops the network from making an infinite number of inferences—forward inferences are made but only as far as there is support from context. For example, when input for *John put the pot inside the dishwasher* (**P1**) is presented to the network, evidential and signature activation reaches the Clean frame but then drops below threshold and stops spreading. While **P1** provides enough evidence to infer that John might have put the pot inside the dishwasher to clean it, there is not enough evidence to make any further inferences as to why he would want to clean it. Further inferences, such as that John might have wanted to clean the pot to get ready for a Dinner-Party (as in **Dinner Party**), require additional evidential activation from the input, such as the convergent evidence from inferences for *company was coming*.

In summary, REMIND is able to avoid most crosstalk problems because of its structure of units and gated connections that allow signature bindings to control the spread of activation. Spurious inferences are avoided because activation only spreads to inference paths that are logically possible interpretations of the input. Highly unlikely inferences are not made because signatures spread only to concepts that have evidential activation. And most important, the virtual structure created by signatures allows it to combine evidence as if the network were hand-built for the current bindings. Because of these interactions between evidential and signature activation, crosstalk is avoided, and REMIND is influenced only by contextually appropriate evidence. Thus the interpretation REMIND constructs of its cues is influenced only by its input activation, the biases of its connection weights, and its inferences.

5.4 Memory Retrieval

In REMIND memory retrieval occurs automatically as a side effect of the spreading-activation understanding process. Representations of previously understood episodes are connected directly to the same semantic network that understood them in the first place. This direct form of indexing causes episodes that share conceptual similarities with the cue to become active as REMIND interprets the cue.

5.4.1 Representation of Long-Term Episodes

Whereas the general world knowledge and inference rules used to initially build REMIND's networks are hand-coded, REMIND is not given any information about the particular episodes it is going to understand and store in long-term memory. The representations used for these target episodes are created entirely by REMIND's spreading-activation understanding process. Input for each episode's text is presented to the network, which then infers an interpretation of it by the spread of signature and evidential activation. Next units and connections are added (by hand) to store the episode's entire resulting interpretation in REMIND's long-term memory. Accordingly each episode's representation includes all aspects of its interpretation, from its disambiguated surface features (e.g., the actors and objects in the story) to the plans and goals that REMIND inferred that the actors were using.

To determine the symbolic representation used to store an episode in memory, the state of the network is examined by hand to determine the interpretation it has settled on. As described previously, the network's interpretation is the most highly activated path of frames and their role-bindings. For example, the representation of **Hiding Pot** that the network would store in long-term memory would include all of the instantiated frames and their disambiguated role-bindings in the dark gray area of figure 5.6, representing the inferred interpretation of John hiding his Marijuana from the police to avoid being arrested.

As a complete example, consider how **Dirty Magazine** (*Billy put the Playboy under his bed so his mother wouldn't see it and spank him*) is processed and stored in the network as a memory episode. First, signature and evidential activations representing its phrasally analyzed input are clamped to the network to start the understanding process. The actual phrasally analyzed input given to the network for **Dirty Magazine** is:

(Phrase ⟨Subject put Direct-Object under Indirect-Object⟩
  (Subject Billy) (Direct-Object Playboy) (Indirect-Object bed))
(Phrase ⟨Subject see Direct-Object⟩
  (Subject Mother) (Direct-Object Playboy))
(Phrase ⟨Subject spank Direct-Object⟩
  (Subject ?) (Direct-Object Billy))

Possessives (*his*), connectives (*so, would*), and negations (*not*) are not included in the phrasally analyzed input given to REMIND. The above input for **Dirty Magazine** could therefore be more accurately be described as follows: *Billy put Playboy under bed. Mother see Playboy.* ⟨*Somebody unmentioned*⟩ *spank Billy*. REMIND is left to infer the relations between the actions described by the individual phrases itself.

As described earlier for **Hiding Pot**, the input is presented to the network by clamping the evidential activations of the input's phrase and word nodes to 1 and clamping the binding units of the phrases' roles to the signatures of their bindings' word meanings. Activation then spreads through the network to infer and disambiguate an interpretation of the input. As in **Hiding Pot**, the network infers that somebody is hiding something (Avoid-Detection) and that it is blocked from sight (Block-See). Here, however, the inferred signatures show that it is Billy hiding a Playboy-Magazine rather than John hiding Marijuana.

The entire representation inferred for **Dirty Magazine** is shown in figure 5.8. The ".1" after each frame name (e.g., Transfer-Under.1 and Bed.1) indicate that they are specific instantiations of concepts in the first episode processed by the network. For example, **Dirty Magazine**'s interpretation includes a surface action inferred directly from the first phrase (*Billy put the Playboy under the bed*), namely that an instance of Transfer-Under, Transfer-Under.1, had occurred. The Actor of this Transfer-Under.1 is Billy.1, the Object is Playboy-Magazine.1, and the Location is Bed.1. The inferred representation also includes instantiations of more distant frames used by the network to understand **Dirty Magazine**, such as Avoid-Detection.1 and Block-See.1. As in **Hiding Pot**, the network's representation of **Dirty Magazine** also includes the possibility of a Punishment taking place, as it inferred for **Hiding Pot** (not shown in figure 5.6)—though in this case the refinement of Punishment.1 is a Spank rather than an In-Jail. These similarities make **Dirty Magazine** a likely candidate for reminding when the network is presented with **Hiding Pot** as a cue.

It is important to note that each episode's representation also includes all of the simple bridging inferences that were necessary to make the plan/goal analysis. Here the bridging inferences for **Dirty Magazine** include that the Playboy was Under.1 the

```
(Instance Transfer-Under.1        0.61              (Instance Possess-Obj.1        0.10
         :Roles (Actor Billy.1)                              :Roles (Actor Billy.1) (Object Playboy.1)
                (Object Playboy.1)                           :Refinement         Possess-Naughty-Obj.1
                (Location Bed.1)                             :Implied-By         Do-Action-To-Obj.1)
         :Phrase <S put DO under IO>.1            (Instance Possess-Naughty-Obj.1 0.32
         :Refinement-Of    Do-Action-To-Obj.1              :Roles (Actor Billy.1) (Object Playboy.1)
         :Results-In       Under.1)                        :Refinement        Naughty-Committed.1
(Instance Under.1                 0.46                     :Refinement-Of     Possess-Obj.1)
         :Roles (Planner Billy.1)                (Instance Naughty-Committed.1 0.72
                (Object Playboy.1)                         :Roles (Actor Billy.1)
                (Location Bed.1)                                  (Evidence Playboy.1)
         :Refinement       Under-Opaque.1                   :Precondition-For  Guardian-Know-Naughty.1
         :Result-of        Transfer-Under.1)                :Refinement-Of     Possess-Naughty-Obj.1)
(Instance Under-Opaque.1          0.32            (Instance Guardian-See-Naughty.1 0.79
         :Roles (Planner Billy.1)                          :Roles (Actor Mother.1) (Evidence Playboy.1)
                (Object Playboy.1)                         :Refinement-Of     See-Object.1
                (Location Bed.1)                           :Plan-For          Guardian-Know-Naughty.1)
         :Refinement-Of    Under.1                (Instance Guardian-Know-Naughty.1 1.00
         :Results-In       Block-See.1)                    :Roles (Actor Mother.1)
(Instance Block-See.1             0.28                            (Object Billy.1)
         :Roles (Planner Billy.1) (Object Playboy.1)               (Evidence Playboy.1)
         :Result-Of        Under-Opaque.1                  :Plan              Guardian-See-Naughty.1
         :Blocks           See-Object.1                    :Precondition      Naughty-Committed.1
         :Plan-For         Avoid-Detection.1)              :Precondition-For  Guardian-Discipline.1)
(Instance Avoid-Detection.1       0.10            (Instance Guardian-Discipline.1 0.89
         :Roles (Planner Billy.1)                          :Roles (Actor Mother.1)
                (Object Playboy.1)                                (Object Billy.1)
         :Plan             Block-See.1)                           (Evidence Playboy.1)
(Instance See-Object.1            0.98                     :Precondition      Guardian-Know-Naughty.1
         :Roles (Actor Mother.1) (Object Playboy.1)        :Results-In        Spank.1)
         :Phrase           <S see DO>.1           (Instance Spank.1              0.71
         :Precondition     Proximity-Of.1                  :Roles (Actor Mother.1) (Object Billy.1)
         :Blocked-By       Block-See.1                     :Phrase            <S spank DO>.1
         :Refinement       Guardian-See-Naughty)           :Result-Of         Guardian-Discipline.1
(Instance Proximity-Of.1          0.48                     :Refinement-Of     Punishment.1)
         :Roles (Actor Mother.1) (Object Playboy.1)(Instance Punishment.1          0.38
         :Precondition-For See-Object.1                    :Roles (Actor Mother.1) (Object Billy.1)
         :Result-Of        Transfer-Self.1)                :Refinement        Spank.1)
(Instance Transfer-Self.1         0.15            (Instance Unhappy-Punished.1   0.19
         :Roles (Actor Mother.1) (Object Playboy.1)        :Roles (Planner Mother.1) (Object Billy.1)
         :Results-In       Proximity-Of.1)                 :Refinement-Of     Unhappy.1
(Instance Do-Action-To-Obj.1 0.31                          :Result-Of         Punishment.1)
         :Roles (Actor Billy.1) (Object Playboy.1)(Instance Unhappy.1             0.14
         :Refinement       Transfer-Under.1                :Roles (Planner Mother.1) (Object Billy.1)
         :Implies          Possess-Obj.1)                  :Refinement        Unhappy-Punished.1)
```

Figure 5.8
Interpretation inferred by spread of signature and evidential activation through the network for *Billy put the Playboy under his bed so his mother wouldn't see it and spank him* (**Dirty Magazine**). Frame names end in ".1" (e.g., Transfer-Under.1) to indicate that they are instantiations of concepts inferred in the first episode stored in the network. Numbers following instance names are final evidential activations of the frame.

Retrieval from Episodic Memory

bed, that Billy possessed the Playboy (Possess-Obj.1), that the salient refinement of this possession was that it was possession of a naughty object (Possess-Naughty-Obj.1), and so on.

Once the full interpretation for an episode has been determined, units and connections representing this interpretation are hand-coded into the network's long-term memory. For **Dirty Magazine**, the units added include (1) nodes representing each instantiated frame of its interpretation in figure 5.8 (e.g., Billy.1, Playboy-Magazine.1, Avoid-Detection.1, and Possess-Obj.1), (2) units to represent their roles, and (3) a unit to stand as a place holder for the entire episode (e.g., Episode.1). These units are then connected to their corresponding local elements in the normal evidential semantic network. They are also interconnected to encode their role-bindings and which episode they are part of.

Figure 5.9 gives an example of the units and connections that are added to the network to represent episodes. The figure shows a simplified part of the network's evidential layer after several episodes have been understood and added to long-term memory. The gray units in the figure are the normal semantic conceptual units originally in the network, including the conceptual units for frames Possess-Obj and Possess-Naughty-Obj and units in part of the physical object refinement (is-a) hierarchy. At this stage, two episodes have been processed that include Possess-Obj or Possess-Naughty-Obj as part of their interpretation: **Dirty Magazine** (Episode.1), and *Betty wanted to smoke a cigarette, so she put it on top of the stove and lit it* (**Cigarette Lighting**; Episode.4). **Cigarette Lighting**'s interpretation includes an instance of Possess-Obj because the network inferred that Betty must have possessed the cigarette to light it.

The white units in figure 5.9 show some of the units added to the network to encode **Dirty Magazine** and **Cigarette Lighting**. For each episode there is a single *episode unit* serving to represent and group all of its elements together, such as Episode.1 and Episode.4 in figure 5.9. In addition there is an *episode instance unit* representing each element of the episode's interpretation. For **Dirty Magazine** there is an episode instance unit for Billy.1, Playboy-Magazine.1, Possess-Obj.1, and Possess-Naughty-Obj.1, along with units (not shown) representing all of the other elements of its representation. These episode instance units are connected both to the general semantic concept of which they are an instantiation (e.g., Billy.1 is connected to Billy) and to the episode unit of which they are part (e.g., Episode.1 for **Dirty Magazine**'s elements). Furthermore each episode instance is connected to units representing its roles (e.g., the Actor and Object unit for Possess-Obj.1), which are in turn connected to the concepts that were bound to them (e.g., Possess-Obj.1's Actor is connected to Billy.1, and its Object is connected to Playboy-Magazine.1). The rest of the interpretation

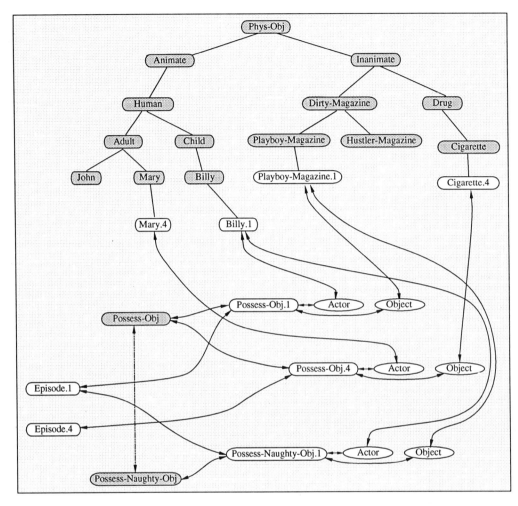

Figure 5.9
Encoding of Possess-Obj and Possess-Naughty-Obj instances for Episode.1 (Dirty Magazine) and Episode.4 (Cigarette Lighting). Gray units are preexisting conceptual nodes. White units are nodes added to represent the episodes.

Retrieval from Episodic Memory

of each episode (e.g., in figure 5.8) is encoded similarly with units and connections that represent all of its other instantiated frames and elements.

As can be seen, REMIND's method of encoding its episodes is different from that of many memory retrieval and case-based reasoning models. Episodes in REMIND are not indexed under any one knowledge structure or important groups of knowledge structures. They are instead indexed under every concept that was an aspect in understanding them in the first place. These concepts include both the surface features of the text (e.g., its direct disambiguated word and phrase meanings) and the abstract inferences that make up the plan/goal analysis of the episode. As will be discussed later, this fully dispersed form of indexing has important implications for the kinds of remindings that the model produces.

5.4.2 Detailed Connectivity of Episodic Units

Unlike the inferencing and understanding portion of the network, the units and connections representing long-term memory episodes reside entirely on the evidential layer of the network. Because the bindings of each individual long-term memory episode are fixed once an episode has been understood and remembered, the bindings can be encoded by direct connections between role units and the elements that are bound to them. Thus, long-term memory episodes do not need the more complex inferencing structure that holds and propagates dynamic signature bindings.

An example of the full set of units and connections used to encode each frame instance in an episode is shown in figure 5.10. As in the normal conceptual units of REMIND, each incoming connection to a concept unit from other concepts goes through an *input branch unit*. Input branch units are analogous to the *input sites* described by Cottrell and Small (1982). They serve both to specify the relationships concepts hold to each other and to control the spread of evidential activation.

Episode instance units have four input branches: an Instance-Of branch, an Element-In branch, a Roles branch, and a Bound-to branch. For example, Possess-Obj.1 has three input branch units in figure 5.10: (1) an Instance-Of input branch that receives activation from Possess-Obj, the concept it is an long-term instance of, (2) an Element-In input branch that receives activation from the episode it is a part of (i.e., Episode.1), and (3) a Roles input branch that receives activation from each of its role units (i.e., its Actor and Object units). The Instance-Of and Element-In branch units calculate their activation as the sum of their single input, since any one instance can only be an instantiation of one general semantic frame. Likewise any one instance can only be an element in one episode. The Roles input branch, on the other hand, calculates its activation as the *average* of its role unit inputs so that frames with multiple roles do not become the most active simply because they have more role-bindings than simpler frames. Episode instance units also have a Bound-To input

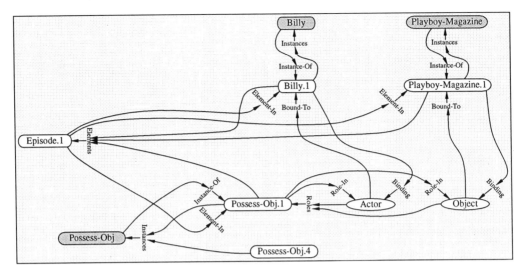

Figure 5.10
Detailed view of units added to represent Possess-Obj.1 of Episode.1. Labels next to nodes (e.g., Instances, Instance-Of) represent their input branch units.

branch that has connections from any of the episode roles they are bound to. For example, Billy.1 is bound to the Actor roles of Possess-Obj.1 and Possess-Naughty-Obj.1 (among others), and so receives activation from those roles through its Bound-To branch. Bound-To input branches calculate their activation as the *maximum* of their inputs so that they receive activation from the most active role they are bound to.

Episode role units, such as Possess-Obj.1's Actor and Object roles, have two input branches: a Role-In branch and a Binding branch. Role-In branches receive activation from the episode instance unit of which the episodic role is part. In figure 5.10 Possess-Obj.1's Actor and Object roles therefore both have Role-In branches that receive activation from Possess-Obj.1. In contrast, Binding branches have a connection from the element that is bound to their role to represent its long-term role-binding. Since Possess-Obj.1's Actor role is bound to Billy.1, it therefore receives activation from Billy.1 through its Binding branch. Similarly the Binding branch of Possess-Obj.1's Object role receives activation from Playboy-Magazine.1.

The episode units themselves have a single Elements branch that receives and sums up the activation of all elements that make up the episode. For example, Episode.1's Elements branch receives activation from Billy.1, Playboy-Magazine.1, Possess-Obj.1, and all the other episode instance elements of its interpretation. This serves two functions: to keep track of all the elements in each episode and to cause episode units to become active when their elements are active.

Finally, all of the concept units in the normal evidential semantic network have an Instances input branch that is used to activate them from each of their instantiations in long-term memory. For instance, Possess-Obj has an Instances branch that receives activation from Possess-Obj.1, Possess-Obj.4, and all of its other episode instances (not shown). This is in addition to the normal conceptual input branches of the network (see Lange and Dyer 1989). An Instances branch unit calculates its activation as the *maximum* of its inputs, since, in general, REMIND can only be reminded of one instantiation of a given frame at a time. An important effect of this activation function is that it also stops concepts that have been seen in many stories before (and therefore have a lot of instances) from dominating concepts that may have more unique (and therefore fewer) instantiations in memory.

All connections in figure 5.10 have unit weight, with the exception of the connections from the episode units (e.g., Episode.1) to the Element-In branches of their episode instances, which have a weight of 0.05. The unit weights from semantic concepts to each of their episode instances make episode instances likely to become active when related concepts are active. On the other hand, the small weights from episode units to the Element-In branches of episode instance units cause their elements to become moderately primed when their episode is active, without becoming too active unless they share other similarities with the reminding cue.

5.4.3 The Process of Episodic Reminding

Retrieval in REMIND begins with presentation of an input cue to the network to be understood. Since episode instance units are connected directly to their corresponding concept units, they become active when the concepts they are instantiations of become activated by the understanding process. The more similarities an episode shares with the inferred interpretation of a cue, the more of the episode's instance units will become active. Episodes having a number of elements in common with the cue's interpretation therefore tend to become highly active. After the network settles, the episode with most highly activated episode unit is retrieved.

Figure 5.11 shows an overview of part of the network after it has understood and encoded the eight different episodes shown in table 5.3. The circled numbers above frame nodes in the figure indicate instantiations in different episodes that are connected to the frames. For example, the episode instance units for Possess-Obj.1 and Possess-Naughty-Obj.1 of Episode.1 (**Dirty Magazine**) shown in figure 5.9 are indicated by the circled 1's above Possess-Obj and Possess-Naughty-Obj in figure 5.11.

Notice that more specific frames tend to have fewer episode instances than less specific frames. This is to be expected, since specific knowledge structures pertaining

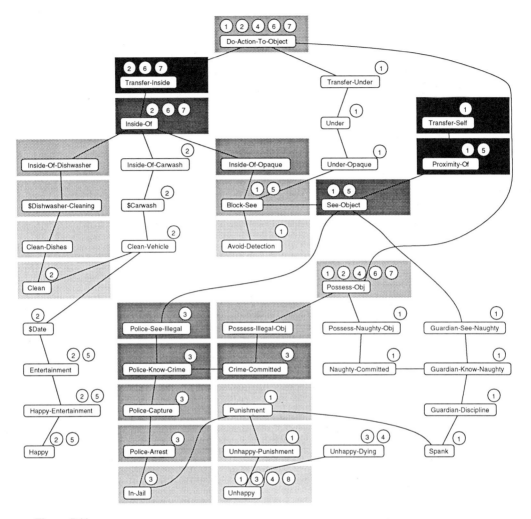

Figure 5.11
Overview of part of the network after activation has settled in processing of **Hiding Pot**. Gray boxes around nodes represent the level of evidential activation on the frame concept nodes (darker = higher activation, no box = no activation). Circles above frames indicate long-term instances connected to them. Numbers within circles indicate which episode the instance is part of in table 5.3.

Table 5.3
Episodes for which input was understood and stored in the network of figure 5.11

Episode number	Episode text	Phrasally parsed input given the network
1	Billy put the Playboy under his bed so his mother wouldn't see it and spank him. (**Dirty Magazine**)	(<S put DO under IO> (S Billy) (DO Playboy) (IO bed)) (<S see DO> (S Mother) (DO Playboy)) (<S spank DO> (DO Billy))
2	Fred put his car inside the car wash before his date with Wilma. (**Car Wash**)	(<S put DO inside IO> (S Fred) (DO car) (IO carwash)) (<S date DO> (S Fred) (DO Wilma))
3	Jane shot Mark with a Colt-45. He died.	(<S shot DO with IO> (S Jane) (DO Mark) (IO Colt-45)) (<S died>) (S Mark))
4	Betty wanted to smoke a cigarette, so she put it on top of the stove and lit it.	(<S smoke DO> (S Betty) (DO cigarette)) (<S put DO on top of IO> (S Betty) (DO cigarette) (IO stove)) (<S lit DO> (DO cigarette))
5	The pleasure boat followed the whales to watch them.	(<S followed> DO> (S pleasure-boat) (DO whales)) (<S watch DO> (DO whales))
6	Barney put the flower in the pot, and then watered it. (**Flower Planting**)	(<S put DO inside IO> (S Barney) (DO flower) (IO pot)) (<S watered DO> (DO flower))
7	Mike was hungry. He ate some fish.	(<S was hungry>) (S Mike)) (<S ate DO> (S Mike) (DO fish))
8	Suzie loved George, but he died. Then Bill proposed to her. She became sad. (**Sad Proposal**)	(<S loved DO> (S Suzie) (DO George)) (<S died>) (S George)) (<S proposed to DO> (S Bill) (DO Suzie)) (<S became sad>) (S Suzie))

to certain situations (e.g., a police search or a parent disciplining a child) represent events that are less frequently encountered than general knowledge structures about simple actions and states (e.g., being inside of something, or possessing an object). As an example, five of the episodes in table 5.3 and figure 5.11 (1, 2, 4, 6, and 7) inferred a Possess-Obj as part of their interpretation, but only one episode (1) involved a Possess-Naughty-Obj or Avoid-Detection. An important consequence of specific frames providing activation evidence for a smaller number of instances is that specific, contentful knowledge structures tend to be stronger reminding indexes than general ones.

Now consider what happens when input for **Hiding Pot** is presented as a cue to the network. Evidential and signature activation spread through the network, dynamically instantiating the competing inference paths as described earlier. Figure 5.12 shows the activation levels of the eight episodes as activation spreads through the network. As can be seen, Episode.6 (*Barney put the flower in the pot, and then watered it*) initially becomes highly active because it shares a number of surface features with **Hiding Pot**, for example, that both involve a Transfer-Inside and have humans, and Planting-Pot receives activation from the word *pot*. Similarly Episode.2 (**Car Wash**) initially becomes active because of shared surface features with **Hiding Pot**. Episode-2's activation continues to climb when the Clean frame is inferred, since a Clean is part of **Car Wash**'s interpretation. However, as REMIND continues to process **Hiding Pot**, the hiding and punishment frames are inferred and become active. Eventually Episode.1's (**Dirty Magazine**) activation climbs and wins because it shares the most surface *and* abstract features of any episode with **Hiding Pot**'s interpretation (see figure 5.11). **Dirty Magazine** is therefore retrieved as the episode most similar to **Hiding Pot**.

An explanation for why **Dirty Magazine** becomes the most highly activated of the eight episodes can be seen in figure 5.11. The gray boxes around nodes in figure 5.11 indicate the final levels of evidential activation of the frames inferred for **Hiding Pot**. Of the eight episodes stored in the network, **Dirty Magazine** has the most instances of its interpretation shared with **Hiding Pot**'s final active interpretation (e.g., instantiations Avoid-Detection.1, Block-See.1, Punishment.1, and Possess-Obj.1). It therefore eventually becomes the most activated of the episodes.

Figures 5.13 and 5.14 show the activation levels of different elements in **Flower Planting** (Episode.6) and **Dirty Magazine** (Episode.1) as **Hiding Pot** is being understood. **Flower Planting** initially becomes the most active of the episodes because it shares a number of superficial similarities with the undisambiguated phrase *John put the pot inside the dishwasher*. As shown in figure 5.13, it quickly receives activation when its element Planting-Pot.6 becomes activated from the Planting-Pot meaning of *pot* at about cycle 25. Additional activation is received when Transfer-Inside.6 becomes activated from Transfer-Inside at about cycle 40. The activation of Episode.6

Retrieval from Episodic Memory

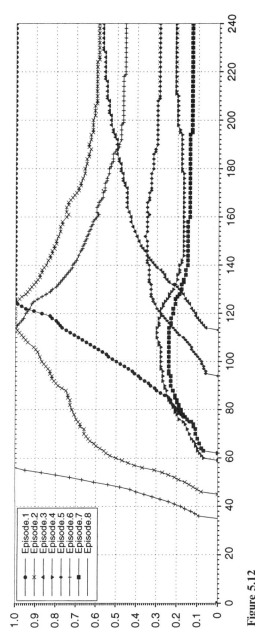

Figure 5.12
Evidential activations of episode units for eight episodes of table 5.3 after presentation of **Hiding Pot**.

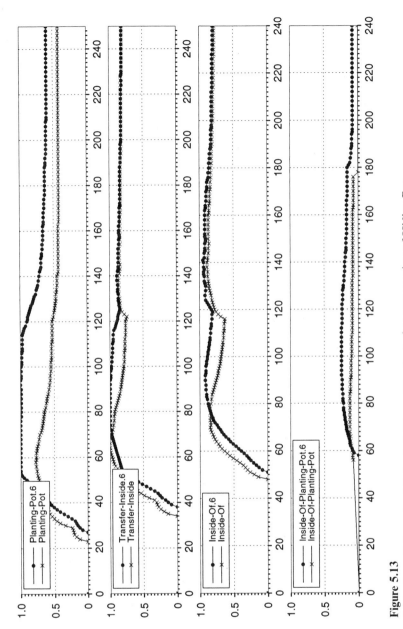

Figure 5.13
Activation of elements of Episode.6 (**Flower Planting**) after presentation of **Hiding Pot**.

continues to climb along with Planting-Pot.6 and Transfer-Inside.6, and gets even more activation when the network infers that the pot is Inside-Of the dishwasher, directly activating Inside-Of.6 at about cycle 50. That, however, is where **Flower Planting**'s similarities with **Hiding Pot**'s inferences end, except for a couple of other shared elements (Do-Action-To-Object.6 and Possess-Obj.6). For example, Inside-Of-Planting-Pot.6, part of **Flower Planting**'s interpretation, does not become significantly active because Inside-Of-Planting-Pot is never inferred by the network (because a pot inside a dishwasher violates its selectional restrictions).

Figure 5.14 shows the activation levels of **Dirty Magazine**'s elements as the network eventually infers the plans and goals of **Hiding Pot** that the two episodes share. One of the first similarities activated is the Possess-Obj.1 instantiation of Episode.1 (see figure 5.9) after about cycle 60. This causes Episode.1's activation to climb above threshold, though its activation is still much lower than that of Episode.6 or Episode.2. However, as time goes on, Block-See, See-Object, Avoid-Detection, Punishment, and the other shared knowledge structures of **Dirty Magazine** are inferred by the spread of signatures and evidential activation for **Hiding Pot**, so that eventually the cumulative evidence from all the shared inferences causes Episode.1 to become the most highly activated episode at around cycle 170 (figure 5.12).

Besides serving as an example of retrieval in REMIND, this example illustrates a number of important points about the model. The first point to notice is that even when the network settles, the losing episodes retain a level of evidential activation relative to the amount of evidence available for them, rather than being driven down to zero. As in the normal evidential semantic network, this is the result of controlling episodes' activations through REMIND's global inhibition rather than normal mutual inhibition.

A second point of interest is that elements and episodes that are superficially similar to the cue tend to become activated *before* elements and episodes that are only abstractly related to the cue (through inferences). This is a direct result of the spreading-activation process, since activation and signature inferences reach closely related concepts before they reach more distant concepts. An example of this was seen in figure 5.12, where the superficially related Episode.6 became activated before the more abstractly related **Dirty Magazine**. As seen, however, the early activation of superficially similar episodes does not stop thematically similar episodes from winning if the thematically similar episodes ultimately share more features and activation with the cue. Because all episodes retain their relative supported levels of activation, thematically similar episodes such as **Dirty Magazine** can climb as inferences reach them and end up with the highest level of activation when the network settles.

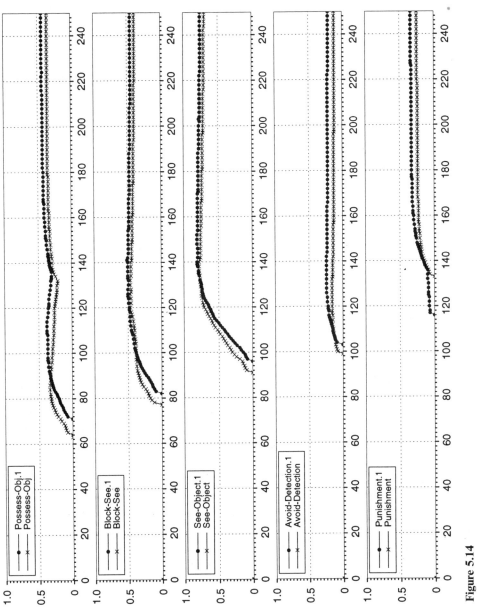

Figure 5.14
Evidential activation of elements of Episode.1 (**Dirty Magazine**) after presentation of **Hiding Pot**.

Retrieval from Episodic Memory

157

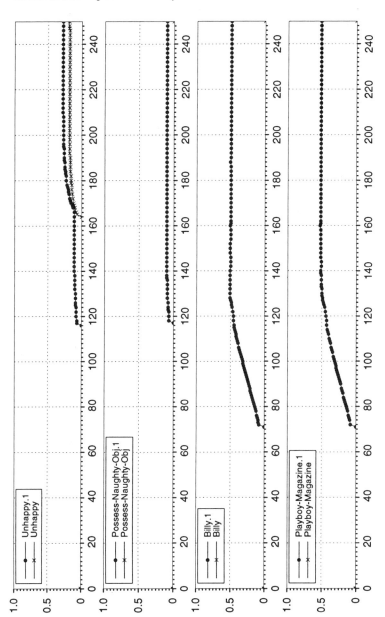

Another important thing to note is that retrieval in REMIND is not all-or-nothing. As in human recall, REMIND often gets *partial* recall in which only subparts of the retrieved episode are activated. Parts of the retrieved episode distant from the current context of inferences may not become activated initially. Possess-Naughty-Obj.1, for example, only becomes partially primed (from its Element-In and Roles branches) because Possess-Naughty-Obj was never activated from the inferences made for **Hiding Pot**. The same is true for most of the other parts of **Dirty Magazine** that differ significantly from **Hiding Pot**'s interpretation (e.g., the Guardian-Discipline and Spank structures, which are relatively distant from anything in **Hiding Pot**). However, the primary actors and objects in episodes, such as Billy.1 and Playboy-Magazine.1 in **Dirty Magazine**, do tend to become active because they play a part in so many of its roles.

5.5 Experiments and Discussion

REMIND has been implemented and tested in the DESCARTES connectionist simulator (Lange et al. 1989). The knowledge base used for the examples in this paper currently includes 206 distinct conceptual frames (e.g., Inside-Of, Avoid-Detection, Cooking-Pot) and 333 inference rules (e.g., R1–R4). It has understood and retrieved the examples presented here (including **Hiding Pot**, **Dinner Party**, and the episodes of table 5.3) and a number of other episodes of similar lengths and complexity.

In this section we discuss three simulations that illustrate (1) the importance of inferences and disambiguation on retrieval in REMIND, (2) the strong influence of superficial feature similarities on retrieval, and (3) the effect of episodic recall on the understanding process. We then compare REMIND to the ARCS and MAC/FAC models of general reminding. Finally we discuss several directions that we are exploring to extend the model.

5.5.1 Importance of Inferences

The retrieval of **Dirty Magazine** when **Hiding Pot** was presented as a cue to REMIND illustrates the importance of inferencing and disambiguation in the retrieval process. **Dirty Magazine** was retrieved over the more superficially similar **Flower Planting** and **Car Wash** episodes because **Dirty Magazine** and **Hiding Pot** were more thematically similar, since both involved someone hiding something to avoid punishment. Without being able to infer these similarities, the model would not have been able to retrieve the most analogous episode.

Another example of how text comprehension affects REMIND's retrieval process is shown when two superficially similar cues that have entirely different interpretations are presented to the network. On the surface the cue *John put the pot inside the dishwasher because company was coming* (**Dinner Party**) is nearly the same as **Hiding Pot**. The only difference is that *company* is coming rather than *the police*. Analogical retrieval models such as ARCS (Thagard et al. 1990) and MAC/FAC (Gentner and Forbus 1991) that do not have inferencing mechanisms would therefore have to predict that the same episode would be retrieved for both cues from among those shown in table 5.3. This would occur for two reasons. First, the only surface feature difference between the two cues does not make a difference in overall surface similarity between the cues and any of the episodes from table 5.3—*company* and *police* are equally similar to all objects in these episodes. Second, the isomorphic structure (structural consistency) of the two cues is the same.

In contrast to ARCS and MAC/FAC, REMIND retrieves different episodes for **Dinner Party** and **Hiding Pot**. This is because REMIND interprets the two cues very differently. Whereas in **Hiding Pot** it appears John is trying to hide marijuana from the police, in **Dinner Party** it appears that he is trying to clean a cooking pot in preparation for company coming over. As such **Dinner Party** is not likely to cause a reminding of **Dirty Magazine** and its hiding event. It seems more likely that **Dinner Party** would cause reminding of another episode involving someone cleaning something in preparation for entertaining, such as the **Car Wash** episode (*Fred put his car in the car wash before his date with Wilma*).

This is exactly what happens in REMIND when episodic memory contains **Dirty Magazine**, **Car Wash**, and the other six episodes of table 5.3. Figure 5.15 shows the evidential activations of the meanings of *pot* and some of the competing refinements of Inside-Of after REMIND is given input for **Dinner Party**. As when **Hiding Pot** is presented, Planting-Pot initially becomes highly activated because the input for *John put the pot inside the dishwasher* (**P1**) contains the word *pot*. After about cycle 60, REMIND infers Inside-Of-Dishwasher and Inside-Of-Opaque. Cooking-Pot's activation therefore starts to climb because of its unmatched activation from Inside-Of-Dishwasher and the other $Dishwasher-Cleaning frames. Input for *company was coming* is presented to REMIND at cycles 51–61. Spreading signature and evidential activation makes candidate inferences for *company was coming* starting from Transfer-Self, through Proximity-Of and then the Dinner-Party frames (representing somebody making dinner for someone else). Activation eventually reaches the Clean-Dishes frame (a *precondition* for Dinner-Party). The cleaning frames were already active after the initial inferences from **P1**, so activation continues to spread and provides added support for the Inside-Of-Dishwasher refinement of Inside-Of at about cycle 130. Inside-Of-Opaque also gets added evidence at about cycle 140 from inferences through the Block-See frames from *company was coming* (since John could still have been hiding the pot). However, Inside-Of-Opaque does not receive enough activation to compete

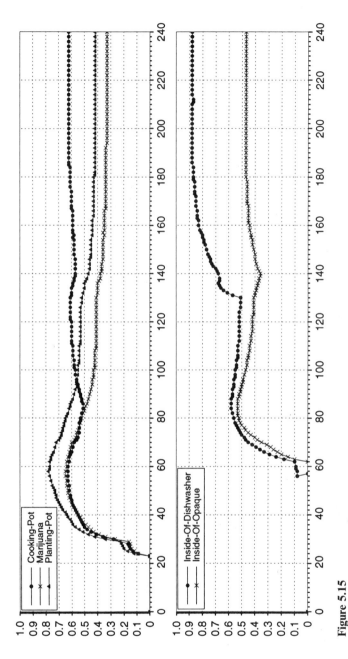

Figure 5.15
Evidential activations for meanings of *pot* and of competing refinements of Inside-Of after presentation of input for *John put the pot inside the dishwasher* (P1) at cycles 1 through 31 and *company was coming* (P2) at cycles 51 through 61 (**Dinner Party**)

Retrieval from Episodic Memory 161

with Inside-Of-Dishwasher. Similarly Marijuana never seriously competes with Cooking-Pot because the Police-Capture and Police-See-Illegal frames that gave it unique activation in **Hiding Pot** are not inferred here (since Company does not match their selectional restrictions). The network's final interpretation of **Dinner Party** is therefore that John was trying to clean a Cooking-Pot to prepare for a Dinner-Party he was giving for Company.

Figure 5.16 shows the activation of the eight episodes and of two of **Car Wash**'s elements as **Dinner Party** is processed. As when **Hiding Pot** is presented, Episode.6 (Mike put the flower in the pot and then watered it) is the first episode to become activated because of its surface similarities with *John put the pot inside the dishwasher*. Episode.2 (**Car Wash**) gets activated after about cycle 45 because of the shared inferences of Transfer-Inside and Inside-Of, and continues to gain more activation when Clean is inferred at around cycle 100. The activation of Episode.1 (**Dirty Magazine**) also starts climbing at around cycle 100 because the network is also activating the hiding and seeing structures as possible inferences for **Dinner Party**. At about cycle 120 the network infers that an Entertainment is being planned (the Dinner Party). This activates Entertainment.2 and provides more evidence for **Car Wash**. At about the same time, the Cleaning frames (including Inside-Of-Dishwasher) get reinforcement from the *company was coming* inferences (cycles 100–140). This boosts the activations of many of the remaining elements of **Car Wash**, such as Clean.2. Accordingly, Episode.2's activation begins to dominate over Episode.1's (**Dirty Magazine**), which gradually loses support starting about cycle 150. Thus REMIND retrieves the **Car Wash** episode when **Dinner Party** is presented as a cue. This demonstrates that even changing a single word in the cue (from *police* to *company*) can completely change the inferences and interpretations REMIND makes and consequently the episode it retrieves.

5.5.2 Superficial Similarities

As mentioned earlier, human reminding seems to be affected strongly by superficial feature overlap between cues and memory episodes. Even when episodes exist in memory that are highly analogous to a cue (and hence useful for problem solving), people may instead get reminded of nonanalogous episodes simply because they are more superficially similar. For example, stories about sharks eating people, such as **Killer Shark**, may remind people of other stories about sharks or other man-eaters devouring people rather than thematically similar stories that do not happen to involve sharks. Superficial remindings therefore often come at the expense of perhaps more valuable cross-contextual remindings.

This characteristic of reminding can be explained quite readily if episodes are remembered by storing all aspects of their interpretation, as in REMIND. Because

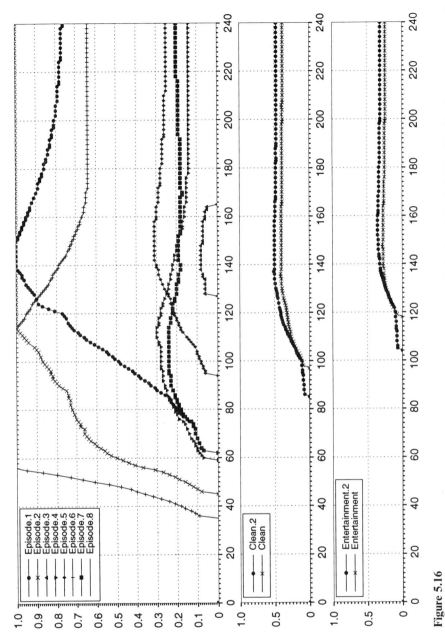

Figure 5.16
Activations of eight episodes of table 5.3 and two of the elements of winning Episode.2 (**Car Wash**) after presentation of **Dinner Party**.

Retrieval from Episodic Memory

REMIND stores all of the knowledge structures used in building an interpretation of the episode, from surface features to abstract inferences, it predicts that episodes that share many surface features with a cue are indeed likely candidates for reminding. For example, consider the sentence:

Cheech put the grass inside the bong because Chong was coming. (**Cheech and Chong**)

Cheech and Chong is an example of a superficially similar episode that can prevent retrieval of an analogous episode. Although **Cheech and Chong** is not analogous to **Hiding Pot**, the two episodes share a number of surface features. Both involve marijuana, marijuana being put inside of something and someone coming near. The plans and goals in the two episodes are completely different, however. In **Cheech and Chong**, the most probable interpretation is that Cheech was readying the marijuana to be smoked with his friend Chong. In **Hiding Pot**, of course, the network's interpretation was that John was hiding the marijuana so that he would not be punished. So if **Cheech and Chong** is understood and stored in memory along with the eight episodes of table 5.3, then **Dirty Magazine** is still the most *analogous* story in memory to **Hiding Pot**. **Cheech and Chong**, however, shares far more *total* features with **Hiding Pot**'s interpretation and is therefore more likely to be retrieved by the model when **Hiding Pot** is presented as a cue.

To test this, input for **Cheech and Chong** was presented to the network to be understood and then remembered. The network disambiguated *grass* to Marijuana (instead of Lawn-Grass) and inferred an interpretation that Cheech put the marijuana inside a Marijuana-Bong to Light it for the Pot-Party that Chong was transferring himself to. **Cheech and Chong**'s interpretation was then added (as Episode.9) to the eight episodes already stored in the network.

Figure 5.17 shows the evidential activations as **Hiding Pot** is being understood in the network containing **Cheech and Chong** and the eight other episodes of table 5.3. Both **Cheech and Chong** (Episode.9) and **Flower Planting** (Episode.6) quickly become activated because of their surface similarities with the undisambiguated *John put the pot inside the dishwasher*. However, Episode.9's activation starts to dominate and Episode.6's starts to fall after *the police were coming* is presented to the network. This occurs because *the police were coming* adds more superficially similar activation to Episode.9's *Chong was coming*. Episode.6's activation drops further when Planting-Pot's activation falls as the network disambiguates *pot* to Cooking-Pot (the cleaning inferences) or Marijuana (the hiding and police capture inferences). Episode.9's activation, on the other hand, remains at its maximum (1.0) until the network settles. **Cheech and Chong** is therefore the episode retrieved for **Hiding Pot**. The other eight

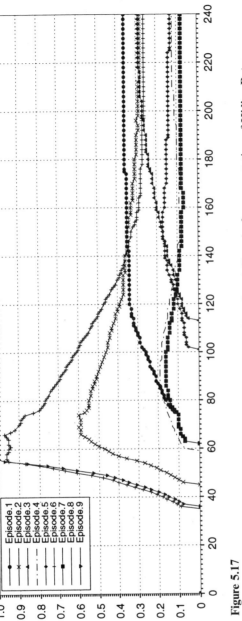

Figure 5.17
Activations of eight episodes of table 5.3 and Episode.9 (**Cheech and Chong**) after presentation of **Hiding Pot**.

episodes end up with relatively little activation, since **Cheech and Chong** is so (superficially) similar to **Hiding Pot** relative to them. As might be expected, **Dirty Magazine** is the most highly activated of the remaining eight episodes, since it was the episode most similar to **Hiding Pot** before **Cheech and Chong** was remembered.

5.5.3 Effect of Reminding on Interpretation

REMIND only models how cues are understood and how episodes are consequently retrieved from memory. Unlike case-based reasoning models, it does not model how the information in those episodes can be used for analogical transfer or applied for problem solving. One of the reasons this would be difficult for REMIND is that the *analogical inferences* that are made by case-based reasoning models are essentially equivalent to applying *novel* rules—such as applying a newly mapped rule from a previous case to the bindings of the new case. Structured connectionist networks such as REMIND cannot currently represent such completely novel rules, because rules connecting concepts are hard-coded with units and links that cannot themselves be dynamically recruited. The possible extensions to signatures' representational and inferencing capabilities discussed in Lange (1992) might solve some of these problems. Eskridge (1994) and Barnden and Srinivas (1992) show that *hybrid* connectionist models that use complex symbolic abilities can perform analogical and case-based transfer from the cases they retrieve.

Though it does not reason from the episodes it recalls, REMIND's integration of the reminding and understanding processes shows that memory retrieval can have pragmatically interesting and useful effects on the understanding process. Episodes that become active during the understanding process feed activation back into the inferencing part of the network. This in effect can prime and bias the interpretation REMIND settles on for a given input. For example, consider the following example:

The star loved the plumber, but he was shot by a thief. Then the astronomer proposed to her. She started to cry. (**Astronomer Proposal**)

There are two possible reasons for the movie star starting to cry after the astronomer proposed to her: Either the proposal made her extremely happy, or the proposal made her extremely sad. Perhaps the most likely reason for her crying was that the proposal reminded her of murdered lover, therefore making her upset and sad. REMIND, however, does not have the complex knowledge about memories and how they affect people's emotions that would be necessary to make that interpretation. However, REMIND is given the knowledge that a person will become sad when someone they love dies (Unhappy-Dead-Friend). The network also knows that marriage proposals can be either happy events (Happy-Proposal) or sad events (Unhappy-Proposal), as in AT-LAST (Eiselt 1987).

When the network is presented with input for **Astronomer Proposal**, the word *star* is quickly disambiguated to Movie-Star because of the selectional restrictions that only Humans can be the Actors of Loves (figure 5.18). REMIND then infers that the $Shooting causes the plumber to be Dead and that the Movie-Star who Loves him will therefore be sad (Unhappy-Dead-Friend leading to Unhappy). After input for the phrase *the astronomer proposed to her* is presented, the network infers at about cycle 120 that there are two possible results from this Marriage-Proposal: that she will consider it a Happy-Proposal or an Unhappy-Proposal. These inferences then instantiate the more general Happy and Unhappy frames, respectively, both of which connect to the Movie-Star's Crying, since Crying can be the result-of states Happy or Unhappy.

As shown in figure 5.18, Happy-Proposal initially becomes more highly activated than Unhappy-Proposal. This is a result of the network being biased to normally consider Marriage-Proposals to be Happy-Proposals—the weight from Marriage-Proposal to Happy-Proposal is 0.6, but the weight from Marriage-Proposal to Unhappy-Proposal is only 0.4. The gap in Happy-Proposal and Unhappy-Proposals activations begins to narrow at about cycle 150 when both begin to receive feedback from Crying (*she started to cry*). This narrowing occurs because (1) Crying has a higher weight to Unhappy than to Happy and (2) Unhappy is already highly active from Unhappy-Dead-Friend. However, REMIND's bias toward Marriage-Proposals being Happy-Proposals is too great, and Happy-Proposal finishes with more activation than Unhappy-Proposal. The final interpretation of **Astronomer Proposal** is therefore that (1) the Movie-Star was made happy by the astronomers proposal and started to cry tears of joy, and (2) she was also sad because her lover the plumber was killed (an active inference path for which REMIND could find no causal connection to the crying of the marriage proposal).

As **Astronomer Proposal** illustrates, REMIND often comes up with counter-intuitive interpretations of stories when the biases of its connection weights are too strong or when it does not have enough knowledge to make the needed inferences for the right interpretation. However, when there is a highly analogous episode (or case) in memory, the influence of episodic retrieval upon text understanding can lead REMIND to a correct interpretation of its input. For example, consider

Suzie loved George, but he died. Then Bill proposed to her. She became sad. (**Sad Proposal**)

Sad Proposal is quite similar to **Astronomer Proposal**, except that the input made it explicit that Suzie became Unhappy after Bill proposed to her. This essentially forces the network to make the correct interpretation, that the Marriage-Proposal after the death of her lover was an Unhappy-Proposal. This interpretation, including the inference Unhappy-Proposal.8, is stored in memory as Episode.8 in table 5.3.

Retrieval from Episodic Memory

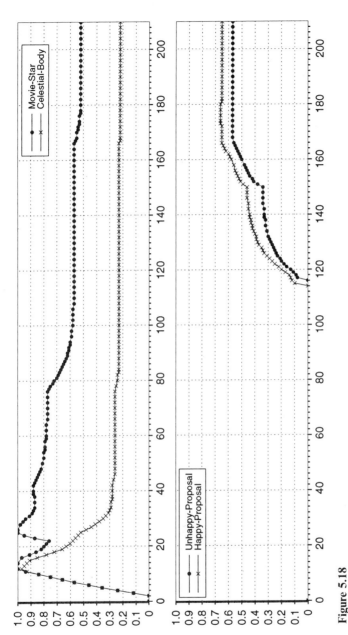

Figure 5.18
Activations of ambiguous meanings of word *star* and of Happy-Proposal and Unhappy-Proposal interpretations of Propose-Marriage after activation is presented for **Astronomer Proposal**.

Figure 5.19 shows the activation levels of **Sad Proposal** (Episode.8) and the other episodes as **Astronomer Proposal** is being understood by REMIND. As expected, **Sad Proposal** quickly dominates most of the other episodes because it is so similar to **Astronomer Proposal**. Episode.3 becomes temporarily active because it also involves somebody shooting somebody to death. However, **Sad Proposal** eventually wins and is retrieved.

The most interesting result shown in figure 5.19 is the activation levels of the competing Happy-Proposal and Unhappy-Proposal frames. As when **Astronomer Proposal** was presented to the network without any episodes in memory, Happy-Proposal initially has more activation than Unhappy-Proposal because of its higher weight from Propose-Marriage. In this case, however, Episode.8 is highly active, and with it Unhappy.8 and Unhappy-Proposal.8. As described in section 5.4, these episode instances feed activation back into their concepts in the understanding network. Unhappy-Proposal therefore gets significant activation from Unhappy-Proposal.8. This added evidence allows its activation to climb over that of Happy-Proposal, which gets no added evidence from any of the episodes in memory. When the network settles, Unhappy-Proposal wins over Happy-Proposal, so REMIND's interpretation is that the astronomer's marriage proposal made the movie star unhappy. The network therefore selects the correct interpretation of **Astronomer Proposal** because of activation feedback from an analogous case in memory, **Sad Proposal**.

REMIND's use of the same spreading-activation mechanism for both language understanding and episodic memory retrieval demonstrates one way memory retrieval can subtly affect the interpretation process. When stored episodes share conceptual similarity with a cue that REMIND is comprehending, these episodes feed evidential activation back into the inferencing network. This feedback can bias REMIND's interpretation to be consistent with the active episodes, a limited form of case-based reasoning. These effects emerge entirely from the integration of language understanding and retrieval within a single spreading-activation network.

5.5.4 Comparison to General Models of Reminding

It is difficult to directly compare REMIND to most case-based reasoning models because they were developed with different goals in mind. As described previously, CBR models are usually models of expert reminding or models built to demonstrate how certain kinds of abstract remindings can occur. Unlike REMIND they are not meant to be models of general, nonexpert human reminding. An advantage of case-based reasoning models over REMIND is that their use of symbolic processing abilities allow them to handle longer and more complex episodes than REMIND (and connectionist models in general) can currently handle. On the other hand, as a model of comprehension and general reminding, REMIND is better able to explain

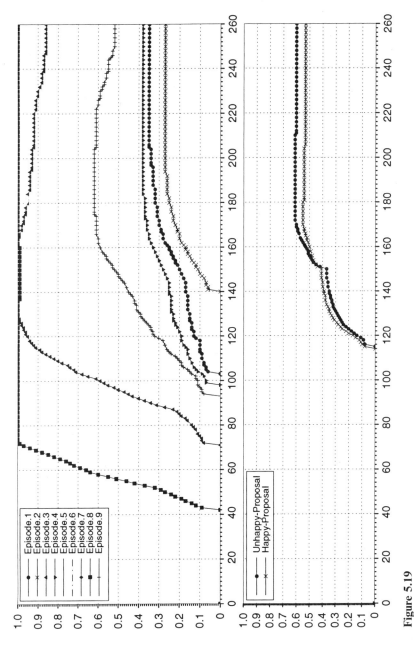

Figure 5.19
Activations of episodes and of Happy-Proposal and Unhappy-Proposal interpretations of Propose-Marriage after activation is presented for **Astronomer Proposal** in network containing **Sad Proposal** episode.

psychological results such as the relatively high prevalence of remindings based on superficial similarities and on how the reminding and language understanding processes interact and effect each other.

The models that REMIND is most directly comparable to are ARCS (Thagard et al. 1990) and MAC/FAC (Gentner and Forbus 1991), two other simulations of general, nonexpert reminding. All three models were built to take into account psychological evidence showing that episodic memory retrieval is strongly influenced by surface feature similarities between a cue and the target episodes in memory, but that deeper analogical or thematic similarities sometimes play an important role. However, there are two important differences between how REMIND explains this evidence compared to ARCS and MAC/FAC.

The most obvious difference is that REMIND is an inferencing-based theory of reminding. Memory retrieval in REMIND results directly from the inferencing and disambiguation process used to understand and form elaborated interpretations of REMIND's cue. ARCS and MAC/FAC, on the other hand, are stand-alone memory retrieval models that are given complete propositional representations of their cues and memory episodes. An advantage of this approach is that it allows ARCS and MAC/FAC to deal with retrieval of much more complicated episodes than does REMIND. ARCS, for example, performed memory retrieval using complex, hand-coded predicate calculate representations of synopses of 24 Shakespearean plays. On the other hand, a major criticism of ARCS and MAC/FAC is that neither model specifies exactly how the representation of its input cues and episodes is formed. More important, neither model specifies what kinds of knowledge those representations should generally include. Should the cue representations include only the surface propositions directly stated in phrases of a cue's text? Or should they include a fully elaborated interpretation of the cue, including a complete causal plan/goal analysis of the text and any abstract themes it involves, as in REMIND?

We believe that many types of memory retrieval cannot be performed without such inferences, as illustrated by some of the examples in this chapter (e.g., sections 5.4.3 and 5.5.1) and some of the examples of case-based reasoning systems. However, even if stand-alone retrieval models such as ARCS and MAC/FAC used fully elaborated interpretations of their cues, we believe that not modeling the *process* by which these interpretations are formed misses an important factor in reminding. People read texts with widely different levels of analysis, ranging from simply skimming the text to reading it carefully and thinking deeply about its ramifications. While there are circumstances under which it is reasonable to assume that subjects make relatively deep thematic inferences, it is misleading to think that this is always the case (e.g., Seifert et al. 1986). Thus, when the process by which the retrieval cue is constructed itself is not modeled, there is no way to simulate the specific circumstances under which understanders infer and can use planning or thematic information in probing memory. In contrast, REMIND explicitly models the cue interpretation process, and so it can potentially explain when elaborated abstract inferences are available to affect reminding.

Another major difference between REMIND and ARCS and MAC/FAC is in how they theorize that analogical similarity exerts an influence on memory retrieval. Both ARCS and MAC/FAC perform memory retrieval in two stages. In their first stage, both search memory to find the episodes in memory sharing the most surface semantic commonalties with the cue. In their second stage, they compute which of the contacted episodes best match the cue and should be retrieved. In addition to counting surface similarities, they calculate the degree of *structural isomorphism* (or *relational consistency*) as an explicit factor in their computation of which episode best matches the cue. Eskridge (1994) describes a hybrid connectionist model of analogical retrieval and transfer that acts in a similar way.

Isomorphism can best be explained by an example from Thagard et al. (1990) for the cue *The dog bit the boy and the boy ran away from the dog* (**Boy Run**). Compare this to the analogues *Fido bit John and John ran away from Fido* (**John Run**) and *Rover bit Fred and Rover ran away from Fred* (**Rover Run**). **John Run** is structurally isomorphic with **Boy Run** because mapped objects play the same roles in mapped predicates. In both cases the dog did the biting and the person it bit did the running. In **Rover Run**, however, it was the dog that ran from the person it bit. **John Run** is therefore more isomorphic, in a purely syntactic sense, to **Boy Run** than is **Rover Run**, and is therefore a better analogue.

Both ARCS and MAC/FAC explicitly compute the level of syntactic isomorphism between a cue and episodes that share surface semantic overlap with the cue. The degree of cue/target isomorphic match is factored into their second stage's matching process. Analogical similarity is hypothesized by these models to exert its effect on memory retrieval as a direct result of this specifically computed degree of syntactic relational consistency between cues and memory episodes. REMIND, on the other hand, never explicitly computes the degree of isomorphism between a cue and memory episodes. In REMIND the influence of such relational consistency is entirely the result of the inferencing process. Relationally consistent targets are retrieved over relationally inconsistent targets in REMIND only when the different syntactic structure of each input *leads to different inferences*. For example, if presented with **John Run**, REMIND would infer that the boy ran away because he was afraid that dog would continue its attack. However, if presented with **Rover Run**, REMIND would infer that the dog ran away because it feared retaliation in the form of anger or a kick from the boy. Because of the different inferences and interpretation of the two episodes, REMIND, like ARCS and MAC/FAC, would therefore retrieve **John Run** when presented with **Boy Run** as a cue. Unlike ARCS and MAC/FAC, however, REMIND does so without having to go through a separate stage to explicitly compute the degree of syntactic isomorphism.

Like ARCS, our earlier model of integrated language understanding and memory retrieval, SAARCS (Lange et al. 1990), included relational consistency as an explicit factor in reminding. SAARCS was a hybrid connectionist model that combined ROBIN (Lange and Dyer 1989) with aspects of ARCS. Like REMIND, SAARCS used the ROBIN portion of the network to infer and disambiguate an interpretation of a cue. Unlike REMIND, SAARCS then explicitly calculated relational consistency to build a constraint satisfaction mapping network like ARCS' to determine which episode was retrieved. Oftentimes SAARCS would not have enough knowledge to make different inferences between cues with cross-mapped bindings, such as for *The boat followed the dolphins* versus *The dolphins followed the boat*. In those cases SAARCS' use of ARCS' explicit influence of relational consistency between cues and targets led SAARCS to retrieve the right analog (Lange et al. 1990). However, when SAARCS had enough knowledge to build a different interpretation for cross-mapped cues (e.g., for *The surfer ate the shark* vs. The *shark ate the surfer*), the explicit effect of relational consistency turned out to be unneeded. As in REMIND the different shared inferences in SAARCS were enough to activate the analogous episode enough to win. It turned out that in every case that we built enough knowledge into the network for it to build different interpretations for disanalogous episodes; the degree of syntactic isomorphism only boosted (confirmed) the analogous episode that had already won due to those different interpretations. This was a primary motivating factor for simplifying the model and moving to REMIND, a purely inferencing-based model of episodic reminding.

We therefore believe that the noted effects of syntactic isomorphism and relational consistency on memory retrieval can be fully explained by the understanding process. Relationally consistent episodes tend to have similar inferences, interpretations, and themes, while relationally inconsistent episodes tend to have different inferences, interpretations, and themes. In REMIND relationally based reminding occurs as a natural side effect of interpreting and disambiguating an input text. Relational consistency only affects reminding to the degree that it changes those inferences.

5.5.5 Future Work

In the future there are three main areas that we would like to explore: (1) improved inferencing abilities, (2) the ability to determine the initial surface role-bindings with additional lexical information in the networks, and (3) automatic learning of the episodes the network has understood.

5.5.5.1 Improved Inferencing REMIND's propagation of signature activations dynamically instantiates candidate inference paths in parallel, in much the same way as marker-passing systems. The use of ROBIN's signatures therefore allows REMIND to perform dynamic inferencing difficult for most connectionist models, while using its evidential activation allows it to perform disambiguation and reinterpretation difficult for most symbolic models. However, REMIND's representation and rule-firing abilities are currently limited relative to those of traditional symbolic models, limiting the length and complexity of the texts the model can understand and therefore remember.

One of the main restrictions of the model as described is that there can be only one dynamic instance of each frame at any given time, since binding units can only hold one signature activation at once. Because of this, REMIND cannot yet represent or interpret texts involving two different seeing or eating events, for instance. Another limitation is that REMIND currently only propagates signatures of *pre-existing* concepts, such as of Cooking-Pot, Marijuana, or John. REMIND does not propagate signatures of the *dynamically* instantiated frames inferred by signatures, such as the dynamic instance of Cooking-Pot or Marijuana being Inside-Of a Dishwasher in figure 5.5. Not being able to propagate signatures of dynamically instantiated frames makes it impossible for REMIND to encode most rules for *general* planning knowledge or complex interactions of goals which generally require the ability to reason over any dynamic plan or goal instance the system might have. These type of rules are needed to understand many complex texts, such as those involving abstract planning failures or themes (see Schank 1982; Dyer 1983).

These and other restrictions on the types of inferencing REMIND performs limit the complexity of the episodes REMIND can currently understand and retrieve relative to many symbolic language understanding and case-based reasoning models. We are currently exploring solutions to some of these problems to allow multiple dynamic instantiations of individual frames and to allow rules that propagate signatures of the novel concepts inferred by the network. A number of different ways to approach these problems and handle more complex text are discussed in Lange (1992). Shastri and Ajjanagadde (1993) discuss an analogous solutions for structured networks that do not perform disambiguation.

5.5.5.2 Lexical Information and Initial Role-Bindings REMIND does not currently address the problem of deciding upon the original syntactic bindings, for example, that *pot* is bound to the Object role of a phrase. Rather, REMIND's networks are given these initial bindings and use them for high-level inferencing. To handle natural language input entered as text, the network must somehow contain and use syntactic and phrasal information to create the initial role-bindings that REMIND is currently given by hand.

5.5.5.3 Automatic Learning of Episode Units The representations that REMIND uses for its memory episodes are created entirely by REMIND's spreading-activation understanding process. To store those representations in the network, however, the units and connections used to encode them must be added by hand. It would be desirable to have those episode units be learned automatically by the network itself. We are currently exploring a mechanism to *recruit* units (see Diederich 1990) to encode the interpretation held by signature and evidential activation in the network and therefore allow episode learning to proceed without intervention.

Another area to explore will be gradual decay of the weights between episode units and the semantic network. Episodes that are not retrieved for a long time should gradually have their weights decay so that they become more difficult to become reminded of as time goes on. This is also a potential solution to the problem of indexing too many episodes under general concepts, such as Possess-Obj and Inside-Of, since connections from them to old episodes could gradually decay away and become available for new ones.

5.6 Conclusions

The process of memory retrieval has generally been explored in isolation from the process of language understanding, even though both activities seem to share many of the same processes. One of the reasons for this is that building an integrated model of language understanding and retrieval requires not only solving the important aspects of each of the processes individually—a difficult enough problem separately—but also finding a parsimonious way to integrate the two processes that can explain the effect they have on each other. Because of their simple processing mechanism and demonstrated abilities to perform disambiguation and model the psychological effects of priming and context, structured spreading-activation networks seem to have a great deal of potential for building such an integrated model.

A number of difficult problems for spreading-activation networks have to be solved to use them for language understanding and memory retrieval. First, language understanding requires the ability to represent variable bindings within the network and to perform dynamic inferencing to explain the plans and goals of actors. Second, problems of disambiguation and frame selection require the ability to combine evidential domain knowledge with the contextual evidence of the network's inferences to select the best interpretation of a text from multiple possible interpretations. In addition ambiguous texts requiring many inferences make the problems of controlling crosstalk between unrelated concepts and inferences especially important to solve. Finally, a method must be developed for representing episodes in the network's long-term memory that allows them to be influenced and retrieved by the spreading-activation understanding process.

This chapter has described REMIND, a structured spreading-activation model that solves many of these problems in an integrated model of language understanding and episodic reminding. In REMIND activation is spread through a semantic network that performs dynamic inferencing and disambiguation to infer a conceptual representation of an input cue. Because stored episodes are associated with concepts used to understand them, the spreading-activation process also activates any memory episodes in the network that share features or knowledge structures with the cue. After the cue's conceptual representation is formed, the network recalls the memory episode having the highest activation. Since the inferences made from a cue often include actors' plans and goals only implied in a cue's text, REMIND is able to get abstract analogical remindings that would not be possible without an integrated understanding and retrieval model.

Theoretically REMIND lies somewhere between case-based reasoning models and general analogical retrieval models such as ARCS and MAC/FAC. Like ARCS and MAC/FAC, REMIND is meant to be a psychologically plausible model of general human reminding, and therefore it takes into account the prevalence of superficial feature similarities in remindings. However, we believe that many of the types of high-level planning and thematic knowledge structures used as indexes in case-based reasoning systems also have an important effect on reminding. REMIND is thus partially an attempt to bridge the gap between case-based and analogical retrieval models. As it turns out, this gap is naturally bridged when the same spreading-activation mechanism is used to both understand cues and to retrieve episodes from memory. Using the same mechanism for both processes causes retrieval to be affected by all levels that a text was understood with. This is the case in REMIND, in which the understanding mechanism is given the superficial features and actions of a text and attempts to explain them by inferring the plans and goals being used, causing long-term memory episodes to be activated by both.

Although being an integrated comprehension and retrieval model makes REMIND more complex than the retrieval mechanisms of case-based reasoning models and ARCS and MAC/FAC, it also allows REMIND to be simpler than them in a couple of significant respects. A large amount of the research in case-based reasoning models is devoted toward discovering the best indexes to store cases under (the *indexing problem*). In REMIND, however, episodes are simply stored (indexed) under all of the concepts that played a part in understanding them. When combined with the comprehension part of the model, this simple connectionist approach to indexing avoids the indexing problem altogether, while still giving the effect of having chosen the proper indexes since the most salient and unique features of an episode in a given context naturally become highly activated as part of the understanding process.

ARCS and MAC/FAC also avoid the indexing problem of CBR models because they both make contact with episodes that share any feature similarities with the cue, in effect using all features as indexes. Where REMIND differs from ARCS and MAC/FAC is that both ARCS and MAC/FAC use separate mechanisms to explicitly factor the degree of syntactic relational consistency (analogical similarity) into retrieval. We believe that psychological effects of analogical similarity on memory retrieval that their separate syntactic mechanisms are meant to model can be fully explained by the understanding process. Relationally consistent episodes tend to have similar inferences, interpretations, and themes, while relationally inconsistent episodes do not. In REMIND analogically based reminding therefore occurs as a natural side effect of understanding an input text rather than as a result of a separate process that explicitly computes it, as in ARCS and MAC/FAC.

A final aspect to note about REMIND concerns how language understanding and retrieval processes come full circle. The episode retrieved depends crucially on the interpretation of the cue from the spreading-activation network's inferences. Once an episode is retrieved, it in turn primes the activation of the evidential spreading-activation network, perhaps leading to a different disambiguation and therefore interpretation of the next cue. Thus we believe that REMIND is able to uniquely provide insights which other current reminding models are not able to show. As such, REMIND represents an entirely new class of reminding models.

Notes

This research was supported by NSF grant DIR-9024251, Army Research Institute contract MDA 903-89-K-0179, and by a grant from the Keck Foundation. We would like to thank John Barnden, Michael Dyer, Keith Holyoak, Eric Melz, and John Reeves for their helpful comments on the model and on earlier drafts of this paper.

1. Partial solutions to these problems have been proposed by several researchers using *hybrid* marker-passing networks that include some aspects of spreading-activation (see Kitano et al. 1989; Hendler 1989).

2. REMIND and ROBIN do not currently address the problem of deciding on the original syntactic bindings, that is, that *pot* is bound to the Object role of phrase **P1**. Rather, their networks are initially given these bindings and then use them for high-level inferencing.

3. The reader may note that he signature for Marijuana did not reach the binding units of Insider-Of-Dishwasher in figure 5.5. This is due to additional structure of gated links that encode knowledge about what kind of concepts can be bound to the roles of particular frames—such that only concepts that are refinements of Cooking-Utensils are prototypically cleaned as the Object in Inside-Of-Dishwasher. These *selectional restrictions* and their importance are described further in section 5.3.7.

4. The network's decision or selection is actually simply the interpretation that the human modeler gives to the levels of activation present in it, as in all connectionist models.

References

Anderson, J. R. 1983. *The Architecture of Cognition*. Cambridge: Harvard University Press.

Barnden, J. 1990. The power of some unusual connectionist data-structuring techniques. In J. A. Barnden and J. B. Pollack, eds., *Advances in Connectionist and Neural Computation Theory*. Norwood, NJ: Ablex.

Barnden, J., and K. Srinivas. 1992. Overcoming rule-based rigidity and connectionist limitations through massively-parallel case-based reasoning. *International Journal of Man-Machine Studies* 36: 221–46.

Charniak, E. 1986. A neat theory of marker passing. In *Proceedings of the Fifth National Conference on Artificial Intelligence*. Menlo Park, CA: AAAI Press.

Cottrell, G., and S. Small. 1982. A connectionist scheme for modeling word-sense disambiguation. *Cognition and Brain Theory* 6: 89–120.

Diederich, J. 1990. Steps toward knowledge-intensive connectionist learning. In J. Barnden and J. Pollack, eds., *Advances in Connnectionist and Neural Computation Theory*. Norwood, NJ: Ablex.

Dolan, C. P., and P. Smolensky. 1989. Tensor product production system: A modular architecture and representation. *Connection Science* 1: 53–68.

Dyer, M. G. 1983. *In-depth Understanding: A Computer Model of Integrated Processing for Narrative Comprehension*. Cambridge: MIT Press.

Eiselt, K. P. 1987. Recovering from erroneous inferences. *Proceedings of the Sixth National Conference on Artificial Intelligence (AAAI-87)*, Seattle, July 1987.

Eskridge, T. C. 1994. A hybrid model of continuous analogical reasoning. In J. Barnden and K. Holyoak, eds., *Advances in Connectionist and Neural Computation Theory*, vol. 2, *Analogical Connections*. Norwood, NJ: Ablex.

Falkenhainer, B., K. D. Forbus, and D. Gentner. 1989. The structure-mapping engine: Algorithm and examples. *Artificial Intelligence* 41: 1–63.

Gentner, D. 1989. The mechanisms of analogical learning. In S. Vosniadou and A. Ortony, eds., *Similarity and Analogical Reasoning*. Cambridge: Cambridge University Press, pp. 199–241.

Gentner, D., and K. D. Forbus. 1991. MAC/FAC: A model of similarity-based retrieval. *Proceedings of the Thirteenth Annual Conference of the Cognitive Science Society*. Hillsdale, NJ: Lawrence Erlbaum, pp. 504–509.

Gentner, D., M. Rattermann, and K. Forbus. 1993. The roles of similarity in transfer: Separating retrievability from inferential soundness. *Cognitive Psychology* 25: 524–75.

Gick, M., and K. J. Holyoak. 1980. Analogical problem solving. *Cognitive Psychology* 12: 306–55.

Gick, M. L., and S. J. McGarry. 1992. Learning from mistakes: Inducing analogous failures to a source problem produces later successes in analogical transfer. *Journal of Experimental Psychology: Learning, Memory, and Cognition*, 18: 623–39.

Glucksberg, S., R. J. Kreuz, and S. H. Rho. 1986. Context can constrain lexical access: Implications for models of language comprehension. *Journal of Experimental Psychology: Learning, Memory, and Cognition* 12: 323–35.

Granger, R. H., K. P. Eiselt, and J. K. Holbrook. 1986. Parsing with parallelism: A spreading activation model of inference processing during text understanding. In J. Kolodner and C. Riesbeck, eds., *Experience, Memory, and Reasoning*. Hillsdale, NJ: Lawrence Erlbaum, pp. 227–46.

Hammond, K. 1989. *Case-Based Planning*. San Diego: Academic Press.

Hammond, K. J., C. M. Seifert, and K. C. Gray. 1991. Functionality in analogical transfer: A hard match is good to find. *Journal of the Learning Sciences* 1: 111–52

Hendler, J. 1989. Marker-passing over microfeatures: Towards a hybrid symbolic/connectionist model. *Cognitive Science* 13: 79–106.

Hofstadter, D., and M. Mitchell. 1994. The copycat project: A model of mental fluidity and analogy-making. In J. Barnden and K. Holyoak, eds., *Advances in Connectionist and Neural Computation Theory, vol. 2, Analogical connections*. Norwood, NJ: Ablex.

Holldobler, S. 1990. A structured connectionist unification algorithm. In *Proceedings of the Ninth National Conference on Artificial Intelligence*. Menlo Park, CA: AAAI Press.

Holyoak, K. J., and K. Koh. 1987. Surface and structural similarity in analogical transfer. *Memory and Cognition* 15: 332–40.

Johnson, H. M., and C. M. Seifert. 1992. The role of predictive features in retrieving analogical cases. *Journal of Memory and Language* 31: 648–67.

Keane, M. 1988. *Analogical Problem Solving*. Chichester, England: Ellis Horwood.

Kintsch, W. 1988. The role of knowledge in discourse comprehension: A construction-integration model. *Psychological Review* 95: 163–82.

Kitano, H., H. Tomabechi, and L. Levin. 1989. Ambiguity resolution in DMTrans Plus. *Proceedings of the Fourth Conference of the European Chapter of the Association of Computational Linguistics*. Manchester, England: Manchester University Press.

Kohonen, T. 1984. *Self-organization and Associative Memory*. New York: Springer Verlag.

Kolodner, J. 1984. *Retrieval and Organizational Strategies in Conceptual Memory: A Computer Model*. Hillsdale, NJ: Lawrence Erlbaum.

Kolodner, J., R. Simpson, and K. Sycara. 1985. A process model of case-based reasoning in problem solving. *Proceedings of the Ninth International Joint Conference on Artificial Intelligence*, Los Angeles.

Lange, T. 1992. Lexical and pragmatic disambiguation and reinterpretation in connectionist networks. *International Journal of Man-Machine Studies* 36: 191–220.

Lange, T., and M. G. Dyer. 1989. High-level inferencing in a connectionist network. *Connection Science* 1: 181–217.

Lange, T., J. Hodges, M. Fuenmayor, and L. Belyaev. 1989. DESCARTES: Development environment for simulating hybrid connectionist architectures. In *Proceedings of the Eleventh Annual Meeting of the Cognitive Science Society*. Hillsdale, NJ: Lawrence Erlbaum, pp. 698–705.

Lange, T., E. Melz, C. Wharton, and K. Holyoak. 1990. Analogical retrieval within a hybrid spreading-activation network. In D. S. Touretzky, J. L. Elman, T. J. Sejnowski, and G. E. Hinton, eds., *Proceedings of the 1990 Connectionist Models Summer School*. San Mateo, CA: Morgan Kaufmann, pp. 265-76.

Lebowitz, M. 1980. *Generalization and Memory in an Integrated Understanding System*. PhD thesis. Research report 186. Yale University, Department of Computer Science, New Haven.

Lytinen, S. 1984. *The Organization of Knowledge in a Multi-lingual Integrated Parser*. PhD thesis. Research report 340. Yale University, Department of Computer Science, New Haven.

McClelland, J. L., and A. H. Kawamoto. 1986. Mechanisms of sentence processing: Assigning roles to constituents of sentences. In J. L. McClelland and D. E. Rumelhart, eds., *Parallel Distributed Processing*, vol. 2, Cambridge: MIT Press, 272-325.

Miikkulainen, R. 1993. *Subsymbolic Natural Language Processing: An Integrated Model of Scripts, Lexicon, and Memory*. Cambridge: MIT Press.

Miikkulainen, R., and M. G. Dyer. 1991. Natural language processing with modular PDP networks and distributed lexicon. *Cognitive Science* 15: 343-99.

Norvig, P. 1989. Marker passing as a weak method for text inferencing. *Cognitive Science* 13: 569-620.

Owens, C. 1989. Integrating feature extraction and memory search. In *Proceedings of the Eleventh Annual Conference of the Cognitive Science Society*. Hillsdale, NJ: Lawrence Erlbaum.

Read, S. J., and I. L. Cesa. 1991. This reminds me of the time when....: Expectation failures in reminding and explanation. *Journal of Experimental Social Psychology* 27: 1-25.

Reeves, J. F. 1991. *Computational Morality: A Process Model of Belief Conflict and Resolution for Story Understanding*. PhD thesis. Tech report UCLA-AI-91-05. Computer Science Department, UCLA.

Riesbeck, C. K., and R. C. Schank. 1989. *Inside Case-Based Reasoning*. Hillsdale, NJ: Lawrence Erlbaum.

Riesbeck, C. K., and C. E. Martin. 1986. Direct memory access parsing. In J. Kolodner and C. Riesbeck, eds., *Experience, Memory, and Reasoning*. Hillsdale, NJ: Lawrence Erlbaum, pp. 209-26.

Ross, B. H. 1987. This is like that: The use of earlier problems and the separation of similarity effects. *Journal of Experimental Psychology: Learning, Memory, and Cognition* 13: 629-39.

Ross, B. H. 1989. Distinguishing types of superficial similarities: Different effects on the access and use of earlier problems. *Journal of Experimental Psychology: Learning, Memory, and Cognition* 15: 456-68.

Ross, B. H, and G. L. Bradshaw. 1994. Encoding effects of remindings. *Memory and Cognition* 22: 591-605.

Rumelhart, D. E., G. E. Hinton, and J. L. McClelland. 1986. A general framework for parallel distributed processing. In J. L. McClelland and D. E. Rumelhart, eds., *Parallel Distributed Processing*, vol. 1, Cambridge: MIT Press, pp. 45-76.

Schank, R. C. 1982. *Dynamic Memory*. Cambridge: Cambridge University Press.

Schank, R. C., and R. Abelson. 1977. *Scripts, Plans, Goals and Understanding*. Hillsdale, NJ: Lawrence Erlbaum.

Schank, R. C., and D. B. Leake. 1989. Creativity and learning in a case-based explainer. *Artificial Intelligence* 40: 353–85.

Seifert, C. M. 1998. The role of goals in retrieving cases. In J. Barnden and K. Holyoak, eds., *Advances in Connectionist and Neural Computation Theory*, vol. 2, *Analogical connections*. Norwood, NJ: Ablex.

Seifert, C. M., G. McKoon, R. P. Abelson, and R. Ratcliff. 1986. Memory connections between thematically similar episodes. *Journal of Experimental Psychology: Human Learning and Memory* 12: 220–31.

Shastri, L., and V. Ajjanagadde. 1993. From simple associations to systematic reasoning: A connectionist representation of rules, variables, and dynamic bindings using temporal synchrony. *Behavioral and Brain Sciences* 16: 417–51.

Spencer, R. M, and R. W. Weisberg. 1986. Context-dependent effects on analogical transfer. *Memory and Cognition* 14: 442–49.

St. John, M. 1992. The story gestalt: A model of knowledge-intensive processes in text comprehension. *Cognitive Science* 16: 271–306.

Sun, R. 1993. Beyond associative memories: Logics and variables in connectionist networks. *Information Sciences*, special issue on AI and neural networks, 70: 49–74.

Swinney, D. A. 1979. Lexical access during sentence comprehension: (Re)consideration of context effects. *Journal of Verbal Learning and Verbal Behavior* 15: 681–89.

Thagard, P., K. J. Holyoak, G. Nelson, and D. Gochfeld. 1990. Analog retrieval by constraint satisfaction. *Artificial Intelligence* 46: 259–310.

Till, R. E., E. F. Mross, and W. Kintsch. 1988. Time course of priming for associate and inference words in a discourse context. *Memory and Cognition* 16: 283–98.

Touretzky, D. 1990. Connectionism and compositional semantics. In J. A. Barnden and J. B. Pollack, eds., *Advances in Connectionist and Neural Computation Theory*, Norwood, NJ: Ablex.

Touretzky, D., and G. Hinton. 1988. A distributed connectionist production system. *Cognitive Science* 12: 423–66.

Waltz, D., and J. Pollack. 1985. Massively parallel parsing: A strongly interactive model of natural language interpretation. *Cognitive Science* 9: 51–74.

Wharton, C. M., K. J. Holyoak, P. E. Downing, T. E. Lange, and T. D. Wickens. 1991. Retrieval competition in memory for analogies. *Proceedings of the Thirteenth Annual Conference of the Cognitive Science Society*. Hillsdale, NJ: Lawrence Erlbaum, 528–33.

Wharton, C. M., K. J. Holyoak, P. E. Downing, T. E. Lange, and T. D. Wickens. 1992. The story with reminding: Memory retrieval is influenced by analogical similarity. *Proceedings of the Fourteenth Annual Conference of the Cognitive Science Society*. Hillsdale, NJ: Lawrence Erlbaum, 576–81.

Wharton, C. M., K. J. Holyoak, P. R. Downing, T. E. Lange, T. D. Wickens, and E. R. Melz. 1994. Below the surface: Analogical similarity and retrieval competition in reminding. *Cognitive Psychology* 26: 64–101.

Wharton, C. M., K. J. Holyoak, and T. E. Lange. 1996. Remote analogical reminding. *Memory and Cognition* 24: 629–43.

Wilensky, R. 1983. *Planning and Understanding*. Reading, MA: Addison-Wesley.

Chapter 6
A Connectionist Model of Narrative Comprehension

Mark C. Langston, Tom Trabasso, and Joseph P. Magliano

In this chapter we explore how a connectionist model can simulate aspects of processing narrative texts. The sentences of the texts are assumed to be connected either by causal inferences made by readers during processing or by the encoding of common word connections between sentences (argument overlap). From a sentence by sentence matrix of the number of connections, the model processes the connections of each sentence and computes several measures. Five processing measures are derived from the model and examined in two ways: (1) the behavior of the measure over the course of versus after processing the text ("on-line" versus "off-line" processing) and (2) the prediction of empirical comprehension data obtained on human readers. The three on-line measures on each sentence were (1) number of cycles to settle, (2) level of working memory activation, and (3) average connection strength. The two off-line measures on each sentence were (1) level of final activation and (2) average connection strength.

The simulations on artificial texts with different connectivity matrices showed that all five measures of the model were sensitive to variation in the number of connections between sentences. However, the sensitivity to connections of the measures differed substantially during and after processing of text. Independence of the measures was assessed by correlation analysis. Independence of these measures is important to making unique and psychological interpretable predictions of empirical data. For the on-line and off-line measures, the average connection strength was the least correlated with the other measures.

Predictions of human, on-line, comprehension data from Magliano, Trabasso, and Langston (1995) were examined for each of the model's measures. The empirical measures of comprehension were (1) reading time per syllable and (2) ratings of how well a sentence fit into the prior context of sentences as it was read. For reading times, when the connections were causal, both off-line measures were the best predictors. When the connections were based on common words, one on-line measure—average connection strength—was the best predictor. For the fit ratings and causal connections, the best measure was average connection strength. For common word connections, the model accounted for less variance in fit ratings and reading times. Even so, connection strength was a significant predictor in two of the three data sets.

On balance, connection strength measures succeeded best in predicting comprehension data, and the model was more successful when the connections were based on potential causal connections rather than on connections that could be established by common words or argument overlap.

The successful measure of a sentence's connection strength provides a quantitative index of the cumulative history of integrating sentences over the course of processing into a long-term memory representation. The larger the average connection strength for a sentence, the better that sentence was integrated into the existing memory representation for the text. When human subjects judge whether a sentence fits into what has been read, they apparently use their knowledge of how well connected that sentence is with all prior sentences. Causal inferences appear to provide the basis for integrating sentences into a coherent and stable text representation.

6.1 On-line versus Off-line Study of Comprehension

Reading comprehension historically has been assessed by having someone read a text and then answer questions or recall what was read. Question answering or recall after reading a text is regarded as postprocessing or *off-line* assessment of comprehension. Off-line measures refer to what was understood after or when all the text had been read. Comprehension measured while the reader is reading and absorbing the text is termed *on-line*. On-line measures include the time taken to read a sentence, to recognize sentences or words, or to name words, and to assign importance or notice how well a sentence fits in with prior text context.

In recent years interest in the study of comprehension has shifted from off-line to on-line assessments (Balota et al. 1990). Of particular interest Keenan et al. (1990) and McKoon and Ratcliff (1990) describe and evaluate several on-line tasks such as word priming, recognition, and naming. On-line comprehension has for the most part been restricted to the use of obtrusive, single-word tasks interspersed here and there during reading of connected discourse or text (Keenan et al. 1990; McKoon and Ratcliff 1990). The use of reading time and judgments of how well a sentence fits into the context read thus far are examples of recent less obtrusive methods that assess processing of sentences during reading (Zwaan and Langston 1995; Magliano, Trabasso, and Langston 1995). Supplementing empirical studies of on-line comprehension are those that involve computer simulations. Here, it is possible to mimic, unobtrusively, human on-line comprehension through the use of mathematical models. These models involve processes that are assumed to occur during comprehension (Just and Carpenter 1991; Goldman and Varma 1995; Kintsch and van Dijk 1978; Kintsch 1988, 1992).

A benchmark in text comprehension was the study by Kintsch and van Dijk (1978). Of interest to on-line comprehension was their proposal that a theory of text comprehension should be able to describe the mental operations that occur during comprehension and in the subsequent recall and summarization of the text. This chapter tests a process model's ability to simulate comprehension as it occurs in line with the goals expressed above by Kintsch and van Dijk's proposal.

Later Kintsch (1988, 1992) presented a computational model, which they called the Construction-Integration model, that formally achieved their aim. The Construction-Integration model takes as input a network representation of a text and produces a long-term memory network representation. This long-term memory representation has *activation values* for each proposition in the text and *values for connections* between the propositions. The model also produces an index of the computation necessary to arrive at these results, called the *settling rate*. These products form the basis for comparison of the model to behavioral measures of comprehension. The validity of the model is assessed by how well its products predict various behavioral measures.

A number of successful empirical tests of the Construction-Integration model have appeared since the Kintsch (1988) paper. These studies include tests of the model's ability to predict the time course of proposition recall (Goldman and Varma 1995; Kintsch 1992; Tapiero and Denhiere 1995), sentence recognition and verification (Kintsch et al. 1990), and word identification (Kintsch 1988). Although these applications of the model had some predictive success, all the comparisons of the model with behavioral measures were on the *final products* of the Construction-Integration model (e.g., final activation values and long-term memory connection strengths) *after* comprehension has occurred. These comparisons support the model in terms of its ability to predict off-line behavior. However, they provide no direct confirmation of the models assumptions for on-line processing.

6.2 Purpose of Present Study

In this chapter we propose a connectionist model that is related to the Construction-Integration model, and it tests the ability of our model to simulate comprehension as it occurs on-line or off-line. Our goals are consonant with those expressed above by Kintsch and van Dijk's proposal (1978). There are two questions of interest here: Can we derive from the model measures that reflect on-line and off-line processing? Do the processing measures predict on-line and off-line comprehension performance of readers?

6.3 Our Approach to Comprehension

In a comprehension study one uses a theory of discourse structure to analyze the relational properties of a text. These relational properties may be used to predict directly how well readers understood the text. Alternatively, one could use a model to process the properties of the text before trying to predict on-line comprehension by readers. The model's processing of the text properties leads to various processing measures that may also be used to predict how readers understood the same text. In this case certain properties of the text and particular processing measures may combine to be the best predictors of what readers do during comprehension. The properties and how they were processed should advance our understanding of how and what readers comprehend as they read a text.

The success of the model in predicting on-line comprehension is a joint result of a discourse analysis of the properties of the text along with the use of a quantitative model of text processing. Thus the model provides us with a quantified theory of processing that integrates inputs during comprehension, but its success in prediction in turn depends on the relational properties of the text given to the model to process. Therefore we will explore quantitative measures from the model that successfully predict on-line comprehension, and by the use of different discourse analyses, we will vary the inputs to the model.

The relationships between discourse analyses of texts, a process model of comprehension, and readers' performance during comprehension of a text are depicted in figure 6.1. We first use discourse analyses to identify text properties (number 1 in figure 6.1). We are interested in two text properties: word level or causal relations between sentences. The identified relations are quantified in terms of the number of

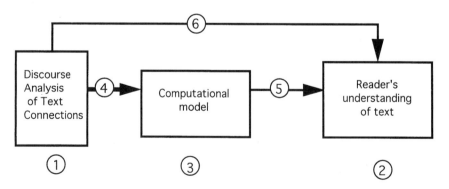

Figure 6.1
Three components and their relationships in comprehending text.

connections that a sentence has with other sentences. The connections are then given to the model in a numerical form (number 4 in figure 6.1).

The theory of discourse analysis enables us to understand variation in the properties, namely how a particular representation of the text affects the model's processing and its output measures (number 3 in figure 6.1). The validity of properties identified by discourse theory (number 1 in figure 6.1) and how they are processed by the model (number 3 in figure 6.1) are estimated by empirical measures of comprehension (number 2 in figure 6.1) based on the resulting model measures of processing (number 5 in figure 6.1). Empirically obtained measures of on-line text comprehension, however, depend on theoretically motivated operational definitions of comprehension. By these empirical indexes of comprehension measures we can learn about reading comprehension and evaluate the validity of discourse theory and a quantitative model.

Alternatively, in figure 6.1, number 6, we can use measures derived from discourse analysis of the text in (1) to predict the readers performance in (2). We can then compare predictions of these empirical measures made by text properties (6 versus 5 in figure 6.1).

To make quantitative predictions of comprehension behavior, we first derive a computational model for on-line and off-line processing of text properties. Using text representations that vary in connectivity among sentences, we simulate the behavior of each quantitative measure over the course of processing the entire text. We compare the sensitivity to variation in connections of three on-line and two off-line quantitative measures. We also assess the statistical independence of the these measures.

Taking representations of texts used in experiments and quantitative measures of the model, we generate predictions for three empirical measures of on-line processing. One set of predictions is based on causal text representations (Trabasso, van den Broek, and Suh 1989), and a second set of predictions is based on proposition, argument overlap (Kintsch and van Dijk 1978). From these predictions we determine the quantitative measure that best accounts for variation in the empirical data. The results are discussed in terms of which measures can relate the current approach to future study of on-line text comprehension.

6.3.1 Presentation of Text Input to Model

On-line processing requires that the processor understand and integrate each sentence as it is read. To model the processing of an entire text sentence by sentence, it is necessary to construct a network representation of a text that contains all the connections between each pair of sentences. This representation can be encoded in an $N \times N$ matrix so that each cell i, j in the matrix represents the measure of the connection between sentences i and j. This matrix is then presented to the model in an incremental form. The first presentation is a 1 × 1 matrix, which shows the connections to the first sentence. The next presentation adds the connections of the second sentence, forming a 2 × 2 matrix, and then the connections to the third sentence in a 3 × 3 matrix, and so on. The model thus receives and processes the connectivity of one additional sentence in succession until the entire $N \times N$ matrix has been presented. The outputs at the processing of the connections of each sentence simulates an on-line, "reading" process. For each presentation, the model computes numerical values for every sentence in a current matrix. These values are used to determine the contents of working memory and to update the contents of long-term memory. After all of the sentences are processed, the numerical values are those that are used to represent off-line measures.

6.3.2 Implementation of the Model

The computational model we use here is based on the general Construction-Integration theory outlined by Kintsch (Kintsch 1988; Kintsch and van Dijk 1978). We have implemented our model using the Construction-Integration software of Kintsch and others (Glavanov 1979; Goldman and Varma 1995; Kintsch 1988, 1992; Kintsch et al. 1990; Tapiero and Denhiere 1995), but our version uses slightly different procedures for processing text representations in working memory (see below). We first present the standard model and then show how we varied it for our purposes.

6.3.3 "Standard" Kintsch Construction-Integration Model

In a standard Construction-Integration model, a text is represented by a network of interconnected nodes. Each node corresponds to a concept, sentence, phrase, proportion, or word in the text. The processed nodes and the connections between them are stored in the model's *long-term memory*, but the nodes are processed in the model's *working memory*. At any given time then, the model contains all the nodes that it has already processed and their connections in the model's long-term memory. Whenever a new node is presented to the model it is entered into its working memory. The working memory is limited to the n most highly active of all the processed nodes. Activation is spread among the nodes in working memory until the activation of each node in working memory becomes stable. This process is called *settling*. Once the activations of the nodes in working memory have settled, the long-term memory representation is adjusted. The long-term memory activation values for the nodes in working memory are increased or decreased depending on their settled activation values. Long-term memory connection strengths are similarly adjusted for the nodes in working memory. The model then determines which nodes should be kept in working memory by a criterion of being among the n most active nodes in working memory. A new node is now entered into the model. The process repeats itself until all of the nodes from the text have been entered and processed.

A crucial assumption in the "standard" Construction-Integration model is that only those nodes in working memory are operated upon during processing. As a consequence long-term memory values can be affected only by nodes that are processed in working memory. This means that if some node in working memory shares a connection with some node stored only in long-term memory, the node in long-term memory will have no effect on the processing of the nodes currently in working memory. In order for a node in long-term memory to have an effect, it has to be reintroduced to working memory before processing occurs for the node that it is to affect.

6.3.4 Modified Construction-Integration Model

The model used in this chapter is nearly identical to the standard model described above. The crucial difference is that the working memory constraint is relaxed. In the standard model only those nodes currently in working memory are involved in processing. Nodes that are stored in long-term memory and are connected to nodes currently in working memory have no effect on working memory processing. In our model we allow all nodes to participate in processing.

Removing the working memory constraint may at first seem counterintuitive, since allowing all nodes to participate in processing would seem to suppress any effects otherwise observable in a model with a limited working memory capacity. However, the "working memory" of the standard model may be viewed as not so much a model of human working memory, but more as a model with a local processing constraint. In the standard model only those nodes with the highest activation values are allowed to remain in working memory. As we will show below, high activation corresponds to a high degree of connectivity and can be construed as a measure of the importance or centrality of a node. In the standard model important nodes are allowed to influence further processing, and unimportant nodes are dropped out of working memory. Removing the working memory constraint, however, does not really change this effect. Important highly connected nodes will continue to have a large impact, and relatively unimportant poorly connected nodes will continue to have little or no impact on processing. The only impact of our change is that nodes not typically contained in the standard working memory buffer will now have an opportunity to influence the processing of the current node, given that the discourse analysis of the text indicates a connection between the nodes. By relaxing the working memory capacity constraint, we provide the model with a "weak retrieval mechanism." Previously processed nodes connected to the current node can have an effect.

However, the extent of that effect will depend on overall connectivity and consequently the activation values.

To illustrate, we move ahead to examine figure 6.6 and table 6.1. Figure 6.6 contains the causal network representation of the story in table 6.1. Consider node A16, which corresponds to the sentence, "That night, Ivan returned back to his village with his mighty sword" in table 6.1. Figure 6.6 indicates that this sentence should be connected to the original goal expressed in node G5, "Ivan was determined to kill the giant." Assume that this text is being processed by the standard model. Node A16 is presented to the model for processing. Unless the working memory size is 12 nodes or greater, node G5 would not be contained in the working memory buffer, and would have no influence on the processing of node A16, even though a discourse causal analysis of the text dictates that it could and empirically readers make this inference frequently (Suh and Trabasso 1993; Trabasso and Suh 1993). Now consider the same situation using our modification of the "standard" Construction-Integration model. When node A16 is presented to the modified model, node G5 is still available and able to affect the processing of node A16. In effect the modified model was able to "retrieve" node G5 where appropriate, whereas the standard Construction-Integration model would not have been able to bring node G5 back into working memory for processing.

6.3.5 Components of the Model

The model contains one main storage area called the *text representation*. The text representation of the model contains nodes, connections between nodes, and quantitative values that change over time as each new node is processed. The nodes in the text representation correspond to clauses or sentences from the discourse being modeled. Each node in the text representation has associated with it some *activation value* that changes over time as the text representation is constructed. Each connection represents the relationship between a pair of sentences in the text, as identified by the discourse analysis. Each connection has associated with it *a connection strength* which also changes over time as new nodes and their connections are integrated into the existing text representation. The activation values and connection strengths reflect, through processing, both the current memory representation of the reader and the history of her comprehension.

The model performs two main computations: It spreads activation among nodes in the text representation, and it adjusts connection strengths based on the results of the activation spread. The spread of activation among concepts in memory as a fundamental psychological process involved in memory retrieval and concept association has been shown to be valid (Goldman and Varma 1995; Just and Carpenter 1992; van den Broek 1990; van Dijk and Kintsch 1983). Spreading activation results in quantities that reflect the overall structure of a network representation, accounting for both direct and indirect connections between nodes. This property allows the use of activation values to modify connection strengths between nodes so that they more accurately reflect the current state of the representation. To achieve this, a correlation learning rule specifies that connection strengths should be modified by the activation of the nodes at either end of the connection. This implies that if two nodes become highly active at the same time, the connection between them will be strengthened to reflect this context-sensitive dependence. In relation to our model, when two sentences become highly active due to some change in the text representation (e.g., the introduction of a consequence that was necessitated by an antecedent sentence), the connection between those two sentences would be strengthened to reflect their relationship to each other as well as their relationship to the rest of the text representation.

Together the spreading activation mechanism and the correlation strength update rule operate over network representations to provide a model capable of accounting for a range of on-line and off-line comprehension measures. The main psychological implication of our model is that the integration of a new sentence and its relations into an existing memory representation changes the entire memory representation. Examining these representational changes, as described by connection strengths over time, provides us with a parsimonious account of the construction of context and the mechanisms implicated in discourse comprehension.

6.3.6 How the Model Integrates a Text

Assume that at time t, the text representation consists of n previously processed nodes, their connections, and the numerical values representing their state at time t. Each node in the representation represents one clause or sentence from the text being processed. At time $t+1$ the next sentence in the text is processed, causing a new node and its connections to be entered into the existing text representation. A new node has an initial activation value of 1.0. Its connections also have initial connection strengths of 7.0. The values associated with the nodes and connections must be updated because the addition of the new node changes the structure of the existing text representation. This update occurs via a spread of activation among the nodes in the current representation. The new activation value for each node is computed according to the strength of its connections and the activation values of the nodes to which it is connected. Formally this may be stated as

$$a_{i(t+1)} = \sum a_{j(t)} w_{ij(t)} \tag{1}$$

where $a_{i(t+1)}$ is the activation of node i at time $t+1$, $a_{j(t)}$ is the activation of node j at time t, and $w_{ij(t)}$ is the strength of the connection between node i and node j at time t. Activation values therefore depend on connection strengths between nodes.

After formula (1) has been applied, the resulting activation values are converted to percentages of total activation. This normalization is needed to keep the activation values from increasing exponentially. This procedure is repeated until the total change between the normalized activation values just computed and the normalized activation values previously computed falls below some arbitrarily small value n. This may be stated as

$$\sum a_{i(x)} - \sum a_{i(x-1)} < n \qquad (2)$$

where $\sum a_{i(x)}$ is the sum of the activation values from the current spread of activation, $\sum a_{i(x-1)}$ is the sum of activation values from the previous spread of activation, and n is an arbitrarily small value. Therefore formula (2) requires that formula (1) be computed at least twice. Once the inequality in formula (2) has been satisfied, the activation values for the text representation are considered to have *settled*.

After the activation values have settled, it is necessary to adjust the text connection strengths to reflect the change in the text representation brought about by the addition of the new node and its connections at time $t + 1$. Just as activation values depend on connection strengths, connection strengths in turn depend on activation values. After the activation values have settled, the connection strengths are updated by adding the product of the activation of two nodes and the strength of the connection between them to the current connection strength. Formally this is written as

$$w_{ij(t+1)} = w_{ij(t)} + (w_{ij(t)} * a_i * a_j) \qquad (3)$$

where $w_{ij(t+1)}$ is the new strength of the connection between node i and node j, $w_{ij(t)}$ is the old strength of the connection between node i and node j, a_i is the activation of node i, and a_j is the activation of node j. Once formula (3) has been applied for all nodes in the text representation, processing is finished for time $t + 1$. If the node just processed was that for the last sentence in the text, processing stops. If not, a new node is entered into the representation and the process repeats.

6.3.7 Assumptions of the Model

There are several computational assumptions that affect how the model processes information. Each assumption is either psychologically or computationally motivated, and together they provide the constraints within which the model operates. When a new node is introduced to the model, each new connection is given an initial strength of 7.0 before any processing occurs. The discourse analysis identifies potential causal or word relationships between sentences. It is therefore assumed that these relationships must have some strength and that 7.0 is simply an arbitrary value. The processing the model performs over the text representation is responsible for adjusting this value to reflect more correctly the strength of association at a given time between any two sentences.

When a new node is introduced to the model, it is assigned an initial activation value of 1.0. This implies that each new sentence comes into memory with some activation with which it may influence other areas of the text representation via the spread of activation among nodes. We also assume that all nodes are allowed to participate in every processing cycle. The number of nodes and connections over which computations are performed is not limited, as is the case in other computational models of text comprehension (Goldman and Varma 1995; Kintsch 1988). This assumption was motivated by recent work by Ericsson and Kintsch (1995), who proposed that expertise in a particular task or domain requires a highly efficient organization of long-term memory. This organization allows retrieval and processing of items from memory that does not reflect the constraints of short-term memory. In our model we assume that the representation being used is that of an expert in narrative comprehension, possessing expert-level knowledge of agent-oriented causation. Further we assume that the data we predict was produced by subjects who are also expert comprehenders.

Activation values are converted to percentages after each iteration of formula (1). This is necessary to constrain activation values to a reasonable range. Without such normalization, activation values would increase exponentially and quickly become unmanageable. We assume that if activation values have not settled after 100 iterations of formula (1), the settling process is halted and the current values are used in formula (3). This assumption was necessitated by the types of networks we modeled. Occasionally the model will receive as input a node that has no connections to the rest of the text representation. When this situation arises, settling cannot be guaranteed. Typically, if the activation values have not settled after 100 iterations, one node is oscillating between two activation values, and the settling criterion will never be satisfied. However, the activation values have reached some minimum, and this minimum provides sufficient values for the modification of connection strengths.

All settled activation values found at time $t-1$ are carried over to the next processing cycle. When a new node is introduced to the model, it receives an initial activation value of 1.0, and all previously existing nodes begin the new processing cycle with the same activation values they had at the end of processing at time $t-1$.

In sum, the model receives a network of connections derived from a discourse analysis of a text. The network is processed one node at a time in order to simulate reading. The model incorporates each new node and its connections into an existing text representation and spreads activation among the nodes. Once activation has settled, the activation values are used to adjust the strengths of the connections between the nodes. At any time during or after this processing, we may extract values from the matrix of connection strengths. These activation values, settling rates, and connection strengths are used to predict behavioral data.

6.4 Simulating On-line Processing with the Connectionist Model

The model produces five sets of output each time a new node (sentence and connections) is presented and processed. First, it computes the *activation* for each node (sentence) contained in the model at that time. This activation value is then used to determine the long-term memory activation values and the long-term memory connection strengths. Additionally the number of computations necessary to compute the activation values, called the settling rate, is available. In the literature, as was pointed out earlier, only two of these data sets have been compared with empirical data: the final long-term memory activation value for each sentence, and the final long-term memory connection strengths between each sentence of the text. One exception is found in the work of Goldman and Varma (1995) who used argument overlap and settling rate from the Construction-Integration model to predict recall. These measures are final products obtained after all nodes in a text have been processed by the model.

6.5 Simulations

On-line processing measures from the model enables one to gain insight into the model's dynamics during the iterative processing of the text. We conducted simulations to determine how the various model measures behave over time. We also wanted to examine how sensitive the measures were to the connectivity of the text. To vary connectivity, we simulated two different representations of a text. One simulation text had a linear representation and is displayed in figure 6.2a.

In figure 6.2 each text representation contains 16 nodes or "sentences." The nodes are numbered 1 through 16 for later reference. In addition each node is labeled with a letter that corresponds to a category of a sentence in a narrative episode according to Trabasso and Suh's (1993) discourse analysis (see table 6.1 for an example). These categories will become more useful in dealing later with real texts. They are included here because of the differences that their number of connections and in their roles for structuring linear and hierarchical texts.

In figure 6.2a and b, each line represents an episode in the narrative text. There are three episodes in each text representation. In episodes 1 and 2 (the first and second strings), there is a setting (represented by S), an event that initiates the episode (E), a goal (G), an attempt (A), and a reaction (R). In episode 3 (the third string) there are two attempts (A), an outcome (O), and a reaction (R).

Connectionist Model of Narrative Comprehension

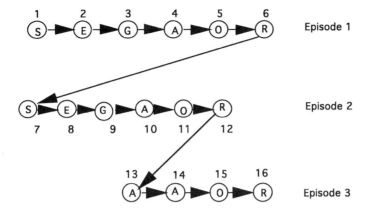

A. Linear Text Representation

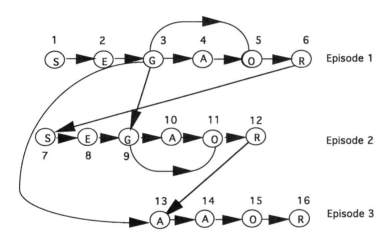

B. Hierarchical Text Representation

Figure 6.2
Artificial connectivity networks used in model simulation of linear and hierarchical text representations.

In figure 6.2a, except for the first and last sentences (nodes), each sentence in the linear representation has one antecedent and one consequent connection. The linear representation provides a means of determining how the model behaves over time for a simple structure with the same number of connections per sentence. Figure 6.2b displays what we call a "hierarchical" representation. Here multiple connections exist between a subset of sentences. Simulating the two networks in figure 6.2 allows us to compare the effect of variation in number of sentence connections. In particular, nodes 3, 5, 9, 11, and 13 differ in the number of connections in the two representations.

In the hierarchical representation (figure 6.2b) there are additional connections among the goal and the outcome in the first episode, the goal of the first episode and the goal in the second episode, the first goal and the first attempt in the third episode, and the second goal and second outcome in the second episode. The representations of the simulation texts in figure 6.2 are based on those for actual narratives studied by Suh and Trabasso (1993) and Trabasso and Suh (1993).

6.5.1 Activation Values

During processing, activation values form the quantitative basis for all other values being computed. For example, the long-term memory activation values are simply the square of the working memory activation values. To simulate the effect of variation in text connectivity on activation values, each text representation was presented to the model one sentence at a time. After each new sentence was entered and its connections processed, its working memory activation value was computed.

Figure 6.3a shows the activation values obtained for sentences just after each sentence has been entered and its connections processed for linear and hierarchical text representations. The on-line activation value of each sentence ranges between 0 and 1.

Figure 6.3a shows that the linear text exhibits a steadily decreasing pattern of on-line activation. The hierarchical representation declines only for the last three nodes. The reason for the decline in the linear representation can be understood in terms of how activation is computed. In the standard Construction-Integration model and in our modification, activation values are normalized after each new sentence is entered. Normalization is obtained by dividing the on-line activation for each sentence by the highest on-line activation value at each step. When the first sentence is entered, it is the only sentence in the model and the normalization procedure creates an on-line activation value of 1.0. After the second sentence is processed, both sentences have the same on-line activation value before normalization (0.5), and thus the second sentence receives a normalized value of 1.0. As more sentences are entered in the linear model, each new sentence has a lower normalized activation value.

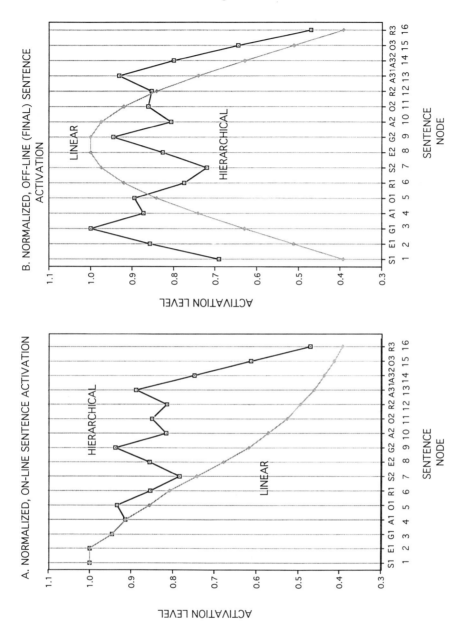

Figure 6.3
Simulated measures on- and off-line levels of activation for sentences in processing artificial texts by a connectionist model.

The hierarchical representation in figure 6.3 indicates that the model was sensitive to differences in sentence connectivity. It behaves identically with the processing of linear text up until the point when the incoming node 5 is entered. Node 5 is the first node that has more than one incoming connection. At this point node 5 receives more on-line activation in the hierarchical text representation than its counterpart in the linear version. The activation values of the subsequent sentences then revert, for a time, to behaving like the linear text until node 9 is entered. Node 9 is the second node in the hierarchical text with two incoming connections. At this point, however, the deviation of the activation values of the hierarchical representation from the linear representation is much greater than it was at node 5. The large change in on-line activation at node 9 in figure 6.3 indicates that "distal" connections with more intervening nodes have a greater impact on increasing the activation values than when nodes are close together or "local." Distal connections operate at nodes 9, 11, and 13 as indicated by spikes in activation in figure 6.3. Following these spikes, there are declines.

When the entire text representation has been entered and processed, the final activation value of each sentence in the representation is obtained. The final activation values produced by the two simulations by our model are shown for hierarchical and linear texts in figure 6.3b. Whereas the on-line activation values in figure 6.3a declined steadily over processing of linear text representations, figure 6.3b shows that final activation values increase than decrease in a inverted U-shaped function over the sixteen sentences. The final activation values for the hierarchical texts in figure 6.3a and b are very similar except for the first three nodes.

As figure 6.3b shows, for the linear text representation the two sentences with the highest final activation (nodes 8 and 9) are in the exact middle of the text. This symmetry is a result of the "spreading activation mechanism" where, in a purely linear structure, final activation tends to pool in the middle. This same mechanism is also responsible for the steady decline of the on-line activation values for the linear text after node 9 in figure 6.3a. As each new sentence is processed, the linear chain is lengthened. The new sentence is at least one-half of the sentences further away from the center of the linear chain, thereby reducing the normalized activation value for that sentence. The inverted-U function demonstrated by the linear text in figure 6.3b is counterintuitive. The final activation levels obtained for linear text representations are opposite that one would expect when there are primacy and recency effects in memory.

The final activation values for sentences in the hierarchical representation in figure 6.3b exhibits markedly different behavior than those for the linear representation. The first points of interest are the three peaks in the graph (nodes 3, 9, and 13). These peaks reflect the sensitivity of this measure to connectivity. The peaks correspond to the sentences that share more and distal connections separated by at least two sentences in hierarchical versus linear texts. In actual texts with similar structures (Magliano, Trabasso, and Langston 1995) we found these sentences were the most likely to be recalled, largely responsible for overall coherence judgments, and key to organizing a text representation in memory.

There is no connection between nodes 6 and 7 which end and begin episodes 1 and 2, respectively. In figure 6.3a and b, there is a dip at node 7. This drop may be accounted for by a decline in activation as a result of reduced connectivity of the text representation. The lack of connections between nodes 6 and 7 are known as "coherence breaks" and have strong psychological effects on processing texts. For example, Trabasso, Suh, and Payton (1994) found that coherence ratings depend on the overall causal connectivity of a narrative and Magliano et al. (1995) found that a drop in the rated coherence occurred for individual sentences in a narrative text where there was an episodic coherence break between sentences.

6.5.2 Cycles to Settle

Figure 6.4 shows the results of the simulations on the number of cycles necessary for a sentence to arrive at a stable activation value. In figure 6.4 the number of cycles to settle steadily increases for the linear representation, whereas cycles for the hierarchical representation rise initially, and then remain relatively constant. The differences between the two representations reflect differences in connectivity. They also demonstrate that connectivity facilitates processing, since the more connections a sentence has, the faster it is processed.

The cycles to settle measures, however, appear to be relatively insensitive to variation in the number of connections for individual nodes. In figure 6.4 there is a sharp rise to node 4 with no peaks thereafter.

6.5.3 Connection Strength

The strength of connections between sentences is one of the most commonly used measures to predict recall (Goldman and Varma 1995; Kintsch 1988, 1992). This measure is the cumulative sum of the product of the connection strengths between each pair of sentences. Those sentences that are highly connected to other sentences will be highly active and their strengths, over time, will tend to increase. As a result in our simulations there should be a pattern of connection strengths that is sensitive to the connections between highly active sentences.

With respect to on-line and off-line measures, there are two ways to analyze the connection strengths. One can measure the mean connection strength for a given sentence over the entire text representation, an off-line measure, or one can measure the mean connection strength for a given sentence over all the preceding sentences,

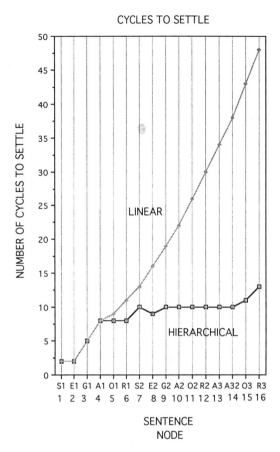

Figure 6.4
Simulated measures of cycles to settle for sentences in processing artificial texts by a connectionist model.

an on-line measure. We obtained an on-line measure of a node's average connection strength in terms of a node's connections to its predecessors. The mean connection strengths of sentences with all their preceding sentences are shown in figure 6.5a. Here the connection strength of a sentence with its predecessors exhibits patterns similar to those found for final activation values (see figure 6.3b). Both functions are inverted-U in shape. These results are not surprising since the formula for computing a sentence's connection strength is a function of activation values. The peak in mean connection strengths are shifted to the left, and these effects are attributable to the use of slightly different values of activation than those in figure 6.3b. The relatively low

Connectionist Model of Narrative Comprehension

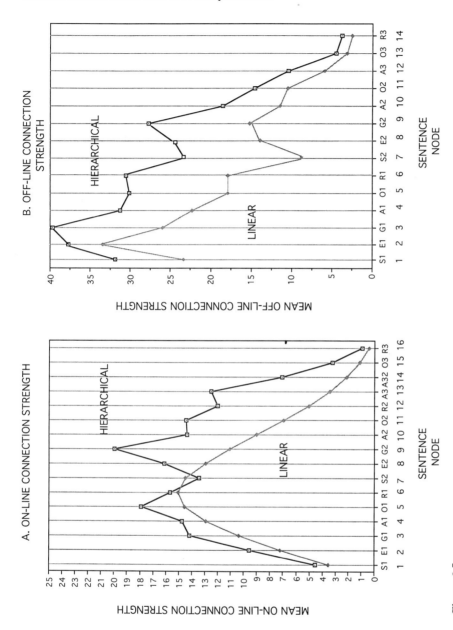

Figure 6.5
Simulated measures of on- and off-line connection strength in processing artificial texts by a connectionist model.

connection strengths near the beginning and end of the two structures in figure 6.3b are related to the lack of overall connectivity of the early and later nodes in both representations.

Figure 6.5a, however, shows that this on-line measure of connection strength was sensitive to variation in connectivity. There are distinct peaks for the hierarchical representation at nodes 3, 5, 9, 11, and 13, and a sharp drop at node 6, the coherence break between episodes.

Figure 6.5a also reflects the effects of distal connections between nodes that are separated by one or more other nodes. Examining nodes 3, 4, and 5, the mean connection strength of node 4 is actually lower than it would be if there were no distal connection between nodes 3 and 5. This same effect if present in node 12, where an identical relationship exists between nodes 11 and 13. As the distance between connected nodes increases, so does this effect. The sharp dip of mean connection strength for node 7 can be explained by the distal connection of length 6 between nodes 3 and 9. If node 11 were not also distally connected to node 3, the entire pattern of data between nodes 3 and 9 would have resembled that of inverted-U shape function.

Figure 6.5b displays the mean connection strength values obtained after processing the entire text (off-line measure) for the hierarchical and linear text representations. Here both the hierarchical and linear measures decrease in value over the course of the text. This effect is, however, not just a result of the sentence's ordinal position in the text. Connection strengths are based on activation values. Earlier sentences that have connections to later sentences will have higher activations than do later sentences. Later sentences, even with more connections, will not be present in long-term memory as long as earlier sentences. As a result, over the course of processing the text, the overall mean connection strength for an early sentences will tend to be higher.

The hierarchical data in figure 6.5b show that the off-line connection strength measure is sensitive to the number of connections, despite the overall decline in value over the course of the text. Nodes 3, 5, and 9, the most highly connected of the sentences, display peaks and exhibit effects similar to those found in other measures of the simulation data. They must, however, be interpreted in light of the steady linear decrease as a function of serial position. We note also that the largest differences occur between the two representations at those sentences with more than one connection, namely at nodes 3, 5, and 9. However, mean connection strength is not differentially sensitive at nodes 11 and 12 which also have more connections.

6.5.4 Summary of Simulation Analyses

The number and distance of connections that a particular sentence has in a text had a profound impact on the measures obtained from the model. Peaks in the measures occurred for those sentences with the most connections and at a distance across other sentences. These peaks were found for hierarchical representations in figure 6.3a and b with the level of activation and in figure 6.5a and b with connection strength, regardless whether the processing was incomplete and on-line or complete and off-line. The only measure that did not show the peaks was that for settling rate, suggesting that this measure is not a good one to use to quantify connectivity of individual sentences.

While on-line activation values decreased with serial position in figure 6.3a, the presence of multiple or distal connections inhibits this tendency. Furthermore there is a linear relationship between the amount of inhibition and the distance of the distal connections. A similar but opposite relationship is evidenced by the examination of mean on-line connection strengths in figures 6.3, 6.4, and 6.5. The number and distance of a sentence's connections tends to reduce the connection strengths of those nodes that lie between the two nodes at either end of the connections, while bolstering the mean connection strength of the connected nodes. Finally the number and distance of connections tends to shorten the processing necessary for the model to achieve stability at a given time in figure 6.4. The amount of time necessary to process the current structure tends to increase linearly as the size of the structure increases unless distal connections are present.

These findings show how the model's outputs behave when processing artificial network representations for idealized texts that vary in connectivity. The next section presents these same analyses on actual rather than artificial representations. The actual texts are hierarchical and linear in structure with respect to causal connections (Suh and Trabasso 1993). To the extent that they are and that their network representations are similar to the artificial ones, we anticipate similar findings on the model's simulations of actual texts.

6.6 Simulating Representations of Actual Stories

The actual texts used are 16 stories, averaging 15 and ranging from 13 to 18 sentences in length, from Suh (1988), and analyzed by Suh and Trabasso (1993) and Trabasso and Suh (1993). There are 8 unique stories comprised of 3 episodes each, with a main character's goals presented in episodes 1 and 2. Each of the 8 stories exists in two versions. In the hierarchical version the goal in the first episode fails, making the second goal a subgoal of the first goal. In the sequential version the first goal succeeds, and the second goal is independent of the first goal. The hierarchical and sequential versions have structural causal connections similar but not identical to those in the above simulations.

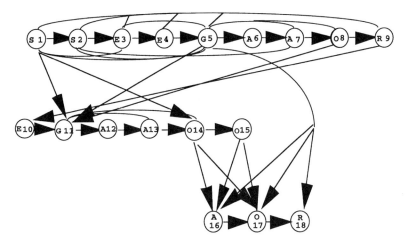

Figure 6.6
An example of a hierarchical, causal connectivity network used in model simulation of an actual text, *Ivan the Warrior* (see table 6.1).

Figure 6.6 contains an example of an hierarchical network graph of one story, *Ivan the Warrior*. Table 6.1 contains text of the story with corresponding sentence categories. One can see in figure 6.6 that this representation is more highly connected that the hierarchical simulation in figure 6.2b.

Each of the 16 stories were constructed to control for argument overlap and local causal connectivity across versions. The connections depicted in figure 6.6 are based on different types of causal relationships between sentences (i.e., physical, motivational, psychological, and enabling; see the taxonomy of Trabasso, van den Broek, and Suh 1989). In our simulation all connections have equal weight. Likewise all types of sentences (i.e., setting, initiating event, goal, attempt, outcome, and reaction) are treated equally. Despite having more connections overall, the hierarchical version of the story in figure 6.6 has a similar structure to the hierarchical structure of the simulated texts in that there are multiple distal connections to G1, including distal connections to O1, G2, and A3, as well as a distal connection between G2 and O2.

The sequential graph of the *Ivan the Warrior* story, while not shown here, is similar to the linear structure used in the above simulations. In the actual linear texts, however, there are some multiple and distal connections. Most of the distal connections are short, usually with two intervening sentences. These small distal connections should not have as great an impact on the model's output as do more distal connections. Therefore the model data from actual text representations should resemble those obtained from the simulated linear structure. Differences in connectivity between

Table 6.1
Ivan the Warrior (hierarchical version)

Story sentence		Episodic category
1.	Ivan was a great warrior.	Setting (S1)
2.	He was the best archer in his village.	Setting (S2)
3.	One day, Ivan heard that a giant had been terrifying people in his village.	Initiating event (E3)
4.	They said that the giant came to the village at night and hurt people.	Initiating event (E4)
5.	Ivan was determined to kill the giant.	Goal (G5)
6.	He waited until dark.	Attempt (A6)
7.	When the giant came, Ivan shot an arrow at him.	Attempt (A7)
8.	Ivan hit him but the arrow could not hurt the giant.	Outcome (O8)
9.	The people were disappointed.	Reaction (R9)
10.	One day, a famous swordsman came to a nearby village.	Initiating event (E10)
11.	Ivan decided to learn how to fight with a sword.	Goal (G11)
12.	He went to the swordsman.	Attempt (A12)
13.	Ivan studied very hard for several weeks.	Attempt (A13)
14.	He became a very skilled swordsman.	Outcome (O14)
15.	Ivan got a powerful sword from his teacher.	Outcome (15)
16.	That night, Ivan returned home to his village with his mighty sword.	Attempt (A16)
17.	He finally killed the giant with his sword.	Outcome (O17)
18.	The people thanked Ivan a hundred times.	Reaction (R18)

hierarchical and sequential actual text representations occur at the same points as in the simulations so that effects on the model's measures, both on-line and off-line, are expected and can be assessed by comparisons between the linear and hierarchical simulations. The simulation data are based on the average of all sentences within a structure. In addition, where there were more than one sentence category in succession, these were averaged across categories.

6.6.1 Activation Values for Actual Texts

The model's output of activation levels for on-line and off-line simulations are shown in figure 6.7. In both graphs the hierarchical data match those of the hierarchical simulation in figure 6.3. There are peaks at nodes 6 (R1), 9 (G2), and 11 (O2), where high connectivity occurred, and valleys at nodes 8 (E2) and 7(S2) where there were

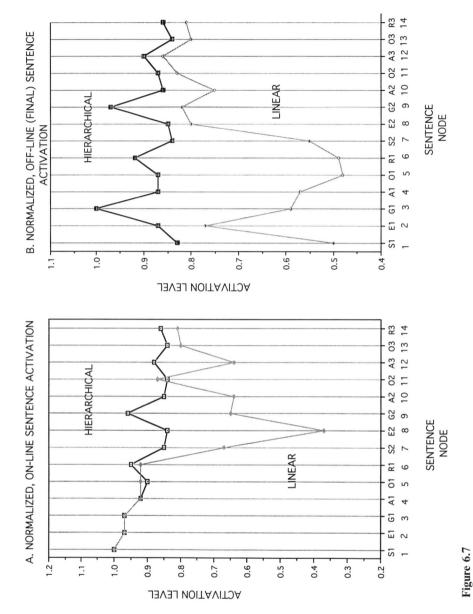

Figure 6.7
Simulated measures on- and off-line levels of activation for sentences in processing actual, narrative texts by a connectionist model.

no connections or coherence breaks. Activation values for the real stories do not drop off near the end of the texts as they did in the simulations of artificial networks. The higher connectivity of the final sets of sentences lead to higher activation levels.

The sequential data in figure 6.7, however, differs substantially from those of the simulated linear structure in figure 6.3. This difference is a result of distal connections in the real sequential story structures. The linear structure of the simulated stories, however, was totally linear with only one local connection between each adjacent "sentence" node. Also the activation values for episodes 2 and 3 of the sequential stories are much lower overall. This is accounted for by the lower frequency of connections as a whole and the relative absence of distal connections in the sequential stories.

6.6.2 Cycles to Settle

Figure 6.8 plots of the mean number of cycles to settle for each type of sentence and story structure. The model processed the stories with a ceiling of 100 cycles to avoid the endless cycling possible when a structure is nonergodic, namely when there is no path between one node and another. These data in figure 6.8 replicate those found for the simulated story structure data reported in figure 6.4. The sequential stories required more processing to reach stability as a function of serial position, whereas the hierarchical stories reached a plateau early and maintained a relatively consistent, low level of processing before achieving stability. The model indicates that the hierarchical stories have coherent structures and should be processed faster or integrated more easily into an existing mental representation. These data also indicate that cycles to settle is one parameter of the model that is not differentially sensitive to connections between sentences in the text. We would not expect that this measure to be a good predictor of behavioral measures of comprehension that are in fact influenced by connections between sentences.

6.6.3 Connection Strength between Sentences

Graphs of the average on-line sentence connection strengths for each version are displayed in figure 6.9a. Figure 6.9b shows this measure as off-line, that is, after processing of the whole text has occurred. These means are computed by summing across a sentence's values in the connectivity matrix and dividing by the total number of sentences in the text minus one. The sentence's self-connection strength is not included in the mean.

For the hierarchical versions, both measures in figure 6.9 are very similar to those in figure 6.5. The actual hierarchical stories thus resemble the simulated hierarchical structures on this measure. As in the simulations the connection strength values decrease over sentence position. Sentences entered later into the model have lower

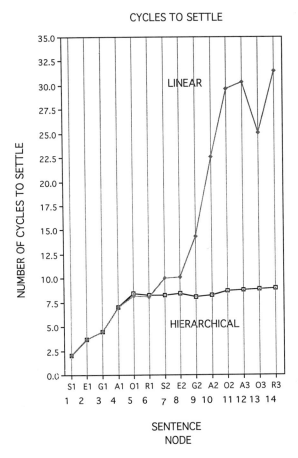

Figure 6.8
Simulated measures of cycles to settle for sentences in processing actual, narrative texts by a connectionist model.

overall connection strength with respect to the preceding text. The peaks and valleys and differences between the versions reflect differences in connections at nodes 3(G1), 5(O1), 9(G2), and 12(A3), as expected on the basis of increased number of connections to and from these sentences.

The sequential data in figure 6.9 are, however, different than those in figure 6.5 for the on-line connection strength measure. The actual sequential text representations provide more structural variation than that of the simulated linear structure in figure 6.5.

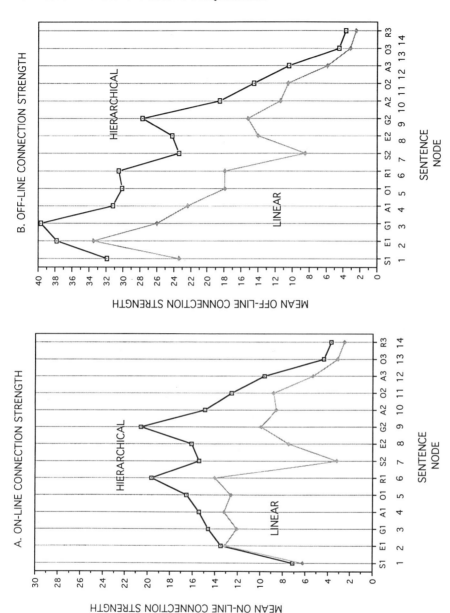

Figure 6.9
Simulated measures of on- and off-line connection strength in processing actual, narrative texts by a connectionist model.

6.6.4 Summary

The results obtained from the model over the sentences of actual texts closely resemble those obtained from the simpler simulated structures, especially on the peaks and valleys of the hierarchical version and on the differences between the two versions. The qualitative patterns exhibited by the simulations occur in the data obtained from the actual story representations. In particular, distance and frequency of connections between sentences affect the activation values and connection strengths of connected sentences and sentences that lay in between them. Since connection strength depends on activation value (see Langston and Trabasso 1998), the common sensitivity to connectivity is not surprising. Cycles to settle differed from these measures substantially in both the simulated and real texts and appear to be independent of activation.

6.7 Validating the Model against Comprehension Data

In this chapter we wish to evaluate the measures of processing obtained from the model to predict *on-line* behavioral measures. Two on-line measures of comprehension are used here: per syllable reading time and goodness-of-fit ratings. The fit rating is a new measure of on-line processing introduced in Magliano et al. (1995). The subject reads a text one sentence at a time and is asked after each sentence to rate how well the sentence "made sense" with respect to the prior sentences. The ratings are on a seven-point scale with 1 being the lowest or least sensible rating. At no time were subjects allowed to re-read prior sentences. However, a second condition was used in which subjects read the entire story before performing the task, allowing them to base their judgments on their previously constructed representation of the entire text.

6.7.1 Predicting Reading Time

Cycles to settle appears intuitively to be a god candidate for processing "effort." Goldman and Varma (1995) used cycles to settle without success to predict reading time per word for adult subjects using argument overlap and another variant of the standard Construction-Integration model. They found that cycles to settle was in fact significantly negatively correlated with reading times. In a regression analysis they found that number of words per sentence accounted for the most variance in processing time and that cycles to settle did not uniquely predict any variance. One reason for their failure to predict variance in reading time using cycles to settle may be that the structures the models used contained implicit processing assumptions (i.e., the creation of the connections themselves) not accounted for by the processes of the model. If these processes were already completed and were not present in the cycles to settle metric, it could not account for reading time. Furthermore, although cycles to settle is sensitive to connectivity, the presence of multiple connections suppresses the tendency of the number of cycles to increase as a function of serial position. Cycles to settle therefore is not sensitive to variation in connectivity or suppression occurs. Thus we have a priori, theoretical, methodological, and empirical reasons to doubt the validity of the cycles to settle metric as a valid predictor of on-line processing.

The fit ratings of Magliano et al. (1995) should be related to measures derived from activation values, since activation values are directly related to number and distance of connections. Magliano et al. (1995) found an empirical relationship between a sentence's fit and connectivity. The frequency of causal connections had a positive correlation with the ratings. With this in mind the various model measures that are sensitive to connections should be considered as likely candidates for predicting both initial and re-reading ratings of a sentence's fit into the prior story context.

The final activation values are not on-line measures. As such, we would not expect them to predict reading time or fit ratings. On the other hand, working memory activation and sentence connection strength with predecessor sentences are on-line measures and should predict these behavioral on-line measures. However, the activation of a sentence in working memory reflects its impact with respect to the current contents of working memory. This property would reduce its value of a predictor of more global integration that occurs when connections are distal.

Long-term memory connection strength reflects a particular sentence's influence on the construction of a situation model and its coherence. The computation of the long-term memory connection strength takes the current strength of the connection between two sentences and modifies it according to the activation values of both sentences being connected. A sentence can thus have a high long-term memory activation, but it may not play a crucial role in the coherence of the long-term memory structure. The sentences to which it is connected may have low activations. If so, this would be reflected in the mean of the long-term memory connection strengths for that sentence. The strength of these connections would be low compared to that of a highly active sentence connected to other highly active sentences. The sentence in question therefore is not only relevant in the current situation but is also important to the coherence of the entire situation model. Because of this unique property, the long-term memory connection strength should predict much more variance in sentence processing than either activation measure.

With respect to the fit ratings obtained after re-reading, the model measures should predict those reported by Magliano et al. (1995). The on-line model processing measures should be predictive of the ratings after reading, at least partially since the same antecedent connections enter into the computation. However, given that the whole text has been processed once, the re-reading should also reflect the reader's prior knowledge of the entire text. In this case, off-line measures, particularly connection strength should predict the fit ratings during re-reading.

6.7.2 Summary

On-line model measures should be the best predictors of on-line empirical data. Mean connection strength to predecessors is a leading candidate as a predictor of empirical reading time measures and fit ratings. In the next section, a series of analyses are presented that evaluate the validity of the various model measures as predictors of comprehension reading operationally defined in terms of reading time or ratings of fit per sentence.

6.8 Validation of Model Measures

Recall from figure 6.1 the set of possible relations among text discourse analyses, the computational model, and measures of comprehension. In this section we examine the relationships either within a component or between components. The only exception is that for the text/understanding relationship. This has been examined in detail by Magliano et al. (1995).

Magliano et al. (1995) found several relationships between fit ratings and structural properties of the text. When subjects had no prior exposure to the text, the initial ratings were directly related to the number of local (the prior sentence) and goal-based causal connections. For example, if a sentence had only one causal connection to the previous sentence and no causal connection to the goal hierarchy, the sentence would receive a relatively low goodness of fit rating, indicating that the subject was sensitive to the lack of causal connectivity for the current sentence. Conversely, if the sentence had a high number of causal connections to one or more distal sentences or goals (particularly G1 in the hierarchical texts), the subject would give the sentence a relatively high fit rating.

Magliano and his colleagues also demonstrated that fit ratings were different, depending on whether or not the reader had read the text before. When the reader read a text for the first time, the fit rating was based on local text information (e.g., argument overlap and local causal connections), whereas readers relied on a global representation (e.g., distal causal connections) of the texts when computing the second fit rating. They found that argument overlap and spatial continuity text variables were significant predictors of fit measures but not of reading times. Furthermore temporal continuity was a significant predictor of reading time but not of fit.

Overall, Magliano et al. (1995) discovered that readers rely mostly on distal and goal-based connections when making fit judgments.

Given the results of Magliano et al. (1995), we investigated whether or not these textual properties would be more predictive if introduced to a computational model capable of providing on-line processing measures for comparison to behavioral measures. Study 1 explores the relationships among the measures available from the model itself. Study 2 examines the relationships among the empirical comprehension measures. Study 3 investigates the predictive power of the model measures with respect to the on-line empirical data. Study 4 replicates study 3 using proposition argument overlap instead of causality as input to the model.

6.8.1 Study 1

The first study examined the relationships among the various model measures. The measures considered were (1) *cycles*, the number of cycles required for a given sentence to reach a stable activation value, a process termed "settling"; (2) *on-line activation* of each sentence, obtained by recording the activation value of a sentence immediately after settling has occurred; (3) *final activation* of each sentence in a text, after all sentences have been processed; (4) *on-line connection strength*, the mean connection strengths for each sentence with all preceding sentences; (5) *off-line connection strength*, the mean long-term memory connection strengths of each sentence, after all sentences have been processed. All the data were derived from runs of the model over eight hierarchical and eight sequential text representations constructed from a causal analysis of the texts studied by Suh and Trabasso (1993). All the data were averaged over sentence categories, adjusted for their frequency.

Table 6.2 reports the intercorrelations for the five model measures. The number of cycles it takes for a particular sentence to settle was negatively correlated with three

Table 6.2
Correlations between model measures for processing causal connections

	On-line activation	Off-line (final) activation	On-line connection strength	Off-line connection strength
Cycles	−0.52*	0.61*	−0.51	−0.92**
On-line activation	—	−0.45	0.19	0.58*
Off-line (final) activation	—	—	−0.18	−0.40
On-line connection strength	—	—	—	0.71**

Note: $*p < 0.05$; $**p < 0.01$.

Table 6.3
Mean percentage of variance accounted for by each measure in the other measures for processing causal connections

	Cycles to settle	On-line activation	On-line connection strength	Off-line connection strength	Off-line (final) activation
Mean R^2	0.35	0.29	0.25	0.42	0.22

measures and positively correlated with one (final activation). Its highest negative correlation was with the off-line connection strength ($r = -0.92$, $p < 0.01$). Sentences that are more strongly associated causally with other sentences in the text are processed more quickly by the model than are sentences weakly associated causally with other sentences in the text.

To assess the degree of independence or dependence among the measures, we computed a multiple correlation for each individual measure by the other four measures. Table 6.3 summarizes the mean R^2 (variation accounted for in one by the other four measures) for each model measure. While the measures were all interrelated and accounted for proportions of variance in one another, the on-line and off-line connection strengths had the lowest R^2s and thus were the least correlated with other measures. Connection strength therefore is less dependent on the other processing measures of the model.

6.8.2 Study 2

This study examines the relationships among three behavioral on-line measures of comprehension: goodness-of-fit ratings and median reading time per syllable from the Magliano et al. (1995) study. There are two different goodness-of-fit ratings, termed fit 1 and fit 2, each being a rating on a six-point scale indicating how well a subject thought a sentence made sense given the prior context of what the subject had already read. The first fit measure was obtained during subjects' first reading of a text, and the second fit measure was obtained durig a re-reading of a text. Correlations were found between the measures by sentence type, for sentences pooled across both hierarchical and sequential versions of the texts. Reading time was not correlated with fit 1 ($r = -0.06$) but was negatively correlated with fit 2 ($r = -0.57$, $p < 0.05$). This correlation suggests that those sentences with more overall connections were read more quickly or were more easily integrated into the context of the story. The two fit measures were positively correlated ($r = 0.46$, $p < 0.05$). Since they share antecedent connections, this correlation is expected. The fact that the correlation is moderate reflects the influence of the number of connections that a sentence had after it itself was processed.

6.8.3 Study 3

This study examines predictions of empirical reading time and fit data by the model measures. Three stepwise regression analyses were performed, with initial goodness-of-fit ratings (fit 1), re-reading fit ratings (fit 2), and reading time per syllable as the respective dependent measures. In addition to the model measures examined in study 1, five auxiliary text variables were included in the regressions, identical to those used by Magliano et al. (1995): serial position, number of causal connections, sentence category, temporal continuity, and spatial continuity. Serial position indexed numerically the position of a sentence in a text from the first to the last. Number of connections was a count of the number of connections a sentence had with other sentences in the causal graph of a text, per Trabasso and Suh (1993). Temporal continuity quantified whether the event(s) described in the current sentence occurred in the same time-frame as those in the immediately prior sentence. If the events in the current sentence either co-occurred or immediately followed those in the prior sentence, the current sentence was coded as having temporal continuity. If the events in the current sentence occur at a time other than that specified or implied by the prior sentence, the sentence was coded as being temporally discontinuous. For example, the sentence "John went home" would be temporally continuous with the prior sentence "John left the theater," since the two events (leaving a theater, going home) may be assumed to occur in a temporal sequence, with no large time-span separating the two events. However, the same sentence would be temporally discontinuous with the prior sentence "John went to see a movie," since one may infer that John saw a movie between the two events. The action of seeing a movie requires several hours to complete; thus going to see a movie and going home are not temporally contiguous and must be coded as discontinuous.

Spatial continuity was coded in a manner similar to temporal continuity. If the events described in the current sentence explicitly or implicitly occur in the same spatial area as those in the immediately prior sentence, the sentence is coded as spatially continuous. For example, the sentence "John fell down" is spatially continuous with the prior sentence "John tripped over a large rock," since both events occur in some implied spatial region, containing John, the rock, and the path John was walking. On the other hand, the prior sentence "John took a nap" is spatially discontinuous with "John fell down," since one action, napping, required a particular location, namely a bed. Falling down, however, required that John was awake and moving about, activities that are mutually exclusive with sleeping.

As one might expect, temporal and spatial continuity overlap to a certain extent with each other and with causal connectivity. Spatial continuity was significantly correlated with both temporal continuity ($r = 0.30$, $p < 0.01$) and causal connectivity ($r = -0.25$, $p < 0.01$). However, these correlations were not high enough to warrant exclusion of these variables from the analyses on grounds of colinearity.

6.8.4 Predictions

The predictors used in this study may be divided into three categories: text-based predictors (serial position, sentence category, causal connections), situation-based predictors (temporal and spatial continuity), and process-based predictors (on-line connection strengths, off-line connection strength, number of cycles to settle, on-line activation, and off-line final activation).

The text-based variables should not be significant predictors for the initial fit ratings but should account for some variance in the re-reading fit and reading time data. The situation-based predictors should account for variance in all three dependent measures (Magliano et al. 1995). The model-derived predictors should account for variance according to their status (on-line versus off-line) and uniqueness (see study 1). Therefore we expect that on-line connection strength should be the best overall predictor, since it is a model measure of on-line processing and is also the most unique measure (study 1). We also expect final activation to become significant predictors for the re-reading fit measure, since it is an off-line model measure and we did not find it to be significantly correlated with the other on-line measures.

6.8.5 Regression Analyses

Table 6.4 reports the results of the first stepwise regression analysis. On-line connection strength accounted for the most variance, a significant 21 percent, in the initial fit ratings. Spatial continuity accounted for an additional 5.6 percent, and on-line activation predicted a further 1.6 percent, for a total of 28.2 percent explained variance in the initial fit ratings. None of the other situation-based, text-based, or model-derived variables accounted for additional unique variance in the fit scores.

As expected, the most unique of the on-line model measures, a sentence's mean connection strength with all predecessor sentences, was the best predictor of empirical on-line fit ratings. This result is comparable to that reported by Magliano et al. (1995), who were able to predict 32 percent of the variance in initial fit ratings using only text-based variables. Other than spatial continuity, the model replaced text variables as predictors. On-line measures derived from the connectionist model reflect quantitatively the structural properties of the text responsible for initial fit ratings.

Table 6.5 describes the results of the second regression, using the re-reading fit ratings as a dependent measure. This time, the text-based variables become signifi-

Table 6.4
Summary of regression analysis on predicting initial fit ratings using the model and causal connections ($N = 236$ sentences)

Unique variable	B	SE B	Beta	Variance accounted for
Text-based				
Serial position				
Sentence category				
Causal connection frequency				
Situation-based				
Temporal continuity				
Spatial continuity	−0.241	0.103	−0.444*	5.6%
Model-derived (on-line)				
Cycles to settle				
On-line activation	0.146	0.233	0.577*	1.6%
On-line connection strength	0.374	0.009	0.056*	21.0%
Model-derived (off-line)				
Final activation				
Off-line connection strength				
Total	28.2%			

Note: The * represents $p < 0.05$. B represents the beta weights in the multiple linear regression, SE B represents the standard error of the beta weights, and beta represents the coefficients of the regression.

cant predictors. This result was of course that found by Magliano et al. (1995) so that these results were expected. On-line connection strength, however, again accounted for large amount of unique variance, 10.5 percent, but spatial continuity now accounted for a larger amount, 15.3 percent, of the unique variance in the ratings. The sentence category also became important in the re-reading fit ratings, accounting for a unique 9.9 percent of the variance. Temporal continuity and serial position did not account for much variance. The total variance accounted for in the re-reading fit ratings was 37.5 percent, an increase of 9.3 percent from that accounted for in the initial fit ratings.

The increased role of the situation and text-based variables may result from readers having comprehended and integrated the text during the first reading. They can thus draw from both the situation model constructed during initial comprehension as well as from knowledge of causal consequences that each sentence has in their contribution to the overall coherence of the story.

Table 6.5
Summary of regression analysis on predicting re-reading fit ratings using the model and causal connections ($N = 236$ sentences)

Variable	B	SE B	Beta	Unique variance accounted for
Text-based				
Serial position	−0.348	0.049	−0.101*	0.8%
Sentence category	0.662	0.056	0.215*	9.9%
Causal connection frequency				
Situation-based				
Temporal continuity	−0.118	0.145	−0.314*	0.9%
Spatial continuity	−0.272	0.152	−0.755*	15.3%
Model-derived (on-line)				
Cycles to settle				
On-line activation				
Connection strength	0.413	0.012	0.094*	10.5%
Model-derived (off-line)				
Final activation				
Connection strength				
Total 37.5%				

Note: The * represents $p < 0.05$. B represents the beta weights in the multiple linear regression, SE B represents the standard error of the beta weights, and beta represents the coefficients of the regression.

These results suggest that the model represents an improvement in prediction over the text-based results reported in Magliano et al. (1995) who accounted for 18 percent of the re-reading fit ratings, whereas the current model captures 37.5 percent of the variance, an improvement of 19.5 percent. As with the initial fit ratings, the computational model captures process-related variation better than those from an analysis of the text.

Table 6.6 summarizes the results obtained from the third regression analysis where text properties and the model's measures are used to predict reading time per syllable. In the prediction of reading time, the only text variable was the serial position of the sentence in the text. Later sentences were processed more quickly than earlier sentences. In the analysis, serial position accounted for 6.6 percent of the variance.

Two model measures accounted for unique variance. Off-line connection strength and final activation values accounted for 3.7 percent and 1.4 percent of the variance, respectively, for a total of 11.7 percent of per syllable reading time variance.

Table 6.6
Summary of regression analysis on predicting median reading time per syllable using the model and causal connections ($N = 236$ sentences)

Unique variable	B	SE B	Beta	Variance accounted for
Text-based				
Serial position	−0.589	2.601	−14.441*	6.6%
Sentence category				
Causal connection frequency				
Situation-based				
Temporal continuity				
Spatial continuity				
Model-derived (on-line)				
Cycles to settle				
On-line activation				
On-line connection strength				
Model-derived (off-line)				
Final activation	0.179	32.700	70.523*	1.4%
Connection strength	−0.424	1.028	−4.015*	3.7%
Total 11.7%				

Note: The * represents $p < 0.05$. B represents the beta weights in the multiple linear regression, SE B represents the standard error of the beta weights, and beta represents the coefficients of the regression.

How could these off-line measures be better predictors of reading time than the on-line measures? One possibility is that sentences that are highly connected to antecedent sentences also tend to have more consequent connections. The antecedent connections enable their faster integration into the text representation. Trabasso and Magliano (1996) found that in thinking aloud, readers anticipate future events in narratives via predictive inferences. These predictive inferences are, in effect, causal consequents of the current sentence. The predictions, when confirmed, would also facilitate processing of new sentences.

6.8.6 Discussion

Study 3 found that one measure of the model, namely connection strength, predicted judgments of sentence fit into the preceding context, over and above text variables and other model measures. This measure predicted uniquely variation in fit ratings when readers read the text for the first time or re-read it a second time and then rated its fit in the context of the story.

The only situation model variable that was consistently predictive was spatial continuity. This variable, which indexes sentence to sentence changes in location factors in the story, accounted for substantial variance in both fit ratings.

Our findings that spatial and causal factors influence a new, on-line measure of processing narrative texts are consistent with those of Zwaan and his colleagues (Zwaan, Langston, and Graesser 1995; Zwaan, Magliano, and Graesser 1995) who studied reading time. However, in our analyses of the reading time data of Magliano et al. (1995), only causal variables processed by the model were predictive. The results on fit ratings, in particular, validate the computational model for predicting on-line processing. The results on the reading time data of Magliano et al. (1995) did not validate the on-line measures of the model but they do validate causal connections.

6.8.7 Study 4

Study 4 explores the consequences of using another text variable, argument overlap (see Kintsch and van Dijk 1978). Argument overlap was measured as the number of common nouns between sentences. The number of connections based on common nouns across sentences were entered into the matrix representation of the text, upon which the model operates. It should be noted that text variables, themselves, come from different theoretical positions, and they are as important in prediction as the model itself. The connectionist model, then, is neutral as to which inputs it receives. Study 4 allows a comparison of different text discourse analyses as valid on-line predictors of comprehension by readers.

The mean number of argument overlap connections for the same texts was 6.4 (standard deviation = 4.2). Even though the amount of argument overlap was controlled by Suh and Trabasso (1993) across the hierarchical and sequential versions of the same texts (i.e., every sentence in a text shared at least one argument with every other sentence), there is considerable variation between sentences with respect to shared nouns. This variation in argument overlap is important, since it allows this variable room to account for variance in fit ratings and reading time. In short, we do not have a restricted range problem with respect to argument overlap as a predictor.

6.8.8 Analyses

Table 6.7 depicts the correlations between the various model measures for text representations of connections established through argument overlap. The patterns of correlations resemble those found for the model where causal connections served as inputs (see table 6.2). On-line connection strength also has the lowest correlation with the other measures. Cycles to settle had the highest correlation. Although the text representations here differ qualitatively from those in the previous study, the measures of the computational model behaved in a similar manner.

Table 6.7
Correlations between model measures on argument overlap

	On-line activation	Off-line (final) activation	On-line connection strength	Off-line connection strength
Cycles	−0.34**	−0.17*	−0.47**	−0.54**
On-line activation	—	0.86**	−0.06	0.17*
Off-line (final) activation	—	—	0.00	0.04
On-line connection strength	—	—	—	0.32**

Note: * for $p < 0.05$; ** for $p < 0.01$.

We next evaluated the ability of the model, coupled with argument overlap, to predict the initial ratings of fit. Table 6.8 reports the results of the regression analysis. The models were able to account for 12.7 percent, overall, of the variance in the fit ratings, a decrease of 15.5 percent from that found when causal connections served as an input in study 3.

When argument overlap was used as the representation of text, the processing measures did not dominate in the regression. Instead, a text variable, spatial continuity accounted uniquely for 9.4 percent of the variance, and the sentence category accounts for an additional 1.5 percent unique variance. The only on-line model measure to contribute to the analysis was on-line connection strength, which accounted uniquely for another 1.6 percent of the variance. The variation in argument overlap for these stories was not as sensitive to processing the text content as was causal reasoning. However, the same model measure, on-line connection strength, was again a significant predictor of initial fit as found is study 3. This replication of the model's prediction across different text representations is encouraging for the model.

Table 6.9 summarizes the regression results on re-reading fit ratings. The total variance accounted for using the argument overlap models in this analysis was 24.2 percent, a decrease of 13.3 percent from the causal models in study 3. Once again, text and situation-based variables predominated. Spatial continuity, sentence category, and temporal continuity accounted uniquely for 15.3, 4.8, and 1.9 percent of the re-reading fit variance, respectively. One model measure, on-line activation, accounted for another 2.2 percent of variance. This finding fails to replicate that of study 3 which used causal connections. Again, the data indicate that the model's measures are inconsistent in prediction when argument overlap is used as a text representation input.

Table 6.8

Summary of regression analysis on predicting initial fit ratings using the model and argument overlap connections ($N = 236$ sentences)

Unique variable	B	SE B	Beta	Variance accounted for
Text-based				
Serial position				
Sentence category	−0.165	0.013	−0.036*	1.5%
Overlap frequency				
Situation-based				
Temporal continuity				
Spatial continuity	−0.328	0.113	−0.604*	9.4%
Model-derived (on-line)				
Cycles to settle				
On-line activation				
On-line connection strength	0.151	0.008	0.020*	1.6%
Model-derived (off-line)				
Off-line (final) activation				
Off-line connection strength				
Total 12.7%				

Note: * for $p < 0.05$. *B* represents the beta weights in the multiple linear regression, SE *B* represents the standard error of the beta weights, and beta represents the coefficients of the regression.

Table 6.10 reports a summary of the results on using an argument overlap-based model to predict empirical on-line comprehension as measured by median reading time per syllable. In this case 10.1 percent of the variance was uniquely accounted for by the statistical model. This is close to the findings using causal connections but is 1.6 percent less. Serial position predicted the same amount of variance, 6.6 percent, as found in study 3. Sentence category accounted for 1.5 percent of the variance. On-line connection strength reappears in this analysis, accounting for an additional 2.0 percent of the reading time variance.

The argument overlap input to the model did not provide off-line measures that were predictive of reading time, as was the case in the study 3. Instead, on-line connection strength was predictive. This result might be due to different relationships shared among the model variables. Comparing to tables 10.2 and 10.8, final activation and on-line connection strength have quite different correlations with argument overlap than they did with causal connections.

Table 6.9
Summary of regression analysis on predicting re-reading fit ratings using the model and argument overlap connections ($N = 236$ sentences)

Unique variable	B	SE B	Beta	Variance accounted for
Text-based				
Serial position				
Sentence category	0.203	0.019	0.066*	4.8%
Overlap frequency				
Situation-based				
Temporal continuity	−0.174	0.160	−0.465*	1.9%
Spatial continuity	−0.330	0.166	−0.159*	15.3%
Model-derived (on-line)				
Cycles to settle				
On-line activation	−0.161	3.152	−8.759*	2.2%
On-line connection strength				
Model-derived (off-line)				
Off-line (final) activation				
Off-line connection strength				
Total	24.2%			

Note: * for $p < 0.05$. B represents the beta weights in the multiple linear regression, SE B represents the standard error of the beta weights, and beta represents the coefficients of the regression.

6.8.9 Discussion

In study 4, using as text input the argument overlap between sentences indexed as shared nouns, the model predicted empirical measures of on-line text comprehension. On-line connection strength and activation were again predictive of fit ratings or reading times. Similar patterns were found in study 4 for situation- and text-based predictors of re-reading fit ratings. The argument overlap model, however, did not account for as much variance as did the models that operated on causal connections.

6.9 Summary Conclusions on Validation Studies

The studies together demonstrate the capacity of a computational model to provide processing measures capable of predicting empirical measures of on-line comprehension. With causal connections as input, one on-line model processing measure in particular, connection strength, was very predictive of initial and re-reading fit measures. Reading time, however, was unexpectedly predicted by off-line model

Table 6.10
Summary of regression analysis on predicting median reading time per syllable using the model and argument overlap connections ($N = 236$ sentences)

Unique variable	B	SE B	Beta	Variance accounted for
Text-based				
Serial position	−0.814	5.079	−19.951*	6.6%
Sentence category	0.596	5.718	16.266*	1.5%
Overlap frequency				
Situation-based				
Temporal continuity				
Spatial continuity				
Model-derived (on-line)				
Cycles to settle				
On-line activation				
On-line connection strength	−0.160	1.077	−2.672*	2.0%
Model-derived (off-line)				
Final activation				
Off-line connection strength				
Total 10.1%				

Note: * for $p < 0.05$. B represents the beta weights in the multiple linear regression, SE B represents the standard error of the beta weights, and beta represents the coefficients of the regression.

measures. Here again, though, connection strength was a valid predictor. The differences between models based on causal versus argument overlap text analyses showed that the causal-based models outperformed argument overlap-based models in predicting reading time and fit ratings.

6.10 General Discussion and Implications

The original Construction-Integration model as proposed by Kintsch (1988; Kintsch and van Dijk 1978) and explored by others (Glavanov 1979; Goldman and Varma 1995; Kintsch 1988, 1992; Kintsch et al. 1990; Tapiero and Denhiere 1995) has had demonstrated success in accounting for off-line measures of comprehension. This chapter examined how a variant of the standard Construction-Integration model, coupled discourse analyses of text relations, accounted for on-line comprehension as measured by reading time or fit judgments.

The present Construction-Integration model assumed a relaxed spreading activation mechanism that performs similarly to resonance models (Dopkins, Klin, and Myers 1993). The present Construction-Integration model simulates the searching of long-term memory for appropriate items to retrieve during processing of a sentence. We derived from the model three on-line and two off-line processing measures. Using causal connections in the text representation, one on-line measure, namely the average connection strength between a sentence and its predecessors, accounted for substantial variation in empirical, on-line comprehension measures.

Connectionist models, such as the one presented here, provide researchers with a platform from which to test various theories of mental representation and organization within a framework of the construction-integration theory. This was demonstrated by study 4 which compared models using text representations based on causal discourse analysis versus text representation based on proposition argument. The kind of text representation input to the model was crucial to the model's success. Causal representation accounted for more unique variance than argument overlap using the same version of the Construction-Integration model.

The Construction-Integration model can also be used to test different theories of retrieval from long-term memory. In this chapter, we examined only one such mechanism for retrieval, using a relaxed spread of activation algorithm to facilitate retrieval of distal items from long-term memory. Other mechanisms are possible, however. For example, one could compare the performance of the model presented here with the "standard" Construction-Integration model software. The latter imposes a fixed size on the working memory buffer. This comparison would be similar to one performed by Goldman et al. (1995) who examined the impact of relaxing the working memory buffer size within the Construction-Integration framework.

Extracting data from a computational model while it is running has been carried out by Rumelhart and McClelland (1986). They explored connectionist learning algorithms with back propagation networks as a means of "training" the model. As the connectionist model is given a new input, the output of the model is compared to a desired output, and changes in the model's architecture are made according to the incorrectness of the current output. A possible extension of the Construction-Integration model presented here would be to one in which a similar process could occur. Instead of extracting processing measures from the model for the purposes of empirical comparison, one could design a mechanism that processed the current input and checked the on-line processing measures as a means of tracking the construction of the text representation. Such a mechanism would be analogous to comprehension monitoring, allowing the model to judge the "correctness" of the overall text representation with respect to the newly added input. Such a mechanism, however, would require much that is not present in the current model but would be feasible.

Considering the current model as a process model of comprehension, one must keep in mind that the structures upon which the model operates are "preprocessed." That is, the networks derived from textual analysis for input to the model contain the products of cognitive processes not accounted for by the model but derived from different discourse analyses that are based on different theories of discourse processing. As such, the process model provides one account of the mechanisms that operate over particular mental representations of a text generated by some other mechanism or mechanisms not present in the current model. However, the studies presented in this chapter demonstrate that the mechanisms that are contained in the model can provide compelling predictions of on-line empirical data. Thus the model can be deemed successful as a process model of these data as well as providing confirmation or disconfirmation of different theories of text representation. Further the model allows one to compare the predictive validity of different theories of text representation.

One further question to be explored is whether all the variables of the situation model, that is, spatial, temporal, character, and causal continuity as well as argument overlap, can be combined into a "hybrid" model to predict the on-line behavioral data. This could be done by inputting successive representations of the text for each input and generating on-line measures after all properties of a sentence have been processed.

References

Balota, D., G. Flores d'Arcais, and K. Rayner, eds. 1990. *Comprehension Processes during Reading*. Hillsdale, NJ: Lawrence Erlbaum, pp. 403–22.

Dopkins, S., C. Klin, and J. L. Myers. 1993. The accessibility of information about goals during the processing of narrative texts. *Journal of Experimental Psychology: Learning, Memory, and Cognition* 19: 70–80.

Ericsson, K. A., and W. Kintsch. 1995. Long-term working memory. *Psychological Review* 102: 211–45.

Goldman, S. R., and S. Varma. 1995. CAPping the construction-integration model of discourse comprehension. In C. A. Weaver III, S. Mannes, and C. R. Fletcher, eds., *Discourse Comprehension: Essays in Honor of Walter Kintsch*. Hillsdale, NJ: Lawrence Erlbaum, pp. 337–58.

Graesser, A. C., M. Singer, and T. Trabasso. 1994. Constructing inferences during narrative text comprehension. *Psychological Review* 101: 375–95.

Just, M. A., and P. A. Carpenter. 1992. A capacity theory of comprehension: Individual differences in working memory. *Psychological Review* 99: 122–49.

Keenan, J. M., G. R. Potts, J. M. Golding, and T. M. Jennings. 1990. Which elaborative inferences are drawn during reading? A question of methodologies. In D. Balota, G. Flores d'Arcais, and K. Rayner, eds., *Comprehension Processes during Reading*. Hillsdale, NJ: Lawrence Erlbaum, pp. 337–402.

Kintsch, W. 1988. The role of knowledge in discourse comprehension: A construction-integration model. *Psychological Review* 95: 163–82.

Kintsch, W. 1992. How readers construct situation models for stories: The role of syntactic cues and causal inferences. In A. F. Healy, S. M. Kosslyn, and R. M. Shiffrin, eds., *Essays in Honor of William K. Estes*. Hillsdale, NJ: Lawrence Erlbaum.

Kintsch, W., and T. A. van Dijk. 1978. Toward a model of text comprehension and production. *Psychological Review* 85: 363–94.

Kintsch, W., D. Welsch, F. Schmalhofer, and S. Zimny. 1990. Sentence memory: A theoretical analysis. *Journal of Memory and Language* 29: 133–59.

Langston, M. C., and T. Trabasso. 1998. Modeling causal integration and availability of information during comprehension of narrative texts. In H. van Oostendorp and S. Goldman, eds., *The Construction of Mental Representations during Reading*. Mahwah, NJ: Lawrence Erlbaum.

Magliano, J., T. Trabasso, and M. Langston. 1995. Cohesion and coherence in sentence and story understanding. Paper presented at the meetings of the Psychonomic Society, November.

McKoon, G., and R. Ratcliff. 1990. Textual inferences: Models and measures. In D. Balota, G. Flores d'Arcais, and K. Rayner, eds., *Comprehension Processes during Reading*. Hillsdale, NJ: Lawrence Erlbaum, pp. 403–22.

Rumelhart, D. E., and J. L. McClelland. 1986. *Parallel Distributed Processing*, vol. 1. Cambridge: MIT Press.

Suh, S. 1988. *Converging Evidence for Causal Inferences during Comprehension*. PhD dissertation. University of Chicago.

Suh, S., and T. Trabasso. 1993. Inferences during reading: Converging evidence from discourse analysis, talk-aloud protocols, and recognition priming. *Journal of Memory and Language* 32: 278–301.

Tapiero, I., and G. Denhiere. 1995. Simulating recall and recognition by using Kintsch's construction-integration model. In C. A. Weaver III, S. Mannes, and C. R. Fletcher, eds., *Discourse Comprehension: Essays in Honor of Walter Kintsch*. Hillsdale, NJ: Lawrence Erlbaum, pp. 211–32.

Trabasso, T., and J. P. Magliano. 1996. Conscious understanding during comprehension. *Discourse Processes* 21: 255–87.

Trabasso, T., and S. Suh. 1993. Understanding text: Achieving explanatory coherence through on-line inferences and mental operations in working memory. *Discourse Processes* 16: 3–34.

Trabasso, T., S. Suh, and P. Payton. 1994. Explanatory coherence in communication about narrative understanding of events. In M. A. Gernsbacher and T. Given, eds., *Text Coherence as a Mental Entity*. Amsterdam: John Benjamins, pp. 189–214.

Trabasso, T., P. van den Broek, and S. Suh. 1989. Logical necessity and transitivity of causal relations in stories. *Discourse Processes* 12: 1–25.

van den Broek, P. 1990. The causal inference marker: Towards a process model of inference generation in text comprehension. In D. Balota, G. Flores d'Arcais, and K. Rayner, eds., *Comprehension Processes in Reading*. Hillsdale, NJ: Lawrence Erlbaum, pp. 423–45.

van den Broek, P., K. Risden, C. R. Fletcher, and R. Thurlow. 1996. A "landscape" view of reading: Fluctuating patterns of activation and the construction of a stable memory representation. In B. K. Britton and A. C. Graesser, eds., *Models of Understanding Text*. Mahwah, NJ: Lawrence Erlbaum, pp. 165–87.

van Dijk, T. A., and W. Kintsch. 1983. *Strategies of Discourse Comprehension*. New York: Academic Press.

Zwaan, R. A., M. C. Langston, and A. C. Graesser. 1995a. The construction of situation models in narrative comprehension: An event-indexing model. *Psychological Science* 6: 292–97.

Zwaan, R. A., J. P. Magliano, and A. C. Graesser. 1995b. Dimensions of situation model construction in narrative comprehension. *Journal of Experimental Psychology: Learning, Memory, and Cognition* 21: 386–97.

Chapter 7
Importance of Text Structure in Everyday Reading
Bonnie J. F. Meyer

For a moment, think about the last novel which you read. Now, consider the latest newspaper article you read. Both of these pieces of texts involved similar comprehension tasks—the reader wanted to understand what ideas the author of the text was communicating. So it is somewhat unusual that the way in which you read the two pieces was very different in each case. For example, most people read the headline and first paragraph of a news article and then skim the rest unless they are especially interested in the subject matter. On the other hand, one tends to read a novel in a different fashion. Chapters provide convenient boundaries for the reading process, with the text within each chapter assumed to be fairly independent. The organization is less defined than in a news article, so while skimming may occur, it is not following the rule of skimming every paragraph after the first. Contrast both of these examples with reading a journal article. This requires yet another style of reader interaction. Here the experienced reader of journal articles knows exactly which part of the article to read for which purposes by utilizing the well-structured sections focusing on the problem, method, findings, and discussion.

Many of the chapters of this book discuss various computational models of the reading process. Unfortunately, few reading models are at the level of complexity that enables them to read more than one genre of text. As a result the kinds of decisions driven by text structure as just described are either not made by the systems or are implicitly made in that the system is capable of reading one style of text well while ignoring all others. For computational models of reading to become more reflective of the human reading process, this awareness of the role that text structure plays in human reading must be better understood (e.g., Carpenter and Alterman 1993; Mandler and Johnson 1977; Meyer 1975).

The purpose of this chapter is to focus on the role of text structure in reading and remembering text. What is the importance of text structure and how does it relate to other factors that influence reading and understanding texts? The chapter examines reasoning about text structure, genre information, and the intent of an author within the context of communication between author and reader during the reading of everyday texts under various task conditions. In this chapter I will examine how readers across the life span can use text structure to identify the main ideas an author is trying to communicate to them.

7.1 Interaction among Strategy, Task, Text, and Reader Characteristics in Reading

The communication between an author and a reader depends on interaction among strategy, task, text, and reader characteristics. The characteristics of texts produced by authors are as variable as the characteristics of readers. Predicting understanding and performance from reading is thus extremely complicated. The individual characteristics of people, such as purposes, strategies, interest, and prior knowledge, interact with characteristics of texts, such as topic, structure, and emphasis. To complicate the situation further, task characteristics interact with these reader, strategy, and text characteristics as depicted in figure 7.1 (Jenkins 1978; Meyer and Rice 1989).

7.2 Strategies

This chapter primarily examines only one of the strategies listed in figure 7.1, the structure or plan strategy. This strategy is discussed in detail because it is a strategy that focuses on and uses text structure. Over the last twenty years my colleagues and I (e.g., Bartlett 1978; Meyer, Young, and Bartlett 1989; Meyer, Talbot, and Poon 1995) have been training readers to identify the structure in text to aid their understanding and memory of their reading. We have been able to double the amount of information readers can recall by teaching them what we call the plan strategy. Our strategy involves two steps. In reading, we find the plan the writer used and the main idea organized by that plan. In recalling, we use the same organization. This is a strategy to improve memory. A key motto of the training program is "choose it, use it, or lose it."

We explain to our participants learning the plan strategy that we know five facts about reading for information as seen in figure 7.2. First, the writer wants to tell you something. Second, you must be told in writing. Third, there are only a small number of broad and basic plans in which to organize information about a topic. Fourth, the writer should organize his or her main ideas about a topic with a plan. Fifth, to find this organizational plan is the key to getting the writer's main ideas or message. We explain that this strategy is a good one to use under certain conditions, but not others. Participants are encouraged to use it when they want to know what a writer is trying to tell them. In addition they are encouraged to use the recall step of

Importance of Text Structure in Everyday Reading

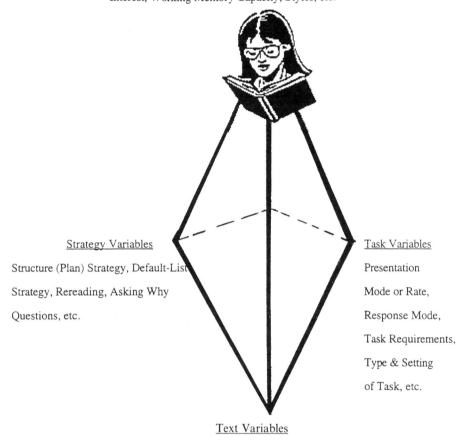

Figure 7.1
Reader, strategy, text, and task variables that influence the communication between readers and authors (adapted from Meyer and Rice 1983).

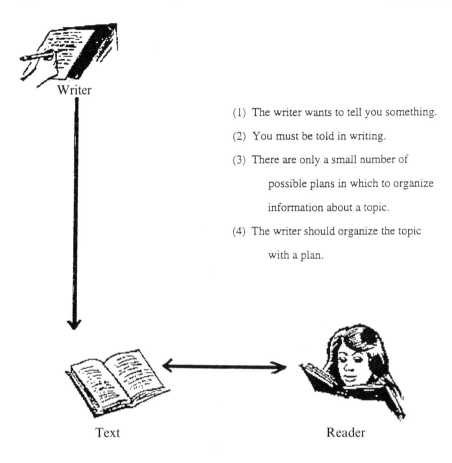

Figure 7.2
The organizational plan is a key to finding the writer's message (adapted from Meyer, Young, and Bartlett 1989).

the strategy when they want to tell someone or write them a letter about what they read in an article. We explain that the plan strategy is not a good strategy to follow if they are just reading to find out a particular detail, such as the date trout fishing begins, and don't have any interest in the point the writer is trying to make. We also explain that the strategy is not as useful for reading information about a very familiar topic (Meyer 1984, 1987; Voss and Silfies 1996).

7.2.1 Communication between the Author and the Reader
First, I am assuming that most writers are trying to communicate something to their readers (e.g., Flower and Hayes 1984; Grice 1975). Constructivists (e.g., Goetz and Armbruster 1980; Spiro 1980) have argued strongly against any idea of "meaning-in-the-text" arguing for meaning as constructed by the reader of the text. Certainly both the writer and the reader contribute to the understanding constructed by a particular reader (e.g., Kintsch 1988). The more ambiguous the text (e.g., Dooling and Lachman 1971; Bransford and Johnson 1972) and the less skilled the reader (e.g., Meyer et al. 1989), the greater the contribution of the reader to this construction of meaning and the less likely the agreement between the coherence of ideas identified by the reader and those identified by the writer. It appears that it is an author's job, as composition teachers can explain, to use linguistic and stylistic devices in the text such as signals (e.g., Lorch and Lorch 1995; Meyer 1975, 1985a), repetition (e.g, Britton and Gulgoz 1991), sequencing of sentences (e.g., Keiras 1980), and headings (e.g., Hartley 1994), to try to help the reader arrive at an interpretation of the text similar to the meaning the author intended.

Writers attempt to interrelate their ideas while producing a coherent text, and readers attempt to construct a coherent representation of the information. A writer gives guidance for a reader to form a similar coherent representation of the information by anticipating some characteristics of their audience of readers and using linguistic devices. However, a portion of readers will not form similar coherent representations due to varying purposes, backgrounds, and skills from those anticipated by the author. Readers intent on understanding a writer's message pay attention to guidance provided by an author, form a similar coherent representation, and often argue back with this representation and modify it to fit their own views. One characteristic of expert readers across the life span is that they describe one of their frequently used reading strategies as "arguing back with what they read" (Meyer and Rice 1983).

Writer's goals have been categorized according to communicative intent to (1) inform, (2) entertain, (3) persuade, and (4) provide an aesthetic experience (Brewer 1980). In my laboratory we have studied the first three categories and students have successfully employed the plan strategy with these types of texts and purposes of authors.

The second point in figure 7.2 focuses on the limitation of writing. Writers have to leave their message in writing and cannot rephrase segments when they detect misunderstandings by their readers. Good communication is difficult between individuals even when dialogue is possible. It is possible that readers sometimes have a false sense of communicating with the ideas of an author; if feedback were possible, readers might be quite surprised to see the difference in their understanding and that of the author.

The third point explains that there are a limited number of ways in which to organize information about a topic. Although there appear to be a limited number of plans, there is not universal agreement about exactly how they should be described or to what degree of specification (e.g., D'Angelo 1979; Hobbs 1990; Mann and Thompson 1988; Meyer 1985b; Sander, Spooren, and Noordman 1992, 1993). Table 7.1 describes the plans understood and used effectively by participants across the life span from our training programs.

The fourth point stresses that it would be ideal if writers organized texts with plans that were readily identifiable. In the first sessions of our training programs, we employ everyday text from advertisements, magazine articles, books, and newspapers that can be clearly classified into one of the five plans identified in table 7.1. It is not a difficult task to find such materials, and our participants appear to easily find examples from their everyday reading to bring into the classroom. In later sessions of our training program, we help readers clarify and reorganize muddled text (session 4, Meyer et al. 1989). For example, a newspaper article with the title formatted as a question asked if molecules could be ambidextrous. The format of the question might cause the reader to expect the question/answer (form of problem/solution) plan shown in table 7.1. However, the text of the article did not answer this question, so a problem/solution plan would not be effective for encoding and retrieval of the most important information in the newspaper article. In addition "ambidextrous" in the title could bring to the readers' minds an incorrect analogy to apply to the text. The body of the text drew an analogy between hand preference in humans and a mirror image phenomena in the molecules of blood pressure medication with one form being more powerful than another. Since ambidextrous refers to using both hands equally well and one form of the medication is 100 times more potent than the other, the author is setting the reader up for some added confusion. For this muddled text, we teach readers to relate the ideas together with the comparison plan seen in table 7.1 and compare the two forms of blood pressure medication with the aid of the hand preference analogy rather than attending to the author's title with its misleading question/answer format and inappropriate use of "ambidextrous."

Table 7.1
Five basic writing plans and signals that cue readers to these plans

Writing plan	Definition	Signals
Description	Descriptive ideas that give attributes, specifics, or setting information about a topic. The main idea is that attributes of a topic are discussed.	for example; such as; for instance e.g., a newspaper article describing who, where, when, and how
Sequence	Ideas grouped on the basis of order or time. The main idea is the procedure or history related.	to begin with; as time passed; later e.g., recipe procedures, history of Civil War battles, growth from birth to 12
Causation	Presents causal or cause and effect relationships between ideas. The main ideas are organized into cause and effect parts. The effect comes before the reason (cause) in explanations.	because; so; caused; reasons; if..., then... e.g., directions: if you want to take good pictures, then you must...; explanations
Problem/solution	The main ideas are organized into two parts: a *problem* part and a *solution* part that responds to the problem by trying to eliminate it, or a *question* part and an *answer* part that responds to the question by trying to answer it.	need to prevent; problem; solution; question; answer e.g., scientific articles often first raise a question or problem and then seek to give an answer or solution
Comparison	Relates ideas on the basis of differences and similarities. The main idea is organized in parts that provide a comparison, contrast, or alternative perspective on a topic.	instead; on the other hand; however; in contrast e.g., political speeches, particularly where one view is clearly favored over the other

Source: From Meyer, Young, and Bartlett (1989).

The fifth point in figure 7.2 states that finding the organizational plan enables readers to understand the writer's main ideas or message. We have found that using the organizational plan in text through the plan strategy helps readers remember more of what they read (e.g., Meyer, Brandt, and Bluth 1980), remember more of the important information in what they read (e.g., Meyer et al. 1989), and remember this information longer (Meyer et al. 1989). Due to the limited processing capacity of readers, they cannot learn and remember everything in a text, so some information must be selected for deeper encoding, more cycles of processing or elaboration than other information. The overall structure or plan of the text can help readers select the most important information for thorough encoding. In addition the structure can help the reader retrieve this information from memory over time.

In our training program we stress the organizational components of various text types for aiding retrieval from memory. For example, the comparison plan often falls under the writer's goals of persuasion particularly for political articles and speeches. The contrastive pattern of the comparison plan is that different points of view are shown in different parts of the passage. It may be that one view tells what did happen and the other tells what did not happen; or, one might tell what exists and the other what does not exist; or, each part might tell opposing arguments. Often when opposing views are compared, they are compared on many of the same issues; for example, one political candidate's views on abortion, taxes, government spending, and defense, and then the other candidate's views on these same issues. Memory will be improved by remembering that a comparison plan was used and the number and name of the issues compared; for the above example remember that the candidates were compared on four issues: abortion, taxes, government spending, and defense.

We also emphasize the usefulness of the structure in a problem/solution text to aid encoding and retrieval. As shown in table 7.1 this plan is often used in scientific articles and frequently for the writer's goal of persuasion. The pattern of the problem/solution plan is that there is part of the passage that tells about a problem (question, puzzle, concern) and another that tells about its solution (answer, reply). In the question/answer version the answer must deal with the ideas discussed in the question and provide some answer. In the problem/solution version often the causes and effects of the problem are discussed first; then, a solution follows that should attempt to block or eliminate at least one of the causes of the problem. When reading a problem/solution text, we encourage readers to look for possible causes of the problems and descriptions of the effects of these causes, the problem itself. Then readers are encouraged to look for a posited solution or solutions that would refer back and eliminate causes of the problem. When recalling the text, the readers are encouraged to write problem/solution at the top of their recall sheet and then a main idea sentence that incorporates both the problem part and solution part of the text. Next, the learners organize their written or oral recall using the problem/solution plan. First, they start off a paragraph with signaling stating that "the problem is. . . ." Then, they write a paragraph(s) about the problem or group of problems remembering to include any causes, effects, or descriptions of the problem. After recalling everything they can remember about what the author stated about the problem, they explicitly signal the solution stating that "the solution is. . . ." Paragraphs about the solution include a description of the solution and an explanation of how it gets rid of causes of the problem or tries to eliminate a cause. Finally, readers check to be sure they have used the plan to organize their recall that they identified in reading and listed at the top of their recall sheet, and then they add anything else they remember.

Through our strategy training program we have been able to increase the communication between an author and a reader by helping readers follow overall text structure or, as Grimes (1975) phrased it, the thread of discourse. Once the readers understand the main points of what the author is trying to tell them, we ask them to evaluate this message. For example, one advertisement used in the first session of a six-session training program has the boldfaced caption, **CLUB MED SHOULD FEEL THIS FREE. HEDONISM II. CLUB MED SHOULD BE THIS GOOD.** The text reads: "In a nutshell, Club Med is *almost* an all-inclusive holiday. But you still have to buy beads to pay for drinks and cigarettes. At Hedonism II, we do things differently. *Everything* is included. Drinks at the bar. Cigarettes. No beads. No membership. No nothing. Like Club Med, we offer all food, wine, entertainment, sailing, tennis, snorkeling, scuba—also included. But the real magic is this: When you need no money for *anything*, you have total freedom to enjoy. And we know that total freedom is the only thing that can be better than Club Med." The plan used is comparison. Hedonism II and Club Med are compared and Hedonism II is favored. The plan strategy focuses on the plan the author used to write the advertisement. Once the reader figures out what the author is communicating then he or she needs to evaluate the message. For example, for the Hedonism II advertisement if I don't smoke or drink, then Hedonism II may be a bad choice for me because I will end up paying for the "free cigarettes and drinks" of the other vacationers. I would need to check and see if Hedonism II is more expensive than Club Med.

Another example of working to understand what an author is trying to communicate and then evaluating this communication comes from the sixth session of the training program (during 1996 we added the sixth session to promote use of the plan strategy to take brief notes in everyday reading). We explain to young and older readers that the plan strategy can be helpful in taking notes about articles related to health issues and then using these notes when visiting a doctor or others in a search to gather more information about a health issue. One article utilized to teach this skill appeared in the November 6, 1995, issue of *U.S. News & World Report* and was entitled "A drug for fragile bones." Participants were encouraged to organize their notes by using a problem/solution plan, a common plan used in health-related materials. The goal of the author appeared to be to persuade readers to be aware of the problem of osteoporosis and alternative solutions to eliminate the problem with an emphasis on a new possible solution, the drug Fosamax. The desirability of each of the alternative solutions depended on the characteristics of the reader in need of such information. Participants made notes, discussed them with a partner, and then examined the structure shown in figure 7.3. We explained that once they understood the information an author was trying to communicate, readers could use this information to make decisions. After finding out the information about osteoporosis and Fosamax shown in figure 7.3 and verifying it through other sources, they could use this information to make a wise health decision. For example, if a reader had been previously diagnosed with breast cancer, she might decide to use Fosamax instead of estrogen; this would protect her from osteoporosis without the danger related to reoccurring breast cancer. However, if a reader had no personal or family history of breast cancer, but a strong family history of heart disease and osteoporosis she might want to take estrogen in order to protect herself from both diseases.

We encourage participants in our training studies to use the plan strategy when they want to know what the author said and remember this information. They are told that they probably would not use the plan strategy when casually looking over the newspaper for enjoyment.

7.2.2 How Successful Is the Communication between Reader and Author?

Brewer (1980) operationalized text type or genre as the writer's communicative goal. Expressive, informative, and persuasive are three types identified. In expressive text the writer's goal is to express feelings and attitudes. For example, in the Aesop fable "Mercury and the Woodsman" (text structure analysis of a version adapted for children in Meyer et al. 1980) the attitude to be conveyed is explicitly signaled by the author with the moral, "honesty is the best policy." The story exemplifies this moral by relating the rewards given to an honest lumberjack versus the punishment given to a scheming, dishonest lumberjack. The communication of this attitude to readers could be assessed with various tasks ranging from recognition of the moral to its application in the everyday life.

For informative texts the writer's goal is to inform the reader about something. Common texts of this type can be found in the encyclopedia. These types of texts focus on relaying semantic information with ideas related on the basis of further specification and description, cause and effects relationships, and contrastive relationships.

For persuasive texts the writer's goal is to persuade the reader of something. Advertisements are common persuasive texts. These texts contain semantic information but also pragmatic problem/solution type information where the writer tries to convince the reader to buy a product or idea for a certain problematic situation.

A good deal of my research has focused on how well readers have been informed or persuaded by expository text. One persuasive text taken from *Scientific American* magazine (Seaborg and Bloom 1970) allots two paragraphs for explaining the problems of meeting demands for electrical energy while at the same time protecting the

Importance of Text Structure in Everyday Reading

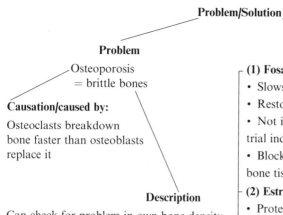

Problem/Solution

Problem
Osteoporosis
= brittle bones

Causation/caused by:
Osteoclasts breakdown bone faster than osteoblasts replace it

Description
Can check for problem in own bone density through a quick, painless bone density scan (cost $125.–$350.; Medicare covers after 65 years; call National Osteoporosis Foundation for Bone-scanning centers 800-464-6700)

Comparison of Solutions

(1) Fosamax
- Slows bone loss
- Restores some of lost bone
- Not increase risk for breast cancer (3 year trial indicated rare/mild side effects)
- Blocks osteoclasts from breaking down bone tissue

(2) Estrogen
- Protects women from bone loss
- Increases risk of breast and uterine cancer
- Relieves menopause symptoms
- Lowers risk of heart disease
- New studies add to confusion: one—decrease risk alzheimers, another—increase risk for asthma

(3) Fosamax and estrogen
- Unusual solution at this point

(4) Medication-free treatments
- Types of exercise and calcium: postmenopausal 1500 mg/day other adults 1000 mg
- Slow-release fluoride + calcium supplements indicated by study with osteoporosis patients
- Preventative for 50% of adolescents and young adults in bone-building years 1200–1500 mg/day

Figure 7.3
Notes taken using the plan strategy to understand the important information presented by an author in a current health-related article about osteoporosis and fosamax.

environment and finite resources. The next three paragraphs present the author's solution, the fast breeder reactor, and explanations for why it is a solution to these problems and how the breeder reactor works (for structural analysis see Meyer 1975, or Meyer, Young, and Bartlett 1989). A young woman recalled this 506-word text for us and her efforts showed little evidence for much communication between the author and reader. She was a high school graduate with average vocabulary and reading comprehension skills. The authors' goals to inform and persuade fell very short as can be seen by her recall reproduced below.

Breeder reactors are the fast growing ideas of how to carry fuel. It was talking about how important gas is becoming because we are getting low on it (Meyer et al. 1989).

The authors persuaded her to view breeder reactors as an up-and-coming idea, although she was confused about their purpose. Also she was informed or reminded about the finite supply of gas. This level of performance was typical of her understanding for this type of expository text. She recalled all the text we gave her (Meyer et al. 1989) regardless of its overall organization as a list of things she remembered without an attempt to interrelate ideas. She participated in one of our training programs and was taught to recognize and use the structure in text to aid her understanding and recall. After the training she was able to apply the strategy we offered and double the amount of information she could remember after reading. She was better able to grasp what an author was trying to tell her. The following is an example of her recall from a text with the same organization and length as the breeder reactor text; it presented problems associated with distributing wealth at one's death with and without a will. These problems included court costs and delays. Then a solution, a trust, was promoted and described (Meyer et al. 1989).

There is a problem about how to divide the money up when a person dies without having a will. If you go to probate court to try to settle it, it might take up to six years to get your money plus all the court costs.
 A solution to this problem is to make a trust. This is a substitute for a will. It avoids going to court. Trusts can never die. The trustor can divide up his money the way he wants, and it will stay that way unless he changes his mind (Meyer et al. 1989).

As can be seen the reader shows evidence of being both persuaded and informed to a much greater extent than before the training. Of course more evidence for her persuasion could involve finding out if she asked her wealthy grandmother to look into trusts, but certainly from this recall it appears more likely that the author's goals for this communication were achieved to a greater extent than in the example from the reactor text. This reader learned to use the plan strategy to increase her ability to communicate with authors. She reported greater interest and enjoyment from her reading after participating in the training. An unsolicited call several years after completion of the program revealed that this learner attributed her willingness to go back to school to train as a paraprofessional to her success in our training program.

These examples of author and reader communication came from a reader with average abilities and skills. What about a reader with exceptional abilities? Could we aid such a reader with our training program focusing on helping readers communicate with author's by identifying the overall structures in text? The following looks at the performance of such an individual who recently participated in a six-session version of the training program. He read and recalled the trust passage on a pretest and over two months later on a post-test. This reader was a young man with 20 years of education who was completing his dissertation in the physical sciences; he scored one standard deviation above our sample mean for young adults on a measure of working memory span and approximately three standard deviations above the means on multiple choice tests of vocabulary and reading comprehension. Many of our young and old participants with such extremely high reading comprehension test scores showed evidence of using the plan strategy prior to instruction, but this individual was particularly interesting because he did not use the strategy prior to instruction as evidenced in his recalls and by his own report. He involved himself wholeheartedly in the training and went beyond the requirements of simply identifying the overall plan in the training materials; in addition he diagrammed the overall structure of each text and produced figures similar to figure 7.2 to show how main sections of texts were interrelated. He reported that he had changed his way of looking at text by learning the plan strategy. His recall performance on the trust text jumped from a good recall of 40 ideas to an unusually excellent recall of 103 ideas, and the way he structured his recall changed so that it better matched the structure used by the author. Without using the plan strategy, he was informed and perhaps persuaded by the text, but clearly the author's goals were achieved to a greater degree when this reader learned to employ the plan strategy. His recall protocols produced before and after instruction are shown below.

On the pretest he used a plan to organize the information, but it was a different plan from that employed by the author. Contrary to the example of the average reader's performance prior to training where ideas were simply listed without any organizing plan, this more expert reader organized the information with a different plan, a comparison: adversative plan, where the advantages of trusts are favored and emphasized over an alternative vehicle for distributing wealth, a will. This plan is compatible with the author's goal of persuasion even though it is not the plan originally employed. Below is the pretest protocol; it contains three confusions about ideas in the text (e.g., forming a trust gives the legal ownership to the trustee, not the person forming the trust) and two confusions from incorrectly integrating the information with some prior knowledge (e.g., a living will deals with a legal document directing that measures of life support not be employed for a signer with an incurable condition; it does not deal with a trust).

A will can involve lengthy probate court time and costs to distribute your property to your heirs after your death while court proceedings go on, your survivors and heirs cannot enjoy the property in the will. Also, this involves paying gift and estate taxes.
   A trust is a good alternative. A trust bypasses court time and costs. When you form a trust for a property, you have legal ownership. You may designate a beneficiary for what is called beneficial ownership. The trust is managed by a trustee, an entity like a bank, in accordance with the will of you, the trustor.
   The beneficiary may enjoy use and income from the property as specified by the trustor. The trustor, through a living will, can control the conditions under which the property is enjoyed. The trustor/trustee may also change beneficial ownership through will clauses.
   These are the advantages of trusts and this is why people like Pep Jackson and Lee Copenhagen promote them.

Compare the pretest to the post-test reproduced below. In the post-test the reader is now following the plan strategy by organizing the information with the same problem/solution plan as used by the author of the text. The coherence of the protocol is higher, and there are no apparent misconceptions. In addition more information has been conveyed, and again we have some evidence that the reader may have been persuaded by the text.

The problem is how to distribute your property as you wish after death, while avoiding the costs of probate courts. If you die intestate (without a will), court delays and management, along with equitable inheritance laws, can be obstacles to your chosen beneficiaries enjoying your estate. Wills to distribute property after death have drawbacks, such as probate court costs or delays.
   One solution is to place your property in a trust. Trusts completely avoid probate courts, with their costs and delays. U.S. gift and inheritance taxes are also avoided. Using a trust with a revocable will, you can control your property after your death, e.g., a trust has no life span.
   How do trusts do this? The property in question, called the corpus, is placed by you the trustor, in care of the trustee—say your bank. The trustee has legal ownership of the corpus. The beneficiary ownership of the corpus allows you to enjoy the corpus in life. After your death, the trustee transfers beneficiary ownership to your chosen heirs. The transfer may be revoked or changed by provisions set by you in your trust control document.
   By dividing the legal and beneficiary ownerships of property, trusts provide a good inheritance mechanism. Some people are promoting trusts. Trusts are a solution that help you control property in life and after death.

Significantly more of our young and old adults receiving instruction with the plan strategy report that they remember more from their everyday reading after instruction than do comparable groups of people involved in alternative instruction with the same texts, but without the plan strategy or a no contact control group. They also report more changes in the type of information they attend to and remember when reading in the laboratory and in everyday life. It appears to be a strategy that can be taught to people with a wide range of abilities with the result of greater communication between authors and readers. For readers it would appear to be an important strategy in their repertoire of reading strategies to use when they desire to really understand an author's viewpoint and message.

Communication between an author and reader involves a complex interaction of strategy, task, text, and reader variables as outlined in figure 7.1. Through this detailed discussion of the structure strategy, I have pointed out how this strategy interacts with different types of texts, such texts organized with varying structures, or even muddled texts. In addition I have pointed to individual differences in readers who learn the structure strategy and how these differences lead to differences in the amount of information remembered as well as the quality of recall. In the examples of the average and superior young adults on reading and vocabulary tests, we saw that both participants at least doubled their pretraining recall performance after instruction with the strategy. Mastery of the strategy did not equalize their performance, but their individual reader differences interacted with the strategy to yield their reading performance. The remainder of the chapter discusses some of the other task, text, and reading variables depicted in figure 7.1.

7.3 Task

As depicted in figure 7.1 task variables are important in understanding reading performance. Task characteristics relevant to the communication between an author and reader deal with how to present the text. Another important aspect of task is how to evaluate a reader's understanding and use of the information. These two aspects will be examined in this section of the chapter.

7.3.1 Mode and Rate of Text Presentation

Concerning presentation of text, computers are becoming an alternative mode to print for text presentation. Computers are now major conveyors of information to persons of all ages. Some recent research in my laboratory (Meyer and Poon 1997) indicated that presentation of information via computer does not handicap young adults' learning but tends to facilitate it, and even make it more efficient in computer-paced versions of presentation. However, this is not the case for older adults (65 years and older); they are more efficient when learning from the traditional media of the printed page. The most plausible explanation for this interaction of mode of presentation and age group is the greater familiarity and use of computers by young people (U.S. Census Bureau 1993), since we held contrast, font size and visual angle of characters constant among the modes of presentation (Legge, Rubin, and Luebker 1987). Older learners are going to need some training and practice in communicating with authors via computers if they are expected to maintain the same level of understanding in reading that they have experienced through a lifetime of reading from the printed page.

Another recent study in my laboratory (Meyer, Talbot, and Poon 1995) combined reading strategy training with the research on reading speed and pointed to the same age by mode (computer or print) interaction. The goal of this study was to equate the recall strategy of young and old adults through training and then to test the limits of the strategy in minimizing age deficits. In order to do this, rates of text presentation were chosen so as to press the old adults' working memory capacity at one speed while allowing enough time for natural reading at another rate of text presentation. The young adults were predicted to show little speed effect because of their larger working memory capacities and higher normal reading rates. Previous research by Mandel and Johnson (1984) indicated no age difference at 102 wpm; however, other research using 120 wpm have found deficits. This suggested that in the range between 102 and 120 wpm lies the critical turning point between efficient discourse processing and deficits for old adults (Meyer and Rice 1989). Meyer and her colleagues (1989) found that in reading several expository texts from scientific magazines and history books that young adults read at an average pace of 144 wpm. In this same study old adults were found to be reading at an average pace of 121 wpm. The intended presentation pace of 130 wpm therefore seemed to be well within the grasp of most of the young, while it might push the limits of the old adults' processing capabilities.

A potential problem was encountered within the research literature on reading speed. Carver (1982) indicated that college students' optimal rate is approximately 300 words per minute when reading for the author's message, rather than recalling facts. Smith (1994) asserts that a reading rate that falls below 200 wpm would be deprived of coherence. The rationale follows that if the text is presented too slowly, the words would not remain in working memory long enough to provide for the organization and integration of ideas to occur. For this reason it was thought that younger adults might be impaired in discourse comprehension when given text at a slow rate.

Meyer, Talbot, and Florencio (in press) examined three rates of text presentation (90, 130, and 300 wpm) with college adults. In contrast to Smith's hypothesis, the fastest presentation rate yielded the poorest recall. Also measured was the participant's most comfortable presentation speed. Only 7 percent of the participants favored the "average" reading speed of 300 wpm, while 47 percent and 46 percent favored the 130 and 90 wpm, respectively. This finding demonstrated that the 90 and

130 wpm speeds were equally favorable to young participants. Contrary to expectations from the theory that limitations in working memory pose a lower limit to reading rate, Meyer, Talbot, and Florencio (in press) found better recall performances at the slowest reading rate.

Young and old adults were trained in the structure strategy (Meyer, Talbot, and Florencio, in press; Meyer et al. 1998), previously found to double recall from prose (e.g., Meyer, Young, and Bartlett 1989). After training these adults were asked to read and recall three passages. Our objective was to alter some parameters of text presentation so as to increase the cognitive load on readers and differentially disable older adults' ability to effectively use the structure strategy. The two variables manipulated in this study were pace (reading speed) and sentence context. The passages were presented on a computer screen one sentence at a time. In order to examine the first variable, pace, each participant received one problem-solution passage presented at 90 wpm and another at 130 wpm.

The second variable on which the presentation of the texts varied was context. The text was presented in one of two formats: sentences in isolation or sentences in context. In the first condition, isolation, each sentence was presented in the vertical center of the screen one sentence at a time. Therefore, each sentence replaced the sentence before it. In the second condition, context, the sentences appeared at the top of the screen with each successive sentence being added in its naturally occurring space. Each new sentence was presented with regular contrast; the old sentences in the context dimmed but were still visible on the screen. The bright displaying of the new sentences was intended to pace the reader's reading speed. The context was available to check in order to clarify comprehension or review if a participant had extra time after reading the highlighted new sentence. The presence of this context was expected to aid in the reading process by allowing the reader to review previous sentences if necessary. This was thought to lessen the working memory load compared to the isolated sentence presentation.

The results indicated that there were no significant effects related to the presentation method: Isolation versus context. The data on the presentation speed indicated that both young and old adults were affected by the increase in pace. There were no age by pace interactions. However, the most important findings from this study indicated that the use of computers in the testing of older adults may have produced spurious effects. According to the recall results from a passage read on paper at each reader's own pace given prior to training, the young and old adults were not significantly different in their ability to read and recall information from text (Meyer et al. 1998). However, after training, the young adults showed a marked improvement in the amount of information recalled, while the old did not. In fact the old adults' recall decreased from the pre-training task to the 90 and 130 wpm conditions.

Almost all of the young and old participants showed signs of mastering the strategy when reading in the traditional manner from the printed page by the end of the last training session. However, while 95 percent of the young showed consistent use of the strategy for all three post-test texts read off a computer screen, only 44 percent of the old performed similarly. Even in considering only those 44 percent of old adults who consistently used the strategy, no training gains in overall recall are found for the old adults.

This finding leads to the explanation of computer interference in reading comprehension and recall. The young adults are very accustomed to the use of computers, but the same cannot be said of the old adults. Thus this research points to the interaction between the reader variables of age and computer knowledge and the task variable of mode of presentation. As depicted in figure 7.3 the communication between authors and readers can be impacted by learner variables interacting with task variables.

7.3.2 Ways of Evaluating Understanding

Another important task variable relates to how reading performance will be assessed. Although actors are no doubt interested in whether a learner can recite verbatim the lines of Shakespeare, few psychologists are interested in verbatim recall of the information to be communicated by a writer. Instead, they want to know if learners can paraphrase that information, answer questions about it, summarize it, or use it to complete a task, solve a problem, or make a decision. For example, Mayer and Gallini (1990) looked at different ways to communicate how a pump worked to students with high or low experience with mechanical systems. They were not interested in their ability to paraphrase this information, but whether they could use it to troubleshoot problems with pumps. One group (complete illustration group) received the information with illustrations that labeled critical parts of the pump and two views of the pump that showed what happened when the pump handle was moved up and down. Another group received only one view of the illustration without explicit labels about how the pump worked, and another group did not receive the illustration. All groups received an identical text about the working of pumps. For students who possessed prior knowledge about mechanical systems, all three groups did equally well on the troubleshooting task. They were also equivalent in performance to the low prior knowledge group who received the complete illustration and text. The complete illustration apparently helped mechanically naive readers create a mental model of the pumping system that could be used to solve pump problems. The high prior knowledge readers already possessed such models or could generate them on their own. Not only author-provided aids in the form of good illustrations but also aids in the form of signals to text structure are particularly helpful to the naive learner in a field (e.g., Voss and Silfies 1996). While some have found such aids in text to help learners with low prior knowledge and not harm those with high knowledge, others have pointed to better learning for students with high prior knowledge when they have to expend more effort in generating these connections themselves (e.g., McNamar et al. 1996; Rabinowitz 1989).

Alexander and colleagues (1994) conducted an interesting study that looked at task in terms of the task created by classroom teachers for the evaluation of learning after middle school students read about Stephen Hawking and his work in physics. The students read the text, rated it on importance and interest, recalled it, and reported what questions they believed the teacher would ask them. Students were found to be quite aware of the information that their teachers would test, but this information was not necessarily the important information presented in a text. Better matches between children's appraisals of information to be tested and important information in the text only occurred in classrooms when a teacher possessed adequate knowledge in the physics domain as well as good pedagogical skills. Thus the learning environment created by a teacher in a classroom also affects how well an author can communicate an important message to children in the classroom.

Unlike writing down all the information one can remember from a text, making a decision based on a body of information does not require all of the information given to the participant to be used. Rather, as the information is read, participants choose which portions are important and which are not according to their own knowledge and biases as well as the emphasis given to the material by the author through text structure and signals.

Meyer, Russo, and Talbot (1995) reported that after having participants make a treatment decision regarding breast cancer, in which there was no significant differences in the decisions made by young and old women, the older adults provided less detailed explanations for their decisions than did younger women. The first study reported by Meyer et al. (1995) involved decisions about treatments for breast cancer in an unfolding hypothetical scenario, while the second study focused on data gathered from a questionnaire about decisions for the treatment of breast cancer given to patients who had actually experienced breast cancer. Similar findings were found for both studies in that older adults sought less information and made their treatment decision faster than younger women, but the types of decisions made did not significantly vary for the different age groups. These data seem to represent some difference in the manner in which young and old adults process information. It could be that old adults are, as Sinnott (1989) indicates, more likely to process the information and make a decision based on their prior knowledge and not on the information given them in the task.

In order to get a better idea about whether or not information attended to while reading affects subsequent decision making, Meyer et al. (1995, study 1) asked participants to underline the seven most important pieces of information given to them in text describing the contrasting treatment views of seven experts (e.g., oncologist, pathologist) and a summary of the research literature. There were numerous pieces of information that could be underlined from this text comprised of 12 paragraphs, but only 13 statements gave information for or against the six treatment options given to the women. After making a treatment decision, participants wrote down all they could recall about the views of the experts and research literature. Items that were underlined or recalled played an important role in the treatment option chosen by the young and old participants. For example, participants underlining statements against radiation were less likely to select the radiation treatment option and more likely to select either lumpectomy or do nothing but checkups every six months. In addition women who underlined "in situ cancer spreads faster under age 50" did not underline statements recommending participation in a national study where participants were randomly assigned to radiation or no treatment, but they did underline statements favoring mastectomy. These individuals were more likely to select a mastectomy as their choice of treatment options. Similarly, if women recalled the faster spread of in situ cancer in women under age 50, they did not select the treatment options of the national study nor radiation but tended to select mastectomy, lumpectomy, or just checkups. Participants who recalled promastectomy statements were more likely to have selected a mastectomy, whereas those who did not recall promastectomy ideas were more likely to select lumpectomy, radiation, or just checkups. In addition recall of one specific fact, near 100 percent cure with mastectomy for in situ cancer, related to a decision for mastctomy. Also analysis of prior knowledge statements provided some limited support for prior knowledge affecting underlining which also affected decision making.

In this study there was evidence that participants were attending to information presented by authors and not just relying on prior knowledge when making decisions. These findings point to the importance of communication between authors and readers on such important health care issues. Since signaling devices in text can emphasize certain ideas and make them more salient to readers (e.g., Lorch and Lorch 1995), a heavy burden is placed on authors to accurately report information as well as their biases to readers.

7.4 Text

Figure 7.1 lists some important text characteristics that influence comprehension from text. The hierarchical structure itself influences what people remember from text (e.g., Meyer 1975). For example, Rice, Meyer, and Miller (1989) rewrote medical information to put important information from physicians' perspectives higher in a content structure analysis of text than originally placed in published medical information with a resultant boost in memory for this information by patients.

Meyer and Freedle (1984) reported superior recall of information presented in certain discourse structures or plans than others. For example, the plan of comparison was more memorable than a plan of description. Whether or not a topic adapts well into a causation plan versus another plan can depend on constraints of the topic (Calfee and Drum 1986). However, there are a number of topics that can be cast into either a description or a comparison plan, such as the Archaeopteryx fossil from the evolutionist perspective or the fossil from an evolutionist perspective compared to a creationist perspective. A topic can be described from one viewpoint, or it can be described and contrasted from two or more viewpoints. Salisbury (1996) recently found a strong effect for type of discourse structure when she examined college students' immediate and delayed test performance assessing knowledge about recent theories of motivation; students who read this information in a comparison structure that compared new views of motivation to old views of motivation performed better than students who read a description of the new views. Vincent's (1985) work indicated that adults across the life span with average vocabulary performance performed at equivalent levels on both structures in contrast to high average and high verbal adults who show facilitative effects with the comparison structure. However, training in the use of text structure might aid such learners. Without training there appears to be an interaction between discourse type and verbal ability.

As mentioned previously, text structure interacts with reading skill and domain knowledge (Voss and Silkies, 1995). In addition emphasis devices (e.g., signals and headings) can support or undermine the text structure and influence learning and memory. Some of the text variables can be seen interacting with capacity limitations of learners. For example, Kemper and colleagues (1989) found that sentences with long phrases coming before the verb (left-branching sentences) are more taxing for older adults presumably because of limitations in working memory capacity.

7.5 Reader

I have already mentioned numerous contributions of reader characteristics, such as domain knowledge and aging, listed in figure 7.1. There are large bodies of research on many of the individual differences listed under reader variables in figure 7.1. For example, there is an increasing body of research dealing with the influence of interest on learning from text (for reviews, see Alexander 1998; Hidi 1990; Schiefele 1992; Wade 1992). Both topic interest (enduring evaluative attitude toward a topic) and text-based (situational, emotional state aroused by specific text features) have been found to relate to learning from text (e.g. Meyer et al. 1998; Schiefele 1991; Schiefele and Krapp 1966).

A recent study in my laboratory (Meyer and Poon 1996; Meyer and Talbot 1998) showed different reading strategies for adults with reduced processing resources. We found that readers who still have sufficient processing resources, either because they were young or highly verbal older adults, read with similar strategies. However, older adults who were both subject to declines in processing speed and showed little expertise in verbal ability spent a greater amount of time on the first two pages of a four page text presented in a self-paced condition on the computer. They apparently required more time for building a framework or structure (Gernsbacher 1996) to interpret the text; on the first two pages of the text taken from *Scientific American* magazine the problems were presented and the solution was introduced, and then the solution was further elaborated on pages three and four. Highly verbal older adults did not appear to allocate time differently than highly verbal young adults, while less verbal older adults may have been attempting to compensate for the processing declines by drastically slowing down their reading at the beginning of a text.

7.6 Conclusion

In this chapter we have seen that communication between readers and authors can be improved by strategy instruction, modifications of tasks, and text design. Reader limitations can often be mediated through strategy training or designing materials to compensate for some memory problem (e.g, help screens on computers) or modifying task constraints (e.g., giving extra time) or expectations (e.g., a reasonable decision versus detailed recall and rationale for a decision). This is extremely important because a good portion of the knowledge and wisdom a person acquires over the life span in a literate society comes from reading text. In addition many of the findings identified with text hold for television broadcasts, and the like. For example, we have found the plan strategy to work quite well for young and older adults watching a persuasive video about nutrition and fats (Meyer et al. 1997). Clear writing and strategic, skilled readers are vital for successful education.

Ram and Moorman in their overview chapter for this book describe various purposes for reading. In this chapter I have mainly dealt with the purpose of communication with an author and information seeking, rather than entertainment. In Ram's chapter of this volume he discusses the effects of purpose on the manner and depth to which text is processed in the context of computational reading systems. In this chapter I have shown how the reader can use the structure of text to support the comprehension of that text. In the future more computational reading systems may want to take advantage of the influence of text structure.

Note

The research reported in this chapter was supported in part by the National Institute of Aging grants AG03438 and AG09957. Correspondence concerning the chapter should be addressed to Bonnie J. F. Meyer, Department of Educational and School Psychology and Special Education, The Pennsylvania State University, 204 Cedar Building, University Park, Pa 16802—e-mail at BJM8@PSU.EDU.

References

Alexander, P. A. 1998. Stages and phases of domain learning: The dynamics of subhect-matter knowledge, strategy knowledge, and motivation. In C. E. Weinstein and B. L. McCombs, eds., *Strategic learning: Skill, will, and self-regulation*. Hillsdale, NJ: Lawrence Erlbaum.

Alexander, P. A., T. L. Jetton, J. M. Kulikowich, and C. A. Woehler. 1994. Contrasting instructional and structural importance: The seductive effect of teacher questions. *Journal of Reading Behavior* 26: 19–45.

Bartlett, B. J. 1978. *Top-level structure as an organizational strategy for recall of classroom text*. Unpublished doctoral dissertation, Arizona State University.

Bransford, J. D., and M. K. Johnson. 1972. Contextual prerequisites for understanding: Some investigations of comprehension and recall. *Journal of Verbal Learning and Verbal Behavior* 61: 717–26.

Brewer, W. F. 1980. Literacy theory, rhetoric, and stylistics: Implications for psychology. In R. J. Spiro, B. C. Bruce, and W. F. Brewer, eds., *Theoretical Issues in Reading Comprehension*. Hillsdale, NJ: Lawrence Erlbaum, pp. 221–44.

Britton, B. K., and S. Gulgoz. 1991. Using Kintsch's computational model to improve instructional text: Effects of repairing inference calls on recall and cognitive structures. *Journal of Educational Psychology* 83: 329–45.

Calfee, R., and P. Drum. 1986. Research on teaching reading. In M. C. Wittrock, ed., *Handbook of Research on Teaching*, 3d ed. New York: Macmillan, pp. 804–50.

Carpenter, T., and R. Alterman. 1993. Reading as a planned activity. *Proceedings of the Fifteenth Annual Conference of the Cognitive Science Society*. Hillsdale, NJ: Lawrence Erlbaum, pp. 300–305.

Carver, R. P. 1982. Optimal rate of reading prose. *Reading Research Quarterly* 18: 56–58.

D'Angelo, F. J. 1979. Paradigms as structural counterparts of topoi. In D. McQuade, ed., *Linguistics, Stylistics, and Teaching of Composition*. Akron, OH: University of Akron Press, pp. 41–51.

Dooling, D. J., and R. Lachman. 1971. Effects of comprehension on retention of prose. *Journal of Experimental Psychology* 88: 216–22.

Flower, L. S., and J. R. Hayes. 1981. A cognitive process theory of writing. *College Composition and Communication* 31: 21–32.

Flower, L. S., and J. R. Hayes. 1984. Images, plans, and prose: The representation of meaning in writing. *Written Communication* 1: 120–60.

Gernsbacher, M. A. 1996. The structure-building framework: What it is, what it might also be, and why. In B. K. Britton and A. C. Grasesser, eds., *Models of Understanding Text*. Mahwah, NJ: Lawrence Erlbaum, pp. 289–312.

Goetz, E. T., and B. B. Armbruster. 1980. Psychological correlates of text structure. In R. J. Spiro, B. C. Bruce, and W. F. Brewer, eds., *Theoretical Issues in Reading Comprehension*. Hillsdale, NJ: Lawrence Erlbaum, 201–20.

Grice, H. 1975. Logic and conversation. In P. Cole and J. Morgan, eds., *Syntax and Semantics, III: Speech Acts*. New York: Academic Press, pp. 41–58.

Grimes, J. E. 1975. *The Thread of Discourse*. The Hague: Mouton.

Hartley, J. 1994. *Designing Instructional Text*, 3d ed. East Brunswick, NJ: Nichols Publishing.

Hidi, S. 1990. Interest and its contribution as a mental resource for learning. *Review of Educational Research* 60: 549–71.

Hobbs, J. R. 1990. *Literature and Cognition*. Menlo Park: Center for the Study of Language and Information.

Jenkins, J. J. 1979. Four points to remember: A tetrahedral model of memory experiments. In L. Cermak and F. Craik, eds., *Levels of Processing in Human Memory*. Hillsdale, NJ: Lawrence Erlbaum.

Kemper, S., D. Kynette, S. Rash, R. Sprott, and K. O'Brien. 1989. Life-span changes to adults' language: Effects of memory and genra. *Applied Psycholinguistics* 10: 49–66.

Kieras, D. E. 1980. Initial mention as a signal to thematic content in technical passages. *Memory and Cognition* 8: 345–53.

Kintsch, W. The role of knowledge in discourse comprehension: A construction-integrated model. *Psychological Review* 95: 163–82.

Legge, G. E., G. S. Rubin, A. Luebker. 1987. Psychophysics of reading—V. The role of contrast in normal vision. *Vision Research* 27: 1165–77.

Lorch, R. F., and E. P. Lorch. 1995. Effects of organizational signals on text-processing strategies. *Journal of Educational Psychology* 87: 537–44.

Mandler, J. M., and N. S. Johnson. 1977. Remembrance of things parsed: Story structure and recall. *Cognitive Psychology* 9: 111–51.

Mann, W. C., and S. A. Thompson. 1988. Rhetorical structure theory: Toward a functional theory of text organization. *Text* 8: 243–81.

Mayer, R. E., and J. K. Gallini. 1990. When is an illustration worth ten thousand words? *Journal of Educational Psychology* 82: 715–26.

McNamara, D. S., E. Kintsch, N. B. Songer, and W. Kintsch. 1996. Are good texts always better? Interactions of text coherence, background knowledge, and levels of understanding in learning from text. *Cognition and Instruction* 14: 1–43.

Meyer, B. J. F. 1975. *The Organization of Prose and Its Effects on Memory*. Amsterdam: North-Holland.

Meyer, B. J. F. 1985a. Signaling the structure of text. In D. H. Jonassen, ed., *The Technology of Text*, vol. 2. Englewood Cliffs, NJ: Educational Technology Publications, pp. 64–89.

Meyer, B. J. F. 1985b. Prose analysis: Purposes, procedures, and problems. In B. K. Britton and J. Black, eds., *Analyzing and Understanding Expository Text*. Hillsdale, NJ: Lawrence Erlbaum, pp. 11–64, 269–304.

Meyer, B. J. F. 1984. Organizational aspects of text: Effects on reading comprehension and applications for the classroom. In J. Flood, ed., *Promoting Reading Comprehension*. Newark, DE: International Reading Association, pp. 113–38.

Meyer, B. J. F. 1987. Following the author's top-level organization: An important skill for reading comprehension. In R. J. Tierney, P. L. Anders, and J. N. Mitchell, eds., *Understanding Readers Understanding*. Hillsdale, NJ: Lawrence Erlbaum, pp. 59–76.

Meyer, B. J. F., D. M. Brandt, and G. J. Bluth. 1980. Use of the top-level structure in text: Key for reading comprehension of ninth-grade students. *Reading Research Quarterly* 16: 72–103.

Meyer, B. J. F., and R. O. Freedle. 1984. The effects of different discourse types on recall. *American Educational Research Journal* 21: 121–43.

Meyer, B. J. F., M. J. Haring, Brandt, and C. H. Walker. 1980. Comprehension of stories and expository text. *Poetics* 9: 203–11.

Meyer, B. J. F., and L. W. Poon. 1996. *Age differences in reading and memory from printed versus two types of computer-displayed text*. Revised Research Report 1 of the Reading and Aging Series. University Park: Pennsylvania State University.

Meyer, B. J. F., and L. W. Poon. 1997. Age differences in efficiency of reading comprehension from printed versus computer-displayed text. *Educational Gerontology* 23: 789–807.

Meyer, B. J. F., and A. P. Talbot. 1998. Adult age differences in reading and remembering text and using this information to make decisions in everyday life. In M. Cecil Smith and T. Pourchot, eds., *Adult Learning and Development: Perspectives from Educational Psychology*. Hillsdale, NJ: Lawrence Erlbaum, pp. 179–200.

Meyer, B. J. F., A. P. Talbot, and D. Florencio. In press. Reading rate and prose retrieval. *Scientific Studies of Reading*.

Meyer, B. J. F., A. P. Talbot, L. W. Poon, K. J. Wright, J. Edmondson, J., C. J. Hetrick, and R. A. Stubblefield. 1997, May. *Reading strategy instruction aids young and old adults' memory for everyday tasks*. Paper presentation at the 1997 Convention of the American Psychological Society in Washington, DC.

Meyer, B. J. F., A. Talbot, R. A. Stubblefield, and L. W. Poon. 1998. Interest and strategies of young and old readers differentially interact with characteristics of texts. *Educational Gerontology* 24, in press.

Meyer, B. J. F., A. P. Talbot, and L. W. Poon. 1995. An exploration of the effects of slow and faster computer-paced reading presented sentence by sentence in isolation or with prior context available for review on the reading comprehension and memory of young and old adults trained in the structure strategy and a long-term follow-up of this strategy training. Research Report 2 of the Reading and Aging Series. University Park: Pennsylvania State University.

Meyer, B. J. F., and G. E. Rice. 1983. Learning and memory from text across the adult life span. In J. Fine and R. O. Freedle, eds., *Developmental Studies in Discourse*. Norwood, NJ: Albex, pp. 291–306.

Meyer, B. J. F., and G. E. Rice. 1989. Prose processing in adulthood: The text, the learner, and the task. In L. W. Poon, D. C. Rubin, and B. A. Wilson, eds., *Everyday Cognition in Adulthood and Late Life*. New York: Cambridge University Press, pp. 151–94.

Meyer, B. J. F., C. J. Young, and B. J. Bartlett. 1989. *Memory Improved: Enhanced Reading Comprehension and Memory Across the Life Span through Strategic Text Structure.* Hillsdale, NJ: Lawrence Erlbaum.

Meyer, B. J. F., C. Russo, and A. Talbot. 1995. Discourse comprehension and problem solving: Decisions about the treatment of breast cancer by women across the life span. *Psychology and Aging* 10: 84–103.

Rabinowitz, J. C. 1989. Judgments of origin and generation effects: Comparisons between young and elderly adults. *Psychology and Aging* 4: 259–68.

Rice, G. E., B. J. F. Meyer, and D. C. Miller. 1989. Using text structure to improve older adults' recall of important medical information. *Educational Gerontology* 15: 527–42.

Salisbury, J. D. 1996. *The effect of text, motivation, self-regulated learning and epistemological beliefs on conceptual change.* Unpublished PhD dissertation. Pennsylvania State University, University Park.

Sanders, T. J. M., W. P. M. Spooren, and L. G. M. Noordman. 1992. Towards a taxonomy of coherence relations. *Discourse Processes* 15: 1–35.

Sanders, T. J. M., W. P. M. Spooren, and L. G. M. Noordman. 1993. Coherence relations in a cognitive theory of discourse representation. *Cognitive Linguistics* 4: 93–133.

Schiefele, U. 1991. Interest, learning, and motivation. *Educational Psychologist* 26: 299–323.

Schiefele, U. 1992. Topic interst and levels of text comprehension. In A. Renninger, S. Hidi, and A. Krapp, eds., *The Role of Interest in Learning and Development.* Hillsdale, NJ: Lawrence Erlbaum, pp. 151–82.

Schiefele, U., and A. Krapp. 1996. Topic interst and free recall of expository text. *Learning and Individual Differences* 8: 141–60.

Seaborg, G. T., and J. L. Bloom. 1970. Fast breeder reactors. *Scientific American* 223: 13.

Sinnott, J. D. 1989. A model for solution of ill-structured problems: Implications for everyday and abstract problem solving. In J. D. Sinnott, ed., *Everyday Problem Solving: Theory and Applications.* New York: Praeger, pp. 72–99.

Smith, F. 1994. *Understanding Reading.* 5th ed. Hillsdale, NJ: Lawrence Erlbaum.

Spiro, R. J. 1980. Constructive processes in prose comprehension and recall. In R. J. Spiro, B. C. Bruce, and W. F. Brewer, eds., *Theoretical Issues in Reading Comprehension.* Hillsdale, NJ: Lawrence Erlbaum, pp. 245–78.

U.S. Census Bureau. 1993. Computer use in the United States: October 1993. *Current Population Reports.* Education and Social Stratification Branch, Population Division U.S. Bureau of the Census (http://www.census.gov/ftp/pub/population/www/compute.html).

Vincent, J. P. 1985. Effects of discourse types on memory of prose by young, middle-age, and old adults with average vocabularies. Unpublished PhD dissertation, Arizona State University.

Voss, J. F., and L. N. Silfies. 1996. Learning from history text: The interaction of knowledge and comprehension skill with text structure. *Cognition and Instruction* 14: 45–68.

Wade, S. E. 1992. How interest affects learning from text. In A. Renninger, S. Hidi, and A. Krapp, eds., *The Role of Interest in Learning and Development.* Hillsdale, NJ: Lawrence Erlbaum, pp. 255–77.

Chapter 8
A Theory of Questions and Question Asking

Ashwin Ram

8.1 Introduction

In this chapter, I discuss a theory of questions, viewed as a basis for understanding and learning. Most teachers have had the experience of thinking that their students understood some material because they were asking the "right questions." Children ask questions constantly in an attempt to understand and learn about the world around them. Even as adults, we express our curiosity in the form of questions, often to ourselves, as we wonder about novel situations, explore new hypotheses, and become interested in various issues. The ability to ask questions, it seems, is central to the processes of reasoning, understanding, and learning. In this chapter I formalize the basis for these processes by developing a theory of questions and question generation. I explore different kinds of questions, how a reasoner might come to ask them, and the effects of having asked these questions. Also presented is a computer program that asks intelligent questions in an attempt to reason and to learn about its domain.

Story understanding programs are often designed to answer questions to demonstrate that they have adequately understood a story (e.g., Lehnert 1978). In contrast, I claim that asking questions is central to understanding. The underlying theme of this research is the goals of the reasoner and the interaction of these goals with reasoning processes. In particular, I focus on *knowledge goals*, that is, the goals of a reasoner in learning by acquiring and organizing new knowledge and by reorganizing existing knowledge in memory. I argue that knowledge goals, often expressed as questions, arise when the reasoner's model of the domain is inadequate in some reasoning situation. This leads the reasoner to focus on what he or she needs to know, to formulate questions in acquiring this knowledge, and to learn by pursuing these questions.

Reprinted from *The Journal of the Learning Sciences*, 1(3–4): 273–318, 1991.

Rather than presenting details of learning algorithms (see Ram 1993), this chapter is concerned more with the relationship between questions and learning and with the nature of the questions themselves. I discuss the sources of questions, the types of questions arising from different reasoning tasks, the process of generating questions, and the process of learning by answering questions. I also discuss a computer model of question-driven understanding and learning, and the model's implementation in a natural language understanding domain. The main point of the research is to create a model of a dynamic understander that is driven by its questions or goals to acquire knowledge. Rather than being "canned," the understander is always changing as its questions change. Such an understander reads similar stories differently and forms different interpretations as its questions and interests evolve. The intent is not to design a system that can acquire the "right" understanding of a topic but one that is able to wonder and to ask questions about the unusual aspects of its input. As it learns more about the domain, the system asks better and more detailed questions. This kind of questioning forms the origins of creativity; rather than being satisfied with available explanations, a creative person asks questions and explores the explanations in novel ways.

In my model, question-driven information-seeking forms the basis for active, goal-based learning processes. Question generation is the process of identifying what the reasoner needs to learn. Learning occurs incrementally as the reasoner's questions are answered through experience. My system's "experience" corresponds to reading newspaper stories. Although the computer model is being used to explore cognitive issues such as the ones previously mentioned, there are also practical benefits of a system that can represent and reason explicitly about its own goals. Such a system can focus its limited resources on relevant aspects of its environment while paying less attention to irrelevant ones. This allows it to spend more time drawing inferences that are relevant and useful to its goals. This is important in reasoning situations in which the reasoner might draw a combinatorially large set of inferences and also in learning situations in which it is impractical to focus attention on every aspect of a situation and remember every novel aspect. The reasoner needs a principled way to determine which inferences are worth drawing or what is worth learning. In order to ensure that the system does not spend its limited resources trying to infer everything it can, its knowledge goals are used to focus the inferencing and learning process on information that is useful to the goals of the system. What the system learns from the story depends on what it needs to learn, that is, on its knowledge goals. The computer system reasons about its own reasons for learning and hence does not need to generalize everything in the hope that it might eventually be useful.

There is an additional benefit to be derived from the study of questions, especially those questions that are asked in novel reasoning situations. A theory of question generation will help us to develop improved theories of teaching. Questions arise from an interaction between the interests and goals of the understander and the information provided by the environment. In an educational situation, the "environment" may be a teaching program. To design educational environments that facilitate learning, we need to pay attention to the question-asking process that students go through when interacting with the teaching program. For example, in Scardamalia and Bereiter's (1991) Teacher C model, the teacher is concerned with "helping students formulate their own goals, do their own activating of prior knowledge, ask their own questions, direct their own inquiry, and do their own monitoring of comprehension" (p. 39). We also need to consider the motivational aspects of teaching. If we can put students into situations in which they *want* to find something out, they will be better motivated and better able to focus their attention on the relevant information. The solution to this problem lies in understanding the nature of the "learning goals" of the student. These goals are often manifested as *questions* and may be thought of as information goals or knowledge goals. This ties into my formulation of questions as expressions of goals to collect knowledge that arise from underlying needs to know that piece of knowledge.

Thus understanding the nature of questions, and their role in learning, is an important and fundamental problem in cognitive science and has implications for theories of learning and education.

8.1.1 Role of Questions in Understanding and Learning

The basic assumption of our theory, which is called *question-driven understanding*, is that asking questions is central to understanding. To illustrate what this means, consider the following story (*New York Times*, April 14, 1985):

S-1: Boy Says Lebanese Recruited Him as Car Bomber
Jerusalem, April 13–A 16-year-old Lebanese was captured by Israeli troops hours before he was supposed to get into an explosive-laden car and go on a suicide bombing mission to blow up the Israeli Army headquarters in Lebanon....

What seems most striking about [Mohammed] Burro's account is that although he is a Shiite Moslem, he comes from a secular family background. He spent his free time not in prayer, he said, but riding his motorcycle and playing pinball. According to his account, he was not a fanatic who wanted to kill himself in the cause of Islam or anti-Zionism, but was recruited for the suicide mission through another means: blackmail. [p. A1]

If one wants to learn more about the motivations of the terrorists in the Middle East, this story is interesting because it is anomalous. The usual stereotype of the Shiite religious fanatic does not hold here. Instead, this story raises many new questions.

Some of the questions that were voiced by a class of graduate students when this story was read to them:

1. Why would someone commit suicide if he was not depressed?
2. Did the kid think he was going to die?
3. Are car bombers motivated like the Kamikaze?
4. Does pinball lead to terrorism?
5. Who blackmailed him?
6. What fate worse than death did they threaten him with?
7. Why are kids chosen for these missions?
8. Why do we hear about Lebanese car bombers and not about Israeli car bombers?
9. Why are they all named Mohammed?
10. How did the Israelis know where to make the raids?
11. How do Lebanese teenagers compare with American teenagers?

Some of these questions seem reasonable, (e.g., "Did the kid think he was going to die?"), but some are rather silly in retrospect (e.g., "Does pinball lead to terrorism?"). Some, though perfectly reasonable, are not central to the story but relate to other issues that a given student was reminded of, was wondering about, or was interested in (e.g., "Why do we hear about Lebanese car bombers and not about Israeli car bombers?").

The claim is that an understander has questions already extant in memory before it begins to read a story. These questions are left over from the understander's previous experiences. As the understander reads the story, it remembers these questions and thinks about them again in a new light. This raises further questions for the understander to think about. Many of these questions seek *explanations*, which are knowledge structures that allow the understander to answer its questions based on a causal understanding of the situation (e.g., "Kids are chosen because they are more gullible"). Explanations, in turn, can give rise to further questions (e.g., "Are Lebanese teenagers more gullible than American teenagers?").

Ultimately the understander is left with several new questions that may or may not have been asked before. Certainly, after reading the blackmail story, one expects to have several questions representing issues one was wondering about that were not resolved by the story. For example, in this story, it turns out that the boy was blackmailed into going on the bombing mission by a terrorist group that was threatening his parents. This makes one think about the question "What are family relations like in Lebanon?" This question remains in memory after reading the story. To the extent that one is interested in this question, one will read stories about the social life in Lebanon, and one will relate other stories to this one. To cite another

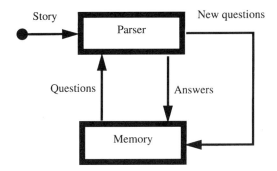

Figure 8.1
Question-driven understanding. In contrast to the traditional view of understanding as a "story-in, representations-out" process, we view understanding as a "questions + story-in, answered questions + new questions-out" process. This process is elaborated in figure 8.2.

example, one of the students in the class repeatedly related the story to his readings on the IRA because he was interested in similar issues about Ireland.

Understanding is a process of relating what one reads to the questions that one already has. These questions represent the knowledge goals of the understander, namely the things that the understander wants to learn (Dehn 1989; Hunter 1989; Ram 1987, 1989, 1990c; Schank 1986; Schank and Ram 1988). The purpose of reading is to find answers to these questions and thus to arrive at a more complete understanding of the issues one is interested in. However, while doing this, many new questions are often raised. These questions are stored in memory, and they in turn guide the understanding of future stories and affect the interpretations that are drawn. This process is shown in figure 8.1.

Although this type of reasoning may not be conscious, learning is motivated by a reasoner's goals and interests. When the reasoner encounters difficulties during understanding, planning, or any other task, it remembers the nature of these difficulties and learns in order to perform its tasks better in the future. The knowledge goals of the reasoner, which arise from these very difficulties, are used to focus the learning process. My model is very different from other approaches that rely on properties of the domain to determine what needs to be learned because it relies on the goals of the reasoner. For example, one might propose a rule, similar to that discussed by DeJong (1983), that the understander generalize a new schema whenever it reads a story in which a preservation goal (P-GOAL) is violated in a novel manner. But this should be so only if noticing violations of this P-GOAL is actually useful to the program. Any such rule must make a statement about the goals of the program, not just about the content of the domain. A similar argument can be made for the use of knowledge goals, or questions, to focus inference generation for understanding, explanation or diagnosis (Ram 1990c; Ram and Hunter 1992; Ram and Leake 1991).

In the following sections I argue that a goal-based model of learning is a plausible account of human behavior, and has computational advantages for the design of learning programs as well. The model raises two sets of issues:

- *Content.* What kinds of questions are there? How does the reasoner know which questions to ask?
- *Process.* What difference do questions make? What effect do they have on the understanding process? How do they affect what one learns? How are questions managed in memory?

These issues are discussed from a cognitive perspective as well as a computational one.

8.1.2 Cognitive Motivations: Questions as a Basis for Learning

When comparing the way people read newspaper stories with the way computer programs typically read them, notice the following differences:

Subjectivity. People are biased. They interpret stories in a manner that suits them. They jump to conclusions. Computer programs, on the other hand, are usually designed to read stories in an objective manner, and to extract the "correct" or "true" interpretation of a story to the extent that they can.

Variable-depth parsing. People do not read everything in great detail. They concentrate on details that they find relevant or interesting and skim over the rest. In contrast, computer programs are designed to attend to every aspect of a story that is within the scope of their knowledge structures. Consequently they either process the entire story in great depth or skim everything in the story. They cannot decide which aspects to process in detail and which ones to ignore.

Learning and change. People change as they read. They never read the same story twice in the same way. They notice different things during the second reading, or they simply get bored. After reading a story, they interpret other similar stories differently. Typical computer programs, in contrast, are not adaptive; they always read a given story the same way.

What makes people different from computer programs? What is the missing element that our theories do not yet account for? The answer is simple: People read newspaper stories for a reason: to learn more about what they are interested in. Computers, on the other hand, do not. In fact computers do not even have interests; there is nothing in particular that they are trying to learn when they read. If a computer program is to be a model of story understanding, it should also read for a "purpose."

Of course people have several goals that cannot be attributed to computers. One might read a restaurant guide in order to eventually satisfy hunger or entertainment goals or to find a good place for a business lunch. Computers do not get hungry, and computers do not have business lunches.

However, these physiological and social goals give rise to several intellectual or cognitive goals. A goal to satisfy hunger gives rise to goals to find information: the name of a restaurant that serves the desired type of food, how expensive the restaurant is, the location of the restaurant, and so on. These are goals to acquire information or knowledge and are knowledge goals. These goals can be held by computers too; a computer might "want" to find out the location of a restaurant and might read a guide in order to do so in the same way as a person would. Although such a goal would not arise out of hunger in the case of the computer, it might well arise out of the "goal" to learn more about restaurants.

In other words, knowledge goals also arise from the desire to learn, to pursue one's intellectual interests, to improve one's model of the world. These goals can be viewed as questions about the domain of interest. To be interested in terrorism, for example, is to have many questions about the various aspects of terrorism and to think about these questions in the context of input data, such as newspaper stories about terrorist incidents. The point of reading these stories is to answer one's questions as well as to reveal flaws or gaps in one's model of terrorism in order to improve this model. These gaps give rise to new questions which in turn stimulate further interest in terrorism. In this sense, both computers and people can be "interested" in terrorism.

In contrast with people, a computer has only one underlying goal: to learn and improve its world model.[1] However, this (and, in the case of people, other physical and social goals) gives rise to knowledge goals that then drive the understanding process. Understanding consists of using questions to focus attention on relevant or interesting aspects of the input, answering these questions using information provided by the input, and asking new questions based on unusual or unexpected aspects of the input. This process is illustrated in figure 8.2.

My theory of questions and question asking is based on a functional account of the role of questions in understanding and learning. However, similar arguments have been made based on empirical results in psychology and education. For example, Ng and Bereiter (1991) identified three types of learning goals in students undergoing a course in BASIC programming: task-completion goals, instructional goals, and knowledge-building goals. Students oriented toward knowledge-building goals (similar to what I am calling *questions*) were distinctive in many ways; they "actively constructed learning agendas for themselves, used prior knowledge to make sense of

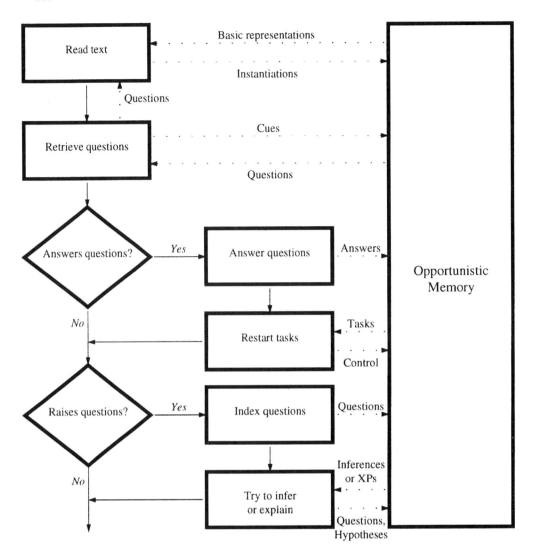

Figure 8.2
Control structure: The understanding cycle. A fact is interesting if it satisfies a knowledge goal currently pending in memory, or if it gives rise to new knowledge goals. Uninteresting facts pass vertically down with minimal processing; interesting facts cause suspended understanding tasks to be restarted or new tasks to be created. New tasks can give rise to new knowledge goals, which are suspended along with the tasks if answers are not yet known and cannot be inferred. This process implements the question-driven understanding model of figure 8.1.

what they were learning, and used their new learning in turn to reconsider their prior knowledge." Scardamalia and Bereiter's (1991) educational environment, CSILE, is based on an analysis of the types of questions asked by students, which is similar to the analysis of questions in this chapter. These empirical results are consistent with my theory of questions and question-driven understanding, and they provide further support for my claim that better question asking leads to better learning.

Although in this chapter I use story understanding as the reasoning task, a similar argument can be made for other reasoning tasks. Understanding, in general, is also subjective and adaptive, as are other cognitive processes such as problem solving and design. A similar functional analysis could be performed for these tasks as well, and yield taxonomies of questions similar to those presented in this chapter. These question taxonomies overlap with the one in this chapter to the extent that the same subtasks (e.g., explanation) are used in different reasoning situations (e.g., diagnosis). Similar questions or knowledge goals can then arise in the service of different reasoning tasks, and similar mechanisms can then be used for question management and learning. For example, Birnbaum (1986) arrived at similar conclusions about the indexing and opportunistic retrieval of pending goals during real-time planning and plan execution, based on an analysis of Zeigarnik's (1927) experiments demonstrating enhanced memorability of unsatisfied goals during the performance of various tasks.

8.1.3 Computational Motivations: What Are the Knowledge Goals of an Understanding Program?

Learning then can be viewed as the pursuit of one's interests or questions. However, it defeats the theoretical purpose to build a "question-asking" or "interest-pursuing" program per se. Instead, questions and interests should arise naturally as cognitive goals of the program during various stages of the reasoning process. This means that the program should ask a question only when it needs to acquire that piece of knowledge. For example, in the case of a story understanding system, a knowledge goal should be formulated only when the system requires the answer for the purposes of understanding the story. In other words, knowledge goals should be functionally useful to the overall goals of the system.

Similarly, if a student is to ask a question or formulate a knowledge goal, the teacher must provide a context in which the student requires the answer for a particular purpose. Again this requires an analysis of the functional role of questions in the context of a learning task involving understanding, problem solving, or design. Although problem solving or design contexts may be more appropriate to some teaching goals (e.g., scientific discovery), the task of understanding novel and unusual situations can also provide interesting contexts (e.g., teaching geography in the context of a mystery story). Understanding and problem-solving tasks may also be combined (e.g., teaching economics in the context of a market situation; Shute et al. 1988). In this chapter I focus on an analysis of understanding tasks from a point of view of question generation. A similar approach could be used for the analysis for problem-solving or design tasks as well.

My theory of questions is based on a theory of *understanding tasks*, the basic tasks of an understander. In addition to parser-level tasks such as noun group connection and pronoun reference, these tasks include higher-level tasks such as the integration of facts with what the understander already knows, the detection of anomalies in the text that identify flaws or gaps in the understander's model of the domain, the formulation of explanations to resolve those anomalies, the confirmation and refutation of potential explanations, and the learning of new explanations for use in understanding future situations. These are the basic tasks that an understander needs to be able to perform.

In order to carry out these tasks, the understander needs to integrate the text, which is often ambiguous, elliptic, and vague, with its world knowledge, which is often incomplete. In formulating an explanation, for example, the understander may need to know more about the situation than is explicitly stated. However, it is impossible to anticipate when a particular piece of knowledge will be available to the understander because the real world (in the case of a story understanding program, the story) will not always provide exactly that piece of knowledge at exactly the time that the understander requires it. Thus the understander must be able to suspend questions in memory and to reactivate them just when the information needed becomes available. In other words, the understander must be able to remember what knowledge is needed and why.

Furthermore the system's understanding of any real-world domain can never be quite complete. Conventional script-, frame-, or schema-based theories assume that understanding means finding an appropriate script, frame, or schema in memory and fitting it to the story. Schemas in memory are assumed to be "correct" in the sense that they are completely understood and constitute a correct model of the domain. If an applicable schema is found, an instance of the schema is created and applied to the story. The story is then assumed to be "understood." However, this model is inadequate because an understander's memory is always incomplete. Knowledge structures often have gaps in them, especially in poorly understood domains. These gaps correspond to what the understander has not yet understood about the domain. Even if a schema appears to be correct, novel experiences or stories may reveal flaws in the schema or a mismatch with the real world. Furthermore the schema may not be indexed correctly in memory.

Understanding tasks, therefore, generate information subgoals or *questions*, which represent what the understander needs to know to perform the current task, be it

A Theory of Questions and Question Asking

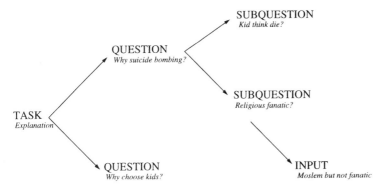

Figure 8.3
Inferences supporting the religious fanatic hypothesis, illustrating the idea of understanding as a process of question transformation.

explanation, learning, or any other cognitive task. These questions constitute the specific knowledge goals of the understander. Learning is a process of seeking answers to these questions in the input, which in turn raises new questions while answering old ones.

For example, in order to understand the blackmail story S-1, the system must understand the motivations of the would-be suicide bomber (an explanation task). In other words, it must formulate the question "Why would the boy have done the suicide bombing?" The desired explanation for the suicide bomber's actions constitutes an answer to this question. The explanation task gives rise to further questions and subquestions. Ultimately the system finds an answer to a question in the input story which enables it to complete its explanation task. Thus understanding can be viewed as a process of question transformation, as shown in figure 8.3.

If novel answers to questions are found, or if standard hypotheses are refuted, the system can learn a new fact or can modify an old belief. When a new piece of information comes in, the understander determines whether a question pending in memory can be answered. If a question is answered, the source of the question determines the further processing that needs to be done on the new piece of information. In other words, the task that gave rise to the question now receives the new information, which is then processed by that task.

For example, consider the following sentence:

S-2: The boy was sixteen years old.

What inferences should be drawn from this sentence? Suppose that this is used to answer the question, "Was the boy a teenager?" This now tells the understander that it was the fact that he was a teenager, as opposed to being male or sixteen years old, that is important. Furthermore the understander also knows why this is important because it knows why the question was asked in the first place. For example, if the question arose from a memory-level similarity-based generalization task, the understander might now try to construct a new generalization in memory, say, that suicide bombers in Lebanon are often teenagers. Alternatively, if the understander was trying to confirm the hypothesis that the boy was recruited because he was a gullible teenager, the understander would then try to confirm that explanation. This requires the understander to determine whether the boy was gullible. Because it is computationally intractable to draw all possible inferences from every fact, it is essential for the understander to be able to focus attention on inferences that are likely to be useful in learning.

This example illustrates how an understander can use its questions to focus the reasoning process. The computational advantage of this approach is that it provides the system with a principled way of determining what it should learn and which inferences it should draw so that its attention can be focused on the knowledge needed for a given task.

8.1.4 Question-Driven Learning

I argued that modeling goal-driven behavior is a reasonable task from the point of view of cognitive modeling and also that the ability to suspend and reactivate questions is essential to deal flexibly with real-world input. This view has strong implications for theories of learning. I view learning as an incremental process of theory formation, involving both case-based reasoning and explanation-based learning processes. In general, any learning system would have incomplete knowledge of its domain because, by definition, it is still learning about that domain. These gaps give rise to difficulties during processing and drive the system to learn. The system learns in an incremental manner, by noticing interesting aspects of novel stories and generating questions and by filling in the gaps in its memory that correspond to questions answered from previous experiences.

Learning can be broadly classified into two types: the acquisition of new knowledge and the reorganization of existing knowledge. Corresponding to these types of learning, we can distinguish between *knowledge acquisition goals* and *knowledge organization goals*, respectively. In the former case, the system learns by acquiring a new piece of knowledge (e.g., by acquiring a new knowledge structure or by acquiring new knowledge that fills a gap in an existing knowledge structure). In the latter case, the system learns by organizing or reorganizing what it already knows (e.g., by learning a new way to index an existing knowledge structure). Each type of knowledge goal corresponds to a class of gaps in the system's knowledge.

What is done with the newly learned information depends on the kind of "knowledge gap" the system is trying to fill. In an explanation-based understander the new piece of knowledge may result in a new explanation in memory; it could be used to fill in a gap in an existing explanation, it could be used to elaborate an existing explanation if that explanation was not detailed enough to deal with the new situation, or it could be used to reorganize or reindex knowledge in memory to allow the reasoner to use what it already knows in novel situations to which that piece of knowledge had not been applied before (Ram 1993). Each type of learning leaves the system a little closer to a complete understanding of its domain. Each type of learning may also result in a new set of questions as the system realizes what else it needs to learn, which in turn drives the system toward further learning.

8.2 Computer Model of Question-Driven Understanding and Learning

I have developed a computational model of this process in a natural language understanding domain. AQUA (asking questions and understanding answers) is a question-driven story understanding program that learns about terrorism by reading newspaper stories covering unusual terrorist incidents in the Middle East (Ram 1987, 1989; Schank and Ram 1988). AQUA builds causal and motivational explanations for the events in the story in order to understand why the characters acted as they did or why certain events did or did not occur.

AQUA's basic goal in reading is to answer its questions and to improve its understanding of the domain (terrorism). AQUA's output consists of answers to old questions about the domain plus, of course, new questions. A specific example illustrating questions generated and answered during the reading of two stories is shown in figure 8.4. AQUA is driven by its questions or knowledge goals. It is a dynamic program, and it reads similar stories differently and forms different interpretations as its questions and interests evolve. AQUA would reread a story differently from the way it first read the story because the questions and explanations generated during the first reading affect the questions raised on the second reading.

My model of question-driven understanding and learning is summarized in table 8.1. The chief aspects of this process are the algorithms for the tasks of text interpretation, inference control, explanation, and learning. These algorithms are integrated using the generation and answering of questions as a unifying framework. Each task is sensitive to the current set of questions of the system and can raise new questions during its execution. Rather than being preprogrammed, questions are generated dynamically based on the requirements of the current task. Questions are indexed in an opportunistic memory, with suspended understanding tasks that are awaiting the answers. This means that the system knows not only what it wants to

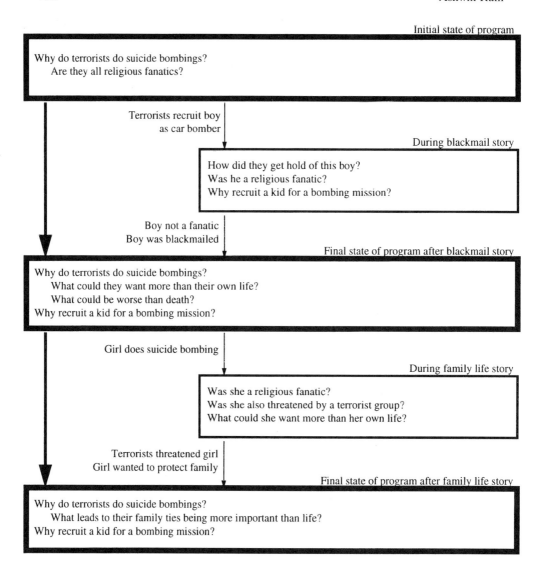

Figure 8.4
Questions in, questions out. Question-driven understanding is a process of asking questions and trying to answer them by reading a story. The understander starts out with a set of questions. At it reads, some of these questions are answered, and new questions are raised. After reading the story, the understander is left with a new set of questions, and these questions are the starting point for reading future stories. Here the understander has read two stories, one about a boy being blackmailed into going on a suicide bombing mission in which no further details are given and another about a girl being "persuaded" to commit a suicidal terrorist attack by a terrorist group who threatened her family.

Table 8.1
Processing cycle in AQUA

Read some text, focusing attention on interesting input as determined below. Build minimal representations in memory.

Determine interestingness of new input based on previous questions (the **retrieve questions** step below) and on new questions (the **ask questions** and **build explanations** steps).

Retrieve questions indexed in memory that might be relevant. Use these questions as an interestingness measure to focus the **read** step above.

Answer questions retrieved in the previous step, and restart the suspended process that was waiting for this piece of information. Learn from novel answers to questions.

Ask questions based on new input. Index new questions in memory, and use these questions as an interestingness measure to focus the **read** step above.

Build explanations to explain anomalous input identified by anomaly detection questions. Index new questions raised by this process in memory, and use these questions as an interestingness measure to focus the **read** step above.

Note: Learning occurs in the **answer questions** step, in which AQUA learns from novel answers to its questions, and in the **ask questions** step, in which AQUA "learns" new questions to ask in different situations.

find out but why it needs that piece of information. The architecture of the system is shown in figure 8.2.

Memory plays an important role in the construction of explanations for the purposes of understanding. As is discussed later in section 8.4, the understander relies on its memory of past experiences to provide potential explanations for new stories. However, the system's memory does not always contain "correct" cases or "correct" explanations, but rather one or more hypotheses about what the correct explanation might have been.[2] These hypotheses often have questions attached to them, representing what is still not understood or verified about those hypotheses. As the system reads new stories, it is reminded of past cases and of old explanations. In attempting to apply these explanations to the new situation, it also remembers previously unanswered questions. The system's understanding of its cases gradually gets refined as these questions get answered (Ram 1989, 1990b, 1993).

Much of real-world learning is an incremental process of this type. A reasoner learns by modifying what it already knows using pieces of new information that it acquires during its experiences. AQUA, the program described in this chapter, implements the model of question generation and learning. The basic process in AQUA is one of question transformation (figure 8.4). The questions that AQUA asks, and the hypotheses that it formulates, change as it reads. As AQUA learns more about the domain, it asks better and more detailed questions, both "basic information questions" and "wonderment questions" (Scardamalia and Bereiter 1991). AQUA also gets "bored" if a story does not raise any new questions that it finds interesting by virtue of its interestingness criteria. Curiosity and interest are fundamental components of human learning; AQUA's question transformation process is an attempt to model this kind of learning.

Although this model was developed in the context of a story understanding task, I expect my theory of active question-driven learning to be applicable to a wide range of cognitive tasks. For example, Hunter presents a theory of learning based on "knowledge acquisition goals" for the diagnosis of lung tumors (Hunter 1989) and for scientific discovery in molecular biology (Hunter 1990). In addition to modeling reasoning tasks, my theory can also help in the design of educational environments. For example, Scardamalia and Bereiter (1991) examine concrete issues that have arisen from their attempts to implement a particular innovative educational environment. The environment they have created, CSILE, encourages students to collaborate with each other as they are learning, and in particular, encourages the asking of questions. Scardamalia and Bereiter examine whether students are capable of creating their own curricula by first asking questions, and then determining which set of questions will be productive to follow up on. The design of such environments depends on a theory of questions. In the AQUA model many interesting questions arise from the detection of anomalies and the formulation of explanations to resolve these anomalies. This suggests, for example, that it may be useful to put students into situations in which they encounter anomalies or unexpected events and to allow them to pose questions in the pursuit of explanations and explore different hypotheses as they try to make sense of the situation.

8.3 Nature of Questions

I argued that questions play a central role in learning, and I presented both cognitive and functional arguments for a theory of question-based understanding and learning. In this section I consider the nature of questions in more detail. Further details of the understanding and explanation aspects of AQUA are presented in the next section.

Much of the discussion here focuses on processing issues in question-asking and learning. In addition I argue that it is important for the understander to ask the "right" questions to make sure that it focuses on relevant issues and does not miss the point of the story. The depth of understanding that the understander achieves depends on the questions that it asks. Thus it is also necessary to develop a content theory of questions and a taxonomy of the types of questions that an understander might ask. Of particular interest to the problem of understanding goal-based stories is the underlying model of motivational explanations, which will be discussed along with the questions associated with this model.

8.3.1 Sources of Knowledge Goals
Questions arise from gaps in a reasoner's domain knowledge. This could happen in three ways:

Novel situation. In a truly novel situation an applicable case or schema may not be available. The reasoner simply does not have a prior experience that provides it with a case that is relevant to the current situation.

Misindexed knowledge. The reasoner may have a case or schema that is applicable to the current situation but may be unable to retrieve it, since the case is not indexed under the cues that the situation provided.

Incorrect or incompletely understood knowledge. Previous experiences, especially in novel and complex domains, may not have been completely understood, so cases or schemas corresponding to them may be incomplete or incorrect.

In all these circumstances the understander has an opportunity to learn by further refining or altering the case or schema, by reindexing it in memory, or by answering the questions attached to it. I consider each situation in turn.

8.3.2 Knowledge Structures Are Not Perfect
Conventional script, frame or schema-based theories assume that understanding means finding an appropriate script, frame or schema[3] in memory and fitting it to the story (e.g., Cullingford 1978; DeJong 1979). Schemas in memory are assumed to be "correct" in the sense that they are completely understood and constitute a correct model of the domain. If an applicable schema is found, it is instantiated and the story is assumed to be "understood."

However, this model is inadequate, since in practice an understander's memory will always be incomplete. Knowledge structures often have gaps in them, especially in poorly understood domains. These gaps correspond to what the understander has not yet understood about the domain. Even if a schema appears to be correct, novel experiences or stories may reveal flaws in the schema or a mismatch with the real world. Furthermore the schema may not be indexed correctly in memory.

8.3.3 Misindexed Knowledge Structures
If a ready-made schema cannot be found that fits the story perfectly because the schema is not indexed correctly in memory, a conventional schema-based understander would simply fail. However, in a realistically sized memory, knowledge

structures would not always be indexed with every conceivable and relevant scenario; also, the understander could not be expected to try all possible structures in every situation. For example, one would not expect the blackmail schema to be associated with suicide bombing a priori, nor would one want to draw on the blackmail hypothesis each time a suicide bombing is encountered.

8.3.4 Gaps in Knowledge Structures

Even if a relevant schema is found, the understander's knowledge of the scenario is often incomplete. Clearly it is impossible to input all knowledge about every situation into our computers. Instead, we expect that many schemas will be incomplete, that many will have questions attached to them representing what the understander did not understand about those situations in the past, or that many will be simply very sketchy.

In the blackmail story, for example, even if one assumes that blackmail was known to be a possible explanation for suicide bombing, it could hardly be a fully fleshed out causal chain. There would be many gaps in that chain, many questions attached to that explanation: How does one blackmail a child? What could anyone want more at the expense of his or her own life? In such a situation there is more to understanding a story than fitting it into a schema; the understander has the opportunity to answer some of these pending questions if the story happens to provide these answers and thus to improve its understanding of the scenario represented by the schema.

8.3.5 Incremental Refinement of Knowledge Structures

Even if the schema appears to be perfectly self-contained and complete, new stories that differ in small but interesting ways can raise other questions about the scenario, questions that the understander could not have anticipated in advance. The religious fanatic explanation for suicide bombings in the Middle East, for example, is one that most people raise and apply automatically, but there are many stories about fanatics that are just a little different from the standard scenario. For example, consider applying the religious fanatic explanation to the following story (*Los Angeles Times*, April 10, 1985):

S-3: 4 Die in Suicide Attack against Israelis

Jerusalem, April 10—A young guerrilla driving a car filled with explosives blew it up in a suicide attack Tuesday against a group of Israeli guards in Lebanon, killing three and wounding two others, an Israeli military source confirmed.

Besides the driver, identified by the guerrilla group as a 16-year-old girl, the blast killed two Israeli soldiers and a Druze member of the Israeli-backed South Lebanon Army. The wounded were Israeli soldiers, the source said....

A spokesman for the group identified the driver as Sana Mohaydaleh. In an interview taped before the incident and shown Tuesday after the attack on Beirut television, a girl identified as Mohaydaleh said: "I hope that my soul will unite with the souls of all the martyrs before me. I decided on martyrdom to free our land because I saw the misery of my countrymen under the occupation. I hope I will be successful and able to kill the highest number possible of our enemies."

Assuming that the understander has previous knowledge about religious fanatics, this story fits pretty well into the mold of a stereotypical scenario. Conventional understanders would be able to apply the schema to the story, but they would ignore the novel aspects of the story that are often the most interesting aspects. Instead, an understander should be able to focus on these aspects of the story and learn from them by modifying its schemas to accommodate these variations. This kind of incremental learning is an essential part of the understanding process.

While reading the story S-3, an understander might think about why these suicide bombers are all teenagers or about the strange fact that a television interview with this girl was videotaped before the mission. Is there something general to be learned by reading this story? Certainly, these issues are more interesting than other more stereotypical facts in the story, such as what kind of car was used or how many people were killed. These are the issues that the understander should focus on in this story.

8.3.6 Interestingness and the Focus of Attention Problem

Combinatorial explosion of inferences has always been one of the classic problems in AI. Resources are limited, and inferences potentially infinite; a reasoner needs to be able to determine which inferences are useful to draw from a given piece of text. However, unless one considers the goals of the reasoner, it is very difficult to give a principled definition of what it means for an inference to be "useful."

The pragmatic need to focus attention provides a functional context in which to develop a theory of questions. Knowledge goals, the goals of a reasoner to acquire some piece of knowledge required for a reasoning task, can be used as the focusing criteria for inference control. Knowledge goals correspond to the interests of the reasoner. This approach then provides the basis for a theory of interestingness that is functionally motivated by consideration of the needs of the reasoner.

A program that uses knowledge goals to guide understanding is an improvement over one that processes everything in equal detail, that is, one that is completely text driven. An understander that is completely text driven processes everything in detail in the hope that it might turn out to be relevant. To avoid this, the understander should draw only those inferences that help it determine what it needs to know. In other words, the understander should use its knowledge goals to focus its attention on the interesting aspects of the story, where "interesting" can be defined as "relating to something the understander wants to find out about."[4] This idea is similar to that of "goal-guided inference" in social cognition (Zukier 1986), to the "goal satisfaction principle" of Hayes-Roth and Lesser (1976), which states that more processing should be given to knowledge sources whose responses are most likely to satisfy processing goals, and to the "relevance principle" of Sperber and Wilson (1986), which states that humans pay attention only to information that seems relevant to them. These principles make sense because cognitive processes are geared to achieving a large cognitive effect for a small effort. To achieve this, the understander must focus its attention on what seems to it to be the most relevant information available (Sperber and Wilson 1986).

Why would an understander need to find something out in the first place? Ultimately the point of reading is to learn more about the world. Questions arise when reading a story reveals gaps or inconsistencies in the world model. It is useful to focus attention on such questions because they arise from a "need to learn." For example, questions arising from anomalous facts are more useful than those arising from routine stereotypical facts because in the former case the understander may learn something new about the world.

There are two basic ways in which a fact can turn out to be worth processing, corresponding to the two diamonds in figure 8.2:

Top-down. A fact that answers a question is worth focusing on because it helps to achieve a knowledge goal of the understander, which in turn allows the understander to continue the reasoning task that was awaiting the answer.

Bottom-up. A fact that raises new questions is worth focusing on if the questions arise from a gap or inconsistency in the understander's knowledge base because the understander may be able to improve its knowledge base by learning something new about the world.

These can be viewed as heuristics for focusing attention. The decision to focus attention corresponds closely with the notion of "interestingness." When an understander focuses on a particular fact and processes it in greater detail, it can be said to be "interested" in that fact.[5] For this reason, focus of attention heuristics can also be thought of as interestingness heuristics. These heuristics provide a functional definition of "interestingness" as a criterion for focusing attention. Interestingness is a guess at what one thinks one might learn from paying attention to a fact or a question. The guess must be made without processing the fact or question in detail because otherwise the purpose of focusing attention to control inferences would be defeated. Thus the interestingness heuristics used in AQUA are indeed heuristics rather than precise measures of the value of thinking about a fact or a question. Readers interested in this aspect of question-driven understanding are referred to Ram (1990c) and Ram and Hunter (1992) for more details.

8.3.7 Opportunism and the Memory Model

It would of course be impractical to maintain a list of "pending questions" and to check every question in that list every time a new fact was encountered. Thus questions, with suspended understanding tasks that gave rise to them, must be indexed in memory. AQUA's memory model is based on the theory of dynamic memory (Kolodner 1984; Lebowitz 1983; Schank 1982). Rather than build an independent representation, which then has to be integrated into memory and related to previous episodes as a separate stage in the understanding process, an understander parses text directly into memory and relates it to its questions. In turn this memory and, in particular, the questions currently in memory are actively used to guide the parser as previously described.

Because questions are indexed in memory, it is quite likely that an understander will find the answers to questions other than the one it is thinking about while reading. In other words, knowledge goals can be satisfied *opportunistically* during the course of understanding. Birnbaum (1986) made a similar argument for the opportunistic pursuit of goals during planning. Questions that are formed during understanding may be ones raised earlier in the same story or even during some other previously read story.

For example, one of the questions that is raised during many suicide bombing stories is: Why are children chosen for these missions? One doesn't actively and constantly think about this question, of course. However, answers to questions like these often are forthcoming even when the question is only "at the back of one's mind." Consider the following story (*New Haven Register*, August 6, 1988):

S-4: 200,000 Children in World's Armed Forces, Study Finds

Geneva, August 6—An estimated 200,000 children are under arms worldwide, most of them forcibly recruited but some urged to enlist by their parents....

According to the survey, examples of the problem reportedly included:

- Illegal street roundups in Afghanistan to recruit youths under 15.
- Abduction of boys under the legal draft age of 18 by army recruiters in El Salvador.
- Lowering of Iran's conscription age to 13, with voluntary enlistment by parental consent for younger children.
- Introduction by South Africa of compulsory military training at age 16....
- Use of volunteers under age 15 in Honduras and Morocco. (p. 5)

This story provides an answer, in fact several possible answers, to questions of why children are recruited for suicide bombing missions in Lebanon. If the understander is interested in and is reminded of this question when reading this story, this opportunity can be used to answer the question or to propose new hypotheses. Thus questions can be answered opportunistically, either within the same story in which they were raised or during future stories.

8.4 Question-Based Model of Interpretation and Explanation

I now turn to the implications of the model for the tasks of text interpretation and explanation in the context of story understanding and learning, and I discuss the implementation of the model in the AQUA program. Methodologically I used AQUA as a test bed for exploring issues of interpretation, learning, explanation, and interestingness in an integrated framework. The domain of AQUA is that of newspaper stories about terrorism. In addition to the "factual" stories that many understanding programs deal with, AQUA reads "human interest" stories in the terrorism domain. It can achieve a better level of understanding of these stories than conventional script- and MOP-based understanders, since its questions need not only be generated from slots in stereotypical scripts or MOPs.[6] In fact many interesting questions about a story arise from the detection of anomalies in the story and from the construction of explanations for those anomalies. These questions are used to guide understanding in the same way as questions from other sources.

Since questions represent the knowledge goals of the understander, they also provide the focus for learning. In addition to asking questions, AQUA can therefore learn from answers to these questions. As implemented, AQUA improves its explanatory knowledge of its domain by incremental refinement of this knowledge using answers to questions that arise from the explanation process (Ram 1990b, 1993). In this section I describe the underlying model of question-driven text interpretation and explanation which form the basis for the AQUA program.

8.4.1 Question-Driven Interpretation of Natural Language Text

In my theory, reading is viewed as a "plan" to learn more about the world. The understander's world model grows more complete as it reads a story and relates it to gaps and questions in memory. Ideally only those inferences should be drawn that lead to conclusions required by the program. In practice, however, this is not always possible. Given that the basic task of a question-based understanding program is to answer questions in its memory by reading stories, there is an obvious choice to be made in the design of the program as characterized by the following extremes:

Text-driven program. A program that is totally text driven will read the text, build representations for it, and then process it to determine whether it addressed any questions in memory.
Question-driven program. A program that is totally question driven will select the most interesting or urgent question in memory and answer it via inference, reading text, or any other available method.

Each of these approaches has its disadvantages. The text- or data-driven method relies completely on bottom-up processes. It processes everything in detail in the hope that everything will be relevant. However, we want the program to concentrate on those aspects that are of immediate interest to it. In other words, we want the process to be driven by the interests or goals of the understander.

The goal- or question-driven method, in the purest sense, relies too heavily on top-down processing. It sees only what it is looking for already. Such a program is not be able to learn from unexpected input. Another disadvantage of the purely question-driven method is that it expends resources in trying to answer a question immediately; therefore it might be advantageous to design a program that indexes the question in memory, to be answered later when the opportunity arises. Last, so as not to overlook obvious information and to be sufficiently sensitive to the exigencies of the input, the process should incorporate some features of the data-driven method. The interaction between these requirements is nontrivial.

This dilemma has long been recognized in theories of text understanding, and various compromises between the two approaches have been proposed. For example, Kintsch's (1988) construction-integration approach involves bottom-up processing to construct a "text base" that is then integrated into a coherent whole. This approach is in contrast to top-down approaches in which language analysis proceeds in a top-down predictive manner, and bottom-up processing is invoked only when expectations fail (e.g., Schank 1978). However, these theories do not take into account the learning goals of the understander. There is a static notion of what it means to "understand" a story, usually defined in terms of coherence relationships at some arbitrary level of detail. Typical story understanding systems are designed either to read stories in depth (e.g., BORIS; see Dyer 1982; Lehnert et al. 1983) or to skim stories (e.g., FRUMP; see DeJong 1979). However, these systems cannot decide the depth to which the story should be processed or which inferences should be drawn during the understanding process because they do not maintain an explicit model of their learning goals. In other words, such systems are not trying to learn about anything in particular; they are merely reading.

At some level, of course, the task of the understanding process is to integrate the components of the text with the relevant components of the understander's memory into a coherent whole, given some suitable definition of coherence, for example, "event concept coherence" (Alterman 1985). In an active reader this integration is directed by the goals, or questions, of the system. Questions then are used to focus attention on those aspects of the story that allow the understander to learn something of interest to its needs. This is the basis of AQUA's question-driven understanding algorithm.

AQUA is designed as a compromise between the bottom-up and top-down approaches. The basic understanding cycle that it uses is as follows: The parser reads the story word by word, trying to build a basic conceptual structure to represent the input. As quickly as possible, this structure is related to the questions in memory. If the new structure answers a question in memory, the inferences that were awaiting that answer are restarted. Thus the program only draws those inferences that are required to match the new structure to the question and those that are demanded by the task that generated the question in the first place.

This method is called *variable-depth parsing*. The process is data driven to the extent that pieces of the input for which there are no explicit expectations but which are likely to be relevant are processed to the extent necessary to determine their relevance. In practice, this means that there is a set of bottom-up questions that the program always asks of incoming text. Further processing of the input is goal driven and is done only if these questions raise other questions that need answers or if the input turns out to answer some question already in memory. These correspond to the two diamonds in figure 8.2. These diamonds attempt to determine which facts the understander should focus on.[7]

8.4.2 Theory of Explanation

The major emphasis in the development of AQUA was on the questions that arise during, and in support of, the explanation process. AQUA's theory of explanation is based on the claim that new explanations are built not by chaining inference rules together but by reusing explanations that have been encountered in previous situations and are already known to the system. Previously encountered explanations are represented as stereotypical patterns of causality, known as *explanation patterns* (XPs; see Schank 1986). AQUA builds on Schank's theory of explanation patterns in three ways. First, a content theory of volitional explanations for motivational analysis is proposed. Second, a graph-based representation of the structure of explanation patterns is introduced. Third, the process of case-based explanation, while similar to that used by the SWALE program (a system using explanation patterns that was developed under Schank; see Kass et al. 1986), is formulated in a question-based framework. My emphasis is on the questions that underly the creation, verification, and learning of explanations, and not on the creative adaptation process described in Kass, Leake, and Owens (1986). The main points of my theory are summarized below; further details may be found in Ram (1989, 1990a).

8.4.2.1 Content Theory of Volitional Explanations The content of explanations is specific to the domain of interest. AQUA's task of understanding human interest stories depends on a theory of motivational analysis, the construction of volitional explanations to describes the planning behavior of agents. The representation of explanatory cases in this domain is based on the theory of decision models, which describes the planning process that an agent goes through in considering whether to perform an action. A decision model relates the actions in which the characters in the story are involved to the outcomes that those actions had for them; to the goals, beliefs, emotional states, social states of the characters, and the priorities or orderings among the goals; and to the decision process that the characters go through in considering their goals, goal-orderings and likely outcomes of the actions before deciding whether to perform those actions. A detailed volitional explanation involving the planning decisions of a character is called a *decision model* and is illustrated in figure 8.5. An example of a decision model representing the stereotypical religious fanatic explanation is shown in figure 8.6.

8.4.2.2 Structure of Explanation Patterns AQUA has several XPs indexed in memory, representing its causal knowledge of the terrorism domain. These XPs are represented as graphs in figures 8.5 and 8.6. The XPs have four main components:

PRE-XP-NODES. Nodes that represent what is known before the XP is applied. One of these nodes, the EXPLAINS node, represents the particular action being explained.
XP-ASSERTED-NODES. Nodes asserted by the XP as the explanation for the EXPLAINS node. These make up the premises of the explanation.
INTERNAL-XP-NODES. Internal nodes asserted by the XP to link the XP-ASSERTED-NODES to the EXPLAINS node.
LINKS. Causal links asserted by the XP. These, together with the INTERNAL-XP-NODES, are also called the internals of the XP.

An explanation pattern states that the XP-ASSERTED-NODES lead to the EXPLAINS node (which is part of a particular configuration of PRE-XP-NODES) via a set of INTERNAL-XP-NODES, the nodes being causally linked together via the LINKS (which in turn can invoke further XPs). In other words, an XP represents a causal chain composed of a set of nodes connected together using a set of LINKS (causal rules or XPs). The "antecedent" (or premise) of this causal chain is the set

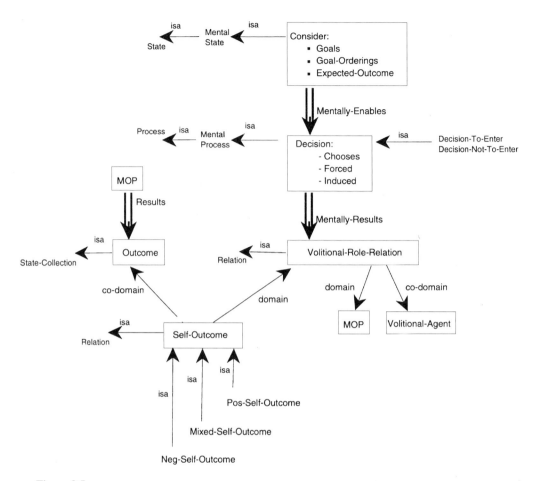

Figure 8.5
Structure of volitional explanations. A volitional-agent participates in some volitional-role in a mop, which then results in an outcome (a collection of states). Before this, the volitional-agent undergoes a decision process in which he considers his goals, goal-orderings, and expected-outcome, which then mentally-results in the volitional-role-relation being considered becoming true (in) or false (out) depending on the outcome of the decision.

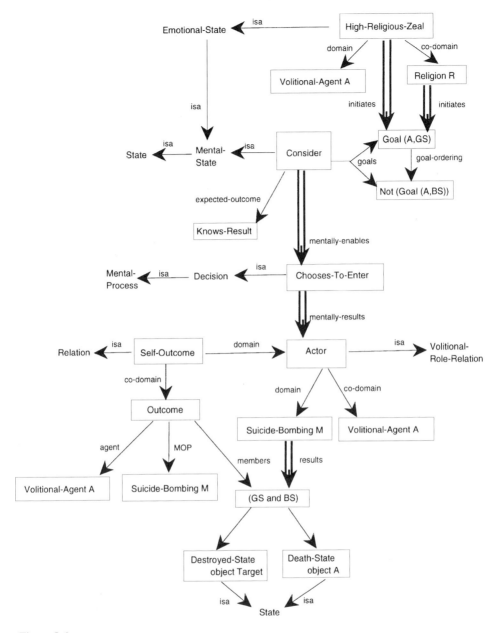

Figure 8.6
Religious fanatic explanation pattern. *A* is the agent, *R* his religion, *M* the action he chooses to do, and *GS* and *BS* the good and bad outcomes for *A* as a result of doing that action. *A* considers his goals to achieve *GS* and to prevent *BS*, the relative priorities of the two goals, and volitionally chooses to perform *M* knowing both expected outcomes of *M*, the `death-state` of *A* and the `destroyed-state` of the `target`.

of XP-ASSERTED-NODES, the "internal nodes" of the causal chain are the INTERNAL-XP-NODES of the XP, and the "consequent" is the EXPLAINS node. The difference between XP-ASSERTED-NODES and INTERNAL-XP-NODES is that the former are merely asserted by the XP without further explanation, whereas the latter have causal antecedents within the XP itself.

8.4.2.3 Process Model for Explanation An explanation-based understander must be able to detect anomalies in the input and resolve them by building motivational and causal explanations for the events in the story. In this way it can understand why the characters acted as they did or why certain events did or did not occur. This process characterizes both "story understanders" that try to achieve a deep understanding of the stories that they read and programs that need to understand their domains in service of other problem-solving tasks. Explanations are constructed by retrieving XPs from memory, applying them to the situation at hand, and verifying or evaluating the resulting hypotheses. This process consists of the following steps:

Anomaly detection. Anomaly detection refers to the process of identifying an unusual fact that needs explanation. The anomalous fact may be unusual in the sense that it violates or contradicts some piece of information in memory. Alternatively, the fact may be unusual because, although there is no explicit contradiction, the reasoner fails to integrate the fact satisfactorily in its memory.

Explanation pattern retrieval. When faced with an anomalous situation, the reasoner tries to retrieve one or more explanation patterns that would explain the situation. Ideally an XP should be indexed in memory so that it is retrieved only in those situations in which it is applicable. In practice, the indexes to an XP represent the system's best guess at characterizing the situations to which the XP is likely to be applicable. In AQUA, indexes to volitional XPs consist of stereotypical situations or contexts in which the XP might be encountered and of stereotypical categories of actors to whom the XPs might be applicable. These are called *situation indexes* and *character stereotype indexes*, respectively. A third type of index, the *anomaly category index*, represents the category of the XP required to explain a given type of anomaly.

Explanation pattern application. Once a set of potentially applicable XPs is retrieved, the reasoner tries to use them to resolve the anomaly. This involves instantiating the XPs, filling in the details through elaboration and specification, and checking the validity of the final explanations. The problem arises when the XP being applied has pending questions attached to it. If this occurs, these questions are instantiated and used to focus the understanding process. If the instantiated questions are answered by reading the story, answers to the questions are generalized and used to modify the original XP by answering the general questions attached to the XP.

Hypothesis verification and evaluation. The final step in the explanation process is the confirmation or refutation of possible explanations, or, if there is more than one hypothesis, discrimination between the alternatives. A hypothesis is a causal graph that connects the premises of the explanation to the conclusions via a set of intermediate assertions. At the end of this step, the reasoner is left with one or more alternative hypotheses and a set of new questions raised by these hypotheses.

8.4.2.4 Questions and Explanations From the point of view of questions, the process model for the task of explanation can be formulated as follows:

Anomaly Detection

- Ask anomaly detection questions based on the goals, goal-orderings, plans, beliefs, and decisions represented in decision models.

XP Retrieval

- Ask XP retrieval questions based on the indexes used by AQUA and attempt to match the current situation to the PRE-XP-NODES of an available XP.
- Retrieve specific XPs based on XP retrieval questions.
- Apply specific XPs or abstract XPs if no specific XPs are found.

XP Application

- Ask XP applicability questions based on the INTERNAL-XP-NODES and LINKS of the XP. Suspend XP application if necessary.
- Instantiate nodes of the XP.
- Instantiate links of the XP.

Hypothesis Confirmation

- Ask hypothesis verification questions (HVQs) based on the XP-ASSERTED-NODES of the XP.
- Suspend hypothesis verification if necessary.
- Confirm/refute hypothesis later when HVQs are answered.

At the end of this process, AQUA is left with one or more alternative hypotheses, each with its own set of HVQs. Partially confirmed hypotheses are maintained in a data dependency network called a *hypothesis tree*, along with questions (HVQs) representing what is required to verify these hypotheses (see figure 8.7).

8.5 Types of Questions

A functional theory of questions, as argued earlier, must be based on a taxonomy of types of knowledge goals that arise from the underlying understanding tasks that the

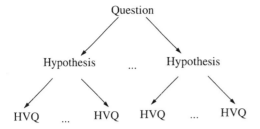

Figure 8.7
Structure of a hypothesis tree.

questions serve. To develop a taxonomy of these knowledge goals, I asked several subjects to voice the questions that occurred to them as stories were read out to them. I then analyzed those questions and grouped them according to the understanding task (e.g., hypothesis verification) that they were relevant to. The groupings were revised based on a functional analysis of the knowledge required for the subtasks in my theory of story understanding and explanation, the subtasks in turn being mutually refined based on my analysis of the question data.

It is interesting to note that although my main taxonomic criteria were functional, the taxonomy fits my data well. Thus I hypothesize that my theory, although intended as a computational model of an active reader, is also a plausible cognitive model. This is supported by the fact that my model is consistent with psychological data on question asking reported by Scardamalia and Bereiter (1991). My goal-based approach is also consistent with psychological data on goal orientation in learning (e.g., Ng and Bereiter 1991) and in focus of attention and inferencing (cf. review by Zukier 1986).

I propose the following taxonomy of knowledge goals for story understanding:

Text goals. Knowledge goals of a text analysis program, arising from text-level tasks. These are the questions that arise from basic syntactic and semantic analysis that needs to be done on the input text, such as noun group attachment or pronoun reference. An example text goal is to find the referent of a pronoun.

Memory goals. Knowledge goals of a dynamic memory program, arising from memory-level tasks. A dynamic memory must be able to notice similarities, match incoming concepts to stereotypes in memory, form generalizations, and so on. An example memory goal might be to look for an event predicted by stored knowledge of a stereotyped action, such as asking what the ransom will be when one hears about a kidnapping.

Table 8.2
Examples of questions

	Questions	Task
Text questions	Was the car the target or the instrument of the bombing?	Interpret the noun phrase "car bombing."
Memory questions	Why are they all named Mohammed?	Notice similarities.
Explanation questions	Did the kid think he was going to die? Why are kids chosen for these missions?	Explain anomalies.
Relevance questions	How does Mohammed Burro compare with a typical American teenager?	Determine personal relevance.

Explanation goals. Goals of an explainer that arise from explanation-level tasks, including the detection and resolution of anomalies and the building of motivational and causal explanations for the events in the story in order to understand why the characters acted as they did or why certain events did or did not occur. An example explanation goal might be to figure out the motivation of a suicide truck bomber mentioned in a story.

Relevance goals. Goals of any intelligent system in the real world, concerning the identification of aspects of the current situation that are "interesting" or relevant to its general goals. An example is looking for the name of an airline in a highjacking story if the understander were contemplating traveling by air soon.

A detailed taxonomy is presented in the appendix. Table 8.2 presents examples of questions corresponding to these types of knowledge goals. Each question focuses on a different aspect of a story. For example, explanation questions focus on different types of anomalies and on explanations for these anomalies. Asking an anomaly detection question is essential to detecting the corresponding anomaly. For example, asking the question "Does the actor want the outcome of this action?" is essential to the detection of a goal violation anomaly in the sense that the program will not notice the anomaly if it does not focus on the goals of the agent, that is, if it does not think of asking the question.

To put this another way, the questions asked by the understander influence its final understanding. Thus it is important for the understander to ask the "right" questions in order to achieve a detailed understanding of the situation. For the purpose of understanding stories involving motivations of people, I developed a taxonomy of motivational questions that focus on those motivational aspects of stories that are needed to build volitional explanations based on decision models. Figure 8.8 illustrates a series of anomaly detection questions based on questioning the goals, plans, beliefs, and decisions of an agent. Each question, if its answer seems anomalous, raises further questions. A more detailed taxonomy of explanation questions is presented in the appendix.

In addition to their theoretical role in my model of inference control and interestingness, knowledge goals have also played an implementational role in my research by providing a uniform mechanism for the integration of various cognitive processes. For example, knowledge goals arising from, say, memory tasks are indexed in memory and used in the same way as knowledge goals arising from explanation tasks. A knowledge goal generated from one task may be suspended and satisfied opportunistically during the pursuit of some other task at a later stage or even during the processing of a different story. Implementational details may be found in Ram (1989).

8.6 Representation of Questions

When an understander is trying to reason about something (e.g., it is trying to explain something that seems anomalous, and it needs some piece of information that is not present in memory), it formulates a question that is indexed in memory where it expected to find the information. The question consists of two parts:

- *Concept specification.* The object of the question, that is, the desired information. This is represented using a memory structure that specifies what is minimally acceptable as an answer to the question. A new piece of knowledge is an answer to a question if it matches the specification completely. The answer can specify more than the question required, of course.
- *Task specification.* What to do with the information once it comes in, which depends on why the question was generated. This may be represented either as a procedure to be run or as a declarative specification of the suspended task. When the question is answered because the program either actively pursued it or opportunistically answered it while processing something else, the suspended process that depends on that information is restarted.

In a sense a question is similar to an open "slot" in a memory structure. AQUA's initial processing could be viewed as being similar to that of typical "script-based" understanders: Words in the input text are used to instantiate memory structures, and open slots in these memory structures are used as predictions for the rest of the story. However, there are three main differences (expressed here in a "slot-filling" terminology for comparison):

A Theory of Questions and Question Asking 285

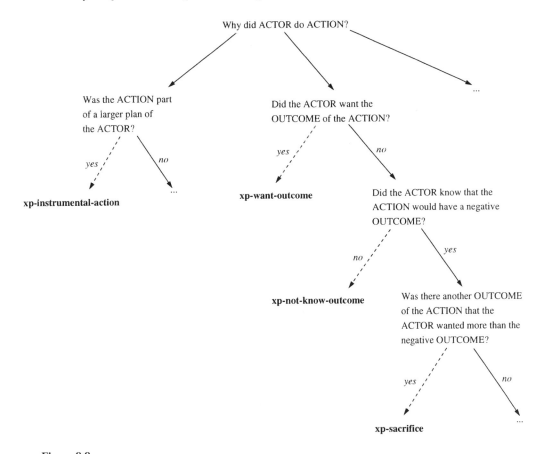

Figure 8.8
Anomaly detection questions arise from questioning different parts of the planning/decision model used to represent volitional explanations. These questions can be viewed as comprising a discrimination net of volitional questions, as shown in simplified form. This net corresponds to the hierarchy of abstract XPs represented in the program; the questions shown here are generated using the PRE-XP-NODES of abstract XPs in this hierarchy. If an anomaly is detected, the discrimination net also determines the category index of the XP required.

1. Typically all open slots in newly instantiated structures are used as "requests" or "predictions" and cause the understander to look for fillers for those slots. AQUA, however, uses its interestingness heuristics to mark interesting slots to be used as predictions or questions. In addition slots can be marked as being interesting by understanding tasks when their values are needed but not yet known.
2. Open slots arise not only from scriptlike knowledge structures but also from causal or explanatory structures.
3. Typically the ultimate task of the understander is to fill in as many of these open slots as possible. However, the action of filling in a slot does not do anything more than provide a value for that slot. In AQUA, however, slots are not filled for their own sake but rather for the sake of performing some kind of reasoning with that value (e.g., confirming a hypothesis).

Thus AQUA subscribes to the basic slot-filling idea but extends this idea by selecting which slots are worth filling, by using different kinds of knowledge structures to provide slots and by remembering why particular slots need to be filled so that it can use the filled values when they become known. The uniform representation of questions generated by different processes allows us to design an integrated system in an easy and natural manner.

AQUA's memory is built on top of an opportunistic memory architecture (Birnbaum 1986; Birnbaum and Collins 1984; Dehn 1989; Hammond 1988; Hayes-Roth and Hayes-Roth 1979; Ram 1989), which provides a uniform way to integrate question-based processing for different types of understanding tasks. The underlying memory model is based on the theory of dynamic memory (Schank 1982), such as that used by IPP (Lebowitz 1983) or CYRUS (Kolodner 1984). In addition to MOP-based episodic structures similar to these programs, AQUA's memory contains XPs indexed by situation, character stereotype, and anomaly category indexes. The memory also contains questions indexed with the concepts in memory, each with its own reason for being asked. When these questions are answered, perhaps opportunistically, AQUA can restart the suspended computation. This requires the following supporting mechanisms:

- *Knowledge goal retrieval.* Finding suspended knowledge goals, even if not currently in "focus," that a new piece of knowledge might satisfy.
- *Knowledge goal indexing.* Storing knowledge goals in memory so that they are found almost only when they are relevant without having to look through long lists of pending questions.
- *Process scheduling.* Suspending tasks when there is insufficient information to execute them and restarting suspended tasks that depend on knowledge goals when the required information becomes available.

- *Hypothesis management.* Deleting alternative knowledge goals and hypotheses when a knowledge goal is satisfied because their likelihood of being useful decreases because an alternative has been found.

Implementation details of these mechanisms are discussed in Ram (1989). These mechanisms allow AQUA to reason about what it knows, pose questions about what it needs to learn during the performance of an understanding task, and manage alternative hypotheses and explanations. These processes are fundamental to what Ng and Bereiter (1991) call the "knowledge-building goal orientation" in learning and are similar to the processes for self-management of learning goals used in their study.

8.7 Conclusions

Question generation and question answering are central to the processes of reasoning, understanding and learning. The point of reading is to answer one's own questions or fill in gaps in one's memory structures, that is, to learn. Based on this premise, I developed a model of questions and question asking in which questions are viewed as goals to learn. Questions are not just open "slots" in memory structures; they are gaps that a reasoner needs to fill, or information that it needs to gather, for the purposes of carrying out various reasoning tasks.

My theory of questions has three components: a content theory describing the nature of questions and the actual questions that a reasoner might ask in a given situation; a computational process theory describing the processes of question generation, management of questions in memory, and interaction of questions with learning and understanding; and an implementational model in which I developed a program that embodies the content and process theories. The model is based on empirical results in psychology, social cognition, and education as well as research in artificial intelligence on case-based reasoning, explanation, machine learning, natural language understanding, and opportunistic planning.

The taxonomy of explanation questions presented in this article is appropriate for domains involving reasoning about goals, plans, and motivations of people. Similar taxonomies may be developed for other domains if explanatory theories are available for the domain. The taxonomy of text level questions is appropriate for natural language understanding tasks and is independent of the domain. The main claims of my process theory are summarized below:

- Questions are subgoals of understanding tasks and arise as knowledge goals when the reasoner needs a piece of knowledge to carry out some task that it does not already have.

- Questions are indexed in memory.
- Questions can be used to focus attention on interesting facts and limit the inferences drawn from them. In story understanding, questions determine what to look for in the story.
- Questions may be answered opportunistically. The explicit representation of questions facilitates the discovery of unexpected opportunities to answer the questions.
- Questions (and memory) are dynamic.
- Learning occurs incrementally through the answering of questions and the generation of new questions.

The ultimate focus of my research is on the relationship between questions and learning. I believe that learning is an active process involving the generation of questions and the pursuit of inferences in the context of these questions. Interestingness is viewed as a heuristic that allows the system to focus its attention on what it needs to learn. Learning, in turn, is viewed an incremental process of both question generation and question answering. I have demonstrated that this model is viable by implementing a computer program, AQUA, whose source of power (to borrow a term from Lenat and Brown 1984) resides in its question-asking capabilities. The learning process in AQUA is incremental and dynamic, involving both goal-driven (top-down or active) and data-driven (bottom-up or opportunistic) processes. AQUA gradually evolves its understanding of a domain through experience with different situations. Its ability to ask questions is central to this process.

The issues in this chapter have implications not only for theories of learning, but for theories of education. While much research has focussed on question answering (e.g., what information to provide a student, how people learn, algorithms for machine learning), question asking is also important and involves issues such as when students ask questions, what kinds of questions they ask, what information to provide students relative to their pending questions, and so on. Research in learning and education needs to focus on the relationship between the learning goals of the student and the information provided by the environment. My theory models active-learning behavior in a dynamic environment and is a step towards understanding this relationship.

Appendix: A Taxonomy of Questions

8A.1 Anomaly Detection Questions

Anomaly detection questions can be categorized as follows:

Decision Questions These questions focus on the decision that the actor took when he decided to do the action. Therefore this is also a taxonomy of the planning decisions one would consider when deciding on an action.

Personal Goals

- Does the actor want the outcome of this action?
- Does the actor want to avoid a negative outcome of not doing this action?
- Does the actor want a positive outcome of this action more than he wants to avoid a negative outcome of doing the same action?
- Does the actor enjoy doing that action?
- Does the actor habitually do this action?

Instrumentality

- Is this action instrumental to another action that the actor wants to carry out?
- Is this action part of a larger plan that the actor is carrying out?

Interpersonal Goals

- Does the actor want a positive outcome of this action for someone he likes?
- Does the actor want to avoid a negative outcome of this action for someone he likes?
- Does the actor want a negative outcome of this action for someone he dislikes?
- Does the actor want a positive outcome of this action for a group that he belongs to?
- Does the actor want to avoid a negative outcome of this action for a group that he belongs to?
- Does the actor feel gratification in doing good for others?

Social Control

- Did someone with social control over the actor ask him to perform the action?
- Did someone with social control over the actor force him to perform that action?

Knowledge and Beliefs

- Did the actor know the probable outcomes of the action?
- Did the actor believe that the action would have a positive outcome for him?
- Did the actor know about the possible negative outcome of the action?

Interference Questions   These questions focus on possible interference from external sources.

- Did someone want to block the actor's goal?
- Did someone want to prevent this state of the world? Would this state of the world violate this person's goals?
- Did someone want the actor to be involved in this action?
- Did the actor accidentally get involved in this action?

Planner Questions These questions concern an action that was planned and executed by different people or groups.

- Did the action result in a positive outcome for both the planner and the actor?
- Did the planner select the actor knowing that the action would result in a negative outcome for the actor?

Physical Anomaly Questions These questions focus on the physical causality underlying the observed events. For example, if this is the first suicide bombing story one has read:

- How can a car be used as a bomb?

8A.2 XP Retrieval Questions

The taxonomy at the level of XPs representing abstract decision models mirrors the taxonomy of anomaly detection questions. Since the particular XP retrieval questions at the level of stereotypical XPs depend on the stereotypes currently in memory, this category is illustrated using examples rather than a taxonomy.

Abstract XP Retrieval Questions

Decision Anomalies

Anomaly **goal-violation**
Situation Actor does action that results in a negative outcome.
Questions
- Did the actor actually want this outcome (i.e., did we misperceive his goals)?
- Did the action result in another outcome that the actor wanted even at the expense of the negative outcome?
- Was the actor forced into doing this action?
- Did the actor know that the action would have this negative outcome?
- Did the actor have enough information about the environment?
- Did the actor project the effects of the action correctly?

Anomaly **goal-violation** or **unusual-goal-ordering**
Situation Actor does action that results in a positive outcome and a negative outcome.
Questions
- Does the actor prefer to achieve the positive outcome even at the expense of the negative outcome?
- Does the actor actually want to avoid the negative outcome?
- Can the goal violated by the negative outcome be pursued later?

XPs
- Goal priority elevation in particular contexts.
- Goal violated by negative outcome can be pursued later.
- Goal of positive outcome is temporarily urgent.
- Short-term goals preferred to longer-term goals.
- Personal goals preferred to group goals.
- Difficult goals postponed.
- New goals from wanting what others have.
- Actor's goal priorities were misperceived.
- Personal differences (individual, parental).
- Group differences.
- Cultural differences.

Anomaly **bad-plan-choice**
Situation Actor does action to achieve a goal even though another action looks better.
Questions
- Did the second action have a negative side effect for the actor?
- Did the actor know about the second action?
- Was the actor capable of performing the second action?
- Is the first action better in the long run?
- Is the cumulative effect of the first action better?
- Does the first action keep more options open?
- Does the actor enjoy doing the first action?

Anomaly **failed-opportunity**
Situation Actor doesn't do action that would have resulted in a positive outcome for actor.
Questions
- Did the actor actually want this outcome (i.e., did we misperceive his goals)?
- Did the actor know that the action would result in the positive outcome?
- Did the action also result in a negative outcome for the actor?
- Was the actor capable of performing that action?

Anomaly **unmotivated-action**
Situation Actor does an action that doesn't satisfy any of his goals.
Questions
- Did the actor think that the action would satisfy one of his goals?
- Does the action actually satisfy a goal (i.e., did we misperceive the situation)?

Planner Anomalies

Anomaly **malicious-intent**
Situation Planner knowingly recruits actor for action that results in negative outcome for actor.
Questions
- Was the planner's real intention to achieve a negative outcome for the actor?
- Did the planner want some other outcome of the action, but also wanted to avoid the negative outcome from happening to himself?
- Was the planner willing to sacrifice the actor's goal to achieve a goal of his own?
- Did the planner want both the outcomes (i.e., was he killing two birds with one stone)?
- Was the planner in turn forced to make this decision?

Stereotypical XP Retrieval Questions

XP **Religious fanatic does suicide bombing**.
Questions
- Was the actor religious?
- (If in the Middle East) Was the actor a Shiite Moslem?

XP **Depressed teenager commits suicide**.
Questions
- Was the actor a stereotypical teenager?
- Was the actor depressed?

8A.3 XP Application and Hypothesis Verification Questions

XP application questions arise from the internal nodes and links of XPs, and hypothesis verification questions arise from XP-ASSERTED-NODES (abductive assumptions). These questions depend on the particular XPs in memory.

8A.4 Text-Level Questions

Actor-Action Identification

- Who was the actor of the action?

Attachment Questions

Noun Group Connection

- Is this a noun phrase?
- How do I connect the two nouns together?

Adjectives, Prepositional Attachment These result in syntactic predictions being made, which are represented as questions. For example, on reading "recruit boy as ...":

- For what purpose did the terrorists recruit the boy?

Reference Questions A referential description could be a pronoun (e.g., "he") or a definite reference (e.g., "the teenage bomber").

- Who or what does this description refer to?

Disambiguation and Specialization Questions These questions try to disambiguate or refine vague descriptions. For example, on reading "get into":

- What is the destination of "get into"? (If the destination turns out to be a car, which is a type of container, "get into" can be specialized to "enter.")

8A.5 Memory-Level Questions

Journalism Questions These questions seek the who, what, when, and where of the story.

Reference Questions At the text level, reference questions are triggered by pronouns and definite noun phrases, but referential cues may be nontextual too. Some examples of reference questions are:

- Is this bombing the same bombing that was predicted?
- Is the sixteen-year-old teenager the same as the boy that was recruited?
- Is the explosive-laden car the same car that was implicitly part of the suicide bombing mentioned in the headline?

Attachment Questions Attachment questions try to determine the connection between two concepts.

Stereotype Activation Questions These questions arise from the activation of stereotypes (stereotypical features of concepts, stereotypical activities and goals of people, or stereotypical motivational explanations for actions).

- Does this instance fit this stereotype?
- Is this a typical role filler for this stereotype?
- Does this person have these stereotypical goals?
- Can I view this instance as one that matches this stereotype?
- Does this group of instances follow a pattern?

MOP and Scene Inference Questions These questions are based on the following tasks:

- **Predicting the scenes of a MOP.** For example, `recruit` predicts `locate` and `persuade`.
- **Finding the correct context for a scene.** For example, `blow-up-bomb` is part of `bombing`.
- **Activating definitional inferences.** For example, `suicide` by definition results in the `death-state of the actor`.
- **Specializing or refining vague descriptions.** For example, a `person` with `age = 16` is a `teenager`; a `ptrans` with `instrument = car` is a `drive`.

For example, on reading about the recruiting of a boy for a suicide bombing mission, AQUA asks:

- How did they locate the boy?
- How did they persuade the boy to do the suicide bombing?

Reminding and Memory Search Questions A dynamic memory must be able to recognize unique combinations, notice similarities (both superficial and structural), and retrieve memory structures given a specification. Some examples of these questions are:

- Why are they all named Mohammed?
- Why do we hear about Lebanese car bombers and not about Israeli car bombers?
- Are there any other instances of teenage suicide bombers in memory?

Analogy and Generalization Questions Remindings give rise to questions that seek generalizations. For example:

- Are car bombers motivated like the Kamikaze?

8A.6 Relevance Questions

All intelligent systems in the real world are, in some sense, constantly asking questions about personal relevance:

Why does this matter to me?
How does this relate to my goals?
Is this story about anyone I know or have heard of?
Is this story about a place that I know of or have been to?
Is this story about goals that I share?

Notes

Research for this article was supported in part by the National Science Foundation under contract IRI-9009710. Part of the research described was conducted while the author was at Yale University, and supported by the Defense Advanced Research Projects Agency and the Office of Naval Research under contract N00014-85-K-0108 and by the Air Force Office of Scientific Research under contracts F49620-88-C-0058 and AFOSR-85-0343.

I thank Roger Schank for his guidance during this research, and Rick Alterman, Jeremiah Faries, and an anonymous reviewer for their detailed comments on an earlier draft of this article.

1. Since computers will eventually be expected to interact with the physical world (e.g., robots) and the social world (e.g., employees), they will also be expected to have some of the physical or social goals that we currently attribute only to people.

2. Actually a single story or episode can provide more than one "case," each case being a particular interpretation or dealing with a particular aspect of the story. In AQUA each anomaly in a story, along with the corresponding set of explanatory hypotheses, can be used as a case.

3. I will use the neutral term *schema* for knowledge structures that encapsulate "canned" or stereotypical information about some situation, when for the purposes of the discussion at hand the distinctions between various kinds of schemas (scripts, frames, memory organization packets [MOPs], explanation patterns [XPs], etc.) or cases are irrelevant.

4. Clearly the author of a story also has control over what the understander finds interesting at any point. There is a tension between the conveyance of the story and the subjective bias of the reader in reading the story (Alterman, personal communication, March 15, 1991). The interaction between the two is complex. For example, there is some evidence that the subjective bias of the reader may cause the reader to perceive biases on the part of the author (e.g., the "hostile media phenomenon"; Vallone et al. 1985). This issue is beyond the scope of this chapter.

5. Since interestingness depends on one's goals, the heuristics implemented in AQUA do not cover interests arising from goals that lie outside the scope of the basic understanding and learning tasks that AQUA performs. For example, a parent would be interested in the report card of his or her child. However, AQUA's goals do not include caring for children, so AQUA does not have any reason to be interested in a report card, unless the report card was anomalous with respect to AQUA's beliefs.

6. A MOP is a memory structure that contains information about how other memory structures are linked together in frequently occurring combinations. MOPs are composed of *scenes* that describe how and where a particular set of actions take place, which in turn can point to *scripts* that embody specific aspects of these scenes (Schank 1982).

7. To improve on this even further, AQUA tries to determine which of its questions are interesting and worth pursuing. This decision is made using a set of interestingness heuristics. Details of these heuristics are beyond the scope of this article (see Ram 1990c). For the purposes of this article, we may assume that AQUA pursues all its questions. Even this simplified heuristic is more efficient than pursuing all possible inferences.

References

Alterman, R. 1985. A dictionary based on concept coherence. *Artificial Intelligence* 25: 153–86.

Birnbaum, L. 1986. *Integrated Processing in Planning and Understanding.* PhD thesis. Research report 489. Yale University, Department of Computer Science, New Haven.

Birnbaum, L., and G. Collins. 1984. Opportunistic planning and Freudian slips. In *Proceedings of the Sixth Annual Conference of the Cognitive Science Society*, pp. 124–27, Boulder, CO. Boulder: Institute of Cognitive Science and University of Colorado.

Cullingford, R. 1978. *Script Application: Computer Understanding of Newspaper Stories.* PhD thesis. Research report 116. Yale University, Department of Computer Science, New Haven.

Dehn, N. 1989. *Computer Story Writing: The Role of Reconstructive and Dynamic Memory.* PhD thesis. Research report 792. Yale University, Department of Computer Science, New Haven.

DeJong, G. F. 1979. Prediction and substantiation: A new approach to natural language understanding. *Cognitive Science* 3: 251–73.

DeJong, G. F. 1983. An approach to learning from observation. In R. S. Michalski, ed., *Proceedings of the 1983 International Machine Learning Workshop*, pp. 171–76, Monticello, IL, June 1983. Department of Computer Science, University of Illinois, Urbana-Champaign.

Dyer, M. G. 1982. *In-depth Understanding: A Computer Model of Integrated Processing for Narrative Comprehension.* PhD thesis. Research report 116. Yale University, Department of Computer Science, New Haven.

Hammond, K. J. 1988. Opportunistic memory: Storing and recalling suspended goals. In J. L. Kolodner, ed., *Proceedings of a Workshop on Case-Based Reasoning*, pp. 154–68, Clearwater Beach, FL, May 1988. San Mateo, CA: Morgan Kaufmann.

Hayes-Roth, B., and F. Hayes-Roth. 1979. A cognitive model of planning. *Cognitive Science* 2: 275–310.

Hayes-Roth, F., and V. Lesser. 1976. Focus of attention in a distributed logic speech understanding system. In *Proceedings of the IEEE International Conference on Accoustics, Speech and Signal Processing*, pp. 416–20, Philadephia, April 1976. New York: IEEE.

Hunter, L. E. 1989. *Knowledge Acquisition Planning: Gaining Expertise through Experience.* PhD thesis. Research report 678. Yale University, Department of Computer Science, New Haven.

Hunter, L. E. 1990. Knowledge acquisition planning for inference from large datasets. In B. D. Shriver, ed., *Proceedings of the Twenty Third Annual Hawaii International Conference on System Sciences*, pp. 35–45, Kona, HI, 1990. Los Alamitos, CA: IEEE Computer Society Press.

Kass, A., D. Leake, and C. Owens. 1986. *SWALE: A Program That Explains.* Hillsdale, NJ: Lawrence Erlbaum, pp. 232–54.

Kintsch, W. 1988. The role of knowledge in discourse comprehension: A construction-integration model. *Psychological Review* 95: 163–82.

Kolodner, J. L. 1984. *Retrieval and Organizational Strategies in Conceptual Memory: A Computer Model.* Hillsdale, NJ: Lawrence Erlbaum.

Lebowitz, M. 1983. Generalization from natural language text. *Cognitive Science* 7: 1–40.

Lehnert, W. G., M. G. Dyer, P. N. Johnson, C. Yang, and S. Harley. 1983. BORIS—An experiment in in-depth understanding of narratives. *Artificial Intelligence* 20: 15–62.

Lehnert, W. G. 1978. *The Process of Question Answering*. Hillsdale, NJ: Lawrence Erlbaum.

Lenat, D. B., and J. S. Brown. 1984. Why AM and EURISKO appear to work. *Artificial Intelligence* 23: 269–94.

Ng, E., and C. Bereiter. 1991. Three levels of goal orientation in learning. *Journal of the Learning Sciences* 1: 243–71.

Ram, A., and L. Hunter. 1992. The use of explicit goals for knowledge to guide inference and learning. *Applied Intelligence* 2: 47–73. also available as Technical Report GIT-CC-92/04, College of Computing, Georgia Institute of Technology, Atlanta.

Ram, A., and D. Leake. 1991. Evaluation of explanatory hypotheses. In *Proceedings of the Tl.irteenth Annual Conference of the Cognitive Science Society*, Chicago, August 1991.

Ram, A. 1987. AQUA: Asking questions and understanding answers. In *Proceedings of the Sixth Annual National Conference on Artificial Intelligence*. Menlo Park, CA: AAAI Press, pp. 312–16.

Ram, A. 1989. *Question-driven understanding: An integrated theory of story understanding, memory and learning*. PhD thesis. Research report 710. Yale University, Department of Computer Science, New Haven.

Ram, A. 1990a. Decision models: A theory of volitional explanation. In *Proceedings of the Twelfth Annual Conference of the Cognitive Science Society*, pp. 198–205, Cambridge, MA, July 1990. Hillsdale, NJ: Lawrence Erlbaum.

Ram, A. 1990b. Incremental learning of explanation patterns and their indices. In B. W. Porter and R. J. Mooney, eds., *Proceedings of the Seventh International Conference on Machine Learning*, pp. 313–20, Austin, TX, June 1990. San Mateo, CA: Morgan Kaufmann.

Ram, A. 1990c. Knowledge goals: A theory of interestingness. In *Proceedings of the Twelfth Annual Conference of the Cognitive Science Society*, pp. 206–14, Cambridge, MA, July 1990. Hillsdale, NJ: Lawrence Erlbaum.

Ram, A. 1993. Indexing, elaboration and refinement: Incremental learning of explanatory cases. *Machine Learning* 10: 201–48. Also available as Technical Report GIT-CC-92/03, College of Computing, Georgia Institute of Technology, Atlanta.

Scardamalia, M., and C. Bereiter. 1991. Higher levels of agency for children in knowledge building: A challenge for the design of new knowledge media. *Journal of the Learning Sciences* 1: 37–68.

Schank, R. C., and A. Ram. 1988. Question-driven parsing: A new approach to natural language understanding. *Journal of Japanese Society for Artificial Intelligence* 3: 260–70.

Schank, R. C. 1978. Predictive understanding. In R. Campbell and P. Smith, eds., *Recent Advances in the Psychology of Language—Formal and Experimental Approaches*. New York: Plenum Press, pp. 91–101.

Schank, R. C. 1982. *Dynamic Memory: A Theory of Learning in Computers and People*. New York: Cambridge University Press.

Schank, R. C. 1986. *Explanation Patterns: Understanding Mechanically and Creatively*. Hillsdale, NJ: Lawrence Erlbaum.

Shute, V., R. Glaser, and K. Raghavan. 1988. Inference and discovery in an exploratory laboratory. Technical report 10. Learning Research and Development Center, University of Pittsburgh, Pittsburgh.

Sperber, D., and D. Wilson. 1986. *Relevance: Communication and Cognition*. Language and Thought Series. Cambridge: Harvard University Press.

Vallone, R. P., L. Ross, and M. R. Lepper. 1985. The hostile media phenomenon: Biased perception and perceptions of media bias in coverage of the Beirut massacre. *Journal of Personality and Social Psychology* 49: 577–85.

Zeigernik, B. 1927. Das Behalten Erledigter und Unerledigter Handlungen. *Psychologische Forschungen* 9: 1–85.

Zukier, H. 1986. The paradigmatic and narrative modes in goal-guided inference. In R. Sorrentino and E. Higgins, eds., *Handbook of Motivation and Cognition: Foundations of Social Behavior*, pp. 465–502. Guilford, CT: Guilford Press.

Chapter 9
Semantic Correspondence Theory

Justin Peterson and Dorrit Billman

9.1 Introduction

Natural language processing of real-world texts highlights the fact that language is a dynamic, changing system. Language is not a closed world where all the words and constructions can be anticipated in advance, and once anticipated will cover all texts. Rather language changes across time and varies across user community. Some aspects of language, such as syntax, change slowly and are relatively stable. Other aspects such as the lexicon change quickly; new terms are introduced frequently, and old terms are used in new constructions. Our work in natural language understanding demonstrates how to use the more stable aspects of language to process the more mutable. We show how information from syntax constrains the meaning of the verb and how this is useful for processing texts with novel verbs and with novel uses of old verbs. Our contribution to processing naturally occurring texts is to provide more robust language processing in the face of unanticipated verbs and verb uses.

Language changes over time and across communities. So, why does this pose a hard problem in the implementation of natural language processing systems? Language novelty presents a problem because this makes it both pragmatically and theoretically impossible to anticipate the necessary lexicon when the system is designed.

Change over time presents a limit in principle: If a term has not yet been added to the language, it is simply impossible to include it as a term in the lexicon. As a system encounters terms that were not in the lexicon when its lexicon was written, it has several broad choices: skip over the term with whatever disruption that entails, request human intervention, or try to use existing knowledge to project as much as possible about the new term. Clearly a system that is able to do something sensible on its own is much to be preferred. Processing of novel verbs would be particularly valuable because the verb is so central to integrating sentence components and specifying the relations among them.

Change across user community or the task presents a pragmatic limit. As the task for which natural language is being processed, or the user community changes, the lexicon shifts as well. Different open class words are needed for processing texts about automobile repair versus financial transactions. It is simply not practical nor desirable to equip a single-domain system with the vocabulary intended to span all domains and all dialects of the whole language. However, it would be very desirable if a large part of the framework were constant and hence portable across different domains, content areas, or user communities. To the extent that reuse was designed to anticipate the need for a flexibly expanding lexicon, this can provide a powerful aid to designers interested in taking a system designed for one task and applying it in another.

In short, it would be valuable for natural language processing systems to generate autonomously a sensible, if partial, interpretation of novel verbs. But is this simply asking for the impossible? A look at human performance shows it is not. People routinely encounter and interpret novel verbs. For example, on hearing

(1) John zorched the book into the fire

a speaker of English knows a great deal about what happened, even though he or she has never encountered the verb before. Reading (1), a speaker can infer that

1. The book moved.
2. It was initially not in the fire.
3. At the end of the event, it was in the fire.
4. John caused something to happen.
5. The thing that John caused was the movement of the book along a path that ends inside the fire.

There are probably multiple sources of information that aid the interpretation of the sentence. But consider the related sentence

(2) The mugglet zorched the diggie into the wabe.

Here the same implications hold, and they cannot be derived from the meanings of the nouns or world knowledge about plausible relations. Rather, the information responsible for the set of implications listed above (though not other inferences, e.g., John's attitude toward the book) must be carried by the information common to the two sentences, namely their syntax.

In this chapter we present the Semantic Correspondence model of sentence interpretation. The Semantic Correspondence model uses information from syntax to constrain sentence meaning. By exploiting syntactically specified constraints, Semantic Correspondence can generate accurate though general meanings of sentences that have novel verbs. This contrasts with many natural language processing systems where interpretation is driven by retrieval of the possible argument structures and associated meanings of familiar verbs listed in the lexicon.

We begin by introducing the task decomposition that is critical to the success of the Semantic Correspondence model. This is followed by a description of the semantic representation used in the model.

9.2 Semantic Correspondence: An Introduction

The task of sentence comprehension is to produce a representation of the conceptual content of a sentence. The "traditional" approach to accomplishing this task is to retrieve the meanings of a sentence's constituent words from a lexicon and combine them into a conceptual representation of the sentence. The specific manner in which these word meanings combine is informed largely by knowledge associated with the sentence's main verb. Of course, in those instances where the main verb is novel, neither the manner of combining constituents nor the meaning of the verb is available. The "traditional" approach cannot begin to understand novel verb sentences.

Semantic Correspondence theory adopts a different approach. Its key insight is that the main verb and syntax of a sentence are mutually supporting sources of sentence meaning. Both tell us about the verb's meaning and how the word meanings of its arguments combine. When the verb is known, both types of information may be used to perform sentence comprehension. When verb information is absent, as in the case of novel verbs, the syntactic source of information may be relied upon to infer the meaning of the verb and combine word meanings into a conceptual representation of the sentence. Thus the Semantic Correspondence model provides a partial solution to the problem of understanding sentences with novel verbs. We begin introducing the theory by presenting the task decomposition that is critical to its success.

In Semantic Correspondence, sentence comprehension is comprised of three subtasks: (1) syntactic parsing, (2) semantic interpretation, and (3) conceptual comprehension. As illustrated in figure 9.1, each of these subtasks derives specific types of information about a sentence and its constituent words. Syntactic parsing produces a parse of the sentence, identifying the syntactic structure of the sentence and the syntactic categories of its constituent words. Semantic interpretation uses this syntactic information and its knowledge of the semantics to infer the semantic interpretations of the constituent words and the semantic interpretation of the sentence. Conceptual comprehension uses the information generated by semantic interpretation along with its knowledge of the concepts evoked by the sentence's constituent words to produce the output of the overall task, a representation of the sentence's conceptual content.

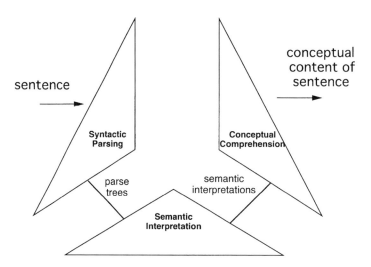

Figure 9.1
Decomposition of the task of sentence comprehension.

Semantic Correspondence theory contributes primarily and directly to the task of semantic interpretation. Its purpose is to identify the grammatically relevant aspects of a sentence's conceptual content (Pinker 1989). Syntactic distinctions between sentences such as *John sent a message to New York* and *John sent New York a message* reflect differences in sentence meanings (e.g., whether a referent is the destination or recipient of a message) (Jackendoff 1990). The task of semantic interpretation is to extract these grammatically relevant distinctions in meaning, leaving those that are not marked by syntax (e.g., the manner in which messages are transmitted) to conceptual comprehension.

Separating semantic interpretation from conceptual comprehension in this way offers an effective, efficient approach to interpreting novel verb sentences. First, it limits the size of the solution space. Semantic interpretation only need consider a subset of the many conceptual distinctions possible. Second, it makes profitable use of processing resources, focusing attention on those distinctions in conceptual content that can be inferred from the syntax of the input. Third, it allows the development of methods and a representation that are specific to the problems of semantic interpretation. For example, Semantic Correspondence employs a representation that is extremely effective for representing correspondences between syntax and semantics. It is unlikely, however, that this semantic representation possesses the universal expressiveness required of a conceptual representation. Separating semantic interpretation from conceptual interpretation allows the use of such semantic representations.

9.3 Representation Levels in Semantic Correspondence Theory

The task decomposition supports a processing model which can integrate information from syntactic, semantic, and conceptual representations. The success of the model depends in large measure on the properties of the semantic representation and on the correspondences between syntactic and semantic form. The focus of this chapter is on presentation of the computational model which uses these representations to construct sentence interpretations, disambiguate verbs, and infer the meaning of novel verbs. Before we present the computational model, we highlight the key assumptions about representation, particularly the semantic representation and the correspondences between syntax and semantics. Here we simply sketch out these assumptions about representation. For justification and rationale, see Peterson (1996).

A fundamental claim of Semantic Correspondence theory is the importance of at least three distinct levels of representation in understanding natural language: syntax, semantics, and conceptual. These levels are related by mappings between syntax and semantics and mappings between semantics and conceptual representation. Our work focuses on semantics and on the syntax-semantics mappings. However, our proposals do depend on certain basic assumptions about syntax and about the semantics-conceptual mapping.

9.3.1 Syntax

Syntactic representation describes the distributional structure of natural languages, articulating the distribution of elements that roughly correspond to words. A number of theories of syntax have been proposed (e.g., government binding theory, Chomsky 1981; head-driven phrase structure grammar, Pollard and Sag 1987; and lexical functional grammar, Kaplan and Bresnan 1982). While these theories disagree on some points, there are many commonalities. Our work requires only a simple and uncontentious grammar. Since the focus of the work is on verbs and their arguments, the grammar is limited to the syntactic structure of verbs and their arguments.

We assume some form of syntactic representation that captures the structural relations between a verb and its arguments in their cannonical positions. As the clearest example, a grammar that assumes distinct representations for surface and deep structure will provide the representation we assume. In general, sentences with the same deep structure have the same meaning with respect to "who did what to whom where." This common meaning can be expressed in different surface forms, such as active and passive, or the *wh*-question and declarative forms.

The correspondences we identify hold between semantics and the deep structure forms of syntax. More specifically, Semantic Correspondence theory assumes that the

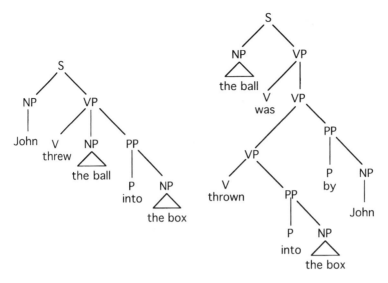

Figure 9.2
Examples of cannonical and noncannonical argument positions: Active and passive forms.

deep structure of syntax identifies equivalences between a sentence with its arguments in cannonical position and its variants in which arguments appear in noncannonical position. For example, in the passive form in (3b), *John* is not in the cannonical subject position but appears as a prepositional object in figure 9.2:

(3) a. John threw the ball into the box.
 b. The ball was thrown into the box by John.

Further we assume that sentences with arguments in different but cannonical positions do not have a common deep structure. The bitransitive examples in (4a) and (4b) use two different but still cannonical configurations of argument position. Therefore we assume that the two bitransitive, surface forms do not have a common deep structure.

(4) a. John sent New York a message.
 b. John sent a message to New York.

It is the deep structure grammar that we use, and this is summarized in figure 9.3. The simple grammar employed in the Semantic Correspondence model is a phrase structure grammar that covers the syntax of verbs and their arguments. The grammar describes the distributions of verbs for a significant portion of English expressions.

```
S -> NP VP
VP -> V NP
VP -> V PP
VP -> V PP PP
VP -> V NP PP
VP -> V NP PP PP
PP -> P NP
NP -> N
NP -> Art N
```

Figure 9.3
Phrase structure rules (for cannonical sentence forms or deep structures) assumed by Semantic Correspondence theory and used in the implemented system.

These rule choices are guided by the work of Chomsky (1981), Pollard and Sag (1987), and Kaplan and Bresnan (1982).

9.3.2 Conceptual Representation and Its Relation to Semantics

Conceptual representation is the medium through which information from perception, memory, and language is pooled, making possible the generation of conceptual inferences that are supported and consistent with the variety of information that is provided by these different sources. It identifies distinctions and equivalences between those concepts that are necessary to behaving successfully in the world, and it may of course include distinctions that are not marked in the syntax of language. Semantic representation, on the other hand, is limited to representing only those aspects of conceptual content that are marked in language. Although we have no specific claims about the structure of conceptual representation, we assume that it is differs from that of semantic representation. The structure of semantic representation is conducive to representing conceptual distinctions as they are marked in language. It is unlikely that conceptual representation has such a structure, since it represents distinctions provided by both language and perception.

Our work does assume that semantic elements, semantic constituents (i.e., combinations of semantic elements), and semantic categories all convey conceptual content. If this is to be the case, each semantic element and semantic constituent must map into some acceptable conceptual entity, and these mappings should be informed by their semantic categories. For example, all members of the semantic category **Place** map into conceptual entities that have something do with regions of space.

This property of the mapping between semantics and conceptual representation guarantees that inferences about the identity of individual semantic elements and semantic categories are inferences about the conceptual content of a natural language expression.

9.3.3 Principles of the Semantic Representation

The semantic representation is a generative representation that expresses a subset of the conceptual content denoted by a verb and its arguments. Its ability to provide the basis for a computational model that interpets both novel verb and known verb sentences as well as its ability to explain certain linguistic phenomena depends on the following properties and correspondences:

1. The semantic representation articulates a subset of the conceptual content of natural language sentences.
2. The semantic representation is a compositional semantics with distributional structure.
3. Its representations maintain significant lexical and structural correspondences with the syntactic representations of the sentences that invoke them.

Below we elaborate on these properties of the semantic representation and its correspondences with syntax.

9.3.3.1 Articulates a Subset of Conceptual Content The semantic representation identifies a critical subset of the conceptual content of natural language sentences, those aspects of a sentence's conceptual content that are grammatically relevant (Pinker 1989). Syntactic distinctions between sentences such as *John sent a message to New York* and *John sent New York a message* reflect differences in sentence meanings (e.g., whether a referent is the recipient or destination of a message; Jackendoff 1990). Semantic interpretations express these grammatically relevant distinctions in meaning, leaving those that are not marked by syntax (e.g., the manner in which messages are transmitted) to conceptual representation.

9.3.3.2 Has a Distributional Structure In Semantic Correspondence, the semantic representation is distributional. This means that the formal properties of its elements, specifically their ability to combine with other elements, determine their semantic identity. A more familiar example of a distributional representation is the phrase structure of syntax: Syntactic categories are defined by the way they combine with other syntactic categories. We claim that the structure of semantics is analogous in this respect. Semantic categories group semantic elements and expressions together into the same category based on how they combine with other elements and expressions. These semantic categories in turn serve to identify differences and equivalences in the semantic identity of their members. This property of the semantic representation allows inferences about the identity of semantic expressions to be generated from evidence about its form.

9.3.3.3 Maintains Correspondences with Syntax The semantic representation maintains two types of correspondences with syntactic representation, lexical correspondences and structural correspondences. Lexical correspondences identify relations between the syntactic categories of words and phrases and the semantic categories of elements and expressions in semantic representation.

Semantic Correspondence theory makes a novel claim that there are structural as well as lexical correspondences. Structural correspondences map the structural relations that hold between the verb arguments in syntax into structural relations that hold between the mappings of these verb arguments in semantic representation. Although these structural correspondences only partially specify the manner in which a given set of semantic elements combine, in many cases they are sufficiently informative to enable complete semantic expressions to be inferred. It is these correspondences along with the distributional structure of semantic representation that endow a computational model with the ability to interpret sentences with novel verbs.

We claim there are four types of structural correspondences, based on the four aspects of the syntactic organization of a verb and its arguments. The four syntactic combinations are as follows: (1) noun phrases are the arguments of the verb, (2) prepositions are complements of the verb, (3) noun phrases are objects of prepositions, and (4) noun phrases maintain remote relations with each other. The first three syntactic relations evoke three structural correspondence rules that maintain local relations. These three structural correspondence rules claim that syntactic arguments of prepositions and verbs designate corresponding semantic arguments: roughly, if x is an argument of y in syntax, then the semantic element designated by x is an argument of the semantic element designated by y in semantics. These three structural correspondences specify important constraints on the local combinations of semantic elements and their arguments, but they tell us little about how these local combinations combine with each other.

Information about remote combinations is provided by the fourth structural correspondence rule, Prominence Correspondence. Simply put, Prominence Correspondence states that the hierarchical relations that arise between verb arguments in syntax preserve aspects of the hierarchical structure of semantic interpretations. We describe this property of syntactic-semantic correspondence in terms of syntactic and semantic *prominence relations*. Prominence relations are hierarchical relations that are defined in terms of nodes and dominance relations, as follows:

Prominence Relation A node *x* is more prominent than another node *y* if and only if the immediate dominator of *x* dominates the immediate dominator of *y*.

Syntactic prominence relations between noun phrase arguments are defined by the syntactic structure of sentences, and semantic prominence relations are defined by the semantic tree structures these sentences invoke. Syntactic prominence relations map into semantic prominence relations by Prominence Correspondence:

Prominence Correspondence Rule Given a set of noun phrase arguments of a verb (i.e., subject, object, prepositional object) and a set of their semantic interpretations, a noun phrase argument *x* is syntactically more prominent than another *y* if and only if the semantic interpretation of *x* is semantically more prominent the semantic interpretation of *y*.

9.3.4 Semantic Representation

The semantic representation employed in the Semantic Correspondence model consists of a set of distributionally defined semantic categories and a set of correspondence rules that relate semantic and syntactic trees. The representation covers spatial expressions, and only these are treated in this chapter. Spatial expressions include sentences that describe the locations of physical objects, changes in the locations of physical objects, and actions that lead to a change in or maintenance of the location of objects. These semantic elements and categories may also be used to represent other types of expressions. (See Peterson 1996 for application to possessional expressions, and see Jackendoff 1983 and Pinker 1989 for application of similar semantic categories to represent epistemological, identificational, as well as other types of expressions.)

There are two types of semantic elements in this semantic representation: simple semantic elements and semantic functions. Semantic functions are argument-taking elements. They project semantic trees in the categories **Place**, **Path**, **State**, **Event**, and **Causal Event**. Simple semantic elements, on other the hand, do not take arguments. **Things** form a category of simple semantic elements that appear only as arguments in semantic functions. Below we enumerate the distributions and conceptual denotations of each of these types of semantic elements.

9.3.4.1 Things Conceptually, **Things** form the semantic category of simple elements. They refer to those entities in the state of affairs being described that have "some spatial and temporal integrity." Consider

(5) John throws the ball into the box.

Semantic Correspondence Theory

The sentence in (5) denotes three **Things**, (**Thing John**), (**Thing the ball**), and (**Thing the box**). Although this sentence describes a number of dynamic events (e.g., John is acting on the ball, the ball is moving, the ball is landing in the box), the spatial and temporal integrity of the **Things** remains intact. The internal properties of (**Thing John**), (**Thing the ball**), and (**Thing the box**) remain unchanged, and each of these **Things** continues to exist after the event has concluded.

Distributionally, the semantic category **Things** contains the simple elements of semantics. In contrast to semantic functions, **Things** accept no arguments. Their distribution is limited to appearing as arguments in semantic functions. **Things** do, however, appear in a wide variety of semantic functions as will be documented below.

9.3.4.2 The Semantic Functions In contrast to **Things**, semantic functions project complex semantic trees (i.e., semantic constituents). These trees denote conceptual entities that are temporally bounded (e.g., **Events**, **States**, **Paths**, **Places**) and often dynamic (e.g., **Causal Events**, **Events**). Semantic functions also evoke semantic inferences that reveal how their arguments contribute to their content. Below we document each of the semantic functions in this semantic representation:

- The function's conceptual mapping (i.e., an informal description of how the function maps into conceptual representation).
- The function's distribution.
- The function's projections (i.e., the semantic categories in which the semantic function appears as a head).
- Its local distribution (i.e., the semantic categories of the arguments it allows).
- The distributions of the function's projections (i.e., the environments in which the semantic function's projection appears).
- Its semantic inference rules (i.e., rules that decompose the semantic function in terms of its arguments and other semantic functions).

9.3.4.3 Place Functions Consider the following sentences, each of which denotes an occurrence of a **Place** function:

(6) a. The ball was on the box.
    b. The ball was in the box.

(7) a. The ball rolled on/onto the box.
    b. The ball rolled in/into the box.

(8) a. John threw the ball on/onto the box.
    b. John threw the ball in/into the box.

(9) a. Snow covered our front lawn.
   b. Tear gas filled our house.

The sentences in (6a), (7a), (8a), and (9a) denote the semantic function **on**, and the sentences in (6b), (7b), (8b), and (9b) denote the function **in**. As demonstrated by these examples, **Place** functions are specified by both prepositions and verbs. In (6) the semantic functions **on** and **in** are denoted by their corresponding prepositions *on* and *in*. In (7a) and (8a) the function **on** is denoted by both the prepositions *on* and *onto*. In (7b) and (8b) the function **in** is denoted by both *in* or *into*. In (9) **on** is denoted by the verb *covered*, and **in** is denoted by the verb *filled*.

Projection's conceptual mapping	Region of space
Distribution	
Projected category	Place
Local distribution	Place $\to$ place-function Thing
Projection's distribution	Path $\to$ path-function Place
	State $\to$ be Thing Place
	State $\to$ be Place
	Event $\to$ be Thing Place
Inferences	None

Figure 9.4
Properties of **Place** functions.

Projection's conceptual mapping	Trajectory in space
Distribution	
Projected category	Path
Local distribution	Path $\to$ path-function Place
	Path $\to$ path-function Thing
Projection's distribution	State $\to$ go_{state} Thing Path
	Event $\to$ go Thing Path
Inferences	None

Figure 9.5
Properties of **Path** functions.

Semantic Correspondence Theory

9.3.4.4 Path Functions   Consider

(10) a. John walked to the house.
 b. John walked from the shed.
 c. John walked into the house.

(11) a. John entered the house.
 b. John left the shed.

(12) a. John walked from the shed to the house.
 b. John walked from the shed into the house.

(13) a. John's trail of muddy footprints extended to the house.
 b. John's trail of muddy footprints extended into the house.
 c. John's trail of muddy footprints extended from the shed to the house.
 d. John's trail of muddy footprints extended from the shed into the house.

Each of the sentences in (10–13) denotes a **Path** function. As the sentences in (10) and (11) demonstrate, both verbs and prepositions specify **Path** functions. In (10a, b), the semantic functions **to** and **from** are denoted by their corresponding prepositions *to* and *from*. In (10c) **to** is denoted by the preposition *into*, which also denotes the **Place** function **in**. In (11b) the verb *entered* denotes the function **to**, and in (11b) *left* denotes the function **from**.

9.3.4.5 Location State Function   Consider the following sentences, each of which denotes the location state function **be**:

(14) a. There is water in the glass.
 b. There is water on the glass.

Projection's conceptual mapping	State in which object occupies a region of space
Distribution	
Projected category	State
Local distribution	State → be Thing Place
	State → be Place
Projection's distribution	State
	Event → Inch State
Inferences	None

Figure 9.6
Properties of the **be** function.

(15) a. Water fills the glass.
  b. The glass fills.

The semantic function **be** is specified by verbs, and cannot be specified by prepositions. In (14) **be** is denoted by the verb *is*, and in (15) **be** is denoted by the verb *fills*.

9.3.4.6 Location Event Function A semantic function that is closely related to the function **be** is the function be_{event} (Jackendoff 1983). Much like **be**, be_{event} describes locations in terms of a located object and its location. The distinction between these two functions is that be_{event} describes location events, locations that persist over time, while **be** denotes location states. Consider the following sentences, each of which describes a location event:

(16) a. John stayed in Mary's house (all day).
  b. John stayed on the couch (all day).
  c. John stayed (all day).

(17) a. The picture sat in the desk (for years).
  b. The picture sat on the desk (for years).

(18) a. The sergeant kept the men in the barracks (all day).
  b. The sergeant kept the men on the parade ground (all day).

In each of these sentences in (16–18), be_{event} is specified by the main verb. Be_{event} is denoted by *stay* in (16) and by *sat* in (17). In (18) it is denoted by *kept*.

Projection's conceptual mapping	Event in which an object occupies a region of space for a period of time
Distribution	
Projected category	Event
Local distribution	Event → be_{event} Thing Place
	Event → be_{event} Thing
Projection's distribution	Event
	Causal-Event → cause Thing Event
Inferences	
(Event be_{event} Thing Place) ⊨ (State be Thing Place) at start	
(Event be_{event} Thing Place) ⊨ (State be Thing Place) at end	

Figure 9.7
Properties of the be_{event} function.

Semantic Correspondence Theory

9.3.4.7 Motion Event Function Consider the following sentences, each of which denotes the the motion event function **go**:

(19) a. The book fell to the floor.
 b. The book fell onto the floor.
 c. The book fell from the shelf.
 d. The book fell.

(20) a. John threw the book to the floor.
 b. John threw the book onto the floor.
 c. John swept the book from the shelf.
 d. John threw the book.

In each of the sentences in (19–20), **go** is denoted by the main verb. In (19) **go** is denoted by the verb *fell*, and in (20a, b, d) it is denoted by the verb *threw*. In (20c) **go** is denoted by the verb *swept*.

9.3.4.8 Motion State Function The relationship between the motion state function go_{state} and the motion event function **go** (Jackendoff 1983) is analogous to the relationship between the **be** and be_{event} functions. Much like **go**, go_{state} describes the trajectory of an object. The distinction between these two functions is that **go** describes the trajectory of motion an object occupies over time while go_{state} describes the trajectory an object occupies at rest. Consider the following sentences, each of which describes a motion state:

Projection's conceptual mapping	Event in which an object in motion occupies a trajectory over time
Distribution	
Projected category	Event
Local distribution	Event → go Thing Path
	Event → go Thing
Projection's distribution	Event
	Casual-Event → cause Thing Event
Inferences	
(Event go Thing (Path from Place) $\models$ (State be Thing Place) at start	
(Event go Thing (Path to Place) $\models$ (State be Thing Place) at end	

Figure 9.8
Properties of the **go** function.

Projection's conceptual mapping	State in which an object occupies a trajectory in space
Distribution	
Projected category	State
Local distribution	State → go_{state} Thing Path
	State → go_{state} Thing
Projection's distribution	State
	Event → Inch State
Inferences	None

Figure 9.9
Properties of the go_{state} function.

(21) a. The highway extends from Los Angeles to Vegas.
    b. The highway extends into town.
    c. The highway extends.

(22) a. The men extended the highway into town.
    b. The men extended the highway.

In each of the sentences in (21–22), go_{state} is denoted by the main verbs *extends* and *extended*.

9.3.4.9 Inchoate Function In sections above we discussed two types of functions that project **Events**: be_{event} and **go**. Of these two functions, only **go** identifies a change in the location of an object. The inchoate function **inch** is the head of another class of trees that denote a change in location. **Inch** projects an **Event** that indicates a change in location, but for both conceptual and distributional reasons, it does not involve a path (Jackendoff 1990). Consider

(23) a. Water (quickly) filled the tank.
    b. Snow (quickly) covered the sidewalk.
    c. *Water filled into the tank.
    d. *Snow covered onto the sidewalk.

(24) a. John filled the tank with water.
    b. John covered the sidewalk with salt.
    c. *John filled water into the tank.
    d. *John covered salt onto the sidewalk.

Semantic Correspondence Theory

Projection's conceptual mapping	Event that results in the occurrence of a state
Distribution	
Projected category	Event
Local distribution	Event → inch State
Projection's distribution	Event Casual-Event → cause Thing Event
Inferences	
(Event inch State) ⊨ State at end	

Figure 9.10
Properties of the **inch** function.

Each of the sentences (23–24) denotes the **inch** function. In (23a, c) and (24a, c), *filled* denotes the function **inch**. In (23b, d) and (24b, d) it is denoted by *covered*.

9.3.4.10 Causal Event Function The semantic function **cause** is the only function that projects semantic trees in the semantic category **Causal Event**. Each of the following sentences denotes the semantic function **cause**:

(25) a. The guard kept the prisoner in the cell.
 b. The guard threw the prisoner into the cell.
 c. The guard filled the prisoner's bowl with broth.

(26) a. The prisoner stretched his hand into the bowl.
 b. The prisoner stretched.

In (25) **cause** is denoted by the verb *kept* and *threw*. And in (26) *stretched* denotes the function **cause**.

9.3.5 Structural Correspondences between Syntax and Semantics
Structural correspondences between syntactic and semantic structure identify relations between the manner in which words and phrases combine in the syntactic tree and the manner in which semantic functions and simple semantic elements combine in the semantic tree. Within the syntactic structure of a verb and its arguments, four different types of combinations of words and phrases occur:

1. *Noun phrases are arguments of the verb.* Noun phrase arguments that combine with the verb appear as subjects, direct objects, indirect objects, and as the objects of prepositional phrases that are sisters to the verb in the syntactic tree.

Projection's conceptual mapping	An causal event in which an agent's actions result in some event
Distribution	
Projected category	Causal-Event
Local distribution	Causal-Event → cause Thing Event
	Causal-Event → cause Thing
Projection's distribution	Causal-Event
Inferences	
(Causal-Event cause Thing Event) $\models$ Event at end	

Figure 9.11
Properties of the **cause** function.

2. *Prepositions are complements of the verb.* Prepositions that are complements of the verbs are the heads of prepositional phrases that are sisters to the verb in the syntactic tree.
3. *Noun phrases are objects of prepositions.* Noun phrases that combine with prepositions are the objects of the prepositional phrase headed by the preposition.
4. *Noun phrase arguments combine with each other remotely.* Their combinations are specified by the syntactic prominence relations that lie between them.

Each of these combinations conveys independent information about the combinations of semantic elements in the semantic interpretation of the verb and its arguments:

1. *Verb-Argument correspondence.* Noun phrase arguments of the verb denote semantic arguments of the verb's semantic interpretation. The semantic interpretations of noun phrases that are not arguments of the verb are not arguments of the verb's semantic interpretation.
2. *Verb-Preposition correspondence.* The semantic interpretations of prepositions that are complements of the verb appear in the semantic arguments of the verb's semantic interpretation. The semantic interpretations of prepositions that are not complements do not appear in the arguments of the verb's semantic interpretation.
3. *Preposition-Object correspondence.* Noun phrases that are objects of a preposition denote semantic arguments of the preposition's semantic interpretation. The semantic interpretations of noun phrases that are not objects of a preposition are not arguments of the preposition's semantic interpretation. Finally, if a noun phrase denotes a semantic argument of a semantic function denoted by some preposition in the

Semantic Correspondence Theory

language, the preposition must appear in the surface form of the sentence if it is syntactically acceptable.

4. *Noun Phrase Prominence correspondence.* The semantic interpretation of a noun phrase argument that is syntactically more prominent than some other noun phrase argument is semantically more prominent than that other noun phrase's semantic interpretation.

In this section we discuss each of these correspondence rules.

9.3.5.1 Verb-Argument Correspondence The Verb-Argument correspondence rule is precisely stated in terms of semantic tree structure in the following way:

Verb-Argument Correspondence A noun phrase is a syntactic argument of the main verb if and only if its semantic interpretation is dominated by the root of the semantic tree denoted by the main verb.

Simply put, the Verb-Argument correspondence rule states that noun phrase arguments of the verb denote arguments of the verb's semantic interpretation.

To make the Verb-Argument correspondence rule a little more tangible, consider the following sentences:

(27) a. Johnny Appleseed shot the apple into the water.
    b. Johnny Appleseed extended the canal into the orchard.

In both sentences in (27) as in other sentences in natural language, the main verb identifies the manner in which semantic interpretations of the noun phrases contribute to the semantic interpretation of the sentence. This is exactly what is stated by the Verb-Argument correspondence rule. For example, in (27a), both the agency of *Johnny Appleseed* and the motion of *the apple* are clearly determined by the verb *shot*. The noun phrase arguments themselves certainly do not indicate the manner in which they contribute nor is their any other word or phrase except for *shot* that might do so. This equally applies to the noun phrase arguments in (27b). The agency of *Johnny Appleseed* as well as the manner in which *the canal* participates in the effect of Johnny's actions are determined by the verb *extended*. The manner in which the prepositional objects *the water* and *the orchard* contribute to the semantic interpretation of these is in part specified by the verb. Certainly *into* significantly determines their contribution, identifying that they are the conclusion of some trajectory. However, both the verbs *shot* and *extended* also play a critical role. They identify how contributions of the prepositional objects differ. In (27a) *the water* is the destination of the *apple*; *the apple travels a path that concludes at an interior region of the water*. In (27b) *the orchard* is a reference point for the location of *the canal*; *the canal itself concludes at an interior region of the orchard.*

In terms of the semantic structure of the verb's interpretation, the Verb-Argument correspondence rule states that the main verb of a sentence identifies the manner in which its arguments contribute to the sentence's semantic interpretation. Consider the syntactic and semantic structures for the sentences in (27) that appear in figure 9.12. As specified by the Verb-Argument correspondence rule, dominance relations connect the root of the verbs' semantic trees to the semantic interpretations of their

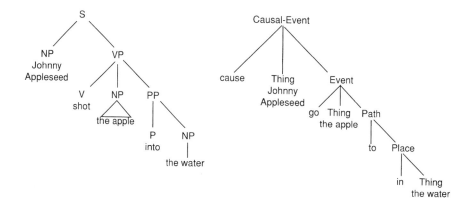

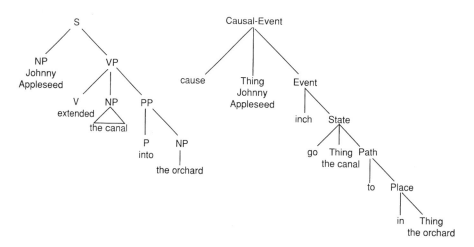

Figure 9.12
Verb-argument correspondence principle. NPs dominated by the verb in syntax must correspond to interpretations dominated (and hence affected) by the interpretation of the verb in semantics. Relative syntactic position is preserved in semantics.

noun phrase arguments. In the semantic interpretation of (27a), the root of semantic tree denoted by *shot*, **Causal Event**, dominates (**Thing Johnny Appleseed**), (**Thing the apple**), and (**Thing the water**). In the semantic interpretation of (27b), the root of the tree denoted by *extended* dominates (**Thing Johnny Appleseed**), (**Thing the canal**), and (**Thing the orchard**).

The verb does not determine the manner in which the semantic denotations of noun phrases that are not arguments of verbs contribute to the semantic interpretation. The manner in which these simple semantic elements contribute is determined by other words in the sentence. As examples consider the following sentences in which prepositional phrases are adjoined to the verb phrases of (27):

(27') a. Johnny Appleseed shot the apple into the water with a slingshot.
   b. Johnny Appleseed extended the canal into the orchard with a shovel.

As indicated by the syntactic trees in figure 9.13, the instrumental *with* phrase is adjoined to the verb phrases of both sentences in (27'). The manner in which the objects of these adjoined prepositional phrases, *a slingshot* and *a shovel*, contribute to the semantic interpretation of the sentence is determined by the instrumental preposition *with*, not by the verbs *shot* and *extended*. Note that contributions of these noun phrases are unaffected by the distinction in the semantics of these two verbs. Although *shot* denotes a motion event and *extended* denotes a motion state, both *a slingshot* and *a shovel* serve equivalent roles; both are the instruments that Johnny employs in achieving these effects.

This characterization of adjoined prepositional phrases is consistent with the other proposed semantic interpretations (e.g., Carlson and Tanenhaus 1988) and befits the modifier status of adjoined prepositional phrases. Adjoined prepositional phrases are always optional, unlike verb arguments, which are required. Furthermore any number of prepositional phrases can be adjoined to a verb phrase. Assuming that the main verb is responsible for determining the manner in which their noun phrases objects contribute to semantic interpretation would lead to computational models that are both inefficient and counterintuitive.

To sum up, whether it be the subject, object, or the object of a prepositional phrase sister to the main verb, the appearance of noun phrase in a verb argument position indicates that the lexical semantics of the main verb identifies the manner in which the noun phrase contributes to the semantic interpretation of the sentence. This is precisely articulated in terms of semantic tree structure by the Verb-Argument correspondence rule.

9.3.5.2 Verb-Preposition Correspondence

Verb-Preposition Correspondence The immediate dominator of a preposition (i.e., PP) is immediately dominated by the immediate dominator of the main verb (i.e.,

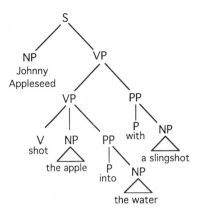

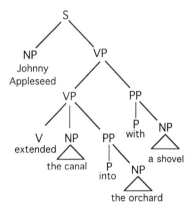

Figure 9.13
Adjuncts versus NP arguments. The interpretation of NPs not dominated by the verb in syntax is not influenced by the semantic interpretation of the verb.

VP) if and only if the root of the semantic tree denoted by the preposition is dominated by the root of the semantic tree denoted by the main verb.

The Verb-Preposition rule is an analogue to the Verb-Argument correspondence rule. Much like the Verb-Argument correspondence rule, the Verb-Preposition correspondence rule provides important information about the lexical semantics of the verb. When a prepositional phrase is a sister to the main verb, then that verb must denote some semantic function that accepts the semantic tree denoted by the preposition. Combining this information with the distributional structure of the semantic

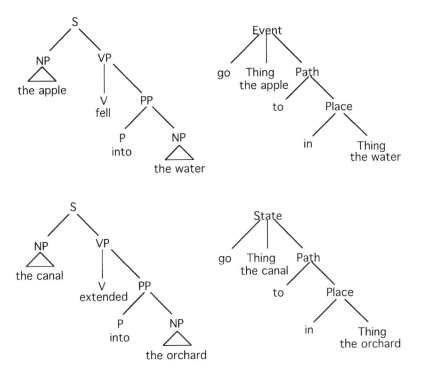

Figure 9.14
Verb-preposition correspondence principle: Path example. The semantic interpretation of PPs dominated by the verb in syntax are dominated (and hence affected) by the interpretation of the verb in semantics.

and the lexical correspondences proves important in inferring the semantics of novel verbs and disambiguating the verb's semantics.

Consider

(28) a. The apple fell into the water.
   b. The canal extended into the orchard.

(29) a. The apple fell in the water.
   b. The apple is in the water.

In both pairs of sentences, the main verbs identify the manner in which the semantic denotation of the preposition contributes to the interpretation of the sentence. *Fell* and *extended* determine whether the **Path** projected by the semantic denotation of *into* refers to a path that some object in motion traverses or a trajectory that some

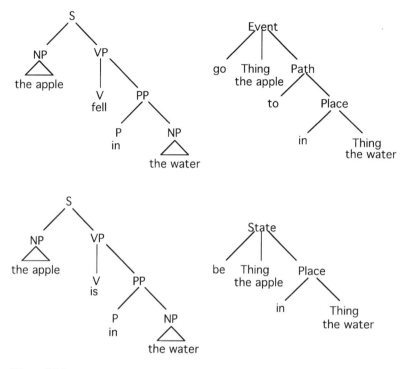

Figure 9.15
Verb-preposition correspondence principle: Place example. The semantic interpretation of those PPs dominated by the verb in syntax are dominated (and hence affected) by the interpretation of the verb in semantics.

object occupies. In (28a) *fell* indicates that *into* specifies the path of *the apple*'s motion. In (28b) *extended* identifies that the **Path** denoted by *into* is a trajectory occupied by *the canal*. *Into* denotes a path that concludes at the interior of some reference object in both sentences. However, the manner in which this path contributes to the semantic interpretation of the sentence is distinguished by whether it combines with *fell* or *extended*. This also occurs in the sentences in (29). When *in* combines with the verb *fell* in (29a), *in* and its object *the water* denote the destination of the *apple*. In contrast, when *in* combines with *be*, as in (29b), it specifies a region of space.

In both pairs of sentences in (28) and (29) as in other sentences with similar syntactic structures, the main verb identifies the manner in which the semantic interpretations of prepositions contribute to the semantics of the sentence. In terms of semantic structure, the root of the semantic tree denoted by the verb dominates the root of the semantic tree denoted by the preposition when the phrase that the preposition heads is sister to the verb. Consider the corresponding syntactic and semantic structures for the sentences in (28) and (29), which appear in figure 9.14 and figure 9.15. All of the preposition phrases in these syntactic trees are sisters to the verbs, and in all cases the root of the semantic tree denoted by the verb dominates the root of the semantic tree denoted by the prepositions. In the semantic interpretation of (28a), the root of semantic tree denoted by *fell*, **Event**, dominates **Path**, and in (28b) **State**, the root of the semantic tree denoted by *extended* dominates **Path**. Similarly, in the semantic interpretations of (29a) and (29b), the roots **Event** and **State** dominate **Place**, the root of the semantic tree denoted by *in*.

Prepositions that head prepositional phrases that are not sisters to the main verb (e.g., prepositional phrases adjoined to the verb phrase) do not appear in the semantic denotation of the verb. Consider the following sentences and the corresponding syntactic trees in figure 9.16.

(30) a. George Washington threw a silver dollar from the east bank of the Potomac to the west bank of the Potomac.
 b. George Washington threw a silver dollar to the west bank of the Potomac from the east bank of the Potomac.

Note that the interpretations of the two sentences in (30) differ. In (30a) the prepositional phrase *from the east bank of the Potomac* specifies the origin of the path traveled by *a silver dollar*; *the silver dollar traversed the trajectory that commenced at the east bank of the Potomac and concluded at the west bank of the Potomac.* In (30b) this same prepositional phrase serves a different function. It modifies the entire causal event articulated by *George Washington threw a silver dollar to the west bank* identifying the location or origin of the event; *from the east bank of the Potomac, a causal event occurred in which George Washington caused the silver dollar to traverse a path that concluded at the west bank of the Potomac.* Correctly, the Preposition-Object correspondence rule states that this *from* phrase offers two different contributions to the semantic interpretations of these sentences. As depicted in figure 9.16, the syntactic tree structures for these two sentences differ. In (30a) the prepositional phrase *from the east bank of the Potomac* is a sister to the verb. In (30b) the same prepositional phrase is adjoined to the verb phrase. The Verb-Preposition correspondence rule states that in (30a) **from**, the semantic function denoted by the preposition *from*, is dominated by **Causal Event**, the root of *throw*, and the semantic denotation of *from* in (30b) is not dominated by **Causal Event**. This distinction in semantic structure is consistent with the differences in interpretation these two sentence evoke.

To sum up, the occurrence of a prepositional phrase that is a sister of the main verb indicates that the lexical semantics of the main verb identifies the manner in

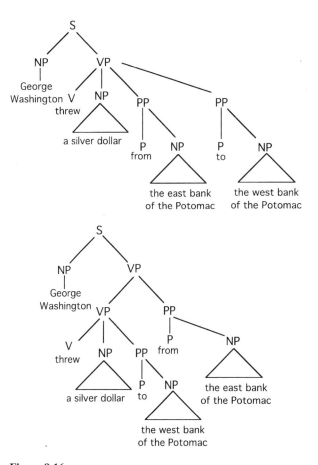

Figure 9.16
Adjuncts versus PP arguments. The interpretation of PPs not dominated by the verb in syntax is not influenced by the semantic interpretation of the verb. Adjuncts and arguments mean different things.

which the semantic interpretation of the preposition that heads this phrase contributes to the semantic interpretation of the sentence. The Prepositional-Object correspondence precisely states this in terms of the dominance relations of syntactic and semantic structure.

9.3.5.3 Preposition-Object Correspondence The correspondence between combinations of prepositions and their noun phrase objects and the combination of their semantic elements in the semantic interpretation can be stated in terms of the immediate dominance relations of syntactic and semantic structure in the following way:

Preposition-Object Correspondence A noun phrase argument is an object of a preposition if and only if the semantic interpretation of the noun phrase is dominated by the root of the semantic tree denoted by the preposition. Furthermore it is immediately dominated by the projection of the least prominent semantic function denoted by the preposition and must appear as a prepositional object if it is immediately dominated by a semantic function that can be denoted by a preposition and the resulting prepositional phrase is syntactically acceptable.

Simply put, within a verb and its arguments, a prepositional object denotes an argument of the preposition's semantic denotation. And there are certain instances where a preposition's semantics cannot be completely incorporated into the lexical semantics of the verb.

The following sentences demonstrate the various properties of the correspondence between the combination of a preposition and the noun phrase in the syntactic tree and the combination of their semantic interpretations in the semantic tree. The corresponding semantic trees for the acceptable sentences appear in figure 9.17.

(31) a. George Washington entered the coin in the Potomac.
 b. George Washington threw the silver dollar in the Potomac.
 c. *George Washington threw the silver dollar the Potomac.
 d. The silver dollar entered the Potomac.
 e. *The silver dollar entered into the Potomac.

Consider (31a). In this sentence the manner in which the prepositional object *the Potomac* contributes to the sentence interpretation is determined in part by the main verb *threw* and in part by the preposition *into*. It is solely *threw*, however, that determines the manner in which the other noun phrase arguments, *George Washington* and *the silver dollar*, contribute to the semantic interpretation. *Into* indicates that *the Potomac* marks the conclusion of a trajectory, and *threw* indicates that this trajectory is a path of motion. The semantic interpretation of *into* does not, however, participate in identifying the contributions of the noun phrase arguments *George Washington* and *the silver*. Regardless of whether the trajectory is left unspecified (e.g., *George Washington threw the silver dollar*) or articulated in terms of its point of commencement (e.g., *George Washington threw the silver dollar from the Potomac*), the agency of *George Washington* and the motion of *the silver dollar* remain intact.

Both of these properties are specified by the Preposition-Object correspondence rule. The Preposition-Object correspondence rule articulates them in terms of the dominance relations of semantic structure, stating that it is only the semantic interpretation of the prepositional object that is dominated by the root of the preposition's semantic tree. Or more informally, the preposition participates only in identifying

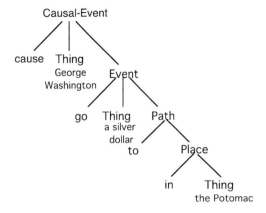

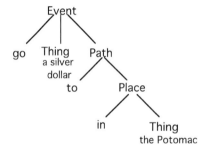

Figure 9.17
Preposition-object correspondence principle. NPs dominated by a preposition in syntax must correspond to interpretations dominated (and hence affected) by the interpretation of the preposition in semantics.

the semantic contribution of its object. This is illustrated in the semantic tree corresponding to (31a) in figure 9.17. The root **Path** dominates (**Thing the Potomac**). It does not dominate either (**Thing George Washington**) or (**Thing the silver dollar**).

Furthermore all of the semantic functions denoted by the preposition participate in identifying the manner in which the prepositional object contributes to the semantic interpretation. In (31a) *George Washington is causing the silver dollar to travel a trajectory that concludes in some interior region of the Potomac.* Both of the semantic functions denoted by the preposition *into*, **to** and **in**, participate in identifying the contribution of (**Thing Potomac**). Some interior region of (**Thing Potomac**) is being selected, and this interior region identifies the conclusion of a trajectory. The Preposition-Object correspondence rule identifies this property by requiring that the semantic element denoted by *the Potomac* be an argument of the least prominent semantic function denoted by *into*. As can easily be seen, this correspondence is satisfied by the semantic trees in figure 9.17. Of the two functions, **in** is less prominent than **to** since the immediate dominator of **to**, **Path**, dominates the immediate dominator of **in**, **Place**.

The Preposition-Object correspondence rule also places limits on semantic incorporation. The acceptable sentences in (31) demonstrate various levels of semantic incorporation. In (31a) no semantic incorporation occurs. In (31b) the semantic function **to** is incorporated into *threw*. In (31d) the combination of the semantic functions **to** and **in** are incorporated into *entered*. Note, however, that some preposition that denotes the semantic function **in**, either *into* or *in*, must appear in the surface form if it is to be syntactically acceptable. When it is syntactically acceptable, leaving it out of the surface form produces a semantically incongruous sentence as illustrated by (31c). The sentence in (31d) illustrates the case where incorporating the least prominent semantic function in the semantics of the verb is admissible. This is admissible in (31d) because placing a preposition in the direct object position would produce the syntactically unacceptable (31e).

To sum up, the semantic interpretations of prepositional objects and only the semantic interpretations of prepositional objects are arguments of their prepositions' semantic interpretations. The semantic elements they denote are the arguments of the least prominent semantic function denoted by the preposition. And some preposition that denotes the least prominent semantic function must appear in the surface form if the resulting prepositional phrase is syntactically acceptable.

9.3.5.4 Prominence Correspondence Prominence correspondence identifies a correspondence between the prominence relations that arise between noun phrase arguments in syntactic structure and the prominence relations that arise between the interpretations of the noun phrases in semantic structure. In syntactic structure, noun phrase arguments combine with each other. These combinations correspond to combinations of their interpretations in semantic structure. Both these combinations of noun phrase arguments and their semantic interpretations and their correspondence to one another can be described in terms of prominence relations, yielding the following correspondence rule:

Prominence Correspondence Rule Given a set of noun phrase arguments of a verb (i.e., subject, object, prepositional object) and a set of their semantic interpretations, a noun phrase argument x is syntactically more prominent than another y if and only if the semantic interpretation of x is semantically more prominent the semantic interpretation of y.

To get a better understanding of how Prominence correspondence operates, let us consider the semantic interpretations of the following sentences:

(32) a. The silver dollar is in the Potomac.
 b. The silver dollar went into the Potomac.
 c. The silver dollar went in the Potomac.
 d. The silver dollar entered the Potomac.
 e. George Washington threw the silver dollar from the east bank of the Potomac to the west bank of the Potomac.

The corresponding syntactic and semantic trees for these sentences appear in figure 9.18 and 9.19. Consider (32a). In this sentence the noun phrase *the silver dollar* is more prominent than the noun phrase *the Potomac*; **S**, the immediate dominator of *the silver dollar*, dominates **PP**, the immediate dominator of *the Potomac*. As specified by the Prominence correspondence rule, the semantic interpretation of *the silver dollar*, (**Thing the silver dollar**), is semantically more prominent than (**Thing the Potomac**); **State**, the immediate dominator of (**Thing the silver dollar**), dominates **Place**, the immediate dominator of (**Thing the Potomac**). The combination of the noun phrases *the silver dollar* and *Potomac* in the syntactic tree structure preserves the semantic dominance relation between **State**, the projection of the semantic function **be**, and **Place**, the projection of the semantic function **in**.

The Prominence correspondence rule is undeterred by semantic incorporation. The sentences in (32b, c, d) are sentences with equivalent semantic interpretations that demonstrate various levels of semantic incorporation. Consider figure 9.19. All three sentences indicate that *the silver dollar traveled a path that concluded at an interior region of the Potomac*. In (32b) no incorporation occurs. In (32c) the semantic function **to** is incorporated into the semantics of *went*. And in (32d) the combination of the semantic functions **to** and **in** are incorporated into the semantics of *entered*. Although these sentences differ with the respect to semantic incorporation, both their syntactic and semantic prominence relations are the same. *The silver dollar* is syntactically more prominent than *the Potomac* in all three sentences. Consistent with the Prominence correspondence rule, (**Thing the silver dollar**) is semantically more prominent than (**Thing the Potomac**) in all three sentences.

The sentence in (32e) provides an example of equally prominent syntactic arguments that correspond to equally prominent semantic elements. Consider the syntactic structure of (32e) in figure 9.18. Both of the prepositional objects, *the east bank of the Potomac* and *the west bank of the Potomac*, are equally prominent in the sentence's syntactic structure. The immediate dominator of *the east bank of the Potomac* is **PP**(*from*), and the immediate dominator of *the west bank of the Potomac* is **PP**(*to*). These prepositional objects are equally prominent, since neither immediate domi-

Semantic Correspondence Theory

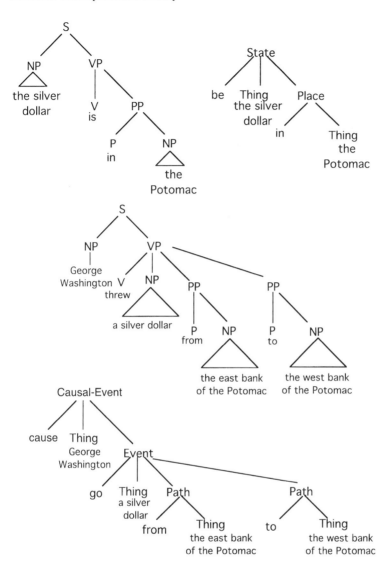

Figure 9.18
Prominence correspondence principle. Prominence relations between NPs in syntax are preserved in the prominence relations between the interpretations of those NPs in syntax.

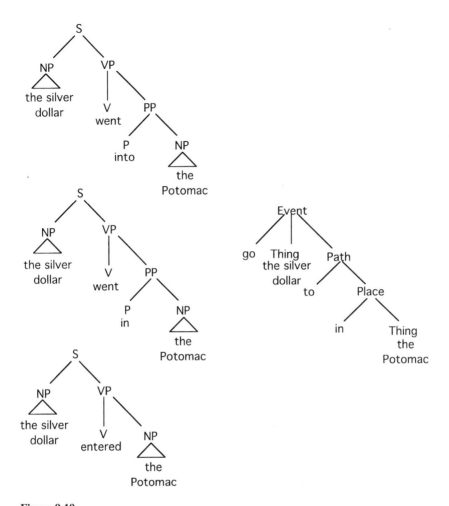

Figure 9.19
Prominence correspondence holds even when semantic elements are lexically incorporated: *Enter* and *Into* examples.

nator dominates the other. In accord with the Prominence correspondence rule, the semantic interpretations of these prepositional objects, (**Thing the east bank of the Potomac**) and (**Thing the west bank of the Potomac**), are equally prominent. Each of these **Things** is dominated by a corresponding **Path**, and neither of these **Paths** dominates the other. Finally it should be noted that the rest of the semantic tree for (32e) is also in line with the Prominence correspondence rule. Syntactically *George Washington* is more prominent than *the silver dollar*, which is more prominent than both prepositional objects, and semantically (**Thing George Washington**) is more prominent than (**Thing the silver dollar**), which is more prominent than both **Path** arguments.

In sum, combinations of noun phrase arguments in the syntactic structure preserve the semantic dominance relations between semantic functions denoted by verbs and prepositions. The Prominence correspondence rule articulates this property of syntactic-semantic correspondence in terms of syntactic and semantic prominence relations.

9.4 Computational Model

We have developed a computational model that produces semantic interpretations of natural language sentences. The purpose of the model is to demonstrate that Semantic Correspondence can be used to interpret sentences with novel verbs, known verbs, and novel uses of known verbs in an efficient, systematic, uniform manner, as well as to investigate other benefits derived from the approach. Of course certain design decisions that fall outside this goal have been made in order to produce a functional model of sentence interpretation, such as the model parses sentences, and it employs a process model. Although both the parsing and the process model are adequate for these purposes, they are not intended to offer an improvement in syntactic parsing technology, nor do they provide a superior account of human sentence processing behavior; in many cases the model will not successfully resolve prepositional-attachment ambiguities nor will it demonstrate garden-path behavior. The computational model does, however, fulfill its purpose: It demonstrates that Semantic Correspondence can be used to generate verb interpretations when the verb is novel, to disambiguate verbs when they are known, and to identify the semantic composition of a verb and its arguments for both novel and known verbs.

Within the model, sentence processing is broken down into syntactic parsing and semantic interpretation. The model generates a syntactic parse given a natural language sentence, and in concert, it constructs a semantic interpretation, combining partial information provided by the lexical correspondences between syntax and semantics and the semantic interpretations of known words. The structural correspondences between syntax and semantics and the restrictions upon the possible combinations of semantic elements inform this process of construction.

To make possible the Semantic Correspondence approach to sentence interpretation, the model's functional architecture must satisfy a number of requirements. First, it must provide a means of communication between syntactic and semantic processing. Second, it must access and use word-specific information when it is available. Third, it must be able to resort to general knowledge about syntax and

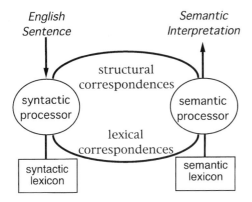

Figure 9.20
Functional architecture of the computational model. The system allows separate syntatic and semantic lexicons, uses two processors, and uses correspondence rules to communicate between syntactic and semantic processing.

semantics when word-specific information is absent, and when it is in conflict with the input (e.g., novel uses of known verbs). This section presents the model's architecture that satisfies these requirements and discusses its operation.

9.4.1 Functional Architecture

The functional architecture of the computational model is displayed in figure 9.20. It is very modular, containing six separate components, each of which performs a unique function in service of the overall task. This high degree of modularity provides the model with considerable flexibility, making possible the investigation of different types of process models for each subtask as well as different types of subtask interaction. For example, one of its unique features is its two lexicons, a syntactic lexicon and a semantic lexicon. These components provide information about the linguistic properties of individual words. The semantic lexicon informs the model about the semantic interpretations of known words, and the syntactic lexicon provides information about their syntactic properties. Typically models of sentence interpretation employ a single lexicon containing both syntactic and semantic information. This feature of their architectures is more often than not a constraint imposed by their approach to sentence interpretation. Semantic Correspondence, makes possible the use of separate syntactic and semantic lexicons. It takes advantage of this feature of the approach in order to allow the investigation of contrasting process models for the syntactic and semantic lexicons as well as contrasting models of lexicon-syntactic processor interaction and lexicon-semantic processor interaction. The flexibility of architecture allows the generation of many different types of sentence processing behaviors.

The model's architecture also contains two main processing modules: a syntactic processor and a semantic processor. The semantic processor produces the final output of the model, semantic interpretations of input sentences. The syntactic processor supports semantic processing by producing a syntactic parse tree for the input. Each of these processing modules contains general knowledge about the linguistic properties of the English language and its constituent words. The semantic processor possesses the primitive elements and distributional structure of the semantic representation, and the syntactic processor possesses a limited grammar of English.

Finally the architecture contains two mapping components, the lexical correspondence component and the structural correspondence component. They provide the means of communication between syntactic and semantic processing. The lexical correspondence component maps the syntactic categories of words onto their respective semantic categories, and the structural correspondence component maps the structure of the syntactic parse tree onto the structure of the semantic interpretation. Below we describe each of these components in detail and describe how they interact.

9.4.1.1 Syntactic Lexicon The purpose of the syntactic lexicon is to provide the syntactic processor with information about the syntactic properties of words with which the lexicon is familiar. The syntactic lexicon describes syntactic properties in terms of lexicalized tree structures (Abeille et al. 1990). Lexicalized tree structures identify the portion of the sentence's syntactic structure that can be inferred given the occurrence of the word in the sentence. They identify the syntactic categories of the relevant word and the types of phrases that the word can head. They also identify the manner in which phrase heads combine with other words. Possible combinations are described in terms of (1) the syntactic categories of words with which a head can combine, (2) the structural relation(s) formed by the combination, and (3) the linear relations that must hold if the combination is to be well formed.

As an illustration of the types of descriptions the syntactic lexicon provides, consider the lexicalized tree structures produced for *the*, *book*, and *threw*. They appear in figure 9.21. The tree structure for *the* simply indicates that *the* is a member of the syntactic category "article" (i.e., "the" has the distribution of an article.).

The tree structure for *book* indicates that the word *book* is in the syntactic category "noun" and that given the occurrence of *book* in the sentence, it is possible that this noun participates in a noun phrase of which it is the head. The lexicalized tree structure also identifies that a noun phrase is formed when *book* is combined with an article. This is indicated by the anchor symbol ↓ and the accompanying specification of the syntactic category "article." Finally the structure indicates that in order for a

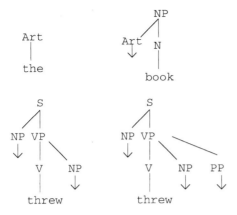

Figure 9.21
Syntatic lexicon: Syntactic entries for *the*, *book*, and *threw*.

combination of *book* and an article to be well formed, the article must precede *book* in the sentence.

Threw appears with multiple syntactic tree structures. Each of these structures represents a different sentence form in which *threw* can appear; *threw* can appear within a sentence that has only a subject and a direct object, and it can appear in a sentence that has a subject, direct object, and a prepositional phrase. The tree structures also indicates that *threw* is member of the syntactic category "verb" and that when combined with the appropriate set of noun phrases and prepositional phrases, it can produce both a verb phrase and a sentence. Finally both tree structures describe the syntactic prominence relations that arises between the subject and direct object of *threw*.

9.4.1.2 Semantic Lexicon The purpose of the semantic lexicon is to provide the semantic processor with the semantic interpretations of known words. The semantic lexicon accepts a word as input and produces semantic interpretation(s) as output. Semantic interpretations are described in terms of the semantic tree structures defined by the primitive elements and distributional structure of the semantic representation. The semantic interpretations for the words *John*, *threw*, and the noun *book* are provided in figure 9.22.

9.4.1.3 Syntactic Processor The syntactic processor is a stack-based processor that uses a lexicalized grammar to perform its task. It accepts a linear string of words as input and produces a syntactic parse tree of the string as output. Words are processed in the order which they appear in the input string.

Figure 9.22
Semantic lexicon: Semantic entries for *the*, *book*, and *threw*.

The syntactic processor pursues multiple parses in parallel. Each word may have multiple tree structures associated with it. When these tree structures are combined with the syntactic tree structures associated with other words, a number of parses of the sentence are produced. The syntactic processor pursues all of these candidate parses in parallel. It eliminates candidates only when the evidence provided by the input sentence dictates it. It does not backtrack nor look ahead.

The syntactic processor begins processing a word by requesting all of the word's associated lexicalized syntactic trees. Once this set has been returned, the syntactic processor attempts to combine each of the tree structures with the current parse(s) of the input. Constraints on the possible combinations of syntactic tree structures are provided by the stack which maintains the linear relations between the words in the input string. Lexicalized tree structures that fail to combine are discarded, while well-formed combinations are retained on the stack. After all of the well-formed combinations have been produced, the constituent words and their lexical categories are sent to the lexical correspondences component, and all relevant structural relations are sent to the structural correspondences component.

The syntactic processor can parse sentences that contain one or more novel open-class words (e.g., noun, verb). Employing the natural language grammar that was shown in figure 9.3, it generates a set of lexicalized tree structures for each novel open-class word. The process of generation is similar to the method, described in the previous section, that is used to generate verb interpretations. As in the case of known words, the syntactic processor attempts to combine each of the generated tree structures with the current parse of the input in parallel.

The syntactic processor has three operations to choose from when it is attempting to combine syntactic structures with the current parse of the input: *attach left*, *attach right*, and *shift*. Each of these operations corresponds to a different combination decision. *Attach left* makes the current word's syntactic tree an argument of the syntactic tree structure on the top of the stack, and *attach right* makes the syntactic tree structure on the top of the stack an argument of the current word's syntactic tree. If neither of these combination operations is successful, the syntactic processor chooses the *shift* operation, which simply puts the current word's tree on the top of the stack.

When all of the words in the input have been processed, the syntactic processor performs postprocessing on the current parse(s). Those parses that do not produce a single parse tree, and those parses that contain argument positions that have not been filled (i.e., empty anchors) are removed. The final parse(s) are then produced as the syntactic output.

As example of how the syntactic processor performs its task, let us isolate it from the rest of the system architecture and consider how it parses the following sentence:

(33) John threw the book.

Let us assume that *John threw* has been already parsed and the partial syntactic parse trees for this sentence fragment are residing on top of the stack as displayed in figure 9.23. Note that there are two structures on the stack, each corresponding to one of the lexicalized syntactic structures associated with *threw*. The current word in the input is *the*.

The syntactic processor begins by requesting the lexicalized tree structures associated with *the*. The lexicon responds by returning the syntactic tree structure that appears in figure 9.23. Once this structure is received, the syntactic processor attempts to make *the* an argument of *threw* (attach left), and it attempts to make *threw* an argument of *the* (attach right). Neither of these operations is successful, so *the*'s tree structure is simply shifted onto the top of the stack as illustrated in figure 9.23. The syntactic processor then moves onto *book*, the next word in the sentence.

Once the relevant tree structure has been received, both attach left and attach right operations are attempted. Since *the* can appear as an argument of *book*, the attach right operation is successful, producing the noun phrase structure that appears in figure 9.23. The syntactic processor sends the noun phrase *the book* to the lexical correspondence component and then attempts to combine this newly formed syntactic tree structure with the current structures on the top of the stack, the syntactic tree structures for the fragment *John threw*. The noun phrase *the book* can be attached left to both of these tree structures, so two new combinations are produced. This leaves two tentative parse trees for the sentence. The syntactic processor concludes its processing of *book* by sending the newly formed syntactic prominence and dominance relations to the structural correspondences component.

In postprocessing, the syntactic processor identifies that the (NP NP PP) form of *threw* has an empty argument, so it is removed from the stack. The alternative parse

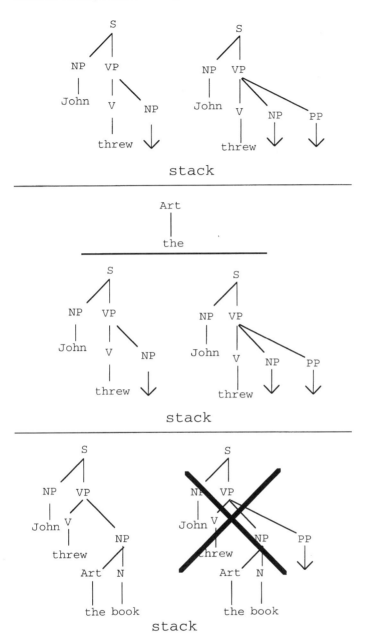

Figure 9.23
Syntactic processing: States of the stack while processing *John threw the book*.

tree, which invokes the (NP NP) form of *threw*, is deemed acceptable and returned as the syntactic output.

9.4.1.4 Semantic Processor The purpose of the semantic processor is to produce a semantic interpretation of the sentence. The semantic processor is a set-based processor; it does not use the linear order of words as a constraint. It accepts a string of words annotated with their semantic categories from the lexical correspondence component and a set of structural relations from the structural correspondence component. Processing word by word and applying the constraints on semantic structure, the semantic processor produces the output of the computational model, a semantic interpretation of the input sentence.

Given a word and its semantic category, the semantic processor requests interpretations of the word from the lexicon. Those interpretations that are inconsistent with the semantic category are immediately discarded. For example, if the semantic processor received two interpretations of the word *man*, an **Event** interpretation (e.g., *strong men man oars*) and a **Thing** interpretation (e.g., *the strong man manned the oars*), and the lexical correspondence component had determined that *man* was a **Thing**, the semantic processor would discard the **Event** interpretation of *man*.

Much like the syntactic processor, the semantic processor pursues interpretations of a sentence in parallel. It attempts all possible combinations of a word's interpretation(s) with the current interpretation(s) of the input. Unlike the stack-based syntactic processor, combinations of semantic elements are not constrained by the linear order of the input. Instead, they are constrained by structural relations provided by the structural correspondence component and the distributional structure of the semantic representation.

When the verb being processed is novel, the semantic processor generates a semantic interpretation autonomously, without recourse to constraints from the semantic lexicon, as described in subsection 9.4.2.3. The semantic processor applies this method incrementally. It generates those interpretations that minimally satisfy the constraints on semantic structure and the distributions of semantic elements for those words in the sentence that have been encountered so far. For example, after encountering the novel verb *zorched* in the sentence *John zorched the book into the fire*, the semantic processor will have generated only those semantic interpretations that minimally satisfy the sentence fragment *John zorched*. The appearance of the noun phrase *the book* requires the semantic processor to add to its semantic interpretation of *zorched* so that it may satisfy the requirements of the sentence fragment *John zorched the book*. This process is continued until of all the words in the input have been processed. This incremental approach to generating verb interpretations will be demonstrated in the novel verb example below.

In postprocessing, the semantic processor removes those interpretations that do not satisfy the constraints on the argument-taking properties of the semantic functions. For example, the distribution of the semantic function **go** also includes a **Thing** argument. In postprocessing, semantic interpretations which include **go** functions without **Thing** arguments are discarded. Once postprocessing has been completed, the semantic processor produces the remaining interpretation(s) as output.

9.4.1.5 Lexical Correspondence Component The purpose of the lexical correspondence component is to identify the semantic categories of words and phrases. Relevant inputs include noun phrases, prepositions, and verbs. The lexical correspondence component receives words and phrases annotated with their respective syntactic categories. It maps the syntactic categories onto categories in the semantic representation (e.g., **Thing**, **Event**) and sends them to the semantic processor, which uses the semantic categories (1) to eliminate irrelevant semantic interpretations returned by the semantic lexicon, and (2) to constrain the generation of novel word interpretations.

To achieve its task, the lexical correspondence component applies the following rules of lexical correspondence:

- Verbs denote semantic tree structures that are complete, such as semantic trees in the categories **Event**, **State**, **Causal Events**.
- Prepositions denote incomplete semantic tree structures, such as semantic trees in the categories **Path** and **Place**.
- Noun phrase denote simple semantic elements, such as semantic elements in the category **Thing**.

9.4.1.6 Structural Correspondence Component The purpose of the structural correspondence component is to identify the semantic dominance and prominence relations invoked by combinations of words and phrases. Relevant combinations are those involving verbs, prepositions, and their noun phrase arguments. After receiving a syntactic combination from the syntactic processor, the structural correspondence component maps the syntactic dominance and prominence relations they contain onto the dominance and prominence relations of the semantic representation. The output is sent to the semantic processor, which uses the semantic dominance relations (1) to disambiguate verb interpretations and (2) to construct sentence interpretations.

There are three relevant syntactic combinations:

- *Verb-Argument combinations.* When a noun phrase or prepositional phrase becomes an argument of a verb, the syntactic processor informs the structural correspondence component and sends the syntactic prominence relations that arise

between the relevant noun phrase (e.g., subject, object, prepositional object) and the other noun phrases in the sentence.
- *Verb-Preposition combinations.* When a preposition appears as a part of a prepositional phrase argument of a verb, the syntactic processor sends the resulting dominance relation between the verb and the preposition to the structural correspondence component.
- *Preposition-Object combinations.* When a noun phrase becomes an object of preposition, the syntactic processor sends the structural correspondence component the resulting dominance relation between the preposition and its object.

When the structural correspondence component receives structural information from the syntactic processor, it applies the following rules of structural correspondence:

- *Verb-Argument correspondence.* Noun phrase arguments of the verb denote semantic arguments of the verb's semantic denotation.
- *Verb-Preposition correspondence.* The semantic denotations of prepositions that appear in propositional phrase arguments of the verb appear in the semantic arguments of the verb's semantic denotation.
- *Preposition-Object correspondence.* Noun phrases that are objects of the preposition are arguments of the preposition's semantic denotation.
- *Noun Phrase Prominence correspondence.* The semantic denotation of a noun phrase argument that is syntactically more prominent than some other noun phrase is semantically more prominent than that other noun phrase's semantic denotation.

9.4.2 Examples

In this section we demonstrate how the model uses correspondences between syntax and semantics to determine the contributions that verb arguments make to sentence interpretation, to disambiguate the semantics of known verbs, and to infer the semantics of novel verbs.

9.4.2.1 Verb-Argument Composition Consider

(34) John threw the book into the fire.

The goal is to produce an interpretation of the sentence in (34). All of the words in the sentence are known, and there are no semantic ambiguities. The task before the model is simply to combine the semantic interpretations of the noun phrases *John*, *the book*, *the fire* and the semantic interpretation of the preposition *into* with the semantic interpretation of the verb *threw*. We use this example to illustrate how the model combines information about verbs, prepositions, and their arguments. The states of the semantic processor, the states of the syntactic processor, and the actions performed by the lexical and structural correspondence components are shown in figure 9.24 and figure 9.25.

The model begins by retrieving the syntactic structure for the first word in the sentence, *John*. Since there are no items on the stack with which the structure can combine, the syntactic processor simply places it on top of the stack and sends the noun phrase *John* to the lexical correspondence component. The lexical correspondence component applies the lexical correspondence rule for noun phrases, determining that the semantic element **John** is a member of the "simple" semantic category, **Thing**. This is consistent with the entry for *John* retrieved by the semantic lexicon. The resulting states of the semantic and syntactic processors appear in figure 9.24.

The model retrieves the syntactic structure for the next word in the input, *threw*, and sends it to the lexical correspondence component. The lexical correspondence component identifies that the verb's interpretation should be a **Causal-Event**, **Event**, or **State**. The semantic processor retrieves the semantic interpretation of the verb *threw*, which projects a **Causal-Event**, a semantic structure consistent with the results of the lexical correspondence component. It then combines (**Thing John**) with the **Causal-Event**. As illustrated in figure 9.24, this produces two semantic interpretations, one in which John is the causal agent and one in which John is the thing undergoing motion. Concurrent with semantic processing, the syntactic processor attaches the noun phrase *John* to the verb *threw*, making *John* the subject of the sentence. This combination is relevant to the semantic processor, so the syntactic processor informs the structural correspondence component that *John* has been made an argument of the verb. The structure correspondence component applies the Verb-Argument correspondence rule, producing a semantic dominance relation between **Causal-Event** and (**Thing John**). Since both semantic interpretations satisfy this constraint, both are maintained in the semantic processor as illustrated in figure 9.24.

Next the model processes *the*. The syntactic tree structure for *the* cannot combine with the current parse of the input, so it is simply placed on the stack. Since *the* is an article, it is not sent to the lexical correspondence component. Note that the state of the semantic processor has been left unchanged.

Then, the model processes *book*. The semantic processor combines the (**Thing the book**) with the current semantic interpretations. As illustrated in figure 9.24, this produces two interpretations, one in which the book is throwing John and another in which John is throwing the book. The syntactic tree structure of *the* attaches to the *book*, producing the noun phrase *the book*. Since the combination of article *the* with the noun *book* was successful, the syntactic processor attempts to combine the noun phrase *the book* with verb phrase, which it does successfully, producing a parse tree in

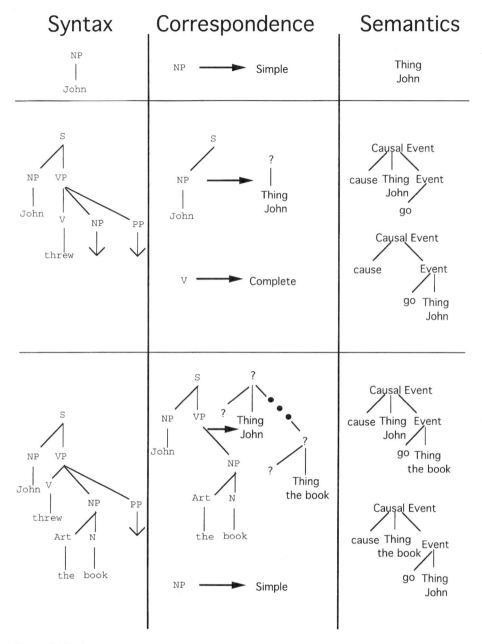

Figure 9.24
Semantic processing with syntax and correspondence rules: Example for a known and unambiguous verb. Each row shows a step in processing *John threw the book...*, with the syntactic representations, semantic representations, and correspondence rules.

Semantic Correspondence Theory

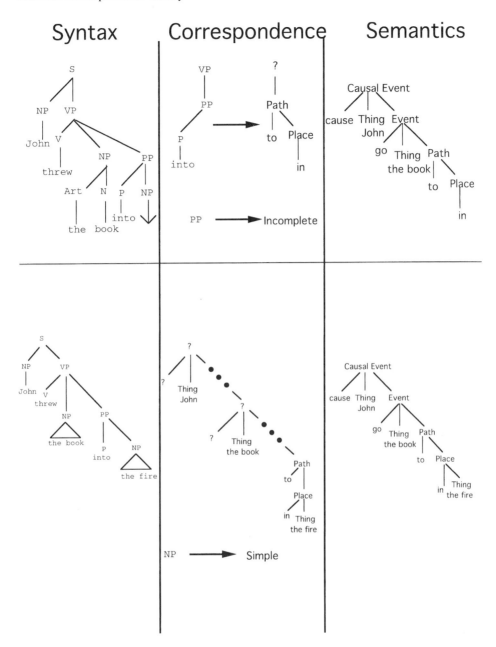

Figure 9.25
Semantic processing with syntax and correspondence rules: Continued processing of *John threw the book into the fire*.

which *the book* is the object of the sentence. This combination invokes two properties of the parse tree that are relevant to semantics. First, *the book* is an argument of the verb, and second, *John* is syntactically more prominent than *the book*. Both of these syntactic relations are sent to the structural correspondence component, which applies the Verb-Argument correspondence rule and the prominence correspondence rule. This produces a semantic dominance relation between **Causal-Event** and (**Thing the book**) and a semantic prominence relation between (**Thing John**) and (**Thing the book**). Applying the prominence relation as a constraint on the semantic interpretation, the model rules out *the book threw John* interpretation. As illustrated in figure 9.25, this leaves only the *John threw the book* interpretation.

The model processes the next word in the sentence, *into*. The semantic processor retrieves the semantic tree structure associated with *into* from the semantic lexicon and combines it with the current interpretation. The syntactic processor attaches the preposition to the current parse tree, creating a dominance relation between the verb phrase and *into*. This syntactic dominance relation is sent to the structural correspondence component which applies the Verb-Preposition correspondence rule. This produces a semantic dominance relation between **Causal-Event** and **Path**. The current semantic interpretation satisfies this constraint as well as the constraints provided by the distributional structure of the semantic representation. The resulting states of the syntactic and semantic processors are illustrated in figure 25.

The model processes the next word in the sentence, *the*. The syntactic tree structure for *the* is retrieved from the syntactic lexicon and placed on top of the stack, and the semantic processor is left unchanged.

Next the model processes *fire*. The syntactic processor retrieves the syntactic tree structure for *fire* and attaches *the* to *fire*, producing a noun phrase, *the fire*, which is sent to the lexical correspondence component. The semantic processor combines (**Thing the fire**) with the current semantic interpretation, making it an argument of the semantic function **in**. The syntactic processor combines the noun phrase *the fire* with the current parse, creating three semantically relevant relations: *the fire* is an argument of *threw*, *John* is syntactically more prominent than *the fire*, and *the book* is syntactically more prominent than *the fire*. These relations map onto a semantic dominance relation between **Causal-Event** and (**Thing the fire**), a semantic prominence relation between (**Thing John**) and (**Thing the fire**), and another semantic prominence relation between (**Thing the book**) and (**Thing the fire**). The semantic interpretation is deemed consistent with these constraints on semantic structure and maintained. Since there are no more words in the input, processing is halted, and the semantic interpretation *John caused the book to go into the fire* is produced as output.

It should be noted that the task of combining verb and verb argument interpretations in the example above was accomplished using a lexically general method.

There are no lexically specific rules, for example, that map the subject of *threw* onto the causal agent argument, the direct object of *threw* onto object in motion argument, and the prepositional object of *threw* onto the destination argument. It is this property of the model that grants it such considerable parsimony.

9.4.2.2 Disambiguating Verbs This parsimony is also apparent in the model's approach to disambiguating the semantics of verbs. Consider

(35) John left the house to Mary.

Unlike the sentence in (34), this sentence does have a semantically ambiguous word, the verb *left*. It may denote either the causal transfer of possession or a departure, as in *John left the house and headed towards the store*. This sentence is particularly interesting because its interpretation involves two implications of the Prominence correspondence rule: (1) Semantic incorporation verbs may exhibit the same grammatical features as other "more straightforward" verbs, and (2) verb arguments that designate equally prominent semantic elements must be equally prominent in the syntactic parse tree. The two uses of *left* are grammatically indistinguishable in the case of *John left the house*. However, when combined with the prepositional phrase *to Mary*, the departure meaning of *left* can be ruled out by Prominence correspondence. In the departure interpretation of (35), the arguments of the semantic elements **from** and **to** are equally prominent in the semantic tree and must correspond to equally prominent noun phrase arguments in the syntactic tree. Since they do not, the departure interpretation can be ruled out.

Consider the state of the semantic processor and the state of the syntactic processor after the model has processed the sentence fragment *John left*. They appear at the top of figure 9.26. Note that in the semantic processor there are four semantic interpretations active: (i) *John caused a causal transfer*, (ii) *the possession of John was transferred*, (iii) *John moved from someplace*, and (iv) *John was the place from which something moved*. All of these semantic interpretations are consistent with the syntactic evidence, which simply indicates that (**Thing John**) is a semantic argument of *left* under either interpretation.

At this point, the model processes the noun phrase *the house*. After producing the combination of the article *the* and the noun *house*, the syntactic processor sends it off to the lexical correspondence component, which identifies the noun phrase *the house* as a **Thing**. The semantic processor combines the (**Thing the house**) with the current semantic interpretations, producing four semantic interpretations: (i) *John caused a causal transfer of the house*, (ii) *the possession of John was transferred by the house*, (iii) *John moved from the house*, and (iv) *John was the place from which the house moved*. Concurrent with semantic processing, the syntactic processor attaches the

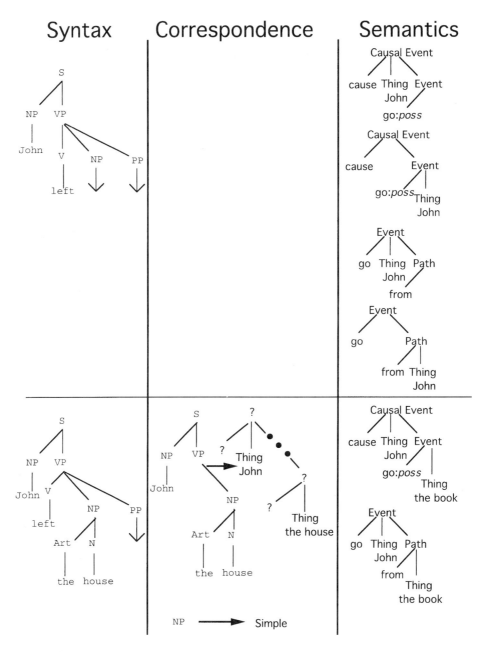

Figure 9.26
Semantic processing with syntax and correspondence rules for a known but ambiguous verb: Distinguishing departure and change of possession senses of *left* in *John left the house....*

noun phrase *the house* to the current parse trees, making the *the house* the direct object. This combination produces two semantically relevant syntactic relations: *the house* is an argument of the verb, and the subject *John* is syntactically more prominent than *the house*. Both of these relations are sent to the structural correspondence component, which maps them onto semantic dominance relations between the roots of *left*'s semantic interpretations and (**Thing the house**) and a prominence relation between (**Thing John**) and (**Thing the house**). Using the semantic prominence relation as a constraint, the semantic processor rules out *the possession of John was transferred by the house* and *John was the place from which the house moved*. As illustrated in figure 9.26, only those interpretations that are consistent with the sentence *John left the house* remain: (i) *John caused the transfer of possession of the house*, and (ii) *John moved from the house*.

Next the model processes *to*. The syntactic processor retrieves the syntactic structure associated with *to* from the syntactic lexicon and sends it to the lexical correspondence component. The semantic processor retrieves the semantic tree for *to* from the semantic lexicon and combines it with the current semantic interpretations. Concurrently the syntactic processor attaches *to*'s syntactic tree to the parse tree, which allows combination with a prepositional phrase. This produces a dominance relation between the verb phrase and the preposition *to*, which is sent to the structural correspondence component. The structural correspondence component maps syntactic dominance relation onto semantic dominance relations between the roots of the two interpretations and the **Path** tree projected by **to**. As illustrated in figure 9.27, both semantic interpretations satisfy this constraint on semantic structure.

The model then processes the next word in the sentence, *Mary*. The syntactic structure associated with *Mary* is retrieved and sent to the lexical correspondence component. The semantic processor combines the (**Thing Mary**) with both semantic interpretations. This produces the two semantic interpretations that appear in figure 9.27: (i) *John caused the transfer of possession of the house to Mary*, and (ii) *John went from the house to Mary*. The syntactic processor attaches the noun phrase *Mary* to the prepositional phrase, making it the object of *to*. Then, the syntactic processor informs the structural correspondence component that *Mary* is an argument of *left* and that *John* and *the house* are syntactically more prominent than *Mary*. The syntactic prominence relations are mapped onto a semantic prominence relation between (**Thing John**) and (**Thing Mary**) and semantic prominence relation between (**Thing the house**) and (**Thing Mary**). Applying these semantic prominence relations, the semantic processor identifies that *John went from the house to Mary* violates the semantic prominence relation between (**Thing the house**) and (**Thing Mary**); the Prominence correspondence rule indicates that (**Thing the house**) should be semantically more prominent than (**Thing Mary**), whereas this semantic interpretation contains an

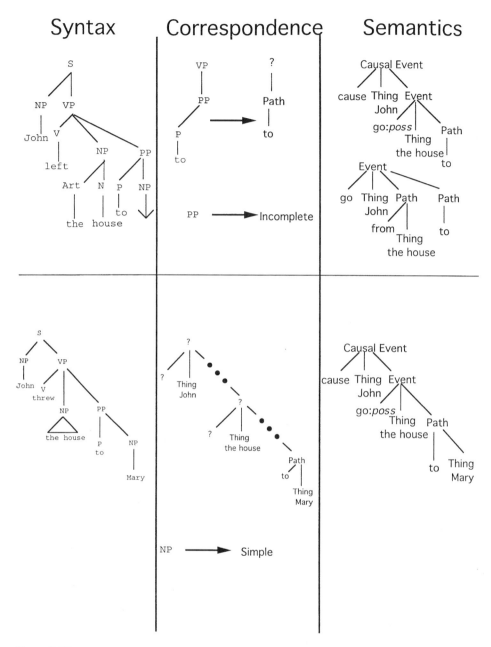

Figure 9.27
Semantic processing with syntax and correspondence rules: Continued processing of *John left the house to Mary*.

Semantic Correspondence Theory

equally prominent (**Thing the house**) and (**Thing Mary**). So the semantic processor excludes the *John went from the house to Mary* interpretation, as illustrated in figure 9.27. The remaining interpretation, *John caused the possession of the house to transfer to Mary*, is produced as the output of the model.

It is important to note that the model resolves semantic ambiguities such as that displayed by the verb *left* by using a lexically general method. There are no lexically specific rules, for example, that indicate that only the causal transfer interpretation of *left* occurs with the verb form (NP NP PP(to)). It is this property of the model that allows it to use a considerably smaller lexicon in performing the task of sentence interpretation.

9.4.2.3 Interpreting Novel Verbs The lexically general properties of both the verb-argument composition and verb disambiguation methods allow them to be used with novel verbs. Consider the following nonsense verb example:

(36) John zorched the book into the fire.

Consider the state of the semantic processor and the state of the syntactic processor illustrated at the top of figure 9.28. Only the word *John* has been processed.

The model then processes the word *zorched*. Since *zorched* is unknown to the syntactic processor, it must identify its syntactic category before communicating with the lexical correspondence component. It begins this process by generating all possible syntactic tree structures for the word. These include syntactic trees in the syntactic category noun and verb. Combining these structures with the noun phrase *John*, it determines that in order to produce a successful combination, *zorched* must be a verb. The syntactic processor informs the lexical correspondence component that *zorched* is a verb. Given this information, the lexical correspondence indicates that *zorched* is a **Causal-Event**, **Event**, or **State**. The semantic processor generates the minimal set of semantic interpretations for the verb. A subset of these are displayed in figure 9.28. These interpretations include *John causes something to happen*, *John is located somewhere for some period of time*, and *John went somewhere*. Concurrently the syntactic process informs the structural correspondence component that *John* is an argument of the verb *zorched*, which in turn informs the semantic processor that (**Thing John**) is a semantic argument of the semantic interpretation of *zorched*. Since all of the interpretations satisfy this constraint, the state of the semantic processor is left unchanged as illustrated in figure 9.28.

The model then processes the noun phrase *the book*. The syntactic processor informs the lexical correspondence component that *the book* is a noun phrase, and in turn the lexical correspondence determines that its semantic interpretation is a **Thing**. (**Thing the book**) cannot be combined with the semantic interpretations that appear in

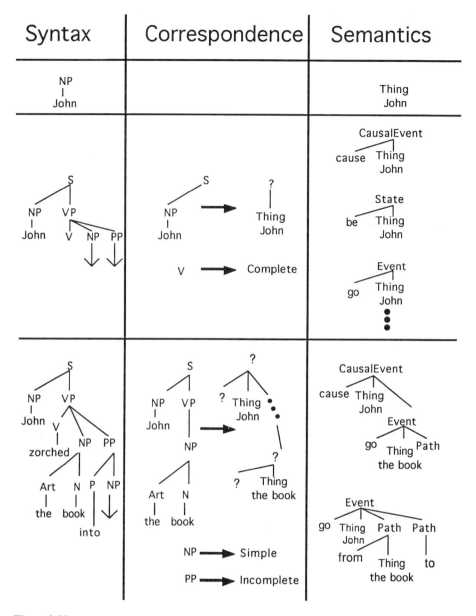

Figure 9.28
Semantic processing with syntax and correspondence rules for a novel verb: *John zorched the book into* . . . .

figure 9.28. So these semantic interpretations of *zorched* must be augmented before (**Thing the book**) can be successfully combined. This produces semantic interpretations of the sentence that include the following: (i) *John entered the book*, (ii) *John left the book*, (iii) *John occupied the book*, (iv) *John has the book*, (v) *John threw the book*, and (vi) *John kept the book someplace*. Concurrent with semantic processing, the syntactic processor combines the noun phrase *the book* with the current parses, making it either the direct object or the indirect object. The syntactic processor informs the structural correspondence component that *the book* is an argument of *zorched* and that *John* is syntactically more prominent than *the book*. The semantic prominence relation between (**Thing John**) and (**Thing the book**) produced by the structural correspondence component is used to rule out interpretations such as *the book threw John* and *the book kept John somewhere*.

The next word processed is the preposition *into*. The syntactic parse tree for *into* is retrieved from the syntactic lexicon and sent to the semantic processor via the lexical correspondence component. The semantic processor combines (**Path to** (**Place in**), the semantic structure retrieved for *into*, with the current interpretations. Employing the distributional structure of the semantic representation, the semantic processor rules out interpretations such as *John occupied the book*, *John has the book*, *John kept the book*, and *John entered the book*. As show in figure 9.28, those remaining interpretations are *John left the book* and *John threw the book*.

As illustrated in figure 9.29, the model then processes the final noun phrase in the sentence, *the fire*. Combining the noun phrase *the fire* with the prepositional phrase headed by *into*, the syntactic processor identifies a syntactic prominence relation between *the book* and *the fire* that maps onto a semantic prominence relation between (**Thing the book**) and (**Thing the fire**). Much like the *left* example, this semantic prominence relation is used to rule out *John left the book into the fire*. Finally the model produces an interpretation of *John zorched the book into the fire* that describes a causal event in which (1) the book was not in the fire at the onset, (2) John caused something to happen, (3) what happened was that the book went along a path leading to the fire, and (4) the result is that the book is now in the fire.

In sum, the model interprets novel verb sentences through a combination of methods. One produces tentative verb interpretations. Another lexically general method combines verb and verb argument interpretations. And a third lexically general method disambiguates verb interpretations.

9.5 Contributions

We have identified previously unappreciated sources of information about the meaning of a sentence and we have implemented a system which exploits this information

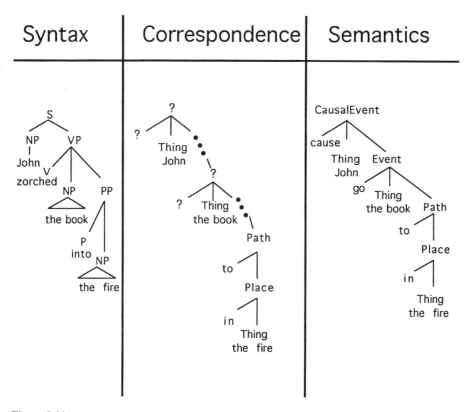

Figure 9.29
Semantic processing with syntax and correspondence: Continued processing of *John zorched the book into the fire*.

in processing. The new information is the distributional, hierarchical character of semantic representation and particularly the correspondences, structural as well as lexical, between this semantic representation and syntax. The new system exploited this information in processing: It decomposed the sentence interpretation task so that information from any available sources can be used. The system is not brought to a halt when one source is missing but can continue its principled use of available information. Because of this, it can apply the same methods in tasks which look quite different.

Semantic Correspondence theory was supported by the successful performance of the implemented system. It generates the appropriate semantic analysis across the range of syntactic structures used in English verbs in the motion domain. The semantic analysis that the system generates provides accurate implicatures about the events or states that the semantic representation entails. It generates appropriate analyses of novel as well as known verbs, and it can provide a semantically equivalent verb (or verbs) that matches the semantic interpretation of the known verb.

The identification of these information sources and the development of an architecture to exploit them provides a variety of benefits. Underlying all these benefits are two sorts of generality that Semantic Correspondence theory provides: Principles of Semantic Correspondence are lexically general, applying across all verbs, and principles from Semantic Correspondence are general across tasks, reliable for a variety of uses which might appear to be unrelated and to require separate processing modules from a naive or system-external perspective. In summarizing these benefits, we first consider the benefits to artificial intelligence work in natural language processing. Next we consider some analogous processing issues from the psychological perspective of understanding human language processing. Then we consider the contribution as a linguistic analysis of structure and remind the reader of some limitations of the current work. Finally we review the particular points of benefit to natural language processing driven by a practical need to use language or texts that were not generated or selected specifically to demonstrate the properties of a natural language processing system.

9.5.1 Benefits to Natural Language Processing in AI

For natural language processing, perhaps the clearest demonstration of merit is whether a new proposal can provide solutions to a problem where none were previously available and thus extend the range of tasks or situations that a system can address. We provide at least one such extention: the ability to derive reliable semantic interpretations of sentences with unknown verbs is not provided by previous systems. This ability directly derives from the lexical generality of the principles that Semantic Correspondence offers. Further the system does not accomplish this by adding in a special "Novel Verb Processing Module" designed just for this situation; rather the same system running on impoverished information can still perform reliably in these circumstances. A second benefit is the reuse of the information and processors for a variety of tasks. Our implemented system demonstrated flexible reuse in three respects. First, it used the same information and processors to determine what verb means (e.g., *stay* versus *throw* versus *keep*) and what role the verb arguments play (e.g., whether *the book* is identifying an agent, a location, or an object in motion). Second, it used the same information and methods to disambiguate the meanings of verbs and to construct a sentence interpretation. Third, the information and method used to interpret known verbs were also used to interpret novel verbs, including matching the novel verb to a semantically identical familiar verb, when one existed. This same system could be run on still other tasks such as explicit identification of paraphrase and partial paraphrase relations between sentences and generation of syntactic form from a semantic representation. Extended implementations of the architecture could equally apply to languages where information becomes available in very different orders. Specifically the same processors could apply to verb-final languages. Such languages are challenges to sentence interpretation systems which are verb driven, since reliance on verb-specific information would imply that no analysis could begin until the verb was encountered.

A second type of contribution to the field of natural language processing is a pragmatic one: tools for facilitating the implementation and extention of large systems. The architecture developed to capitalize on Semantic Correspondence principles is modular, allows use of the same components for a variety of tasks, and stipulates what must be changed if the system is extended to a new task, a new content domain, or even a new language. In particular, it directly simplifies implementation of the lexicon, compared to traditional approaches. First, since the principles are lexically general, less information needs to be in each lexical entry; the system developer is spared redundantly specifying the information captured in the principles in the lexical items. Second, the principles identify which information will need to be encoded in new lexical entries. The theory provides very clear stipulation of what information is carried in the syntactic representation, the semantic representation, and by exclusion what residual information must be in the conceptual representation for it to influence natural language processing at all. Thus, by working within the Semantic Correspondence framework, the information for the syntactic and semantic lexicon is both reduced and organized. The aspects of inference which, by default, must be driven by general world knowledge are distinguished.

9.5.2 Benefits to Psychology

The first contribution to psychology is recognition of an unappreciated human ability, namely the extent of comprehension of sentences with novel verbs. While this ability was capitalized on by Lewis Carroll in poems such as "Jabberwocki", it has generally escaped attention (but see Cabrera and Billman 1996). A related phenomena in acquisition has been discussed as syntactic bootstrapping (Landau and Gleitman 1985), though verb learning is assumed to be guided by exposure to a conspiracy of forms. But people also make clear interpretations from a single use, with the detail of the implications varying with the syntactic form. The informal findings and intuitions here deserve more detailed exploration. Semantic Correspondence theory also provides a broad framework for understanding the flexible array of language tasks people accomplish, from unimpaired comprehension in verb final languages to the ability to paraphrase.

Language acquisition is an aspect of language processing much more in focus for human that computer users of language. Computers, after all, can be programmed with much knowledge about language. We have already pointed out that this framework helps explain how individual verb meanings and argument structures might be learned from only a few exposures. But there is a deeper and more surprising implication for language acquisition. Where a rich set of semantic categories is proposed (Pinker 1989), it is generally assumed to be innate. However, within our framework much of the semantic structure of a language could be learned. If Semantic Correspondence is correct, and semantic representation does have the strong distributional character and the strong correspondences with syntax, these regularities provide a basis from which a learner could make inductions about the semantic categories of their particular language. Little evidence germain to this idea is available. However, recent work by Choi and Bowerman (1991) suggests that children's semantic categories are importantly different for Korean and English-learning children, and these differences project distinctions in the semantic organization of Korean versus English verbs.

9.5.3 Linguistics

Semantic Correspondence also benefits linguistics. The explanatory power of the semantic representation and its correspondences with syntax is greater than that of previous approaches (Rappaport and Levin 1988; Pinker 1989; Jackendoff 1990; Grimshaw 1990; Goldberg 1995). In particular, it explains the mappings of semantic arguments (e.g., causal agents) into syntactic positions (e.g., subject) rather than simply stipulating the mappings as has been done previously.

Semantic Correspondence also offers a fruitful approach for studying verb semantics. Performing a linguistic analysis of verb semantics is an extremely difficult endeavor. This is largely due to the limited evidence about semantics that is really available. Semantic Correspondence makes two claims about semantic representation that improve our ability to perform an effective analysis of verb semantics. First, it posits **structural** correspondences between syntax and semantic. Second, it offers a **direct** mapping between syntactic and semantic arguments. These two properties magnify the implications of solutions to specific problems in syntactic-semantic correspondence and provide alternative sources of evidence for making hypothesis about the properties of semantic representation.

In Semantic Correspondence the critical correspondences between syntax and semantics are structural correspondences; namely the critical correspondences are articulated in terms of the structure of the semantic interpretation. Solutions to specific correspondence problems are inherently general since they must range over all combinations of semantic elements. Thus solutions to one class of correspondence problems have direct implications for the entire theory of syntactic-semantic correspondence. For example, the correspondences used to map the semantic arguments of *throw* into syntax give us some idea of how the semantic arguments of *be*, *go*, and *have* are mapped into syntactic arguments. Narrowly constructed solutions that identify individual correspondences between specific elements of syntax and specific semantic elements do not have this property; they cannot be used to derive hypotheses concerning correspondence properties of other semantic elements.

Employing both structural correspondences and a direct mapping between syntactic arguments and semantic arguments allows us to use syntactic-semantic correspondence phenomena to derive hypotheses about the structure and primitive elements of semantic interpretation. In Semantic Correspondence, semantic arguments with similar mappings into syntax must have structurally similar semantic representations. So knowing the uses and meaning of one semantic element, we can make inferences about the uses of other semantic elements. For example, given both objects in motion and objects at a location have similar mappings into syntactic structure, we can conjecture that they have similar uses (e.g., both are involved in the results of causal events). The distributional structure of the semantic representation allows us to refine these hypotheses by identifying similarities and distinctions in meaning. For example, since objects in motion and objects at a location combine with two semantically distinct classes of prepositions, they themselves must be semantically distinguished.

9.5.4 Current Limitations

Semantic interpretations do not tell all you want to know about a sentence. The manner by which John caused the book to move is simply not part of the semantic representation in English, nor is information about what happened to the book once in the fire. The information provided in the semantic representation must be extended in at least two ways. For one thing, it is elaborated with inferences drawing on conceptual knowledge about the world. For another, it is elaborated by conceptual information carried by the verb, such as manner of motion. The information in semantic representation is limited, and the information that syntax provides about the semantic representation is further limited. However, the information from syntax, though partial, is reliable. Each subsystem does what it can with whatever relevant information is available and makes available the result of its analysis.

Some syntactic forms provide more constraints on semantic form than do others. Broadly, more articulated argument structure provides more information. While (NP V NP PP) sentence forms map onto a unique semantic representation, (NP V NP) sentences are less constraining and map onto several possible semantic representations. This is a fact about English, not a failing of the analysis of correspondences. However, it illustrates again that syntax-semantics correspondences are limited in the information about semantics that they provide and that some syntactic forms provide more information than others.

Within our work, we have restricted our focus to sentences that describe states of affairs within the spatial and possessional semantic fields. Following the thematic relations hypothesis (Jackendoff 1983), we assume that a careful analysis of the spatial semantics and its correspondences with syntactic form will provide a semantics and a set of correspondence rules that may be applied equally for both spatial and nonspatial semantic fields.

9.5.5 Benefits to the Processing of Unrestricted Texts

The discussion above lays out our contributions to natural language processing, and by implication to natural language processing systems dealing with input, which was not artificially selected nor designed to demonstrate the properties of a particular system. However, the implemented system deals with a modest range of surface forms and a considerably restricted verb vocabulary. Perhaps the greatest limitation of the implemented system is its simple parser which only deals with simple syntactic forms. Clearly our work would need to be joined with a much more sophisticated parser that can deal with a wide variety of surface forms, including noncannonical ones. Thus it is worth reiterating how the principles demonstrated in this system will contribute to the processing of a less restricted set of actual inputs.

Perhaps most clearly, our system provides the capability to interpret sentences with novel verbs. This is critical for dealing with naturally occurring text streams, where no designer can anticipate the full set of verbs that might appear, and the effort to encode rare forms even if known might not be worth the benefit. Further new uses of old verbs occur as well. Semantic Correspondence principles offer two other sorts of benefits besides extending the class of tasks that can be performed, both having to do with the ease of implementation and extention.

Semantic Correspondence provides a reduced and principled verb lexicon, making initial development and subsequent extention to new domains easier. It employs a modular architecture that can operate flexibility across a variety of tasks, depending on the information provided and the information needed. The same information base is organized in a way to allow its use in tasks that range from identification of paraphrases to generation (or translation) of sentences from a semantic form, as well as the sentence interpretation tasks to which we have already applied it.

In short, we identified new general sources of information that constrain the semantic representation of a sentence, and we provided a modular architecture that allows flexible use of this information in a variety of tasks.

References

Abeille, A., K. Bishop, S. Cote, and Y. Schabes. 1990. A lexicalized tree adjoining grammar for English. Technical report MS-CIS-90-24, University of Pennsylvania.

Cabrera, B., and D. Billman. 1996. Language-driven concept learning: Deciphering Jabberwocky. *Journal of Experimental Psychology: Learning, Memory, and Cognition* 22: 539–555.

Carlson, G., and M. Tannenhaus. 1988. Thematic roles and language comprehension. In W. Wilkins, ed., *Syntax and Semantics*, vol. 21: *Thematic Relations*. New York: Academic Press.

Choi, S., and M. Bowerman. 1991. Learning to express motion events in English and Korean: The influence of language-specific lexicalization patterns. In B. Levin and S. Pinker, eds., *Lexical and Conceptual Semantics*. Oxford: Blackwell.

Chomsky, N. 1981. *Lectures on Government and Binding*. Dordrecht: Foris.

Grimshaw, J. 1990. *Argument Structure*. Cambridge: MIT Press.

Goldberg, A. 1995. *Constructions*. Chicago: University of Chicago Press.

Jackendoff, R. 1983. *Semantics and Cognition*. Cambridge: MIT Press.

Jackendoff, R. 1990. *Semantic Structures*. Cambridge: MIT Press.

Kaplan, R., and J. Bresnan. 1982. Lexical-functional grammar: A formal system for grammatical representation. In J. Bresnan, ed., *The Mental Representation of Grammatical Relations*. Cambridge: MIT Press.

Landau, B., and L. Gleitman., 1985. *Language and Experience*. Cambridge: Harvard University Press.

Peterson, J. 1996. *Making Novelty Normal: a Theory of Sentence Processing*. PhD dissertation. Georgia Institute of Technology.

Pinker, S. 1989. *Learnability and the Cognition*. Cambridge: MIT Press.

Pollard, C., and I. Sag. 1987. *An Information-based Syntax and Semantics*, vol. 1: *Fundamentals*. Stanford, CA: Center for the Study of Language and Information.

Rappaport, M., and B. Levin. 1988. What to do with theta-roles. In W. Wilkins, ed., *Syntax and Semantics*, vol. 21: *Thematic Relations*. New York: Academic Press.

Chapter 10
Creativity in Reading: Understanding Novel Concepts

Kenneth Moorman and Ashwin Ram

10.1 Motivations

Reading is such a ubiquitous skill that it is easy to forget just how complex it really is. One of the goals of this book has been to demonstrate just how many underlying processes have to exist for even basic reading to occur. However, as with many cognitive processes, an analysis of the base components often produces a model that, while accurate, is lacking some of the higher-level aspects of the cognitive reasoning in question. In some sense these higher-level aspects are emergent qualities; that is, they are not the result of any particular component but come about from the interaction of all the components of the cognitive system. The ability to perform *creative reading* is such an aspect.

In the simplest terms, creative reading is the ability to comprehend texts containing novel concepts. This basic definition immediately raises the following question: Is there *mundane reading* as well? Do two reading processes exist—one that is utilized when texts containing known concepts are encountered and one that is activated when novel concepts are discovered? Simplicity would argue otherwise, and this is the approach we will take in this chapter. We use the term "creative reading" to indicate that reading is inherently a creative process. While texts containing novel concepts are the clearest examples of a medium that require creativity, texts containing known concepts in novel combinations also require some level of creativity for reading to be successful; in other words, all reading is a creative act.

By closely examining reading and other cognitive activities, we propose that there is a general purpose process that allows the understanding of novel concepts to occur. These concepts may be used in a text, in which case the behavior we call creative reading will result. Or, the novel concepts may simply be new things in the world around the reasoner. Regardless of the source the understanding of these novel concepts is a key aspect in a reasoner successfully interacting with the world. This basic ability to understand novel concepts is what we call *creative understanding*.

This chapter will explore the issues dealing with creative understanding within the context of the entire reading process. It will present the motivations behind our research, the knowledge representation used in the theory, and the functioning algorithm we have developed. Additionally the chapter will discuss issues concerning the computer model instantiation of the theory, including the examples on which it works and the evaluation of the model and the theory that it embodies. Along the way we will explore exactly how creative understanding fits into the general reading process, how it is controlled, and what it contributes to comprehension.

To demonstrate, consider the following short story, *Lycanthrope*[1] (Hartman 1992):

"I tell you, Norm, there really are such things as werewolves!"

"You're crazy, Ed. And even if there were any, how would you go about proving it?"

We were at it again. Ed and I. The same old favorite of his. Lycanthropy, the ages old belief that a man or woman could turn into an animal. According to Ed the kind of animal depended on the cultural background and ancestry of the person involved.

"A lot of people believe in witchcraft and werewolves, more every day if you believe what you read in some of these magazines. Why, I heard just the other day about a book that tells you how to do all sorts of things like summoning demons and casting spells. It's supposed to be as accurate as possible, even giving the reasoning behind each part of the spell as it goes along."

"You believe everything you read in those crazy magazines of yours, Ed. If we had a copy of that book I'd soon prove to you that those spells won't work by actually trying them out."

"I'll just call you on that! The book review in *Playboy* said that it's being reprinted in England and tells where to send for it. It's twenty-five bucks and it's going to be a good investment for me because if the spells work you'll be the one who pays for the book!"

"It's a deal! You look up that book review and I'll type up the order."

The letter ordering one copy of Van der Camp's *Witchcraft in Central Europe* went out in the next day's mail, and Ed and I spent the next few weeks reading up on necromancy and related subjects in the library at State U. We kidded the librarian into letting us read some volumes from shelves normally closed to any but accredited researchers. The books were old and dusty, some of them in archaic English, but while they were very interesting in places none of them was very much help to a couple of beginners.

Then the book finally arrived. It was all that we had hoped for, and then some. It gave complete formulas, rituals, and incantations; correct times for gathering and processing ingredients; and most important the right phases of the moon to the minute necessary for reliable results. In order to give the spells a proper trial we had to follow the book's instructions in every minute detail, so it was some time before we were ready but at last we were prepared. The materials were at hand and we had rehearsed the rituals and incantations until we knew them by heart.

"Are you sure you want to go through with this, Ed? There's no telling what you might turn into if the spell should really work." I was really uneasy. The logic behind this spell seemed so logical, somehow.

"Of course I want to go through with it. I didn't spend my money and come this far just to turn around and quit. Just think, I might become a lion or a tiger or an eagle. Anyway, no matter what I turn into I'm sure to be able to make the proper ritual motions in order to return to my original form."

"Yeah, but what if you can't? Remember, these spells were devised back in the days when people lived close to the soil. They were supposed to change people into forms that represented the major destructive forces of their times. In Europe, and England, they tried to turn into wolves and vampire bats, while in Scandinavia it was were-bears. In Malaya and India, it was were-tigers and snakes, but in Africa it was were-hyenas, buffalos, and leopards. In each case it was the creature that took the greatest toll of the common people's life and property," I reasoned with him. "We have different fears these days than back in the Dark Ages, and different things to menace our daily lives."

"And what if we do? Those old fears are ingrained into the heredity of mankind by a million years of fleeing in terror from animals fiercer and stronger than they were. What they feared then, we still fear today. I would be scared to death of a wolf or a bear, even though I've never met one fact to face."

It was a cold, windy night. A sickly gibbous moon gleamed fitfully through rents in the ragged clouds. We traced interlocking pentacles in the raw dirt of a new grave, lit the Coleman stove and began to concoct the unholy brew called for by the book.

"You're sure that you want to go through with this?"

"For the last time, YES!"

We hastily mumbled the incantation. Ed picked up the saucepan of evil-smelling liquid and quaffed it at a single gulp. There was a flash! A crash! An opaque cloud of smoke!

When people admire my new sports car I tell them that it's European, custom-made, . . . but where in Hell am I going to get spare parts?

With the above story in mind, two statements can be made with a high degree of certainty:

1. Most of you reading this story comprehended it without much difficulty.
2. Most of you reading this story had no a priori idea of what a were-car might be.

And, yet, if a reader has no existing idea of what a were-car is, how are they able to read a story that hinges on this concept? It is not simply a peripheral concept in the story; it is the core of comprehending the tale. Furthermore it is more than just an unfamiliar concept—if the novel concept was unknown but "possible" in the mind of the reasoner, then understanding can be achieved without much effort. For example, a person may not be familiar with the idea of an electric car intended for city travel, but there's nothing in that concept that is impossible. In this story, however, the idea of a were-car violates the reader's (or rather, most readers') view of the world—it is not simply unfamiliar; rather, the reader has reason to suspect that it is completely impossible. As a result there is a limit to how much existing knowledge can be directly applied to the problem. But, again, most people are able to read this story without a high degree of trouble. Even those who do not predict the ending are not so confused by it that they are unable to comprehend the story.

This ability to read and comprehend a text containing novel concepts is one of the defining features of the human reading process. One result of this is that a human reader does not need to possess every concept used in a text before undertaking the reading of that text; in fact, reading is one method used to explicitly learn new concepts. However, most of the models of the reading process that exist in artificial intelligence, especially those which attempt to do so-called deep comprehension, do require that all the concepts needed to comprehend a text exist in the system's memory prior to reading. This leads to massive knowledge engineering problems, since thousands of concepts must be provided to the system before the simplest stories can be read. New stories require a few more thousand concepts to be added. And so on.

A theory of creative understanding and how it relates to the overall reading process would allow models of reading to be built that possess two features:

- The models would be able to bootstrap with fewer concepts than previous theories would allow. In particular, it would often be possible to define only one core meaning of a concept and allow the model to learn the nexus of associated real-world meanings. For example, if provided with the concept of *robot-as-industrial-tool*, a creative understander could develop associated concepts as needed, such as *intelligent-robot* or *alien-robot-as-industrial-tool*.
- The models resulting from such a theory would be more closely related to how humans actually read and comprehend texts. Thus, as a cognitive model, the creative understanding approach is more accurate.[2]

Both of these reasons provide strong motivations for this research; the practical and the theoretical goals interact to drive us toward the theory of creative understanding. But, before going farther, we need to examine exactly what creative understanding is and define the term more precisely.

10.2 Creative Understanding Defined

Informally, creative understanding is the understanding of novel concepts. This definition, however, is vacuous for any serious research effort—two questions immediately raised rather than answered are *what is understanding* and *what does it mean for a concept to be novel*? Both of these terms, *understanding* and *novel*, carry connotational meanings that are shared among many researchers. However, this tends to make the situation more problematic—since this work is motivated by a wide range of crossdisciplinary research, any connotations carried in one field will cause confusion in the others. Thus a more exact definition is required. To do so, we need to examine each key component of the original definition attempt.

10.2.1 Defining Understanding

To realize what creative understanding is, we must first realize what understanding means. For the purposes of our research, *understanding* is the task of examining a concept and either *predicting* future states and events based on it or *abducing* prior states and events from it. Both of these processes are used in providing an *explanation* of how that concept fits into the entire set of concepts being dealt with in the current reasoning experience. To illustrate, consider the concept of a science-fiction robot. One can make predictions about it such as the actions it will perform; for example, a robot may be used to explore the surface of an alien planet. Or, one can perform abduction and understand why it exists. In the robot example it may exist in order to act as a strong, reliable tool. Finally one can explain aspects of the robot with respect to itself and to other concepts. Notice that this may include elements of both prediction and abduction; for instance, a particular robot is made of metal because it must work in environments that are detrimental to plastics. It is this explanation that allows a reasoner to judge how coherent a specific concept is—concepts that are coherent will be explainable without much cognitive effort; less coherent ones will require more explanation or be impossible to explain. This ability to tell if a concept "makes sense" is also the way in which the term *understanding* is often used in the vernacular—you understand something precisely at the moment when it does cohere in your mind.

10.2.2 Defining Novelty

If creative understanding is the understanding of novel concepts, the next step is to determine what is meant by *novel*, a feat that is somewhat difficult. What is novel to one person may be mundane to another. What is merely novel may not be creative. And, what is ultimately novel and creative may end up having limited impact while other novel concepts have historical repercussions (e.g., see Boden's [1991] discussion of *Psychological-Creativity* versus *Historical-Creativity*).

In this research, novelty is considered useful only when considered with respect to a particular point of view. This means that it will always be important to define the background of the reasoner in question; what is novel to one reasoner may be a mundane fact to another. To this end, then, a concept is defined to be novel with respect to a particular reasoner and with respect to the other (similar) concepts which that reasoner is familiar with. Each concept known to a reasoner will possess a function or purpose.[3] The novelty of a new concept will be judged in relation to the known concepts and their functions. Ultimately there are four broad ways in which a concept (M) may be novel with respect to a given function (F):

- *Absolute novelty (A-Novel)*. M is defined to be A-Novel iff M is unknown to the reasoner whose point of view is being considered.

- *Instantiation novelty (I-Novel)*. M is defined to be I-Novel iff M is unknown to the reasoner whose point of view is being considered, and if M accomplishes F in a way that is similar or identical to other concepts that also accomplish F.
- *Evolutionary novelty (E-Novel)*. M is defined to be E-Novel iff M is A-Novel and M accomplishes F in a better way than other examples of concepts that accomplish F.
- *Revolutionary novelty (R-Novel)*. M is defined to be R-Novel iff M is A-Novel and M accomplishes F in a new way than other examples of concepts which accomplish F.

We will return to this breakdown of novelty in the section concerning knowledge representation (section 10.3), where we will describe precisely how the modifications which will produce novel concepts may occur. Meanwhile, in order to illustrate these differences, consider a black longsword. Without question, a red longsword will perform the same function as the black longsword. The red sword, in this scenario, would be described as I-Novel—it accomplishes the same purpose and in the same way as the black longsword. On the other hand, within a range of possibilities, a short sword, a bastard sword, and a two-handed sword are all capable of performing the same function as the original longsword, just in a better fashion for different situations. Therefore these are concepts that are E-novel. Finally the light saber from the *Star Wars* series is also capable of performing the same function as the original longsword. In this case the light saber is an example of R-novelty. All of these examples would also be classified as A-Novel if they were unknown to the reasoner being considered.

10.2.3 Defining Useful

There is only one missing piece of the definition of creative understanding. In creative design and invention, researchers discuss the issue of *usefulness*—any random creation, while novel, is not necessarily creative; creativeness is achieved only when the novel creation possesses usefulness. Is such a distinction beneficial when considering creative understanding?

Any achieved understanding that allows comprehension to continue can be defined to be useful. The only danger is ensuring that all such understandings are not allowed with equal possibility. Some understandings may allow comprehension to continue at the present time but run into difficulties later. For example, consider the following narrative:

Mary slapped John. He ran into his house, crying. A few minutes later, John's mother came out with a grim look on her face.

Part of comprehending this story would be to explain why Mary slapped John. One possible answer is that aliens from the Vegan system took over control of her mind and forced her to do this, since they were undertaking a study of human emotional response to violence. That understanding is achievable, does not violate anything which is currently presented in the story, and allows reading to continue. Yet it is somehow unsettling. Of course that could be the explanation; it just seems premature to arrive at that understanding at this point in the story (after all, it is more likely that this is not the proper explanation and will have to be "retracted" in some fashion later in the comprehension of the text). Useful then, in the context of understanding, should be defined as the minimum level of understanding that can be achieved so that further comprehension can occur. It makes the least assumptions about facts not in evidence and has a high degree of internal coherence.

10.2.4 Definition, Revisited

With the above clarifications and elaborations, we are able to return to the original definition of creative understanding and present it in a more rigorous fashion:

Creative understanding is the understanding of concepts that are novel to the reasoning agent doing the understanding, such that the understanding is useful and allows reading to continue.

But a definition is not a theory, it merely allows us to precisely talk about what we are modeling. Before describing the theory and model, we need to outline the methodological assumptions that underly this work. Our theory of creative understanding and reading is a functional one. This approach to theory creation presumes that a cognitive *behavior* may be explained by appealing to an information processing formalism. In doing so, the behavior in question is defined by describing the *function* of each of its *tasks*, the *relationships* between them, the *mechanisms* that accomplish the tasks, and the *knowledge* needed. The resulting *functional theory* can then be used as a guide to the implementation of a cognitive model of the behavior. The theory itself does not explicitly tie the researcher to a particular method of implementation; instead, it describes the behavior at a higher level, the functional level. The program produced is used only to evaluate the original theory of the cognitive behavior, thereby allowing it to be refined in a cyclical manner. Using this methodology, it is possible to clearly see how a theory is broken into its *knowledge* components and *process* components. The knowledge components together make up the *knowledge system* to which the theory is appealing. In particular, there will be a specific *knowledge representation* formalism; this is the set of rules and conventions that describes how knowledge is allowed to be represented in the system. In addition to the representation of knowledge, the theory can also describe the organization of that knowledge, or the *ontology*. The process side of the theory is the set of tasks and their mechanisms that act on the knowledge. This methodology allows a researcher to specify which tasks and mechanisms make use of what knowledge in the system; this makes it clearer as to where the power in the system originates. Finally it is possible to group a set of related tasks together into a *supertask*; this helps to identify and to model the major cognitive behaviors of the system. The next two sections will describe our theory, within this framework.

10.3 Creative Understanding: Knowledge Issues

As a process, creative understanding can be described as a set of tasks, their mechanisms, and how the tasks interact; indeed, that is what will be done in the next section. However, our theory of creative understanding tightly couples the process with the underlying knowledge representation used. In particular, we employ a set of ontological commitments that greatly aids the understanding process. Before we can comprehend the process, then, we must first comprehend the knowledge system.

10.3.1 Representation of Concepts

In order for creative understanding to occur, existing concepts may have to be combined with other concepts. More accurately, bits and pieces of existing concepts will need to be recombined with other concepts. This means that a flexible knowledge representation system is required. We begin with the ideas of standard semantic networks using framelike representations (e.g., see Quillian 1966 and Minsky 1975). In this formalism, concepts are represented as entities known as *frames*. Frames are connected to each other, usually in terms of a *supergroup-group-subgroup* hierarchy. That is, **dog** is a frame representing the concept of "dogginess." A **dog** is-a **animal**, which is another frame-concept. A **doberman** is-a **dog**. A concept may also have multiple parents (e.g., dogs are also pets). Information known about concepts is stored on those frames in *slots*. The number of legs an animal possesses would be the kind of information you would expect to find in a slot. Other concepts will fill these slots; these are known as *fillers*. So a **dog** may have a slot representing communication which is filled with the concept **barking**.

All concepts, whether they refer to objects, people, actions, or anything else, can be represented in this *frame-slot-filler* style of notation. For example, see the **robot** concept in figure 10.1. More power, however, can be achieved by requiring that every entity in the knowledge system be a frame-concept. In the previous example, the slots were simply names. But a reasoner knows information concerning things like *communication*. If the knowledge system contains a **communication** frame-concept, then additional reasoning power can be achieved. In doing this, one can then represent the frames themselves as *nodes* in a large, connected *knowledge graph* (e.g., see Barsalou 1992; Sowa 1984; Wilensky 1986). What would traditionally be represented as slots

ROBOT-12	
:IS-A	ROBOT
:ROLES	{INDUSTRIAL-TOOL WEAPON TRANSPORT}
:FUNCTION	INDUSTRIAL-TOOL-5
:IS-MADE-OF	TITANIUM-7
:IS-POWERED-BY	ELECTRICITY-6
:CAN-LIFT	WEIGHT-10
:COLOR-IS	GRAY-8
:HEIGHT-IS	HEIGHT-11
:P-ATTRIBUTES	{:IS-MADE-OF :IS-POWERED-BY :CAN-LIFT}
:S-ATTRIBUTES	{:COLOR-IS :HEIGHT-IS}
:EXPLANATION	EXPLANATION-9

Figure 10.1
Represented concept in frame notation.

and fillers exist in this system as other nodes in the graph, connected to the original concept node via links. Figure 10.2 shows part of the same **robot** concept represented in this graph formalism.

This representation means that every "thing" in the frame-slot-filler version of the concept actually exists as an instantiated node within the knowledge system. The frame itself exists as a node, the slot names map onto other nodes in the knowledge base representing state relationships, and the filler for the slots are still other nodes. This extreme interconnectedness does raise an interesting question: Where does the knowledge base "ground" itself? One approach would be to have only internal consistency, with no piece of the knowledge base referring to anything other than other nodes. However, we are able to ground the representation in something external to the knowledge base. Since we are dealing with texts, the answer is to ground the system at the actual textual level—certain concepts map directly onto the English words that represent them. In this fashion every concept in the knowledge base can be tied to a textual description.

A further feature of the knowledge representation we are using is that there are limitations on exactly what sorts of concepts can be used for slot names. In some earlier knowledge systems the choices of slot-names were completely unconstrained. This led to an interesting position where in the observer of such a system may attribute too much power to the system by bringing in their own biases as to what the labels on the slots actually meant (see McDermott 1981). The limitation that everything in the knowledge system, including slots, actually exists as a knowledge node is one way to lessen this problem. The other way is by restricting slots to being *relationships* or *states* that exist between concepts. For example, consider the concept of

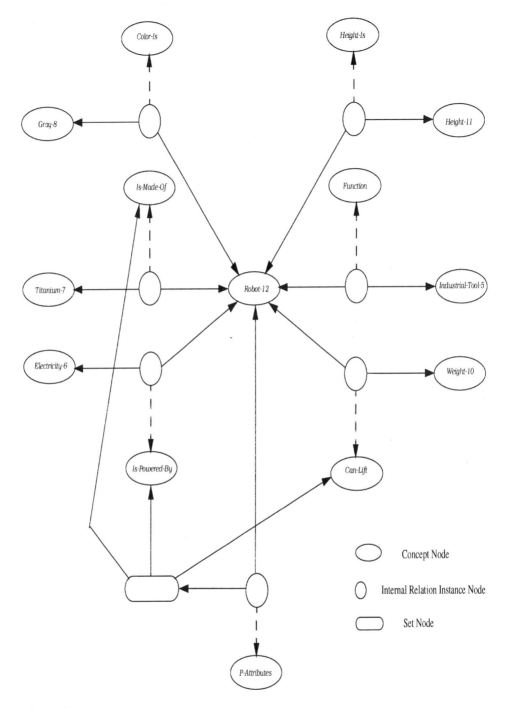

Figure 10.2
Represented concept as a graph.

car which might contain a slot named wheels. It would seem perfectly reasonable to have the filler of this slot be 4, thereby capturing the fact that the car possesses four wheels. Unfortunately, it is also reasonable for the filler to be yes, indicating that the car possesses wheels.[4] In our knowledge representation scheme, however, wheels is a meaningless slot name because it refers to an object and not a relationship. To remedy the problem, the proper slot name would need to be something like number-of-wheels-possessed, which should refer to a concept representing some state.[5]

The final aspect of the knowledge representation is that each concept is tagged with the current function it is being viewed as performing, as well as a set of possible functions it is known to be capable of performing. This fact is utilized to achieve flexible memory retrieval—during one search through memory, a car and a horse might be similar; with a different function in mind, a horse and a zebra would be more closely related. The process of function tagging follows the work of Barsalou on *ad hoc categories* (1989); rather than having all categories predefined, a reasoner can create temporary categories by collecting concepts with similar functions. The *primary attributes* of a concept are those features that determine how it achieves its function; together, these attributes provide an explanation of how the function is accomplished. Meanwhile the *secondary attributes* represent additional information; while this knowledge may be important, it does not directly contribute to the achievement of the current function. If the function of a concept is changed (e.g., a reasoner stops viewing the horse as an animal and starts viewing it as a mode of transportation), it might be necessary to repartition the primary and secondary attributes. By considering novel combinations of primary and secondary attributes, it is possible to hypothesize novel functions for a concept.

10.3.2 Novelty, Revisited

The function, primary attributes, and secondary attributes view of a concept can be directly related to the earlier discussion of the types of novelty (section 10.2.2). A concept that is I-Novel with respect to a known concept will simply differ in terms of the secondary attributes. More complex novelty is achieved by considering a concept that differs from a known one by possessing new values for the primary attributes; this is an example of an E-Novel concept. Finally, if the primary attributes and secondary attributes are completely altered, perhaps shifting some into or out of focus, the new concept will possibly be R-Novel. Of course, through all of these alterations, it is important that explainability be maintained. That is, random changes will result in potentially impossible concepts being formed; to restrict this, changes must maintain the explanation that exists between the primary attributes and the function of the concept in question.

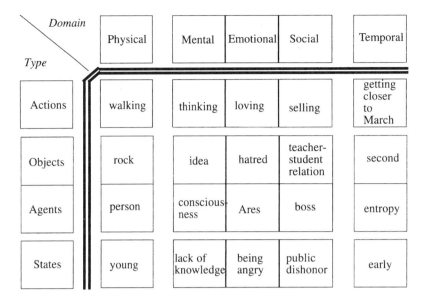

Figure 10.3
Knowledge grid.

10.3.3 Ontological Grid

In addition to representing individual concepts, a knowledge system must also represent the relationships between those concepts. Some of these relationships are captured by the relations embodied by the *frame-slot-filler* structure. The remaining relationships can be described by recognizing that the concepts within the knowledge system are organized into a specific ontology. At the topmost level, all knowledge is grouped with respect to an ontological grid. Figure 10.3 shows the breakdown of knowledge and example concepts from each category. The vertical axis of the grid represents the possible *types* of concepts. These are *action*, *agent*, *state*, and *object* (Domeshek 1992; Schank and Abelson 1977). Objects and agents inhabit the world; these are described by sets of state relationships between objects. Objects are non-volitional entities that participate in actions; for example, a ball can be thrown. However, objects cannot initiate action; for that to occur, an agent is required. The boy, for instance, can throw the ball. Agents then are volitional entities in the world; the set of agents would include things such as dogs, adults, and children. The actions in which objects and agents participate also occur in the world; they are preceded by a state description of the objects involved, and they result in a modified state description.

The horizontal axes of the ontological grid represents the *domain* of a concept. These five possible domains are *physical*, *mental*, *social*, *emotional*, and *temporal*. The physical domain is the one we are most familiar with; it is the one in which we exist. The mental domain represents the landscape of the mind, including ideas and thought. Closely related to the mental domain is the emotional one. This is the domain concerned with feelings, emotions, and attitudes. Next the social domain is made up of our interactions with society and other members of it. Finally, the temporal domain is the milieu of time, including the elements of time (e.g., seconds) and various movements through time (e.g., approaching tomorrow).

By crossing the domain and type, the twenty ontological categories seen in the figure are created. Consider *Lycanthrope* again. *Ed* and *Norm* are *physical agents*. A *book* is a *physical object*. *Crazy* is a *mental state*. *Believe* is a *mental action*. The state of being *uneasy* is an *emotional state*. And so on. Every concept in the story could be matched to one of the twenty ontological categories.

A reasoner will possess knowledge concerning the cells of the grid themselves, knowledge concerning the concepts that fall into each of these, and knowledge about the particular rows and columns (e.g., knowledge about physical types in general, or knowledge of objects in general). While performing creative understanding, a concept may need to be *transitioned* from one cell to another (e.g., it might be necessary to view a person as an object in order to understand a particular event; for more complex examples; see section 10.3.4). The level of effort required to understand a particular novel concept can be determined by how much transitioning is required of the current concepts in the memory system.

The design of our ontology was driven by two necessities. First, there was a need to measure how much "effort" was needed for a particular concept manipulation to occur. Second, there was a requirement that similar concepts be "close together" in the organization; this helps in the manipulation process. The ontology we developed fulfills both of these requirements. Beyond the necessities of the theory, however, we have also been motivated by prior psychological research concerning ontology. This has mainly been studied by developmental psychologists who attempt to explain the changes that take place to a child's ontology as they mature, as well as attempting to explain what, if any, ontology may exist from birth.

The first issue to consider is that of what ontologies exist. Two important ontological distinctions have been studied by a number of researchers. The *physical-immaterial distinction* is an important one that arises relatively early in the development pattern of normal children, although it continues to be refined and sophisticated as they age (Carey 1992; Carey and Spelke 1994). Another major ontological division is the *object-event distinction*—some things in the world are objects (rocks, people, etc.) while other things are events (e.g., walking) (Carey 1992).

The second aspect of the previous research to note is the recognition that shifting basic ontological categories is difficult. Numerous researchers have noticed and theorized about this (e.g., Carey 1992; Chi 1993). One of the best descriptions of the possible range of changes comes from Thagard (1992). In his framework there are nine degrees to conceptual change, ranging from the simple addition of new instances of known concepts to the complete reorganization of the ontological hierarchy. The lower levels are far easier to perform; it is only with growing ability and sophistication that a reasoner will achieve the reorganization level.

Finally, viewing various ontological experiments over the course of the research has prompted some researchers to claim that certain types of ontological categories are fundamental to human reasoning and would therefore need to be accurately modeled. For example, Brewer (1993) suggests that a rich ontology is needed, consisting of (at least) natural kinds, nonexisting natural kinds, artifacts, social entities, psychological entities, and abstract entities. While our approach does not duplicate this exactly, the basic ideas are consistent.

10.3.4 Manipulations of Concepts

When an existing concept needs to be manipulated during the course of a creative understanding episode, there are three basic outcomes with respect to the grid. The concept can be manipulated, yet remain in the same grid cell as when it started. For example, a reasoner may use a *horse* to understand the concept of a *zebra*. Second, a concept may transition along a row or a column. If a reasoner uses their knowledge of physical concepts in order to understand social ones (e.g., a boss blocking your promotion), this is an example of this shift. Finally a transition may occur that moves the concept in terms of both axes. A reasoner understanding something like *His mind was a steel trap* is making use of this dual transition—a physical object is transitioned to a mental state. These three possibilities represent a simple ordering of the amount of cognitive work required to manipulate any given concept. Finally a set of high-level heuristics is needed to bound the possible motion within the grid (Moorman and Ram 1996). These are as follows:

- Physical types can become transitioned to other domains more easily than other domain types can be transitioned to physical. Since humans are physical entities with a great deal of experience with other physical entities, it is "easier" to believe in the existence of a novel, nonphysical entity formed from a physical analogue than it is to accept the creation of a new type of physical entity. Consider, *John saw the days fly by*. Is this a novel use of *saw* and *fly* created by altering physical concepts into the temporal domain, or is it a novel use of *days* created by considering a temporal object as a physical one?
- An object may transition to an action by creating an action that captures a function of that object, and vice versa. English, in particular, tends to have many lexical

examples of this. A fax is the thing you send when you fax someone. A (*Star Trek*) transporter is the device used to transport material from one location to another.
- An object may transition to a state by creating a state which captures a primary attribute for that object, and vice versa. Through this transition, we get many common similes and metaphors, such as *Hungry as a bear* and *As good as gold*.
- Agents and objects can easily transition between each other. This results from two observations. First, agents exist as embodied entities in the world (Johnson 1987), explaining the agent to object transition. For example, one may treat John as a physical object. Second, it is possible to view objects as though they possess intention (Newell 1981), enabling the object to agent transition. For instance, a thermostat may be thought of in terms of agency; namely it *wants* to keep the house at a constant temperature.
- Concepts from the three so-called psychological domains, which are *emotional*, *mental*, and *social*, can transition between those three domains easier than into or out of the other domains.
- Make the minimal changes necessary. This is simply a general rule, à la Occam's razor. It results from the earlier discussed idea of satisfaction ultimately driving the creative understanding process—stop the process once you have a "good enough" understanding to allow the higher cognitive task to continue.

By combining the three basic movement types with the high-level heuristics, we get an ordering of the amount of *cognitive effort* required to manipulate concepts (from easiest to most difficult):

1. Concepts may transition within a single cell.
2. Agents may be treated as objects, and objects may be treated as agents.
3. Concepts may vertically transition according to the modification heuristics.
4. Mental, emotional, and social concepts may horizontally transition between those domains easier than into the other domains.
5. Physical domain concepts may transition to other domains (horizontal motion).
6. Other domain types may transition to the physical domain (horizontal motion).
7. Combinations of 2–5 may occur.

Within this ordering, however, operations that result in the minimal changes are preferred over those that are more complex.

10.4 Creative Understanding: Algorithmic Issues

With a firm comprehension of the knowledge representation issues, we are ready to address the actual creative understanding algorithm. Since this research studies creative understanding within the context of the reading process, it is first necessary to realize exactly what tasks make up reading. This will provide a framework in which to explore the creative understanding algorithm.

10.4.1 Reading Decomposition

The numerous tasks that go into the reading process can be grouped into six *supertasks*, or collections of related tasks. There are three primary supertasks, CONTROL, SCENARIO COMPREHENSION, and STORY STRUCTURE COMPREHENSION. These function to produce a troika of representations that, when taken together, capture what the reader has comprehended from a given text.

- *CONTROL.* CONTROL integrates the other supertasks. It includes the tasks of *focus control*, which manages the depth of reading based on interest and understanding; *time management*, which allows the reader to make decisions based on time resources; and *suspension of disbelief*, which enables a reader to accept, at least temporarily, a text that violates their world view. This last function is particularly important in the case of reading a story containing unfamiliar concepts. A rational reader of *Lycanthrope* knows that the story cannot be true. Witchcraft does not allow the transmutation of humans into any sort of were-creature, no matter how elaborate the ceremony. In order to read, understand, and enjoy the story, however, the reader must be willing to accept the unfamiliar ideas for the duration of the reading experience. Other aspects of control are important in all reading episodes, whether creative or not. Readers are cognitive agents involved in numerous ongoing tasks. They must decide how much effort to expend on each task as a whole, as well as on each part of an individual task. As part of this resource management, the reader must also decide in how much depth they wish to read the given material. With *Lycanthrope*, for example, an average reader will not read each and every word; instead, some sections will be read closely, others will be skimmed, and some may be skipped entirely. *Interest management* controls the reader's level of interest in the story. An avid science fiction fan, for instance, would be more interested in the example story than a fan of Westerns. *Belief management* reasons about the beliefs of the agents involved in the scenario. Did the narrator really believe that his friend would transform? If so, why? These are questions that will be handled by the belief management task as *Lycanthrope* is being read. Finally the *metareasoning* task reflects on the reader's own actions during the reading process; this information is used by other supertasks for learning and explanation.

- *SCENARIO COMPREHENSION.* The tasks making up the SCENARIO COMPREHENDER are the *event parser*, which identifies various components such as agents, actions, states, objects, and locations; the *agent modeler*, which maintains descriptions of the agents, including their goals, knowledge, and beliefs; and the *action modeler*, which maintains descriptions of the acts with which the agents are involved. This supertask would be used in any experience in which the reasoner had to understand the actions of agents around it. As such, it is equally useful in day-to-day encounters with other reasoners as it is in the comprehension of text. Generally, texts are intended to relate a scenario to the reader. *Lycanthrope* is not just a story; it tells the reader about events that could potentially happen, some more likely than others. A reader can understand the relationship between the two friends using some of the same processes that they would in an attempt to understand the relationship if it were occurring in the physical world.

- *STORY STRUCTURE COMPREHENSION*. This supertask handles the details of the text that relate to the story structure. Tasks include *character identification*, including protagonist and antagonist; *setting identification*, made up of time and location; *plot description*, which builds a coherent summary of the story's plot; and *genre identification*, which specifies in which category of text the story is. The inclusion of this supertask is largely the result of the way in which reading is taught in this country for the types of text which are most familiar in the Western tradition (Smith 1986). While this area of the reading process may not be in-born or even learned at an early age, it does become automatic through our educational system. As such, it acts as a valuable aid in controlling and focusing the overall reading process. Realizing, for example, that *Lycanthrope* takes place in the present with fantasy elements interwoven in the story acts as an aid to comprehending the story.

For the purposes of the reading process, these three supertasks are supported by a secondary one, SENTENCE PROCESSING. Of course SENTENCE PROCESSING will be used in oral communication as well as in reading.

- *SENTENCE PROCESSING*. This supertask is responsible for low-level (mainly intrasentential) understanding and includes tasks such as *pronoun reference*, *syntactic parsing*, and *lexical retrieval*. Other tasks are *punctuation analysis*, which reasons about punctuation of phrases and *tense analysis*, which attempts to discover the text's tense. In many texts, low-level understanding issues will prove to be extremely helpful in gaining an overall understanding of the material.

Finally, from the perspective of the reading process, there are two tertiary supertasks, UNDERSTANDING and MEMORY. The term tertiary is not intended to imply that these supertasks are somehow more "simple" than the others. Instead, the hierarchy of primary, secondary, and tertiary is defined in terms of how reading-centric each supertask is. UNDERSTANDING and MEMORY are extremely general-purpose supertasks and are the least bound to the reading process.

- *UNDERSTANDING.* This supertask performs high-level reasoning and learning. The *prediction*, *abduction*, and *explanation* tasks build the inferences needed to connect the events of the story, enabling the reader to learn from the material.[6] Explanation provides reasoning for why two concepts are related. Abduction allows backward inferencing to take place. Finally prediction permits forward inferencing.
- *MEMORY.* This supertask handles general memory storage and retrieval, including spontaneous reminding. It is made up of *reminding*, which uses the current situation to provide spontaneous remembrances; *retrieval*, which returns information from memory which the reasoner needs if explicit indices are known; and *storage*, which places new information and cases into memory. In addition to the conscious requests to store or retrieve elements in memory, the memory supertask should also handle the unconscious storing of material and spontaneous remindings. During the reading of *Lycanthrope*, the reader will constantly be retrieving and storing concepts related to the material in the text. Some of these may be spontaneous; for example, the story may trigger memories of other stories which concern were-creatures, or other stories written by Norman Hartman. Other memory processes will be more deliberate; the reader may decide, for example, to try to remember the last story they read about witchcraft.

10.4.2 Suspension of Disbelief

Since the need for creative understanding exists on a continuum, as suggested by the novelty breakdown, it is necessary for the creative understanding process to be capable of producing such a continuum of levels of understanding. This means that so-called mundane understanding cannot be separated from creative understanding. Instead, there is a single understanding process that acts on concepts given to it. Based on the novelty of the concept with respect to the reasoner's background knowledge, different levels of effort will be required to reach the understanding goal. Simply, the more novel something is, the more effort required.

Before the process can begin, however, the reasoner must make a decision to attempt such an understanding. After all, the understanding process extracts a cognitive price from the reasoner; in some situations it might be better to *not* attempt understanding.[7] Scholars of literature and the dramatic arts refer to this decision as the *willful suspension of disbelief*, a term introduced by Coleridge (1926). A reasoner must be willing to accept concepts that seem unbelievable, given the current state of the reasoner's background knowledge. It is only then that a reasoner will be able to attempt the understanding process on those concepts. Otherwise, the reasoner could simply elect to ignore the text, for the fact that it contains "unbelievable" concepts.[8] And, once the decision is made, there is no reason it cannot be retracted—if a reader feels that a story is failing to pull together, the cognitive load required may cause the comprehension task to be abandoned.

10.4.3 Tasks of Creative Understanding

While the ability to perform creative reading is distributed across the supertasks of reading, the core of the process lies within the UNDERSTANDING supertask, extensively supported by the rest of the system. It is here that concepts encountered in the text being read are integrated into the mind of the reader. Four tasks act together to produce the understanding behavior:

- Memory retrieval permits concepts to be retrieved from the long term memory of the reasoner, by requesting this behavior from the MEMORY supertask.
- Analogical mapping allows the reasoner to see the functional relationships between two concepts—the encountered one being understood and an existing concept that may allow this understanding to succeed.
- Base-constructive analogy gives the reasoner the ability to dynamically create new concepts from existing ones, concepts that can then be used to understand the novel one being encountered.
- Problem reformulation forces the reasoner to "re-think" the concept being understood if something indicates that the current approach is treating the concept incorrectly.

Each of these tasks represents more willingness to suspend disbelief as each one moves the possible understanding farther away from what is known to be true.

10.4.3.1 Memory Retrieval *Memory retrieval* is the most basic level of all understanding. Even if we eliminate the need for the understanding of novel concepts, memory retrieval would still be needed; to only perform recognition-based understanding (i.e., understanding that hinges on remembering a known concept when presented with it) would require the ability to retrieve known concepts from some sort of memory system. As concepts enter the understanding supertask, a routine memory retrieval request is sent to the memory supertask. The memory supertask then returns the best set of matches that it can find. If an exact match is found, then the concept being considered is a known one, and a very mundane style of understanding can be said to have occurred. Another possibility is that a similar object will be returned, perhaps one that differs in terms of secondary attributes only. This would indicate that the considered concept is I-Novel. Finally it might be the case that some concepts are returned that were judged in some way to be similar to the concept in question but that do not provide enough of a match for the understanding process to be satisfied. If this happens, then memory retrieval is said to have failed, for the purposes of understanding. It is not the responsibility of the memory system to attempt to make alterations to the concepts being retrieved in order to make them "fit" with the novel concept being understood; that aspect of the creativity cycle lies in the later stages.[9]

Last it is important to realize, before moving on to the next task, that the memory supertask may fail to retrieve the proper concept, even if the "novel" concept being considered is a known one. Humanlike memory is not perfect; our memory supertask is a cognitively driven theory of memory. As a result it is not perfect either. Correct concepts may exist that fail to be retrieved at the initial time a memory request is made. This is balanced by the fact that the memory supertask also contains the ability to asynchronously continue to process retrieval requests (Francis and Ram 1993; Ram and Francis 1996). Thus at some later point the memory supertask may inform the understanding supertask that a previously failed retrieval request has actually succeeded.

10.4.3.2 Analogical Mapping The next task making up creative understanding is that of *analogical mapping*. *Analogy* is the process by which two concepts are seen to be related in some way (e.g., Falkenhainer 1987; Gentner 1989; Holyoak and Thagard 1995). A well-known analogy is that of the atomic structure being analogous to the solar system. In analogy terms the object that a reasoner is attempting to explain is called the *target* and the known analogue is the *base*; the reasoner discovers the relationships that exist between base and target. In the atom example, the atom is the target and the solar system is the base. This framework can be the springboard on which creative ideas are based. If a reasoner can find and make use of an appropriate analogue, then the resulting behavior and/or product will at least appear to be externally creative. On the other hand, analogical mapping can also appear to be a mundane sort of behavior; this is the case if the retrieved analogue is so familiar that no novelty is generated through the analogical mapping process.

In the creative understanding process, memory retrieval may have returned concepts that were not considered "good enough" matches by the understanding supertask. But the memory supertask was using some set of matching criteria that determined that these retrieved concepts were in some way similar to the concept being understood. If this is the case, analogical mapping can be called upon to determine if any of the retrieved concepts can be determined to be an analogue of the concept the reasoner is interested in. Analogical mapping can fail if elements of the base concept and target concept that have to be in alignment are determined to be functionally nonequivalent.

By utilizing this task, a reasoner can add the ability to understand concepts that are E-Novel to them. Additionally known concepts and I-Novel ones can be understood through the use of analogical mapping. This is useful if the memory supertask has not managed to find a suitable match for a concept but has managed to find a suitable analogue.

10.4.3.3 Base-Constructive Analogy There are times when an analogylike process is needed but no base exists with which to draw the analogy. Consider the following story:

There was once a large area of the City which was a desolate wasteland of condemned buildings, known simply as the Neighborhood. The New Boys, a street gang, currently control the Neighborhood and have their headquarters in the exact center of the wasteland. Lately, a new gang calling itself the Elected Ones has shown an interest in acquiring control of the Neighborhood. Fearing the loss of control, the New Boys decide that they need to bring in an outside gang to aid their cause. The New Boys learn that the blood enemies of the Elected Ones are a group of men known simply as the Pros. The Elected Ones and Pros so fear each other that as long as one Pro is in the New Boys' territory for each Elected One there will be no violence. So, the New Boys bring in the exact number of Pros as there are Elected Ones. Frustrated in their takeover attempts, the Elected Ones are forced to stay outside the Neighborhood and only circle it. After a while, all three gangs decide to change their names to include "-tron" in their names. So, the Elected Ones become the Elec-trons, the Pros become the Pro-tons, and the New Boys become the New-trons. The Elec-trons continually circle a vast area of open space. At the center is a group of Pro-tons and New-trons. Notice that there is always the same number of Pro-tons as there are Elec-trons. (WKRP Episode 1980)

It is quite possible to describe atomic structure by appealing to ideas from the domain of gang warfare. And yet this is not quite the same as appealing to the solar system model. The solar system model is a preexisting concept that acts immediately as a base; there is no preexisting model of the Pros, New Boys, and Elected Ones that can act as an atomic base. Rather, the reasoner constructs the necessary base dynamically, driven by the constraints of the problem and by existing domain knowledge (e.g., Clement 1989; Moorman and Ram 1994; Nersessian 1992).

10.4.3.4 Problem Reformulation The final task to consider in the creative understanding of novel concepts is that of problem reformulation. It may be possible that the reasoner has been mistaken about what they are trying to understand; at this point the reasoner can elect to reconsider the concept under consideration. For example, in the story *Men Are Different* (Bloch 1963), the reader is presented with a first-person narrative. It is quite acceptable to assume that the narrator is a human. This is reinforced by the narrator informing the reader that he is an archaeologist. However, the fact that the narrator is studying the "lost" civilization of Mankind leads the reader to suspect that their understanding of *narrator-as-human* is flawed;

problem reformulation is needed to see if any other explanation "fits" the available data. In this case the narrator turns out to be a robot.

Within our theoretical framework for creative understanding, there are two mechanisms by which problem reformulation can occur. The first mechanism hinges on the fact that we are using reading as the domain in which to study the creative understanding process. There is a communicative agreement between the author of a text and the reader—that is, the author is expecting the reader to be able to understand what is being presented in the text. The author may select to delay the presentation of all the relevant facts (e.g., in a mystery story), but if readers have the prerequisite knowledge, they should be able to comprehend the text. So a conservative approach to problem reformulation is to simply delay reformulation until the text indicates a specific problem with the understanding that has been achieved up to that point. In *Men Are Different*, for instance, the narrator continually talks about lost Mankind and eventually describes itself as a robot. These explicit text pointers indicate to the reader that the initial *narrator-as-human* understanding is flawed; problem reformulation must occur.

Other, more general purpose, techniques have also been studied for allowing problem reformulation to occur. For example, Jones (1992) and Bhatta (1995) both make use of abstraction; that is, reformulation can occur if the problem can be abstracted to a higher level. While we do not explicitly make use of this in our theory, we achieve a similar effect through the use of *spontaneous retrieval*. Since the memory system is working in parallel with understanding, previous indexes and cues still active in memory may trigger a new memory that can then interrupt the process and force a problem reformulation to occur. For example, consider the story *Zoo* (Hoch 1978). In this story an intergalactic zoo visits the Earth each year. The reader eventually learns that the "creatures" in the zoo are intelligent beings that view themselves as going on a great adventure to many foreign worlds; they are in the cages in order to protect themselves from the dangerous natives. One way to understand the novel use of *zoo* is to perform an analogy between the standard idea and the novel one. Another possibility, however, relies on problem reformulation via spontaneous retrieval. As the story is being read, memory retrieval is continuing based on the original specification. If the memory system is given enough time, it can return the concept of *safari* in addition to the original concept of *zoo*. The understanding process can then use the newly retrieved concept to perform the understanding of the zoo in the story. Nothing explicit has triggered this reformulation; rather, the change was brought about by the memory system's discovery of a better match than the one originally retrieved.

Creativity in Reading

- Consider a concept in the world, designated as M.
- Let f be defined as the function which returns the function of a concept.
- Let C be the class of functions which alter an object, including:
  1. Add a new attribute
  2. Remove an attribute
  3. Change the value of an attribute
  4. Change the allowable values of an attribute
  5. Make a primary attribute a secondary one
  6. Make a secondary attribute a primary one
- C_1 through C_n are a set of n such functions.
- Thus, a set of objects S_{all} can be created by $\bigcup_{i=1,...,n} C_i$.
- Consider the subset, S_f defined as $\{s \mid s \in S_{all} \text{ and } f(s) = f(M)\}$.
- Finally, consider the subset S_c defined as $\{s \mid s \in S_f \text{ where } s \text{ is unknown}\}$.
- Items in S_c are useful (they fulfill the same role as the original object M), and they are novel to the reasoner. Therefore they are creative.

Figure 10.4
Function-driven morphological synthesis.

10.4.4 Where Do "New" Concepts Originate?

In section 10.4.3.3 we presented the idea that base-constructive analogy could be used to dynamically create a proper base if none exists in memory (or is able to be retrieved). The mechanism that allows this creation to occur is *function-driven morphological synthesis*, or FMS. The basic outline of this mechanism can be seen in figure 10.4.

It is assumed that the reasoner has encountered a concept that needs to be understood. The reasoner applies a set of manipulator functions to the concept, altering its attributes and producing new concepts. These manipulator functions include altering the value for a particular attribute, changing the restrictions that exist for the allowable values of an attribute, eliminating an attribute, adding a new attribute, and changing primary attributes to secondary ones, and vice versa. The concepts that possess the original functionality and are novel to the reasoner are considered as creative ones. The FMS technique was inspired by Allen's *morphological synthesis* (cited in Finke et al. 1992), in which a reasoner manipulates combinations of primary attributes to produce potentially creative results. Since only primary attributes were modified, Allen's technique could not result in an R-Novel item. By removing this restriction, FMS *is* able to produce such novelty.

FMS can exist in two forms. *Strong-FMS* performs the needed manipulations by examining other concepts with the same functionality. In this form several concepts are considered and "mixed and matched" until a proper concept is formed. It might happen, though, that a single concept is all that exists when the need to create a new one arises. If this situation occurs, then *weak-FMS* is utilized. This mechanism uses general background knowledge to perform the needed manipulations.

Consider the *Lycanthrope* story once more. If the reader already possesses the concepts of **car** and **lycanthropy**, then the novel concept of **were-car** can be understood through base-constructive analogy, by utilizing strong-FMS. One possible sequence of tasks is the following:

1. The concept that needs to be understood is **were-car**.
2. Consider known concepts that fulfill the same functional role as the novel concept seems to be. This set would include concepts such as **were-wolf**, **were-tiger**, and **were-hyena**.
3. None of these will succeed in an analogical mapping attempt; there is a functional restriction that what form is assumed is an animal form. **car** fails to meet this functional requirement.
4. The reasoner may elect to modify the concept of **were-creature** or the concept of **car**.
  a. Modifying **were-creature** requires relaxing the functional constraint.
  b. Modifying **car** requires transitioning the concept from the physical-object category into the physical-agent one.
5. Of these two possibilities, the first is preferred because it makes fewer changes to the existing knowledge system.
6. The reasoner therefore creates a new concept of **were-creature** that subsumes the previous one.
7. This allows the reasoner to understand the novel concept of **were-car**.

Another story, *Experiment* (Brown 1954), demonstrates the need for weak-FMS. In this story a professor has invented a time machine. Without the time travel concept, a reader must dynamically create the concepts needed in order to comprehend the story. Unlike the *Lycanthrope* example, however, there is not a set of concepts that can be merged to develop the necessary concept. Rather, a reasoner must start with a particular single concept, that of **physical-travel**, and some knowledge about the temporal column of the ontology grid. Properly manipulating the information will result in the concept of **temporal-travel** being created. One possible reasoning path is:

- Start with the concept being understood, **temporal-travel**.
- Find concepts that are related functionally to this one; in this case **physical-travel** is a good candidate.
- Analogical mapping fails, since there is no way to relate the physical locations to **temporal-travel**.

- The understanding process now begins to modify the concept of **physical-travel**, attempting to bring it to a point where it can be used to understand the time traveling in the story.
- The purpose of **physical-travel** is to allow a physical agent to transport a physical object from one physical location to another one, which is different from the starting location. The purpose of the time travel depicted in the story is for a physical agent to transport a physical object from one temporal location to another.
- To alter **physical-travel** requires that the restrictions on starting and ending locations be modified from physical locations to temporal locations.
- A new problem is introduced if the reasoner does not possess the concept of **temporal-location**. Then creative understanding is used to develop an understanding of **temporal-location** before continuing.
- With the modifications in place, the reasoner has transitioned the original concept from the *physical action* category into the *temporal action* category. However, while this is a relatively "large" modification, it still represents the minimal one that can be made in order to understand the time-travel story.

10.4.5 Control of Creative Understanding

With the tasks defined, it is time to see how they fit together and how they fit into the overall structure of the reading process. We begin with the general description of how reading proceeds.

CONTROL selects the next sentence to read and informs SENTENCE PROCESSING, which takes in the English sentence and converts it into an intermediate conceptual representation. The conceptual entity formed is then passed to UNDERSTANDING. The understood concept is then given to SCENARIO COMPREHENSION and STORY STRUCTURE COMPREHENSION in order to allow them to build their internal models of the text.

The question, then, is what happens in the UNDERSTANDING supertask? The four tasks of the theory act together to produce an understanding, if one is possible. In earlier versions of our work, we hypothesized that the four tasks acted in an iterative looping fashion, proceeding in the order presented. That is, memory retrieval was called; if it failed, then analogical mapping was tried; upon its failure, base-constructive analogy was utilized; finally, problem reformulation was attempted if all else fails. However, continued development of the theory revealed that this single path through the four tasks was not the only one possible. For example, a reader may fail at memory retrieval but receive a cue that problem reformulation is needed, skipping the analogy steps. While the process is still iterative, the control path is slightly more complicated than the initial approach:

- Memory retrieval is the entry point into the creative understanding process; as stated earlier, all understanding attempts begin here. If the memory retrieval is successful, then understanding is successful. On the other hand, if memory retrieval fails, two possibilities could be the result. (1) An analogue (or set of analogues) may have been discovered. At this point, analogical mapping can be executed. (2) Evidence may have been returned that enables the understanding supertask to determine that problem reformulation is needed.

- The task of analogical mapping will be followed by a memory retrieval request if it is successful. If the mapping fails, the understanding supertask can elect to attempt to dynamically create a new base with base-constructive analogy. Or, it might be the case that the failed analogy indicates that a problem reformulation is required. Finally the understanding supertask can decide to attempt another memory retrieval upon a mapping failure.
- If base-constructive analogy fails, it can be followed by a new memory retrieval attempt, thereby starting a new cycle. Or, the failure can indicate that a problem reformulation needs to occur.
- Problem reformulation, if unsuccessful, can be followed by memory retrieval.

The current view interprets creative understanding as a search task with the operators being the four tasks. However, there is not unrestricted movement between the four tasks. A task may succeed, thereby triggering the next understanding cycle that will begin with a memory retrieval. If a given task fails, then the failure will indicate which task to attempt next, as outlined in the above list of tasks. The possible search space can be compactly represented (due to the redundant nature of possibilities), as seen in figure 10.5.

Given the general cyclic nature of the algorithm, some metric must exist that enables the reasoner to limit the amount of creative understanding performed. Up to a certain point, the understanding achieved will be useful and creative. It has the potential, though, to become bizarre. It is possible for the researcher to enforce bounds on the level of bizarreness allowed to occur, but this seems to restrict the outcomes in an unreasonable fashion. Alternatively, arbitrary choices could be made. Both of these options have been argued against from a theoretical perspective (Birnbaum 1986). We prefer to have reasonable bounds on the process. To accomplish this, all understanding must be directed toward an ultimate goal. Three factors combine to provide this necessary limit: the *satisfaction of the reasoner*, the *interest level of the reader*, and the *knowledge ontology*. Each provides a different sort of bound; acting together, principled understanding is the result.

10.4.5.1 Satisfaction The *satisfaction* solution bounds the creative understanding process by virtue of it existing within a larger cognitive task—in our case, reading. Understanding can be said to be successful as soon as the quality of explanation or

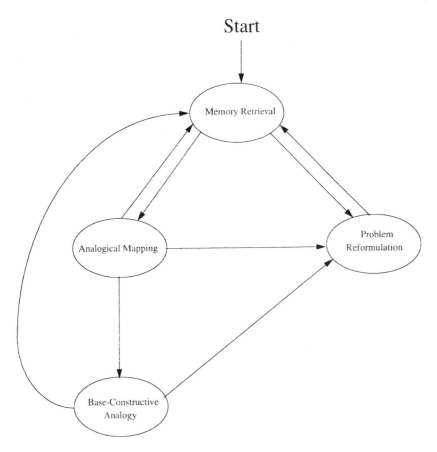

Figure 10.5
Search space for creative understanding.

prediction provided is high enough to allow the reading process to continue. As an example, consider the world of *Star Trek*. The *warp drive* is an example of a concept that must be understood to comprehend the stories. But, if a particular story has the warp drive functioning normally, then the reader can be satisfied by simply understanding that it provides a way to get from point A to point B very quickly. On the other hand, if a story involves the breakdown of the antimatter in the warp core, a reader has to reach a higher level of understanding with respect to the warp drive, or the comprehension of the story will be impaired.

10.4.5.2 Interest Reader interest will also act as an important factor in determining when to "say when" regarding the creative understanding process (e.g., Ram

1991). This factor is somewhat in opposition to the satisfaction criterion. Rather than stop as soon as reading can progress, interest will drive the reader to continue until they are satisfied. Consider the warp drive example, again. Readers with an interest in faster-than-light travel, for instance, may try to extend their understanding of the warp drive even if a more in-depth understanding is not needed for a particular story. Of course this means that some potentially bizarre understandings may result and be in place longer before having to be abandoned; that is simply the price that must be paid for interest-driven understanding.

10.4.5.3 Ontology As described extensively in the knowledge representation section (section 10.3), the ontology acts as an important bound to the creative understanding process. If creative understanding requires that a concept move from one grid cell to another, this is considered a more radical change than if the process leaves all concepts in their original cells; this provides bounding. Additionally function tagging aids in bounding by allowing only concepts with similar functionality to be reasoned about interchangeably.

10.5 ISAAC: A Model of Creative Reading

The theory described in this chapter has been implemented in a computer model known as the ISAAC (integrated story analysis and creativity) system. The ISAAC system is programmed in Common LISP, consisting of approximately 40,000 lines of core code.[10] The basic knowledge representation system utilized in the research is the KR package, which is part of the GARNET development system (which also provides a graphical interface to the ISAAC system; Myers 1988).

The focus of our work has been on theorizing a process that can explain creative reading. As a result we have focused our model building on those features of the overall theory that directly support the creative reading behavior. However, it was also necessary to accurately model the remaining aspects of the theory, to the best degree possible, in order to make our own model of creative reading complete. To accomplish these goals, we elected to make use of other research projects to provide us with the functionality of some of the supertasks. In particular, our research interests did not lie in the area of sentence processing, yet we recognized the importance of having a cognitive model of sentence processing underlying our overall model. We achieved this through the COMPERE system (Mahesh 1993). This model, with some modifications, provides the functionality of the SENTENCE PROCESSING supertask. In a similar fashion we have made use of the MOORE memory system (Francis and Ram 1993; Ram and Francis 1996). This model of context-driven, spontaneous memory retrieval gives the ISAAC system the capability of the memory supertask.

Creativity in Reading

The system can read five short science fiction stories and numerous *Star Trek: The Original Series* episodes (Asherman 1989). The *Star Trek* stories ranges from one paragraph to three, while the five short stories range from one page to four pages. The ISAAC system reads the stories in the original English form from the published sources. As a result of the reading process, three interlocking representations are created. A scenario model is built that contains the representation of the events occurring in the text. A story structure model is developed that contains information about the characters, setting, and so forth. Finally a metareasoning model is created that represents the tasks that the system undertook in order to arrive at its comprehension of the text. Also the postreading memory of the system has been altered to include the information gleaned from the reading episode. During the reading process, or after it is completed, the system may be queried in order to determine its level of comprehension. Additionally various metrics of performance with respect to internal functioning can be examined.

10.6 Examples of Creative Understanding

To see the power of creative understanding, we will now consider a number of examples, at different levels of complexity. Remember that we are striving for a general purpose process, so all levels of complexity should ultimately be handled by the same process.

10.6.1 A Bear Example

First, consider the extremely simple sentence:

John was a bear.

This sentence could be understood in a number of ways. John could be a human male who is always gruff before his morning cup of coffee. On the other hand, the understanding could also be that John became a were-bear under a full moon some time recently. Yet another understanding could be that John is the name of a particular bear. Each of these are possible interpretations for the sentence.

If all of these readings are possible, which is the most probable one? If the reader is familiar with the metaphor of "bearness" representing anger, then the first interpretation would be preferred. This would be arrived at simply by memory retrieval. If the reader only knows about bears as animals, though, the most reasonable interpretation to arrive at is that there is a bear named John, again by memory retrieval. If this proves to be incorrect, then base-constructive analogy could be used to get at either of the other interpretations. If the reasoner is familiar with were-wolves in actuality, then analogy would allow the interpretation of were-bear to be developed.

Now, wait a minute. Here we have a simple sentence and two things have been made fairly obvious. First, there are no "simple" sentences; most sentences can have a myriad number of *possible* interpretations, especially as a stand-alone entity (or the starting sentence of a text). Second, it seems that creative understanding is being driven by the preexisting knowledge of the reasoner. This will always be the case—the use of the various tasks in the creative understanding process breakdown will be determined by the background knowledge of the reader. Obviously, if a reader already possesses a particular concept, then memory retrieval is all that is needed. If other readers lack that concept, they will have to make use of the remaining three tasks in order to understand the concept. This fact is also why is becomes "easier" to read stories from a particular genre as readers gain experience with that genre. The tenth Robert Heinlein novel one reads should be easier to comprehend than the first; the reader will have built up concepts that are unique to Heinlein's style of writing. This allows less base-constructive analogy to be needed as more understanding shifts to analogical mapping or memory retrieval.

10.6.2 Barking Dog

A second example comes from the Meta-AQUA system (Ram and Cox 1994) which uses an example of a drug-sniffing dog. Meta-AQUA initially knows only that dogs will bark at agents that threaten them. But in the story a dog is barking at a suitcase. With ISAAC, the system is presented with two possibilities—its knowledge of dogs is wrong or its knowledge of suitcases is. The first involves altering an existing physical agent to create a variant of it, an intracellular movement. The second involves shifting a physical object to the physical agent cell, a vertical movement. The intracellular movement is therefore preferred.

10.6.3 Robots and Archaeologists

In the story *Men Are Different* (Bloch 1963), a robotic archaeologist is studying the destroyed civilization of mankind. The story is presented as a first-person narrative. ISAAC is aware that narrators, archaeologists, and protagonists are all known to be human; robots are industrial tools; but the narrator, archaeologist, and protagonist of the story is known to be a robot. ISAAC can create a new type of robot that embodies agentlike aspects (by using base-constructive analogy), or it can change the definitions of narrators, archaeologists, protagonists, and the actions in which they may participate. The new robot concept represents a more minimal change.

10.6.4 Interplanetary Zoos

The final example involves the story *Zoo* (Hoch 1978) in which the reader is presented with an intergalactic zoo that travels from planet to planet, giving the inhabitants of those planets a chance to view exotic creatures. At the end of story, however, the reader is shown that the true nature of the intergalactic ship—it is an opportunity for the "creatures" on the ship to visit exotic planets, protected from the dangerous inhabitants by the cages they are in. To understand the new zoo, ISAAC forms an analogy between the known zoo and the novel one. The result then is simply a shift from one physical object to another physical one.

10.7   Evaluation Issues

An important issue to deal with is how to evaluate a model of creative reading. ISAAC seems to read and comprehend several science fiction stories that contain concepts novel to the system. As the examples of the last section showed, the theory and model handles a wide range of levels of understanding. But a motivated evaluation of the theory and model would be more illuminating.

Traditional artificial intelligence reading systems were evaluated in a fashion analogous to how human readers would be evaluated—the programs would generate summaries of the stories they read or they would answer questions created by the researcher that were designed to evaluate the level of comprehension achieved. When we first began to consider evaluation, we knew that something beyond that level was required to fully demonstrate our theory. Initially, and somewhat naively, we felt that we would be able to appeal to the reading education literature and "pull out" a set of guidelines to use in developing a motivated evaluation of the reading capabilities of ISAAC. It was unfortunate, then, when we discovered that the reading education literature left precise evaluation issues up to the individual teacher; only general guidelines were given. Our problem was that we did not possess the experience necessary to produce accurate evaluation criteria. Second, the literature of the field where we would expect to find such expertise was lacking. However, we had access to experienced reading educators.

The technique we eventually settled on was a modification of the classic Turing Test (Turing 1950). We would give the stories being read to a group of reading experts. They would provide us with a set of questions that they felt was sufficient for testing a person's comprehension of the material. So we would have a group of humans read the stories and answer the questions. At the same time, we would allow ISAAC to read the stories and answer the questions. Then the human teachers would be given the answered questions and asked to grade them, unaware of which were of human origin and which were by ISAAC. By examining the final scores, we felt that we would be able to discover how well ISAAC was as a reader. By analyzing the knowledge it had to work with, we would be able to substantiate our claims to its creative understanding abilities.

We made use of a number of human evaluators in our methodology. There were two high school English teachers with years of experience dealing with the teaching of literature and evaluation of reading comprehension. One evaluator was a university-level computer science professor with a strong research background in natural language processing. The final evaluator was a postdoctoral position with a background in linguistics and teaching English as a second language.

The participants in the study were twenty-five students from a sophomore-level college course in Knowledge Representation and Processing. The students received extra credit in the course for their willingness to participate.

Finally we made use of three of the longer stories which ISAAC is capable of reading. These were:

- *Men Are Different* (Bloch 1963). A future robot archaeologist is studying the lost race of Mankind, which now exists only in legends.
- *Zoo* (Hoch 1978). An interplanetary zoo visits the Earth each year, bringing bizarre creatures from around the galaxy.
- *Lycanthrope* (Hartman 1992). Two friends discuss the plausibility of lycanthropy and send off for an "authentic" book on witchcraft, guaranteed to transform one of the duo into a modern-day were-creature.

The activity of ISAAC while reading each of these stories is based on the information that is provided to the system prior to the reading event:

- In *Men Are Different*, the system knows only that robots are industrial tools. They are stationary machines that are programmed to perform a specific task, often in a repetitive fashion. ISAAC uses base-constructive analogy through strong-FMS to arrive at a concept of story-robot. By dynamically merging the concepts of human and industrial-robot, an intelligent robot concept is created that allows the system to read the story.
- In *Zoo*, ISAAC knows about standard zoos. However, the interplanetary zoo in the story turns out to be one in which the bars are protecting the exhibits from the "fierce" inhabitants of the planets being visited. ISAAC is able to use analogical mapping to arrive at the proper understanding of "zoo-ness" and comprehend the story correctly.
- In *Lycanthrope*, ISAAC is given the standard mythological concept of lycanthropy. The system is able to use base-constructive analogy to create the concept of a were-car, thereby enabling the story to be comprehended.

Three facts come together at this point. First, we know that ISAAC lacked the crucial concepts it needed to comprehend the stories before reading them. Second, the initial evaluation performed indicates that ISAAC is reading and comprehending

Creativity in Reading 391

the stories at the same level as the human participants. Third, we are able to examine ISAAC's memory after the reading episodes as well as the concepts created during the course of reading—in each case the model successfully creates concepts that allow it to comprehend the stories without creating unnecessary concepts or bizarre concepts. Together, these facts provide strong evidence that ISAAC is performing creative understanding at a level sufficient to support the general reading process.

10.8 Conclusions

Reading is a complex process. As we have shown, it is also an amazingly creative one. A reader must possess the ability to handle novel concepts in a text being comprehended. "Handle" can be anything from simply not giving up at the first novel concept to learning the meaning of the novel concept via an understanding process, such as the one described here. If computer models of human reading behavior are to move out of narrow toy domains and into the realm of real-world texts, then building a successful model of creative understanding is an important first step.

Beyond the theory itself, we have also presented a method of evaluation that removes the researcher from the direct loop of evaluation. This helps to eliminate any potential biases, whether intentional or not. Of course this method of evaluation is only possible if a model exists that is at a sufficient level of development to permit humanlike evaluation to be performed. It also depends on there existing a set of experts in the field being evaluated who are willing to donate their time and expertise.

Although the theory of creative understanding we have developed has proved robust within the context of reading, there are several areas we would like to explore. First, we are interested in adapting the creative understanding algorithm to non-reading domains. We have theorized in the past that there is a tight link between creative understanding and creative invention in much the same way that there is a strong connection between understanding and problem solving (e.g., Wilensky 1983; Birnbaum 1986). So we would like to explore the use of the creative understanding process in both other comprehension areas and in design areas.

Second, we wish to continue to expand the theory within the context of reading, particularly the aspect of weak-FMS. One facet that needs further research is the determination of exactly where a modified concept should exist in the knowledge grid. For example, consider the time travel example again. If a reasoner modifies physical travel to arrive at temporal travel, then a physical action has been transitioned to a temporal action. On the other hand, consider modifying a physical transport device in order to arrive at a temporal transport device. In this case one physical object has been transformed into another physical object. Exactly how a reasoner should determine when to transition versus when to leave a concept in the same grid cell is an area of research that needs further refinement.

Artificial intelligence systems have tended to trade off so-called "deep" understanding for wide coverage of texts, largely due to the knowledge engineering problem. The creative understanding theory presented in this chapter is a step toward eliminating this trade-off. With the ability to learn new interpretations for existing concepts, reading systems can maintain a deep level of comprehension while still being able to handle real-world texts. The theory also represents a form of reading that is closer to human reading behavior. The work is a blending of practical goals with cognitive modeling ones. The result is a theory of creative understanding which has allowed us to produce a robust reading model which can read published science-fiction stories.

Notes

This work was supported by the Fannie and John Hertz Foundation and by the Georgia Institute of Technology. The authors would like to thank the members of the IGOR research group for their constant source of provocative ideas, invaluable feedback, and constant monitoring. The authors would also like to thank the people who have assisted with the development of various pieces of the theory and the model: James Riechel, Gordon Shippey, Tommy Smith, Thomas Tiller, Laurie Bare, and Rajagopal Lakshminarayan.

1. Copyright © 1992. Reprinted by permission of the author, Norman E. Hartman.

2. Notice that this does not mean that our theory of creative understanding is a "correct" one with respect to what humans do—only detailed future evaluation will allow that to be determined. However, the elements of a theory of creative understanding that permitted the reading of novel concepts are *sufficient* to explain the process, although not really *necessary*.

3. Most concepts actually possess multiple possible functions, but only one will be considered to be the current primary function of the concept.

4. A fact made humorously evident by an episode of the sitcom *Taxi*. The character Jim is taking the exam in order to become a taxicab driver. While filling out the initial paperwork, he fills in 2 for the line on the form asking eyes.

5. Of course, the slot could still be called wheels if the concept **wheels** existed as a state and not as an object; the thing to keep in mind is that slots should be relationships between objects and therefore must be states. The actual name of a concept is irrelevant; the interconnections possess the representational power. The name *number-of-wheels-possessed* is preferred over the name *wheels* simply as an aid to a human reader of the knowledge system.

6. These three aspects of understanding are the same ones discussed in our original definition of the term in section 10.2.1.

7. Note that this requires a high-level of metacognitive awareness.

8. Many high school English and literature teachers have anecdotal evidence of this. Students have been known to refuse to read certain stories or novels because they "make no sense" or just "aren't possible."

9. Other theories do place more emphasis on the memory system itself. Kolodner's *reconstructive memory* theory (1984) suggests that novel concepts can be retrieved from a memory. Turner's (1992) MINSTREL system creatively writes short stories by making use of *imaginative memory*, a theory of memory that permits memory requests to be altered dynamically according to a set of modification heuristics in order to find better matches. Our memory retrieval, in contrast, is a more traditional model, with alterations to existing concepts occurring outside the memory retrieval process.

10. Not including the code contained in the GARNET package, the COMPERE system, or the MOORE system.

References

Asherman, A. 1989. *The Star Trek Compendium*. New York: Pocket Books.

Barsalou, L. W. 1989. Intraconcept similarity and its implications for interconcept similarity. In S. Vosniadou and A. Ortony, eds., *Similarity and Analogical Reasoning*. Cambridge: Cambridge University Press.

Barsalou, L. W. 1992. Frames, concepts, and conceptual fields. In A. Lehrer and E. F. Kittay, eds., *Frames, Fields, and Contrasts*. Hillsdale, NJ: Lawrence Erlbaum.

Bhatta, S. 1995. *Model-Based Analogy in Innovative Device Design*. PhD thesis. Georgia Institute of Technology, Atlanta.

Birnbaum, L. 1986. *Integrated Processing in Planning and Understanding*. PhD thesis. Research report 489. Yale University, New Haven.

Bloch, A. 1963. *Men Are Different*. In I. Asimov and G. Conklin, eds., *50 Short Science Fiction Tales*. New York: Macmillan.

Boden, M. A. 1991. *The Creative Mind: Myths and Mechanisms*. New York: Basic Books.

Brewer, W. F. 1993. What are concepts? Issues of representation and ontology. In G. V. Nakamura, R. Taraban, and D. L. Medin, eds., *Categorization by Humans and Machines*. San Diego: Academic Press.

Brown, F. 1954. Experiment. In *The Best of Fredric Brown*. Garden City, NY: Doubleday.

Carey, S. 1992. The origin and evolution of everyday concepts. In R. N. Giere, ed., *Cognitive Models of Science*. Minneapolis: University of Minnesota Press.

Carey, S., and E. Spelke. 1994. Dmain-specific knowledge and conceptual change. In L. A. Hirshfeld and S. A. Gelman, eds., *Mapping the Mind: Domain Specificity in Cognition and Culture*. Cambridge: Cambridge University Press, 169–200.

Chi, M. T. H. 1993. Barriers to conceptual change in learning science concepts: A theoretical conjecture. In *Proceedings of the Fifteenth Annual Conference of the Cognitive Science Society*. Hillsdale, NJ: Lawrence Erlbaum, pp. 312–17.

Clement, J. 1989. Learning via model construction and criticism: Protocol evidence on sources of creativity in science. In J. A. Glover, R. R. Ronning, and C. R. Reynolds, eds, *Handbook of Creativity*. New York: Plenum Press.

Coleridge, S. T. 1926. *Biographia Literaria; or, Biographical Sketches of My Literary Life and Opinions*, ed. and intro. by J. C. Metcalf. New York: Macmillan.

Domeshek, E. 1992. *Do the Right Thing: A Component Theory of Indexing Stories for Social Advice*. PhD thesis. Yale University, New Haven.

Falkenhainer, B. 1987. Scientific theory formation through analogical reasoning. In *Proceedings of the Fourth International Workshop on Machine Learning*. San Mateo, CA: Morgan Kaufmann.

Finke, R. A., T. B. Ward, and S. M. Smith. 1992. *Creative Cognition: Theory, Research, and Applications*. Cambridge: MIT Press.

Francis Jr., A. G., and Ram, A. 1993. Conquering the untility problem: Designing a memory module for all seasons. Unpublished draft.

Gentner, D. 1989. Mechanisms of analogical learning. In S. Vosniadou and A. Ortony, eds., *Similarity and Analogical Reasoning*. Cambridge: Cambridge University Press.

Hartman, N. E. 1992. Lycanthrope. In I. Asimov, M. H. Greensberg, and J. D. Olander, eds., *Microcosmic Tales: 100 Wondrous Science Fiction Short-Short Stories*. New York: Daw Printing.

Hoch, E. D. 1978. Zoo. In I. Asimov, M. H. Greenberg, and J. D. Olander, eds., *100 Great Science Fiction Short Short Stories*. Garden City, NY: Doubleday.

Holyoak, K. J., and P. Thagard. 1995. *Mental Leaps: Analogy in Creative Thought*. Cambridge: MIT Press.

Johnson, M. 1987. *The Body in the Mind: Bodily Basis of Meaning, Imagination, and Reason*. Chicago: University of Chicago Press.

Jones, E. K. 1992. The flexible use of of abstract knowledge in planning. Technical report 28, Institute for the Learning Sciences, Northwestern University, Euanston, IL.

Kolodner, J. L. 1984. *Retrieval and Organization Strategies in Conceptual Memory: A Computer Model*. Hillsdale, NJ: Lawrence Erlbaum.

Mahesh, K. 1993. A theory of interaction and independence in sentenc understanding. Technical report GIT-CC-93/34, Georgia Institute of Technology, Atlanta.

McDermott, D. V. 1981. Artificial intelligence meets natural stupidity. In J. Haugeland, ed., *Mind Design*. Cambridge: MIT Press.

Minsky, M. L. 1975. A framework for representing knowledge. In P. H. Winston, ed., *The Psychology of Computer Vision*. New York: McGraw-Hill.

Moorman, K. and A. Ram. 1994. A model of creative understanding. In *Proceedings of the Twelfth National Conference on Artificial Intelligence*. Menlo Park, CA: AAAI Press, pp. 74–79.

Moorman, K., and A. Ram. 1996. The role of ontology in creative understanding. In *Proceedings of the Sixteenth Annual Cognitive Science Conference*, Hillsdale, NJ: Lawrence Erlbaum.

Myers, B. A. 1988. The GARNET user interface development environment: A proposal. Technical report CMU-CS-88-153. Carnegie-Mellon University, Pittsburgh.

Nersessian, N. 1992. How do scientists think? Capturing the dynamics of conceptual change in science. In R. N. Giere, ed., *Cognitive Models of Science*. Minneapolis: University of Minnesota Press.

Newell, A. 1981. The knowledge level. *AI Magazine* 2: 1–20.

Quillian, M. R. 1966. Semantic memory. In M. Minsky, ed., *Semantic Information Processing*. Cambridge: MIT Press, pp. 227–70.

Ram, A. 1991. A theory of questions and question asking. *Journal of the Learning Sciences* 1: 273–318.

Ram, A., and M. Cox. 1994. Introspective reasoning using meta-explanations for multistrategy learning. In R. Michalski and G. Tecuci, eds., *Machine Learning: A Multistrategy Approach*, vol. 4. San Mateo, CA: Morgan Kaufman.

Ram, A., and Jr. A. G. Francis 1996. Multi-plan retrieval and adaptation in an experience-based agent. In D. B. Leake, ed., *Case-Based Reasoning: Experiences, Lessons, and Future Directions*. Menlo Park, CA: AAAI Press.

Schank, R., and R. Abelson. 1977. *Scripts, Plans, Goals, and Understanding*. Hillsdale, NJ: Lawrence Erlbaum.

Smith, N. B. 1986. *American Reading Instrauction*. Newark, DE: International Reading Association.

Sowa, J. F. 1984. *Conceptual Structures: Information Processing in Mind and Machine*. Reading, MA: Addison-Wesley.

Thagard, P. 1992. *Conceptual Revolutions*. Princeton: Princeton University Press.

Turing, A. M. 1950. Can a machine think? *Mind* (October): 433–60.

Turner, S. 1992. *MINSTREL: A Computer Model of Creativity and Storytelling*. PhD thesis. University of California, Los Angeles.

Wilensky, R. 1983. *Planning and Understanding*. Reading, MA: Addison-Wesley.

Wilensky, R. 1986. Knowledge representation—A critique and a proposal. In J. L. Kolodner and C. K. Riesbeck, eds., *Experience, Memory and Reasoning*. Hilldale, NJ: Lawrence Erlbaum, ch. 2, pp. 15–28.

WKRP Episode 60. 1980. Venus and the Man. Written by Hugh Wilson, Directed by Rod Daniel.

Chapter 11
On the Intersection of Story Understanding and Learning

Michael T. Cox and Ashwin Ram

11.1 Introduction

Problem solving, comprehension (i.e., understanding), and learning are distinct processes that assume an integral role in a cognitive milieu. For the most part these processes have been studied separately in artificial intelligence and cognitive science (with some notable exceptions; e.g., see Birnbaum, 1986; Wilensky, 1983). As we intend to show, however, the relationship between these reasoning processes can be quite intimate. For example, both problem solving and comprehension must be at least partially transparent to learning if the learning process is to explain and understand failures in these reasoning components. Here we begin to outline an interrelated theory of these cognitive functions and show some of the linkages between them in a multistrategy framework.

Figure 11.1 shows a hierarchical decomposition of the relationships among problem solving, comprehension, and learning. These reasoning processes share a number of intersecting characteristics. As indicated by the stripe-filled intersection on the left, learning can be thought of as a planning task. Cox and Ram (1995) discuss this analogy at length.[1] This chapter examines the similarity between learning and story understanding as indicated by the filled intersection on the right in figure 11.1.

Our theory of introspective multistrategy learning (IML) and story understanding is implemented in a computational system called Meta-AQUA (Cox 1996b; Ram and Cox 1994). Although Meta-AQUA is an integrated system, it is useful to distinguish between its *performance task*, the externally observable task that the overall system carries out, and its *learning task*, the internal task that the system must carry out in order to improve its ability to execute the performance task. Meta-AQUA's performance task is story understanding. The task is to build a coherent conceptual interpretation of an input story in its foreground knowledge (FK). When the performance task fails, Meta-AQUA's learning task is to make changes to its background knowledge (BK)[2] so that story understanding failures are not repeated when

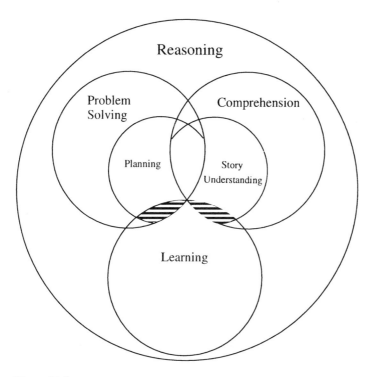

Figure 11.1
Hierarchical decomposition of reasoning.

processing similar stories in the future. In IML theory, learning has three major subtasks:

1. *Failure explanation (blame assignment)*. Determining the underling cause of the failure.
2. *Learning goal specification*. Deciding what to learn in response to the failure.
3. *Learning-strategy construction*. Deciding how to perform the necessary learning.

As illustrated in figure 11.2, blame assignment requires a system to circumscribe the source of reasoning failure. Deciding what to learn entails the explicit specification of desired changes to the BK in service of failure repair. Given such learning goals, the changes can be achieved by constructing a strategy or plan that achieves the learning specification. To generate the changes to the BK then, the system need only execute the learning strategy.

Likewise we view story understanding as the generation of changes to the story model in the FK in response to interesting input. In our theory it also has three major subtasks:

Figure 11.2
Major process components of learning changes.

1. *Concept elaboration.* Determining the underling source of the interest.
2. *Question specification.* Deciding what to ask in response to the interest.
3. *Explanation-strategy construction.* Deciding how to perform the necessary explanation in order to answer the question.

To explain an anomalous or otherwise interesting input in a story, a system should elaborate the source of the interest, specify a knowledge goal (pose a question) to explain the interesting part of the story, choose or construct a strategy to formulate the explanation, and finally execute the explanation strategy. This process causes changes to the representation of the story in the FK that refines the interpretation as new information is encountered by a reader. In addition an insightful reader will be aware of the current level of comprehension and will use this evaluation to invoke learning. That is, the perceptive reader can distinguish between those conditions under which the knowledge used to interpret the story needs refinement and the conditions under which the model of the story needs refinement.

Section 11.2 begins to describe our theory by presenting a generalized process model for multistrategy reasoning that applies to both problem-solving and comprehension tasks. Section 11.3 refines the process model specifically to comprehension tasks and then specializes it further to account for the task of story understanding. Section 11.4 develops a process model of learning that parallels the model of understanding. Section 11.5 then compares the model of understanding from section 11.3 with the learning model of section 11.4. The chapter concludes with a discussion in section 11.6.

11.2 Multistrategy Reasoning

In a classic study of human problem-solving, Newell and Simon (1972) outline a model that humans follow when engaged in reasoning about complex tasks. An initial process first translates the perception of the external environment into an internal representation of the problem. Second, the reasoner selects a method such as recognition or heuristic search by which to solve the problem.[3] Third, the method is applied to the problem. Finally, if the problem is not solved, then the reasoner either chooses another method, reformulates the problem, or quits. In their framework the emphases are on the cognitive representation of the problem and on the multiple problem-solving methods among which the reasoner must select.

Although the cognitive science community has almost universally recognized representation as crucial to intelligent behavior, the issues of strategy selection and construction has received much less attention. The research that does exist often scopes the issue much narrower than did Newell and Simon (e.g., Brigham and Pressley 1988; McDermott 1988; Puerta et al. 1992; Punch, Goel, and Brown 1996; Reder 1987). An operational definition of the generalized reasoning task that subsumes both understanding and problem solving, however, can be cast in a multistrategy framework, assuming problem-solving goals and comprehension goals. Problem-solving goals are typically specified as states in the world desired by the reasoner, whereas comprehension goals are desires to understand an input (i.e., to relate the input to the knowledge the reasoner already possesses). Given such goals, both problem solving and comprehension can be operationalized as follows:

Given some input from the world (e.g., preprocessed perceptual input or text from a story) and a current context (including contextual goals and knowledge), if the input is anomalous, or otherwise interesting,[4] choose or construct a reasoning strategy with which to explain the input while, at the same time, furthering the goals.

The outermost level of computation focuses on the choice (or construction) of a reasoning strategy rather than on the choice of a domain-specific solution operator. The outermost control is thus a second-order (executive) process at the meta-level; the first-order explanation process is at the object level. This multi-level reasoning approach is reminiscent of the MOLGEN system (Stefik 1981), in which a plane of reasoning exists in both the design plane (the reasoning task in MOLGEN's domain) and the meta-plane (the task of choosing an operator in the design plane). As a result of this division, to choose a reasoning strategy, the system should understand and model its own first-order algorithms.

In our formulation, reasoning at the object level is a variant of a heuristic generate-and-test paradigm (Newell and Simon 1976), with the enhancement of a front-end identification process to filter interesting input (see figure 11.3). If no unusual input to the system exists, no significant resources will be expended on reasoning. Therefore, in the absence of interesting input, an understander will skim its data; a problem-solver will simply act reactively or habitually. In such situations there is no great

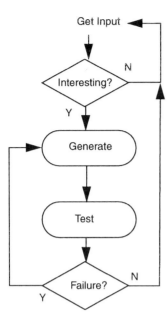

Figure 11.3
Basic reasoning model.

deliberation in pursuit of the contextual goals. With interesting input, however, a reasoner should construct and execute a strategy, thus generating some response that resolves the anomaly that sparked the interest. Subsequently the result is verified by some means constructed by the reasoner. If the result is falsified, then the generation process begins anew.

Reasoning at the meta-level (i.e., multistrategy reasoning) concerns either choosing the right strategy from among alternatives or constructing a strategy by assembling a sequence of methods that together can accomplish a desired state. It does not matter whether the desired state is a solution to a problem-solving task, a state of understanding for a comprehension task, or a state of knowledge to be acquired or modified during a learned learning task. The framework persists in all three.

11.3 Process Model of Comprehension

Comprehension (understanding) involves building causal explanations of an input, whether that input is a visual scene, spoken language, or written text. These explanations provide conceptual coherence by incorporating the current input into pieces of the previous input and by generating expectations about subsequent input. The understander skims a stream of input by instantiating schemas to fit each input item and linking it into the model of previous input, unless the current input is anomalous or unusual. If an anomalous situation is identified, then the understander must explain the input by elaborating it beyond simple schema instantiation. This is what it means for an agent to achieve a comprehension goal.

Consider the goal an art critic has when viewing a painting in a recently opened show. The critic wishes to achieve some internal mental state that relates the symbols and images in the painting to the current understanding of the genre, thus enabling an evaluation of the object. That is, the painting must be interpreted with respect to information already present in the critic's BK. A mental comparison is made between what the critic expects of such paintings with the images and emotions actually invoked by the current painting. Note that a surprising or unexpected image may be interpreted either as an exemplar of a new, creative category or as a discordant failure. Both judgments are with respect to what the critic has previously experienced, but in either case, unusual objects that violate the agent's expectations are the ones that garner the most attention because they are interesting.

Figure 11.4 provides a more detailed specification of this understanding process. Given some input and a current context (including a comprehension goal, the system's BK, and within the FK_1, a current model of the previous input), if the input is interesting, choose or construct a strategy with which to explain the input; otherwise, incorporate the input into FK_1. Upon execution of the explanation strategy, output a new representation (FK_2) of the input that has no anomaly and is coherent with

Input
- Comprehension goal
- Input
- BK (includes library of explanation strategies)
- FK1

If the input is interesting, then
Construct or select an explanation strategy to elaborate the input
Execute strategy
Incorporate story input into FK1
else skim the input.

Output
- FK2
- Trace

The input is understood if, given future input, FK2 remains consistent and coherent.

Figure 11.4
Understanding specification.

respect to the BK. The input is understood given that it remains consistent and coherent in the face of future input. Also output a representational trace of the reasoning that produced the understanding.

The explanation of interesting input should further the overall goal of understanding the entire story. The explanation is a good one if it helps to incorporate the new input with previous input and it needs little or no re-explanation when given further input concerning the same topic. The explanation is also good if it addresses the particular features that made it interesting to begin with (Ram 1989; Ram and Leake 1991).

Although not all understanding goals of are as specific as those of the art critic (i.e., the need for a critical judgment is not always present), the general process outlined above conforms to the constraints of many comprehension tasks, including the task of reading a story.

11.3.1 Understanding Elvis's Behavior: An Example

The model of comprehension presented in this chapter is a modification of the reasoning method used by the AQUA question-driven story-understanding system (Ram 1991, 1993, 1994). This model is implemented in a program called Meta-AQUA. Meta-AQUA is a multistrategy learning system that chooses and combines learning methods from a toolbox of algorithms in order to repair faulty components responsible for story-understanding failures encountered during the system's performance task.

As an example of the story understanding task, Meta-AQUA might process a story about a polite, Memphis musician named Elvis boarding with a young, Southern family (see figure 11.5).[5] While processing the story, Meta-AQUA constructs a model of the characters and the actions involved in the story. When the story reveals that Elvis occasionally smokes ganja (marijuana) in the house, endangering his safety and freedom, as well as that of the family's with which he lives, the system detects an anomaly that must be explained to fully understand the story. The event is anomalous (and hence interesting) because the model of Elvis constructed before the point of his taking drugs was one of a law-abiding citizen. A conflict occurs as a result of trying to unify the picture of Elvis as a typical, adult male (assumed to be happy) with the picture of him as an individual likely to commit a crime (thus, apt to be desperate).

To explain the incongruity, the system must understand the anomaly. Meta-AQUA accomplishes this by consulting a decision model (Ram 1990a) that describes the planning process an agent such as Elvis performs when considering a choice of actions in the world. The objective of the analysis is to refine the nature of the anomaly and to identify the parts of the story that bear on the anomaly, so as to

```
Elvis pushed cupboard-door away from the cupboard1. The cupboard1 was
open. He took the pipe2 from the cupboard1. He had the pipe2. The
cupboard1 didn't have the pipe2. He pushed cupboard-door to the
cupboard1. The cupboard1 wasn't open. He pushed fridge-door away from
the fridge1. The fridge1 was open. He took the ganja1 from the fridge1.
He had the ganja1. The fridge1 didn't have the ganja1. He pushed fridge-
door to the fridge1. The fridge1 wasn't open. He poured the ganja1 into
the pipe2. The pipe2 was filled with the ganja1. He took the lighter1
from the table2. He had the lighter1. The table2 didn't have the
lighter1. He pushed the lighter1. The lighter1 was on. He moved the
lighter1 to the ganja1. The ganja1 was burning. He pushed the lighter1.
The lighter1 wasn't on. He smoked the ganja1. The pipe2 wasn't filled
with the ganja1. The pipe2 was dirty. He exhaled the smoke1 into the
air1. He pushed hot-faucet-handle away from the hot-faucet. The hot-
faucet was flowing. He moved the pipe2 to the hot-faucet. The pipe2
wasn't dirty. He pushed hot-faucet-handle to the hot-faucet. The hot-
faucet wasn't flowing. He smoked the ganja1 because he didn't want to
be withdrawing.
                        --- The End ---
```

Figure 11.5
Elvis does the unexpected.

more clearly ascertain what needs to be explained to resolve the anomaly. An analysis of the story yields the facts that Elvis is not desperate, yet at the same time he performs an act that threatens the loss of his liberty. This situation is certainly anomalous because the decision model asserts that people value the goal of preserving their own freedom above most other goals they possess, other than the goal of preserving their lives. A goal competition (Wilensky 1983) therefore exists that Meta-AQUA must explain.

Subsequently Meta-AQUA poses a series of questions about the anomaly and the context of the story surrounding the anomaly. In this case the system asks what would cause a man to carry out an action he knew could result in his own arrest. If this question can be answered, then the anomaly would likely be resolved, and the story would be considered understood.

To explain events in a story, Meta-AQUA can generate two types of explanations.[6] *Physical explanations* give a causal account of events according to a model of the way things work in the world, whereas *volitional explanations* give a causal account of why people perform the acts they do in the world (Ram 1990a).[7] The former class links physical events (e.g., the burning of flammable materials) with probable causes (e.g., the lighting of materials with combustible devices). The latter type of explanation links the actions of agents in a story to their goals and beliefs, thus providing a motivation for story characters. In the Elvis scenario, Meta-AQUA retrieves, instantiates, and adapts a cigarette-smoking explanation, which produces expectations in the story (e.g., that the smoking will relieve a nervous emotional state). It can either look for verification of the explanation by tying it into the story or suspend the explanation until a later point in time. The explanation can be verified when subsequent sentences in the story confirm the hypothesis.

11.3.2 Question-Driven Story Understanding

Figure 11.6 shows three processes in the general understanding task used to process the Elvis example. First, the understander needs to identify anomalous (or otherwise interesting) input. In the absence of interesting story passages, the reader skims the input by passing it to a simplified version of SAM, a script application program (Cullingford 1978, 1981).[8] Second, given interesting input, the reader generates a hypothetical explanation for the text. Third, it verifies the generated explanation. Both explanation generation and verification involve strategy construction (selection). The understander must construct (or select) a method to generate an explanation and to construct (or select) a method to test the veracity of the explanation. With respect to the more generic model shown in figure 11.3, the two understanding subprocesses of constructing hypothetical explanations and verifying hypotheses correspond to the generate and test processes, respectively.[9]

11.3.2.1 Interest Identification
The first step the system performs is a simple interest detection. As previously mentioned, a concept is interesting if it is anomalous, intrinsically interesting, or about which something recently learned. In the first case, an anomaly is signaled when the input conflicts with known facts in the BK, or when the system is otherwise unable to successfully incorporate the representation of the input into the current story model in the FK. This is often detected by a unification mismatch during story processing. When a new instance is input from a story, the conceptual frame is unified with a story template or schema from the BK. If unification fails, a mismatch has occurred, and a pointer to the location of the mismatch is returned as the paths value of the anomaly (see figure 11.7). For example, the act of Elvis smoking pot does not unify with a pipe-smoking script because the value of ganja1 does not match the tobacco constraint on the object role-filler of the script (see figure 11.8).[10]

In the second case an input is determined as interesting if it is inherently interesting; that is, it is interesting if it pertains to the intrinsic goals of the reasoner. Intrinsic, or innate, goals such as the desire to maintain a state of personal safety, are associated with loud noises and violent actions, for example. In a simple way, then, Meta-AQUA, categorizes as intrinsically interesting, any concept that inherits features from among the following: loud-action, violent-action, and sexual-action.

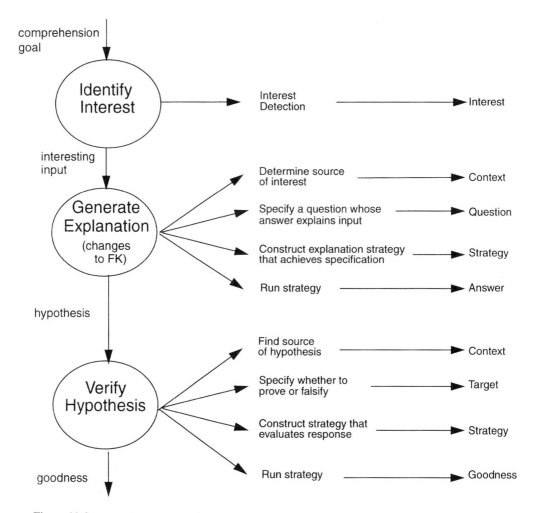

Figure 11.6
Question-driven understanding.

Finally in the third case, when Meta-AQUA has performed some learning on a particular class of objects or actions, it assigns that conceptual type an "interestingness marker." Therefore, when Meta-AQUA encounters new input pertaining to that concept, it will again be considered interesting and receive closer processing. Such an approach allows the system to form hypotheses in one story and verify it in another. The interestingness marker is amortized across time so that, after repeated encounters with the concept, the reader will no longer exhibit interest in the subject.

Intersection of Story Understanding and Learning

```
(define-frame ANOMALY
    (isa (value (commission-error)))      ; As opposed to an error of omission.
    (expected-outcome (value (entity)))   ; Obtained from some conceptual definition.
    (actual-outcome (value (entity)))     ; Obtained from some input.
    (action (value (mop)))                ; Memory organization packet.
    (paths (value (literal))))            ; Path points from outermost frame in input to
                                          ; sub-frame where contradiction occurred.
```

Figure 11.7
Frame definition for anomaly.

```
define-frame SMOKING-SCRIPT
    (isa (value (script)))
    (actor (value (volitional-agent)))
    (object (constraint (tobacco)))
    (instrumental-object (constraint (pipe)))
    (lighting-object (constraint (ignition-device)))
    (instrumental-scene
        (value (gain-control-of-contained-object
                (actor (value =actor))
                (object (value =instrumental-object))
                (containing-object (constraint (container))))))
    (scene1
        (value (fill-pipe
                (actor (value =actor))
                (object (value =instrumental-object)))))
    (goal-scene
        (value (smoke-pipe
                (actor (value =actor))
                (object (value =object))
                (instrumental-object (value =instrumental-object))
                (lighting-object (value =lighting-object))
                (goal-scene
                    (value (ingest
                            (actor (value =actor))
                            (object (value =object))))))))
    (post-completion-scene
        (value (wash-item
                (actor (value =actor))
                (object (value =instrumental-object)))))
    (scenes (value (=instrumental-scene =scene1 =goal-scene =post-completion-scene))))
```

Figure 11.8
Smoking script definition.

11.3.2.2 Explanation Generation Once an input is determined to be interesting, an explanation process attempts to resolve the anomaly by constructing a causal account of the input with respect to both the story and the reader's knowledge. Given some anomalous state the reader encounters, if the reader is to fully understand the story, the following questions must be answered:

- How did the anomaly occur?
- What needs to be explained?
- How can I explain this?

Subsequently it will resolve the anomaly by generating an explanation.

Concept Elaboration The initial step is to elaborate the anomaly in order to provide a relevant context for determining what occurred within the story. The reasoner refines the anomaly in such a way that a specific question can be posed. Since the specification of the explanation process must be more precise than simply "explain the anomaly," simply asking what the reason is for the anomaly adds little benefit. Although it may be clear that some representation for a character like Elvis indicates that he is a typical-person.0, that a later representation of him is a criminal-person.0, and that the two representations will not unify in the program internals, a better characterization of the anomaly provides specific circumstances (motivations, states, goals, beliefs, etc.) in terms of both a model of normative decisions and a model of the current story that point to possible locations of the anomaly. Moreover, by providing a story context, a system avoids much search, since the context should contain only the pertinent details known so far. A talented programmer can set up the anomalies that its system knows about in such a way that resolution is all but guaranteed. It is better to have some process that attempts to focus the anomaly so that conditions not envisioned by the programmer can also be addressed.

Question Specification Given the context provided by the previous step, the function of the next step is to provide a set of questions that represents gaps in the model of the story with respect to the anomaly. Any such question can be viewed as a *knowledge goal* (Cox and Ram 1995; Ram 1991; Ram and Hunter 1992), since it specifies the knowledge states that, if achieved, would provide coherence to both the story and what the system knows (its BK). The function of such knowledge goals, is to focus the resources and processing of the reasoner so that the combinatoric explosion of inferences is mitigated. For example, by asking the question "Why did Elvis smoke ganja in the pipe?" the reader of the Elvis episode will concentrate inference on the problem that is most relevant in the story. Without a causal explanation to the question, the story will be only partially understood.

```
Compute index as characterization of input
Retrieve Explanation Pattern (XP)
Apply XP to input representation
If XP application is successful then
   Check XP antecedents
   If one or more nodes not believed then
      Recursive questioning
```

Figure 11.9
Example explanation strategy.

Explanation-Strategy Construction Following this specification the system can pick an explanation method that will answer the focal questions (i.e., achieve the knowledge goals). Depending on the given situation and the organization of the BK (i.e., how memory is indexed), a system may choose from case-based reasoning (CBR), analogy, explanation application, or any number of reasoning methods for generation. For example, if a reader is reminded of prior case, CBR may be used, whereas if the reader is reminded of an old *explanation pattern* (XP), explanation application may be used. Figure 11.9 shows an example explanation strategy using XP Application (Ram 1991; Schank 1986).[11] Once a strategy is determined, the program can generate the explanation by executing the strategy.

11.3.2.3 Hypothesis Verification The resulting hypothesis is then tested for degree of fit or believability. To verify the hypothesized explanation, the verification process makes a similar four-step analysis. The first step, however, that of finding the source of the hypothesis, is known to follow from the generation process.[12] Step two is to determine whether to attempt to prove or disprove the hypothesis. Given a target approach, the system then needs to choose an algorithm best suited to achieving the goal. To perform a test of the resulting hypothesis, a reasoner may devise an experiment, ask someone, or simply wait, in the hope that the answer will be provided by future input. Once the algorithms have been selected and ordered, the hypothesis can then be evaluated.

Assuming such a model for the story-understanding performance task, traces of system performance can be specified and recorded at run-time in declarative structures. These knowledge structures are used by learning mechanisms to reason about processing failures, if and when failure occurs. A trace contains a decide-compute node (D-C-NODE) for each of the subprocesses of an understanding task; that is, it records the decision and the reasons behind each decision in every step of figure 11.6. Both the generation and verification processes have four steps, each of which correspond to a process field in a D-C-NODE. The four fields are input analysis, goal specification, strategy decision, and strategy execution. For each field the record stores both the enabling conditions and the resulting state. For the first three fields, the D-C-NODE records the decision basis, and for the last field, it records the side effects of the process.

If a failure occurs (as detected by the algorithm to be presented in the forthcoming section), the system suspends the understanding performance task and invokes the learning task. When this happens, the trace of the reasoning along with a characterization of the failure (as determined by the failure detection algorithm) is passed to the learning process for introspective explanation. When learning abates, the system resumes the story-understanding performance task.

11.4 Process Model of Learning

In contrast to the first-order performance task that seeks to understand events in a story, a model of the second-order learning task defines a process that seeks to understand events in the story-understanding process. When a failure occurs, the learning process inspects a trace of the system performance in order to explain the failure and decide what to learn; that is, the learning is in the domain of story-understanding failures. Upon understanding the failure, a learning strategy can be assembled and executed. This section places this model into a context of multi-strategy approaches and overviews the IML algorithm underlying such a model of learning.

Simon (1983) defines learning as "changes in the system that are adaptive in the sense that they enable the system to do the same task or tasks drawn from the same population more efficiently and more effectively the next time" (p. 28). Thus some performance task exists that receives an input and acts upon it given its knowledge dealing with that class of data. A measure of this performance is then passed to a learning task, whereupon it makes changes to the knowledge used by the performance system, depending on the success or failure of the performance. This general view of learning is diagrammed in figure 11.10.

For instance, students often learn to program computers in LISP when previously knowing another language such as Pascal. But as LISP novices, the code that results from their problem-solving is usually overextenuated, inefficient, buggy, and written in an imperative style with loops and block control-structures. As students learn to debug their programs better and acquire mastery of more LISP functions, the code becomes much more compact, efficient, bug-free, and written recursively within a functional programming style. The difference in performance is due to a change in the knowledge and skills used by the programmer both to understand and solve problems and to implement the resulting solutions. These conceptual changes come

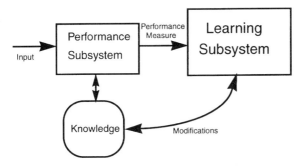

Figure 11.10
Tradition model of learning.

about from a removal of rigid, Pascal-like coding habits, an acquisition of new LISP techniques, and a reorganization of the applicability conditions for much of the knowledge relevant to the task of computer programming.

In contrast to Simon's definition, the inferential learning theory of Michalski (1991, 1994)[13] defines a learning task as consisting of three components: some input (information), the BK, and a learning goal. Even though this description does not explicitly refer to the performance of a reasoning system, and so differs from IML theory, the concept of a learning goal is central to both Michalski's model and the model of learning presented here. The learning goal determines the relevant pieces of the input, the knowledge to be acquired, and the criteria for evaluating the learning. The model of learning presented here is consistent with these constraints and, as championed by Michalski, concentrates on a multistrategy approach to learning whereby more than one learning strategy can be brought to bear upon a given learning task. Because the multistrategy approach applies equally well to both reasoning (in the form of either problem solving or understanding) and to learning, this framework is a natural one for integrating the learning and the performance tasks.

11.4.1 Multistrategy Learning

Recent attention to multistrategy learning systems is evident from numerous sources in the machine learning literature (e.g., Carbonell, Knoblock, and Minton 1991; Michalski 1993; Michalski and Tecuci 1994) and in the psychological literature (e.g., Anderson 1983, 1993; Medin et al. 1996; Wisniewski and Medin 1991). Such research constitutes a functional approach that designates the kinds of strategies a learning architecture needs to perform and the conditions for applying each. Multistrategy learning systems are those that integrate several learning algorithms into a unified whole and thus contrast with single-strategy systems such as Soar (Newell 1990;

Laird, Rosenbloom, and Newell 1986; Rosenbloom, Laird, and Newell 1993) in which all learning is performed by a single learning mechanism. Whereas any learning in Soar reduces to the chunking mechanism, methods as disparate as explanation-based learning, similarity-based learning, deduction, abduction, constructive induction, and analogy can be directly included in the same multistrategy framework. In Soar, such learning strategies must be built up from the chunking mechanism via a production implementation (Steier et al. 1987/1993).[14]

Approaches to multistrategy learning fall into three broad categories, which we call strategy selection models, toolbox models, and cascade models. The common element in all these approaches is the use of multiple learning methods to allow the reasoning system to learn in multiple types of learning situations. In *strategy selection models* the reasoner has access to several learning strategies, each represented as a separate algorithm or method. Learning involves an explicit decision stage in which the appropriate learning strategy is identified, followed by a strategy application stage in which the corresponding algorithm is executed. Methods for strategy selection also differ. The Meta-AQUA system uses characterizations of reasoning failures to determine what to learn and, in turn, the learning strategies to use when building a learning plan. *Toolbox models* are similar to strategy selection models in that they too incorporate several learning strategies in a single system. The difference is that these strategies are viewed as tools that can be invoked by the user to perform different types of learning. The tools themselves are available for use by other tools; thus learning strategies may be organized as co-routines. In *cascade models* two or more learning strategies are cascaded sequentially, with the output of one strategy serving as the input to another. Clearly these categories of models are not exclusive of each other (e.g., a strategy selection system may choose to cascade learning strategies in certain circumstances), but they serve to characterize the major ways in which learning strategies may be integrated.

Research into multistrategy learning is useful on pragmatic grounds when complex worlds are the domains of learning systems. Such approaches allow for maximal flexibility. Significant interactions are present in multistrategy systems, however, that are not apparent in isolated systems. For example, if two algorithms modify the domain knowledge of the system, and a dependency exists between the two, such that one strategy modifies a part of the domain knowledge that the second one uses, then an implied sequencing must be enforced; that is, the first strategy must be applied before the second. Such dependencies do not exist in single-strategy systems.

The general model of learning from figure 11.10 can be refined to a multistrategy framework as seen in figure 11.11. The problem generation module outputs a story to the story understanding performance system with the initial goal to understand the input. The performance module uses schemas from the BK to explain the story and

Intersection of Story Understanding and Learning

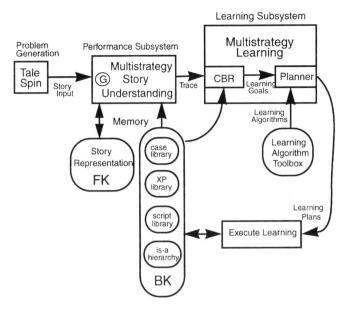

Figure 11.11
Model of introspective multistrategy learning.

to build a representation for it in the FK. If this task fails, then a trace of the reasoning that preceded the failure is passed to the learning subsystem.

A CBR subsystem within the learner uses past cases of introspective reasoning from the BK to explain the comprehension failure and to generate a set of learning goals. These goals, along with the trace, are then passed to a nonlinear planner. The planner subsequently builds a learning strategy from its toolbox of learning methods. The learning plan is passed to an execution system that examines and changes items in the BK. These changes enable improved future performance on the performance task (i.e., story understanding). Although Meta-AQUA's algorithms and knowledge structures have been reported in detail elsewhere (e.g., Cox 1994, 1996b; Cox and Ram 1995; Ram and Cox 1994; Ram, Cox, and Narayanan 1995), the following two sections provide a short example and an outline of the learning algorithm in order to provide context for the comparison between learning and story understanding.

11.4.2 Explaining an Explanation Failure: Why Did Elvis Strike the Ball?

Figure 11.12 illustrates a short story generated by Tale-Spin and input to the story-understanding module of Meta-AQUA. In the story, Meta-AQUA finds it unusual for Lynn to strike a ball because the program's conceptual definition of the "hit"

```
Elvis asked Lynn, "Would you push the ball2 to me away from you?"
Lynn went to the garage. She picked up the ball2. She had the
ball2. She went to outside. He went to outside. He played with the
ball2. She hit the ball2. She hit the ball2 because she wanted to
move the ball2 to him. He hit the ball2. He hit the ball2 because
he wanted to move the ball2 to her. He played with the ball2
because he didn't want to be bored.

                        --- The End ---
```

Figure 11.12
Elvis plays ball.

predicate constrains the object attribute to animate objects. It tries to explain the action by presupposing that Lynn tried to hurt the ball (a volitional explanation pattern, or XP, retrieved from the BK instantiates this hypothesis). In a following sentence, however, the story provides an alternate explanation (i.e., the hit action is intended to move the ball to the opposing person). This input causes an expectation failure because the system had expected one explanation to be true, but another proved true instead.

When the Meta-AQUA system detects an explanation failure, the performance module passes a trace of the reasoning to the learning subsystem. At this time the learner needs to explain why the failure occurred (assign blame) by applying an introspective explanation to the trace. A *meta-explanation pattern* (Meta-XP)[15] is retrieved using the failure symptom as a probe into memory. Meta-AQUA instantiates the retrieved meta-explanation and binds it to the trace of reasoning that preceded the failure. The resulting structure is then checked for applicability. If the Meta-XP does not apply correctly, then another probe is attempted. An accepted Meta-XP either provides a set of learning goals (determines what to learn) that are designed to modify the system's BK or generates additional questions to be posed about the failure. Once a set of learning goals are posted, they are passed to the nonlinear planner for building a learning plan (strategy construction).

Figure 11.13 lists the major state transitions that the three learning processes produce. The learning plan is fully ordered to avoid interactions. For example, the abstraction step must precede the other steps because a knowledge dependency exists between the changes on the hit concept as a result of the abstraction step and the use of the hit concept by both the generalization and indexing steps.[16] After the learning is executed and control returns to sentence processing, subsequent sentences concerning the hit predicate causes no anomaly. Instead, Meta-AQUA predicts the proper explanation when Elvis hit the ball.

Failure symptoms
Contradiction between input and background knowledge
Contradiction between expected explanation and actual explanation

Faults
Incorrect domain knowledge
Novel situation
Erroneous association

Learning goals
Reconcile input with conceptual definition
Differentiate two explanations

Learning plan
Abstraction on concept of hit
Generalization on hit explanation
Index new explanation
Mutually re-index two explanations

Figure 11.13
Learning from explanation failure.

11.4.3 Process Divisions within the Model of Learning

During the processing of stories such as these, Meta-AQUA records its reasoning in a trace structure as described earlier so that it can pass relevant information to the learner upon failure. These knowledge structures contain representations for each of the reasoning subprocesses: interest identification, explanation formation, and verification (see figure 11.6). For each the structure records the considerations that prompted the process, the bases for making a reasoning strategy decision, and the result of strategy execution. Using information from the trace, learning is divided into three similar subprocesses: failure identification, learning generation, and verification.

The first process performs failure detection. Five types of failures can occur. Failure detection inputs two structures (an expected outcome E and the actual outcome A) and the trace of the reasoning producing these knowledge structures. The algorithm for this process is shown in figure 11.14.[17] The detection process occurs either during the verification phase of the performance task of the system or during the generation phase after a resumption of a suspended generation goal. This second condition occurs after the performance system tried unsuccessfully to generate a hypothesis. The generation phase suspends the goal, and new input later provides the answer. See the impasse condition in figure 11.14. Along with the trace the process outputs a determination of which of the failures exist (if any) to the next phase. While reading the story from figure 11.12, the detection process returns a contradiction

Detect-failure (E, A, trace)
begin
If (A (out_{FK}) and trace indicates time to event expired)
or (A (out_{FK}) and impossible (goal (generate, E))) then
        return *false expectation*
If E(in_{FK}) then
    if E ≠ A then
        return *contradiction*
    else if E = A then
        If expected to fail then
            return *unexpected success*
        else return *success*
else if ∃ goal (generate, E) then
    return *impasse*
    else return *surprise*
end

Figure 11.14
Failure detection algorithm.

between the input instance of Lynn hitting the ball, thus the conceptual definition of hit in the BK, and another contradiction between the expected explanation for this event and the one provided by the story.

The second phase concerns the actual determination of the causes of failure and the construction of a learning strategy then executed. Figure 11.15 defines this learning task and shows the overall information flow to and from the learning process. The strategies from which it may construct a learning plan is dependent on the Meta-XP structures in memory. Although this phase will be covered in some detail by the next sections, alternate strategies that may result include combinations of fine-grained knowledge transmutations or more global approaches such as a student's strategy of re-reading instructions when all else fails. The output of the phase is an implicit hypothesis that the learning was correct along with an augmented trace. The changes to the BK from learning are attached to a set of D-C-Nodes and are indexed in memory where the changes occur.

The third phase concerns verification. Although beyond the scope of this chapter and more suitable for future research, verifying the learning could involve either of two strategies. The system could be reminded of a change to the BK (as associated with the D-C-Nodes and described above) at some future time when the changed knowledge is reused. The learning can then be checked as to whether it is effective. Alternatively, the system could actually make a deliberate test of the newly learned knowledge by trying to falsify the information. When either of these processes finishes, the verification phase would output an evaluation of the quality of learning.

Input
- Learning goal
- Reasoning trace
- FK
- BK1

If a failure occurred during the trace, then
Construct a learning strategy to repair BK1
Execute strategy
Store reasoning trace

Output
- BK2

The knowledge is repaired if, given a similar future situation, the failure will not recur

Figure 11.15
Learning specification.

The most critical of the three phases above, and the one upon which we place the most emphasis, is the second phase that generates changes to the BK. The remainder of this section offers additional details concerning its decomposition. Ram and Cox (1994) have argued that three fundamental learning-processes must be performed if learning is to be effective in an open world where many sources of failure exist. The processes are referred to as *blame assignment* (Birnbaum et al. 1990; Minsky 1961–1963; Stroulia et al. 1992; Weintraub 1991), *deciding what to learn* (Cox and Ram 1995; Hunter 1989, 1990; Keller 1986; Krulwich 1991; Leake and Ram 1993; Ram and Hunter 1992; Ram and Leake 1991, 1995), and *learning-strategy construction* (Cox and Ram 1991; Ram and Cox 1994; Michalski 1991). In the event of a performance failure, these processes answer the following three questions:[18]

- How did the failure occur?
- What must be learned?
- How can this be learned?

Subsequently the learner will repair the background knowledge.

To justify our process decomposition that answers these three questions, we advance the following argument: To construct a strategy, a system needs to know what is supposed to be learned; to decide what needs to be learned, it must know the cause of failure; to determine the cause of the failure, it must perform blame assignment; and to perform complete blame assignment in many situations, it must reflect upon its own reasoning. The subsections to follow presents an overview of the algorithm that instantiates these processes, and figure 11.16 sketches it in brief. The system records a trace of the reasoning used in the performance task in a number of trace meta-explanation structures. Each trace is inspected to detect a failure. When

0. Perform and Record Reasoning in Trace
1. Failure Detection on Reasoning Trace
2. If Failure Then
   Learn from Mistake:
   - 2 a. Blame Assignment
     Compute index as characterization of failure
     Retrieve Meta-XP
     Apply Meta-XP to trace of reasoning
     If Meta-XP application is successful then
       Check Meta-XP antecedents
       If one or more nodes not believed then
         Introspective questioning
         GOTO step 0
     Else GOTO step 0
   - 2 b. Create Learning Goals
     Compute tentative goal priorities
   - 2 c. Choose Learning Algorithm(s)
     Translate Meta-XP and goals to predicates
     Pass goals and Meta-XP to planner (Nonlin)
     Translate resultant plan into frames
   - 2 d. Apply Learning Algorithm(s)
     Interpret plan as partially ordered network of actions such that primitive actions are algorithm calls
3. Evaluate Learning (not implemented)

Figure 11.16
IML learning algorithm.

the system detects a failure, it invokes learning. During learning the system constructs a learning strategy via the three process steps: blame assignment, deciding what to learn, and strategy construction. Subsequently the system executes the learning strategy to perform the necessary knowledge repairs.

11.4.3.1 Blame Assignment (step 2a, figure 11.16)

Take as input a trace of the mental and physical events that preceded a reasoning failure; produce as output an explanation of how and why the failure occurred, in terms of the causal factors responsible for the failure.

Blame assignment is a matter of determining what was responsible for a given failure. Thus the function of blame assignment is to identify which causal factors could have led to the reasoning failure as determined from the output of the performance task and contained in the reasoning trace. That is, blame assignment is like troubleshooting; it is a mapping function from failure symptom to failure cause. The purpose is the same whether the troubleshooter is explaining a broken device or itself (Stroulia 1994).

The input trace describes how results or conclusions were produced by specifying the prior causal chain (both of mental and physical states and events). The learner retrieves an abstract meta-explanation pattern, or Meta-XP, from memory and applies it to the trace in order to produce a specific description of why these conclusions were wrong or inappropriate. This instantiation specifies the causal links that would have been responsible for a correct conclusion, and enumerates the difference between the two chains and two conclusions (what was produced and what should have been produced). Finally the learner outputs the instantiated explanation(s). The Meta-XP that explains the symptoms of our earlier story asserts that the expectation-failure between competing explanations is due to three factors: incorrect domain knowledge (overly restrictive definition of the hit predicate), novel situation (never encountered the explanation that people hit objects to make them change locations), and erroneous association (the hurt explanation was associated with the actor that performed the hitting rather than the object hit). See again figure 11.13.

11.4.3.2 Deciding What to Learn (step 2b, figure 11.16)

Take as input a causal explanation of how and why failure occurred; generate as output a set of learning goals which, if achieved, can reduce the likelihood of the failure repeating. Include, with the output, both tentative goal-dependencies and priority orderings on the goals.

The previously instantiated Meta-XP assists in this process by specifying points in the reasoning trace most likely to be responsible for the failure. The Meta-XP also specifies the suggested type of learning goal to be spawned by this stage. Because these goals are tentative, it may be necessary to retract, decompose, or otherwise adapt the learning goals dynamically during run-time. This stage of learning mediates between the case-based approach of blame assignment and the nonlinear planning approach of strategy construction. The learner includes with the output learning goals both tentative goal-dependencies and priority orderings on the goals. The trace is passed as output as well.

In the case of the hit anomaly, the Meta-XP focuses the learner on two learning goals. The story instance of hitting needs to be reconciled with the hit definition, and the two explanations need to be differentiated. These two learning goals determine the kinds of changes to the BK necessary for effective learning. They operationalize the effects that matter and localize the inferences required for instantiating the changes.

11.4.3.3 Learning-Strategy Construction (step 2c, figure 11.16)

Take as input a trace of how and why a failure occurred and a set of learning goals along with their dependencies; produce as output an ordered set of learning strategies to apply that will accomplish the goals along with updated dependencies on the set of goals.

The final learning-strategies are organized as plans to accomplish the learning goals. The plans are sequences of steps representing calls to standard learning algorithms. The plans are created by a Common LISP version of Tate's (1976) Nonlin planner (Ghosh et al. 1992). To use the nonlinear planner, the learning module translates the learning goals and the relevant context of the program environment to a predicate representation. In this form Nonlin assembles a learning plan just as if it were creating a plan to stack a series of labeled blocks. The only difference is that the planner is given a set of learning operators that describe actions that modify the mental world (i.e., the BK) instead of the blocks world (see Cox and Ram 1995 for full details of the planning analogy and implementation used in strategy construction).

The learner instantiates the plan, translates it back into a frame representation, and then executes the learning plans (in step 2d, figure 11.16). In the case of Lynn and Elvis's game of ball, the reconciliation goal is achieved by performing abstraction on the concept of hit. Thus the constraint on the object slot is raised to physical object (the parent of animate and inanimate), rather than being limited to animate ones. The goal of differentiating the two explanations is solved by running EBG on the new explanation, indexing the new explanation, and then reindexing the two explanation with respect to each other to achieve discrimination. Nonlin generates a full order for the plan steps that achieves the conjunctive learning goals and avoids goal interactions. At the termination of the plan execution, control is returned to the performance system, and story understanding is resumed.

11.4.4 Evaluation

In an empirical study of the effects of this learning method on explanation performance, Cox, (1996a) demonstrates that Meta-AQUA performs significantly better under a fully introspective mode than under a reflexive mode that ablates learning goals. Figure 11.17 shows Meta-AQUA's cumulative improvement in performance (as measured by an evaluation function rating question answering ability) given one 24-story sequence of problems randomly generated by the Tale-Spin program. The lower curve represents Meta-AQUA without learning, the middle curve represents the system without learning goals, and the upper curve includes all three transformations.

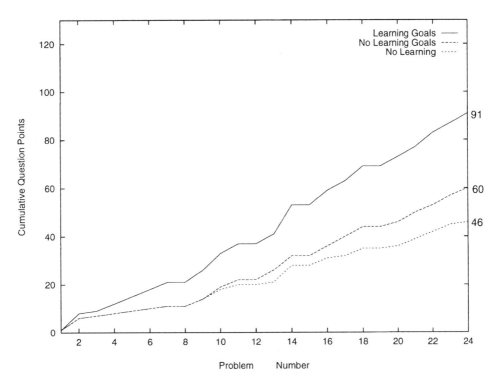

Figure 11.17
Effects of learning goals.

To serve as experimental trials and to minimize order effects, Tale-Spin generated six such random sequences of stories. On each of these runs, Meta-AQUA processed a sequence three times, once for each experimental manipulation. The system begins all runs with the same initial conditions. For a given experimental condition, it processed all of the stories in the sequence while maintaining the learned knowledge between stories. At the end of the sequence, the system resets the BK. The input size for a run varies in length but averages 27.67 stories per run. The corpus for the six runs included 166 stories, comprising a total of 4,884 sentences. The stories varied in size depending on the actions of the story and Tale-Spin's randomness parameters, but they averaged 29.42 sentences.

Across all six experimental runs, the expected gain in learning (i.e., the differential between the average "learning goal" improvement of 102.7 and the average "no learning goal" improvement of 65.7) is a 56.38 percent difference. That is, across a number of input conditions, the use of learning goals to order and combine learning choices should show about 1.5 times the improvement in performance than will a straight mapping of faults to repairs when interactions are present. In general, these data lead to the conclusion that the process which posts learning goals (deciding what to learn) is a necessary transformation if negative interactions between learning methods are to be avoided and if learning is to remain effective. Moreover we showed that because learning algorithms can negatively interact, the arbitrary ordering of learning methods can actually lead to worse system performance than no learning at all.

11.5 Comparison of Learning and Story Understanding

Throughout this exposition numerous parallels have been drawn between introspective learning and understanding. Compare figure 11.4 with figure 11.15, for example, which shows the general specifications of understanding and learning, respectively, as modeled by this research. Note also the correspondences between figure 11.2 and the "generate explanation" node of figure 11.6. This chapter has argued, given a multi-strategy approach, that a good strategy for both learning and story-understanding is to identify anomalies, generate some response to the anomaly, and then test the response. The augmented generate-and-test paradigm fits both equally well. Both are concerned with selecting or combining a strategy, rather than applying a particular one. Both models are highly top-down and goal-driven; goals are essential for both focus and direction.

Both the form and the function of the generation phases in learning and understanding are similar (see figure 11.18). The structure of both is to take some unusual input (reasoning failure or incongruous story concept), elaborate the input, generate some goal that provides focus for the process, and then change some knowledge base to achieve the function of the process. Changes during story understanding take place in the FK, whereas changes during learning take place in the BK.

A number of differences, however, exist between learning and understanding. For example, as understanding can be likened to **recovery**, so too, learning can be likened to *repair*. In the planning literature a number of researchers have made the distinction between recovery and repair (e.g., see Owens 1991; Hammond 1989). When a plan fails, the planner must recover from the error so additional progress can be made toward the goal. After recovery the plan needs to be repaired and stored again in memory so that the plan failure will not recur.

For example, if an autonomous robot vehicle finds an expected fuel cache missing and thereby runs out of gasoline, it must first recover from the potentially threatening situation by obtaining fuel (example taken from Owens 1991). Therefore the explanation of the failure will dictate the means of recovery. If the robot concludes that it

Intersection of Story Understanding and Learning

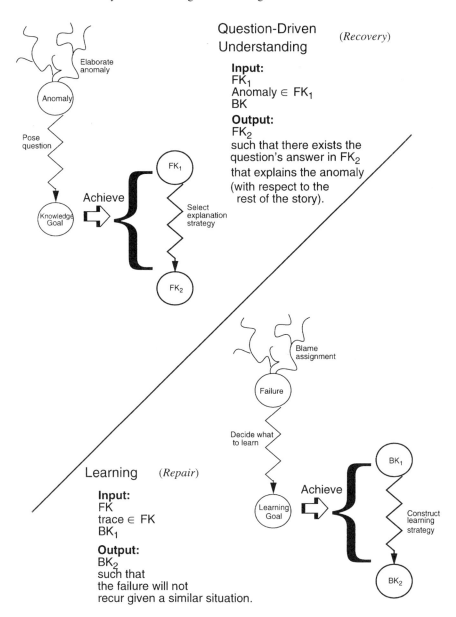

Figure 11.18
Parallels between learning and understanding.

cannot find the gasoline because it is lost, then it should recover by obtaining orientation information, whereas if it explains the fuel's absence because of theft, then the recovery taken will involve turning back or calling for assistance. The repair (to adjust its plans and the information on which the plan was based) also follows from the explanation of the failure. For instance, if the robot previously considered taking on extra fuel, but did not because it assumed that the fuel cache would be at the proper location and easy to find, then this explanation of its decision would lead the system to modify its knowledge concerning the persistence of fuel caches. This modification would bias it toward conservative decisions in the future and thus make it less likely to repeat the failure.

The difference between recovery and repair can be applied in an analogous manner to the processes of understanding and learning. The understanding process requires a recovery phase when it fails. If some explanation does not work, first there is a need to create a new explanation or somehow to seek one out. Once the correct (or more useful) explanation has been derived, the system needs to learn from the experience by repairing its knowledge, so as not to repeat the failure. Thus, as seen in figure 11.18, the understanding process operates on the FK to instill the change that removes the anomaly (thus constituting the recovery), whereas the learning process operates on the BK, producing a repaired knowledge base with which the failure will not be as likely in future similar situations. The recovery is a system's response to anomalous input from the outside world that its knowledge could not adequately understand, whereas the learning is a response to the inadequacy in the reasoner's world.

Functional reasons exist for having an explicit input analysis stage in both learning and understanding (i.e., concept elaboration, or more specifically anomaly elaboration, in understanding and failure explanation, or more specifically blame assignment, in learning). Most programs accept cleanly defined problems as input, such that little ambiguity and sharp distinctions concerning what needs to be done exist. In more practical systems, problem elaboration is necessary to clarify what may actually be ill-defined tasks. For example, planning tasks in artificial intelligence are often structured and circumscribed by the programmer or user, not the planner. A planner may be given operational goal specifications from which a state, such as one block being on top of another, may be achieved. The tasks of recognizing that a problem exists for which a plan is required and establishing the goal specifications, however, are not considered a part of the planner's reasoning process. In comprehension tasks such as story-understanding, the problems are not usually so well defined. In learning, the problem of recovery is to modify the story representation in such a way that the anomaly is coherent with respect to the rest of the story and the system's BK. This specification is so broad that either the programmer must include the specifications implicitly or the explanation must be somewhat trivial. To narrow the range of behaviors appropriate for recovery, then, is to elaborate the input anomaly, so as to identify what went wrong and why.[19]

11.6 Discussion

This chapter presented a first-order process theory for understanding and second-order process theory of learning by defining the phases of each, by outlining what steps are used to accomplish such functions, and by arguing why each phase is required by the theories. IML theory holds that both understanding and learning consist of three basic phases. The first stage is an identification phase, the second is a generation phase, and the final phase is verification. Although each stage is important, this research has concentrated on the generation stage of each. For both types of generation, the phase has three steps: input elaboration, goal generation, and strategy construction/selection. In both learnings and story understanding, the resultant strategy is simply executed to accomplish the desired goal. We have also placed both the reasoning and learning processes within a multistrategy framework. Many methods may exist with which a reasoner can solve a problem, an understander can comprehend an input, and a learner can improve its performance. The choice of a best set of methods and the combination of such methods represent challenging decisions for any intelligent system.

Although the relationship between text comprehension and metacognitive activities has been studied since the turn of the century albeit under the guise of differing technical terms (Brown 1987), more recent research examining the relationship between metacognitive skills and educational instruction have made significant progress. For example, Forrest-Pressley, MacKinnon, and Waller (1985) and Garner (1987) report successful instruction procedures related to both problem-solving and reading comprehension (see also Ram and Leake, 1995, for a related discussion). Chi (1995; Chi et al. 1989) reports that improved learning is correlated with human subjects who generate their own questions and explain the answers themselves (see also Pressley and Forrest-Pressley 1985). This is the so-called self-explanation effect. Thus the ability of a system to pose self-generated questions both indexes actual understanding and simultaneously reduces the probability of asking only the easy questions.

Consider the following quote from Gavelek and Raphael (1985):

> One form of metacognition—metacomprehension—addresses the abilities of individuals to adjust their cognitive activity in order to promote more effective comprehension. We have been interested in a specific aspect of metacomprehension—namely, the manner in which questions generated by sources external to the learner (i.e., from the teacher or text), as well as those questions generated by the learners themselves, serve to promote their comprehension of text. (p. 104)

The ability to adjust cognition in order to improve comprehension is at the heart of the research presented here. Thus simply being able to recognize that a gap exists in one's own knowledge, and to therefore ask the question "Why don't I understand this?" (Ram 1991), is the first step to improving the understanding rather than actually giving an answer. So, to evaluate the ability of the performance of the Meta-AQUA system, credit should be given for simply posing a question that deserves asking.

Garner (1987) has argued that metacognition and comprehension monitoring are important factors in the understanding of written text. Reading comprehension is therefore considered to be chiefly an interaction between a reader's expectations and the textual information.[20] Psychological studies have also confirmed a positive correlation between meta-memory and memory performance in cognitive monitoring situations (Miner and Reder 1994; Schneider 1985; Wellman 1983) and between the use of metacognitive abilities with standard measures of intelligence (Davidson, Deuser, and Sternberg 1994). This evidence, along with results from the studies above linking problem-solving performance with metacognitive abilities, directly supports the conviction that there must be a second-order introspective process that reflects to some degree on the performance element in an intelligent system, especially a learning system involved in tasks such as story understanding.

Notes

This research is supported by AFOSR under contract F49620-94-1-0092 and by the Georgia Institute of Technology. The authors thank Kenny Moorman for insights and comments on an earlier draft of this chapter.

1. Cox (1996b, pp. 294–99) discusses some of the intersections between problem-solving and comprehension represented in the top-center of the figure. For example, a problem-solver must be able to monitor the execution of a solution to confirm that it achieves its goal. If the comprehension process determines that the goal pursuit is not proceeding as planned, then the planning failure must be addressed and the plan changed.

2. The system's background knowledge, or BK, contains more that just the domain theory of the performance task. It represents all long-term knowledge including metaknowledge, heuristic knowledge, associative knowledge, and knowledge of process. In contrast to the BK, the FK constitutes the current model of the input that has been constructed, and the memory of the reasoning with which such a model was built.

3. See Simon (1979) for a discussion of alternative strategies given a single problem representation.

4. Interesting input is either an anomalous conceptualization or something pertaining to the intrinsic goal of the reasoner. For example, sex, violence, and loud noises are intrinsically interesting (Schank 1979). In addition anything concerning a concept about which something has been learned recently will be categorized as interesting. For a more detailed set of interestingness heuristics, see Ram (1990b).

5. Figure 11.5 was produced by a modified version of the Tale-Spin story-generation program (Meehan 1981). This program provides automatically generated, albeit stylized, input to the Meta-AQUA system.

6. For a far more exhaustive taxonomy, see Kass and Leake (1987).

7. To explain story-understanding events (e.g., the process of explanation itself), Meta-AQUA can generate a third type of explanation. *Meta-explanations* give a causal account of mental events according to our model of the way things work in the story-understanding process. This class will be briefly discussed in section 11.4.

8. The script applier understands a story by matching input sentences to stereotypical sequences of events (i.e., to scripts). For example, a simple pipe-smoking script consists of sub-scenes to get the pipe, put tobacco into it, smoke it, then clean it, and hierarchically these scenes are composed of subscenes (see figure 11.8). Although scripts omit many of the causal relations between events in a story, they can help an understander interpret a story by providing details not explicitly mentioned in the story.

9. This is not unlike Klahr and Dunbar's (1988) model of scientific discovery, where there is a hypothesis generation phase followed by hypothesis verification and evidence testing phases. The major difference, though, is that IML theory assumes no explicit exploration of a hypothesis space via search. Instead, a simple indexed memory provides suggestions that constitute hypotheses.

10. In the frame definition, =X is a variable binding to the outermost slot named X.

11. An XP is a directed graph with nodes that are either states or processes and links that are ENABLES links (connecting states with the processes for which they are preconditions), RESULTS links (connecting a process with a result), or INITIATE links (connecting two states). The XP provides a causal justification for a distinguished node called the EXPLAINS node by providing its causal antecedents.

12. Yet, in instances where a hypothesis is not self-generated but provided to the reasoner as input, step one would indeed require significant computation.

13. See also Michalski and Ram (1995) for a more detailed inspection of the relation between views presented here and those of Michalski.

14. A more critical evaluation of the single-strategy approach is that learning is actually a melange of several mechanisms of the architecture (Pylyshyn 1991). Learning can be obtained as a result of goal-driven problem solving (as is with the Soar framework), or by the passive exposure to experience or goal-orientations (e.g., see Barsalou 1995), or by instruction, trial and error, perceptual reorganization, insight, or numerous other mechanisms. The position here is that learning is best modeled as a multistrategy process, even if different learning strategies are ultimately implemented by a single underlying mechanism.

15. Unlike volitional or physical XPs that explain why persons perform particular actions and how object behave and function, a Meta-XP explains how and why mental actions (e.g., the explanation process itself) occur. For instance, the EXPLAINS node of IMXP-NOVEL-SITUATION-ALTERNATIVE-REFUTED points to an Expectation Failure (the reader expected one explanation to be true, while another explanation proved to be better), and the Meta-XP provides the causal antecedents that led to the failure (i.e., an erroneous association indexed the first explanation in the BK, whereas the second explanation was missing from the BK). Both Ram and Cox (1994) and Cox (1996b) provide representational details.

16. During mutual re-indexing, the explanations are differentiated based on the object attribute-value of the hit. However, the abstraction transmutation changes this attribute. The generalization method applied to the new explanation also uses this attribute. See Cox and Ram (1995) for a more complete analysis.

17. The notation $X(out_{FK})$ means that the concept X is out of the set of beliefs with respect to the FK. The semantics of such notation is further explained in Cox (1996b) and Cox and Ram (1992).

18. Note the similarity to the analogous questions pertaining to comprehension section 11.3.2.2.

19. Kolodner (1993) also speaks of *situation assessment* (or elaboration) of new input in preparation for case retrieval. The function is the same as input analysis above. In nontrivial systems a significant part of the problem is to massage the input into a form that is most useful for both processing and retrieval.

20. A special relation exists between metacognition, question asking and text understanding (see Gavelek and Raphael 1985; Pressley and Forrest-Pressley 1985). In effect, human learners use question-asking and question-answering strategies to provide an index into their level of comprehension of a given piece of text. This metacognitive feedback helps readers find areas where their understanding of the story is deficient, and thus where greater processing is necessary. Such a perspective supports our ancillary claim that question generation is a key activity in text comprehension and also that meta-level processing is important in such a learning context. As a final tangent, not only is metacognition important in language understanding, it is also important in language generation (i.e., in metalinguistic development; see Gombert 1992).

References

Anderson, J. R. 1983. *The Architecture of Cognition*. Cambridge: Harvard University Press.

Anderson, J. R. 1993. *Rules of the Mind*. Hillsdale, NJ: Lawrence Erlbaum.

Barsalou, L. W. 1995. Storage side effects: Studying processing to understand learning. In A. Ram and D. B. Leake, eds., *Goal-Driven Learning*. Cambridge: MIT Press, pp. 407–19.

Birnbaum, L. 1986. *Integrated Processing in Planning and Understanding*. PhD dissertation. Technical report 489. Yale University, Department of Computer Science, New Haven.

Birnbaum, L., G. Collins, M. Freed, and B. Krulwich. 1990. Model-based diagnosis of planning failures. In *Proceedings of the Eighth National Conference on Artificial Intelligence*. Menlo Park, CA: AAAI Press, pp. 318–23.

Brigham, M. C., and M. Pressley. 1988. Cognitive monitoring and strategy choice in younger and older adults. *Psychology and Aging* 3: 249–57.

Brown, A. 1987. Metacognition, executive control, self-regulation, and other more mysterious mechanisms. In F. E. Weinert and R. H. Kluwe, eds., *Metacognition, Motivation, and Understanding*. Hillsdale, NJ: Lawrence Erlbaum, pp. 65–116.

Carbonell, J. G., C. A. Knoblock, and S. Minton. 1991. PRODIGY: An integrated architecture for planning and learning. In K. VanLehn, ed., *Architectures for Intelligence: The 22nd Carnegie Mellon Symposium on Cognition*. Hillsdale, NJ: Lawrence Erlbaum, pp. 241–78.

Chi, M. T. H. 1995. Revising the mental model as one learns. Plenary address to the Seventeenth Annual Conference of the Cognitive Science Society, Pittsburgh, July 23.

Chi, M. T. H., M. Bassok, M. Lewis, P. Reimann, and R. Glasser. 1989. Self-explanations: How students study and use examples in learning to solve problems. *Cognitive Science* 13: 145–82.

Cox, M. T. 1994. Machines that forget: Learning from retrieval failure of mis-indexed explanations. In A. Ram and K. Eiselt, eds., *Proceedings of the Sixteenth Annual Conference of the Cognitive Science Society*. Hillsdale, NJ: Lawrence Erlbaum, pp. 225–30.

Cox, M. T. 1996a. An empirical study of computational introspection: Evaluating introspective multistrategy learning in the Meta-AQUA system. In R. S. Michalski and J. Wnek, eds., *Proceedings of the Third International Workshop on Multistrategy Learning*. Menlo Park, CA: AAAI Press, pp. 135–46.

Cox, M. T. 1996b. *Introspective Multistrategy Learning: Constructing a Learning Strategy under Reasoning Failure*. PhD dissertation. Technical report GIT-CC-96-06. Georgia Institute of Technology, College of Computing, Atlanta. Available URL: ftp://ftp.cc.gatech.edu/pub/ai/ram/git-cc-96-06.html

Cox, M. T., and A. Ram. 1991. Using introspective reasoning to select learning strategies. In R. S. Michalski and G. Tecuci, eds., *Proceedings of the First International Workshop on Multistrategy Learning*. Washington, DC: George Mason University, Artificial Intelligence Center, pp. 217–30.

Cox, M. T., and A. Ram. 1992. An explicit representation of forgetting. In J. W. Brahan and G. E. Lasker, eds., *Proceedings of the Sixth International Conference on Systems Research, Informatics and Cybernetics*, vol. 2: *Advances in Artificial Intelligence—Theory and Application*. Windsor, Ontario, Canada: International Institute for Advanced Studies in Systems Research and Cybernetics, pp. 115–20.

Cox, M. T., and A. Ram. 1995. Interacting learning-goals: Treating learning as a planning task. In J.-P. Haton, M. Keane, and M. Manago, eds., *Advances in Case-Based Reasoning*. Berlin: Springer-Verlag, pp. 60–74.

Cullingford, R. 1978. *Script Application: Computer Understanding of Newspaper Stories*. PhD dissertation. Technical report 116. Yale University, Department of Computer Science, New Haven.

Cullingford, R. 1981. Micro SAM. In R. C. Schank and C. Riesbeck, eds., *Inside Computer Understanding: Five programs plus Miniatures*. Hillsdale, NJ: Lawrence Erlbaum, pp. 120–35.

Forrest-Pressley, D. L., G. E. MacKinnon, and T. G. Waller, eds. 1985. *Metacognition, Cognition and Human Performance*, vol. 2: *Instructional Practices*. New York: Academic Press.

Garner, R. 1987. *Metacognition and Reading Comprehension*. Norwood, NJ: Ablex Publishing.

Gavelek, J. R., and T. E. Raphael. 1985. Metacognition, instruction, and the role of questioning activities. In D. L. Forrest-Pressley, G. E. MacKinnon, and T. G. Waller, eds., *Metacognition, Cognition and Human Performance*, vol. 2: *Instructional Practices*. New York: Academic Press, pp. 103–36.

Ghosh, S., J. Hendler, S. Kambhampati, and B. Kettler. 1992. *UM Nonlin* [a common Lisp implementation of A. Tate's Nonlin planner]. Available FTP: Hostname: cs.umd.edu Directory: /pub/nonlin Files: nonlin-files.tar.Z

Gombert, J. E. 1992. *Metalinguistic Development*. Chicago: University of Chicago Press.

Hammond, K. J. 1989. *Case-Based Planning: Viewing Planning as a Memory Task*, vol. 1: *Perspectives in Artificial Intelligence*. San Diego, CA: Academic Press.

Hunter, L. E. 1989. *Knowledge Acquisition Planning: Gaining Experience through Experience*. PhD dissertation. Technical report 678. Yale University, Department of Computer Science, New Haven.

Hunter, L. E. 1990. Planning to learn. In *Proceedings of Twelfth Annual Conference of the Cognitive Science Society*. Hillsdale, NJ: Lawrence Erlbaum, pp. 261–76.

Kass, A., and D. Leake. 1987. Types of explanations. Technical report 523. Yale University, Department of Computer Science, New Haven.

Keller, R. M. 1986. Deciding what to learn. Technical report ML-TR-6. Rutgers University, Department of Computer Science, New Brunswick, NJ.

Klahr, D., and K. Dunbar. 1988. Dual space search during scientific reasoning. *Cognitive Science* 12: 1–48.

Kolodner, J. L. 1993. *Case-Based Reasoning*. San Mateo, CA: Morgan Kaufmann.

Krulwich, B. 1991. Determining what to learn in a multi-component planning system. In *Proceedings of the Thirteenth Annual Conference of the Cognitive Science Society*, August 7–10, Chicago, pp. 102–107.

Laird J. E., P. S. Rosenbloom, and A. Newell. 1986. Chunking in Soar: The anatomy of a general learning mechanism. *Machine Learning* 1: 11–46.

Leake, D., and A. Ram. 1993. Goal-driven learning: Fundamental issues and symposium report. *AI Magazine* 14: 67–72.

McDermott, J. 1988. Preliminary steps toward a taxonomy of problem-solving methods. In S. Marcus, ed., *Automating Knowledge Acquisition for Expert Systems*. Boston: Kluwer, pp. 225–56.

Medin, D. L., E. B. Lynch, J. D. Coley, and S. Atran. 1996. The basic level and privilege in relation to goals, theories, and similarity. In R. S. Michalski and J. Wnek, eds., *Proceedings of the Third International Workshop on Multistrategy Learning*. Menlo Park, CA: AAAI Press, pp. 71–83.

Meehan, J. 1981. Talespin. In R. C. Schank and C. Riesbeck, eds., *Inside Computer Understanding: Five Programs plus Miniatures*. Hillsdale, NJ: Lawrence Erlbaum, pp. 197–258.

Michalski, R. S. 1991. Inferential learning theory as a basis for multistrategy task-adaptive learning. In R. S. Michalski and G. Tecuci, eds., *Proceedings of the First International Workshop on Multistrategy Learning*. Washington, DC: George Mason University, Artificial Intelligence Center, pp. 3–18.

Michalski, R. S., ed. 1993. Multistrategy learning. *Machine Learning* 11 (Special issue).

Michalski, R. S. 1994. Inferential theory of learning: Developing foundations for multistrategy learning. In R. S. Michalski and G. Tecuci, eds., *Machine Learning IV: A Multistrategy Approach*. San Francisco: Morgan Kaufmann, pp. 3–61.

Michalski, R. S., and A. Ram. 1995. Learning as goal-driven inference. In A. Ram and D. Leake, eds., *Goal-Driven Learning*. Cambridge: MIT Press, pp. 479–90.

Michalski, R. S., and G. Tecuci, eds. 1994. *Machine Learning IV: A Multistrategy Approach*. San Francisco: Morgan Kaufmann.

Miner, A. C., and L. M. Reder. 1994. A new look at feeling of knowing: Its metacognitive role in regulating question answering. In J. Metcalfe and A. P. Shimamura, eds., *Metacognition: Knowing about Knowing*. Cambridge: MIT Press, pp. 47–70.

Minsky, M. L. 1963. Steps towards artificial intelligence. In E. A. Feigenbaum and J. Feldman, eds., *Computers and Thought*. New York: McGraw Hill, pp. 406–50. (Original work published 1961.)

Newell, A. 1990. *Unified Theories of Cognition*. Cambridge: Harvard University Press.

Newell, A., and H. A. Simon. 1972. *Human Problem Solving*. Englewood Cliffs, NJ: Prentice-Hall.

Newell, A., and H. A. Simon. 1976. Computer science as empirical inquiry: Symbols and search. (The 1976 ACM Turing Lecture.) *Communications of the ACM* 19: 113–26.

Owens, C. 1991. A functional taxonomy of abstract plan failures. In *Proceedings of the Thirteenth Annual Conference of the Cognitive Science Society*. Hillsdale, NJ: Lawrence Erlbaum, pp. 167–72.

Pressley, M., and D. ... essley. 1985. Questions and children's cognitive processing. In A. C. Graesser ... eds., *The Psychology of Questions*. Hillsdale, NJ: Lawrence Erlbaum ...

Puerta, ... Musen. 1992. A multiple-method knowledge-acquisition shell ... of knowledge-acquisition tools. *Knowledge Acquisition* 4: 171–96.

Punch, W. ... C. Brown. 1996. A knowledge-based selection mechanism for ... ion in design, diagnosis and planning. *International Journal of ...* 4: 323–48.

Pylyshyn, Z. ... .e role of cognitive architecture in theories of cognition. In K. VanLehn, ed., *Ar... .ctures of Cognition: The 22nd Carnegie Mellon Symposium on Cognition*. Hillsdale, NJ: Lawrence Erlbaum, pp. 189–223.

Ram, A. 1989. *Question-Driven Understanding: An Integrated Theory of Story Understanding, Memory and Learning*. PhD dissertation. Technical report 710. Yale University, Department of Computer Science, New Haven.

Ram, A. 1990a. Decision models: A theory of volitional explanation. In *Proceedings of Twelfth Annual Conference of the Cognitive Science Society*. Hillsdale, NJ: Lawrence Erlbaum, pp. 198–205.

Ram, A. 1990b. Knowledge goals: A theory of interestingness. In *Proceedings of Twelfth Annual Conference of the Cognitive Science Society*. Hillsdale, NJ: Lawrence Erlbaum, pp. 206–14.

Ram, A. 1991. A theory of questions and question asking. *Journal of the Learning Sciences* 1: 273–318.

Ram, A. 1993. Indexing, elaboration and refinement: Incremental learning of explanatory cases. *Machine Learning* 10: 201–48.

Ram, A. 1994. AQUA: Questions that drive the understanding process. In R. C. Schank, A. Kass, and C. K. Riesbeck, eds., *Inside Case-Based Explanation*. Hillsdale, NJ: Lawrence Erlbaum, pp. 207–61.

Ram, A., and M. T. Cox. 1994. Introspective reasoning using meta-explanations for multistrategy learning. In R. S. Michalski and G. Tecuci, eds., *Machine Learning IV: A Multistrategy Approach*. San Francisco: Morgan Kaufmann, pp. 349–77.

Ram, A., M. T. Cox, and S. Narayanan. 1995. Goal-driven learning in multistrategy reasoning and learning systems. In A. Ram and D. Leake, eds., *Goal-Driven Learning*. Cambridge: MIT Press, pp. 421–37.

Ram, A., and L. Hunter. 1992. The use of explicit goals for knowledge to guide inference and learning. *Applied Intelligence* 2: 47–73.

Ram, A., and D. Leake. 1991. Evaluation of explanatory hypotheses. In *Proceedings of the Thirteenth Annual Conference of the Cognitive Science Society*. Hillsdale, NJ: Lawrence Erlbaum, pp. 867–71.

Ram, A., and D. Leake. 1995. Learning, goals, and learning goals. In A. Ram and D. Leake, eds., *Goal-Driven Learning*. Cambridge MIT Press, pp. 1–37.

Reder, L. M. 1987. Strategy selection in question answering. *Cognitive Psychology* 19: 90–138.

Rosenbloom, P. S., J. E. Laird, and A. Newell, eds. 1993. *The Soar Papers: Research on Integrated Intelligence*. Cambridge: MIT Press.

Schank, R. C. 1979. Interestingness: Controlling inferences. *Artificial Intelligence* 12: 273–97.

Schank, R. C. 1986. *Explanation Patterns: Understanding Mechanically and Creatively*. Hillsdale, NJ: Lawrence Erlbaum.

Schneider, W. 1985. Developmental trends in the metamemory-memory behavior relationship: An integrative review. In D. L. Forrest-Pressley, G. E. MacKinnon, and T. G. Waller, eds., *Metacognition, Cognition and Human Performance*, vol. 1, *Theoretical Perspectives*. New York: Academic Press, pp. 57–109.

Simon, H. A. 1979. What the knower knows: Alternative strategies for problem-solving tasks. In F. Klix, ed., *Human and Artificial Intelligence*. Amsterdam: North Holland, pp. 89–100.

Simon, H. A. 1983. Why should machines learn? In R. S. Michalski, J. G. Carbonell, and T. M. Mitchell, eds., *Machine Learning I: An Artificial Intelligence Approach*. Los Altos, CA: Morgan Kaufmann, pp. 25–37.

Stefik, M. 1981. Planning and metaplanning (MOLGEN: Part 2). *Artificial Intelligence* 16: 141–69.

Steier, D. M., J. E. Laird, A. Newell, P. S. Rosenbloom, R. Flynn, A. Golding, T. A. Polk, O. G. Shivers, A. Unruh, and G. R. Yost. 1993. Varieties of learning in Soar: 1987. In P. S. Rosenbloom, J. E. Laird, and A. Newell, eds., *The Soar Papers: Research on Integrated Intelligence*, vol. 1. Cambridge: MIT Press, pp. 537–48. (Original work published in 1987.)

Davidson, J. E., R. Deuser, and R. J. Sternberg. 1994. The role of metacognition in problem solving. In J. Metcalfe and A. P. Shimamura, eds., *Metacognition: Knowing about Knowing*. Cambridge: MIT Press, pp. 207–26.

Stroulia, E. 1994. *Failure-Driven Learning as Model-Based Self-redesign*. PhD dissertation. Georgia Institute of Technology, College of Computing, Atlanta.

Stroulia, E., M. Shankar, A. Goel, and L. Penberthy. 1992. A model-based approach to blame assignment in design. In J. S. Gero, ed., *Proceedings of AID92: Second International Conference on AI in Design*. Boston: Kluwer Academic Press, pp. 519–37.

Tate, A. 1976. Project planning using a hierarchic non-linear planner. Technical report 25. University of Edinburgh, Department of Artificial Intelligence, Edinburgh, UK.

Weintraub, M. A. 1991. *An Explanation-Based Approach to Assigning Credit*. PhD dissertation. Ohio State University, Columbus.

Wellman, H. M. 1983. Metamemory revisited. In M. T. H. Chi, ed., *Contributions to Human Development*. vol. 9. *Trends in Memory Development Research*. Basel, Switzerland: S. Karger, AG.

Wilensky, R. 1983. *Planning and Understanding: A Computational Approach to Human Reasoning*. Reading, MA: Addison-Wesley.

Wisniewski, E. J., and D. L. Medin. 1991. Harpoons and long sticks: The interaction of theory and similarity in rule induction. In D. H. Fisher, M. J. Pazzani, and P. Langley, eds., *Concept formation: Knowledge and Experience in Unsupervised Learning*. San Mateo, CA: Morgan Kaufmann, pp. 237–78.

Chapter 12
Information Extraction as a Stepping Stone toward Story Understanding

Ellen Riloff

Historically story understanding systems have depended on a great deal of handcrafted knowledge. Natural language understanding systems that use conceptual knowledge structures (Schank and Abelson 1977; Cullingford 1978; Wilensky 1978; Carbonell 1979; Lehnert 1981; Kolodner 1983) typically rely on enormous amounts of manual knowledge engineering. While much of the work on conceptual knowledge structures has been hailed as pioneering research in cognitive modeling and narrative understanding, from a practical perspective it has also been viewed with skepticism because of the underlying knowledge engineering bottleneck. The thought of building a large-scale conceptual natural language processing (NLP) system that can understand open-ended text is daunting even to the most ardent enthusiasts. So must we grit our collective teeth and assume that story understanding will be limited to prototype systems in the foreseeable future? Or will conceptual natural language processing ultimately depend on a massive, broad-scale manual knowledge engineering effort, such as CYC (Lenat, Prakash, and Shepherd 1986)?

Perhaps the answer lies in the current trends of *information extraction* research. Information extraction (IE) is a form of natural language processing in which certain types of information must be recognized and extracted from text. Although IE systems are typically designed for a single domain, there is a great deal of interest in building systems that are easily portable to new domains. Many researchers are developing methods to acquire the necessary domain-specific knowledge automatically. The goal is not necessarily to produce a general-purpose information extraction system but to create tools that would allow users to build customized information extraction systems quickly.

If the IE researchers are ultimately successful, one could imagine being able to create, quite literally, an IE system "du jour" that is tailored to our interests on any given day. Another possible future scenario is to assemble a large suite of IE systems, each being a specialist in extracting information pertaining to its own area of expertise. Collectively the suite of systems could support conceptual natural language understanding capabilities, if not for every subject then at least for a wide variety of subjects.

On the surface, information extraction might appear to be fundamentally different from story understanding. And there are some important differences between these tasks. But I will argue that the challenges and difficulties underlying them are largely the same. A corollary of this view is that automated knowledge acquisition techniques developed for information extraction are likely to be applicable to story understanding as well. In this chapter I will explain how research in information extraction may be a significant stepping stone toward progress in story understanding. I will discuss emerging trends in the information extraction community, draw parallels between the two types of natural language understanding, and describe recent research in automated case frame generation for information extraction.

12.1 Information Extraction

12.1.1 What Is Information Extraction?

Information extraction is a subfield of natural language processing that is concerned with identifying predefined types of information from text. For example, an information extraction system designed for a terrorism domain might extract the names of perpetrators, victims, physical targets, weapons, dates, and locations of terrorist events. Or an information extraction system designed for a business domain might extract the names of companies, products, facilities, and financial figures associated with business activities.

Natural language understanding is crucial for most information extraction tasks because the desired information can only be identified by recognizing conceptual roles. I use the term "conceptual role" to refer to semantic relationships that are defined by the role that an item plays in context. For example, extracting noun phrases that refer to people can be done without regard to context by searching for person names, titles, and personal pronouns, such as "Mary," "John," "Smith," "Mr.," "she," and "him." Contextual information may be necessary for word sense disambiguation (e.g., distinguishing the person "John Hancock" from the company "John Hancock"), but that is a separate issue.

In contrast, some semantic relationships are defined by the role that an item plays in a larger concept. For example, "perpetrator" and "victim" are conceptual roles related to the concept of crime. One cannot identify perpetrators and victims simply by looking at names. "John Doe" could be a perpetrator in one context but a victim in another. In both cases "John Doe" is a person, but his role as perpetrator or victim depends entirely on the surrounding context.

Name:	%MURDERED%
Event Type:	MURDER
Trigger Word:	murdered
Activating Conditions:	passive-verb
Slots:	VICTIM <subject> (*human*)
	PERPETRATOR <prep-phrase, by> (*human*)
	INSTRUMENT <prep-phrase, with> (*weapon*)

Figure 12.1
Case frame for information extraction.

Similarly one can identify many companies by searching for known company names such as "IBM," and capitalized noun phrases ending with "Inc.," "Co.," or "Corp." But it is impossible to identify companies involved in a merger simply by searching for company names. The surrounding context determines the conceptual role of the company. For example, "XYZ Corp." might be involved in a merger, a joint venture, an acquisition, or a charity event depending on its role in the larger context. Understanding conceptual roles is essential for these types of problems.[1]

Most information extraction systems use some form of extraction pattern to identify potentially relevant information. For example, the pattern ⟨**subject**⟩ **was bombed** might be used to identify bombing targets. Whenever a passive form of the verb "bombed" is encountered, this pattern extracts the subject of the verb as a bombing target. Some extraction patterns are more complicated than others, but most extraction patterns can be viewed as simple case frames. Each case frame is activated by specific linguistic expressions and then extracts surrounding phrases as slot fillers.

To illustrate, figure 12.1 shows a murder case frame with multiple slots. This case frame is activated by the word "murdered" whenever it appears as a passive verb. The case frame contains three slots to extract a victim, perpetrator, and weapon (instrument). Each item is extracted from a different syntactic constituent in the clause. For example, the subject of the verb is extracted as the murder victim and the object of the preposition "by" is extracted as the perpetrator. Selectional restrictions are often used to check that an extracted item satisfies certain semantic constraints. For example, the %MURDERED% case frame requires victims and perpetrators to be human. Throughout the rest of this article, we will refer to extraction patterns and case frames interchangeably, with the understanding that case frames for other tasks may be significantly more complex.

The components of an information extraction system vary depending on the approach that is used, but most IE systems perform part-of-speech tagging, partial parsing, semantic interpretation, case frame instantiation, and some sort of discourse analysis. Much of the work on information extraction has been fostered through a series of message understanding conferences (MUCs) sponsored by the U.S. government (e.g., see DoD 1991, 1992, 1993).

12.1.2 Message Understanding Conferences

Since the late 1980s the U.S. government has been sponsoring MUCs to evaluate and advance the state-of-the-art in information extraction. In the last few years, these message understanding conferences have grown in participation, scope, and visibility. The MUCs are competitive performance evaluations involving a set of participants from different sites, usually a mix of academic and industrial research labs. Each participating site builds an IE system for a predetermined domain. The IE systems are all evaluated on the same domain and text collection, and the results are scored using an official scoring program developed by the MUC organizers.

The message understanding conferences are especially noteworthy because they represent the first large-scale effort to evaluate natural language processing systems. The question of *how* to evaluate an NLP system is a nontrivial issue, so the development of standard scoring criteria was a worthwhile contribution in its own right. Evaluation is a complicated and sometimes controversial issue, but the MUC scoring program and criteria represents an important first step in confronting this problem.

The MUC meetings are also important as a forum for comparing the performance of different NLP techniques on a uniform task and text collection. Until these conferences most NLP systems were developed in isolation and designed for their developer's favorite domain. The message understanding conferences have served as a platform for comparing and contrasting different NLP approaches on equal footing. Furthermore the MUC tasks involve real, unconstrained text—primarily news wire articles. The message understanding conferences have played an important role in pushing the NLP community toward realistic text applications.

One of the most interesting aspects of these conferences has been the evolution of IE systems over the years. Initially there was a great deal of variation across systems, representing a broad range of natural language processing techniques. But over time the IE systems converged so that most IE systems today share relatively similar architectures and approaches. Many lessons have been learned about the strengths and weaknesses of various techniques. In the next section I survey some of the most notable trends in the information extraction community and explain their relationship to issues in story understanding.

12.2 Trends in Information Extraction

As historians well know, watching the evolution of a field often provides valuable insights into the nature of its problems and possible solutions. So it is useful to take a

Information Extraction as a Stepping Stone 439

step back every once in a while and reflect on general directions that have emerged over time. I will discuss three such trends in information extraction: a convergence toward partial parsing, a healthy respect for discourse analysis, and an emphasis on automated knowledge acquisition. It would be presumptuous to claim that these are the only trends that have taken place in the field, but these three are particularly interesting from the perspective of conceptual natural language processing and story understanding.

12.2.1 Partial Parsing

One of the most obvious trends in the IE community has been a convergence toward partial parsing techniques. In 1991 the systems presented at the Third Message Understanding Conference (MUC-3) reflected a wide variety of parsing techniques. Some systems were grounded in linguistic theory and attempted to generate a complete parse tree for each sentence in a text (e.g., Dahlgren et al. 1991; Grishman, Sterling, and Macleod 1991; Montgomery 1991). At the other end of the spectrum, the TTS system (Dolan et al. 1991) did virtually no syntactic analysis at all. The diversity of syntactic approaches was quite remarkable, running the gamut from full syntactic parsing to practically no syntactic parsing and everything in between.

As the field matured, the syntactic components began to look increasingly alike. Today almost all IE systems use partial parsing techniques. Even the most linguistically oriented IE researchers have reluctantly accepted that for the information extraction task at least, the potential benefits of full parsing are usually overwhelmed by the extra overhead and lack of robustness. Real news articles pose major challenges for syntactic parsing because of ungrammatical text, complex and lengthy grammatical constructs, and massive ambiguity.

For information extraction, the information being sought can often be identified by searching a single clause or phrase. The remaining clauses and phrases may be ignored because they do not contain relevant information. For example, consider the sentence below, which is the first sentence of a MUC-3 text.

In an action that is unprecedented in Colombia's history of violence, unidentified persons kidnapped 31 people in the strife-torn banana-growing region of Uraba, the Antioquia governor's office reported today.

The relevant information in this sentence is that unidentified persons kidnapped 31 people in the region of Uraba. The rest of the sentence can be effectively ignored. Simply looking for the pattern ⟨X⟩ **kidnapped** ⟨Y⟩ **in** ⟨Z⟩ will identify the perpetrators, victims, and location.

For information extraction, generating complete parse trees has had minimal reward thus far. Researchers committed to full syntactic parsing might offer the explanation that information extraction does not require full natural language processing capabilities because only specific types of information need to be recognized. There is some validity to this argument since, by definition, information that is not relevant to the domain can be safely ignored. However, determining which information is relevant is not always easy, and simple pattern recognition is not enough. For example, consider the following sentences:

1. The mayor was killed by FMLN guerrillas.
2. The mayor was killed by a burglar.
3. The mayor was killed by armed men.
4. The mayor was killed by armed men belonging to the FMLN.
5. The mayor was killed by armed men during a holdup in a convenience store.
6. The mayor was killed by armed men in retaliation for the arrest of a prominent FMLN leader.
7. The mayor was killed and the FMLN claimed responsibility for the murder.

In the first six sentences the perpetrator can be extracted using the simple pattern **killed by** $\langle X \rangle$. In sentence 1 the word "FMLN" identifies the perpetrators as terrorists, so this murder was clearly terrorist in nature. In sentence 2 the word "burglar" suggests a criminal robbery that was probably not terrorist in nature. But the perpetrators in sentences 3, 4, 5, and 6 are described only as "armed men." Determining whether they are terrorists or not requires information from elsewhere in the sentence. And in sentence 7 there is no specific reference to a perpetrator at all, but the second clause states that a terrorist organization has claimed responsibility for the murder, so one can infer that the FMLN is the perpetrator. These sentences illustrate that identifying relevant information can be quite complicated. In many cases local patterns are not enough, and the entire sentence must be understood. And sometimes inferences must be generated across sentences or even paragraphs. Inference can be essential in determining the relevance of an event or a piece of information.

Given these difficulties, one might think that more syntactic analysis is needed. But syntactic analysis has been relegated to a relatively minor role in most information extraction systems. Concept activation and instantiation are the central activities. Syntax is used to map syntactic roles to conceptual roles in case frames, but this is usually accomplished with a fairly shallow syntactic analysis. The domain-specific expressions that activate a case frame and the conceptual roles defined by a case frame are the key elements that identify potentially relevant portions of text. The case frames are arguably the most crucial component of an IE system; without the case frames, no information would be extracted at all.

For most IE tasks, discourse processing is also crucially important to the success of the system. As I will describe in the next section, discourse processing can be espe-

Information Extraction as a Stepping Stone   441

cially challenging when the discourse analyzer has only partial information to work with. Full parse trees and deeper syntactic analysis would surely provide more clues to aid discourse analysis. But conceptual analysis, domain knowledge, and memory organization are still at the heart of the discourse problem.

12.2.2 Discourse Analysis

Perhaps one of the most sobering results of the message understanding conferences has been the realization that discourse analysis of written text is a wide open problem. While there has been substantial work on analyzing spoken discourse, there has been much less work on written discourse. Furthermore most discourse theories depend on large amounts of world knowledge, and have not been tested empirically on large text collections. Real texts are typically more irregular and arbitrary than most discourse theories expect.

In general, discourse processing of written text involves tracking events and objects and understanding the relationships between them. Anaphora resolution is one such problem, which includes resolving pronouns, proper nouns, and definite noun phrases. Topic recognition and segmentation is another key problem. For example, consider the MUC-4 text shown in figure 12.2.

This text describes a series of terrorist attacks in protest of the murder of the group's leader, Bernardo Jaramillo Ossa. The first paragraph mentions both the terrorist attacks and Jaramillo's murder, so it is important to recognize that his murder is a separate incident. The second paragraph describes the terrorist attacks, which include bombings and burnings in several locations. Whether these bombings and burnings are distinct incidents or a single, collective incident is an interesting question as well. The third and fifth paragraphs again mention both the terrorist attacks and Jaramillo's murder. This text illustrates how even relatively short cohesive texts can reference multiple events that may be easily confused. Keeping track of the separate incidents requires event tracking to assign each piece of information to the appropriate incident and consolidation to combine different pieces of information and merge multiple references to the same information.

At first glance it might appear that discourse analysis is simpler for information extraction than for general story understanding because only certain types of objects and events need to be tracked. But in some ways the problem is more challenging because the discourse analyzer has to do its job without complete knowledge. Most IE systems extract information in a piecemeal fashion so that only relevant text segments are recognized and saved. Consequently the output representation may not include information that is crucial to distinguish events. For example, consider the first paragraph of the text in figure 12.2. An IE system might extract the following pieces of information:

(1) MEMBERS OF THE 8TH FRONT OF THE SELF-STYLED REVOLUTIONARY ARMED FORCES OF COLOMBIA [FARC] HAVE CARRIED OUT TERRORIST ATTACKS IN SOUTHERN CAUCA DEPARTMENT TO PROTEST PATRIOTIC UNION [UP] PRESIDENTIAL CANDIDATE BERNARDO JARAMILLO OSSA'S MURDER.

(2) THE FARC MEMBERS BLEW UP A POWER SUBSTATION AND A POWER PYLON IN SAJANDI, LA FONDA CORREGIMIENTO. THE GUERRILLAS ALSO BURNED THREE VEHICLES ON THE PAN-AMERICAN HIGHWAY– A BALBOA HOSPITAL AMBULANCE, A FUEL TRUCK CARRYING 3,000 GALLONS OF GASOLINE, AND A STATION WAGON. A LARGE SECTION OF EL PATIA VALLEY WAS LEFT WITHOUT ELECTRICITY.

(3) THROUGH SEVERAL TELEPHONE CALLS TO THE POPAYAN MEDIA, THE 8TH FARC FRONT DECLARED THE PAN-AMERICAN HIGHWAY A MILITARY TARGET DURING THE NEXT 48 HOURS IN ORDER TO DEMAND THAT THE GOVERNMENT INVESTIGATE AND ARREST THOSE WHO ARE TRULY RESPONSIBLE FOR JARAMILLO'S MURDER.

(4) TRANSPORTATION SERVICES BETWEEN [WORD INDISTINCT] AND PASTO IN SOUTHERN COLOMBIA HAVE BEEN SUSPENDED AS A RESULT OF THE TERRORIST ATTACKS, WHICH BEGAN AT 0300 TODAY.

(5) POLICE AND 3D INFANTRY BRIGADE MEMBERS WERE DEPLOYED TO THE AREAS WHERE THE 8TH FRONT OF THE SELF-STYLED REVOLUTIONARY ARMED FORCES OF COLOMBIA BLOCKED TRAFFIC. THE 8TH FARC FRONT MEMBERS SAID THEIR MILITARY ACTIONS ARE AIMED AT DEMANDING THE CLARIFICATION OF UP PRESIDENTIAL CANDIDATE BERNARDO JARAMILLO'S MURDER.

(6) THE POPAYAN POLICE DEPARTMENT CONFIRMED THAT THE ATTACKS TOOK PLACE ON THE PAN-AMERICAN HIGHWAY AND AT LA FONDA CORREGIMIENTO, PATIA MUNICIPALITY.

(7) GOVERNOR FERNANDO IRACONI SAID THAT THE REGIONAL SECURITY COUNCIL WILL MEET IN POPAYAN IN A FEW MINUTES TO ASSESS THE MOST RECENT TERRORIST ATTACKS AND TO ADOPT THE NECESSARY MEASURES.

Figure 12.2
Sample MUC-4 text.

(a) Members of the 8th Front of the Self-styled Revolutionary Armed Forces of Colombia [FARC] have carried out terrorist attacks
(b) Terrorist attacks in southern Cauca Department
(c) Patriotic Union [UP] presidential candidate Bernardo Jaramillo Ossa's murder

Given only these sentence fragments, one could easily infer that Jaramillo's murder was one of the terrorist attacks. The key phrase "to protest" would probably not be extracted because protesting is not usually associated with terrorism. It is unlikely that a terrorism dictionary would contain a case frame to recognize this expression.

But the phrase "to protest" is essential to understand that the murder happened prior to the attacks reported in the article.

These examples emphasize the fine line between information extraction and general story understanding. It is easy to argue that IE systems will always suffer from a ceiling effect if they operate with tunnel vision and do not process portions of the text that do not appear to be directly relevant to the domain. On the other hand, it would be self-defeating to adopt the attitude that we should not attempt to build IE systems until the natural language understanding problem has been completely solved. There is a wide spectrum of language processing techniques, with shallow text understanding at one end and deep text understanding at the other. Choosing where one wants to sit on this spectrum is a central issue when designing a text analyzer.

Part of the difficulty with discourse processing stems from the fact that it depends heavily on world knowledge. So it is not surprising that one of the emerging trends in information extraction involves developing techniques to automate the acquisition of discourse knowledge. In the next section I discuss the general trend toward automated knowledge acquisition for information extraction systems.

12.2.3 Automated Knowledge Acquisition

The first generation of information extraction systems relied on a tremendous amount of hand-coded knowledge. Consider the UMass/MUC-3 system (Lehnert et al. 1991a), which was designed for the MUC-3 terrorism domain. The UMass/MUC-3 system used three primary knowledge bases: a hand-coded lexicon, hand-coded case frames, and hand-coded discourse rules. The lexicon contained over 5,000 words which were tagged with parts-of-speech, semantic features, and a few other types of linguistic information. The lexicon was engineered specifically for the terrorism domain, so only tags associated with terrorism were used. For example, the word "party" was tagged as a noun but not as a verb, and its only semantic tag corresponded to the political party word sense and not the celebration sense.

The dictionary of extraction patterns contained 389 case frames designed to extract perpetrators, victims, targets, and weapons. Initially the case frames represented simple patterns and phrases, but over time some of them became quite complex. For example, the %KIDNAP-CAPTURE% case frame originally represented the expression $\langle X \rangle$ **captured** $\langle Y \rangle$, where X is extracted as the perpetrator of a kidnapping and Y is extracted as the victim. However, this case frame frequently misfired for events such as police arrests and prisoner escapes. After repeated modifications the activating conditions for this case frame evolved into a complex function that required X to be a terrorist or an organization, but not a civilian or a law enforcement agent, and required Y not to be a terrorist, a prisoner, or an organization.[2]

Another major component of the UMass/MUC-3 system was a rule base for discourse analysis. The UMass/MUC-3 system was organized as a pipelined system consisting of two main modules: sentence analysis and discourse analysis. The sentence analyzer, CIRCUS (Lehnert 1991), performed a shallow syntactic analysis of each sentence and produced instantiated case frames. Each sentence was processed independently of the others. The discourse analyzer was then responsible for putting the pieces back together. Since CIRCUS extracts information in a piecemeal fashion, discourse processing involves not only figuring out how one sentence relates to another but also how case frames activated in the same sentence relate to one another. The discourse analyzer had many jobs, including coreference resolution (pronouns and noun phrases), case frame merging, event segmentation, and relevance filtering. Domain-specific rules for all of these problems were manually encoded in the system.

The UMass/MUC-3 system was an exercise in manual knowledge engineering. While the system performed well in MUC-3 (Lehnert et al. 1991b), it took a tremendous amount of time, energy, and expertise to make it work as well as it did. And the UMass system was no exception—virtually all of the systems that performed well in MUC-3 required many person-months of manual labor.

So it is not surprising that there is strong interest in developing techniques to acquire the necessary domain-specific knowledge automatically. Several systems have been developed to generate domain-specific extraction patterns automatically or semiautomatically (Kim and Moldovan 1993; Huffman 1996a; Soderland et al. 1995; Riloff 1996a). There have also been efforts to automate various aspects of discourse processing (Soderland and Lehnert 1994; Aone and Bennett 1996; McCarthy and Lehnert 1995). And some researchers have used the information extraction framework to focus on general issues associated with lexical acquisition (Cardie 1993; Hastings and Lytinen 1994).

In the next section I present current efforts to automatically generate case frames for information extraction. I describe a system called AutoSlog that was one of the first dictionary construction systems developed for information extraction. AutoSlog generates extraction patterns using a specially annotated training corpus as input. I then explain how AutoSlog evolved into its successor, AutoSlog-TS, which generates extraction patterns without an annotated training corpus. AutoSlog-TS needs only a preclassified text corpus consisting of relevant and irrelevant sample texts. AutoSlog-TS represents a major step toward building conceptual dictionaries from raw text. The case frames generated by AutoSlog-TS were used for both information extraction and text classification tasks to demonstrate that tools and techniques developed for information extraction can be useful for other natural language processing tasks as well.

12.3 Automatically Generating Case Frames for Information Extraction

One of the most substantial bottlenecks in building an information extraction system is creating the dictionary of domain-specific extraction patterns. Almost all of the IE systems presented at the message understanding conferences have relied on hand-crafted case frames. Recently, however, there have been several efforts to automate the acquisition of extraction patterns.

Two of the earliest systems to generate extraction patterns automatically were AutoSlog (Riloff 1993) and PALKA (Kim and Moldovan 1993). More recently CRYSTAL (Soderland et al. 1995) and LIEP (Huffman 1996b) have been developed. All of these systems use some form of manually tagged training data or user input. For example, AutoSlog requires text with specially tagged noun phrases. CRYSTAL requires text with specially tagged noun phrases as well as a semantic hierarchy and associated lexicon. PALKA requires manually defined frames (including keywords), plus a semantic hierarchy and associated lexicon, and user input is sometimes needed to resolve competing hypotheses. LIEP uses predefined keywords and object recognizers, and depends on user interaction to assign an event type to each relevant sentence.

Defining extraction patterns by hand is time-consuming, tedious, and prone to errors and omissions, so all of these systems represent important contributions to automated dictionary construction. The knowledge-engineering bottleneck has not been eliminated yet, but it has been greatly reduced and simplified. For example, it took approximately 1,500 person-hours to build the UMass/MUC-3 dictionary by hand, but it took only 5 person-hours to build a comparable dictionary using AutoSlog, given an appropriate training corpus (Riloff 1996a). Furthermore only minimal expertise is needed to generate a dictionary. Defining case frames by hand requires working knowledge of the domain, natural language processing, and the underlying sentence analyzer, but generating a training corpus requires only knowledge of the domain. In essence the knowledge-engineering effort has shifted from the hands of NLP specialists to the hands of domain experts, which is more realistic for most applications.

First, I describe the AutoSlog dictionary construction system that creates domain-specific extraction patterns using an annotated training corpus. Next, I describe its successor, AutoSlog-TS, which creates extraction patterns using only raw text. AutoSlog-TS reduces the knowledge-engineering bottleneck even further by eliminating the need for specialized training data. Finally, I describe experimental results with AutoSlog-TS for both information extraction and text classification.

12.3.1 AutoSlog: Generating Case Frames from Annotated Text

In retrospect, it was realized that the manual dictionary construction effort for the UMass/MUC-3 system was remarkably straightforward. The process generally involved two basic steps:

1. Observe a gap in the dictionary by identifying a noun phrase that should have been extracted but was not.
2. Find a key word in the sentence that identifies the conceptual role of the noun phrase and define a case frame that is activated by that word in the same linguistic context.

For example, consider the following sentence:

The governor was kidnapped by terrorist commandos.

The governor should be extracted as a kidnapping victim, and the terrorist commandos should be extracted as the perpetrators. If either of these noun phrases is not extracted by a case frame, then there must be a gap in the dictionary.

Suppose that the governor is not extracted. Then the key question is what expression should have extracted it? The word "kidnapped" clearly suggests a relevant incident (a kidnapping) so "kidnapped" should trigger a kidnapping case frame. To recognize that the governor played the conceptual role of the victim, the kidnapping case frame must have a victim slot that is filled by the subject of the passive verb "kidnapped." In essence the case frame must represent the expression: $\langle X \rangle$ **was kidnapped**.

Similarly suppose that the terrorist commandos were not extracted. Again the word "kidnapped" is the key word that suggests a relevant incident and should trigger a kidnapping case frame. The terrorist commandos should be assigned to the conceptual role of the perpetrator, and since "terrorist commandos" is the object of the preposition "by," the case frame should represent the expression **was kidnapped by** $\langle Y \rangle$.

AutoSlog was designed to mimic this process. As input, AutoSlog needs a set of texts and noun phrases that should be extracted from those texts.[3] The noun phrases must be labeled with their conceptual role and event type. For example, in the previous example "the governor" should be labeled as a *victim* in a *kidnapping* event and the "terrorist commandos" should be labeled as a *perpetrator* in a *kidnapping* event. Figure 12.3 shows what an annotated text would look like.

Given this training data, AutoSlog generates a case frame to extract each tagged noun phrase. In theory, it would make sense for case frames to extract more than one object, but for simplicity AutoSlog is restricted to single-slot case frames that extract only a single object. AutoSlog uses a small set of heuristic rules to decide what

Information Extraction as a Stepping Stone 447

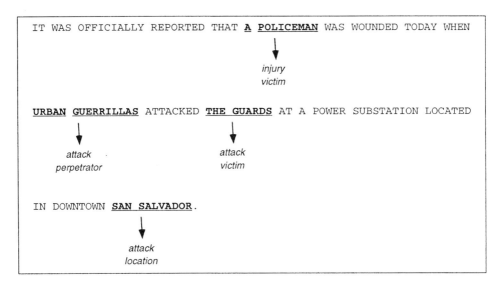

Figure 12.3
Annotated sentence for AutoSlog.

expression should activate the case frame and from which syntactic constituent the slot should be filled. Figure 12.4 shows the heuristic rules used by AutoSlog, with examples from the terrorism domain.

Given a sentence and a tagged noun phrase, AutoSlog first calls a sentence analyzer, CIRCUS (Lehnert 1991), to analyze the sentence syntactically. AutoSlog needs only a flat syntactic analysis that recognizes clause boundaries and identifies the subject, verb, direct object, and prepositional phrases of each clause. So almost any parser could be used. AutoSlog finds the clause that contains the targeted noun phrase and determines whether it was the subject, the direct object, or in a prepositional phrase. The heuristic rules are divided into three sets, depending on the syntactic type of the targeted noun phrase. The appropriate rules are invoked, and the rule that most closely matches the current context is allowed to fire (i.e., the rule with the longest pattern). For example, consider the following sentence:

The *U.S. embassy* in Bogota was bombed yesterday by *FMLN guerrillas*.

Suppose that *U.S. embassy* was tagged as a bombing target and that *FMLN guerrillas* was tagged as a perpetrator. Given *U.S. embassy* as the targeted noun phrase, AutoSlog first calls CIRCUS and determines that *U.S. embassy* is the subject of the sentence. The subject rules are invoked and the pattern ⟨**subject**⟩ **passive-verb** fires. This pattern is matched against the input sentence and a case frame is constructed to

Linguistic Pattern	Example
<subject> active-verb	<perpetrator> bombed
<subject> passive-verb	<victim> was murdered
<subject> verb infinitive	<perpetrator> attempted to kill
<subject> auxiliary noun	<victim> was victim
active-verb <direct-object>	bombed <target>
infinitive <direct-object>	to kill <victim>
verb infinitive <direct-object>	threatened to attack <target>
gerund <direct-object>	killing <victim>
noun auxiliary <direct-object>	fatality was <victim>
noun preposition <noun-phrase>	bomb against <target>
active-verb preposition <noun-phrase>	killed with <instrument>
passive-verb preposition <noun-phrase>	was aimed at <target>

Figure 12.4
AutoSlog heuristics and examples from the terrorism domain.

represent the expression ⟨**target**⟩ **was bombed**. This case frame is activated by passive forms of the verb "bombed" and extracts the subject as a bombing target. Similarly, given *FMLN guerrillas* as the targeted noun phrase, AutoSlog determines that it was in a prepositional phrase, and the prepositional phrase rules are invoked. AutoSlog uses its own simple pp-attachment algorithm to decide where a prepositional phrase should be attached. In this case *FMLN guerrillas* should attach to the verb "bombed," and AutoSlog generates a case frame to represent the expression **was bombed by** ⟨**perpetrator**⟩. This case frame is activated by passive forms of the verb "bombed" and extracts the object of the preposition "by" as a bombing perpetrator.

It is important to note that the input consists of a sentence and tagged noun phrases, while the output consists of case frames that represent linguistic expressions. For example, the case frame generated by *U.S. embassy* will be activated by a variety of expressions such as "X was bombed," "X and Y were bombed," "X has been bombed," and "X and Y have been bombed." These words do not have to be adjacent because the natural language processing system uses syntactic information to activate the case frames. For example, the case frame ⟨**target**⟩ **was bombed** will be activated by the sentence below in which the verb ("bombed") and the subject ("Telecom") have many words between them.

Telecom, Colombia's second largest telecommunication utility, was mercilessly bombed yesterday afternoon.

However, many of the case frames generated by AutoSlog will not reliably extract relevant information. AutoSlog can create bizarre or overly general patterns for a variety of reasons, including faulty sentence analysis, incorrect prepositional phrase attachment, or insufficient context. So a person must manually review the case frames and decide which ones are reliable enough for the domain. A simple user interface allows a user to scan each pattern and click an *accept* or *reject* button. The manual review process is very fast; it took a user only five person hours to filter 1237 case frames generated by AutoSlog for the MUC-4 terrorism domain (Riloff 1996a). The case frames accepted by the user become the final dictionary for the domain.

AutoSlog has been used to generate case frames for three domains: terrorism, joint ventures, and microelectronics (Riloff 1996a). In the MUC-4 terrorism domain, a dictionary of case frames created by AutoSlog achieved 98 percent of the performance of the hand-crafted dictionary that achieved good results in the MUC-4 evaluation (Riloff 1993).

AutoSlog was a major contribution toward reducing the knowledge-engineering bottleneck for information extraction systems. Previously case frames had to be manually defined by people who had experience with natural language processing, the domain, and the sentence analyzer. Using AutoSlog, a dictionary of domain-specific case frames could be constructed automatically, given an annotated training corpus and a few hours of time for manual review.

But there is still a substantial bottleneck lurking underneath AutoSlog: the need for a specially annotated training corpus. Generating the training corpus is both time-consuming and difficult. The annotation process can be deceptively tricky. The user needs to tag relevant noun phrases, but what is a noun phrase? Even simple NPs may include noun modifiers, as in "the heavily armed FMLN guerrillas." Should the user include all of the modifiers, only the relevant modifiers, or just the head noun? Noun phrases can also be quite complex, including conjunctions, appositives, and prepositional phrases. Should the user tag all conjuncts and appositives or just some of them? If not all of them, then which ones? Prepositional phrases can substantially change the meaning of the concept that they modify. For example, "the president of San Salvador" is different from "the president of Colombia." How do you dictate which prepositional phrases are essential and which ones are not? The annotation process can be confusing and arbitrary, resulting in inconsistencies in the tagged training corpus. While the annotation process is less demanding than generating case frames by hand, it is still a major undertaking.

In the next section I describe the successor to AutoSlog, called AutoSlog-TS, which creates case frames for information extraction without the need for an annotated training corpus. AutoSlog-TS needs only a *preclassified* training corpus consisting of relevant and irrelevant sample texts for the domain.

12.3.2 AutoSlog-TS: Generating Case Frames from Untagged Text

The AutoSlog-TS dictionary construction system is designed to create dictionaries of case frames using only a *preclassified* text corpus. As input, AutoSlog-TS needs two piles of texts: one pile of texts that are relevant to the target domain, and one pile of texts that are irrelevant to the domain. Nothing inside the texts needs to be tagged in any way. The motivation behind this approach is that it is relatively easy for a person to generate such a training corpus. The user simply needs to be able to identify relevant and irrelevant sample texts. Anyone familiar with the domain should be able to generate a training corpus with minimal effort. The goal of AutoSlog-TS is to exploit this very coarse level of domain knowledge to generate case frames that represent important domain-specific expressions.

AutoSlog-TS is essentially an exhaustive version of AutoSlog combined with statistical feedback. The dictionary construction process consists of two stages: pattern generation and statistical filtering. Figure 12.5 illustrates this process.[4]

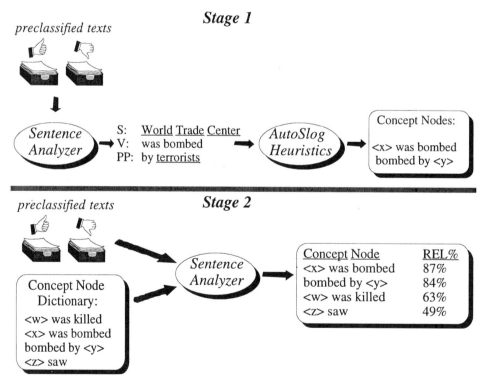

Figure 12.5
AutoSlog-TS flowchart.

In stage 1, AutoSlog-TS pretends that every noun phrase is a candidate for extraction. A sentence analyzer, CIRCUS, is used to identify all of the simple NPs in a text. For each noun phrase the heuristic rules shown in figure 12.4 are applied to generate extraction patterns. One difference between AutoSlog and AutoSlog-TS is that AutoSlog-TS allows <u>all</u> applicable rules to fire. For example, given the sentence "terrorists attacked the U.S. embassy" and the noun phrase "terrorists," both the ⟨**subject**⟩ **active-verb** and ⟨**subject**⟩ **verb direct-object** rules would apply. Two extraction patterns would be generated: ⟨**perpetrator**⟩ **attacked** and ⟨**perpetrator**⟩ **attacked embassy**.

Allowing multiple rules to fire gives AutoSlog-TS additional flexibility. AutoSlog-TS can create several patterns of varying length to extract the same information. Ultimately the statistics will reveal whether the shorter, more general pattern has sufficient reliability or whether the longer, more specific pattern is needed. One could have allowed the original AutoSlog system to fire multiple rules as well, but it would have multiplied the number of case frames that had to be manually reviewed. As I will explain shortly, AutoSlog-TS uses statistical information to rank order the case frames so only the most promising case frames need to be reviewed.

The purpose of stage 1 is to create a giant dictionary of case frames that are literally capable of extracting every noun phrase in the training corpus. In experiments with 1,500 texts from the MUC-4 terrorism corpus, AutoSlog-TS created 32,345 unique case frames (Riloff 1996). Some of these case frames represent domain-specific patterns, but most of them represent general expressions that are not specific to the domain.

In stage 2, statistical feedback is used to separate the domain-specific case frames from the general ones. This step takes advantage of the preclassified nature of the training corpus to generate relevance statistics for each case frame. The first step is to load all of the case frames into the sentence analyzer and reprocess the training corpus. Each time a case frame is activated, the system records whether it was activated in a relevant text or in an irrelevant text. When the entire training corpus has been reprocessed, the final relevance statistics are generated for each case frame. For each case frame, the system estimates the conditional probability that a text is relevant given that it activated the case frame. The formula is

$$\Pr(\text{relevant text} \mid \text{text contains case frame}_j) = \frac{\text{rel} - \text{freq}_i}{\text{total} - \text{freq}_i},$$

where $\text{rel} - \text{freq}_i$ is the number of instances of case frame$_i$ that were activated in relevant texts and $\text{total} - \text{freq}_i$ is the total number of instances of case frame$_i$ that were activated in the training corpus. For simplicity, we will refer to this probability estimate as a case frame's *relevance rate*.

Note that case frames representing general expressions will be activated in both relevant and irrelevant texts. For example, expressions like "was reported" will appear in a wide variety of texts. If the corpus contains a 50/50 split of relevant and irrelevant texts, then one would expect general case frames to have about a 50 percent relevance rate. This approach is based on the intuition that the domain-specific expressions will be much more common in relevant texts than in irrelevant texts, so the domain-specific case frames will have higher relevance rates.

After the corpus has been processed a second time, the case frames are ranked in order of relevance to the domain. In recent experiments (Riloff 1996b) the following ranking function was used:

$$\text{score}_i = \text{relevance rate}_i * \log_2(\text{frequency}_i).$$

One exception is that case frames with a relevance rate ≤ 0.5 received a score of zero, since they were negatively correlated with the domain (the training corpus was 50 percent relevant). The ranking function gives weight to both a case frame's relevance rate as well as its overall frequency in the training corpus. For example, if a case frame is activated only twice in a large corpus, then it is probably not very important. On the other hand, case frames that are activated frequently but have only a moderate relevance rate (e.g., 70 percent) may in fact be very important to the domain. For example, the expression "X was killed" is a crucial pattern for the terrorism domain because people are often killed in terrorist incidents. But people are also killed in many other types of events, so this pattern will appear in irrelevant texts as well. This ranking function gives preference to case frames with either a high frequency and a moderate relevance rate, or a moderate frequency and a high relevance rate. I do not claim that this is the best possible ranking function, but it seemed to work fairly well in these experiments.

If the ranking function does its job, then the domain-specific case frames should float to the top. The ranking function is crucial because the dictionary of case frames is so large that it would be unreasonable to expect a person to review them all by hand. Once the case frames are ranked, a person can skim the "best" case frames off the top. One of the main advantages of the ranking scheme is that it prioritizes the case frames for manual review so that the strongest case frames are reviewed first, and the user can review those further down on the list as time permits.

AutoSlog-TS was applied to the 1500 MUC-4 development texts (DoD 1992), of which about 50 percent was relevant. AutoSlog-TS generated 32,345 unique case frames. Due to memory constraints, all case frames that were proposed only once were thrown away, since they were not likely to be very important.[5] This left 11,225 unique case frames, which were loaded into the system for stage 2. The relevance rate for each of these case frames was then computed, and the case frames were ranked

1. <subj> exploded	14. <subj> occurred
2. murder of <np>	15. <subj> was located
3. assassination of <np>	16. took_place on <np>
4. <subj> was killed	17. responsibility for <np>
5. <subj> was kidnapped	18. occurred on <np>
6. attack on <np>	19. was wounded in <np>
7. <subj> was injured	20. destroyed <dobj>
8. exploded in <np>	21. <subj> was murdered
9. death of <np>	22. one of <np>
10. <subj> took_place	23. <subj> kidnapped
11. caused <dobj>	24. exploded on <np>
12. claimed <dobj>	25. <subj> died
13. <subj> was wounded	

Figure 12.6
Top 25 extraction patterns.

using the scoring function just described. The 25 top-ranked patterns (in the list of 11,225 ranked case frames) appear in figure 12.6.

Most of these expressions are clearly associated with terrorism, so the ranking function appears to be doing a good job of pulling the domain-specific expressions up to the top. The next step is to have a person review the most highly ranked patterns. The manual review process serves two purposes: (1) as confirmation that a pattern is relevant to the domain, and (2) to label the case frame with an event type and a conceptual role for the extracted item. For example, the first case frame in figure 12.6, ⟨**subj**⟩ **exploded**, should be labeled as a bombing case frame that will probably extract an instrument, as in "a car bomb exploded." The second case frame, **murder of** ⟨**np**⟩, should be labeled as a murder case frame that will likely extract a victim, as in "the murder of the mayor." The 22nd case frame, **one of** ⟨**np**⟩, is an example of a case frame that the user would probably reject as a statistical artifact. Although it may have had a high relevance rate in the training corpus, the expression **one of** ⟨**np**⟩ is not specific to terrorism and would probably extract too much irrelevant information.

The top 1970 case frames in the ranked list were manually reviewed and 210 were retained for the final dictionary. The manual review process took approximately 85 minutes. The relatively low number of acceptable case frames is somewhat misleading because the acceptance rate dropped off sharply after the first few hundred. The fast manual review time is also due to the ranking scheme. Most of the good case frames clustered at the top, so after the first few hundred case frames the review

Table 12.1
Comparative results

Slot	AutoSlog			AutoSlog-TS		
	Recall	Precision	F	Recall	Precision	F
Perpetrator	0.62	0.27	0.38	0.53	0.30	0.38
Victim	0.63	0.33	0.43	0.62	0.39	0.48
Target	0.67	0.33	0.44	0.58	0.39	0.47
Total	0.64	0.31	0.42	0.58	0.36	0.44

process mainly consisted of clicking the reject button to dismiss obviously irrelevant patterns.

12.3.3 Experiments with AutoSlog-TS

AutoSlog-TS was designed to be an extension of AutoSlog that substantially reduces the human effort needed to generate appropriate training texts, while still producing a good dictionary of extraction patterns. The goal was to show that the dictionaries produced by AutoSlog and AutoSlog-TS achieve comparable performance.

Dictionaries created by AutoSlog and AutoSlog-TS for the MUC-4 terrorism domain were compared. Details of this experiment can be found in Riloff (1996b). Both dictionaries were evaluated by manually reviewing their output on 100 blind texts from the MUC-4 test set. Recall, precision, and F-measure scores were then computed for each dictionary. The results appear in table 12.1.

The results show that the AutoSlog dictionary achieved slightly higher recall, and the AutoSlog-TS dictionary achieved slightly higher precision and F-measure scores. Analysis of the raw data showed that the differences in correct and missing output were not statistically significant even at the $p < 0.20$ significance level, but the difference in spurious output was statistically significant at the $p < 0.05$ significance level. It was concluded that there was no significant difference between AutoSlog and AutoSlog-TS in terms of recall but that AutoSlog-TS was significantly more effective at reducing spurious extractions.

While the absolute differences in correct and missing output were not significant, AutoSlog did slightly outperform AutoSlog-TS in recall. One possible explanation is that AutoSlog-TS is at the mercy of the ranking function because a human cannot reasonably be expected to review all of the 11,000+ extraction patterns produced by AutoSlog-TS. The most important domain-specific patterns must be ranked highly in order to be considered for manual review. I believe that there were many good

was assassinated in X	assassination in X	X ordered assassination
was captured by X	capture of X	X managed to escape
was exploded in X	damage in X	X expressed solidarity
was injured by X	headquarters of X	perpetrated on X
was kidnapped in X	targets of X	hurled at X
was perpetrated on X	went_off on X	carried_out X
was shot in X	X blamed	suspected X
was shot_to_death on X	X defused	to protest X
X was hit	X injured	to arrest X

Figure 12.7
Patterns found by AutoSlog-TS but not by AutoSlog.

extraction patterns buried deep in the ranked list that did not get reviewed. If so, then AutoSlog-TS is ultimately capable of producing higher recall than AutoSlog.

As further evidence of this, AutoSlog-TS was observed to produce 158 case frames with a relevance rate ≥ 90 percent and frequency ≥ 5, but only 45 of them were in the AutoSlog dictionary. Figure 12.7 shows some of the case frames that clearly represent patterns associated with terrorism.[6] However, many of these patterns had relatively low frequency counts and were not ranked highly.

Another objective was to demonstrate that AutoSlog-TS could be used for tasks other than information extraction. So the case frames generated by AutoSlog-TS were used for a text classification task. In previous research, Riloff and Lehnert (1994) developed a text classification algorithm called the *relevancy signatures algorithm* that uses extraction patterns to recognize key phrases for classification. The task is to automatically classify new texts as relevant or irrelevant to a specific domain. We used the hand-crafted dictionary of extraction patterns in these previous text classification experiments (Riloff and Lehnert 1994), but AutoSlog-TS provides a new opportunity to seed the algorithm with a much larger set of potential patterns. The statistics should ultimately decide which ones are most useful for making domain discriminations.

We gave the relevancy signatures algorithm the same set of 11,225 case frames generated by AutoSlog-TS for the terrorism domain, and trained the algorithm using the 1,500 development texts from the MUC-4 corpus. We evaluated the algorithm on two blind sets of 100 texts each. On the first test set, the AutoSlog-TS dictionary and the hand-crafted dictionary achieved similar results. On the second test set, however, the AutoSlog-TS dictionary produced several data points with 100 percent precision, while the hand-crafted dictionary did not produce any. Overall, the AutoSlog-TS dictionary performed at least as well as the AutoSlog dictionary. Details of this experiment can be found in Riloff and Shoen (1995).

In summary, AutoSlog-TS has been used to create a dictionary of case frames for the MUC-4 terrorism domain that performed well on both information extraction and text classification tasks. AutoSlog-TS appears to be at least as effective as AutoSlog at producing useful extraction patterns, although more experiments need to be done with different ranking functions and additional domains. Perhaps most important, AutoSlog-TS sharply reduces the amount of manual knowledge engineering required to create a dictionary of domain-specific extraction patterns. AutoSlog-TS is the first system that can generate domain-specific case frames using only raw text as input. So far these case frames have been applied to information extraction and text classification tasks, but perhaps AutoSlog-TS or similar systems will ultimately be able to produce more complex case frames for other natural language processing tasks as well.

12.4 Information Extraction and Story Understanding: Bridging the Gap

Research in information extraction has made good progress in recent years, but will it have any impact on computational models of story understanding? Only time will tell, but perhaps some comparisons will shed light on the issue.

For one, both information extraction and story understanding require natural language understanding. This might seem like a trivial statement, but it is important to remember that they are both subject to the same problems of ambiguity, idiosyncracy, and a strong dependence on world knowledge. Research in both fields has tried to minimize these problems by focusing on narrow domains. An information extraction task, by definition, specifies the domain of interest and the types of information that must be extracted. The restricted domain and the focused nature of the task can greatly simplify dictionary construction, ambiguity resolution, and discourse processing. Similarly story understanding systems usually focus on a single domain or certain aspects of the world in order to minimize the knowledge-engineering effort.

A key difference between information extraction and story understanding is that the latter strives to understand the entire story. These two paradigms represent a trade-off between depth and scalability. Information extraction systems limit depth by focusing on certain types of information and a specific domain. In exchange for limited depth, IE systems can effectively process a wide variety of texts within the domain. Story understanding systems, on the other hand, aim for deep understanding of whole texts, but they usually cannot effectively process arbitrary texts without additional knowledge engineering. One notable attempt to bridge this gap was the FRUMP system (DeJong 1982), which had its origins in the story understanding community but could be viewed as an early information extraction system that could recognize certain types of events in unrestricted text.

The depth/scalability trade-off reflects the knowledge engineering bottleneck associated with building natural language processing systems. The growing interest in automated knowledge acquisition should bring the two communities closer together. Information extraction researchers and story understanding researchers could learn a lot from each other. The information extraction community has learned a great deal about robust parsing, case frame generation, and discourse analysis. At least as important is the experience that comes with processing large amounts of real text. Building an IE system is typically an empirical endeavor, and IE researchers have come to appreciate that some well-known NLP problems and phenomena do not appear very often in real text, while other problems are much more common than one might expect.

On the other side of the fence, story understanding researchers have a long history of expertise with complex knowledge structures and inference generation. Ultimately continued progress in information extraction will depend on richer semantics, knowledge structures, and inference mechanisms. Although restricting the domain simplifies many aspects of language processing, it is not a panacea for language understanding. The performance of current IE technology will likely run up against a ceiling effect unless more conceptual knowledge is brought to bear on the problem.

If future IE systems will need to use more conceptual knowledge, where will this knowledge come from? The information extraction paradigm revolves around practical applications and large text collections, so it is imperative that the necessary knowledge can be acquired with little effort. From this vantage point, perhaps the most pragmatic approach is to build gradually upon current IE technology. For example, can extraction patterns be mapped into conceptual primitives? Can combinations of extraction patterns (or primitives) be used to represent more complex knowledge structures? Can automated dictionary construction systems like AutoSlog-TS be used to learn more complex structures? By exploiting the practical nature of IE technology and the insights and theories developed by story understanding researchers, we can entertain the exciting possibility of building increasingly intelligent NLP systems that are practical for large-scale applications. Although the grand challenge of developing a broad-coverage, in-depth natural language understanding system may still be a long way off, an effective synergy between information extraction and story understanding may prove to be a promising starting point for real progress in that direction.

Notes

Thanks to Claire Cardie for providing helpful comments on an earlier draft of this chapter. This work was supported in part by NSF grant MIP-9023174 and NSF grant IRI-9509820.

1. An anecdote from an early message understanding conference nicely illustrates this point. Many of the news articles in the corpus mentioned a particular spokesperson, but he was almost always mentioned in texts that were not relevant to the terrorism domain of interest. His name was so common, that one site began using his name as a keyword to identify irrelevant texts. But one day the spokesperson was killed in a terrorist incident, thus becoming a victim himself. From that point on, virtually every text containing his name was relevant.

2. These activating conditions are domain-specific and would likely be prone to false hits if the case frame was applied to a more general corpus.

3. In these experiments AutoSlog used the MUC templates as input, but an annotated training corpus would have been sufficient.

4. Figure 12.5 refers to *concept nodes*, which are the case frame structures used by CIRCUS.

5. AutoSlog often proposes the same case frame multiple times when different noun phrases spawn the same extraction pattern. For example, the case frame representing the expression **murder of** ⟨**victim**⟩ was proposed in response to many different sentences.

6. The connected words represent phrases in the CIRCUS lexicon.

References

Aone, C., and S. W. Bennett. 1996. Applying machine learning to anaphora resolution. In S. Wermter, E. Riloff, and G. Scheler, eds., *Connectionist, Statistical, and Symbolic Approaches to Learning for Natural Language Processing*. Berlin: Springer-Verlag, pp. 302–14.

Carbonell, J. G. 1979. *Subjective Understanding: Computer Models of Belief Systems*. PhD thesis. Technical report 150. Department of Computer Science, Yale University, New Haven.

Cardie, C. 1993. A case-based approach to knowledge acquisition for domain-specific sentence analysis. In *Proceedings of the Eleventh National Conference on Artificial Intelligence*. Cambridge: AAAI Press/MIT Press, pp. 798–803.

Cullingford, R. E. 1978. *Script Application: Computer Understanding of Newspaper Stories*. PhD thesis, Technical report 116. Department of Computer Science, Yale University, New Haven.

Dahlgren, K., C. Lord, H. Wada, J. McDowell, and E. P. Stabler Jr. 1991. ITP: Description of the interpretext system as used for MUC-3. In *Proceedings of the Third Message Understanding Conference (MUC-3)*. San Mateo, CA: Morgan Kaufmann, pp. 163–70.

DeJong, G. 1982. An Overview of the FRUMP System. In W. Lehnert and M. Ringle, eds., *Strategies for Natural Language Processing*. Hillsdale, NJ: Lawrence Erlbaum, Associates, pp. 149–77.

Dolan, C. P., S. R. Goldman, T. V. Cuda, and A. M. Nakamura. 1991. Hughes trainable text skimmer: Description of the TTS system as used for MUC-3. In *Proceedings of the Third Message Understanding Conference (MUC-3)*. San Mateo, CA: Morgan Kaufmann, pp. 155–62.

Grishman, R., J. Sterling, and C. Macleod. New York University: Description of the Proteus system as used for MUC-3. In *Proceedings of the Third Message Understanding Conference (MUC-3)*. San Mateo, CA: Morgan Kaufmann, pp. 183–90.

Hastings, P., and S. Lytinen. 1994. The ups and downs of lexical acquisition. In *Proceedings of the Twelfth National Conference on Artificial Intelligence*. Cambridge: AAAI Press/MIT Press, pp. 754–59.

Huffman, S. 1996. Learning information extraction patterns from examples. In S. Wermter, E. Riloff, and G. Scheler, eds., *Connectionist, Statistical, and Symbolic Approaches to Learning for Natural Language Processing*. Berlin: Springer-Verlag, pp. 246–60.

Kim, J., and D. Moldovan. 1993. Acquisition of semantic patterns for information extraction from Corpora. In *Proceedings of the Ninth IEEE Conference on Artificial Intelligence for Applications*. Los Alamitos, CA: IEEE Computer Society Press, pp. 171–76.

Kolodner, J. 1983. Maintaining organization in a dynamic long-term memory. *Cognitive Science* 7: 243–80.

Lehnert, W. G. 1981. Plot units and narrative summarization. *Cognitive Science* 5: 293–331.

Lehnert, W. 1991. Symbolic/subsymbolic sentence analysis: Exploiting the best of two worlds. In J. Barnden and J. Pollack, eds., *Advances in Connectionist and Neural Computation Theory*, vol. 1. Norwood, NJ: Ablex Publishers, pp. 135–64.

Lehnert, W., C. Cardie, D. Fisher, E. Riloff, and R. Williams. 1991a. University of Massachusetts: Description of the CIRCUS system as used for MUC-3. In *Proceedings of the Third Message Understanding Conference (MUC-3)*. San Mateo, CA: Morgan Kaufmann, pp. 223–33.

Lehnert, W., C. Cardie, D. Fisher, E. Riloff, and R. Williams. 1991b. University of Massachusetts: MUC-3 test results and analysis. In *Proceedings of the Third Message Understanding Conference (MUC-3)*. San Mateo, CA: Morgan Kaufmann, pp. 116–19.

Lenat, D. B., M. Prakash, and M. Shepherd. 1986. CYC: Using common sense knowledge to overcome brittleness and knowledge-acquisition bottlenecks. *AI Magazine* 6: 65–85.

McCarthy, J. F., and W. G. Lehnert. 1995. Using decision trees for coreference resolution. In *Proceedings of the Fourteenth International Joint Conference on Artificial Intelligence*. San Mateo, CA: Morgan Kaufmann, pp. 1050–55.

Montgomery, C. A., B. G. Stalls, R. S. Belvin, and R. E. Stumberger. 1991. Language Systems, Inc.: Description of the DBG system as used for MUC-3. In *Proceedings of the Third Message Understanding Conference (MUC-3)*. San Mateo, CA: Morgan Kaufmann, pp. 171–77.

E. Riloff. 1993. Automatically constructing a dictionary for information extraction tasks. In *Proceedings of the Eleventh National conference on Artificial Intelligence*. Cambridge: AAAI Press/MIT Press, pp. 811–16

E. Riloff. 1996a. An empirical study of automated dictionary construction for information extraction in three domains. *Artificial Intelligence* 85: 101–34.

E. Riloff. 1996b. Automatically generating extraction patterns from untagged text. In *Proceedings of the Thirteenth National Conference on Artificial Intelligence*. Cambridge: AAAI Press/MIT Press, pp. 1044–49.

Riloff, E., and W. Lehnert. 1994. Information extraction as a basis for high-precision text classification. *ACM Transactions on Information Systems* 12: 296–333.

Riloff, E., and J. Shoen. 1995. Automatically acquiring conceptual patterns without an annotated corpus. In *Proceedings of the Third Workshop on Very Large Corpora*, pp. 148–61.

Schank, R., and R. Abelson. 1977. *Scripts, Plans, Goals and Understanding*. Hillsdale, NJ: Lawrence Erlbaum.

Soderland, S., D. Fisher, J. Aseltine, and W. Lehnert. 1995. CRYSTAL: Inducing a conceptual dictionary. In *Proceedings of the Fourteenth International Joint Conference on Artificial Intelligence*. San Mateo, CA: Morgan Kaufmann, pp. 1314–19.

Soderland, S., and W. Lehnert. 1994. Wrap-Up: A trainable discourse module for information extraction. *Journal of Artificial Intelligence Research (JAIR)* 2: 131–58.

United States, Department of Defense, Defense Advanced Research Projects Agency. 1991. *Proceedings of the Third Message Understanding Conference (MUC-3)*. San Mateo, CA: Morgan Kaufmann.

United States, Department of Defense, Defense Advanced Research Projects Agency. 1992. *Proceedings of the Fourth Message Understanding Conference (MUC-4)*. San Mateo, CA: Morgan Kaufmann.

United States, Department of Defense, Defense Advanced Research Projects Agency. 1993. *Proceedings of the Fifth Message Understanding Conference (MUC-5)*. San Mateo, CA: Morgan Kaufmann.

Wilensky, R. 1978. *Understanding Goal-Based Stories*. PhD thesis. Technical Report 140. Department of Computer Science, Yale University, New Haven.

Chapter 13
Text Processing and Narrative Worlds

Richard J. Gerrig

In her novel *The Infinite Plan*, Isabel Allende describes the day-to-day life her hero, Gregory Reeves, shared with the Vietnamese people in whose village he lived (p. 199):

> What they most esteemed was the ability to tell a story. There was among them an aged story-teller who could transport his listeners to heaven or hell; he could soften the heart of the bravest men with his love stories, his complex tales of maidens in danger and sons in disgrace. When the story ended, everyone would sit suspended in silence, and then the old man himself would laugh, mocking his audience, who had listened like children spellbound by his words.

What is salient in this excerpt is the phenomenology of the experience of a narrative. The aged story-teller could "transport" his audience away to another world, and keep them there until he broke the silence and signaled that it was time for their return to their here and now reality.

In this chapter I consider the ramifications of this experience of being transported with respect to theories of text processing. I first explore some ways in which readers contribute to the experience. I suggest that many narrative effects rely on readers' active participation in response to particular text structures. (Note that I will use "reader" as a shorthand for all the situations in which language users experience narratives. A theory of the experience of narrative worlds should, ideally, apply to circumstances in which people read novels, hear stories, watch movies, and so on.) In the second part of the chapter, I consider some consequences of the phenomenology of being transported. I discuss, in particular, some ways in which narrative worlds are insulated from the real world.

13.1 Participation in Narrative Worlds

To exemplify readers' participation in their experiences of being transported, I begin with an excerpt from Oscar Hijuelos's novel *Mr. Ives' Christmas*. At the very beginning of the book, Hijuelos describes the scene in which Ives's seventeen-year-old son Robert is gunned down on the street (p. 8):

God had timed things so that his murderer, his face scowling, came walking down the street just as his son and a friend were standing around talking. *Pop, pop, pop*, three shots in the belly because his son had simply turned his head to watch his murderer's exaggerated and comic gait as he went by. A fourteen-year-old kid, who'd reeled around asking, "What chew looking at?" his gun out before an answer.

Traditional theories of text processing might begin an analysis of this text by identifying propositions, and then specifying how a reader would draw those units together to form, for example, casual structures or situation models (for reviews, see Fletcher 1994; Kintsch 1994; Singer 1994; van den Broek 1994). An analysis of the text would also, almost certainly, make reference to the inferences readers must draw: the gaps in the text they must themselves fill in. For this excerpt, it is up to the reader to find the equivalence of the "fourteen-year-old kid" and the "murderer" and to repair the temporal order of the kid drawing his gun and the shots to the belly. Over the course of the study of text processing, the process and products of inferencing has, almost certainly, been the topic afforded the greatest research effort. Any full account of the experience of being transported would surely take note of the importance of inferences.

The experience of this passage, however, engages something more than inferential responses. Placed, as it is, at the beginning of the novel, it creates a context in which the reader comes to have strong feelings about many of the other events of the book and, in particular, many of the choices Ives makes in his life that ultimately lead to the circumstances of Robert's murder. The book is a long exercise in making the reader wish that things could be otherwise. Consider the scene in which Robert's death is, at last, fully given (p. 156):

Then this other kid, a brawny teenager in an army jacket, came walking along, jitterbugging, his stride so exaggerated and dancelike that Robert could not prevent his blue eyes from widening or his forehead from crinkling at the humorous affectation. Finding it amusing, he began to smile in a friendly, well-intended way, and, just like that, the teenager said something that Robert did not quite have the time to digest, and then pulled out his pistol and fired three shots, *pop, pop, pop* . . . .

It seems almost inevitable that, while reading this paragraph, people will mentally call out, "Don't stare!" or "Don't smile!" or otherwise express the desire that something be changed. Hijuelos's choice of words reinforces this activity: "Robert could not prevent..." ("Try harder!"). These thoughts emerging from the mental voice are not themselves inferences (though they rely on an inferential connection to earlier parts of the text). Rather, they are members of the class of *participatory responses* (or, for short, *p-responses*), readers' responses engendered by involvement in a narrative (Allbritton and Gerrig 1991; Gerrig 1993).

Although p-responses, as defined, are all noninferential, they otherwise form a diverse class. The examples I've given so far fall into the category of *as if* responses (Gerrig and Prentice 1996). These responses emerge *as if* the reader were really participating in the narrative's events. *As if* responses are highly relevant to analyses of the experience of being transported because they provide evidence that the reader has, in some sense, become involved in the world of the text (cf. Walton 1978a). How else can we explain mental advice to the characters? Another prominent type of p-response represents a more distanced type of participation. In many cases readers respond with comments on their aesthetic experience—"This story is dull"—and consequently make mental suggestions about how a plot could be improved—"It would be better if Jesse just died already." In these cases the reader participates more as a critic than as someone who has entered the world of the narrative. In this chapter the bulk of my discussion will focus on *as if* participatory responses.

Participatory responses are very much a part of readers' phenomenological experience of narratives. Even so, it is important to document the impact they have on the potential adequacy of theories of text processing, with respect to the traditional goals of theories in this domain. For example, theories of text understanding often emphasize the ways in which readers recover the causal structures that lead toward goals or outcomes (e.g., Bloom, Fletcher, van den Broek, Reitz, and Shapiro 1990; Fletcher and Bloom 1988; Trabasso and Sperry 1985; Trabasso and van den Broek 1985). However, p-responses also often concern themselves exactly with goals and outcomes. When, for example, Robert Ives is about to be shot, readers appear to work quite hard (mentally) to deflect the story from that outcome. How might such thoughts influence readers' ability to verify what actually took place?

To address this question, Allbritton and I (Allbritton and Gerrig 1991) wrote brief stories that manipulated readers' preferences about story outcomes. Each story began with a statement of the outcome, which for some readers was positive (for "The Pharoh's Tomb," "When he entered the tomb, Jack was astounded by the treasures it held") and for some readers negative ("When Jack entered the tomb, he found it completely empty"). The story continued in versions that created preferences with respect to this outcome. Some readers were led to develop a preference in favor of the positive outcome:

He [Jack] planned to bring rare artifacts back to the Smithsonian Institute. He only hoped that a band of looters would not beat him to the tomb.

Others were led to a preference for the negative outcome:

It would be Jack's most profitable graverobbing yet if he found it. He only hoped he could beat the museum's archeologists to the loot.

Our goal was to demonstrate the way in which the development of a preference interfered with readers' ability to verify the story outcomes. We predicted, based on analyses from social psychology of people's responses to nonnormative situations (Kahneman and Miller 1986), that readers would emit a greater number of p-responses when the text encouraged them to develop a preference for the negative outcome. Our intuition was that such a nonnormative preference would motivate readers to consider more alternative scenarios than would the ordinary positive preference.

The data revealed exactly such an asymmetry. Negative preferences reliably impaired readers' ability to verify the outcomes, by comparison to positive preferences. Moreover the impairment was specific only to the verification of outcomes. The existence of a positive or negative preference did not affect readers' ability to confirm or disconfirm other story information (e.g., the name of the Pharoh buried in the tomb).

These experiments were designed specifically with an eye to traditional theories of text comprehension. The data suggest that the theories will fail to make correct predictions about, for example, representations of narrative outcomes if they do not make reference to reliable noninferential responses. As is no doubt true for some inferences, some p-responses will be idiosyncratic to individual readers. However, our experiments suggest that some types of p-responses are sufficiently general to warrant attention in theories of text processing.

Many circumstances of text processing will moreover reflect complex moment-by-moment interactions of inferences and p-responses. Consider a scene from Paul West's novel *The Women of Whitechapel and Jack the Ripper*. Walter Sickert is trying to entice Annie Chapman into a carriage. The reader knows that once in, should Annie enter, she will be murdered by Sickert's accomplice (pp. 256–57):

Once again Sickert had to officiate, this time beginning with more of an argument: "You look weary, my dear, and none too well," hating himself for doing it. "We are all weary tonight, it has been a long journey for us. May we drop you at your convenience?"...

"Nah," Annie Chapman said, "I'll walk it Keptin."

Despite Annie's reluctance, Sickert prevails. She enters the carriage and becomes the next victim of "Jack the Ripper." Potential p-responses throughout this scene are many. First, we have the global response "I don't want Annie to die." This response relies on an inference because the belief that she will die, should she enter the carriage, is based on earlier parts of the text. "I don't want Annie to die" can next set in action a course of inferencing as readers struggle to keep Chapman from her fate. The outcome of this inferencing could be another round of p-responses: "Don't let Sickert fool you! Don't get in the carriage!" The readers know that Sickert is participating in this scene unwillingly ("... hating himself for doing it"). They might infer that something about his discomfort could possibly penetrate to Annie's awareness: "Notice that Sickert's not being normal!" What we see here is inferences giving rise to p-responses and p-responses directing or motivating inferences, and so on—to the limits of the reader's penchant for participation.

This example illustrates the way in which an analysis of p-responses must be integrated into an overall theory of text processing. Despite the head start the study of inferencing has, there's every reason to believe that p-responses exert equal force in determining the course of processing and the details of text representations. Accordingly it seems likely that the study of p-responses should encompass many of the types of questions that have dominated the literature on inferences (see Graesser, Singer, and Trabasso 1994; McKoon and Ratcliff 1992): What aspects of a text reliably give rise to p-responses? Are some classes of p-responses produced automatically? How do long-term memory structures play a role in the formation of p-responses? In the next two sections I discuss two specific phenomena, suspense and perspective, to show how we can begin to answer these types of questions.

13.1.1 Suspense

The experience of suspense provides a strong example of why a complete account of narrative processing must make mention of the ways in which text structures give rise to participatory responses. Consider another passage from *The Infinite Plan* which describes Gregory Reeves's childhood spent in theaters, watching serial movies (p. 75):

The episode seemed always to end with the protagonist bound hand and foot in a shed filled with dynamite and the villain lighting the fuse; at the climatic moment the screen would go black and a voice would invite the audience to come back in a week for the next installment. Sometimes Gregory was so miserable he wanted to die but postponed his suicide until the following week: how could he quit this world without knowing how the devil his hero had escaped the trap?

What we see here is that the movie (i.e., the text) provides the dilemma—it "creates" suspense—but Gregory himself creates the misery. It is his own meditation on the lack of knowledge that intensifies his feelings of distress. In this section I discuss participatory responses that heighten experiences of suspense.

It is not difficult to enunciate the type of text structure that gives rise to suspense (Brewer and Lichtenstein 1982, p. 481):

In a suspense discourse organization the initiating event occurs early in the discourse. The initiating event causes the reader to become concerned about the consequences for the relevant character and this produces suspense. Typically, additional discourse material is placed between the initiating event and the outcome event, to encourage the build up of suspense. The suspense is resolved when the outcome is presented in the discourse.

Note that this definition somewhat captures Gregory's experience at the movies. He is concerned that the hero will be snuffed out by the villain. This produces suspense. However, Gregory's suspense does not build up as a consequence of additional discourse material. The period of time in which suspense grows is filled only by Gregory's thoughts. A more adequate characterization of suspense, beyond a trivial analysis of structure, requires a careful appreciation of how readers' thoughts—that is, their inferences and p-responses—contribute to the experience. (See Moorman and Ram 1994, for a computational model that provides a similar perspective on the *creative reading* of science fiction stories.)

Consider this "minimal suspense discourse" (Brewer and Lichtenstein 1982, p. 481):

The sniper was waiting outside the house. Charles got up from the chair. He walked slowly toward the window. There was the sound of a shot and the window broke. Charles fell dead.

How much suspense does this passage engender? Readers' experiences will depend, in large part, on how hard they work to keep Charles away from the window. That is, if a reader emits the p-response, "Don't go near the window!" she's likely to experience marginally more suspense. If the p-responses become more heroic—"Remember, someone's trying to kill you!" "Don't you notice the shadow outside?"—suspense could grow even more intense. Suppose we enhance the story by adding as a second sentence, "His [i.e., the sniper's] mission was to kill the president, Randolph Charles." To the extent that this makes the potential outcome of the sniper's actions even less desirable, we might find readers motivated to work harder to find reasons that it may not obtain. They may emit the same types of "warning" p-responses but also take advantage of the greater resources of the situation—"Maybe a secret service agent will see the sniper!" The "minimal suspense discourse" hardly seems to support all of this p-responding, but it makes the general claim quite visible: Within the confines of the suspense structure, readers do much to enhance their own discomfort.

Professional suspense-makers seem well aware of the contributions readers make to the intensity of suspense. Alfred Hitchcock, for example, was quite explicit in an interview about his movie *Psycho* about how he gets the public "participating in the scene" (Truffaut 1984, p. 269):

You know the public always likes to be one jump ahead of the story; they like to feel they know what's coming next. So you deliberately play upon this fact to control their thoughts. The more we go into the details of the girl's [Janet Leigh, as Marion] journey, the more the audience becomes absorbed in her flight. That's why so much is made of the motorcycle cop and the change of cars. When Anthony Perkins [as Norman Bates] tells the girl of his life in the motel, and they exchange views, you still play upon the girl's problem. It seems as if she's decided to go back to Phoenix and give the money back, and it's possible the public anticipates by thinking, "Ah, this young man is influencing her to change her mind." You turn the viewer in one direction and then in another; you keep him as far as possible from what's actually going to happen....

Psycho has a very interesting construction and that game with the audience was fascinating. I was directing the viewers. You might say I was playing them, like an organ.

Hitchcock's analysis makes explicit reference to what I have called p-responses: "Directing the viewers" suggests getting them to have the right thoughts at the right times.

In fact Hitchcock's comments represent the strong belief that p-responses can be predicted with sufficient accuracy to be useful. Accordingly researchers should be able to look to successful instances of professional suspense to see what types of text structures reliably give rise to appropriate p-responses. Consider the way in which writers often manipulate the readers' evaluations of the solutions available to characters in peril. For example, this passage from Ian Fleming's novel *Casino Royale* occurs after James Bond has been captured by his enemy, Le Chiffre (p. 105):

He [Bond] felt thoroughly dispirited and weak in resolve as well as in his body. He had had to take too much in the past twenty-four hours and now this last stroke by the enemy seemed almost too final. This time there could be no miracles. No one knew where he was and no one would miss him until well on into the morning. The wreck of his car would be found before very long, but it would take hours to trace ownership to him.

Fleming has put the reader inside Bond's head, and modeled a process in which paths to escape are being pared away. The logical elimination of solutions has the effect, it seems, of heightening feelings of suspense.

To test this view that readers experience suspense in proportion to their evaluations as problem solvers Bernardo and I (Gerrig and Bernardo 1994) asked readers to report their levels of suspense in response to story excerpts about James Bond. In one experiment the excerpt had Bond captured by Le Chiffre. As Bond made a thwarted effort to escape, readers encountered either a version of the story that mentioned Bond's pen ("As he crashed to the ground, Bond rolled agilely and, with a motion that he hoped went unnoticed, moved his fountain pen deeper into his breast pocket.") or one that did not ("As he crashed to the ground, Bond rolled agilely and, with a motion in which he took great pride, he righted himself with minimal damage.") Later, some of the people for whom the pen had been mentioned read that

Le Chiffre took it away ("he crossed the room and snatched the pen away"). Readers reported reliably more suspense when Bond's pen was mentioned and removed. Presumably they had no concrete idea of what value it had to him, but the knowledge that Bond wanted to keep the pen made the feeling that a solution had been removed quite strong.

This result may not be particularly surprising, but it makes an important contrast to a purely structural account of suspense. The sequence that enhances suspense itself has a suspense structure: Will Bond keep his pen? No, it is taken away. This nested event increases feelings of suspense via p-responses ("Now how will Bond get away?") rather than by affecting, for example, some initiating event. By attending to p-responses, we can predict something more specific than the absolute presence or absence of suspense.

A second experiment adds weight to this analysis. Bernardo and I created a textual analog to the problem-solving phenomenon of *functional fixedness*. In a classic experiment Duncker (1945) demonstrated that people were not able to find a solution to a problem when the solution required them to overcome their fixation on the ordinary function of an object. In our experiment, once again we had Le Chiffre relieve Bond of an object, his pocket comb. However, for some readers the comb had previously been introduced being put to its ordinary use: "[Bond] noticed that his hair was just the least bit mussed, so he extracted his comb from his pocket and smoothed his wandering locks back into place." Other readers saw only a control passage: "[Bond] noticed that he had a white thread on his lapel, and removed it." If functional fixedness applies to textual circumstances, readers should only have felt as if a solution was being removed from Bond ("Le Chiffre pulled out Bond's pocket comb ... and flipped [it] well out of Bond's reach.") when the comb had not been described serving its ordinary function. In fact readers' reports of suspense confirmed the predictions based on functional fixedness. In this experiment Bond's objective state is identical at the end of each version of the story: He is comb-less. We can only attribute readers' different experiences of suspense to the p-responses otherwise provoked by one version but not the other.

These experiments straightforwardly suggest the limitations of purely structural theories of suspense. Although the minimal structure may serve to set the readers' thoughts in motion, we need to know something about the identity of those thoughts. We can also wonder, with respect to the traditional goals of text processing research, whether some of those p-responses become incorporated into the text representation. (Note that this analysis of suspense has presupposed that suspense only occurs when readers don't know an outcome. In the second section of the chapter, I challenge that assumption.) I now turn to another domain in which a p-response analysis proves fruitful, reader perspectives.

Text Processing and Narrative Worlds 469

13.1.2 Perspective as Participation

Let's return to the text that describes Robert Ives's death:

> Then this other kid, a brawny teenager in an army jacket, came walking along, jitterbugging, his stride so exaggerated and dancelike that Robert could not prevent his blue eyes from widening or his forehead from crinkling at the humorous affectation.

I suggested earlier that readers are likely to emit p-responses such as "Don't stare!" or "Don't smile!" Why would a reader feel compelled to respond in this way? These p-responses reflect an awareness that the reader possesses some information that Robert does not. That is, the readers and Robert have different perspectives on the unfolding events. My suggestion is that readers must often discover that they have a unique perspective on the events of a text, and that participation and p-responses are critical to such discoveries (Gerrig 1999). I will discuss two types of perspectives, *external perspectives* and *difference perspectives*.

External perspectives are the perspectives readers bring with them from the outside world. To exemplify the way in which readers discover the identities of some of those perspectives, I will use passages from John Updike's memoir, *Self-Consciousness*. Throughout the memoir, Updike invokes his experiences as an only child to explain the shape his life has taken:

> Lacking brothers and sisters, I was shy and clumsy in the give and take and push and pull of human interchange. That slight roughness, that certainty of contact we ask for from others, was hard for me to administer; I either fled, or was cruel. (p. 12)

> My debits [as a novelist] include many varieties of ignorance, including an only child's tentativeness in the human grapple.... (p. 109)

These passages suggest Updike's beliefs about the typical fate of only children. Research, however, suggests that Updike is misinformed. Fablo and Polit (1986) reviewed 115 studies comparing only children to other children and concluded, "in achievement, intelligence, and character, only borns excelled beyond their peers with siblings, especially those with many or older siblings" (p. 185). (The studies reviewed included ones from the decades of Updike's childhood.) A reader who is in possession of the research evidence on only children will likely have a rather different perspective on Updike's life than the one Updike himself takes. Rather, that is, than attributing Updike's experiences to "only childness," an informed reader might consider what other aspects of Updike's formative experiences could better explain the details of his life; an informed reader might consider the ways in which Updike's sense of only childness might allow him to overlook other causal forces in his life.

Note how the discovery of a perspective alternative to Updike's relies on participatory responses. An initial p-response, "That's not quite right," potentially gives rise to a sustained bout of participation. If readers wish to carry their perspectives through, they must focus their attention strategically, to construct a representation of the text that is dominated by their own external knowledge.

To demonstrate the impact of external perspectives on the experience of narratives, Prentice, Bailis, and I (Prentice, Gerrig, and Bailis 1997) wrote a short story in which the characters drew conclusions about topics that were clearly false with respect to the real world. One passage, for example, addressed the probability of catching cold after being doused in a downpour:

> Brad interrupted, "In fact, in some ways, getting totally soaked will help you avoid getting a cold. When you get soaked, your body has to pump itself up to help keep you warm. When you increase your body's internal temperature, that also makes it harder for viruses to live within you. So, by getting soaked you can help kill the virus that might cause a cold—how does that sound? Getting soaked actually helps prevent colds."

What made external perspectives relevant to the experience of the overall story was the college Brad and the other characters attended. For some readers, Brad and his peers were Yale students; for others, the characters attended Princeton. In our experiment, half of the readers were themselves Yale students and half were Princeton students. Researchers in social psychology have demonstrated that readers tend to evaluate more critically information relevant to issues that are of personal importance (for reviews, see Johnson and Eagly 1989; Petty and Cacioppo 1986). We hypothesized that readers of stories set at their home school (e.g., a Yalie reading about Yale students) would appraise information more carefully. Accordingly we predicted that attitude change in the direction of our counterfactual arguments would be more likely for the away school.

Readers' attitude ratings toward statements such as "Getting soaked in a rainstorm decreases your chances of catching a cold" supported the prediction of persuasion for the away school. What is important here is that both Yale and Princeton students read exactly the same texts, word for word. The differences we found in changes in attitudes cannot therefore be attributed to the texts. They can only be attributed to the cognitive activities the students carried out with respect to the texts. Presumably p-responses to the home school version (e.g., "A Yalie wouldn't believe that") focused scrutiny on the counterfactual arguments. In that way an external perspective had a major impact on the effect the text had on the reader.

Consider now cases in which readers discover that their perspective differs internally from those of the characters within a narrative. I illustrated an instance of *difference perspectives* when I alluded earlier to Robert Ives's murder. That example supports the notion of discovery via participatory responses. When readers p-respond "Don't stare," that thought provides evidence to them that they know something that the character does not. Similarly the p-responses readers emit while Walter Sickert tries to lure Annie Chapman to her doom make quite plain how much their perspective on events differs from Sickert's (and Chapman's) perspective. It seems likely that a majority of the perspectives most relevant to narrative experiences represent exactly such circumstances in which what readers expect, or predict, or desire, based on their own knowledge diverges noticeably (i.e., via p-responses) from what narrators or other characters expect, predict, or desire. Difference perspectives encourage participation because the difference will matter most when readers work through the consequences.

I devised a simple experiment to demonstrate the ease with which people become aware of difference perspectives (Gerrig 1999). Consider one version of the opening passage of a story written for this purpose, "The Eyewitness:"

When I heard the sirens, I carefully tucked the small gun into the deep pocket of my overcoat. Then I ran in the direction of the police car. When the first cop jumped out of the car, I called out, "It happened over here." I then led the pair of cops into the corner of the parking lot where the body lay sprawling.

A second version of the opening sentence read, "When I heard the sirens, I ran in the direction of the police car," making no mention of the gun. Both versions were otherwise identical, with the two cops examining the body, which lay dead from a bullet to the heart, and the narrator offering an account of the murder:

"Let me tell you what happened," I said. Cortez looked up, so I went on. "I was walking toward my car (I pointed at my car, which was at the other end of the lot), when I heard what sounded like a fire cracker going off. Then I saw one guy running like hell away from here.

The *gun* and *no gun* versions of the opening should produce very different experiences of this later text. Presumably the gun readers should be more suspicious, and p-respond accordingly: which should prompt them, in particular, to note a difference between their own perspective on the events and what the police officers might come to believe.

To test the hypothesis that gun readers would experience more of a difference in perspectives, I asked a pair of questions:

How much do you think the cops will believe the narrator's account of the crime?

How much do you believe the narrator's account of the crime?

In one version of the study, each reader answered both questions; in the other, readers answered only one question. In both cases the difference between answers was about 1.5 rating points greater (on a 9-point rating scale) for the gun readers. That is, participants reported a considerably larger gap between their beliefs and the cops' beliefs when the narrator hid the gun. This result is not surprising, but it does demonstrate once again the way in which p-responses transform the experience of a text.

As soon as readers have drawn the important inference that the gun the narrator has hidden is the same one that produced the "small caliber bullet" the corpse received "right to the heart," they can follow through to discover how their perspective differs from that of the police.

Theories of text comprehension have not traditionally addressed the consequences of difference perspectives. Most theories assume, at least implicitly, that readers adopt the protagonist's perspective. Research reveals, however, that readers often do not naturally adopt such a perspective (Albrecht et al. 1995; O'Brien and Albrecht 1992). The data suggest that people are more likely to construct a model of the text from their own perspective, separate from the character's. The "Eyewitness" experiment suggests another limitation of traditional theories. Gun readers have a perspective that is different from that of the police officer's (who are more likely to believe the narrator) and also from the narrator (who is motivated to fool the cops). The existence of these separate perspectives is an important aspect of the experience of the text.

Traditional psychological theories of text processing have not addressed the possibility or likelihood that readers maintain separate threads of representation to encode different perspectives. We can, however, look to artificial intelligence models as touchstones for computationally feasible theories of the encoding of multiple perspectives. For example, Ram (1991) has developed the AQUA system, which is a question-driven program for story understanding. AQUA is able to produce explanations for the goals and motivations of story characters from different points of view. Although this type of model does not immediately capture the participatory aspects of the discovery of perspective, it provides strong constraints on the computational requirements for perspective building.

13.2 Consequences of Being Transported

I began this chapter with an invocation of the metaphor that readers are transported to narrative worlds. My discussion so far has been focused on the participatory responses readers produce that actively aid and abet the text in transporting them. P-responses, particularly *as if* responses, also provide evidence that readers are, in some way, involved in the world to which they have journeyed. In this section of the chapter, I consider more formally the sense in which readers who have been transported lose phenomenological access to certain aspects of the real world. In this view, readers who have been transported have genuinely left aspects of their day-to-day world behind.

To pursue an argument in favor of the "reality" of being transported, I begin with a phenomenon called *anomalous suspense*. Walton (1978b, p. 26) offered this description:

[S]uspense may remain a crucial element in our response to a work almost no matter how familiar we are with it. One may "worry" just as intensely about Tom and Becky while rereading *The Adventures of Tom Sawyer*, despite one's knowledge of the outcome, as would a person reading it for the first time. A child listening to *Jack and the Beanstalk* for the umpteenth time, long after she has memorized it word for word, may feel much the same excitement when the giant discovers Jack and goes after him, the same gripping suspense, that she felt when she first heard the story.

We saw earlier that suspense is typically defined in terms of uncertainty. What makes the cases Walton describes "anomalous" is that suspense perseveres in the absence of uncertainty. In strictly cognitive terms, readers act as if they are not in possession of knowledge that is clearly within their competence.

My own analyses of anomalous suspense have been intended to illuminate this "strict" cognitive analysis of the phenomenon (Gerrig 1989a, 1989b, 1993). Other accounts of what has also been called the "paradox of suspense" (e.g., Carroll 1996; Walton 1990; Yanal 1996), have mostly ignored the basic memory puzzle: Why doesn't information that is entirely relevant to the unfolding of the narrative world (e.g., the outcome), and should be highly associated with other aspects of the story (e.g., as the culmination of a causal structure), not come rushing in to consciousness (see Gerrig 1997)? Why, that is, doesn't the memory system of a child hearing *Jack and the Beanstalk* for the umpteenth time not automatically provide information about the conclusion of the story? Text processing theories have largely focused on all the ways in which information from long-term memory enhances and supplements (e.g., in the form of inferences) the on-going experiences of narratives. How can we characterize this striking instance in which information remains unavailable?

A major goal of my experiments on anomalous suspense (Gerrig 1989b) was to define its parameters as a memory phenomenon. I began with nonfictional outcomes that were well within the competence of the undergraduates who participated in the experiments:

The Eiffel Tower is in the city of Paris, France.

The United States dropped an atomic bomb on Japan.

The Beatles recorded the song "I Wanna Hold Your Hand."

For each outcome I wrote a brief story that created a hint of uncertainty. Consider the case of the atomic bomb:

The United States has invented several new types of weapons. Throughout World War II, Americans worked on a new super bomb. Scientists had hoped that the bomb would be ready to drop on Germany. But the European war ended before the atomic bomb was ready. Production of the bomb was several years behind schedule. Strategists doubted that it would even be ready to use in Japan.

The prediction, based on the everyday experience of anomalous suspense, was that readers would find it somewhat more difficult to verify the statement "The United States dropped an atomic bomb on Japan" after being transported to this narrative world. The comparison was to control circumstances in which no suspense was induced:

The United States has invented several new types of weapons. Throughout World War II, Americans worked on a new super bomb. Scientists had hoped that the bomb would be ready to drop on Germany. But the European war ended before the atomic bomb was ready. Factory workers labored round-the-clock to prepare the bomb for Japan. They shipped the bombs out, hoping that they would end the war.

In fact readers were reliably faster verifying the stories' target facts (e.g., "The United States dropped an atomic bomb on Japan") when they had not entered a world in which suspense reigned.

We have not yet arrived, however, at the strongest test of anomalous suspense as a memory phenomenon. We need to confirm that the target information was indeed easily accessible in readers' memories, and yet this easy accessibility failed to moderate the experience of suspense. To provide such confirmation, I added *prior warnings*. In these cases (which constituted half of the stories each participant read), the story began with the exact sentence that served as the target for verification. Consider:

The United States dropped an atomic bomb on Japan. Throughout World War II, Americans worked on a new super bomb. Scientists had hoped that the bomb would be ready to drop on Germany. But the European war ended before the atomic bomb was ready. Production of the bomb was several years behind schedule. Strategists doubted that it would even be ready to use in Japan.

In this case there can be no doubt that readers had recently considered the fact that was the target for anomalous suspense.

Prior warning had the overall effect of speeding readers' verification decisions by about 400 milliseconds. This is clear evidence that the prior warning had increased the momentary accessibility of the target facts in readers' memories. Even so, prior warning had virtually no impact on the size of the suspense effect. When prior warning was present, the difference in verification time for the suspense condition minus the control condition was 260 milliseconds. When prior warning was absent, this difference was 238 milliseconds. This result captures the most interesting and important aspect of anomalous suspense: Even when the information is easily accessible in memory, it fails to overwhelm the suspense generated by the unfolding narrative.

Two supplementary experiments examined the way in which anomalous suspense endures over time. In the original study, readers were required to verify the target statements immediately after reading the texts. In a second experiment, the verification task was delayed for a period of about ten minutes. When first reading the stories, participants were just asked to "think of a title" for each one. The verification task therefore came as a surprise. Across this brief delay, prior warning ceased to have a facilitatory effect on verification. Even so, anomalous suspense still reliably slowed verification times. Note that it is quite possible that the verification task itself helped to transport the subjects back to the narrative worlds. When participants read statements such as "The United States dropped an atomic bomb on Japan," that experience may have reactivated the uncertainty that had been evoked by the original story. Whatever facts may have been re-discovered in a real-world consideration of the topics of the stories, the narrative worlds' facts prevailed when readers re-entered them.

The third experiment demonstrated that when suspense had been resolved within the narrative world, no verification deficit accrued. Consider:

The United States has invented several new types of weapons. Throughout World War II, Americans worked on a new super bomb. Scientists had hoped that the bomb would be ready to drop on Germany. But the European war ended before the atomic bomb was ready. Production of the bomb was several years behind schedule. Strategists doubted that it would even be ready to use in Japan. Against all expectations, the bombs were produced in time. Hiroshima and Nagasaki were devastated by the effects of the bombs.

Response times when readers verified target facts for stories with resolved suspense were virtually identical to those for which no suspense had originally been introduced. These data rule out the possibility that this experimental demonstration of anomalous suspense relies on the introduction of counterfactual information, with a related increase in memory load (Anderson 1976; Lewis and Anderson 1976). Rather, the effect appears to rely on the way in which the narrative unfolds—independent of the facts of the real world. Taken together, these experiments provide a strong constraint on theories of text processing: Information highly relevant to the narrative world fails to penetrate to the experience of that narrative.

How might we offer a formal model of anomalous suspense? For a starting point, we can look to an analysis given by Bharucha and Todd (1989; Todd 1988) of a comparable phenomenon that I call *musical suspense*: Bharucha and Todd observed that listeners often remain surprised by particular sequences of notes in very familiar pieces of music. In analogy to anomalous suspense, knowledge of the outcome of a piece does not, apparently, change the experience as the piece unfolds. To explain this phenomenon, Bharucha and Todd make a distinction between *veridical* and *schematic* expectancies (see Bharucha 1987). Veridical expectancies are those listeners develop through experience of a particular piece of music; schematic expectancies reflect regularities in the overall body of a culture's music. Bharucha and Todd suggest that musical suspense relies on the different time courses with which veridical and schematic expectancies function in the experience of a passage of music.

To support this conclusion, they developed a connectionist model of music perception and production. As a function of the input context, the model produces output over a series of units representing notes of the scale. This context specificity enables the network to learn particular melodic sequences; appropriate output units are activated at each point in a sequence of notes. This sequential network therefore reproduces veridical expectancies when acquiring individual melodies. However, depending on the overall population of melodies (i.e., schematic expectancies), activation on the output units approaches the threshold criterion with differing speed. For example, in one simulation the sequential network was trained with eight melodies, six of which included the sequence D–E (Todd 1988). Five of those melodies continued with an A (i.e., D–E–A). Only one included the progression D–E–G. When the network was tested, it always produced the continuation appropriate to the melodies (recall that the D–E–A and D–E–G sequences were components of longer melodies). However, the output unit for the A reached threshold much more quickly than the output unit for the G. The delayed activation of the G arises from the opposition of schematic and veridical expectancies.

We can begin to understand anomalous suspense as a similar interplay between schematic and veridical expectations. Consider the atomic bomb story which read, in part, "Production of the bomb was several years behind schedule. Strategists doubted that it would even be ready to use in Japan." Based on this text, the schematic expectancy would be that the United States would not be able to use the bomb as part of their war effort. The veridical expectancy, based on a reader's historical knowledge, would be that the difficulties were overcome, and the bomb was dropped. As with the analogy to music, we can imagine manipulating the time course with which each of these types of information would become available to produce anomalous suspense. (The time course analysis has particular appeal with respect to my series of experiments because they demonstrated delayed verification times.)

However, the analogy to musical suspense also reaffirms what is particularly salient about anomalous suspense. Recall, for example, the finding that prior warning did not reduce the impact of the suspense text. This suggests how easily and swiftly the veridical expectancy is backgrounded as the story unfolds. Furthermore the veridical expectancy rarely feels as though it crosses a threshold to consciousness. The core experience is that the child never, in some sense, becomes aware of Jack's eventual rescue. Any formal model of anomalous suspense therefore must capture the phenomenological insularity of the experience of being transported.

Finally the decomposition of anomalous suspense into veridical and schematic expectancies does not address the question of why the system behaves in this fashion. Discussions of anomalous suspense have often taken as a starting point the seeming incoherence of experiencing suspense in the face of a known outcome (for reviews, see Carroll 1996; Gerrig 1989a, 1993; Walton 1990). Why should the system act in this manner? This question becomes even more pressing when we factor in the moderate to extreme aversiveness of suspense states. Why doesn't the system reduce this state of tension automatically, by making the relevant information available? To answer these sorts of questions, I have suggested that the system incorporates an *expectation of uniqueness* (Gerrig 1993, p. 170):

Because life presents repeated types, but not repeated tokens, readers do not ordinarily have cause to search memory for *literal* repetitions of experiences.

My claim is that anomalous suspense results from an optimization of cognitive resources. In the (general) absence of literal repetitions, it makes little sense for the system to search for stories' outcomes as they unfold. Reexperiences of narratives therefore provide a violation of uniqueness for which the system is not inherently prepared.

I want to illustrate briefly a second phenomenon that also gives evidence of the consequences of being transported to narrative worlds. In parallel to anomalous suspense, I call this phenomenon *anomalous replotting* (Gerrig 1989a, 1993) because it represents readers' attempts to change a plot in the face of certain knowledge of the outcome. Consider a scene from the movie *Smoke*. Harvey Keitel plays Auggie, the proprietor of a smoke shop. He is describing the death of a writer, Paul's, wife as an innocent bystander in a bank robbery.

The funny thing was, she stopped in here just before it happened, to stock up on cigars for him. She was a nice lady, Ellen. Four or five months pregnant at the time. Which means that when she got killed, the baby got killed too.

One of the store customers comments, "It's a bad day at Black Rock, eh Auggie?" Auggie continues:

It was bad alright. You know sometimes I think that, if she hadn't give me exact change that day. Or, if the store had been a little more crowded, then maybe [it] woulda taken a few more seconds to get out of here and she wouldn't have stepped in front of that bullet. She'd still be alive, the baby woulda been born....

At this instant Auggie notices a teenager shoplifting a magazine. He shouts, "Hey whatta you doin' there kid!" and the moment is over. In this short period of time, however, it was quite easy to get caught up in Auggie's replotting—his "ifs"—and follow the story to the world in which Ellen and her child would survive.

What makes anomalous replotting particularly compelling is the way in which it encapsulates the tension between affect and cognition in readers' experiences of narratives. Most instances of anomalous replotting appear to arise when the reader (or in Auggie's case, the experiencer) is uncomfortable with an outcome (Gerrig 1993). It appears to be trivially easy for the replotter to locate the minimal change that would be necessary to avert that outcome, and to be transported to the narrative world in which that change existed. What is salient here is the recursion: Special urgency is focused on the speed with which Ellen left the smoke shop only because of its consequence. We could imagine repeatedly retelling these events (or, perhaps, watching them in a movie) and p-responding, "Slow down!" each time Ellen prepared to leave the store. "Slow down!" is only relevant—and urgent—because it is impossible.

This brief look at replotting also illustrates the final inadequacy of purely structural approaches to suspense. Both anomalous replotting and anomalous suspense provide evidence that suspense is often not destroyed when an outcome becomes known. Replotting suggests, in addition, that a revelation of the outcome may actually enhance suspense. If the outcome is undesirable, readers may marshal all their mental resources to try to identify the moments at which it could be undone. The ensuing slate of participatory responses would enhance and transform the experience of the narrative.

13.3 Conclusions

I began this chapter by introducing the metaphor that readers are transported to the worlds of narratives. I invoked Gregory Reeves, spellbound by the words of an aged Vietnamese story-teller. I suggested along the way that readers contribute to the power of narrative experiences by mentally participating in a variety of ways. In most visits to narrative worlds, these types of mental participation, which I have called participatory responses, will both follow from and lead to the inferences that have been the traditional subject of theories of text processing. As much as researchers have made progress delimiting the parameters of inferencing, theories will be incomplete if they cannot capture with appropriate complexity the interactions of inferences and p-responses.

Theories of text processing should also capture the ways in which experiences of being transported create for readers some genuine isolation from their everyday world. The bulk of text processing research has focused on the ways in which information from long-term memory provides the foundation for narrative experiences. We must, however, expand the range of inquiry to understand how narrative worlds really are worlds apart. We can examine, for example, how reader immersion yields affective responses that are relatively immune to longstanding knowledge. The adequacy of theories of text processing is imperiled if they ignore compelling aspects of the phenomenology of the experience of narrative worlds.

References

Albrecht, J. E., E. J. O'Brien, R. A. Mason, and J. L. Myers. 1995. The role of perspective in the accessibility of goals during reading. *Journal of Experimental Psychology: Learning, Memory, and Cognition* 21: 364–72.

Allbritton, D. W., and R. J. Gerrig. 1991. Participatory responses in prose understanding. *Journal of Memory and Language* 30: 603–26.

Allende, I. 1993. *The Infinite Plan* (M. Sayers, trans.). New York: HarperCollins.

Anderson, J. R. 1976. *Language, Memory, and Thought*. Hillsdale, NJ: Lawrence Erlbaum.

Bharucha, J. J. 1987. Music cognition and perceptual facilitation: A connectionist framework. *Music Perception* 5: 1–30.

Bharucha, J. J., and P. M. Todd. 1989. Modeling the perception of tonal structure with neural nets. *Computer Music Journal* 13: 44–53.

Bloom, C. P., C. R. Fletcher, P. van den Broek, L. Reitz, and B. P. Shapiro. 1990. An on-line assessment of causal reasoning during comprehension. *Memory and Cognition* 18: 65–71.

Brewer, W. F., and E. H. Lichtenstein. 1982. Stories are to entertain: A structural-affect theory of stories. *Journal of Pragmatics* 6: 473–86.

Carroll, N. 1996. The paradox of suspense. In P. Vorderer, H. J. Wulff, and M. Friedrichsen, eds., *Suspense: Conceptualizations, Theoretical Analyses, and Empirical Explorations*. Hillsdale, NJ: Lawrence Erlbaum, pp. 71–91.

Duncker, K. 1945. On problem solving. *Psychological Monographs* 58 (5, Whole no. 270).

Fablo, T., and D. F. Polit. 1986. Quantitative review of the only child literature: Research evidence and theory development. *Psychological Bulletin* 100: 176–89.

Fleming, I. 1954. *Casino Royale*. New York: Macmillan.

Fletcher, C. R. 1994. Levels of representation in memory for discourse. In M. A. Gernsbacher, ed., *Handbook of Psycholinguistics*. San Diego: Academic Press, pp. 589–607.

Fletcher, C. R., and C. P. Bloom. 1988. Causal reasoning in the comprehension of simple narrative texts. *Journal of Memory and Language* 27: 235–44.

Gerrig, R. J. 1989a. Reexperiencing fiction and non-fiction. *Journal of Aesthetics and Art Criticism* 47: 277–80.

Gerrig, R. J. 1989b. Suspense in the absence of uncertainty. *Journal of Memory and Language* 28: 633–48.

Gerrig, R. J. 1993. *Experiencing Narrative Worlds*. New Haven: Yale University Press.

Gerrig, R. J. 1997. Is there a paradox of suspense? A reply to Yanal. *British Journal of Aesthetics* 37: 168–74.

Gerrig, R. J. 1999. Perspective as participation. In S. Chatman and W. van Peer, eds., *New Perspectives on Narrative Perspective.* Albany, NY: SUNY Press, in press.

Gerrig, R. J., and A. B. I. Bernardo. 1994. Readers as problem-solvers in the experience of suspense. *Poetics* 22: 459–72.

Gerrig, R. J., and D. A. Prentice. 1996. Notes on audience response. In D. Bordwell and N. Carroll, eds., *Post-theory: Reconstructing Film Studies.* Madison, WI: University of Wisconsin Press, pp. 388–403.

Graesser, A. C., M. Singer, and T. Trabasso. 1994. Constructing inferences during narrative text comprehension. *Psychological Review* 101: 371–95.

Hijuelos, O. 1995. *Mr. Ives' Christmas.* New York: HarperCollins.

Johnson, B. T., and A. H. Eagly. 1989. Effects of involvement on persuasion: A metaanalysis. *Psychological Bulletin* 106: 290–314.

Kahneman, D., and D. T. Miller. 1986. Norm theory: Comparing reality to its alternatives. *Psychological Review* 93: 136–53.

Kintsch, W. 1994. The psychology of discourse processing. In M. A. Gernsbacher, ed., *Handbook of Psycholinguistics.* San Diego: Academic Press, pp. 721–39.

Lewis, C. H., and J. R. Anderson. 1976. Interferences with real world knowledge. *Cognitive Psychology* 83: 311–35.

McKoon, G., and R. Ratcliff. 1992. Inference during reading. *Psychological Review* 99: 440–66.

Moorman, K., and A. Ram. 1994. Integrating creativity and reading: A functional approach. In A. Ram and K. Eiselt, eds., *Proceedings of the Sixteenth Annual Conference of the Cognitive Science Society.* Hillsdale, NJ: Lawrence Erlbaum.

O'Brien, E. J., and J. E. Albrecht. 1992. Comprehension strategies in the development of a mental model. *Journal of Experimental Psychology: Learning, Memory, and Cognition* 18: 777–84.

Petty, R. E., and J. T. Cacioppo. 1986. The elaboration likelihood model of persuasion. In L. Berkowitz, ed., *Advances in Experimental Social Psychology*, vol. 19. Orlando, FL: Academic Press, pp. 123–205.

Prentice, D. A., R. J. Gerrig, and D. S. Bailis. 1997. What readers bring to the processing of fictional texts. *Psychonomic Bulletin and Review* 4: 416–20.

Ram, A. 1991. A theory of questions and question asking. *Journal of the Learning Sciences* 1: 273–318.

Singer, M. 1994. Discourse inference processes. In M. A. Gernsbacher, ed., *Handbook of Psycholinguistics.* San Diego: Academic Press, pp. 479–515.

Todd, P. M. 1988. A sequential network design for musical applications. In D. Touretzky, G. Hinton, and T. Sejnowski, eds., *Proceedings of the 1988 Connectionist Models Summer School.* San Mateo, CA: Morgan Kaufmann, pp. 76–84.

Trabasso, T., and L. Sperry. 1985. Causal relatedness and importance of story events. *Journal of Memory and Language* 24: 595–611.

Trabasso, T., and P. van den Broek. 1985. Causal thinking and the representation of narrative events. *Journal of Memory and Language* 24: 612–30.

Truffaut, F. 1984. *Hitchcock*, rev. ed. New York: Simon and Schuster.

Updike, J. 1989. *Self-consciousness*. New York: Knopf.

van den Broek, P. 1994. Comprehension and memory of narrative texts: Inferences and coherence. In M. A. Gernsbacher, ed., *Handbook of Psycholinguistics*. San Diego: Academic Press, pp. 539–88.

Walton, K. L. 1978a. How remote are fictional worlds from the real world? *Journal of Aesthetics and Art Criticism* 37: 11–23.

Walton, K. L. 1978b. Fearing fictions. *Journal of Philosophy* 75: 5–27.

Walton, K. L. 1990. *Mimesis as Make-believe*. Cambridge: Harvard University Press.

West, P. 1992. *The Women of Whitechapel and Jack the Ripper*. Woodstock, NY: Overlook Press.

Yanal, R. J. 1996. The paradox of suspense. *British Journal of Aesthetics* 36: 146–58.

Chapter 14
Computational Models of Reading and Understanding: What Good Are They?

Charles R. Fletcher

This book describes eight computer programs that simulate some of the cognitive processes involved in reading and understanding. Each program represents somewhere between a few hundred (Langston, Trabasso, and Magliano, chapter 6) and 40,000 plus (Moorman and Ram, chapter 10) lines of code, untold hours of writing, testing and maintaining that code, a substantial investment of research funds, and an equally substantial opportunity cost. The goal of this chapter is to take a step back and ask, Was it worth the effort? In order to answer this question, I will consider the following criteria:

1. Do these programs demonstrate the computational sufficiency of the theories they implement?
2. Do they allow us to explore and understand the theories in ways that would not otherwise be possible?
3. Do they make it easier to compare the underlying theories with human performance?
4. Are they useful for solving "real-world" problems?

These are certainly not the only criteria one could use to evaluate the models in this volume, but they are among the most commonly cited reasons for constructing computer models of cognitive processes (see table 14.1), and I believe they support the conclusion that the resources invested in these models have been well spent! This is a conclusion I am delighted to reach, since, like the other authors of this volume, I have invested substantial time and resources developing, maintaining, and testing computer models of reading and understanding.

14.1 Demonstrating Sufficiency

To study processes like reading, cognitive scientists typically begin by breaking it down into constituent parts, such as lexical access, syntactic processing, semantic analysis, retrieval from long-term memory, inference generation, and knowledge

Table 14.1
Programs described in this volume

Model	Sufficiency?	Computational experiments?	Predict human performance?	Perform useful work?
Mahesh, Eiselt, and Holbrook (chapter 3)	Yes	No	No	No
Lange and Wharton (chapter 5)	Yes	No	No	No
Langston, Trabasso, and Magliano (chapter 6)	Yes	No	Yes	No
Ram (chapter 8)	Yes	No	No	No
Peterson and Billman (chapter 9)	Yes	No	No	No
Moorman and Ram (chapter 10)	Yes	No	Yes	No
Cox and Ram (chapter 11)	Yes	Yes	No	No
Riloff (chapter 12)	No	Yes	No	Yes

Note: Seven of the eight programs described in this volume are used by the authors to argue that the theories they implement are computationally sufficient (column 2), two are used to carry out computational experiments (column 3), two are used to predict human performance (column 4), and one does useful work (column 5).

acquisition. To some observers this may seem counterproductive. We have taken one homunculus and replaced it with several. The key to success with this approach is that the several homunculi are "dumber" than the one they replaced. Each dumb homunculus can then be replaced, in turn, by even dumber homunculi until the total set of homunculi are sufficiently simple that we can replace them with a set of data structures and algorithms that can be executed on a computer. At this point the homunculi have been "discharged" in the words of Dennett (1978, ch. 7). In principle, we can then reassemble the parts into a fully functioning simulation with enough computational power to explain reading and understanding.

Clearly none of the authors in this volume have succeeded in reassembling all the parts, or even in discharging all the homunculi, yet most claim (see table 14.1) that by running successfully, their programs demonstrate the computational sufficiency of the theories that they implement. This is probably the most often cited reason for constructing computer models of cognitive processes. But does a running simulation necessarily imply computational sufficiency? Does it prove that all the homunculi have been discharged? The answer, sadly, is not always. At least four potential problems stand in the way (e.g., see Neches 1982):

1. Programs can be designed with a specific set of inputs (e.g., texts or sentences) in mind. The fact that the program works with this restricted set of inputs does not guarantee broader success.
2. Difficult examples can be withheld from a program.
3. Programs often involve simplifying assumptions. These assumptions are usually necessary for the program to run, but they may not be consistent with the theory the program is supposed to implement. Neches (1982) cites Lenat's (1977) AM as an example of a program whose actual implementation appears inconsistent at times with the theory it is supposed to implement.
4. Programs are sometimes provided with inputs that act as nonnumerical parameters. The operators and table of differences in Newell and Simon's (1972) general problem solver are well-known examples. This is problematic when it is unclear where this information would come from were it not provided by the programmer.

An author can demonstrate that the first two factors do not limit his or her claims of computational sufficiency by testing a program against a large number of randomly selected examples that were not utilized during the program's development. An excellent example is provided by Cox and Ram (chapter 11). These authors test the sufficiency of their Meta-AQUA learning and story understanding system by presenting it with six random sequences of 24 stories each, where all stories were generated by Meehan's (1981) Tale-Spin story-telling program. The program's success with this large set of clearly defined, randomly selected test stories strongly suggests that similar performance would be observed with any narratives of the type created by Tale-Spin. Similar testing by Langston, Trabasso, and Magliano (chapter 6) lend strong support to their claims of computational sufficiency.

It is more difficult, or at least less common, to show that a program's apparent computational sufficiency is not inflated by simplifying assumptions or psychologically implausible inputs. Fortunately, as a model becomes successful, it generally becomes more widely available (e.g., see Anderson 1993; McClelland and Rumelhart 1988). Scholars other than those who implemented the model obtain copies to study, run, test, modify, and retest for their own purposes. Any shortcomings the model may have are soon brought to light. The model presented by Langston, Trabasso, and Magliano (chapter 6) has an interesting history that illustrates this process. This model is a relatively straightforward modification of the Construction-Integration model that was originally developed by Kintsch (1988). This model was well received and widely cited, leading other scholars to request copies of the program that implements it. This, in turn, led to the creation of a well-documented, easy-to-use version of the program by two of Kintsch's associates (Mross and Roberts 1992). This program made it possible for researchers like Langston and his colleagues to adapt the model to their own purposes. In doing so, they have both uncovered potential problems with the original implementation and offered solutions for those problems. As an example, Goldman and Varma (1995) identified a significant simplifying assumption in Kintsch's original implementation of the Construction-Integration model—that the number of nodes retained in short-term memory for reprocessing along with the following sentence is constant. These authors were able to demonstrate that this assumption is psychologically implausible and to modify the model in a way that makes this assumption unnecessary. Efforts such as this have increased the scientific community's confidence in the computational sufficiency of this model!

14.2 Operationalized Thought Experiments

Anyone who has ever graded programming assignments knows that it is difficult to understand another person's source code. This unfortunate fact undermines one of the traditional advantages of formal models—clear and unambiguous communication. It is simply not possible to understand a theory in cognitive science by examining the code that implements it. Nevertheless, computer models do facilitate our ability to understand and communicate a theory by enabling what Dennett (1978, ch. 7) calls "operationalized thought experiments." The basic idea is simple, but very powerful. If you wish to know how some component contributes to your program's success, disable that component and observe its effect on the program's performance. As an example, consider the computational experiment described by Cox and Ram (chapter 11). Figure 11.17 illustrates Meta-AQUA's ability to answer questions about stories when its "learning goals" are both enabled and disabled. The striking difference in performance makes a compelling case for the importance of these learning goals. In a slight variation on this approach, Riloff (chapter 12) uses an operationalized thought experiment to show that AutoSlog-TS performs as well with untagged texts as its predecessor, AutoSlog, does with manually annotated texts. This provides a strong validation of the learning heuristics that differentiate AutoSlog from the earlier program. As shown by table 14.1, these are the only examples of operationalized thought experiments presented in this volume. Nevertheless, any computer model can be used for this purpose, and to my mind, this provides a major motivation for constructing such models.

14.3 Predicting Human Performance

Another oft cited reason for simulating cognitive processes is to reproduce or, even better, predict human performance. The goal is to demonstrate that a model achieves its computational sufficiency by implementing the same knowledge structures and processes found in nature. Efforts of this type usually take one of two forms. First, we can compare responses generated by a program to those generated by human subjects. This approach is illustrated by Moorman and Ram (chapter 10) who used their ISSAC model to answer comprehension questions about several complex stories and then asked a panel of college and high school teachers to grade those answers along with those given by a group of college sophomores, without knowing which responses came from each source. The results suggest that ISAAC understands the stories as well (and presumably in the same way) as the students do. This finding is made all the more impressive by the fact that the questions require "creative understanding" such as generalizing the concept "werewolf" to create the new concept "were-car." The other common technique for comparing a computer model to human performance is to demonstrate a correspondence between the computational effort expended by a model and the time expended by human subjects. This approach is nicely illustrated by Langston, Trabasso, and Magliano (chapter 6) who demonstrate a systematic relationship between the number of cycles that their model requires to process sentences in specific contexts and the time that human subjects spend reading the same sentences in the same contexts. For an excellent discussion of how to implement this approach, see Kieras (1984).

But what role does the computer model play in these empirical comparisons? Consider, as an example, the model described by Langston et al. (chapter 6). Computationally this is one of the simpler models in this volume. Yet figures 6.4 and 6.8 indicate that a minimum of 135 and a maximum of 330 processing cycles are required to simulate comprehension of a single text. During an "average" cycle the model must calculate an output value for each of eight nodes (one-half of the nodes in a 16-sentence text), the activation or inhibition that passes between 56 pairs of nodes (eight ways to choose the first node times seven ways to choose the second), the total activation and inhibition acting on eight nodes, and new activation levels for eight nodes. This, in turn, suggests that the number of calculations needed to predict reading times for a single text lies somewhere between a minimum of 10,800 (135 cycles $\times (8 + 56 + 8 + 8)$ calculations per cycle) and a maximum of 26,400 (330 cycles $\times (8 + 56 + 8 + 8)$ calculations per cycle). Performing these calculations by hand would be inconvenient at the very least, and without them Langston et al. would be hard-pressed to connect the reading times of their human subjects to the model's underlying theoretical assumptions. This is a strong argument for the usefulness of this model! The argument is even stronger for a more computationally complex, less tractable model like Moorman and Ram (chapter 10).

14.4 Solving Practical Problems

A complete, realistic model of reading and understanding should be able to recommend a good book, reject junk e-mail, grade essay exams, and perform other useful tasks. This has long been recognized by computer scientists. As much as twenty years ago Schank and his colleagues (e.g., DeJong 1982; Schank and Abelson 1977) were building psychologically plausible models of story understanding that could translate simple narratives and news articles from English into Chinese, Russian, Dutch, and Spanish. Psychologists have shown less interest in the practical applications of their models, but exceptions do exist. Britton and Eisenhart (1993), for example, showed that Kintsch and van Dijk's (1978) simulation of text comprehension and recall can be used to diagnose and repair readability problems in expository texts.

In practice, attempts to use computer models of human understanding to solve practical problems have been limited by at least two factors. First, far more attention has been paid to decomposing comprehension into its constituent parts and implementing the parts than to reassembling them into a "complete" and useful model. Thus in Britton and Eisenhart's application of the Kintsch and van Dijk model, they were forced to propositionalize each text by hand before submitting it to the model for analysis. This is a difficult and time-consuming process that will never be adopted by composition students, newspaper editors, or textbook publishers. It is also a shortcoming that could be overcome by combining Kintsch and van Dijk's model of higher-level comprehension processes with a parser that can take a printed (or ASCII) text as input and generate a propositional representation of the text as output. It is therefore encouraging that several chapters in this volume report attempts to move toward a more complete simulation of reading and understanding by combining models of syntax and semantics (Mahesh, Eiselt, and Holbrook, chapter 3), comprehension and retrieval from long-term memory (Lange and Wharton, chapter 5), and comprehension, problem solving, and learning (Cox and Ram, chapter 11).

A second factor that has limited the practical usefulness of computer models of human reading and understanding is knowledge. As noted by Riloff, most such models depend on "enormous amounts of manual knowledge engineering" (chapter 12). Consider the programs of Schank and Abelson (1977) and DeJong (1982). These programs include large collections of handcrafted "scripts" which represent, in detail, the people, objects, and events associated with stereotyped activities (e.g., robbing a bank or visiting a doctor's office) and can only process texts for which they have an appropriate script. This limits their use to those texts for which someone has taken the time and effort to handcraft an appropriate script. A model that develops its own representations from experience would soon have a much larger knowledge base to draw on, making it much more useful. Given that learning plays a central role in half of the models described in this volume (Ram, chapter 8; Moorman and Ram, chapter 10; Cox and Ram, chapter 11; Riloff, chapter 12), this appears to be the direction in which the field is headed.

Because of the limitations inherent in traditional computer models of human reading and understanding, scholars interested in practical problems of natural language processing have tended to ignore human performance and take a more pragmatic approach. This is nicely illustrated by Riloff's research on information extraction (chapter 12). Her AutoSlog and AutoSlog-TS programs are designed to extract predefined information from texts (e.g., the perpetrators, victims, targets, weapons, dates, and locations of terrorist acts) as accurately as possible. No attempt is made to simulate the processes that human readers would employ to accomplish this goal. Yet, accurate performance seems to require a fairly deep level of understanding, and programs that begin as engineering projects sometimes converge on very human-like solutions (e.g., see Landauer and Dumias, 1997). As a result at the same time that cognitive models are becoming more useful, useful models are becoming more cognitive.

4.5 Conclusions

I began this chapter by asking whether anything was gained by implementing the computer models of reading and understanding described in this volume. In my opinion, the answer is unambiguous. First of all, these programs allow us to evaluate the theories they implement in ways that would not otherwise be possible. This, in turn, makes it far easier to judge the computational sufficiency of these theories. Second, the programs allow us to perform operationalized thought experiments. This simplifies the task of understanding and communicating the contributions of different elements of a theory. Third, the programs make it possible to derive testable psychological predictions from theories that would otherwise be intractable. Fourth and last, computer models of reading and understanding are reaching the point where they may be useful for solving real-world problems. Outcomes such as these suggest that the programs in this volume have earned their keep.

References

Anderson, J. R. 1993. *Rules of the Mind*. Hillsdale, NJ: Lawrence Erlbaum.

Britton, B. K., and F. J. Eisenhart. 1993. Expertise, text coherence, and constraint satisfaction: Effects on harmony and settling rate. *Proceedings of the Cognitive Science Society* 15: 266–71.

DeJong, G. 1982. An overview of the FRUMP system. In W. Lehnert and M. Ringle, eds., *Strategies for Natural Language Processing*. Hillsdale, NJ: Lawrence Erlbaum.

Dennett, D. C. 1978. *Brainstorms*. Cambridge: MIT Press.

Goldman, S. R., and S. Varma. 1995. CAPing the construction-integration model of discourse comprehension. In C. A. Weaver, III, S. Mannes, and C. R. Fletcher, eds., *Discourse Comprehension: Essays in Honor of Walter Kintsch*. Hillsdale, NJ: Lawrence Erlbaum, pp. 337–58.

Kieras, D. E. 1984. A method for comparing a simulation to reading time data. In D. E. Kieras and M. A. Just, eds., *New Methods in Reading Comprehension Research*. Hillsdale, NJ: Lawrence Erlbaum.

Kintsch, W. 1988. The role of knowledge in discourse comprehension: A construction-integration model. *Psychological Review* 95: 163–82.

Kintsch, W., and T. A. van Dijk. 1978. Toward a model of text comprehension and production. *Psychological Review* 85: 363–94.

Landauer, T. K., and S. T. Dumias. 1997. A solution to Plato's problem: The latent semantic analysis theory of the acquisition, induction, and representation of knowledge. *Psychological Review*, 104: 211–40.

Lenat, D. B. 1977. Automated theory formation in mathematics. *Proceedings of the Fifth International Joint Conference on Artificial Intelligence*. San Mateo, CA: Morgan Kaufmann, pp. 833–42.

McClelland, D. L., and D. E. Rumelhart. 1988. *Explorations in Parallel Distributed Processing: A Handbook of Models, Programs, and Exercises*. Cambridge: MIT Press.

Meehan, J. 1981. Talespin. In R. C. Schank and C. Riesbeck, eds., *Inside Computer Understanding: Five Programs plus Miniatures*. Hillsdale, NJ: Lawrence Erlbaum, pp. 197–258.

Mross, E. F., and J. O. Roberts. 1992. *The Construction-Integration Model: A Program and Manual*. Technical Report ICS 92-14. Boulder, CO: Institute for Cognitive Science, University of Colorado.

Neches, R. 1982. Simulation systems for cognitive psychology. *Behavior Research Methods and Instrumentation* 14: 77–91.

Newell, A., and H. A. Simon. 1972. *Human Problem Solving*. Englewood Cliffs, NJ: Prentice Hall.

Schank, R., and R. Ableson. *Scripts, Plans, Goals and Understanding: An Inquiry into Human Knowledge Structures*. Hillsdale, NJ: Lawrence Erlbaum.

Index

Abduction, 6, 376, 412
Abductive matching, 100
Absolute novelty (A-Novel), 363
Abstraction, 414, 415, 420, 428
Abstraction hierarchy, 84
ACT, 124
Action, 90–91, 370
Activation control, 137–38
Activation values, 183, 191, 194–97, 203–205
AELC parsing (arc eager left-corner parsing), 46, 48–52
Agent, 12–13, 370
AI (artificial intelligence), 73, 76, 77, 80, 88, 353–54
Alien-robot-as-industrial-tool, 362
AM, 485
Ambiguity, 32–33
  lexical semantic, resolution of, 63–64
  representational content and, 82–83
  resolution, 33, 37
Analogical inferences, 165
Analogical mapping, 378–79
Analogical similarity, 108
Analogy, 378, 409, 412
Anomaly, 401, 403–408, 414, 419, 424, 425
Anomaly category index, 280
Anomaly detection, 280, 281, 284, 285
A-Novel (absolute novelty), 363
AQUA, 265–68, 274–76, 280, 284–88, 295n, 403–405
Arbitration, 57–58, 61–63
Arc eager left-corner parsing (AELC), 46, 48–52
ARCS, 126, 158, 159, 170, 171, 175, 176
Arc standard left-corner parsing (ASLC), 46, 48, 49
Artificial intelligence (AI), 73, 76, 77, 80, 88, 353–54
Ascription, 17–18
ASLC (arc standard left-corner parsing), 46, 48, 49, 52
Aspect, 55
ATN (Augmented Transition Network), 39
Attachment ambiguity, 33

Attachment questions, 292–93
Augmented Transition Network (ATN), 39
Author, communication with reader, 231–41
Automated knowledge acquisition, 443–44
AutoSlog dictionary construction system, 445, 446–49
AutoSlog-TS, 445, 450–56

Background beliefs, 14–15, 20
Background knowledge, 12, 397, 398, 402, 405, 408, 409–24, 426n, 427n
Base-constructive analogy, 379
Bayesian reasoning, 100
Beliefs, 89, 91
Belief spaces, 18–19
Binding units, 130, 132–33
Blame assignment, 398, 414, 417–19, 424
Blocks World, 424
BORIS, 117–18, 275
Bottom-up processing, 272

Canonical form, 75
Canonical representations, 83
Cascade models, 412
Case-based reasoning (CBR), 109–10, 125, 409, 413, 419
Case-based understanding, 99
Case frames, 446–54
Casino Royale (Fleming), 467–68
Castañeda's theory of guises and consubstantiation, 12–15
Causal account, 408
Causal event function, 315
Causal explanation, 401
Causal justification, 427n
Causation, 89
Causation writing plan, 233
Causes of failure, 416
CBR (case-based reasoning), 109–10, 125, 409, 413, 419
CD (conceptual dependency), 79–80, 87

Chain of inferences, 120
Change, learning and, 258
Characters, fictional, 11, 17–18
Character stereotype indexes, 280
Chunking mechanism, 412
CIRCUS, 447
Cognitive economy, 74
Cognitive effort, 373
Cognitive Model of Parsing and Error Recovery, 69n
Cognitive monitoring, 426
Cognitive motivations, 258–61
Cognitive resources, 233, 247–48
Cognitive structure, 28
Coherence, 408
Coherent interpretation, 403
Combinatorial explosion, 81, 408
Commensurable representation, 83–84
Compactness, of representation, 87
Comparison organization, 233–34
COMPERE, 29, 31, 42, 46, 55–68, 69n, 70n, 386
Compositional representation, 84
Compositional semantics, 75
Composition failure, 64–65
Comprehension, 1, 425, 426n
 episodic reminding and, 111
 failure, 413
 goal, 402
 models, 117–26 (*see also* specific comprehension models)
 on-line vs. off-line study, 182–83
 problem solving, learning, and, 397, 398
 study, 184–85
Computational models, 29, 331–32
 functional architecture, 332–33
 lexical correspondence component, 339
 semantic lexicon, 334
 semantic processor, 338–39
 structural correspondence component, 339–40
 syntactic lexicon, 333–34
 syntactic processor, 334–38
Computational motivations, 261–64
Computer models, 3–4, 265–68. *See also* specific computer models
Computers, 73, 74, 76, 89, 259
Concept
 content, 306
 definitions, 83
 elaboration, 399, 408, 424
 manipulation of, 372–73
 refinement, 116
 representation of, 366–69
 specification, 284
Conceptual analyzers, expectation-based, 118
Conceptual coherence, 401
Conceptual dependency (CD), 79–80, 87

Conceptual frame, 405
Conceptual knowledge, 34, 59, 70n
Conceptual type, 406
Conflict resolution, 57–58
Conjunctive learning goal, 420
Connectionist model, 118–19
Connection strength, 188, 211
Consistent interpretation, 403
Consociation, 14
Constraint, 47, 405, 407
Construction-Integration model, 183, 185, 222–24, 485–86
 activation values, 194–97, 203, 205
 actual stories, simulating, 201–208
 components, 188–89
 connection strength, 197–200, 205–207
 cycles to settle, 105, 197, 198
 measures, validation of, 210–22
 modified, 187–88
 simulations, 192–94, 200–201
 standard, 186–87
 text integration, 189–90
 validating against comprehension data, 208–10
Constructive induction, 412
Consubstatiation, 12–15
Content, 258
 needing representation, 88–91
 representational, 77–88
Content theory, 79–81, 86–87, 277
Context, 20
Contradiction, 415, 416
Control, of reading process, 7
Control structure, 260
Control supertask, 374
COPYCAT, 125
Co-reference, 83
Core semantic analysis, 54–58
Correspondence rules, 340–51
Coverage, 86
Creative reading, 359
Creative understanding, 359
 algorithm issues, 373–86
 control of, 383–84
 defined, 362–66
 examples, 387–89
 knowledge issues, 366–73
 tasks, 377
Crosstalk, elimination of, 138–42
CRYSTAL, 445
CSILE, 261, 268
Cues, 113, 127

Deactivate meanings, 63
Decide-compute node (D-C-NODE), 409, 410, 416
Deciding what to learn, 398, 410, 414, 417–19, 422
Decision anomalies, 290–91

Index 493

Decision model, 91, 277, 403, 404
Decision questions, 288–89
Decontextualized meaning, 54
Deduction, 412
Deictic center, 12
DESCARTES, 158
Description writing plan, 233
Determinism, 38–39
Difference perspectives, 470–71
Disambiguation, 121, 134–37
DISCERN, 125
Discourse analysis, 184–85, 190, 441–43
Distributed connectionist networks, 119–21
Distributional structure, 306–307
Domain, ontological grid, 370–71
Domain theories, 80
Dynamic inference, 120–21

Eager selection, 37
Early commitment, 37
Educational instruction, 425
Efficiency, 87–88
Elaboration, 84–85, 428
ELIZA, 4
Elvis, 403–405, 408, 414, 420
Emotional domain, 370–71, 373
Emotional states, 91
Empirical evaluation, 420
ENABLES link, 427n
E-Novel (evolutionary novelty), 364, 369
Entries, 54
Episodic reminding, 109–12, 149–58
Episodic units, 147–49
Epistemological interpretative issues, 12
Epistemological ontology, 12–13
Erroneous association, 415, 419, 427n
Error recovery, 36, 64–66
Errors, 30–31, 70n
Evaluation, 389–91, 420
Events, 54, 90
Evidential activation, 134–37, 140–41, 144, 153, 156–60
Evolutionary novelty (E-Novel), 364, 369
Executive process, 400
Expectation, 402, 426
Expectation failure, 414, 427n
Experiment, 382
EXPLAINS node, 277, 427n
Explanation, 281, 403, 405, 427n
  application, 409
  generation, 405, 406, 408, 415
  goals, 283
  questions, 283
  volitional, content theory of, 277
Explanation-based generalization (EBG), 420
Explanation-based learning, 412

Explanation pattern (XP), 276, 414, 427n
  application, 280, 281, 292, 409
  AQUA, 277
  retrieval, 280, 281
  retrieval questions, 290–92
  structure, 277–80
Explanation process model, 280–81
Explanation-strategy construction, 399, 409
External perspectives, 469–70
"The Eyewitness," 472–73

Failure, 397–98, 409, 414–16, 422, 424, 427n
Failure detection, 410, 415, 416, 418
False expectation, 416
Fiction, 11, 13–18
Fictional objects, 12, 17–18
Fillers, 366
Final activation, 211
First analysis principle, 37
First-order process theory, 425
Fit ratings, 209, 210
Focus of attention, 7
Focus of attention problem, 271–73
Foreground knowledge, 397, 398, 402, 405, 413, 417, 422–26
Form, representational, 77, 78–79
Formalism, 78–79
Frame commitment, 116–17
Frames, 366
Frame selection, 116, 127, 128
Freedom preservation goal, 404
FRUMP, 275, 456
Functional-computational-representational model, 2–5
Functional-driven morphological synthesis, 381–83
Functional fixedness, 468
Functional independence, 38

Generalization, 414, 415, 428
General problem solver, 485
Generate-and-test, 400, 405, 422
Gifts of the Magi, 6
Global inhibition, 137
Goal/goals, 89, 91, 92. *See also* specific goals
  competition, 404
  generation, 425
  interaction, 420, 422
  learning, 259, 261
  selection, 92
  specification, 409
  writer's, 231–32
Goal-dependency, 419
Goal-driven problem solving, 427n
Goal-guided inference, 272
Goal-orientation, 427n
Goodness of explanation, 403

Grammar, 34, 44
Grammatical meaning, 54
Guises, theory of, 13–15

Head, 47, 48
Head-driven parsing, 47
Head-signaled left-corner parsing (HSLC), 46, 47, 50–54, 69n
Heuristics, 92, 400, 426n
High-level inferencing, 114–17
Homunculus, 484
The Hound of the Baskervilles (Holmes), 17
HSLC parsing (head-signaled left-corner parsing), 46, 47, 50–54, 69n
HVQs (hypothesis verification questions), 281, 292
Hypothesis, 281, 287, 427n
Hypothesis tree, 281
Hypothesis verification, 281, 405, 406, 409–10, 415, 427n
Hypothesis verification questions (HVQs), 281, 292

ILT learning task, 411
IML (introspective multistrategy learning), 397, 410, 411, 418, 425, 427n
Immediacy of interpretation, 38
Immediate semantic decision hypothesis, 38
Immigrant fictional objects, 17
Immigrant objects, 17
Impasse, 415, 416
Inchoate function, 314–15
Incompleteness, 32
Incompleteness failure, 65–66
Incorrect domain knowledge, 419
Incremental comprehension, 38
Incremental interpretation, 37–38
Incrementality, 37–38
Incremental selection, 69n
Indexes, 92, 99, 125, 126
Indexical information, 12
Indexing problem, 99–101, 175–76
Index label, 99
Induction, 412
Inference chains, 81, 120
Inference questions, 289
Inferences, 6, 75–77, 81, 114–15, 139, 254, 263
Inferencing, 114–17, 131–34, 173
Inferential Learning Theory, 411
The Infinite Plan (Allende), 461, 465–66
Information extraction (IE)
  automatically generating case frames for, 444–56
  case frames, 437–38
  defined, 436
  examples of, 436
  research, 435–36
  story understanding and, 456–57
  trends, 438–44

INITIATE link, 427n
Innate goal, 405
I-Novel (instantiation novelty), 364, 369
Input
  analysis, 409
  branch unit, 147
  elaboration, 425
  selection, 92
  of sentence understanding, 31
  sites, 147
Insight, 427n
Instantiation novelty (I-Novel), 364, 369
Instrinsic interest, 405
Integrated architecture, 42
Integrated model, 111, 113–14
Integrated processing, 38
Integrated representations, 40–41
Integration process hypothesis, 29
Intelligence, 426
Intelligent-robot, 362
Intensional objects, 13–14
Interaction, 42, 43
Interactive theory, 29
Interest, 385–86
Interest identification, 405–406, 415
Interestingness, 271–73, 406, 426n
Internal representation of text, 27
INTERNAL-XP-NODES, 277
Interpretation, 165–68, 274–76
Intrinsic goal, 405, 426
Introspective explanation, 410, 414
Introspective learning, 422
Introspective mode, 420
Introspective multistrategy learning (IML), 397, 410, 411, 418, 425, 427n
Introspective reasoning, 413
ISAAC, 67, 68, 386–87, 392
Ivan the Warrior, 202–203

Knowledge, 488. *See also* specific types of knowledge
  ambiguity resolution and, 33
  dependency, 414
  gap, 265
  graph, 366–68
  repair, 418
  representation, 6, 11, 73, 74, 77, 85, 366–69
  selection, 92
  in sentence interpretation, 30–31
  structures, 269–71
  syntactic or grammatical, 34, 44
  transmutations, 416
  types of, 34
Knowledge goals, 253, 271, 399, 408, 409
  acquisition, 264
  indexing, 286

organization, 264
retrieval, 286
sources of, 269
for story understanding, 282–84
of understanding program, 261–64
Knowledge sources, 69n
independent, 39–41
justifying syntactic commitments, 46–47
in sentence understanding, 33–34

Language acquisition, 355
Language generation, 428
Language processing, constraints, 39
Language understanding, 397, 400–405, 409, 422–25, 428
computational model of, 28
high-level inferencing and, 114–17
integrated with reminding, 110–12
levels of, 27–28
multilingual aspects, 28
in REMIND, 126–27
Learning
comprehension, problem solving and, 397, 398
generation, 415
goals, 259, 261, 398, 411, 413–22
plan, 413–16, 420
questions as basis for, 258–61
strategy, 413, 417, 420
task, 397
types of, 264
vs. story understanding, 422–26
Learning model, process divisions, 415–18
Learning operator, 420
Left-corner parsing, 45–49, 54
Lewis's theory of fiction, 15–16
Lexal semantic, 33
Lexical correspondence, 339
Lexical disambiguation, 120
Lexical entry retrieval, 35
Lexical knowledge, 34, 58
LIEP, 445
Life preservation goal, 404
Linguistics, Semantic Corresponence theory and, 355–56
LINKS, 277
LISP learning and programming, 410, 411
Literal meaning, 54
Literary criticism, theoretical entities of, 17
Local ambiguities, 47
Location event function, 312
Location state function, 311–12
Long-term memory, 113, 142–47, 183, 186, 209, 426n
Loud noises, 405, 426
Lovelace questions, 3–5
LUNAR, 39

Lycanthrope (Hartman), 360–61, 371, 374, 375, 382, 390

MAC/FAC, 126, 158, 170, 171, 175, 176
Machine learning, 411
Main ideas, understanding, 233
MARGIE, 80–81, 93
Marker-passing networks, 119, 134
Memory, 6, 267
comprehension and, 107–108
goals, 282
improvement after strategy instruction, 238–41
model, 273–74
organization, 94, 95, 100
questions, 283
requirements, 47
retrieval, 108–109, 114, 142, 377–78, 383–84
supertask, 376
Memory-level questions, 293–294
Memory organization packet (MOP), 97–98, 100, 274, 407
Men Are Different, 379–80, 390
Mental domain, 370–71
Mental event, 427n
Mental knowledge, 88
Mental processes, 92
Mental representation, 74–75
Mental states, 92
Message understanding conference (MUC), 97–98, 438
Meta-AQUA, 397, 403–406, 413–15, 420, 427n
Metacognition, 425, 426, 428
Metacomprehension, 425, 426
Meta-explanation pattern (Meta-XP), 414–19, 427n
Meta-knowledge, 90, 91–93, 426n
Meta-level process, 400, 401, 428
Metalinguistic development, 428
Meta-memory, 426
Meta-plane, 400
Meta-reasoning, 7
Meta-XP (meta explanation pattern), 414–19, 427n
Migration, between stories, 11, 12, 19
Modality, 55
Modeling reasoning, 92–93
Modification, 55
Modularity debate, 29
Modules, 29
MOLGEN, 400
MOORE, 386
MOP (memory organization packet), 97–98, 100, 274, 407
MOPTRANS, 42
Motion event function, 313
Motion state function, 313–14
Motivations, 359–62

Mr. Ives' Christmas (Hijuelos), 461–64
MUC (message understanding conference), 97–98, 438
Multi-level reasoning, 400
Multiple inferences, 113
Multistrategy learning, 399–401, 403, 411–13, 422
Mundane reading, 359
Mutual reindexing, 420, 428

Narrative, 12
Native fictional objects, 17
Native objects, 17
Natural language, 27, 32, 33
Natural language processing (NLP), 2, 73, 80, 299, 435
  message understanding conferences and, 438
  problems, 457
  Semantic Corresponence theory and, 353–54
Negation, 55
Negative learning goal interaction, 422
NLP. *See* Natural language processing
Nonexistent objects, 16–17
Nonlexical knowledge, 34
Nonlin, 418, 420
Nonlinear planner, 413, 414, 419, 420
Normative decisions, 408
Noun phrase prominence correspondence, 340
Noun phrases, 315, 316, 317
Novel situation, 419
Novelty, 6–7, 363–64, 369
Numerical parameters, 485

Object-centered design, 94–95
Objects, 12–14, 17, 54, 370, 373
Occam's razor, 87
Off-line assessment, 182–83
On-line principle, 38
On-line processing, 182–83, 185, 192, 209–210
Ontological grid, 370–72
Ontological theories, 12–18
Ontology, 371, 386
Opportunism, 273–74
Opportunistic reasoning, 415
Organization, representational, 77, 80–81, 93–94
Outcomes, 91, 93
Output, of sentence understanding, 31–32

PALKA, 445
PAM, 98
Parallel architecture, 42–43
Parsing strategies, 45–48, 50
Parsons' theory of fiction, 16–17
Partial matching, 99
Partial parsing, 439–41
Participation, 469–72
Pascal programming, 410, 411
Path functions, 311

PDP networks, 119–21
Performing task, 397
Perspective, 11
Philosophy, computational, 11–12
Phrase structure rules, 305
Physical anomaly questions, 290
Physical domain, 370–71
Physical explanation, 404, 427n
Physical knowledge, 88
Physical symbol systems, 75
Physical XP, 404, 427n
Place functions, 309–10
Plan failure, 422
Plan/goal analysis, 116
Planner anomalies, 292
Planner questions, 290
Planning, 424
Plans, 89
Plan strategy, 91–93, 228, 234–41
Point of view, 11
Practical problems, 486–87
Predication, 11–18
Prediction, 363
Preposition-object correspondence, 316–17, 324–27, 340
Prepositions, 316
Presentation mode, 241, 243
Preservation goal (P-GOAL), 257–58, 404
PRE-XP-NODES, 277
Priorities, 89, 91
Problem elaboration, 424
Problem reformulation, 379–80, 400
Problem/solution organization, 233–34
Problem-solving, 397–400, 426
Processing/computational/interpretative issues, 12
Processing cycles, 487
Processing failure, 409
Process model for explanation, 280–81
Process model of comprehension, 401–403
Process scheduling, 286
Production systems, 412
Prominence correspondence, 308, 327–31
Prominence relations, 307–308
Psycho (Hitchcock), 466–67
Psycholinguistic theories of sentence processing, 29
Psychological (cognitive) models, 29

Question-answering strategy, 428
Question-based interpretation, 274–76
Question-driven information seeking, 253–54
Question-driven learning, 264–65
Question-driven program, 275
Question-driven story-understanding, 403, 405, 406
Question-driven understanding, 255–58, 404, 406, 408, 423
Question-driven understanding and learning computer model. *See* AQUA

Questions, 253–54, 281, 283, 287–88, 428
  anomaly detection, 285
  as basis for learning, 258–61
  nature of, 268–74
  representation of, 284–87
  taxonomy of, 288–94
  types of, 281–84
Question specification, 399, 408

Rate of presentation, 242–43
Reactivate retained meanings, 63–64
Reactive behavior, 400
Readers
  characteristics, task, strategy, text and, 228, 229
  communication with author, 231–41
  exceptional, 239
  interest, 247
  participation, 469–72
  participation in narrative worlds, 461–65
  processing resources, 247–48
  strategies, 228
  transportation to narrative world, 472–78
Reading. *See also* Tasks of reading
  comprehension (*see* Comprehension)
  controlling, 7
  decomposition, 374–77
  defined, 1
Reading process theory, 1–5
Reading time prediction, 208–10
Reasoning
  failure, 422
  hierarchical decomposition, 397, 398
  meta-level, 401
  model, 401
  multistrategy, 401
  object level, 400–401
  success, 93
  trace, 417
Recognition, 400
Reconciliation goal, 420
Recovery, 422, 424, 425
Recovery induced errors, 66
Recurrent networks, 120
Reder, 400, 426
Reference questions, 293
Reflexive mode, 420
Regression analysis, 214–17
Reification, 82, 85–86
Reinterpretation, 116–17, 134–37
Relevance goals, 283
Relevance principle, 272
Relevance questions, 283, 294
REMIND, 108
  knowledge given to, 127–29
  language understanding in, 126–27
  overview, 112–14

retrieval from episodic memory, 133–42, 147, 152–59, 165–76
  structure of, 129–30
Reminding
  aspects of, 108–10
  effect on interpretation, 165–68
  general models of, 168–72
  integrating with understanding, 110–12
  questions, 294
Repair, 422, 424
Representation, 11–12, 73–78, 101–102, 284–87
Representational form, 77, 78–79
Representational organization, 77, 80–81
Re-reading instructions strategy, 416
RESULTS link, 427n
Retrieval, 113
Revolutionary novelty (R-Novel), 364, 369
ROBIN, 124, 126, 133, 135, 140, 176
Robot-as-industrial-tool, 362
Role assignment, 56
Role-binding, 131–32, 134, 145, 173–74
Role-filler, 405
Rule-based systems, 117–19, 121

SAARCS, 172
SAM, 96
Satisfaction, 384–85
Scenario supertask, 374–75
Schema instantiation, 402
Schemas, 98–99, 262, 269, 295n
Scientific discovery, 427n
Script application, 405
Script applier, 427n
Scripts, 96–97, 427n, 488
Search, 408
Secondary attribute, 369
Second-order process, 400, 425, 426
Selection, 37
Selectional preferences, 54
Selection restrictions, 139–40, 141, 176n
Self-Consciousness (Updike), 469–70
Self-explanation effect, 425
Self-generated questions, 425
Semantic context, 33
Semantic Correspondence theory, 300–302
  artificial intelligence and, 353–54
  computational models (*see* Computational models)
  conceptual representation and, 305–306
  contributions, 351–53
  limitations, current, 356–57
  linguistics, benefits to, 355–56
  natural language processing and, 353–54
  psychology, benefits to, 354–55
  syntax and, 303–305
  unrestricted texts processing, 357
Semantic functions, 308, 309

Semantic head, 48
Semantic knowledge, 34, 58–59
Semantic processing, 44–45, 55–56, 338–39
  disambiguating verbs and, 345–49
  novel verb interpretation and, 349–51
  verb-argument composition and, 340–45
Semantic representation, 306–15
Semantic roles, 55
Semantics, 32, 36, 45, 305–306, 315–17
Semantic similarity, 125–26
Sentence comprehension
  independent knowledge sources and, 38–41
  Semantic Correspondence theory and, 301–302
Sentence processing, 6, 27–28, 44
  architectures, 41–43
  errors, 30–31
  psycholinguistic theories, 29
  psychological modeling of, 29
  supertask, 375–76
  in text understander, 67–68
  time, 30
Sentence understanding, 28–31
  functional constraints, 36–39
  knowledge sources in, 33–34
  problems in, 32–33
  task, 31–32, 34–36
Sequence writing plan, 233
Sequential architecture, 41
Settling, 186, 190
Short-circuitry inhibitory nodes, 138
Signaling, 233–34
Signal words, 233–34
Signatures, 124, 130–34, 144
Similarity-based learning, 412
Simplifying assumptions, 485
Single-strategy learning, 411, 412
Situated reading, 7
Situation assessment, 428
Situation indexes, 280
Slots, 366, 367
Smoking script definition, 407
SNePS, 13, 14, 18–22
SNePS Belief Revision system (SNeBR), 19
Social domain, 370–71, 373
Social knowledge, 88
Social-situations, 90
Social-units, 90
Source code, 486
Spatial continuity, 213, 214
Spatial roles, 54
Spontaneous retrieval, 380
Spreading-activation, 121–24, 126, 138. *See also* REMIND
Star Trek, 387
State, 90, 370
Statistical information, 70n

Story, 89
Story operator, 13–16, 20, 22
Story space, 11, 12, 18–21
Story structure supertask, 375
Story understanding, 397, 410, 422, 427n
  information extraction and, 456–57
  knowledge goals for, 282–84
  programs, 253
Story world, 11
Strategy, 90, 228, 230–31
  construction, 405, 414, 418, 419, 425
  decision and execution, 409, 415
  plan, 228, 234–41
  reader, 228
  selection, 412
  structure strategy training program, 234–41
  task, text, reader characteristics and, 228, 229
Strong-FMS, 381–82
Structural correspondence, 307–308, 315–17
Structural isomorphism, 171
Structural syntactic, 33
Structured connectionist networks, 121–24
Structure strategy training program, 234–36, 238–41
Subjectivity, 258
Subtractive inhibitor nodes, 137–38
Sufficiency, 483–86
Superficial similarity, 108, 161–65
Supertask, 374–76
Surprise, 416
Surrogate fictional objects, 17
Surrogate objects, 17
Suspense, 465–68
Suspension of disbelief, 374, 376–77
SWALE, 276
Symbolic rule-based systems, 117–19
Syntactic analysis, 35, 44–46
Syntactic guidance, 56
Syntactic knowledge, 58
Syntactic lexicon, 333–34
Syntactic processor, 334–38
Syntactic structure (grammar), 34, 44
Syntax, 45, 315–17
  disambiguating verbs and, 345–49
  novel verb interpretation and, 349–51
  Semantic Correspondence theory and, 303–305
  semantic representation and, 307–308
  verb-argument composition and, 340–45
Syntax-semantics, 56–57
Syntax-semantics communication, 43–44
Syntax-semantics interactions, 39–44

Tacitus system, 93–94
Tale-Spin, 413, 420, 427n, 485
Target, 378

Tasks of reading, 5–7
  assessing comprehension, 244
  characteristics of, 245
  mode of presentation, 241–44
  rate of presentation, 242–44
  strategy, text, reader characteristics and, 228, 229
Task specification, 284
Template-based approaches, 95–99
Temporal domain, 370–71
Tense, 55
Text base, 275
Text-based predictors, 214
Text characteristics, 241, 246–47
Text comprehension, 111–12
Text-driven program, 275
Text goals, 282
Text input, 185–86
Text-level questions, 292–93
Text organization, 232–34
Text processing, 461–65
  assessing comprehension, 244
  characteristics of reading task, 245
  cognitive resources, 233, 247–48
  comprehension and, 245–46
  decision making after reading, 245–46
  representation of text, 231
  text characteristics and, 241, 246–47
Text questions, 283
Text recall, 241–43, 246–47
Text representation, 188, 196
Text structure, 227–28
Textual information, 426
Text understanding, 428
Thematic roles, 54
Thematic similarity, 108, 109
Themes, 89, 111
Things, as semantic elements, 308–309
Thought experiments, 486
Time, 55, 69n
TMXP (trace meta-explanation), 409
Toolbox models, 412
Top-down processing, 272
Trace meta-explanation (TMXP), 409
Troubleshooting, 418
Type, on ontological grid, 371
Type contraction, 83
Type expansion, 85

UMass/MUC-3 system, 443–44, 445
Uncontrolled interaction, 42
Understanding, 363. *See also* Creative understanding; Language understanding; Sentence understanding
  cycle, 260
  goal, 403
  program, knowledge goals of, 261–64

supertask, 376
system, 27
tasks, 262–63
Unexpected success, 416
Unification mismatch, 405
Usability, of representation, 87
Usefulness, 86, 364–65

Vagueness, 32, 82
Van Inwagen's theory of fictional objects, 17–18
Variable binding, 130–31, 427n
Variable-depth parsing, 258, 276
Verb-argument combinations, 339–40
Verb-argument composition, 340–45
Verb-argument correspondence, 317–19, 340
Verb-preposition combinations, 340
Verb-preposition correspondence, 316, 319–24
Verb-preposition corrspondence, 340
Verbs
  disambiguating, 345–49
  novel, interpreting, 349–51
  syntactic structure, 315–16
Verification process, 409
Violence, 405, 426
Virtual structure, 140
Volitional explanation, 277, 278, 404, 427n
Volitional explanation pattern, 414

Weak-FMS, 382, 391
Were-car, 382
Winner-take-all, 137
WKRP in Cincinnati, 379
The Women of Whitechapel and Jack the Ripper (West), 464–65
Word category information, 34
Word meaning composition, 56
Word meanings, 34
Word processing, 6
Word sense ambiguity, 33
Word-sense disambiguation, 55–56, 116–18
Working memory, 59, 60, 186, 187
Writing plans, 232–33

XP. *See* Explanation pattern
XP-ASSERTED-NODES, 277

Zoo, 380, 390